'Some of the subplots narrated in this fascinating assemblage would challenge the pen of Dostoevsky ... addictively readable' John Sutherland, *Sunday Times*

'This is a Faberge egg of a book ... The final release, after three-quarters of a century, of the love letters of the last Tsar and Tsarina of Russia really do constitute that rare event – genuine publishing history ... This beautifully produced and expertly edited book is not primarily political, however, but a love story which – now those of Burton and Taylor, JFK and Jackie O and Charles and Di have been exploded – must rate as the most romantic of the century' Andrew Roberts, *Mail on Sunday*

'Magnificent, tiresome, candid, absurd and terribly moving' Duncan Fallowell, *Spectator*

'This is a huge book, hard to pick up, equally hard to put down. It is fascinating from the first page to the last' Hugo Vickers, *Sunday Express*

'It is the chorus of contemporary voices – those of crowned heads and foreign ambassadors, Grand Dukes and Duchesses, revolution-aries and murderers – in official documents, letters and memoirs, which really give the book its sense of gripping immediacy, and turn it into such an engrossing drama' Mark Bostridge, *Independent on Sunday*

'This volume is a treasure' *Publishers Weekly*

Andrei Maylunas, author and historian, conceived and compiled *Nicholas and Alexandra: the Family Albums* by Prince Michael of Greece, published in 1992. He lives in an Alpine village.

Sergei Mironenko, author and historian, Director of the State Archive of the Russian Federation, lives in Moscow, and has written books about Russia under Nicholas I and Alexander I.

A LIFELONG PASSION

NICHOLAS AND ALEXANDRA

Their Own Story

Andrei Maylunas
& Sergei Mironenko

*Translations from
original documents
by Darya Galy*

A PHOENIX GIANT PAPERBACK

First published in Great Britain by Weidenfeld & Nicolson in 1996
This abridged paperback edition, abridged by the authors, published in 1997
by Phoenix, a division of Orion Books Ltd, Orion House,
5 Upper St Martin's Lane, London WC2H 9EA

A CIP catalogue record for this book is available
from the British Library.

ISBN 0 75380 044 6

Typeset by Selwood Systems,
Midsomer Norton

Printed and bound in Great Britain by
Clays Ltd, St Ives plc

To my grandmother, Bee
and my wife Clarisse – A.M.

To my wife Masha – S.M.

For many decades after the 1917 revolution, the major part of the archive materials used in this book were inaccessible. They were kept securely hidden from sight in the archive repositories. But contrary to a widely-held belief, nothing was destroyed. And this is why we are now able to read the authentic diaries of Nicholas II, Alexandra, Xenia, KR and the imperial children, and enjoy the sometimes artless letters between the different members of the imperial family, yet which are full of merit and feeling.

This has been made possible by the democratic reforms taking place today in Russia and which have enabled the doors of the archives to be thrown wide open.

SERGEI MIRONENKO

CONTENTS

ILLUSTRATIONS

THE FAMILIES OF
EMPEROR NICHOLAS II
AND HIS WIFE ALEXANDRA

Only the characters mentioned
in the book are shown here.

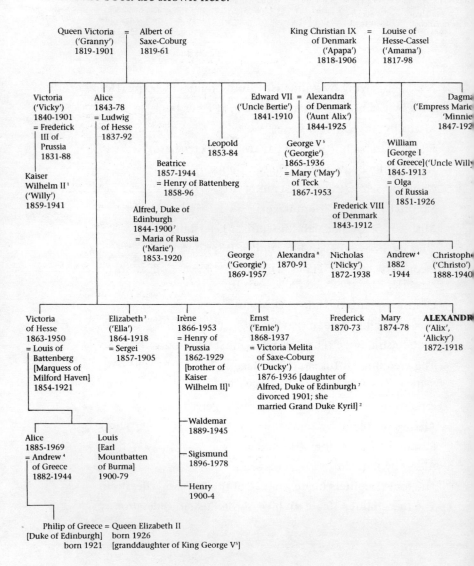

Queen Victoria = Albert of
('Granny') Saxe-Coburg
1819-1901 1819-61

King Christian IX = Louise of
of Denmark Hesse-Cassel
('Apapa') ('Amama')
1818-1906 1817-98

Victoria
('Vicky')
1840-1901
= Frederick
III of
Prussia
1831-88

Alice
1843-78
= Ludwig
of Hesse
1837-92

Kaiser
Wilhelm II [1]
('Willy')
1859-1941

Leopold
1853-84

Beatrice
1857-1944
= Henry of Battenberg
1858-96

Alfred, Duke of
Edinburgh
1844-1900 [7]
= Maria of Russia
('Marie')
1853-1920

Edward VII = Alexandra
('Uncle Bertie') of Denmark
1841-1910 ('Aunt Alix')
1844-1925

George V [5]
('Georgie')
1865-1936
= Mary ('May')
of Teck
1867-1953

Dagma
('Empress Marie
'Minnie'
1847-192

William
[George I
of Greece]('Uncle Willy
1845-1913
= Olga
of Russia
1851-1926

Frederick VIII
of Denmark
1843-1912

George
('Georgie')
1869-1957

Alexandra [8]
1870-91

Nicholas
('Nicky')
1872-1938

Andrew [4]
1882
-1944

Christoph
('Christo')
1888-1940

Victoria
of Hesse
1863-1950
= Louis of
Battenberg
[Marquess of
Milford Haven]
1854-1921

Elizabeth [3]
('Ella')
1864-1918
= Sergei
1857-1905

Irène
1866-1953
= Henry of
Prussia
1862-1929
[brother of
Kaiser
Wilhelm II] [1]

Ernst
('Ernie')
1868-1937
= Victoria Melita
of Saxe-Coburg
('Ducky')
1876-1936 [daughter of
Alfred, Duke of Edinburgh [7]
divorced 1901; she
married Grand Duke Kyril] [2]

Frederick
1870-73

Mary
1874-78

ALEXANDR
('Alix',
'Alicky')
1872-1918

Waldemar
1889-1945

Sigismund
1896-1978

Henry
1900-4

Alice
1885-1969
= Andrew [4]
of Greece
1882-1944

Louis
[Earl
Mountbatten
of Burma]
1900-79

Philip of Greece = Queen Elizabeth II
[Duke of Edinburgh] born 1926
born 1921 [granddaughter of King George V [5]]

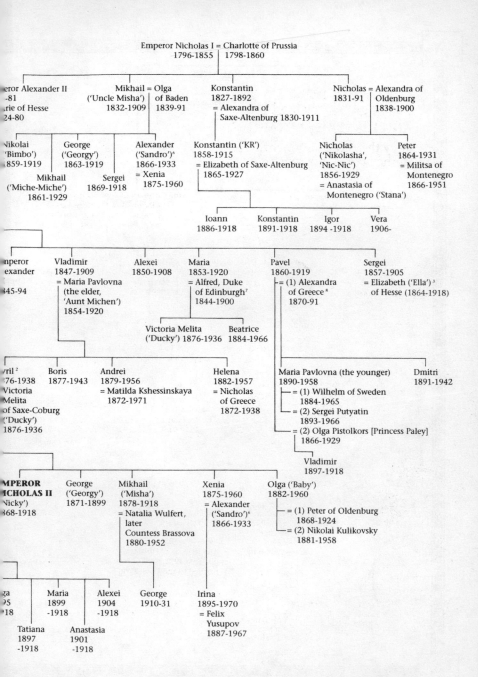

Emperor Nicholas I = Charlotte of Prussia
1796-1855 | 1798-1860

Emperor Alexander II
-81
Marie of Hesse
24-80

Mikhail = Olga
('Uncle Misha') | of Baden
1832-1909 | 1839-91

Konstantin
1827-1892
= Alexandra of
Saxe-Altenburg 1830-1911

Nicholas = Alexandra of
1831-91 | Oldenburg
1838-1900

Nikolai
('Bimbo')
1859-1919

George
('Georgy')
1863-1919

Alexander
('Sandro')[6]
1866-1933
= Xenia
1875-1960

Konstantin ('KR')
1858-1915
= Elizabeth of Saxe-Altenburg
1865-1927

Nicholas
('Nikolasha',
'Nic-Nic')
1856-1929
= Anastasia of
Montenegro ('Stana')

Peter
1864-1931
= Militsa of
Montenegro
1866-1951

Mikhail
('Miche-Miche')
1861-1929

Sergei
1869-1918

Ioann
1886-1918

Konstantin
1891-1918

Igor
1894-1918

Vera
1906-

Emperor
Alexander
845-94

Vladimir
1847-1909
= Maria Pavlovna
(the elder,
'Aunt Michen')
1854-1920

Alexei
1850-1908

Maria
1853-1920
= Alfred, Duke
of Edinburgh[7]
1844-1900

Pavel
1860-1919
= (1) Alexandra
of Greece[8]
1870-91

Sergei
1857-1905
= Elizabeth ('Ella')[3]
of Hesse (1864-1918)

Victoria Melita
('Ducky') 1876-1936

Beatrice
1884-1966

Cyril[2]
1876-1938
= Victoria
Melita
of Saxe-Coburg
('Ducky')
1876-1936

Boris
1877-1943

Andrei
1879-1956
= Matilda Kshessinskaya
1872-1971

Helena
1882-1957
= Nicholas
of Greece
1872-1938

Maria Pavlovna (the younger)
1890-1958
= (1) Wilhelm of Sweden
1884-1965
= (2) Sergei Putyatin
1893-1966
= (2) Olga Pistolkors [Princess Paley]
1866-1929

Dmitri
1891-1942

Vladimir
1897-1918

EMPEROR
NICHOLAS II
('Nicky')
868-1918

George
('Georgy')
1871-1899

Mikhail
('Misha')
1878-1918
= Natalia Wulfert,
later
Countess Brassova
1880-1952

Xenia
1875-1960
= Alexander
('Sandro')[6]
1866-1933

Olga ('Baby')
1882-1960
= (1) Peter of Oldenburg
1868-1924
= (2) Nikolai Kulikovsky
1881-1958

Olga
95
18

Maria
1899
-1918

Alexei
1904
-1918

George
1910-31

Irina
1895-1970
= Felix
Yusupov
1887-1967

Tatiana
1897
-1918

Anastasia
1901
-1918

[Superior numbers indicate more than one appearance]

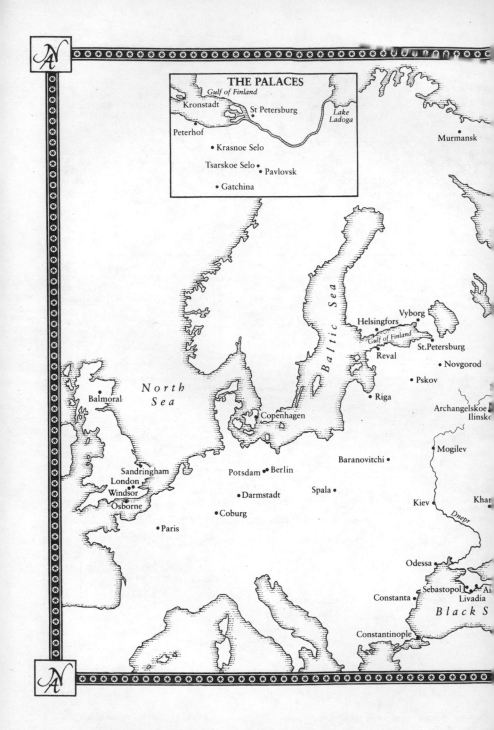

THE PALACES

Gulf of Finland

Kronstadt
St Petersburg

Peterhof

Lake Ladoga

• Krasnoe Selo

Tsarskoe Selo •
• Pavlovsk

• Gatchina

Murmansk

Baltic Sea

Vyborg

Helsingfors
Gulf of Finland

St.Petersburg

Reval
• Novgorod

• Pskov

Riga

Archangelskoe
Ilinsko

*North
Sea*

Balmoral

Copenhagen

Mogilev

Baranovitchi •

Potsdam • Berlin

Sandringham
London
Windsor
Osborne

• Darmstadt

Spala •

Kiev

Khar

Dnepr

• Coburg

• Paris

Odessa

Sebastopol •
Constanta •
Livadia

Ai

Black S

Constantinople

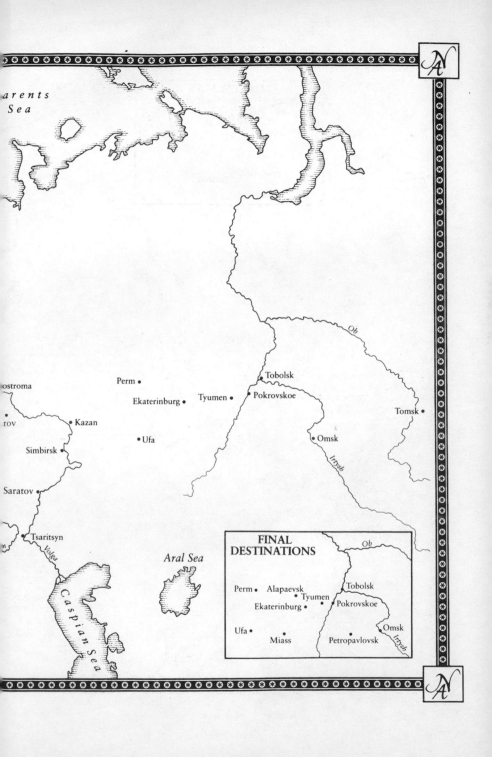

arents Sea

Barents Sea

ostroma

Perm •

• Ekaterinburg • Tyumen • • Tobolsk
• Pokrovskoe

rov • Kazan

• Ufa

Simbirsk •

• Omsk

Saratov •

Tomsk •

Ob

Irtysh

• Tsaritsyn

Volga

Aral Sea

Caspian Sea

FINAL DESTINATIONS

Perm • Alapaevsk
• Tyumen
Ekaterinburg •

Ufa • • Miass

Ob

Tobolsk •
• Pokrovskoe

• Omsk

Petropavlovsk •

Irtysh

INTRODUCTION

by Andrei Maylunas

Our story goes like this: once upon a time, there lived a charming and kind young prince, the heir to a large and rich kingdom, covering one sixth of the world. He fell in love with a beautiful faraway princess. He married her and became king. They loved each other passionately and had five children. One would expect them to live happily ever after. But they could not escape their fate. They were doomed, their bloodline was cursed. The fairy tale turned into tragedy.

This is the story of a family, a very special family and a very special story. The last Romanovs to rule Russia are among the best-documented people in history. Their lives coincided with the beginnings of the age of mass media, and being the rulers of one sixth of the world, they were of course the focus of attention for the then young media. Tabloids, postcards, illustrated magazines, countless books (every one of their contemporaries who knew them – or not – seems to have published a book), early cinema (we sat through thirty hours of live footage of the family, most official and formal, but some private and moving). As for themselves – for people who lived a hundred years ago, they were surprisingly modern. Being an international couple, they spoke and wrote English to each other, they played tennis and took photos (theirs is among the first do-it-yourself snap-shot photography). Every member of the family, children included, had a camera and being rich – photography was then a very expensive hobby – they left us about 150,000 photographs of themselves, not counting all the pictures taken of them by others.

One might argue that with the great strides technology has taken since then, with the advent of audio and video recordings, more recent families – and we don't mean mere mortals, but families like the Kennedys or today's Windsors – are even better documented. We disagree: here, because of the unique timing of our story, we have much, much more. The Romanovs lived at the crossroads of two eras and in spite of all the modern novelties of their day all of them still had the absolutely wonderful nineteenth-century habit: they kept diaries. And though all of our characters had telephones, they wrote to each other daily and very often sincerely. Even a terrorist and a murderer, Kalyaev, writes a letter to the beautiful Grand Duchess Ella, the widow of the man he has blown to bits; she comes to visit him in jail; the terrorist then writes a poem about the visit of his victim's wife; we have it. All of our characters write to each other and they all were literate, and most of what they wrote has survived in the various archives (God bless them). So we have had – just for this short period of history – almost total access to both the outer and, much more importantly, the inner world of our heroes.

This is first and foremost a documentary book, a book which would not have been possible without modern means of communication – computers, modems, faxes, aeroplanes. In a relatively short space of time, and despite living in different countries, the two of us were able to go through literally hundreds of thousands of documents, letters, diaries, police records, published and unpublished memoirs. Many of the documents were unique, previously unread, some even unheard of. But they all combined to make a story which needed no direct comment. They blended into a budding myth, in the form and shape of a classical tragedy.

What makes a myth? We detect in our characters and in the events surrounding them all the makings of mythological tradition. Let us take a closer look at this: one of our protagonists has already been canonized; another seven of our characters are in the process (and already canonized by the Russian church-in-exile). For the last eighty years there have been animated front-page debates on who is dead and who is alive. A plethora of spectacular imposters and the longest ever lawsuit. Active grave-digging, world-wide royal blood collection for DNA tests, science gets involved. Several Hollywood films made and an Anastasia cartoon on its way. In modern times it doesn't take a blind poet to create a myth, but a Broadway musical producer. In any case the process by which an event enters the realm of mythology happens despite the will of historians and laws of academia.

The structure of Greek tragedy drew us like a magnet; whichever way we looked at our story, we were confronted with the formal structural characteristics of antique tragedy. The difference between tragedy and drama is that while drama is based on everyday characters, those of tragedy are mythological or heroic. We think this is the case with the Romanovs. This book is also a tragedy because it is about suffering and passion. It is also about fate, and an inherited curse. In Greek tragedy the Chorus consisted of twelve to fifteen men, the head of the Chorus was the *Coryphaeus*. Our *Coryphaeus* changes in different chapters of the book. Sometimes it is KR – Grand Duke Konstantin Romanov – Nicholas's cousin, a poet and intellectual who translated *Hamlet* into Russian, sometimes the Emperor's sister, the Grand Duchess Xenia, sometimes the French Ambassador to St Petersburg and even sometimes one of the many murderers. And murderers proliferate in this book, which begins and ends with the mix of sulphur and nitrate. All the rest – parents, relatives, sisters, brothers, kings and queens, teachers – make up our Chorus. Since the story spans almost forty years, members of the Chorus come and go.

We were compelled to seek further analogies, and started by looking at Aeschylus. He was the first to increase the number of actors from one to two (in our case Nicholas plus Alexandra), reduce the part of the Chorus and give priority to dialogue. Bloodline curse (haemophilia here), inherited guilt and the perception of suffering as a weapon of divine justice: Aeschylus has it all. So do we. To two excited authors, the prophecies of Cassandra to Agamemnon foreshadowed those of Rasputin. Next Sophocles presents the making of a choice as submitting to the will of the gods while following the traditional ethical norms; a false choice arises not only from consciously breaking these norms, but also from ignorance and the limitations of individual knowledge. This leads to error, self-deception, and justified suffering. Yet it is in the midst of suffering that the best human qualities reveal themselves. The highest form of suffering is suffering in the name of duty. And of course in the end all the characters in our story are doomed and there is no way to avoid the catastrophic climax.

The parallels with mythology and ancient tragedy became clearer and clearer. So we, the authors, at last defined the genre of book we were trying to achieve: a tragedy in documents. As this is a non-academic work, we indulged ourselves. The first title of this book was *The Goat Song*. In Greek *tragos* is a male goat and *ode* is a song – which is where the word tragedy and our title came from (our pragmatic publishers told us to forget it at once).

Thus, although the fireplace is still just warm and there are still a few venerable witnesses around, this book is an exercise in mythologizing, an attempt to speed up by modern means of narration a process already well under way. At the end it is for our readers to judge if we managed this rather awkward reverse transition – from document to myth; from non-fiction to fiction.

And now a few words about our characters, the sources we drew upon and our relationship to them. Nicholas and Alexandra, our two main voices, wrote hundreds of letters to each other. They both kept diaries, Alix intermittently, Nicky every day of his life until a few days before his death. We also quote extensively from the diaries and letters of Xenia, KR, the imperial children and many others, as well as from some extraordinary documents which reveal the truth about the death of the imperial family. Most of the documents mentioned above are being published for the first time.

But we also drew from known published sources, among them the memoirs of Grand Duke Alexander Mikhailovich (Sandro), Prince Yusupov, and Maurice Paléologue. These memoirs were published several years after the events and, though picturesque and rich in detail, sometimes evoke the Russian proverb: 'If you don't lie, you don't tell a story.'

And now for our own sins: everything in this book is the truth, nothing but the truth, but not the whole truth. Our primary sin is that of omission: we have not used a great many important historical documents that we had in our hands, and have mercilessly cut some we did use without indicating our cuts. We have made some sacrifices for the sake of style, narration and counterpoint; and in two or three cases we have interfered with the otherwise strictly observed chronology of the documents.

For ease of reading we have replaced the abbreviations typical of turn-of-the-century documents with full words. We have also made an attempt – not always successful – to bring the numerous and very complicated Russian names to a common denominator. Our characters spoke and wrote in many different languages – English, Russian, French and German. Nicholas, who kept his diary in Russian, spoke and corresponded with his wife in English. The language with his mother was French and Danish. Most of our characters were multilingual, as was the first draft of our book, and to harmonize this tower of Babel was almost an impossible task. This was brilliantly accomplished by Darya Galy, our charming translator, who suffered as much for the last two years as any character from antique tragedy.

Perhaps our biggest problem was the sheer magnitude of the material available to us. As the book progressed and started to assume colossal proportions (the first draft was over 2,500 pages long) it became essential to draw a boundary; this was painful. We had to let go the early youth of Nicholas, his first loves, the virtuoso *entre-chats* of Matilda Kshessinskaya, the trip round the world – including tiger hunting in India and Sandro's adventures with geishas in Japan –

innumerable rumours, anecdotes, gossip, intrigues, the eccentricities of royal uncles and aunts, the extraordinary reforms of Nicholas's grandfather Alexander II and much more.

The vista which opened up – of greed, cupidity, sexual intrigues, financial follies, homosexuality, envy, wrangling over money, power, more power, murder, more murder, horrible death and ever-present doom – started to threaten to turn the story of this large, wealthy, powerful international family into the worst sort of television soap opera. So we drew the line. Unfortunately behind it we also lost many important historical events, politics, court intrigues and many other things which our critics will doubtless draw to our attention.

We had to lose the sympathetic Greek cousins and the Danish grandparents. What a pity it was to lose Grand Duke Nikolai Mikhailovich (Uncle Bimbo), a brilliant historian, author of many famous works and monographs and the number one liberal in the family. There is almost nothing left of him in the book. After the revolution he was incarcerated with his cat in the Peter and Paul fortress in St Petersburg. While discussing his death sentence with Gorky (who came as a deputy of the intelligentsia to beg for his pardon) Lenin said: 'The Revolution does not need historians.' Unfortunately we decided we did not need him in this book either. He was killed. So were others. As for Kings and Queens, they have been killed before; sometimes it comes with the job. Louis XVI and Marie Antoinette were publicly beheaded – after a trial – so was Charles I. There is nothing new about it.

But the way this family met their end, the actual mechanics of their murder, the way they were dragged into a cellar with the maid, the cook, the doctor and the dog, and what happened to them there; the way Ella (by then an elderly nun) was pushed with others into a mine shaft, grenaded and left to die there, the way Nicholas's brother Misha met his end in a forest: this gives a flavour of the nascent twentieth century, it marks its beginning. Dostoyevsky's demons were finally unleashed.

We think there is magic to this family, there is magic in the way they lived and died. And now let them tell their story themselves, in their own words.

London
April 1, 1996

NOTES TO THE READER

HISTORICAL BACKGROUND
Sergei Mironenko examines the historical background to the events covered in this book in the Afterword, pages 679–688.

EDITORS' NOTE
All the correspondence between Nicholas, Alexandra, Ella, Kaiser Wilhelm, Queen Victoria and George V was in English, as were Alix's diaries. Empress Marie's letters to Nicholas were mainly in French.

Before each year or group of years, the principal voices and events are listed.

RUSSIAN CALENDAR
In February 1918 Russia changed from the old Julian Calendar to the Gregorian Calendar already used in the rest of Europe. The gap between the two had widened from ten days (in the seventeenth century) to twelve (in the nineteenth) and thirteen (in the twentieth). Thus February 1, 1918 (Old Style) became February 14, 1918 (New Style). As a result the Bolshevik Revolution was from then on celebrated on November 7 (New Style) instead of October 25 (Old Style) when under the Julian Calendar it actually took place.

For ease in reading the narrative, all dates are given in the Old Style – including letters written from outside Russia – except where otherwise noted.

PROLOGUE

1881–1892

Nicky – Heir to the Russian throne

Sandro – Grand Duke Alexander [Mikhailovich]

Emperor Alexander III – Nicky's father

Alix – Princess of Hesse-Darmstadt

Ella – Grand Duchess Elizabeth, Alix's sister who marries
Nicky's uncle, Grand Duke Sergei

1881

MURDER OF A GRANDFATHER

Nicky's grandfather, Emperor Alexander II, assassinated by a terrorist bomb on March 1 – Famous for the liberation of the serfs in 1861 as well as many other reforms, Alexander is killed on the eve of signing a constitution for Russia – The document lies on his desk as he sets out for his fateful carriage drive – In the midst of the outrage caused by his murder, all plans for a constitution are shelved – Nicky, twelve years old, and Sandro, fourteen, witness the death of the Emperor – Nicky's father, now Alexander III, publishes a manifesto

Bill of Indictment, 1 March 1881 – St Petersburg
At around two o'clock in the afternoon, His late Imperial Majesty[1] drove out of the Mikhailovsky Palace with his usual escort. At a distance of some fifty yards from the corner of Engineer Street there was a terrible explosion, which seemed to fan out from right under the carriage.

Jumping out of the sleigh, and seeing in the same instant that the soldiers had seized a man on the pavement at the side of the canal, Colonel Dvorzhitsky[2] ran towards the imperial carriage, flung open the door, and seeing that His Imperial Majesty was about to emerge from the carriage unscathed, informed His Majesty that the criminal had been apprehended.

At the Emperor's request, the witness led him along the pavement to the place where the detained man was standing, already sur-

---

[1] Emperor Alexander II.
[2] The chief of police of St Petersburg.

rounded by a crowd of people, subsequently he turned out to be Nikolai Rysakov.[3] His Majesty the Emperor was pleased to remark: 'Thank God I am unhurt, but look!', pointing to an injured cossack lying near the carriage, and nearby a wounded boy who was crying out in pain.

Hearing the Emperor's words, Rysakov said: 'Don't thank God yet.'

Just as His Imperial Majesty decided to inspect the location of the explosion and had made a few steps along the canal pavement in the direction of the carriage, another deafening explosion occurred at his very feet, after which for a few moments the whole area was engulfed in a mass of smoke and pieces of clothing.

When it cleared – all those present, both the unscathed and those who had been injured, were struck by a terrifying spectacle: among those thrown down and injured by the blast was His Majesty the Emperor himself. The beloved monarch was half-sitting on the pavement, leaning against the railings of the canal and propping himself up with his arms, covered with blood, but still breathing. The uncovered legs of the August Martyr were smashed and pouring blood, the body hung in pieces, the face was bleeding. There too lay His Majesty's coat, of which only singed and bloody fragments remained. Colonel Dvorzhitsky, who was injured along with His Majesty the Emperor, but was able to raise himself from the ground, heard His Majesty's hardly audible words: 'Help me'. Turning his face towards him, His Majesty said in a feeble voice: 'It's cold, cold.'

In the presence of the Grand Duke Mikhail Nikolaevich,[4] who had hurried to the scene, they carried him to the sleigh.

In reply to the Grand Duke's inquiry as to his health, His Majesty the Emperor replied indistinctly, 'Take me to the palace ... there ... to die ...' These were the last words of the dying monarch.

Sandro, Memoirs – 1 March
At three o'clock sharp we heard the sound of a strong explosion.

'That was a bomb all right,' said my brother George, 'no mistake about that sound.'

At this moment a still stronger explosion shattered the windows in our room. Just then a servant rushed in, all out of breath.

'The Emperor has been killed,' he screamed.

Thousands of people were already surrounding the palace. The

---

[3] A terrorist.
[4] A brother of Alexander II and father of Sandro.

women cried hysterically. We entered by the side door. There was no need to ask questions: large drops of black blood showed us the way up the marble steps of the stairs and then along a corridor into the study of the Emperor. Our father stood at the door giving orders to a group of officials. He had to lift mother[5] in his arms. She had fainted on seeing him alive.

The Emperor lay on the couch near the desk. He was unconscious. Three doctors were fussing around but science was obviously helpless. It was a question of minutes. He presented a terrible sight, his right leg torn off, his left leg shattered, innumerable wounds all over his head and face. One eye was shut, the other expressionless.

Every instant members of the imperial family came in. The room was packed. I clung to the arm of Nicky, deathly pale in his blue sailor's suit. His mother,[6] stunned by the catastrophe, was still holding a pair of skates in her trembling hands.

'Silence, please,' said a hoarse voice, 'the end is near.'

We came closer to the couch. The expressionless eye was still staring fixedly. The chief court surgeon, who was feeling the Tsar's pulse, nodded and let the blood-covered hand drop.

'The Emperor is dead,' he announced loudly. Princess Yurevskaya[7] gave one shriek and dropped on the floor like a felled tree. Her pink-and-white negligee was soaked in blood.

We all knelt and prayed.

MANIFESTO OF ALEXANDER III

The voice of God commands Us to place Ourself with assurance at the head of the absolute power. Confident in the Divine Providence and in His supreme wisdom, full of faith in the justice and strength of the autocracy which We are called to maintain, **We shall preside serenely over the destinies of Our empire, which henceforward will be discussed between God and Ourself alone.**

---

[5] Sandro's mother, born Princess Olga of Baden.

[6] Nicky's mother, afterwards known as Empress Marie, was born Princess Dagmar, daughter of King Christian IX of Denmark. Her sister Alexandra married the Prince of Wales, later Edward VII of England.

[7] Princess Yurevskaya was the morganatic second wife of Alexander II.

1884

FIRST MEETING

Russia is now ruled by Nicky's father Emperor Alexander III – The Emperor's younger brother Sergei marries Princess Elizabeth of Hesse-Darmstadt – Ella is accompanied to Russia by her family, and the sixteen-year-old Nicky meets Ella's twelve-year-old sister Alix for the first time

Nicky, Diary – 27 May – Peterhof
In the morning we washed the mast. We went to church alone; Mama and Papa went to Petersburg. After a little while Aunt Marie[1] and Uncle Pitz[2] arrived. We then went and met Uncle Gega's[3] bride, the beautiful *Ella*, and her sisters and brother. At half-past seven the whole family dined together.

I sat next to little twelve-year-old Alix, whom I really liked a lot; Ella even more; her brother Ernie[4] also.

28 May At half past eight we went to Petersburg. We visited the imperial library in order to improve our poor minds.

When we got back we had luncheon. We found Papa and Mama having luncheon with the Darmstadts.[5] We all romped around a lot on the net. I played with Ernie and Alix. Papa and Mama went to

---

[1] Grand Duchess Maria Pavlovna, wife of Nicky's uncle Grand Duke Vladimir. Also known as Aunt Michen.
[2] Nicky's uncle, Grand Duke Pavel.
[3] Nicky's uncle, Grand Duke Sergei.
[4] Ernst Ludwig, Grand Duke of Hesse-Darmstadt, Alix's brother.
[5] Alix's family.

meet Uncle Willy.[6] We had dinner here with everyone, it was great
fun. I am to be a *best man* at Uncle Gega's wedding.

30 May   This morning Mama went to Petersburg. It has got colder
today. Lunched alone with Papa. Went out with Ernie and Alix in the
break, with Papa driving. Went for a walk. Met Mama at the pier.
Everyone had dinner together at half past six. The others all went off
in the eighteen-place char-à-banc. We hoped they would take us too,
as they took Ernie and Alix; but they left us at home and we felt very
insulted.

31 May   The weather today was wonderful. We lunched as always
with all the Darmstadts. We jumped about with them on the net. At
3 o'clock I went out with them in the four-horse break. Papa drove
in front in the family char-à-banc with Aunt Marie and Victoria.[7] We
looked at Oserki and everyone signed their name in the book at the
mill. We drank fresh milk and ate black bread.

We dined with: Ernest, pretty little Alix and Sergei. Alix and I wrote
our names on the rear window of the Italian house (we love each
other).

1 June   No lessons. Sent a letter to Alix. Went to church. Put on the
uniform of the Preobrajensky [regiment] and went to the parade of
the horse-grenadiers and uhlans. Lunched in the great palace.

Alix and Ernie came to see us. We jumped about together on the
net. Ernie, Alix and I told each other secrets. We had a terrific romp
around the rooms of the Italian House. We had dinner all together. I
sat and chatted to darling little Alix. Wrestled with Ernie.

6 June   I had two lessons. At a quarter past ten Uncle Pitz came for
me and we went to the harbour. From there we set off with Ernie on
the *Marie*.[8] We went to the Winter Palace to see Uncle Pitz's rooms.
Then to the new palace of Uncle Gega and Ella. Luncheon was just
for the best men and our dear hosts. It was very gay. Uncle Willy,
Aunt Olga,[9] Uncles Alexei[10] and Pitz, Ernie and I went to Peterhof.

---

[6] King George I of Greece (the Danish prince Christian Wilhelm Georg, brother
of Empress Marie and therefore Nicky's uncle).

[7] Alix's elder sister, married to Prince Louis of Battenberg.

[8] The imperial yacht.

[9] Queen of Greece.

[10] Nicky's uncle, Grand Duke Alexei, a younger brother of Tsar Alexander III.

When we got back I did some reading. We all dined together. I again sat with dear Alix after dinner. I fooled around with her.

7 June   At last it was so warm that we were able to put on white shirts and shoes. Everyone had luncheon as usual. We boarded the *Duke of Edinburgh* and were shown all over. It was a wonderful lesson on artillery and sailing. We came back on the *Osborne* to Peterhof, where we ate a huge tea. We returned at seven and had dinner with Alix and Ernie. We fooled around a lot on the swings. Papa turned on the hose then we ran through the jet and got terribly wet.

8 June   We had luncheon with Papa, Ernie, Alix, Xenia,[11] Misha[12] and Count Olsufiev. We went completely wild on the maypole. Everyone roared with laughter at the sight of Xenia running with her skirts hitched up. We got covered in sand when we slid through hoops onto the ground. We returned home exhausted, filthy and soaked through with sweat.

We had dinner together in my rooms. We jumped on the net and told each other secrets in the Italian Pavilion. We romped around in the wigwam on Xenia's balcony. I am very very sad that the Darmstadts are going tomorrow and even more so that dearest Alix is leaving me.

19 November   The desire to get married lasted until luncheon, and then went away. At luncheon Perovsky imitated a butterfly and a sparrow taking a sand bath, which surprised Aunt Ella very much. Because of the awful weather we stayed at home. I sat at Mama's lombardy table and wrote out my catechism. After dinner we went round the arsenal. In the evening I did some drawing.

21 December   We slept very late. While cleaning out the birds, we heard a noise in the next room so we went in with a candle and started to search about. Suddenly a mouse jumped out from under the cupboard and ran into a hole in the corner. I decided to go for a walk.

But I had to rush home from the skating rink as my stomach went berserk. Because of this I did not dance with Georgy[13] and Xenia. This evening there was a performance here in the theatre by Russian and French artists.

---

[11] Grand Duchess Xenia, Nicky's younger sister, aged nine.

[12] Grand Duke Mikhail, Nicky's youngest brother, aged five.

[13] Grand Duke Georgy, Nicky's brother, aged thirteen.

22 December Slept rather longer than usual. Georgy got up and dressed in his study earlier than I did. I had my tea while he cleaned out the birds. I have been put on a strict diet today. For luncheon and dinner I had soup and semolina. I read Turgenev instead of going for a walk.

We had tea and dinner with Papa and Mama. No more lessons until Friday! Hourray!!!!!!!

1889

SKATING IN ST PETERSBURG

Seventeen-year-old Alix comes to St Petersburg to spend a winter with her sister Ella, now wife of Grand Duke Sergei – Nicky, now twenty, falls in love with her – Alix recounts her dreams – She and Nicky exchange notes

Alix's dream, recorded in her notebook
That a large party of us were going on a steamer, but before getting onto it, had to jump down a bit – my turn came, I jumped, remained high in the air, held my petticoats tight around me, not that they were flying about, and shrieked that someone was willing me ... but just that moment Gretchen stopped me, and told me not to use such strong language in speaking to the people.

Alix, Diary – 18 January – St Petersburg
Ella and Sergei met us at Tsarskoe. Arrived, all Grand Dukes and Emperor and Nicky at the station. Drove to Anichkov [Imperial Palace] to see Aunt Minnie[1]and the other cousins, and took tea there.

Nicky, Diary – 18 January – St Petersburg
At the skating rink we could hardly move for the wind. Afterwards I went in uniform with Papa to Warsaw Station. We met Uncle Louis,[2] Ernie and Alix.

---

[1] Family name for Empress Marie, Nicky's mother.
[2] Grand Duke Ludwig IV of Hesse-Darmstadt, Alix's father.

She has grown up a lot and become prettier. Received the news of the death of the Austrian crown prince Rudolf.[3]

19 January   I don't know how to explain it, but I'm in a strange kind of a mood, neither sad, nor happy! It seems I am not going to the funeral in Vienna.

Alix, Diary – 21 January – St Petersburg
Breakfast in bed, because of bad cold. Ella and Miss Kitty had their singing lessons, next door. Papa came, Xenia came from 3½–5. Had tea together. Then Papa and Ella came and he read to us in French. The others went to Anichkov for supper, and then Papa, Ernie and Nicky to the Circus. Played a little on the piano, and then to bed.

Nicky, Diary – 22 January – St Petersburg
Dined with the family and the Hesses: Alix sat opposite me. At 9.30 we went to a little *sauterie* and *petits jeux* [dancing party and society games] with supper. It was great fun. I only left at 2.30. It took place at the Vorontsovs'.

Alix, Diary – 29 January – St Petersburg
I skated and slid down the hills in the afternoon in the Anichkov garden. Supper at 7½, then Ella and I went to the Winter Palace where we dressed for the Ball (white diamonds, white flowers and sash).

1. Quadrille with Paul	Round dances with:
2. " "	Derfelden, Costi
3. " "	Paul, Nicky, Toll
Cotillon " Nicky	Gadon, Schilling
Mazurka " Sergei	etc

The Ball was quite delightful, and did not last very long.

Nicky, Diary – 30 January – St Petersburg
At the skating rink we again fooled around a lot with Aunt Ella and

---

[3] Crown Prince Rudolf (son of Austrian Emperor Franz-Josef) committed suicide at Mayerling.

Alix. After the *zakuska* [a light snack] I went with Papa and Mama to the *Mikado*, where we had a lot of fun and laughed a great deal.

Alix's dream
We are in a sort of hospital. Louis in bed. Victoria standing,[4] two men dying in the room, all of a sudden Grandmama comes in and a shot is fired at her. I discover a man sitting in a tree, who did it. He gets down, walks slowly away. I look out of the window, he smiles and bows and I recognize one of the young men who skated with us at Anichkov.

Nicky, Diary – 31 January – St Petersburg
It was fun at the skating rink. Aunt Ella and Alix came. Played ball with them and slid down the hill.

3 February   We had supper as always at our own table. The cotillion was excellent! Went to sleep at 4 o'clock. We lunched alone. There was a concert by Count Sura with one hand; our orchestra played his piece.

Slid down the hill with Aunt Ella and Alix. She visited us after tea and we showed her our rooms. We went to *Eugene Onegin*. It was remarkably good.

4 February   At the skating rink there were: Aunt Ella, Alix and Sergei. We dined at 6.30. Went to the French theatre to see Zola's play *L'Assommoir*, a terrible drama.

12 February   Went skating with my friends. Family dinner was at 7 o'clock. Went to Uncle Sergei's where we danced until we dropped and had a wonderful time. Danced the mazurka with Alix.

14 February   Got up on time at last. Was in a very animated mood, I don't know quite why?

25 February   After lunch, went with Papa and Mama to the Alexander-Nevsky monastery. It was great at the skating rink. Had tea with Aunt Ella, Alix and Sergei. After dinner at their house we played badminton and hide-and-seek. Returned home after tea.

---

[4] Louis and Victoria – Alix's eldest sister, aged twenty-five, and her husband, Louis of Battenberg (later Marquess of Milford Haven).

27 February   A reception for the Bokhara embassy, who were sent with presents, including for me. After luncheon we went to the manège to see the horses they had also brought. Alix and Ernie came skating for the last time. Played chess with Alix. Was in a sad mood!

Alix to Nicky – 17 March – Darmstadt
Dearest Nicky

So many thanks for your note enclosed in Xenia's letter. It was so good of you to write and it gave me great pleasure. My mad letter amused you then all – well I have been cracked enough to write another. We went last night to see the 'Rheingold' and I hope next week to see the 'Walküre's Siegfried'.

But now I must say goodbye as I am going out driving.

Ever your loving Alix

Many messages to the Weeping Willow.[5] We have quite warm weather, Papa and Ernie are gone now out shooting.

Nicky to Alix – 2 April – Gatchina
Dearest Alix,

Thank you so much for your dear little letter, which was such an agreeable surprise to me. I just returned from town yesterday in the night, when it came.

We also saw *Siegfried* with Ella, I like it so awfully especially the melody of the bird and the fire! Now the *Niebelungen* are all over and I think it a great pity.

The other day I also got a frame from Ella with her, you and Ernie in it. I find it charming and she painted round the photo the best remembrances of the winter.

There is the ice, the big hall, the skates, a clown, *the* window with 3 lights, a cotillon-ribbon and a basket with flowers from Aunt Sacha Narychkine's ball, the badminton articles, a branch of pink flowers from the *folle journée* [Shrove Tuesday/mardi gras festival] and best of all *the* Mikado, squinting in his famous way. She gave me too you and her together in Tsarskoe Selo ball-dresses a charming photo, which is constantly before me.

The last week there was a concert at Uncle Sergei and Ella's. I saw the Vorontsovs, Dolgorukys and the little arrangement. I thought of

---

[5] The nickname for Nicky's brother, Georgy.

the goat the whole time. Please tell Ernie I shot my first bear today!

With much love, ever your loving Nicky

Nicky to Alix – 23 May – Tsarskoe Selo
Darling Alix,

Just a wee line to send you my very best wishes on your birthday which is in two days. I am now here in the Hussars serving with delight. I see Ella rather often and we always speak about your stay in Petersburg. It seems to have been so long ago!

I don't remember such a spring with such heats! Have you heard about the betrothal of the eldest Montenegran with Petioucha?[6] – The Shah of Persia was too funny during his stay in Russia. God bless you dearest Alix!

One of the Pelly[7] party, Nicky

Alix to Nicky – 9 June
Dearest Nicky,

So many thanks for your dear letter, which gave me great pleasure. It was so kind of you to remember the Old Toad's Birthday. Yes, it does seem like a long time since we were at Petersburg.

Ella to Nicky – 19 June – St Petersburg
Darling Nicky,

The whole day I have been thinking and thinking about our conversation and your little note I have just received gave me such pleasure, most hearty thanks – of course I told Sergei, but nobody else will know a word of it. Do you know that I was told that if one prayed well in a church going to be consecrated, God would hear one's prayers – well, in Jerusalem and in Paul's house I prayed so deeply for you both to bring you together in love for each other – I wrote today to Alix and told her we had a long chat yesterday and also about her and that you recall with such *pleasure* the visit of this winter and the pleasure of having seen *her* and might I give you kind messages from her. More distinctively, I dared not say, you will do that once – God grant all will go well. Faith and love go very far and

---

[6] Grand Duke Pyotr Nikolaevich, son of Grand Duke Nicholas. He had just become engaged to Militsa, daughter of the King of Montenegro.

[7] Pelly I and Pelly II: private nicknames they gave to each other, Pelly I being Alix and Pelly II Nicky.

if you have in Him and each other all will be for the best. Many affectionate kisses from Sergei and your loving Aunty.

Nicky to Alix – October [no date] – St Petersburg

Just a line or two, darling Alix, as Toria[8] finished her letter on the other page to show the 'Goat' that I have not quite forgotten it.

I am also going to Greece for Tino's wedding[9] I am sure it will be charming. Passing through Kiel on my way to Hanover I lunched with dear Irène[10] at the Schloss and saw the sweet baby. How is the squirrel? So now goodbye, with best love

I remain your loving Nicky (one of the Pelly party)

Kiss Ernie from me!

Alix's dream

Now I am changed into the Baboon out of 'She', but never lonesome and have lovely gold curls. I am called Edward. Two men passing said, I gave him such hard strokes with my hammer across his head that he had to remain in the air. Then I hid.

---

[8] Victoria, daughter of the Prince and Princess of Wales, future King Edward VII and Queen Alexandra. She was a cousin of both Alix and Nicky.

[9] Nicky's cousin Constantine, crown prince and later King of Greece. He was marrying Sophie of Prussia, a sister of Kaiser Wilhelm.

[10] Alix's sister, married to Prince Henry of Prussia. The baby is her son Waldemar.

1891–1892

NICKY'S DREAMS; GIRLS

Nicky hopes to marry Alix one day despite her reluctance to change religion – Nicky's parents think it is about time for him to marry – Nicky writes of his love life

Nicky, Diary – 21 December 1891 – Gatchina
In the evening I sat with Mama and Aprak[1] discussing the family life of the young people of society today.

Inevitably this conversation touched the most sensitive string of my heart, and touched that *dream* and that *hope* I live with from day to day.

It is already a year and a half since I talked about it to Papa at Peterhof, and since then nothing has changed either for better or worse!

My dream – one day to marry Alix H[esse]. I have loved her for a long time, but more deeply and strongly since 1889 when she spent six weeks in Petersburg during the winter! For a long time I resisted my feelings, and tried to deceive myself about the impossibility of achieving my most cherished wish! But now that Eddy has withdrawn or been rejected,[2] the only obstacle or gulf between us – is the question of religion!

It is the one and only barrier; I am almost certain that our feelings are mutual! Everything is the will of God. Relying on His mercy I resign myself to the future with equanimity.

---

[1] Princess A. Obolensky (born Countess Apraksine), lady-in-waiting and close friend of the imperial family.

[2] Prince Albert Victor (Eddy), the Duke of Clarence, elder surviving son of the Prince of Wales, had, with his grandmother Queen Victoria's consent, asked Alix to marry him, but was turned down.

Nicky, Diary – 29 January 1892 – St Petersburg
While I was talking to Mama this morning she made several hints about Helene, the daughter of the Comte de Paris,[1] which puts me in an awkward position. I am at the crossing of two paths; I myself want to go in the other direction, while Mama obviously wants me to take this one! What will happen?

After tea I crept into Xenia's room and watched from behind the curtain as she had her gymnastic lesson with a certain young and attractive person.

1 April – Gatchina   Sandro's birthday, he is twenty-six! And I am following close on his heels, there are only two years between us.

I have noticed something very strange within myself: I never thought that two similar feelings, two loves could co-exist at one time within one heart.

I have already loved Alix H[esse] for three years and constantly hope to marry her one day, God willing! The following year I fell very much in love with Olga D,[2] but that however has now passed! And since the camp of 1890 until now I have been madly (platonically) in love with little K.[3] What a surprising thing our heart is! At the same time I never stop thinking of Alix!

Would it be right to conclude from all this that I am very amorous? To a certain extent: yes; but I must add that I am a severe judge and very choosy! This is the reason for the mood I described yesterday as not very pious.

---

[1] Hélène, second daughter of the Comte de Paris (Louis Philippe d'Orléans).
[2] Princess Olga Dolgorukaya, whom Nicky was in love with for a short time.
[3] Matilda Kshessinskaya, a famous Russian ballerina. Nicky was her first love.

1893

Nicky – Heir to the Russian throne

Alix – Princess of Hesse-Darmstadt

1893

A YEAR OF WEDDINGS

Nicky goes to Berlin for the marriage of Mossy (Margaret), youngest sister of Kaiser Wilhelm II of Germany, to Prince Friedrich Karl of Hesse-Kassel – Alix is also at the wedding, but Nicky never manages to speak to her – In June Nicky travels to London, for the marriage of his cousin George, Duke of York (the future King George V) to Princess May of Teck – Alix has been invited, but explains to her grandmother that the trip would be too expensive – Alix writes a letter of rejection to Nicky, saying she cannot change her religion – Nicky is devastated, but refuses to give up hope

Nicky, Diary – 10 January – St Petersburg
Family dinner, after which nearly everyone went to the ballet. In the evening I had a talk alone with Papa and Mama; I have been permitted to start finding out about Alix – when I am in Berlin! I never expected such a suggestion, especially not from Mama.

13 January – Berlin Got up at 9.30 and after coffee went visiting accompanied by my general. I only called in on Wilhelm and the Empress Victoria, with whom I found Vicky, Mossy and her fiancé. For the other princes and envoys I just left visiting cards. At four o'clock we all went to the castle for Mossy's wedding, and for this Wilhelm presented me with the order of the black eagle, and I had to put on a particularly uncomfortable red cloak – I nearly died of heat in it!

I saw Alix for the first time since the winter of 1889. For the procession to and from the church we walked three-abreast. I did not like the service. There was some singing, a little music from a string choir, the pastor gave a sermon – and that was it – there was nothing to convey that marriage is a sacrament! In the great hall, the newly-weds received congratulations in the most tiresome way: each lady and each man had to come up to them and bow – this pleasure lasted for two hours.

15 January   The Emperor's birthday. A whole crowd of princes, princesses and foreign guests went to the palace to present their con-gratulations.

After the reception of about half an hour, we all went to the same church for a service; the singing and the choir's silver trumpets were magnificent, only absolutely deafening under that cupola! I dropped in on the Anhalts where Henry, Irène, Ernie and Alix were having tea. At six there was a family dinner.

25 January – St Petersburg   In the evening I dashed off to see my M.K. [Matilda Kshessinskaya] and spent the best evening with her yet. I am still under her spell – the pen keeps trembling in my hand!

Alix to Queen Victoria – 2 June – Darmstadt
Darling Grandmama,

Many loving thanks for Your dear letter, I received yesterday. It is *too* kind of You asking me to come to the Wedding, but I fear it is impossible, as we have been about so much this year already, and as Ernie cannot stop very long in England, the journey would be scarcely worth the while for me, would it, and then it is so expensive also. A gentleman does not need so much luggage and really our journey to Italy and Ernie's official ones and Berlin were very expensive.

Excuse my writing so openly, but I thought it was only right You should know the reason of my not accepting your *awfully* kind invi-tation – and hope You will not mind it, and let me come perhaps next year with Ernie.

Nicky, Diary – 18 June – Marlborough House, London
In the morning we crossed over to the landing stage at Port Victoria, where a naval guard of honour was waiting. Colonel Clarke, Uncle Bertie's adjutant, arrived and is attached to us. At 10 o'clock we got into the train in full uniform and set off for London. It is the same wonderful hot weather as in Moscow.

An hour later we drew into Charing Cross. There we were met by: Uncle Bertie, Aunt Alix, Georgie, Louise, Victoria and Maud;[1] the Embassy and a guard of honour of the Scots Guards.

We went straight to Marlborough House, where I was given a cosy room upstairs between the girls and Georgie.

Two hours later Apapa, Amama[2] and Uncle Valdemar[3] arrived. It is wonderful to have so many of our family gathered together. All the Tecks came to lunch, and I met the bride – May[4] – whom I liked very much. We looked at the presents for her and Georgie which have been laid out in a corner room, an amazing amount of things!

At 4.30 I went to see Aunt Marie[5] at Clarence House and had tea in the garden with her, Uncle Alfred and Ducky.[6] Uncle Bertie has sent me a whole bevy of tailors, shoe makers and hatters! He is very funny in that respect, but he has always been extremely attentive and kind to me.

Aunt Alix is as sweet and wonderful as ever, but sorrow has left its mark on her; she is always dressed in black. Victoria has got much thinner and unfortunately does not look well; Maud on the other hand has put on weight. We had a family dinner at 8.30. At around 11 o'clock we went in uniform to a state ball at Buckingham Palace. The hall is magnificent, there were a mass of people I did not know, but not much in the way of attractive women!

19 June Slept wonderfully and took turns to have a bath, since there is only one between Uncle Valdemar, Georgie and I. After breakfast all together we drove round a good part of London; a wonderful town, I particularly liked Hyde Park, where there are a lot of people riding in the morning. At one o'clock I again changed into

---

[1] 'Uncle Bertie', Edward, Prince of Wales, eldest son of Queen Victoria and future King Edward VII; 'Aunt Alix', Alexandra, was the sister of Nicky's mother, the Empress Marie; 'Georgie', George, Duke of York, later King George V, second son of the Prince and Princess of Wales; Louise, Victoria and Maud were the daughters of Uncle Bertie and Aunt Alix.

[2] 'Apapa', King Christian IX of Denmark, and 'Amama', Queen Louise, Nicky's maternal grandparents.

[3] Prince of Denmark and brother of Empress Marie.

[4] May of Teck had previously been engaged to the Prince of Wales's elder surviving son, Eddy, who had himself been rejected by Alix. Eddy died of influenza at Sandringham early in 1892. Early in 1893 she became engaged to Eddy's younger brother, Georgie.

[5] Grand Duchess Maria Alexandrovna, daughter of Emperor Alexander II, who had married Queen Victoria's second son, Alfred, Duke of Edinburgh.

[6] Princess Victoria Melita of Edinburgh, daughter of Uncle Alfred and Aunt Marie.

full uniform, and set out with Uncle Alfred and the rest of the family for Windsor by train, to see the Queen. There was again a formal welcome: an escort of the King's own Dragoons, already familiar from India, and a guard of honour in the inner courtyard of the castle. A typical old building – the best of its kind.

The Queen – a round ball on unsteady legs – was remarkably kind to me. We lunched with her and the Battenbergs, the music was playing in the courtyard. She is attended by two Indians. Then she presented me with the Order of the Garter, which I certainly had not expected!

After taking my leave of her, I looked around the castle, and went into the chapel where poor Eddy's body has been laid to rest. Returned to London at 5 o'clock for tea. After dinner we went to the Drury Lane theatre. The Comédie Française were playing *Les Effrontés* – excellent. Uncle Bertie took Uncle Valdemar and I to the Marlborough Club, to which we were elected as members on the day of our arrival.

20 June Got up late, Uncle Valdemar and Georgie took turns to come and see me while I was lying in bed. After coffee I went with Aunt Marie to our church; the service and singing were very good, the choir having been sent from Paris. Read until luncheon.

The heat was terrible, the sun like some red spot and the air was hazy, presumably from the London fumes. At 2 o'clock we all gathered for luncheon at Uncle Alfred and Aunt Marie's. I made the acquaintance of the Mecklenburgs.[7] After changing into light clothes, we drove by carriage beyond the town. The outing turned out to be a long one, as we went to visit the Teck family at their residence – White Lodge. We had tea with them in the garden. People kept arriving the whole time to congratulate May. We returned to Marlborough House and an hour later set off for a family dinner with old man Cambridge.

A string orchestra was playing. Everyone finds a great resemblance between Georgie and myself – I am getting quite tired of hearing the same thing all the time.[8]

---

[7] Augusta, wife of Frederick, Grand Duke of Mecklenburg-Strelitz, was the sister of May of Teck's mother, Mary Adelaide, Duchess of Teck.

[8] Baroness Buxhoeveden, lady-in-waiting to Alix, recorded in her memoirs that the likeness was such that at a garden party many guests shook Nicky warmly by the hand, taking him for his cousin the bridegroom. 'The greatest joke, however, was when one of the gentlemen of the Court made the contrary mistake, and coming up to the Duke, whom he took for the Tsarevich [Nicky], begged him not to be late for the wedding the next day.'

21 June After coffee, had my picture taken with Georgie in the garden. At about 11 o'clock went into town with Clarke in a 'handsome' – a splendid vehicle – to look at the sights of London. We saw Westminster Abbey, St Paul's Cathedral and the Tower. We returned home just in time for luncheon.

Visited Georgie's new home, where he will live as a married man – St James's Palace; the rooms are not yet completely furnished. From the outside the building looks like a prison. After that I went with Uncle Bertie and Uncle Valdemar to Hurlingham Park, where there is a club and every possible outdoor activity and game: polo, lawn-tennis, cricket, clay pigeon shooting etc., I was fascinated to watch the first of these games, it reminded me of India. At 8.30 there was a dinner at our Embassy with Staal,[9] and afterwards a reception upstairs, what they call here a 'party' – what a crush, not to mention the heat. Luckily it did not last too long.

25 June The day was even hotter than yesterday. I went with Uncle Bertie to Buckingham Palace to say goodbye to the Queen. At about two I went with him to have luncheon with the Marquess of Londonderry. There were quite a lot of people and a string orchestra was playing. The house is not big, but the rooms are beautiful and filled with a mass of magnificent pictures and objects. Our hostess was delightful but a terrible flirt. We left soaked through as we had been sitting in frock coats. Half an hour later I set off with Clarke for the House of Lords and the House of Commons. I heard Gladstone[10] speaking in the latter. Returned home for tea and then went riding in the garden on three-wheeled bicycles with Victoria and Uncle Valdemar. At 8 o'clock went to dine with Fife.[11] A lot more people arrived during the evening and there was a concert. Returned home at 12.30.

26 June It was still very stuffy in the morning. After coffee I received: Lord Rosebery, Mackenzie Wallace and said goodbye to Uncle Alfred. At 12.43 we all (that is the inhabitants of Marlborough House) set off for the City in state coaches with an escort of the Blues. The Lord Mayor met us at the entrance, surrounded by his aldermen in wigs and the most amazing gowns.

In the council chamber he gave a speech for Apapa on the freedom

---

[9] Russian Ambassador.
[10] W. E. Gladstone, enjoying his fourth term as Prime Minister.
[11] The Duke of Fife married Louise, daughter of Edward VII.

of the City, but I simply could not understand what it was. Then we went to another hall, where luncheon was laid for 700 people. After a very bad meal there were toasts; for the first time in my life I had to make quite a long speech, in English of course; they clapped loudly and banged their knives to show their spontaneous appreciation – I was dripping with sweat – but then I was dressed in a cossack coat. Luckily we returned sooner than expected and at around 4 o'clock, in the simplest clothes, we set off in two cabs – I with Victoria and Uncle Valdemar with Maud – to see Captain Boyton's World's Watershow for a second time. We dined and then went to the opera at Covent Garden theatre, where there was a gala performance. The Reshke brothers were singing. It dragged on until 12 o'clock.

28 June   Got up early in order to have time to put away my last things. At 10 o'clock the whole family gathered for breakfast, and an hour later I was accompanied to the station by Apapa and all the Waleses.

I took the same way back to Port Victoria. I took my leave of Clarke on the yacht, and when the luggage had been loaded, we started up and passed out into the sea.

It was remarkably calm, the sun was warm and in general the crossing was remarkably good. We met a mass of ships. I read a lot to dispel my sadness.

26 October – St Petersburg
A great misfortune happened yesterday – our wonderful composer Tchaikovsky died!

Nicky to Alix – 31 October – Gatchina
Dearest Alix

Please excuse this boldness of mine of writing a few lines to tell you how sorry I was and how I deeply regret not to have been able to come and see you while Ella stayed with you. But after our returning from Denmark, a lot of important matters – one about Georgy [brother] – who luckily is quite well now, kept me back from going. You may well imagine my disappointment at losing such a splendid and easy chance of flying off to [you], after such a long long time ...

Berlin and all those ceremonies and functions for Mossy [Margaret of Prussia]'s wedding, where we generally used to be about half a mile off from each other, cannot be called a pleasant meeting. And for you poor thing especially it must be of a disagreeable recollection, as you suffered so from an ear-ache!

I do hope you are quite well and that awful pain has not come back.

If you don't mind wouldn't you send me a photo of yours, one of the new ones, like those you sent to Xenia lately? I would be so happy to have one near me. Whenever I look into our garden at Anichkov I always think of that lovely time on the ice, which seems now to be a dream.

And now goodbye my darling Pelly. God bless you and help you in all the troubles of life.

Ever your devoted Nicky

Alix to Xenia – 8 November – Darmstadt
Darling Xenia

A good kiss and fondest thanks for your dear letter.

It was such a pleasure hearing again from you. Yes, do continue writing to me, don't let what I am going to tell you, put a stop to our friendship and correspondence. My photo and a letter I have sent through Ella to Nicky. In it he will see, that I cannot change my decision, – I cannot become untrue to my own confession – do not believe that my love is less, why that has made it so far more hard and difficult to me, and I have been torturing myself. To hurt one whom one loves is fearful, and yet I don't want him to go on hoping, as I can *never* change my Religion. God bless the dear, and may he not think ill of his old Pelly. I feel too upset to write any more.

Your old Alix

Let me hear sometimes from you, may I? Don't let us quite drift apart, that would be too hard.

Alix to Nicky – 8 November – Darmstadt
Dearest Nicky,

I send you my very best thanks for your dear letter, and enclose the photograph you wished to have and which Ella will forward to you.

I believe it must have been a stronger will than ours which ordained that we should not meet at Coburg, for like this it gives me the chance to write to you all my innermost feelings which perhaps on the spur of the moment I might not have said, so that you may have misunderstood me.

You know what my feelings are as Ella has told them to you already, but I feel it my duty to tell them to you myself. I thought everything for a long time, and I only beg you not to think that I take it lightly for it grieves me terribly and makes me very unhappy.

I have tried to look at it in every light that is possible, but I always return to one thing. I cannot do it against my conscience. You, dear Nicky, who have also such a strong belief will understand me that I think it is a sin to change my belief, and I should be miserable all the days of my life, knowing that I had done a wrongful thing.

I am certain that you would not wish me to change against my conviction. What happiness can come from a marriage which begins without the real blessing of God? For I feel it a sin to change that belief in which I have been brought up and which I love. I should never find my peace of mind again, and like that I should never be your real companion who should help you on in life; for there always should be something between us two, in my not having the real conviction of the belief I had taken, and in the regret for the one I *had* left.

It would be acting a lie to you, your Religion and to God. This is my feeling of right and wrong, and one's innermost religious convictions and one's peace of conscience toward God before all one's earthly wishes. As all these years have not made it possible for me to change my resolution in acting thus, I feel that now is the moment to tell you again that I can *never* change my confession.

I am certain that you will understand this clearly and see as I do, that we are only torturing ourselves, about something impossible and it would not be a kindness to let you go on having vain hopes, which will never be realized.

And now Goodbye my darling Nicky, and may God bless and protect you.

Ever your loving Alix

Nicky, Diary – 17 November – St Petersburg

We left Ropsha in wonderful weather and complete stillness. There were 3 degrees of frost. I killed: 1 black grouse, 2 white partridges (for the first time), 6 grey hares and 8 white hares – 17 in all. The whole result was much inferior to previous times – 285 pieces.

Changed at Sandro's, dined with Uncle Misha [Sandro's father] and then went to see a marvellous *Sleeping Beauty*; it was danced by M. Kshessinskaya. At night there was fog.

18 November This morning I opened the packet which had been lying on my table since last night, and in a letter from Alix from Darmstadt I learned that everything is over between us – it is impossible for her to change religion, and all my hopes are shattered by this implacable obstacle, my best dreams and my most cherished wishes for the future. Such a short time ago, I perceived it as bright, attractive and imminently attainable – yet now it appears indifferent!!!

Yes, it is hard sometimes to submit to the will of God! All day I went about in a daze, it is terribly difficult to appear calm and carefree when the question affecting your whole future life is suddenly decided in this way!

The weather during our walk corresponded to my state of being: it was thawing and a gale was blowing. We dined downstairs.

25 November At eight o'clock went to the first battery of His Majesty's, for their celebration dinner. The singers and the gypsies took turns.

26 November To my surprise I got up feeling quite fresh, and that after a four-day binge!

7 December Woke up at 11.30. For a long time could not decide whether to go to the Council of State or not. All the same I went – and for this reason stayed in town. At 3 o'clock left for the regiment, having wormed my way out of the Committee of Ministers.

15 December Slept late. Found out that the Cavalry Guard had left at 9 o'clock in the morning. The weather is not brilliant for the crossing: 4 degrees of frost and a strong wind blowing straight into their faces. Went to *Petersburg* at 5 o'clock; had tea with Aprak in the train. Dined at 7 o'clock at Countess Vorontsov's. We sat down to a game of 'poker'; and then were joined by the Trubetskoys and Ferden. All the old friends are already married!!! Returned to Anichkov for the night.

17 December Walked in the menagerie. It was warm but terribly dark. After tea, with my face in a sweat, I finished a letter to Alix – in answer to the letter, in which I received her refusal! We dined upstairs at 8 o'clock – the same people as at luncheon.

We listened to the string orchestra in the arsenal – they played divinely. Uncle Alexei came in the evening – we played *makashka* [*macao*, card game].

Nicky to Alix – 17 December – Gatchina
My dearest Alix

Please excuse my not having answered your letter sooner, but you may well imagine what a blow it proved to me.

I could not write to you all these days on account of the sad state of mind I was in. Now that my restlessness has passed I feel more calm and am able to answer your letter quietly. Let me thank you first of all for the frank and open way in which you spoke to me in that letter! There is nothing worse in the world than things misunderstood and not brought to the point.

I knew from the beginning what an obstacle there rose between us and I felt so deeply for you all these years, knowing perfectly the great difficulties you would have had to overcome! But still it is so awfully hard, when you have cherished a dream for many a year and think – now you are near to its being realized – then suddenly the curtain is drawn and – you see only an empty space and feel oh! so lonely and so beaten down!!

I cannot deny the reasons you give me, dear Alix; but I have got one which is also true: you hardly know the depth of our religion. If you only could have learnt it with somebody, who knows it, and could have read books, where you might see the likeness and difference of the two – perhaps then! it would not have troubled you in the same way as it does now!

Your living quite alone without anyone's help in such a matter, is also a sad circumstance in the barrier that apparently stands between us! It is too sad for words to know that that barrier is – religion!

Don't you think, dearest, that the five years, since we know each other, have passed in vain and with no result? Certainly not – for me at least. And how am I to change my feelings after waiting and wishing for so long, even now after that sad letter you sent me? I trust in God's mercy; maybe it is His will that we both, but you especially should suffer long – maybe after helping us through all these miseries and trials – He will yet guide my darling along the path that I daily pray for!

Oh! do not say 'no' directly, my dearest Alix, do not ruin my life already! Do you think there can exist any happiness in the whole world without you! After having *involuntarily!* kept me waiting and hoping, can this end in such a way?

Oh! do not get angry with me if I am beginning to say silly things, though I promised in this letter to be calm! Your heart is too kind not to understand what tortures I am going through now.

But I have spoken enough and must end this epistle of mine. Thank you so much for your charming photo.

Let me wish, dearest Alix, that the coming Year may bring you peace, happiness, comfort and the fulfilment of your wishes. God bless you and protect you!

                                        Ever your loving and devoted Nicky

Alix to Queen Victoria – 26 December – Königliches Schloss, Kiel
My darling Grandmama,

I cannot help always dreading the coming of the New Year, as one never knows what is in store for one, God grant that it may be full of joy and happiness for my darling Ernie and the sweet little Wife whom he is soon going to fetch.[12] Now I long for my precious One[13] more than ever, how happy he would have been to see Ernie happy, and what a comfort it would have been to me, as life indeed will be very different for me, as I shall be feeling myself *de trop*. But I must not bother You with a long letter, as I am sure You have a lot to do.

Kissing Your dear hand most tenderly, and again wish you much joy,

I remain, Darling Grandmama dear,

Ever Your very loving, grateful and dutiful Child, Alix.

Nicky, Diary – 31 December – Gatchina
We saw the new Year in with Mama. For this, and according to the twenty-seven-year-old custom, a hot punch was served with apple pies.

And so each of us, like it or not, has to add yet another year to their life. I have to say in conclusion that 1893 passed off well, thank God, but that personally I had hoped no longer to be a bachelor by now. But everything is the will of God Almighty alone.

---

[12] Princess Victoria Melita, daughter of Alfred, Duke of Saxe-Coburg-Gotha (the Duke of Edinburgh, second son of Queen Victoria) and his wife Maria of Russia, sister of Emperor Alexander III.

[13] Ludwig IV, Grand Duke of Hesse-Darmstadt, had died the previous year aged fifty-five.

1894

Nicky – Heir to the Russian throne

Alix – Princess of Hesse-Darmstadt

Emperor Alexander III – Nicky's father

Empress Marie – Nicky's mother

Xenia – Grand Duchess Xenia, Nicky's sister

Sandro – Grand Duke Alexander Mikhailovich, Nicky's best friend

Olga – Grand Duchess Olga Alexandrovna, Nicky's youngest sister

Georgy – Grand Duke Georgy Alexandrovich, Nicky's brother

Ella – Grand Duchess Elizabeth, Alix's elder sister

KR (Kostia) – Grand Duke Konstantin Romanov, Nicky's cousin, Head of Regiment and well-known poet; his *nom-de-plume* was KR

Queen Victoria – of England

Georgie – George, Duke of York, later King George V of England, first cousin of both Nicky and Alix

Willy – Kaiser Wilhelm II of Germany

1894

ENGAGEMENT, DEATH IN THE FAMILY, MARRIAGE

Nicky's parents at last consent to Xenia's betrothal to Sandro – Alix's brother Ernie is to marry Victoria Melita ('Ducky'), daughter of Alfred Duke of Edinburgh and Grand Duchess Marie of Russia – Alix accepts Nicky's proposal – Nicky and Alix spend twelve days together – Nicky returns to Russia, while Alix goes to England to stay with her grandmother Queen Victoria – They arrange to meet in England where they spend an idyllic month – On his return journey Nicky stops in Denmark to visit his grandparents – The wedding of Xenia and Sandro takes place in July at Peterhof – Nicky's father is unwell – Nicky abandons plans to join Alix in Germany and accompanies his parents to the Crimea, where his father's health continues to decline – Emperor Alexander III dies a few days later on 20 October – Nicky is now Emperor – Two days later Alix is received into the Orthodox Church – The late Emperor's body is conveyed back to St Petersburg – Nicky and Alix are married shortly after the funeral – Overwhelmed by the responsibilities of his new rank, Nicky finds support and comfort in his wife

Nicky, Diary – 12 January – St Petersburg
A beautiful, wonderful day! What a difference between the morning and the evening. At 11 o'clock went as usual to the battalion. Uncle Misha [Sandro's father] had luncheon with us. After this, when we had left, he asked Papa and Mama for Xenia's hand on behalf of Sandro. It all turned out in the best possible way: Papa and Mama

consented. At 4.30 Sandro came to see Xenia and they went up together to see Papa and Mama. Uncle Misha was sitting with me at the time. We also went up and blessed them there in the bedroom by the icons.

After an agonizing wait of three years, Xenia and Sandro's engagement happened in such an unexpected way. I am thrilled! They both look very happy. Telegrams flew to all corners of the world.

At 7.30 we went to church and then had dinner with the Mikhailoviches.[1] In the evening the bride and groom (strange to write it thus) stayed alone with Mama. Uncle Vladimir dragged me to supper in a new club where I got rather tipsy!

Sandro, Memoirs
'When are you going to be married?' father asked me on my return to St Petersburg.

'I have to wait for a definite answer from the Emperor and the Empress.'

'Waiting and travelling seems the best you can do nowadays,' said father impatiently. 'Positively ridiculous! You must settle down. A full year has passed since you have talked to the Emperor. Go and see him again. Tell him you wish to have a definite answer.'

'I won't do that, father. I would not think of annoying the Emperor. He may get very cross with me.'

'Very well, Sandro. If such is the case, I am going to handle this matter in my own way.'

I knew the Empress. She hated to be contradicted or rushed, and I feared she might say 'no' in a manner precluding any further attempts on my part.

I remember having broken a dozen pencils in father's study awaiting his return. It seemed hours and hours since he left the house.

A bell rang in the room of father's valet, then I heard the familiar firm steps ... He nearly choked me in his arms.

'Everything is arranged. You are to go and see Xenia at half past four this afternoon.'

'What did the Empress say? Was she furious?'

'Furious? It is too mild a word to describe her rage ... She said I was trying to break her happiness. That I had no right to steal her daughter. That she would never speak to me again.'

---

[1] Mikhailovich, family name for all the offspring of Grand Duke Mikhail Nikolaevich, for example Sandro, Nikolai, Sergei, Miche-Miche, Georgy.

After so many years spent in timid hopes of marrying Xenia, I was stunned by the suddenness with which my dream had become a reality.

At quarter past four I entered the Anichkov Palace. I could not wait any longer. I looked at the guardsmen on duty and blushed. I had a feeling they already knew of my happiness.

Xenia's valet sat in a chair reading the newspaper.

'Will you please announce me to Her Imperial Highness.'

[He] opened his eyes in astonishment. It was something new for him as I always went in unannounced. Only yesterday we all had a gay tea party in this beautifully furnished room, but today everything seemed different. I stood watching the door of Xenia's bedroom. 'How funny,' I thought, 'that she should make me wait so long.' She came in with her eyes fixed on the floor. A simple white silk blouse, blue skirt, brown stockings and brown shoes. She stopped in front of the window next to the door and waited. I took her hand and led her toward two large soft chairs. We talked in a whisper. I think we both talked at the same time. We used to kiss each other before but those were cousins' kisses. Now it was a kiss of possession.

The day of our wedding was set for the end of July. I tried to argue against this delay of nearly six months but was told to keep quiet and pray to God that the dressmakers would deliver Xenia's trousseau by that time. The honeymoon was to be spent in my beloved Ai-Todor, left to me in mother's will.

Olga (sister), Memoirs

It was my father's fault. He would not even have Nicky sit in Council of State until 1893. I can't tell you why. I know how my father disliked the mere idea of state matters encroaching on our family life – but, after all, Nicky was his heir. And what a ghastly price was later paid for the mistake. Of course, my father had always enjoyed an athlete's health.

Nicky, Diary – 17 January – St Petersburg

Thank God, we were able to breathe again today: Papa is better! This morning his temperature was the same as yesterday evening; his eyes and face had a more normal expression. During the day, Papa fell asleep twice. I was able to leave the house for an hour and a half.

I visited the regiment and the Council of State. The day was sunny.

At Papa's request I read a report and orders from the Ministry of Defence. After going for a walk we had tea upstairs and then sat with Papa for quite a long time. From time to time he had violent attacks of coughing; with this he brought up a lot of phlegm. Temp. was 38.1.

24 January   In honour of Xenia's name day I wore the uniform of the Guards Corps to church. All the close family were at the service; there were relatively few guests and ladies. For the first time since Papa's illness, there was music at luncheon in both reception rooms. Read a navy report, as Papa is still not back at work. Went for a drive with Xenia. It was warm, but snow was falling. After tea looked through the post and papers of the Siberian Committee.

Had supper with Sandro and Kotia Obolensky (on duty); they have recently returned from France. The three of us played hide and seek like little children. We had tea with Mama.

26 January   Slept like the dead; Sergei[2] told some details about myself which made me laugh terribly. I have to admit I did not feel at all well this morning.

Sat at luncheon but did not touch anything; nor did Sandro. For my misfortune there was a reception today and I had to go through this ordeal, after which I went to sleep.

Got up at tea time feeling alert and hungry, and then had some *zakuski*. At 8 o'clock I went with Mama, Xenia and Sandro to the theatre. It was Leniana's benefit performance in a wonderful *Coppélia*. The uncles and I took her a brooch.

Escorted Xenia home and then went on to supper with Montebello.[3] The company consisted of the very best ladies of the capital. We again sang Hungarian songs, but not the same ones as yesterday. Returned home at 2 o'clock.

21 February   Went to the regiment in the morning and had luncheon there. The meeting of the Council of State did not last long.

The weather was foul, frost and no snow. Did not feel like going out at all. Wrote out all the tactical exercises – a real bore.

In the evening I dressed up as a falconer from the time of Alexei Mikhailovich,[4] Xenia as a boyar's lady, and Sandro as a

---

[2] Sandro's brother, Grand Duke Sergei Mikhailovich, Nicky's friend.

[3] French Ambassador to St Petersburg.

[4] Russian Tsar of the seventeenth century and father of Peter the Great.

strelets[5] commander. We went together to the costume ball given by Count Sheremetev ('the fireman').

At first they said that everyone had to wear masks, but when the ball began we took them off – indeed, they do not go with many costumes. Danced the mazurka with the lovely Vestphalen; Mama left after supper, while I stayed on to dance the cotillion.

I sat until 4.30 cooling down with a few glasses of champagne. I was very satisfied with my costume. Xenia gave me the good idea, and it is very well made as well as being extremely comfortable!

24 February   At 11 o'clock went to the official photographer in the Marinsky Theatre and had my picture taken in my falconer costume after Sergei. After that we had a group photograph in frock-coats. For luncheon: Sandro and the Vorontsovs. At 2 o'clock went to the ballet. There was a wonderful *Sleeping Beauty* with M. Kshessinskaya. After going for a drive, returned home for tea. Read.

We then went to the Winter Palace for the second concert ball, which was very friendly and gay, because everyone has already had time to dance together and get to know each other! Returned from the Winter (Palace) at 2.30.

27 February   At 1 o'clock I flew to put in an appearance at the ballet. They were doing *Coppélia*. I was not even able to stay to the end and had to leave before the third act. In the Anichkov the *folle journée* started. Sandro and I called ourselves martyrs, as in all honesty dancing for nine hours in a row is no joke!

At 6.30 we sat down to dinner and then, after an interval of half an hour, the second ball started up with renewed vigour and energy. I was disappointed by the boring sample of the female sex. Supper ended at 1 o'clock at night and the season faded into oblivion.

8 March   It was a wonderful day. I went to a soirée at Aunt Michen's.[6] It was the most elegant gathering – nine ladies and slightly more men. A choir of 70 gypsies sang. They drank well, and they all had to keep up with each other. I had a lot of fun and I chatted a lot with Countess Pototsky. At 2 o'clock we went downstairs to supper and continued talking as dawn was breaking.

---

[5] A soldier in the Russian regular army of the sixteenth and seventeenth centuries.

[6] Grand Duchess Maria Pavlovna, wife of Nicky's uncle Vladimir.

11 March Slept well. Went to the regiment at 11 o'clock, and was present for the end of the company's activities.

Having lost at billiards, I returned home to luncheon with Aunt Katia, whose dress was exactly the same as that of Margarita in *Mephistopheles*! Received people and then went for a drive with Xenia. Understandably there were a lot of people; everyone came out to warm themselves in the sun.

At 9 o'clock went to a German play at the Alexandrinsky theatre; Mama, Xenia and Sandro were already sitting there. Uncle Vladimir, Aunt Michen and their sons also. Sandro and I got very tired of the German play, but luckily it ended and we immediately went home.

25 March Woke up to a lovely warm day. Xenia is already nineteen, it does not seem so long ago that I was the same age!

Took her a bouquet from the Preobrajensky, together with the regimental adjutant. Went to church at 10.30; it was terribly hot inside.

At 4 o'clock went to visit Uncle Alexei, having bought 20 birds and which were let loose from their cage into the garden; all the Uncles also brought birds with them. This custom is carried out every year for the Annunciation in the Adjutant-General's garden. Having drunk Hungarian wine instead of tea, I returned home and then went with Xenia to the Vorontsovs. After we had left they all went to the country. Slept until 8 o'clock. Had some *zakuski* with Sandro and Kostia [KR] (on duty). Went with them to the cavalry gala supper. Thanks to the presence of the gypsies the time passed quickly.

Alix to Xenia – 30 March – Darmstadt
Darling Xenia

A tender kiss, best thanks for your dear letter and the charming photos. It seems too funny to think that you are about to be married – God bless you, my sweet Child, and may you have every possible happiness.

Darling, why did you speak about *that* subject, which we never wanted to mention again? It is cruel as you know it *never* can be – all along I have said so, do you think it is not already hard enough, to know you are hurting first the person whom of all others you would long to please. But it cannot be – he knows it – and so do not I pray you, speak of it again. I know Ella will begin again, but what is the good of it, and it is cruel always to say I am ruining his life – can I help it, when to make him happy I should be committing a sin in my conscience. It is hard enough as it is, and beginning about it again is so unkind – You, who have found what your heart has desired, think only kindly of me, tho' I am grieving you too.

One worry and sorrow follows the other – in 5 days we are off to Coburg for Ernie's wedding[7] – what my feelings are you can imagine. God grant they may be happy – she is such a dear.

I am going to England for two or three months, as I would only be in their way here. The heat is great, but everything is so green and lovely and all the fruit trees in bloom – too beautiful, we spend many hours in the woods.

Goodbye, my little Chicken, many a loving kiss from your ever devoted old Alix.

Best love to Sandro.

Nicky, Diary – 2 April – Gatchina

Ideal weather. Went for a walk with Mama, Xenia and Sandro. The three of us went boating and revelled in the tranquillity and the quiet air. It was possible to sit with the windows open. At 3 o'clock we again went out round the lake and got into various boats. We were very successful at breaking up the ice and pulled large blocks into the middle of the lake. We had tea at 5 o'clock. At 10 o'clock I said goodbye to dear Papa and Mama and went with Sandro to the station. The train had already arrived from town with Uncle Vladimir, Aunt Michen, Uncle Sergei, Aunt Ella, Uncle Pavel and their ladies-in-waiting and adjutants. At 10.30 we set off for Coburg. We had supper; it was very pleasant to travel in the dining car in such company.

KR, Diary – 3 April

Here I learnt from the Empress that on the day of Nicky's departure Xenia received a telegram from Alix in which she warned that she remained adamant, that is to say that she did not agree to convert to Orthodoxy.

Nicky was very upset and wanted to stay, but the Empress insisted that he go. She advised him to turn for help to Queen Victoria, who has a great influence on her granddaughter.

---

[7] The marriage of Alix's brother Ernie to Nicky's cousin Ducky took place at Coburg, the family seat of the Dukes of Saxe-Coburg-Gotha in southern Germany. Ducky's father, Alfred, Duke of Edinburgh, had assumed the title of Duke of Saxe-Coburg-Gotha in 1893.

Nicky, Diary – 3 April – Imperial train
It was very hot in the compartment. I sweated and read a lot. At 6.30 we arrived at the border and flew ahead at full steam in three sleeping cars: Uncle Vladimir and Aunt Michen, Uncle Sergei and Aunt Ella, Uncle Pavel and I, all with our adjutants and staff. In Königsberg we had our *zakuska* on the train.

4 April – Coburg   Was still sleeping when we went through Berlin. It was another wonderful day and we were boiling in the train. We had luncheon at a station in Bavaria. Got dressed in my uniform half an hour before arrival and at five o'clock we drew into Coburg.

There was a whole welcoming committee at the station, Uncle Alfred, Aunt Marie,[8] Alix, Ernie, Missy,[9] Ducky, Alfred[10] and other less exalted persons, the guard of honour was from the local battalion of the 95th regiment: after the review and the presentation of various personages, we were driven by carriage to the Schloss, where we were put next to each other in magnificent apartments. The burgomaster made a very amiable speech in the street; the populace received us well, perhaps the accord with Germany has something to do with it. Having unpacked my things, I went to Aunt Marie and Uncle Alfred's charming house for a family dinner. Afterwards we walked to the theatre, where we saw an excellent operetta *Vogelhändler*. Sat a little with Aunt Marie and returned at 12 o'clock.

5 April   My God! What a day! After coffee Ernie and Alix came to Aunt Ella's rooms. She has grown noticeably prettier, but looked extremely sad. They left us alone together, and then we began the conversation which I have so longed for and yet so feared. We talked until 12 o'clock, but without success, she is still against changing religion.

She cried a lot, poor thing. We parted feeling calmer. Went to luncheon with Aunt Marie.

Went with Auntie and Uncle Sergei to visit the widowed Duchess,[11] the sister of Aunt Olga F,[12] who lives in a beautiful castle outside the

---

[8] Wife of Uncle Alfred, born Grand Duchess Maria Alexandrovna of Russia, Nicky's aunt.

[9] Marie ('Missy'), eldest daughter of Uncle Alfred and Aunt Marie.

[10] Son of Uncle Alfred and Aunt Marie and heir to the dukedom of Saxe-Coburg-Gotha.

[11] The widow of Ernst II, Duke of Saxe-Coburg-Gotha, born Princess of Baden.

[12] Sandro's mother, Grand Duchess Olga Feodorovna, born Princess Olga of Baden.

town, and also Philip of Coburg[13] and his wife. Walked up the hill
with Uncle Vladimir towards the old fortress.

Queen Victoria arrived with great pomp: a squadron of her dragoon guards in front and a whole battalion behind the carriage as
guard of honour. They all trooped past her on the square with Uncle
Alfred at their head. We all watched in full uniform from the windows of her own rooms. Having presented ourselves to her, we
returned to our quarters for tea. Half the family dined with her at 9
o'clock and the rest with Aunt Marie at 7 o'clock. We went to the theatre, where an amusing play *Das Stiftungsfest* was being given. We sat
in the billiard room for a while and then went home. I am weary to
my bones today.

6 April Got up early and walked up the same hill with Uncle
Vladimir right to the fortress, whose castle has been transformed into
a museum of ancient armoury. Returned and had coffee in our communal drawing room. Alix then arrived.

I touched as little as possible on yesterday's question, it was
enough she still agreed to see me and talk to me. We went to have
luncheon with Aunt Marie, the others had to wait until two for luncheon with the Queen.

Meeting again after a short wait, we went in two carriages to
Rosenau, which belongs to Uncle Alfred. There we walked, visited the
orangerie and the house itself, and had tea on the grass next to the
lawn-tennis. We had a good laugh when the chief footman was at
last persuaded to sing two or three songs; he started in the tower and
ended behind the bushes.

On the return journey we met the Queen, Empress Frederick, and
Beatrice.[14] Everyone got out and embraced on the road. Having
changed into Prussian uniforms, we went to the station to meet
Wilhelm [Kaiser Willy]. He arrived at 6 o'clock and also moved into
our castle.

At 8 o'clock we gathered for a family dinner; after which there was
a performance upstairs; they put on two beautifully acted plays, the
tiny stage was in one of the halls. We all dispersed after having tea
together. Wilhelm sat with us until 1 o'clock.

---

[13] Brother of the future King Ferdinand of Bulgaria.
[14] Empress Frederick, otherwise Princess Victoria, eldest daughter of Queen
Victoria. Widow of the German Emperor, Frederick III. Their son Willy was now
Emperor Wilhelm II. Princess Beatrice, Queen Victoria's youngest daughter, mar-
ried to Prince Henry of Battenberg ('Liko'), was mother of the future Queen of
Spain.

7 April   The day of Ernie and Ducky's wedding. I began by being half an hour late for breakfast at Aunt Marie's, where the whole family had gathered, and I had to walk alone in front of the crowd in the square. We all gathered in the upstairs galleries, and after the civil marriage contract had been signed, we went to the church. The service did not last long. Ernie and Ducky make a lovely couple. The pastor gave a splendid sermon, which surprisingly went straight to the heart of my own problem. At that moment I terribly wanted to be able to look into Alix's soul! After the wedding there was a family luncheon, and the young couple left for Darmstadt. Went for a walk with Uncle Vladimir; in the end we reached the fortress and made a detailed tour of the armoury museum. We had just arrived home when a storm broke and it poured with rain all night. We dined with Aunt Marie, in uniform because of the Emperor, who never wears civilian clothes, and then walked, or rather ran because of the downpour, to the theatre. They were performing the first act of *The Clowns* and a good play. Drank beer and champagne in the billiard room.

8 April – Coburg   A wonderful, unforgettable day in my life – the day of my betrothal to my dear beloved Alix. She came to Aunt Michen after 10 o'clock, and after they had talked, she and I had our discussion.

God, what a mountain has fallen from my shoulders; with what joy have I been able to delight dear Papa and Mama! I spent the whole day in a haze, not quite knowing what had happened to me!

Wilhelm sat in the next room with the uncles and aunts and waited for the outcome of our talk. I have just been with Alix to the Queen and from there to Aunt Marie's, where for a long while the whole family embraced each other in joy.

After luncheon we went to Aunt Marie's church for a service of thanksgiving.[15] Then we all went to Rosenau, where a ball had been arranged for the little baby 'Bee', on the occasion of her birthday. I did not feel like dancing, but walked and talked in the garden with my bride. I still cannot believe that I have a bride. Returned home at 6.15. There was already a pile of telegrams. We had dinner. We drove to the illuminations and then went upstairs for a court concert. The Bavarian regimental string orchestra played brilliantly. In the evening we sat again together in our sitting room.

---

[15]   Marie, Duchess of Edinburgh, sister of Tsar Alexander III. She remained Orthodox and therefore had her own private chapel.

9 April This morning the Queen's dragoon guards played a whole programme under my windows – very touching! At 10 o'clock wonderful Alix arrived and we went together to have coffee with the Queen. The day was cold and grey but our souls were light and joyful. At Uncle Bertie's insistence the whole family posed in a group in the garden. After lunch, I sat with Alix answering telegrams. We went together by char-à-banc to Rosenau. I drove.

What a delight! It was not particularly fun there, we just wandered around not knowing what to do, while at home there were goodness knows how many telegrams. On the other hand I did not move from Alix's side, so I should not complain, except perhaps for the cold. Returned home in time for Palm-Saturday vespers. I again sat with my bride, because of which I was nearly late for dinner with the Queen. We wore evening dress as Wilhelm had already left. In the evening there was another court concert. Sat together until 1 o'clock.

George, Duke of York to Nicky – 9 April – York Cottage, Sandringham

My dear, old Nicky!

I wish you and dear Alix every possible joy and happiness now and in the future. I am indeed delighted to think that everything is settled at last and that the great wish of your heart is at last accomplished, as I well know that for some years you have loved Alix and wished to marry her. I am quite certain, that she will make you an excellent wife and she is charming, lovely and accomplished.

I am also so glad that your engagement has taken place at Coburg and I know it will have given Grandmama the greatest possible pleasure to be present on this happy occasion, she is very fond of Alix and has always told me how much she hoped that some day she would marry you. So Ernie and Ducky are married and Xenia and Sandro are engaged, what a lot of weddings there will be this year, you are all following my good example you see.

God bless you, dear Nicky.

Ever your most loving cousin Georgie.

Nicky to Empress Marie – 10 April – Palais Edinburg, Coburg

My dearest darling Mama

I do not know how to start this letter, as there is so much I want to say that the thoughts are all mixed up in my head. So this is how my affair turned out, thanks to the mercy of our Lord God, when I was convinced the outcome was completely hopeless!

The day after our arrival here, I had a long and extremely difficult conversation with Alix, during which I tried to explain to her that she could not do otherwise than to give her consent! She was crying the whole time, and only answered from time to time in a whisper: 'No! I cannot.'

I just kept on repeating and insisting on what I had already said earlier. Although this conversation went on for more than two hours, it ended in nothing, because neither of us would give in to the other.

The next morning we talked more calmly; I gave her your letter and after that she could not say anything. This was already a sign for me of the final stage of the conflict which had arisen within her from our first conversation. The marriage of Ernie and Ducky was the final drop in her cup of suffering and hesitations. She decided to talk to Aunt Michen; this was also Ernie's advice. As he was leaving, he whispered to me that there was hope of a happy outcome.

I have to say here that during the whole of those three days I suffered terrible anxiety; all the relatives kept asking me in confidence about her and, expressing their sympathy in the most touching way, wished me all the best. But all this provoked in me even greater fears and doubts that perhaps things would not be resolved.

The Emperor [Wilhelm] also tried, he even had a talk with Alix and on that morning of 8th April brought her to us at home. She then went to Aunt Michen and soon afterwards came into the room where I was sitting with the Uncles, Aunt Ella and Wilhelm. They left us alone and ... the first thing she said was ... that she agreed! Oh God, what happened to me then! I started to cry like a child, and so did she, only her expression immediately changed: her face brightened and took on an aura of peace.

No! I cannot tell you how happy I am and yet how sad that I am not with you and that I cannot embrace you and dear Papa at this moment. My whole world has been transformed, and everything, nature, people, places, all seem attractive, good and full of joy. I simply was not able to write, my hands were trembling and from then on, in fact, I did not have a single moment free.

We had to do what the rest of the family were doing, there were *hundreds* of telegrams to be answered and – I was dying just to sit alone in a corner with my dear bride. She has completely changed and become gay, amusing, talkative and *tender*. I do not know how to thank God for His great mercy.

That same day we went to a service in Aunt Marie's church. She and all the sisters were present. At Alix's request we will go to Darmstadt for one night, now she will see her native land with quite other feelings. I had asked you if I could stay for two weeks, but now I think I will come earlier, towards the middle of Easter week. I so want to spend a little more time quietly with her.

But now, my dear Mama, I must finish. I am enclosing her letter to you. I embrace dear Papa and all the others,

Your Nicky

Nicky, Diary – 10 April – Palais Edinburg, Coburg

Celebrated Uncle Vladimir's name day; for the first time Alix and I took him a present together. Went upstairs with her to have coffee with the Queen. Made it to church in the middle of the service, and from there to Alix and the endless quantities of telegrams, which seem to increase rather than diminish. All the Russian gentlemen brought my bride a bouquet. Had luncheon at one. Today is simply cold with rain from time to time. Said goodbye to the Queen and Uncle Bertie. At 4.30 Victoria, Aunt Ella, Irène,[16] Alix, Uncle Sergei, Ludwig[17] and I left for Darmstadt. Travelled by special train for precisely five hours. We changed into full uniform and pulled into Alix's native town. There was a triumphant welcome; Ducky and Ernie were our hosts for the first time. A guard of honour, a four-in-hand escort, illuminations and crowds of people. As soon as we reached the palace, we sat down to supper as we were very hungry. How strange and yet pleasant to find oneself here. Sat in Alix's rooms and examined them in detail. It is even a shame to part for the night.

Empress Marie to Nicky – 10 April – Gatchina

My dear sweet Nicky!

Words cannot express with what *delight* and *great* joy I received this happy news! I almost felt *faint* I was so overjoyed! But how sad not to be with you my beloved Nicky at this great moment in your life! Not to be able to kiss you and bless you from the depths of my soul! May God shower you both with his blessings and grant you every possible happiness on this earth; this is my most fervent and ardent prayer for you my Nicky. I was *so* happy, and shed tears of *joy* and *emotion* and ran to announce this happy news to Papa first of all then to Xenia and Sandro and there were nothing but shouts of joy and real jubilation!

---

[16] Alix's sister.

[17] Louis of Battenberg, married to Alix's eldest sister Victoria. They lived at Elm Grove, Walton-on-Thames.

We had parted with such a bad and desperate feeling on the evening of your departure that my heart bled as I saw you go and my thoughts and prayers never left you. But thank God the Good Lord has arranged everything for the best and now you are happy and content and we are overcome with joy knowing you to be so happy. Your greatest wish has been granted *at last* after *so many* vicissitudes. Also we are waiting with an almost *febrile impatience* for the first letter with the details of how it all happened. You cannot imagine how awful and painful it is to be separated from you at a moment like this and how envious and *furious* I am that the uncles and aunts were present while *Papa* and *myself* who are *closest* to you were excluded! It's horribly sad and hard for us. I kiss you both my dear children with all my heart and pray that God will bless and always keep you in under his sacred protection. I hope dearest Alix will look upon me as a loving mother who'll receive her with open arms like her own dear child. Papa embraces you warmly and lovingly and wishes you both happiness and every good thing. May God keep you!

Your ever-loving Mama

Xenia to Nicky – 10 April – Gatchina

Darling Nicky

You cannot imagine my joy, I am terribly happy and you will understand why ...

Imagine, when I last asked Mama yesterday when our wedding was going to be, and Mama answered 'I don't know' and repeated it twice, I was simply mad, it's unbelievable, you can't treat people like things. But when I asked her about your wedding, Mama replied that there was no reason to wait, in other words the sooner the better, now tell me where there is any justice, but I am of course overjoyed for you.

KR, Diary – 10 April, Palm Sunday – Gatchina

There was a church service at Gatchina. I had not seen the Empress so radiant in a long time. Nicky's betrothal has delighted all Russians, who have been waiting for a long time for him to settle down to married life. I personally rejoice for him with all my heart, as I know his most cherished wish has come true. But my joy is tempered by some reservations: I imagine that he will no longer be able to serve in the regiment as he himself would have wished, and it seems certain that he will often be distracted from his military obligations.

Nicky, Diary – 11 April – Palais Edinburg, Coburg
Slept splendidly in Uncle Alfred's rooms downstairs to the left of the
entrance. The weather was much warmer than in Coburg, everything
was in full bloom and the scent wonderful. After coffee with the
whole family, sat with Alix answering telegrams. Her attitude towards
me has changed so much during the last few days, I am utterly
entranced.

This morning she wrote three sentences in Russian without a single
mistake! At 11.30 we went together by char-à-banc to Rosenau, where
her late parents, a brother and sister, are buried in a pavilion.[18] Picked
flowers and lilac everywhere. Returned to town at about two and had
luncheon with those of our relatives who were in Darmstadt.
Afterwards we had our picture taken, as a group and in pairs – I with
Alix. The public broke through into the garden, which made for a
funny spectacle.

12 April   Woke up to a beautiful day. Went with Alix to have coffee
with the Queen; now I must call her Granny. The infantry played
under my windows like the dragoons. Wrote telegrams with Alix. At
11 o'clock went to church. Lunched at 3 o'clock with the Queen.
Looked at the group photographs taken before and after Ducky and
Ernie's wedding.

Alix and I went together to Rosenau by char-à-banc. Quite a number of people had gathered to play lawn-tennis and drink tea.
Returned with her and went straight to church. Sat with my delightful bride. With Aunt Marie's permission have moved from the castle
into the cottage in her garden, next to the villa where Alix is staying.
I am in Alfred's rooms, as he left today for Potsdam. It's very cosy,
convenient and, most importantly, near to her. At 9 o'clock we went
to dine with the Queen also; but were allowed to miss the concert
because of Holy week. We sat for a very long time in our former communal sitting room.

13 April   From the morning it was a wonderful day. Went with Alix
to have coffee with the Queen. It is not very convenient to keep to
Lent abroad, and I had to refuse many things. After church a crowd
of us went to visit Princess Clementine Coburg; she is so deaf that she

---

[18] Alix's mother, second daughter of Queen Victoria, had died in 1878 aged
thirty-five; her father, Grand Duke Ludwig IV of Hesse, died in 1892; her brother
Frederick died aged two in 1873; her sister Mary in 1878 aged four.

always carries a hearing aid. At 3 o'clock Alix and I drove with the same horse up the hill past the fortress, and then along a beautiful roundabout road as far as Rosenau, where the rest of the family were preparing to have tea. Walked with my Alix, gathered flowers and sat with her for a long time on the bench by the pond – a delightful little corner.

Empress Marie to Nicky – 14 April – Gatchina
My sweet dearest darling Nicky,

I thank you with all my heart for your *dear kind* letter which I received yesterday with Aunt Michen and which moved me to tears.

Thank you thank you for each affectionate word which goes straight, straight to my heart which is so full of love for you and which has opened like a flower to receive your dear Alix whom I already regard as my own daughter and whom I await with such impatience. It was *such* a joy yesterday morning to receive your two dearest letters!

Tell Alix that I was *so* touched by hers – only she must not call me *Auntie* – Mama or *Motherdear*, this is what I am for her now. Poor children, what moral tortures you have both been through – it was a real battle! But God helped you to prevail and to win this great victory and now He will bless you both I am sure. May He hear your prayers and grant you every happiness in this world, and thereby our happiness and that of all our dear land! I am sending you a very little Easter egg.

Forever your Loving Mama

Emperor Alexander III to Nicky – 14 April – Gatchina
My dear sweet Nicky

You can imagine the feeling of joy and gratitude towards the Lord with which we learnt of your engagement! I have to admit that I did not believe the possibility of such an outcome and was sure your attempt would fail completely, but the Lord guided you, gave you strength and blessed you, many thanks to Him for His mercy. If only you had seen the happiness and rejoicing with which everyone greeted the news: we immediately started to receive a mass of telegrams, and are still being overwhelmed by them.

I am sure that you are doubly happy, and everything that happened, although forgotten, will surely have been useful in showing that not everything is so easy, particularly such an enormous step, which will decide your whole future and your ensuing family life.

I cannot imagine you as a fiancé, how strange and unusual! How sad it was for Mama and I not to be with you at such a time, not to embrace you, not to talk to you or know anything, just to wait for letters with the details.

Please tell your dear fiancée from me, how much I thank her for at last consenting, and how I wish her to flourish for the joy, comfort and peace she has given us by deciding to agree to be your wife!

I embrace and congratulate you, my dear sweet Nicky; we are happy for your happiness, and may the Lord bless your future life, as he has blessed it from the beginning!

Sandro to Nicky – 14 April – Gatchina

From the day of your engagement we have been pushed into the background, nobody thinks of us any more, the wedding is not being planned, nor our house bought. Write or tell Mama when you come that our wedding should be arranged quickly – after all we are tired of waiting. It is easy for you to do.

I've just returned from tea, during which I asked Papa when our wedding will be. The Emperor said in July. At this point Papa started to talk about your wedding, saying that it would be desirable to arrange it for August. You are lucky, you will only be engaged for 4 months in all. For Xenia and I it will be 6 months, on top of it she will have to go to the Crimea, all this upsets me very much.

Nicky to Georgie, Duke of York – 14 April – Palais Edinburg, Coburg

My dearest old Georgie,

Let me thank you my dear boy for those kind lines you wrote to me for my engagement. Truly it does seem strange to use that word for one's own account! But so it is!

Of course you can judge of my joy of the state of happiness I am in now. I am delighted to be here at Coburg and find this place beautiful. Only the time is so taken up by the family (as in Denmark) that I find it even cruel to be torn away from my beloved Alix for a few hours, as I would prefer spending them with my own little bride! She is going over to England to join Grandmama and I think there will be much chance for me to come over too and see you all dears again.

I shall be so very happy to see London once more. I liked my stay last summer and I have kept the pleasantest recollection of your wedding. I hope dear May is all right, please give her my best love. I must

finish this scribble by giving you Alix's best love, and dearest Georgie
sending every possible wish of happiness and pleasure I remain
            Ever your most loving cousin and devoted friend, Nicky

Xenia to Nicky – 14 April – Gatchina

Sandro and I are depressed that still nothing has been decided about
the wedding. You must understand, Nicky, that it's a terrible bore and
quite impossible to bear! Please will you mention it to both Mama and
Papa when you return, as they will of course talk to you about your
wedding. You are still only *newly* betrothed, but when *three months*
have gone by you will also begin to get tired, as I do, and to feel that
it simply *isn't possible to hold back any longer*, especially when there
isn't even any mention of a wedding.

Nicky, Diary – 15 April, Good Friday – Coburg

At 10 o'clock went with Alix to breakfast with the Queen; it is so
strange to be able to drive and walk alone with her, without feeling
at all embarrassed, as if there was nothing unusual in it! The dragoons were again playing. On my way to see Charles-Alexandre of
Weimar, I came back for the carrying out of the Shroud. The old man
had arrived yesterday to visit the Queen.

The weather started to deteriorate, but we nevertheless set out on
foot to the antiquary and to the wicker shop, where I bought a number of baskets for mushroom picking as well as a chaise-longue for
the camp. Alix gave me a ring. How funny it seemed to put it on my
finger for the first time! Went with my darling bride to Rosenau by
char-à-banc. We gathered flowers along the way and walked up to the
house. Learned that the Queen would remain a further day because
of the brisk weather in the Channel! During the service I carried the
Shroud with Uncle Sergei. Dined with the Queen at 9 o'clock.
Afterwards there was music, while some people sat in the adjoining
room and talked. Returned home, sat for a further hour with dear
Alix, she is calm and happy. Poured with rain.

Alix to Empress Marie – 18 April – Palais Edinburg, Coburg

Darling Motherdear,

Nicky tells me I may call you so, oh thank you so much – you are
too kind and good to me. How can I thank you and dear Uncle
enough for the magnificent present you were so awfully kind as to

send me. It is much too beautiful for me! It gave me quite a shock when I opened up the case – saw those beautiful stones. I thank you ever so much for it, and kiss your hands most tenderly.

I feel so proud to have your lovely order, and am most grateful and thankful for it, and the sweet egg and dear letter – all touched me deeply.

Only two days still, and then darling Nicky and I have to part, it makes me feel miserable, but I am sure that his little Motherdear is longing for him. You will let him come to England this summer, won't you, because it would be too hard to be parted so long, and Grandmama is looking forward to his visit so much. He has quite won her heart, as he has of all those who know him. He is in Church now, and whilst he is kneeling there, my thoughts and prayers are with him. With God's help I will soon learn to love his Religion too, and I am sure he will help me. But I will not bother you with a long letter.

With very fondest love to dear Father, I am, Darling little Motherdear,

Your deeply affectionate and Dutiful Child, Alix

Alix to Xenia – 18 April – Palais Edinburg, Coburg
My darling little Xenia

I send you my most tender thanks for the sweet little egg and lovely little brooch; I was deeply touched at your having thought of me.

The others are all in Church, and I am sitting alone, so use the opportunity for writing to my Chicken.

Alas! Only two days and then we part, I feel miserable at the idea – but what can't be cured must be endured. You are to be envied seeing Sandro every day, and I shall not see my Nicky for over a month.

I cannot describe my happiness – it is too great, I can only thank God on my knees for having guided me thus. And what an angel the dear boy is; how glad you will be to have him back again. You will write to me sometimes, won't you, if Sandro is not the whole day with you. Give him my love.

We went for a drive yesterday in the rain, but not to the Rosenau, today I have no doubt we shall go there.

I am going to spend a night at Darmstadt on my way to England, so shall see the young couple again – they look so happy and content, but it does seem too funny Ernie being married. It is so damp today that I have had to have a fire made.

Now enough for today.

With many a loving kiss I remain ever your very loving old Hen Alix

Nicky to Empress Marie – 18 April – Palais Edinburg, Coburg

My dearest darling Mama,

Words cannot express how happy your kind letter made me, above all you are both happy and pleased.

Now I also am completely happy and calm.

Alix is delightful and has been completely transformed from her state of constant sadness. She is so touchingly sweet with me that I am utterly enchanted. We spend whole days sitting together, and when the family goes on an outing, we follow on behind alone, in a little char-à-banc with one horse; either she or I drive.

She nearly fainted when I gave her your wonderful present. She wore it for the first time last night when there were guests for dinner. I have written to you so little and so seldom, dear Mama, partly because we will soon see each other, but also because there is really no free time. We are completely worn out by the telegrams, Alix and I write them together and help each other: up to now we have received 220 of them! We spent the day in Darmstadt quietly with Ducky and Ernie, the reception the previous night was very grand and yet quite touching! – certainly they all love her there, and they all have the fondest memories of her.

But now I must end my dear Mama.

Alix and I embrace you warmly and tenderly. Once again I thank you for your dear letter and the little eggs.

May the Lord keep you both. Until our next meeting.

Your Nicky

Nicky, Diary – 18 April – Palais Edinburg, Coburg

The day was cold with intermittent rain. Nevertheless we still went to Rosenau, Alix and I of course!

We picked a mass of flowers, which we carried as custom demands in the folds of Alix's dress and in my coat. On returning home we had tea with Aunt Marie. We had dinner at 7 o'clock and then went to the theatre, where they were again giving that charming opera *Der Vogelhändler* (Alix also loves the nightingale aria). We drank tea and beer in the billiard room and then went upstairs to her room. We sat for a long time together, she was unbelievably touching with me!

19 April   Got up at about nine and was slightly late for coffee with Aunt Marie. The family split up for the day: Aunt Ella, Victoria, Missy, Sandro and Ferdinand [of Bulgaria] went to the toy factory. I understandably stayed at home and sat the whole time with Alix. Helped her catch up with her diary. At 3 o'clock Alix and I drove by carriage beyond the town, where we looked at an old house that belongs to the Belgian king. Spent the evening with my dear Alix in her room; it's terribly sad that we will have to part for a long time! How wonderful to be together – bliss!

20 April   Awoke with the melancholy feeling that the end had arrived of our soul to soul existence. After coffee I went with Alix to visit the widowed Duchess, who lives quite alone in her castle on the hill.

At 12.45 I went with Alix to the station and said goodbye to her. She is going to Darmstadt and from there to England with Victoria [her eldest sister] to visit the Queen. How sad it seemed when I returned home! As if on purpose the weather had started to clear up and the sun broke through. We went to Rosenau: all along the way, and there in particular, at every step were memories of Alix. Yes, it's no fun without her! And so, we will have to spend a month and a half apart. I wandered alone in those familiar and now dear to me places, and gathered her favourite flowers which I sent to her by letter in the evening. There was thunder again and then it again cleared. At 9 o'clock, having said goodbye to all my relatives at the station, I set off home.

Nicky to Alix – 20 April, this sad Wednesday – Palais Edinburg, Coburg

My sweet darling beloved Alix!

Oh! it was too awful saying goodbye like that, with a lot of people looking on from all sides! I shall never forget the sweet sad and yet smiling expression of your angelic face looking out of the window as the train was beginning to move!

To know that you had to spend 9 hours in that small compartment nearly by yourself – was cruel to me and especially the thought that I was of no help any more! The coming home was more than unpleasant and when I came into my room, where you had just been a few minutes before, I could not keep back my tears. But then oh! what a delightful surprise – on my table in the bedroom there lay a note from you, my darling little girl. Thank you and thank you for the soothing comforting words that you wrote in it. Oh! really those few lines did me good! Certainly, my love, I shall speak with Papa about that question and I beg you always to remember that in every-thing where you shall need my help, you may be sure that I shall be there by your side and that also a deeply loving and thankful heart wherever it is, will always beat in time with yours my sweet one!

All these days I was so overcome with joy and happiness, being by my darling's side, that I could not say or tell you the hundredth part of what I might have spoken. I feel very deeply and then I cannot get the words out; it is stupid and tiresome, but so it is. I hope that this shyness or whatever it is will pass, for next time we meet we shall know more of each other than in the beginning.

Oh! how impatient I am for the moment when I can again press my lips to your sweet soft face! Alix, my own darling, you don't know how you have changed me by stretching out a fond hand and by making me rise up to you – the emblem of real pure love and faith! No! Do not think that these are vain words, no they come from my innermost feeling of admiration, trust and love that you have inspired me with. I must repeat again the same words I told you my precious little girl, the day of our engagement, that all my life belonged to you and that I could never be enough thankful to you dearest, for all you have done, are doing and are going to do, for me! May God help and protect you on the difficult beginning of your path! My prayers, blessings and thoughts are constantly with my dar-ling little thing!

Of course they all went to Rosenau and I was dragged with the rest. Ella and Sandro drove in our pony-carriage. We drove up our nice road along the hill down to Rosenau where we took tea. Before that we took a walk, I saw our bench where the hare came once, then I went along the stream, looked at the grotto, found these primroses on the side of the hill – and felt suddenly that I loved that place dearly! The weather was too fine for the occasion, the sun was bright, but I was so lonely!!!

I do hope the passage was a smooth one and that my sweet little owl did not suffer and is not too much tried by her journey. Give my best love to Granny. And now good-bye my own darling beloved Alix. God bless you once more! +

For ever your own deeply loving and thankful Nicky

Alix to Nicky – 20 April – Darmstadt
My own precious Nicky Darling,
   I am lying in bed, but cannot go to sleep before I have written to

you, as speak alas, we cannot. Oh, how I miss you, it is not to be described and I long for the two hours all alone with you. No goodnight kiss and blessing, it is hard. But our thoughts will meet won't they?

Your dear telegram made my heart rejoice, and I have got it lying near me. What a delight it will be to find your letter in Windsor. .

And there you are rattling away in the beastly train, whilst I am comfortably installed in my bed in my own 'sweet house' – It reminds me all so much of last week – how glad I am that you have been here and know my rooms a bit. I want you *badly*.

Forever and ever your dear photo stands before me, and makes me feel lonely. I shall write tomorrow from Windsor.

Nicky, Diary – 21 April – on the train

However sad it seems now, nevertheless at the thought of what has happened, my heart involuntarily rejoices and turns to God with a prayer of thanks! The weather is wonderful, even too hot for the train!

I had an old picture of Alix among my things, with her surrounded by the usual pink flowers. I was very touched by the buffet attendant, who asked for her to be brought into the car. At 7 o'clock we crossed the border. While they were moving the luggage, I wrote my dear bride a letter. As soon as we had set off in our train, we sat down to dinner. What a joyful feeling to be going home! In the evening I took a vivifying bath.

Queen Victoria to Nicky – 22 April – Windsor Castle

Dear Nicky,

I must thank you very much for so kindly sending me that splendid copy of your Travels which I shall value very much. I need not say how much my thoughts [have] been with you and my sweet Alicky [Alix] since we left dearest Coburg and I am sure the parting from her will have been very painful for both.

We are looking forward with such pleasure to her arrival on Friday and I shall watch over her most anxiously and carefully that she should get rest and quiet and do all to get strong which she has not been for some time. While she is here, alone without you, I think she ought to go about and out as little as possible as she would be stared at and made an object of curiosity which in her present position as *your Bride* would be both unpleasant and improper.

As she has no Parents, I feel I am the only person who can really be answerable for her. All her dear Sisters after their beloved Mother's death looked to *me* as their second Mother, but *they* had *still* their dear *Father*.

Now poor dear Alicky is an Orphan and has *no one* but me *at all* in that position. Anything you wish, I hope you will tell *me direct*. I am so sorry not to be able to take her to Balmoral, which is the finest air in the world, but it was rather too bracing for her 2 years ago. I hope in the autumn she might be able to do so.

Believe me with true affection, dear Nicky, your devoted (future) Grandmama

Victoria RI

Alix to Nicky – 22 April – Windsor Castle

My own precious Nicky dear,

I have just arrived and had breakfast with Granny. How it reminded me of Coburg and made me miss you more than ever. But there the delight at finding your sweet letter for which many tender kisses and thanks for the flowers. I am going to put them in my Bible and Prayerbook – they smell still excellently. The comfort of having your letter is great and I don't know how often I have read it in these few minutes and covered it with kisses. How I miss your kisses and blessing.

The journey went off well and the crossing was splendid, not a movement and I do not feel very tired. Everything is so beautifully green-bright of flowers. Granny has a tiresome cough. The whole journey I kept your coin in my hand and played with it and looked at the photo – a little comfort. Not only that I miss you, but Ernie too, everything reminds me of a few weeks ago where we were here together and I feel quite lost without him. Granny tells me she has written to you – she wrote to me even to Darmstadt. Aunt Beatrice is going up to London for some function, so Granny, I and the children will be left to ourselves.

Your letter has made me too awfully happy. I also feel shy to express my feelings. I had such a lot I wanted to tell you and ask and speak about and I felt too shy. We shall have to conquer this weakness, don't you think so? Oh, I want you ever so badly my own beloved One my own and all. Oh dear, oh dear ...

So here I am again. I have been trying to arrange the room a bit, and have been standing up all my photos and frog. I have unpacked my music and as soon as I can, I intend playing, as I have neglected the piano too shamefully lately. All your photos are looking at me with their beautiful big eyes. Oh, were you but here. I could press you to my heart. And to think you are still rattling along, poor dear. I shall anxiously wait your telegram this evening. You will write often, won't you, as your letters will be my greatest joy, and what I shall look forward to the most in the day. I have used a little of your scent, but the smell makes me sad.

Yes, sweet one, it was having to say goodbye so coldly at the station before everyone. I had to think of when you arrived. I shall never forget those first days and what a beast I was to you, forgive me, my love. Oh, if you only knew how I adore you and the years have made my affection for you grow stronger and deeper; I wish only I were worthier of your love and tenderness. You are much too good for me. But I must stop, otherwise this letter won't reach the post in time.

God bless you, my own true love. Many a tender kiss,

Ever deeply devoted little girl, Alix.
Your bride – how funny it sounds. Sweet one I cannot stop thinking of you.

Same day   As soon as I have finished one letter to you, I want to begin another. I am an old chatterbox, and when you are near me, I get numb like an old owl. If you could mention any nice book, a translation from the Russian, you would like your stupid frog to read, do tell me.

I went out driving with Grandmama this afternoon. She began by asking me so many questions, when, how, and where, and what had made me change my decision and so on, till I no longer knew what to say. She is very fond of you, my Love, you know. Then she dropped off to sleep, and I admired the beautiful nature. Windsor Castle through the dark trees in the distance, with sunshine on it and brighter blue shades – like a beautiful vision. Then I took tea with her and the children came in and made a shocking noise. Now I am sitting all alone, after having stuck four of your photos in an alas, not very elegant red leather frame bought here.

What the post will think of me if I write so often to you, I cannot imagine, so I think I had better keep to one letter a day, but no, sometimes I must write more, because when I sit alone in my room my thoughts run madder than ever to you – so if I bore you with chattering, forgive me, my own sweet Nicky dear.

If you know of any little books about your Religion, do tell me, so that I might read more about it, before you ring the Priest. One book in French which belongs to Sergei and he sent me since 1890, I have with me. Oh, I wish you were here, you could help me, and you are so religious, you must understand how nervous it makes me, but God will help me, you too, my love, won't you, so as that I may always get a better Christian and serve my God as truly as hitherto and more. How can I thank him enough for having given me such a heart, as my Boysy, to call my own. May He bless and protect you – now and evermore. It is so sad sitting all alone, no Nicky, no Ernie; I could cry. I sit and gaze at your photos and wonder what you are doing and have read your sweet letter over and over again, and kiss you for it.

Now my own precious darling Nicky I must say goodbye. God bless you. Many a tender kiss.

I am, ever your loving and deeply devoted Alix

Today is a big drawing room. Georgie and May are coming to luncheon tomorrow, how I wish you were here. We are only Ladies for supper – not lively and I am tired. I must play the piano to wake me up a bit.

Sleep well my angel and dream of your 'little girly' who is praying to God for your happiness.

Nicky to Alix – 23 April – Gatchina
My own sweet beloved darling Alix,

We arrived yesterday 4.20 in the afternoon; fancy dear Papa and Mama came to the station and they seemed so happy. Of course I told them all what you wanted me to say and they gave in at once and said you would not have to *abschwören* [renounce] the old belief, but that it would be like with Ella. You don't know my darling how happy I felt that they understood your reason and that they consented at once; I am only too glad to be the first one who may comfort you by that. Everybody here is really touching, all the servants and people of the house came flying into my room and each has got a kind word to say. Oh! how happy I am to have taken such a lot of your dear photos, the writing-table and cupboards are covered with them and wherever I look I see my sweet little girly-dear looking back at me, sometimes with a sly look, which makes me think of a certain house on the road from Coburg to Ketchendorf on the left!!!!

24 April Good morning my own precious one! I am just aroused from my slumber, which had been disturbed at 3.0 in the night by an insolent bat. My man, my dog and myself hunted the beast for nearly half an hour before we at last managed to catch the brute in a corner.

'Noch einmal, noch einmal, noch einmal – nachtigal! [Once more, once more, once more – nightingale!]'

Oh! that delightful sweet melody. For ever shall I love and remember those golden days in Coburg!

Alix to Nicky – 24 April – Windsor Castle
Dorogoy mili Nicky,

I have just come back from service, we had lovely singing and a fine sermon. I prayed most earnestly for you my darling – I wish you had been there, I think you would like the English service – the prayers are beautiful and elevating. This moment a letter has arrived from Aunt Alix, full of your praise and so kind. She wants me to go with them to Sandringham from Saturday to Monday – whether Granny can spare me I don't know, as she does not care for one going on visits whilst one is living with her. I shall ask her afterwards. I would have much rather waited and gone with you, it would have been less shy, as they have always such a large party, into which I so little belong.

I forgot to say yesterday that foolish Georgie says I am to insist upon you wearing high heels and that I am to have quite low ones. May, he says, won't change hers, but he wears much higher ones. At first they had been uncomfortable, now he did not mind it any more. I can see your face when you read this – really too mad! As if the higher made any difference, and a gentleman with high heels looks too absurd, and I am sure you would never do it.

Granny is alas very lame today, which depresses her, poor dear. I am also not to go to Ascot races without you, it would not be proper, well honestly I much prefer not going to the latter. Last night I played to Granny some things of Grieg, which she liked. Thora is coming this afternoon and I want her to go to Church with me. I have had such idiotical dreams, I who usually never dream, that it was a mistake, I was not engaged to you, thus I loved you awfully, but to your Uncle Alexei. You and I were always together skating and I was in despair as I only cared for you and did not know how to get out of it – too absurd.

Nicky to Alix – 24 April – Gatchina
My own beloved little darling,

The evenings specially I miss you darling so awfully – that the only

comfort I find is to sit down and begin to scribble off a letter to you!
Today I felt very disappointed in not receiving a few dear lines from my
girly-darling; every time I came into my room I rushed up to my table
– but alas! it was desolate and the much wanted envelope was missing!

I got another letter though instead – and that was from Granny a
very kind one too. But not knowing her handwriting it took me a
good deal of trouble to decipher it. She was very impatient to see you
arrive at Windsor. One thing I am particularly glad of, she said she
wants you to remain quiet during the season, that means you won't
be pulled about to the balls and drawing-rooms etc. Well and so
much the better!

Oh! sweety it is hard to be separated, never did I imagine on the
spur of those happy days that it would be so awful as it seems now. I
told the first couple [Sandro and Xenia] that for them it is much
better, as they always see each other and they agreed especially after
it had been at last decided yesterday that their wedding is going to
be in the middle of July (in the end of your month).

I must tell you one thing my beloved little girly-dear, that it is both
Papa's and Mama's great wish to see you here at home. We might
come together in July over from England for Xenia's wedding which
is going to be celebrated at Peterhof. We would spend a nice fortnight
together and then you would go back to Darmstadt.

26 April – St Petersburg
Naughty, naughty, little girly-dear, I am again reading line by line
your letter and what do I see you have put in the end, what do you
mean by it! Sweet one, it is me who is not worthy of your love and
such sacrifice that you leave your 'sweet home' for me! No! The
thought of possessing such an affection is really too heavenly a
thing, which no words in no language could ever express! That is also
why I was often dumb sitting with you.

Nicky

Nicky to Georgy [brother] – 27 April – Gatchina
So you wanted to hear about my engagement; I have to tell you that
I went there in despair and without hope, relying only on the grace
of God. I am only just beginning to get used to the term fiancé. But
you cannot begin to imagine what difficulties I had to contend with
and what I went through for four days until she at last gave her consent. At that moment I felt as if the whole Caucasus chain had fallen
from my shoulders!

Once she had made the decision, my wonderful Alix was changed as if by magic: she was completely transformed, she became gay, talkative and not at all shy with the others. From that day on the most blissful existence started for me, unfortunately though short-lived – 12 days in all. But however long we had spent together, time would still have passed too quickly! She is now at Windsor with the Queen.

I am planning to go there from camp at the beginning of June. I have not yet discussed the wedding, but there is no way it can be before October, even November. I am so happy that dear Mama and Papa are relieved and delighted for me. I believe what I am experiencing now is a happiness not of this earth. May God grant that with time you also find this happiness! I wish this for you with all my heart – Alix and I write to each other every day; she keeps remembering the winter of 1889 and calls you as then 'the Weeping Willow'! But I do rather miss her – there's no way I can bear it!

KR, Diary – 28 April – St Petersburg

Nicky talked to me a great deal about his bride. The first four days in Coburg were very difficult for him when she would not agree to change faith. He twice tried for some two hours to convince her, with a heavy heart as such a change was against his own conscience. But in this particular instance it was required by absolute necessity. In the end, on the day after her brother's wedding, and finding herself all alone in the world, she went to see Michen, then walked into the room where he was sitting, sat down in silence next to him and from that moment on they said not another word. Finally, marshalling his remaining strength and feeling that he was taking a final and decisive step, he asked her, did she consent? And she replied yes. They then both shed tears of joy.

A week later she was already complaining that she did not yet belong to his faith and could not participate in its celebration of the sacred days of Holy week.

Nicky to Alix – 30 April – Gatchina

Now as it is so warm and lovely we go out for long rows on the lake and generally make the whole tour, coming home at half past 5 for tea. The quantities of strawberries which we then devour is simply shocking, but Xenia certainly might have the first prize for that task. After dinner I generally go to Xenia and play the piano. After tea at

11.0 they generally play those detestable patience, while I read *The Times*. That paper is useful in different occasions; for instance, I remember the name, let me see ... oh! yes the Viscount Drumlanrig! Ha! Ha! Is he as handsome as R. Already two dangerous creatures in a fortnight; what, if it goes on at this rate???? Oh! Oh! Oh!

Alix to Nicky – 30 April – Windsor Castle
Oh, Nicky sweet, do you really not get frightened when you think what a creature is to become your wife, will she not drive you mad?

I shall do all in my power to get my legs in order till next year, but it is not so easy and you who are so fond of walking, oh dear, what could I do? The post has brought me nothing from you, let's hope tonight a letter may still come, or else I shall be so sad. Beloved Boysy, my thoughts are always with you and I long impatiently for the hour of your arrival! If the weather is fine we must have some fun then.

Aunt Beatrice was saying that we must go up the river then, which would be delightful, as I have never done it, and it is said to be lovely. Sweet one, I must say goodbye now. God bless you and may his angels watch over you.

Many a tender kiss.

Nicky, Diary – 2 May – Anichkov Palace, St Petersburg
I am sitting in nothing else but my shirt all the windows wide open though it's night and bad perfumes make my nostrils dilate for a bit of fresh air! I ran about through our future apartments in the Winter Palace (a killing sight), returned home for 5 minutes and drove to Ella. We two dined together and she (the poor governess) had to sit indoors with a sore throat and a rotten eye. Ella gave me some excellent ideas about arranging our rooms – and we talked away till 11. I was glad to see her as of all the sisters she reminds me mostly of my sweet darling. Isn't it so?

2 May – Gatchina   I have received my birthday presents from dear Papa and Mama and Xenia and Sandro. Two pairs of lovely buttons and a heavenly green stone 'frog' (Fabergé) like those animals Ella had in her saloon in the Schloss! Lots of books besides, that I love so – and some French poetry. Misha [brother] also gets his presents on the same day as me, because his birthday and nameday are together on 22 November! so it was considered unfair to give him presents only once a year!

6 May   And so today I am 26! Already nearer to 30, than to 20 – but then thank God I am engaged, and what's more, to whom? To such a jewel, to such a divine being as Alix! The telegrams started to flood in after midday. The weather cleared up completely. Alix sent me congratulations from Windsor and I received the usual letter from her. We walked round the lake and sat in the pavilion of love. After tea sat down to those foul telegrams and managed to answer them all before dinner.

Nicky to Queen Victoria – 7 May – Gatchina
My dearest Grandmama,

Let me thank you deeply for your kind letter, that was a charming surprise and it gave me great pleasure! But I am so touched that you thought of me now, when I separated from my darling little bride, which was really very trying, as we had only spent 12 days together after our engagement. I thank you so much for all your kindness at Coburg which you showed me there: I shall never forget our breakfasts in your room and the music playing outside. It is very kind of you, dear Grandmama, to watch over her yourself and I am most pleased to hear it from you, that she shall remain quiet and not go about. I wrote her yesterday and told her exactly the same, only of course that was said in the form of a wish!

My Parents felt so touched and grateful when I told them all the events of our stay at Coburg that they wish me to express their feelings of joy and gratitude for your attention and kindness bestowed upon me. I am already looking forward with such a pleasure and impatience for the day when I will be able to come and see you and my darling Alix at Windsor. I hope the stay in Balmoral will do you the best possible good: that your precious help will make us happy when we meet again in Windsor. I really don't know how to thank you enough for having taken the trouble of writing to me such a charming letter.

With my very best love to you dearest Grandmama, believe me your most affectionate and devoted (future) grandson.

Nicky

Nicky to Alix – 8 May – Gatchina
Papa is always so dear and kind to me – today I asked whether he would allow me to go over to England in his lovely yacht the *Polar Star* – and he at once consented, adding he was sure I am delighted not to have to go through Berlin!

I should think I *am* mad at the idea of going over to see my sweety by sea and on board that ship. Oh! you ought to see her – she is a beauty and so comfortable, but the best is her engines – she steams 18 knots easily an hour!

Nicky

Nicky to Georgy [brother] – 9 May – Gatchina
With all my heart I share your joy at the prospect of seeing dear Mama and the happy couple! [Sandro and Xenia] They have become quite impossible, presumably from prolonged yearning and being so used to each other. They spend the whole day kissing, embracing and lying around on the furniture in the most improper manner. Xenia in particular is completely impossible, you wouldn't recognize her she has changed so much since becoming engaged!

My dear bride writes to me every day, and I to her; she has asked me to send you her love. She still hasn't forgotten about 'Weeping Willow'. Papa has given me permission to go to England on the *Polar Star* at the beginning of June, you can imagine how happy I am to miss out on awful Berlin!

The old Queen (belly woman) often writes to me – that's nice, isn't it?

Alix to Nicky – 10 May – Harrogate
I had my first sulphur bath this morning, it did not smell lovely, and made my silver bracelet, which I never take off quite black, but that one can clean with the powder one uses for cleaning up one's silver things.

11 May   Before slipping into bed I am going to read your sweet letter over again, and it makes me happy. Oh, what an indescribable joy it is, one is loved and longed for – and I pray on my knees that I may become daily worthier of your great love. Oh, my Nicky, my own sweet Boysy dear God bless you now and for ever. I could cry for love for you. Not only do I miss you but I long also for Ernie, who used to be always running into my room at every hour of the day – *und ich gönne es ihm vom Herzen* [and I was always happy for him to do so]. A kinder, dearer brother never was, except my old cow [Nicky] – And beloved Papa, oh, it is terrible to know that I shall nevermore see him in this world. I miss him daily more and more especially now that through you my heart is so full. Tomorrow my little sister May would have been 20, think only, quite grown up. Sweet little Child that she was. But my love I think I better go to bed, as my legs have been so painful today and as I had my first bath, it is also getting on for eleven.

13 May   Then I had my head washed, which takes an hour, as one's hair will never dry. Shall I cut it off and appear like you? Eh? Would that not look imposing? Of course it is in all the papers that I am here, and all the trades people send epistles and beg of one to order things, even a piano and tea were offered. The rude people stand at the corner and stare; I shall stick my tongue out at them another time.

   Now my beloved Child, I must say goodbye.

                              Ever your own true, loving and devoted girly. Alix
Many loving kisses.

Nicky to Alix – 13 May – Krasnoe Selo[19]

I am glad you saw such an excellent performance of *Faust*, it is a lovely divine and ever young fresh music! I must again answer a letter from Granny, if you knew what trouble they give me. Of course I try to write in a very grand and old-fashioned like style – had you seen one of them you would be quite upset.

   But her letters are so awfully difficult to read, she has got a way of shortening her sentences and words in such a manner that I could not make out for a long time.   Nicky

Nicky, Diary – 14 May – Gatchina

I am on duty today (Lord in waiting) as my Father's a.d.c. and have to appear in church or at the meals in uniform; all my cousins do just the same, we take it in turns with the simple adjutants, having to be on service once a fortnight. Of course, you know, we have nothing hardly to do except sending petitions off to Papa and having to be present at receptions! That's all! In town one duty more is added: we have to go to all the fires whether in the day or in the night and on coming back must report to Papa what has happened!

Alix to Nicky – 16 May – Harrogate

My own deeply beloved Nicky,

   Sweetest of sweet Pets, I press you to my heart and kiss you on *those*

---

[19] A military camp outside St Petersburg.

lovely eyes with deep expression, and how mischievous they can also twinkle!

The people are obvious here, now that they have found me out. They stand in a mass to see me drive out and tho' I now get in at the backyard, they watch the door and then stream to see me and some follow too. One obvious woman, who comes quite close too, and stares; I thought perhaps it might be the mad correspondent (wife) of yours, you remember the letter at Coburg you showed me?

Then when I go into a shop to buy flowers, girls stand and stare in at the window. The Chemist told Madeleine that he had sent in a petition that a policeman should stand near the house to keep people off, as he saw how they stared. Most kind, but it makes no difference. 'That's her,' one said behind me. If I were not in the bathchair I should not mind. When Gretchen was in a shop this morning, a little girl came in and the man asked her whether she had seen me. She said yes only once as I had my carriage in the courtyard, as I did not seem to like being looked at. I wish the others would remark it too and keep away and not stare with opera glasses through their windows. It is too unpleasant!

Nicky, Diary – 19 May – St Petersburg
Wrote, wrote, wrote to my bride!

Nicky to Alix – 20 May – Krasnoe Selo
Your letters are such a comfort to me my own beloved Alix! Well! fancy, just this moment my man brought me your sweet long loving letter N29[20] – for which I must kiss my beloved little bride separately from the birthday kisses I owe you!

Sweet one, but you write Russian beautifully, so many words and not one fault – good little school-girl.

                                                                    Nicky

Sandro to Nicky – 20 May – Abas Tuman
I'm tired of Georgy [Nicky's brother] saying that Xenia and I kiss too much, he's always saying 'stop it, it doesn't help'. Tell Misha that I did not mean to make fun of his letter, Xenia is sitting next to me

---

[20] Nicky's twenty-ninth letter to Alix. They continued to number their letters throughout their engagement and marriage.

looking in the dictionary. Try to make sure that Alix comes to our wedding, it would be wonderful.

Alix to Nicky – 25 May – Harrogate

Good morning my own precious Boysy – my Birthday! 22! Oh, how I wish you were here, beloved Darling! And your glorious bracelet, you naughty monkey, how could you dare to give me such a magnificent thing – I feel quite shy and your telegram. You do spoil one. I must flee to my water, and Goodbye. We have been arranging flowers all the morning, which some kind angel has sent me. More tonight.

Queen Victoria to Nicky – 25 May – Balmoral Castle

Dear Nicky,

I write to you on this dear day, our darling Alicky's birthday which I am sure must be very dear to you and I also wish you many happy returns. Thank you for your very kind letter of the 20 May, for my birthday. It was the only very warm day since we came here. The weather has been quite unusually cold to last so long. And we had a great deal of rain. But it is much warmer . . .

The accounts of dear Alicky are upon the whole satisfactory, but she requires great quiet and rest and I send you the copy of a letter from the Doctor at Harrogate who is [a] very clever, nice man. She keeps a strict regime of life as well as diet. She has to lie down a great deal. This ought to have been done long ago but the family doctor in whom [the family] unfortunately have great faith is a stupid man, who never will do anything and says yes to all they ask. Last autumn and winter she ought to have done what she is doing now.

Her dear Father's death, her anxiety about her brother, and the struggle about her future have all tried her *nerves very much*. You will I hope, therefore *not* hurry on the marriage as she *ought* for *your* as well as *her* sake to be strong and *well before* that.

You had better not arrive till 30 or 1 of July as we shall not arrive till the 21 or 22 and then Alicky would come to us and still rest a good deal.

Pray offer my affectionate respects to your Parents and believe me always your most affectionate (future) Grandmama.

Nicky, Diary – 25 May – Krasnoe Selo

Dear Alix's birthday. How much I thought of her all day, how terribly I wanted to embrace her and spend this day together with her!

The officers and all the companies came to the barracks to congratulate me – I was very touched! There were no works or drill today – I
gave the day off to everyone as well as a glass of vodka.

Alix to Nicky – 26 May – Harrogate
Love-love – what is greater! Kissy kissy. Ta ta!

Alix to Queen Victoria – 28 May – Harrogate
My darling Grandmama,

I send you my very fondest thanks for Your dear letter and kind
wishes, which touched me deeply. Please accept also my best thanks
for the nice photo: of You and Uncle Bertie, and for the delightful
teabasket with which I am quite enchanted. The sun shone on purpose so that we could go for a long drive and use it. It is a most useful present, and I have long wished for such a thing. Victoria being
here for my birthday, was a great pleasure, as it would have been too
sad to have spent my Birthday without one relation. I have never
been away like this without one before.

You must kindly excuse my writing so seldom, dear Grandmama,
but the baths make one tired and I have to rest a great deal. As yet
the pains are no better, but I hope in time that the good effect of the
baths will show itself. It is pouring again today, which is distressing.

I will go to Walton and dear Nicky would then join me there. His
father is lending him his yacht, so he can go the whole way by sea,
which is certainly the more agreeable way of travelling. Yes, darling
Grandmama, the new position I am sure will be full of trials and difficulties, but with God's help and that of a loving husband it will be
easier than we now picture it to ourselves. The distance is great, but
yet in three days one can get to England. I am sure his parents will
often allow us to come over to You. Why I could not bear the idea of
not seeing You again, after the kind Angel You have been to me, ever
since dear Mama died, and I cling to You more than ever, now that I
am quite an Orphan. God bless You for all Your kindness to me,
beloved Grandmama dear. I have no words to thank you enough for
all. Please do not think that my marrying will make a difference in
my love to You – *certainly it will not*, and when I am far away, I shall
long to think that there is One, the dearest and kindest Woman alive,
who loves me a little bit.

Goodbye dearest Grandmama,

Ever Your very loving, affectionate and dutiful Child, Alix

Alix to Nicky – 28 May – Harrogate
Dear Nicky,

Today 10 years ago we arrived at Peterhof, and I for the first time saw and kissed my sweet *Lausbub* [rascal]. How dear and always kind you were to me then – our windowpanes.[21] After we left Russia that year 84, I used for some time to pray for you and then after 89 of course too, as soon as I like anyone I cannot help praying for them. To think that I know you already 10 years, a long time, is it not? I see you still at the Wedding service holding the crown over Sergei – how much has changed and happened since then, it makes one quite melancholy.

Nicky to Queen Victoria – 2 June – Peterhof
Dearest Grandmama,

Your third kind letter gave me such great pleasure which I thank you for most heartily. I leave tomorrow in the afternoon on board Papa's new yacht the *Polar Star* that he kindly lent me for coming to England.

You don't know, dearest Grandmama, how *happy* I am to come and spend some time with you and my beloved little bride. What a different impression for me this time – with my stay in London last year for Georgie's wedding. This separation from Alix has made my love for her still far stronger and deeper than it was before! Now, dearest Grandmama, I must end; with fondest thanks for your kind letter and hoping to see you very soon again believe me your most loving and devoted (future) grandson.

                                                                    Nicky

Nicky to Alix – 2 June – Peterhof
My own darling Alix,

I enclose a small photo of 'the monstrous cow' [Nicky himself] – the rest I bring with me! I wrote to Granny today explaining to her in detail about our plans for Walton. I hope it shall make her understand the reason why I could not come to Balmoral – but now that becomes quite impossible as she intends leaving about the same date for Windsor. So far it is all right – good!

Sweety, you don't know how sly I can be – I coaxed Granny in the

---

[21] On 31 May 1884, ten years before, Nicky recorded 'Alix and I wrote our names on the rear window of the Italian house (we love each other).'

most shameful way possible – try and read it, when we are in
Windsor, then you can judge and see what a creature you have been
unlucky enough to be engaged to! I cannot stop reading your sweet
letter over and over oh! you are the sweetest kindest angelic little
girly in the whole world! And that I should possess such a treasure
and be allowed to love you – no! that is *too heavenly* for words. In all
my life I have never dreamt that such happiness was possible – as this
now. I feel completely changed, one's life seems useful, there is an
object in living for others and for oneself too! Oh! my sweet one – all
that I learnt through you!

I hung out of the window and breathed deeply and pulled the
lovely warm pure sea-air, the wind brought in gushes to me – and I
thought of my sweet girly-dear, it seemed as if the air brought me
your tender kisses from so far off. But though I seem cold as a stone,
I love you, my own darling, as few persons *can* only love! *Quel est
l'amour véritable? Celui qui aime et ne parle pas*! [What is true love?
That which loves and does not speak!] That is so perfectly true and is
so exactly my case. I love you too deeply and too strongly for me to
show it; it is such a sacred feeling, I don't want to let it out in words,
that seem meek and poor and vain! But now I will try and break that
habit of hiding my feelings, because I think it wrong and selfish in
some occasions. You also do not know, my precious one, how long
my whole heart belonged to you and what sufferings it has gone
through these dreary years! Darling primrosy-mine, I love you my
darling!!!!!

3 June   My pet, to think that I am coming to you and if God grants,
shall soon clasp you, my beloved little girly, to my heart! oh what
bliss, what joy, what happiness! Though the sea passage takes two
days more than going by rail, you will understand what a difference
it is to me to be able to sail in Papa's lovely yacht leaving Berlin aside.

Georgy [brother] to Nicky – 9 June – Goderski Pass
Do you remember how you wrote to me about the appalling
behaviour of Xenia and Sandro; I was indeed amazed at the gymnas-
tics, sucking, sniffing and similar activities which these two persons
indulged in all day long. They almost broke the ottoman and generally behaved in the most improper way; for instance they would lie
down on top of each other, even in my presence, in what you might
call an attempt to play Papa and Mama. To the point where I got
angry at such impudence.

It's really not possible! It's a good thing there isn't long left until the wedding, otherwise it could all end badly! I tried to shame them, but to no avail. They just continued their frenzied antics. Well, that's people for you!

Nicky, Diary – 9 June – Walton-on-Thames
Slept splendidly in my cosy little room. What joy I experienced when I woke up in the morning and remembered that I am staying under the same roof as my darling Alix! Had breakfast at about 9 o'clock. After sitting for an hour or so in the drawing room, went with Alix and Victoria's two daughters for a drive around the Walton area. The weather was divine, tranquil and hot. The little girls jumped around terribly in the carriage. Sat with Alix until luncheon and played the piano. At 3 o'clock the six of us went down the Thames by electric boat, passing through two locks. The trip was wonderful, the banks remarkably beautiful, we met a mass of other boaters, mostly ladies. I loved all the buildings along the river bank. We had tea, which we had brought with us, in a rowing boat.

10 June Another wonderful, peaceful day like yesterday; in truth, what blissful existence! Sat all morning in the garden with my dear Alix, on an old rug under the chestnut trees: she worked, while I read Loti's *Matelot* to her.

11 June – Windsor Castle Unfortunately we have had to pack our things and leave behind the carefree life of Elm Grove. Victoria, Alix, Ludwig and I set out for Windsor in the Queen's tandem carriage, and arrived an hour later. We awaited Granny's arrival at Frogmore [near Windsor Castle], where we all had tea together. Returned to the castle on foot. I am staying in rooms upstairs, not far from my darling bride, and which give onto the gallery where we gather before and after dinner. We dined at 9, there were 14 of us, we wore stockings; my shoes rubbed my feet terribly! Spent a divine evening with dear Alix!

13 June Yesterday at 10 o'clock in the evening a son was born to George and May, there was general happiness and rejoicing.[22] Returning with Granny, I was struck by the size of the rhododendron bushes. Had dinner at 9.30. For the first time I wore the Windsor tailcoat with red collar and cuffs.

---

[22] The birth of the future King Edward VIII.

Nicky to Empress Marie – 14 June – Windsor Castle
Darling Mama

She [Queen Victoria] insisted I order a tail-coat with a red collar and cuffs, and that I wear it like the others for dinner, with stockings and shoes. I am in the same rooms you stayed in previously. Your portrait (!) by Angeli hangs on the wall.

It was a joy to see dear Aunt Alix and the cousins on the third day – she looks remarkably well – better than last year.

Your Nicky who loves you with all his heart

Nicky, Diary – 14 June – Windsor Castle
The day was close, as usual at 10 o'clock we went to Frogmore for coffee. Walked a little with Alix around the pond; instead of being able to read the papers quietly, by some mishap I got locked into a certain place, and there was no way I could get out for over half an hour. Alix at last managed to open the door from the outside, although I shouted long and loud, and tried to open the door myself as the key was on my side. Alix met Yanyshev[23] for the first time. The Duc d'Aumale lunched with us. At 4.45 we took the train to Richmond, and from there went by carriage to White Lodge, where Georgie and May are living at the present time. They showed us their new born son. Aunt Alix, Victoria and Maud[24] also arrived to see them.

Alix to Xenia – 16 June – Windsor Castle
Darling Xenia,

As I am sitting here all alone, Nicky having left for Sandringham, I want to send you a few lines. He had breakfast with me here in my little room, and now is off – but returns tomorrow afternoon – yet I feel low he is gone, only they had begged so hard he should come, so off he went. It is such unutterable joy having the dear Boy here and he is so awfully good and kind. Now I suppose you are back home again – it must have been delightful at Abas Tuman – your letter to Nicky killed us, you mad Chicken!

It is beautifully sunny today, and looks as tho' it would be very hot; at 10 we drive down to Frogmore to breakfast.

You must excuse a short letter.

A good kiss for your dear little self, and best love to Sandro
                                        Your loving Old Hen, Alix

---

[23] An orthodox priest, Nicky's confessor, who was brought to England by Nicky to instruct Alix.

[24] Second daughter of the Prince and Princess of Wales.

Nicky to Alix – 16 June – Sandringham[25]
My own sweet precious beloved Darling,

Here I am sitting in my room, scribbling to you in by no means a merry mood! I have got a strong neuralgia (that never happens to me) and I miss my little girly-dear most awfully!

I was happy to have caught a glimpse of your sweet face looking out of the window, as I drove down to the station. As long as I could, I tried not to lose the castle out of my sight, until at a curve some naughty tree shut it quite out. The heat in the train was abominable.

Aunt Alix and the girls met me and brought me to their house. The drive through their woods was charming, there blew such a delightful fresh breeze from the sea. I rushed through the house, looked hurriedly at the rooms and then we all left for the horse-sale near Kings Lynn. Uncle Bertie was as funny as usual and in the carriage there were two or three misunderstandings between him and Aunt Alix. That always happens, because she does not hear what he says and he hates to repeat his own words.

We soon arrived at that place and went into an enormous tent where about 200 farmers and horse dealers were eating. We all sat down at a table higher than the others and had our lunch, quite like on the stage. I thought so of you my precious one and how you would have laughed looking at all those people walking, sitting and eating away.

After that began the horse sale. We sat in a sort of box, as one sits in for the races – and everywhere round there were crowds of people gaping more at us, than at the horses. 50 horses were sold at auction and just fancy *Lausbub* [Nicky] let himself be tempted by two beauties of chestnuts (mares). The foolish people thumped with their sticks and cheered when it was proclaimed I had bought two. But towards the end it became perfectly intolerable as it never seemed to finish and the weather suddenly got cold and very windy. Oh! how I bored myself then and how I wished I were comfortably seated near my darling in her tiny room at Windsor. We drove home for tea, then it was that the neuralgia came on. It was vile! The right eye ran with tears, as strong was the pain. And so I had to walk about the garden, admire the stables, the dogs, two goats and other objects. I pretty nearly went mad, when I came home. Victoria gave me something to soothe the pain, which really helped.

During dinner I got your second telegram. Oh! my sweet darling! I

---

[25] The home in west Norfolk of the Prince and Princess of Wales. Their second son, Georgie, Duke of York, and his wife May moved into York Cottage in the grounds in 1893.

love you, I love you – is all that I can say!!!!!! I miss you now in the
evening so dreadfully, when the others are gone to bed.

I suppose you shall get this letter a little before I turn up which
shall be after the Arch-Duke's[26] arrival. Toria's and Maud's rooms are
sweet and so prettily arranged; they have done everything afresh
after the fire in 1891. We two are invited to a family lunch, before the
garden-party, at Marlborough House. Now my own precious sweet
little Alix I must end. Many a blessing and a kiss do I send you my
true love.   Adoring old Nicky

Nicky, Diary – 17 June – Windsor Castle

Woke up to a divine morning, and after bathing had coffee with Uncle
Bertie downstairs. After arriving in London, I changed to another station and flew back to Windsor by special train. Was overjoyed by my
reunion with dear Alix, even such a separation from her seems long.
In the evening the Arch-Duke Ferdinand arrived. In his honour there
was a grand dinner in uniform and to music. Sweated a lot.

26 June   Today I was allowed to rest, and slept until 9.30. At exactly
10 o'clock went to Frogmore with Granny and Alix; after breakfast,
there was a service in the mausoleum. The Queen's confessor gave a
very good sermon. Sat with Alix until luncheon. I have become very
lazy and cannot bring myself to write home, although I should send
them some news! Every hour with my dear Alix is so precious to me
that I don't want to waste it! The weather has turned grey with rain.
Empress Eugenie[27] arrived with her nephew Napoleon, who was with
us in Petersburg this winter. They were received by Granny in the
Queen's Closet, which is where I received the Order of the Garter last
year. We had dinner at 9, sat next to the Empress. We talked until 11,
and I was driven to total exhaustion both by the standing and by not
being able to smoke.

Nicky to Empress Marie – 27 June – Windsor Castle

My dearest darling Mama

I fear you must be extremely displeased with me because of my
long silence; I myself feel very guilty, nevertheless you can see that I

---

[26] Archduke Franz-Ferdinand, later shot in Sarajevo, the assassination which pre-
cipitated the First World War.
[27] The former Empress of France, widow of Emperor Napoleon III.

am more than happy staying here near my Alix. I treasure every free hour that I can spend with her. I started to write several times in her room, but my efforts to write a good letter came to nothing, as at every moment I felt the imperious and irresistible need to jump up from the chair and embrace her!

The christening of Georgie and May's son has been arranged for 4/16[28] July at White Lodge, where we went to visit them a few days after his birth. A lovely healthy baby!

I am glad I will be able to spend two or three days in Osborne and am thinking of leaving on the 9th, as Granny has asked me to stay until that date! By then I will have been in England exactly one month and one day! I must end here as it is time for luncheon. I hope you have good weather and that all is well. I embrace you, my dearest darling Mama, and dear Papa and the others. Best love from Alix! May the Lord protect you!

With all my heart, your Nicky

Nicky to Georgy [brother] – 29 June – Windsor Castle

I either sit at home with Alix, or go for a drive with her and the Queen. It seems funny to me, all this life here and the extent to which I have become part of the English family. I have become almost as indispensable to my future grandmother as her two Indians and her Scotsman;[29] I am, as it were, attached to her and the best thing is that she does not like me to leave her side.

As far as our wedding goes, nothing has been decided, but we both think it will be difficult to arrange before January. She does not want to hurry learning our faith and our language, which I entirely agree with and am very pleased about, as it shows how seriously she treats this matter.

For dinner here I have to appear in a tail coat with red collar and cuffs, and stockings and pumps – how ghastly!

Nicky

Nicky and Alix to Xenia and Sandro – 30 June – Aldershot

Dearest Xenia and Sandro

We have just come here to the camp, to the English 'Krasnoe Selo'

---

[28] Nicky was avoiding confusion by using both the Julian and Gregorian calendars.
[29] Queen Victoria in old age had several Indian servants. She also relied on Abdul Karim (the `Munshi') from Afghanistan and on a Scottish servant, John Brown.

which is a charming place. The house is a wooden one, one hears every sound or poops through the walls and we live all in the same corridor! It has only one storey and is exactly like an Indian bungalow!

We are sitting together in her room and we love each other very much! Not less than you old birds. For dinner I am going to put on a red Circassian coat, which will absolutely drive Granny wild – she has already asked me several times when I am going to wear a cossack uniform, and so for dinner I shall appear in it. Afterwards there will be reveille with a ceremony, which the locals call a 'tattoo'!

N.

[in Alix's hand] *I found this so I thought I must send it you – does not it remind you of that evening we sat together, you in white, looking more sweet than words can express that I longed to cover your face the whole time with kisses; that tiny little room, it was gemütlich [cosy] no, how I want to see you in that uniform again in the red dress over it, sweet manykins very many kisses, all alone. A big kiss A.*

Nicky, Diary – 3 July – Windsor Castle

After breakfast we went to church. The Bishop of Ripon gave an excellent sermon. Dinner was at 9.15 with only the court officials. The little Lord in Waiting, Lord Playfair mistook me for the Windsor priest and summoned me to the Queen, which made all those present laugh loud and long. Sat with dear Alix.

4 July At 5 o'clock the infant son of Georgie and May was christened at White Lodge in the presence of the whole family. Granny gave him seven names.[30] I was among the godfathers. Instead of immersing him, the Archbishop wet his fingers and touched the baby's head.[31] Then we had tea in a marquee in the garden. Four generations had their photograph taken together. There was no rain on the way back. An officer was almost killed because his horse stumbled. Arrived in Windsor at 7.45. *Lausbub!** [rascal] Dined later. Sat for a long time with! *Shpitsbub** [scamp]

5 July After having coffee with dear Alix, went to the station to go

---

[30] He was named Edward Albert Christian George Andrew Patrick David, and was known in his family as David. He succeeded his father as King Edward VIII in 1936.
[31] In an Orthodox christening the baby is immersed in the font.
* in Alix's hand.

to London. Visited Staal and his wife. Went into an antique furniture shop, where I bought a beautiful Empire bed, wash stand, table and mirror, which I was very pleased with! Spent an hour and a half at Marlborough House; said goodbye to Uncle Bertie, Aunt Alix, Victoria and Maud. Unfortunately they will not be coming to us in Petersburg for Sandro and Xenia's wedding! Returned to Windsor for luncheon.

Two jewellers had laid out their wares in my room and I took a trinket from each. We had tea at Frogmore and then went for a long drive, we were even cold. On the way back we stopped at the chapel where Eddy is buried, and on whose tomb Granny told Alix to lay a wreath. Spent a wonderful evening with my darling bride. I am dying of love for her!

8 July – Osborne, Isle of Wight   Granny's life here is the same, transposed from Windsor – but not for us, as the sea is near. [in Alix's hand] *My own Boysy Boysy dear, never changing, always true. Have confidence and faith in your girly dear who loves more deeply and devotedly than she can ever say. Words are too poor to express my love and admiration and respect – what is past, is past, and will never return and we can look back on it with calm – we are all tempted in this world and when we are young we cannot always fight and hold our own against the temptation, but as long as we repent and come back to the good and on to the straight path, God forgives us. 'If we confess our sins, He is faithful and just to forgive us our sin.' God pardons those who confess their faults. Forgive my writing so much but I want you to be quite sure of my love for you and that I love you even more since you told me that little story,[32] your confidence in me touched me, oh, so deeply, and I pray to God that I may always show myself worthy of it. God bless you beloved Nicky!*

11 July – Polar Star   A sad day – parting – after more than a month of blissful existence! There was rain in the morning, which then turned into mist. I became sadder and sadder as the hour of our separation approached! I did not leave my sweet dear bride for a single moment. *Sweet Nicky love.** After tea I drove with her and Granny for a last time in the direction of the town of Ryde. We had dinner a little before 9 o'clock; the Portsmouth marines were playing. I said goodbye to the ladies and gentlemen and to Munshi; I changed into

---

[32] Nicky had this day confessed to her his affair with M. Kschessinska.
* in Alix's hand.

the uniform of the Guard Corps and after saying goodbye to dear
Granny, I went to the landing stage with Alix. After parting from my
darling bride, I boarded the cutter. Once on the *Polar Star* I received
a long letter from Alix. Was exhausted from sadness and longing.

KR, Diary – 10 July – Krasnoe Selo
Nicky is painting a fan for Xenia for her wedding. He is doing it from
a French book with pictures. The picture shows a frightened hen
which has laid several eggs out of which are hatching a whole army
of paper cockerels. Nicky draws very well and has a lot of taste.

Alix to Nicky – 10–11 July – Osborne, Isle of Wight
My own precious darling Nicky dear,

As I left you a few lines in your room at Coburg, so that you should
find them when I was gone, so I am going to write again and give this
to your servant to give you when you have parted. It makes me too
miserable to think about it tomorrow morning, goodbye! Oh, sweety
love, what shall I do without you, I am so accustomed now to have
you always near me, that I shall feel quite lost.

Sundays, Granny is punctual and I am not washed or anything.

Could I but slip into your pocket instead of the thermometer, what
unspeakable joy, to be ever near you, and watch for every little wish
to try and fulfil it – but someday I may do it – and then no more parting – always with you. With what passion I love you, like a fire burning, and consuming me, and to feel this love returned. What bliss
could be greater?

When your man goes in to wake you tomorrow morning, I hope
that he will bring you this so that at least a good morning kiss may
reach you. I press it here.

Nicky to Alix – 11 July – *Polar Star*
My own beloved precious little darling,

This parting was too awful for words; if it went on more often I
would not live long! My sweet one I have just read your dearest long
letter through, which the old man gave me on arriving on board! I
followed you with my eyes as long as I could from the launch until
such a lump came up my throat that I had to turn away and I sobbed
in the boat like I did this afternoon. Luckily it was dark and the men
were busy rowing.

Alix to Nicky – 12 July – Osborne, Isle of Wight
Sweet Love,

Whenever I have a moment's time I feel I must immediately sit down and write to you. Every moment I think that the door will open and your sweet face appear, but no – lovy is far away from me sailing on the big sea, bless the pet. Could I but fly over to you, and throw my arms round your neck and press you to my beating heart and gently kiss you on the brow. Those *lovely big eyes* – who is there now to gaze into them? How sweet the wind and may it rest upon your lips. I can only kiss your photos and the ring you gave me on board. I am like a dead beat fly, as the air is stifling, not a breath of wind, like a very hard conservatory, everything grey and foggy, my hair hangs on my face and I feel hot and sticky. Nicky, Nicky, Nicky, *I love you, love you, love you.*

God bless you. Alix

Nicky to Alix – 13 July – *Polar Star*
My own sweet darling little Alix,

I had such a longing yesterday to jump into the old pilot's boat, go ashore, take a train to Portsmouth and cross quickly to Osborne, I might have been in my sweety's arms after tea on that afternoon!

Nicky, Diary – 14 July – *Polar Star*
We arrived at Copenhagen and dropped anchor in our old place. Went ashore in full uniform. At Tolboden I was met by Apapa [King Christian], my uncles and cousins. Went to Amalienborg, where I saw Amama [Queen Louise]. I have been put in the rooms right at the top, where Victoria stayed during the jubilee of 1888. I feel that I am only dreaming I am here in Denmark. But I am invaded by sadness, I can't help looking for Alix and being surprised that she is not there. I was very pleased to see little Georgie of Greece [first cousin].

Alix to Nicky – 14 July – Osborne, Isle of Wight
My own precious Nicky dear,

I have just returned from a solitary drive with Granny. She was talkative till a dreadful spasm of pain came on, which made her pale, and cry. She says she can't help it, it gets on her nerves when the pain is so great. I rubbed her leg for a quarter of an hour and then it got better by degrees. Poor dear, it is horrid seeing her suffer so. I am young so it does not matter so, suffering pain. I daresay it is even good to have to bear pain – but she, an old lady, that is hard, and it makes one sad to see it, and it frightens me. We drove as gently as we could. Granny dictated her diary to me this afternoon, she wanted me to do it so much again – and she is still as far back as when the Arch-Duke left, so she is hastening to catch it up again. She makes notes every day, but so indistinctly that she can scarcely read them herself.

Lovy, dear, I must say goodnight. Now sleep well, my precious love. God bless and protect you. Many tender kisses. I miss your sweet blessings so much.

Alix

Nicky, Diary – 15 July – Copenhagen
Had coffee downstairs with Amama, after which Uncle Valdemar, Georgie and I went to Uncle Freddie,[33] who was having a large reception. At one o'clock I went with Apapa to the landing stage, where a crowd of people are awaiting the Swedish King.

He arrived on his repulsive yacht *Drot* accompanied by two warships.

Nicky to Empress Marie – 16 July – Copenhagen
My dearest darling Mama

Yesterday all day there was an appalling din on the landing stage – in the morning Henry [of Prussia] arrived on his warship *Sachsen*. The Swedish King arrived on his awful steamship with two frigates. He always licks and slobbers on everyone.

Uncle Freddie and Swan received delegations all day. That evening they gave a big dinner, at which Apapa, the King and Uncle Freddie gave long speeches. In the morning the whole family accompanied them – with Apapa and Amama in their golden coach – to a church service.

Alix to Nicky – 18 July – Osborne, Isle of Wight
Aunt B[eatrice] has gone to Southampton for some function or other – no opening or shutting this time however. I played on two pianos

---

[33] Frederick, who would become King of Denmark in 1906, was married to Princess Louise of Sweden (`Swan').

with Thora, which was nice. Then we two went down to the beach, I drove the two ponies but they pulled vilely.

We watched the children bathe with the sailors and learn to swim and then we went into the boat and I rowed with heavy oars in the broiling sun – the result is that I look like a vulgar poppy and have big blisters on my hands which stick out like a red lump. Pooh – it is hot, such a change from the wind this morning. How I long for you! What are you doing, I wonder, probably playing Bull with the officers.

I have been for a drive with Granny and Aunt Louise[34] and am now resting on the sofa. The sunset was glorious, like a fiery red-ball. We are so many ladies that it is difficult to find any Gentlemen, most could not come.

19 July Good Morning Darling. It is very warm and fair. We have first come back from bathing in the large swimming bath.

The sailor held Thora from a bridge, with a cord to a belt around her waist and told her the movements, then he fastened a cord to me, made me try, and let it loose afterwards. I swam without anything through the place. 11 years ago I had three lessons in France and fancy I could do it, I was muchly frightened at first – but am delighted I can do it.

Nicky, Diary – 21 July – Peterhof
From the landing stage we went to the palace to look at Xenia's trousseau. The robes and linen were laid out in four halls in huge quantities! Rode my bicycle while Mama and Papa walked. Nicky [of Greece] arrived from Krasnoe, where he is living with Kostia [KR] at the regiment. The family dined together; Uncle Sergei and Aunt Ella arrived from Moscow. I was overjoyed to see them, as she reminds me of my beloved Alix, and of course she was all we talked about together!

Sandro, Memoirs
On 20 July we returned to the capital to attend the 'exhibition of the trousseau' in one of the larger halls of the palace.

Dresses: morning, sports, afternoon, evening, and 'grande soirée'.

---

[34] Princess Louise, daughter of Queen Victoria, married the Marquess of Lorne, heir to the Duke of Argyll. She was an artist and sculptor.

Coats: winter, spring, summer, and fall.

Fur coats and fur wraps: ermine, chinchilla, beaver, mink, seal, astrakhan.

Stockings, gloves, hats, umbrellas, and the mountains of accessories I do not pretend to know the exact names of.

Huge tables packed with dozens of sets of linen.

Silver plate for ninety-six persons. A gold toilette set of one hundred and forty-four articles. Gold-rimmed glass-ware, gold-rimmed cups, gold-rimmed dishes, etc., etc., eight dozens of each of these articles.

Jewellery: a pearl necklace consisting of five rows of pearls, a diamond necklace, a ruby necklace, an emerald necklace, and a sapphire necklace; emerald-and-ruby diadems, diamond-and-emerald bracelets, diamond breast ornaments, brooches, etc. All jewellery was made by Bolin, the best craftsman of St Petersburg. It represented, no doubt, a stupendous outlay of money, but in those days we judged the jewellery by the beauty of its design and colours, not by its value.

At the end of the hall stood a table covered with men's articles. I did not expect to be taken care of in Xenia's trousseau and was surprised. It appeared, however, that according to the tradition in the family the Emperor had to present me with a certain amount of apparel. There were four dozens of day shirts, four dozens of evening shirts, etc. Four dozens of everything. My particular attention was attracted by a silver dressing gown and a pair of silver slippers. The former struck me as being enormously heavy.

'Sixteen pounds,' explained the master of ceremonies.

'Sixteen pounds? Who is going to wear it?'

My ignorance pained him. He explained that a bridegroom, belonging to the imperial family, must wear that monstrous gown and silver slippers before entering the bridal chambers on the wedding night. This ridiculous rule was included in the same set of regulations which forbade me seeing Xenia the day before the wedding. I sighed. What else could I do? The House of Romanov had no intention of changing its three centuries old traditions for the sake of pleasing poor Sandro.

Alix to Nicky – 21 July – Wolfsgarten
Ernie fetched me at the station in pouring rain. We had my four little horses, and drove for an hour through the wood. It cleared up when we came here. The Gentlemen and the Ladies were there and Ducky stood at the top of the steps, looking sweet in white. We had

breakfast, then washed in a nice cool bath and then we promenaded a bit and looked for mushrooms, went and fed the horses with carrots and sugar. I do hope you can manage to come here, sweetykins!

Same day Seeing Ernie and Ducky together always makes me long too madly for you, my own precious Nicky dear. How much I shall think of you at Xenia's wedding – that shrimp marrying before her elder brother – too bad really but our turn will come – and then – oh Nicky sweet, then forever one – no separation, always yours and more even than now. You must come to us still here and sit here in my little house with me.

Nicky, Diary – 22 July – Peterhof
Kostia [KR] had tea with me. It is pleasant to find myself once more in my barracks. Everything here reminds me so vividly of the time before my heavenly stay in England at the side of my bride!

Nicky to Alix – 22 July – Peterhof
You have got me entirely and for ever, soul and spirit, body and heart, everything is *yours*, yours; I would like to scream it out loud for the world to hear it. It is me who am proud to belong to such a sweet angel as you are and to venture to claim for your love to be returned – is more than being greedy and selfish.

Ever your deeply loving and faithful Boysy, Pelly Nicky

Alix to Nicky – 23 July – Wolfsgarten
My sweet lovy dear

It is the third time today that I sit down to write to you. I never can forget [Aldershot] and what an angel you looked – I could have gazed for ever, you were too enjoyable and that dear expression and little movement of head and the deep big eyes, I so madly adore, oh! for the moment to press my lips on them and to whisper words of love and utter contentment into my Nicky's ears.

It must indeed have been a moving scene when Xenia and Sandro went to the Lord's Supper together. I think the idea a lovely one, their going together before their marriage. What a moment of emotions it always is! Sweety dear, that day for me, it will be *quite* in *private*, won't it, like it was for Ella, otherwise it would be fearful – a religious act like that must be quiet, otherwise one cannot think of what one is doing or saying.

Ernie played then lawn tennis and Ducky sat and read to me whilst I lay on the sofa and worked; but the reading did not progress much, as we began talking. She is such a dear thing – in her open way she speaks about everything [which] touches me deeply.

I being so much older, she can speak to me about things I know and younger girls would not, I think that does her good. I cannot say how old I sometimes feel – as a child I knew things, others don't till they are grown up and married. I don't know how it came! Then being alone so much with dear Papa and going with them everywhere and to the Theatre always made me get old early – I have gone through much in different respects – and so I don't mind speaking about things to her. She too has married Ernie to whom I should not mind telling anything, and that helped her at *first*, when she was so shy with him. It does one good to see how they love each other, but it makes me greedily long for you.

Ever your own deeply loving, very devoted and ever true bridy, Alix

KR, Diary – 25 July – St Petersburg

Sandro and Xenia's wedding takes place today at 3 o'clock. May God grant them happiness and may God grant that relations between them and her parents improve. The Empress was never that well disposed towards her daughter's fiancé, but recently there has been a real split between them, albeit a silent one. They say Sandro is very demanding and tactless.

Accommodation has been prepared for them in Ropsha for the first two days after the wedding; then the young couple will leave for the Crimea. The rooms are downstairs, to the right of the entrance; in the past other members of the family have stayed there with their wives during manoeuvres, and have not complained. Sandro, having been to look at them, declared that they simply would not do, and demanded the apartments of the Emperor and Empress. Of course this does not appear tactful on his part. In the Winter Palace, the rooms which are being prepared for the young couple were previously occupied by the Tsars and then in the 80s by Sergei and Pavel, between the Saltykov and Sobstvenny entrances.

Here again Sandro often expressed discontent with the decoration, although he will only have to live there one winter, as the Emperor has bought them Princess Vorontsov's house on the Moika, which will have been completely redecorated in a year's time. All this is upsetting and of course does nothing to bring parents and son-in-law closer.

Xenia suffers because of this discord and finds herself as it were between two fires: by pleasing her fiancé she fears upsetting her parents and vice versa. The family is very critical of Sandro. Of course their Majesties do have one trait which is difficult to cope with; should a decision about anything be needed, one has to wait for a very long time, everything is decided at the very last minute, so that their entourage, being completely uninformed as to any plans, can make no preparations. For example, for a full 5 months after Sandro and Xenia's betrothal, nothing was heard as to the time and place of their wedding. The engaged couple were in difficulty: if they asked. any questions about plans for their future life, this was construed as a challenge to parental authority. Of course such traits of character on the part of the Emperor and Empress do not excuse Sandro's lack of discretion in any way. In short there has been a lot of unpleasantness and bad feeling. I repeat: please God that this should all pass and turn out for the best.

Nicky, Diary – 25 July, the day of Xenia and Sandro's wedding – Peterhof

In the morning there was breakfast as usual with Mama in the sitting room. Afterwards I returned to my own house by bicycle to save time. We lunched at 12.30, as the ladies needed to get ready early, so as to be present for the finishing of Xenia's toilette. I went with Papa to the Great Palace. It was terribly hot in the church, as it was in the halls. Xenia's stewards were: Christian,[35] Nicky, Misha and myself; on Sandro's side stood his four brothers. Xenia's face bore a happy, even animated expression and she looked lovely in her wedding attire!

KR, Diary – 25 July – Krasnoe Selo

I must write of the day of the wedding. It was pitiful to see the Empress. Despite her self control, tears welled in her eyes and her face was very red. Xenia was crushed under the weight of a diadem with a huge pink diamond, a crown of large diamonds and her robe; she appeared even smaller than usual. I could not help but admire the Princess of Wales. She is 51 years old but looks 30. She is marvellously slim and her bright kind smile creates an enchanting impression.

---

[35] Son of Frederick and Louise. On the death of his father, in 1912, he became King Christian X of Denmark.

It was stifling hot; in the church Ella felt faint and had to sit down. Sergei came up to her and pinched her hand hard, after that she was all right. The young couple stood beneath the crowns meekly and reverently. Between the wedding and dinner there was an interval of about an hour.

Sandro, Memoirs – same day

Going back to the palace we marched in the same order as before, except that I changed places with the Emperor and was walking with Xenia on my arm.

'I cannot wait to get rid of this silly dress,' she complained to me in a whisper, 'it must weigh pounds and pounds. I wish we did not have to sit through that dinner. Look at Papa, he is all in.'

We all could see how worn out the Emperor was, but even he could not order the cancellation of the boring gala dinner.

Only at eleven p.m. were we able to change into more comfortable clothes, and off we drove in a court carriage to the suburban Ropsha Palace to spend our wedding night. On our way we had to change horses as the coachman was not able to control them.

The Palace of Ropsha and the adjoining villages were brilliantly illuminated, so much so that our nervous coachman, blinded by the lights, overlooked a small bridge and landed us – three horses, carriage and two newlyweds – flat in the brook. Xenia fell at the bottom of the carriage, I on top of her, while the coachman and the footman were thrown into the water. Fortunately nobody was hurt and we were rescued promptly by the second carriage occupied by Xenia's servants. My wife's gorgeous ostrich-feathered hat and ermine-trimmed coat were covered with mud, my face and hands were absolutely black.

We were alone, for the first time since our engagement. We could hardly believe our luck. Could it be possible that we would be permitted to eat our supper undisturbed? We glanced at the door suspiciously and then burst out laughing. Nobody. Just ourselves. I took the box containing the jewellery of my mother and presented it to Xenia. As little as she cared about jewellery, she did admire a beautiful diamond diadem and a set of sapphires.

We parted at one in the morning to don our 'wedding night uniforms'. On my way to the bridal chambers I saw my figure, moulded in silver, reflected in the mirror, and that ridiculous sight caused me another gale of laughter. I resembled an operatic Sultan in the grand finale.

Alix to Nicky – 27 July – Wolfsgarten
Oh, lovy, had I but got you with me, I want you too badly – a mad
longing takes hold of me, and I don't know how to keep quiet. I am
burning for a kiss and to feel myself clasped tightly in your arms, safe
and protected by the most loving of all beings.

Ella to Queen Victoria – 3 August – Ilinskoe
Alix I think makes such progress with her Russian she writes so nicely
to Nicky making very few faults and the 'tournure des phrases' [turn-
ing of phrases] is quite correct he told me she was rather shy about
speaking. About the wedding nothing seems to be settled. Ducky will
I suppose not be able to come and that deranges all plans. I am so
very very glad she is expecting a Baby if only it could be a Boy the
idea of our branch of the Hessian family dying out made me so sad.
                                                                Ella

Alix to Nicky – 6 August – Wolfsgarten
My own sweet darling
    Do you know the great excitement here is to see a wild cow. Since
5:00 she is in the woods and now every evening comes quite close in
the grounds. She ran away from her people near the Main. The others
saw her yesterday. To their joy, she has a chain around her neck. 100
mark reward for the person who catches her alive, but she is so shy
and frightened that as soon as anybody approaches her she dashes
off again.

Nicky to Alix – 9 August – Peterhof
My own darling Alix,
    I was simply enchanted to get your dear no. 75 this afternoon!
Thank you fondly for it and the violets, which smelt still deliciously.
I can't make out what you call a wild cow. Is it sort of like a simple
cow or something else? If you had a few cossacks there, they would
certainly have caught it in a few hours – it must certainly be easier to
catch an old cow than a wild horse!

11 August
Poor Papa is in very low spirits having to give himself up into the
hands of the doctors, which is of itself a bore, not always, alas, to be
avoided. He feels it more than the others do, having been ill only

twice in his life – 22 years ago, and this winter! We try to cheer him up as much as we can, and now he is pleased to go to that place Bielovejie; the Weeping Willow is also coming there – Greek Nicky too!

Oh! My Sunny, were you only here, I would feel quite else than I do now. But enough of this! Now I must run downstairs and fly on horseback to the other house.

A tender kiss from your own loving and devoted old boysy, Nicky

Nicky, Diary – 11 August – Peterhof

Woke to a wonderful morning. After drinking my coffee I finished a letter to my dear Alix. Zakharin [doctor] spent a long time with Papa, but could not find anything seriously wrong, thank God: he needs rest and a dry climate! But Papa himself is depressed by the thought that a cure is essential.

12 August We stopped at the old mill and signed the book, in which I also found the name of my dear bride when she was twelve years old – in 1884, when they were all staying here after Ella's wedding.

19 August – Bielovejie We arrived at the new hunting lodge. Its position on top of a hill is absolutely beautiful; the river which flows in front of the house has been dammed like a lake. As for the interior, the decoration of the rooms leaves nothing more to be desired in terms of simplicity, taste and comfort.

Count Rochefort, the architect who built the house, also furnished the interior down to the smallest detail, in which he has achieved complete perfection. I have four delightful rooms – almost too luxurious. Sank with delight into the enormous heavenly bath, like a swimming pool, next to my bedroom.

20 August Got up to a wonderful morning, then inadvertently fell back to sleep, and only woke again at 9.15, as Nicky [of Greece] was splashing around in my wonderful bath. Had coffee with Mama at 10.30. Poor Papa was unable to shut his eyes all night because of the heat, and therefore felt tired all day!

27 August Learnt of the death of the Comte de Paris.

Alix to Nicky – 28 August – Schloss Heiligenberg
So you had a nice splash in your big bath and felt quite happy afterwards; you old baby; but I too enjoy having a nice big one. I should
like to have been there when you were suddenly in utter darkness,
you would not have had a quiet moment! Are you not counting the
seconds till a certain somebody dares cruelly to tickle you again;
besides I would have smothered you with kisses.

Nicky to Alix – 1 September – Bielovejie
My own darling Sunny,
   I get in a mad state of excitement when they bring me your letters,
and I don't know what I would have given, to be able to fly over to you
and to cover your sweet face with greedy, burning and loving kisses.
   We have got exactly the same rotten weather as you – I'll say more,
it all comes from Germany as it is the west wind that brings it
straight to us! When I came to England, if you remember, I brought
beautiful weather with me.
   What an idea, love, to wish to have my idiotic bust as a baby. But
I really don't know where I can get one. We have two of them at the
Anichkov – one belonging to Papa and the other to Mama. I cannot
understand their making a bust of me, a frog-like child! If it were of
a child like little Alice – that is another thing. A sweet face like hers
is certainly worth having a remembrance of that kind, but me – what
was the use of it? Did Granny ever tell you that she had wanted your
portrait to be painted by Angeli, and mine too, while we were in
England, but luckily she left us in peace.

Alix to Nicky – 2 September – Wolfsgarten
I felt so funny putting on such smart undergarments and night-
gowns, don't be shocked my mentioning them. – Seeing things
which are being got for the trousseau is the only thing really to
remind me of the Wedding, as everything else remains exactly the
same as always. Gretchen would be shocked if she knew my mentioning such clothings to you. I suppose I ought to be shyer and
primmer with you, like with others, but somehow I can't.

Nicky, Diary – 5 September – Spala
Received a letter from dear Alix – I'm burning now with impatience
to see her again – it's only a few more days! I'm dying to embrace her!

Alix to Nicky – 11 September

You old monkey, how dare you say you will kiss me without my permission as much as you like! I never heard of such impudence before! You better not try it, otherwise my revenge will be most terrible. Oh, dear one, I long for you more and more, especially now that you could not come as soon as intended. What joy when we then at last do meet and I can clasp you in my arms and gaze into your precious face and beautiful tender eyes, and kiss you gently, always more and more, till there is no escaping for you any more. When once I have got you, you will not be free again so soon. I shall smother you with kisses!

Nicky to Alix – 11 September – Spala

Why would you look at me at the balls so sternly in 1889 – I can't forget the impression that constant gaze of the 'oceans' made upon me. I remember not being able to make out what it meant? Joy, despair, astonishment, shyness – overcame me, but still the gaze went on piercing me through and through a burning me, stirring up hope and fear, joy and sorrow! You were an enchantress then, my sweet one.

The state I'm in – a sort of gelatine!

Nicky, Diary – 15 September – Spala

For the whole day I wrestled with my feelings, torn between my duty to stay with my dear parents and go with them to the Crimea, and my terrible desire to fly to Wolfsgarten to my dear Alix!

The first feeling prevailed and, having told Mama – I immediately felt calmer! Leyden found that Papa is suffering from an inflammation of the kidneys, but also from nervous exhaustion – brought on by his enormous and unceasing mental work. Thank God, Papa agreed to all his demands and has decided to obey his advice! I have had to change my plans and write about it all to Alix!

Nicky to Alix – 15 September – Spala

My own sweet darling,

How I wish I were not obliged to write you the following lines. As you must have seen or heard from the papers, you will probably know by this time that Dr Leyden from Berlin has been sent for. The doctor is very nice and comforting – he said he found Papa's condition better than he had thought, and that except for the illness (something in the kidneys), his weakness came from the nerves!

I wanted to tell you this before, when we had met, but now I could not have explained to you otherwise the reason why I am not coming so soon and why I am going with my parents to the Crimea. But you will understand that I could not do otherwise than to sacrifice my own happiness for some time. Of course, it is too hard, not to be able to fly over to you. I could not do otherwise than this, my decision that I had taken after a whole day's violent struggle, as a devoted son and my Father's first faithful servant – I have to be with him wherever he needs me. And then how could I have left darling Mother at such a moment.

Alix to Nicky – 16 September – Wolfsgarten
My own precious darling,

I cannot tell you the state I am in, I feel *too miserable for words*.

What a blow that telegram gave me and a douche fell upon all. I could only laugh when I deciphered your telegram and chatter away and play the piano madly, but when I was alone in the dark in my bed, then it was finished and the suppressed tears streamed with all their might. I can only laugh gently.

No, it is *too hard* – really one must never look forward to anything in this world, one is so quickly disappointed.

Nicky to Alix – 21 September – Sebastopol
My own precious Sunny,

I hoped to have finished with this letter before our arrival at Sebastopol this morning, but unluckily had no time to do so and had to take it here with me! We got there at 11 with a bright sunny weather. Sebastopol does look lovely, on a fine day, with the Black Sea fleet in the middle of the gulf, drawn up in two huge columns. The churches and houses of the town are so white, it reminds you of the south of Italy, the lovely blue sky above all! I particularly like one place there – the cemetery after the Crimean war – the so called 'Brothers' cemetery' where a 100 thousand of our poor sailors and soldiers are buried all together.

I am sure, sweety mine, when you have visited that place, you will understand the feelings one has got (every Russian) whenever one comes to Sebastopol. I feel that I can go off mad with my awful longing and yearning for a kiss from your sweet lips!

Nicky, Diary – 21 September – Livadia[36]
The weather was colder than in the morning in Sebastopol. Papa was tired and felt worse. Georgy, Nicky and I are staying in the other house, in our old rooms. We dined alone with Papa and Mama upstairs in their rooms. I am terribly sad.

25 September At 2 o'clock we rode over to Ai-Todor, where Papa and Mama had gone earlier. It was funny to visit Xenia's apartments in the new house, where she received us as hostess and served us tea! She and Sandro look so happy, that one could not wish for more! Your heart feels glad just looking at them both! But seeing their happiness, I can't help thinking of my own – that which could have been if I had also got married this summer?

Nicky to Alix – 27 September – Livadia
My own sweet precious Darling
    There is no change for the better yet in Father's condition.
    We had an excellent ride to Sandro's and Xenia's place. Too amusing seeing Xenia play the part of the mistress, having to pour out the tea etc. Her rooms are very simply and prettily arranged, lots of photographs and pictures hanging about. But the funniest thing of all is to see Xenia in the midst of her own court – a lady and two gentlemen! Killing! Before us, of course, she is shy – but of one thing she certainly is not shy – that is in kissing her husband – whenever she can she flies at him, her arms round his neck! Quite right too – eh? All this, my beloved Sunny dear makes my heart ache still more about our separation!
    My very own adored darling – I want you, I want you madly! It is impossible to endure this any longer. Tenderly loving and deeply devoted Boysy

Nicky

Nicky, Diary – 5 October – Livadia
The post arrived late last night, bringing two letters from Alix! The day was clear, but a very fresh wind was blowing from the mountains. Papa and Mama have permitted me to send for my Alix from Darmstadt – Ella and Uncle Sergei will bring her here! I am deeply touched by their love and their wish to see her! What a joy to meet

---

[36] Imperial residence in the Crimea.

again so unexpectedly – but sad that it should be in such circumstances.

8 October Received a wonderful telegram from my dear darling Alix, already from Russia, saying that she wishes to be received into the faith upon her arrival – I was so moved and so struck by this that for a long time I could not come to my senses! Uncles Sergei and Pavel arrived from Moscow. Dear Papa felt a little better and ate more! Read reports and documents.

Nicky to Alix – 9 October – Livadia – Telegram
TO PRINCESS ALICE OF HESSE
   TOMORROW GOD GRANT IT WE SHALL MEET HALF-WAY FROM SIMFEROPOL TO YALTA WHERE WE SHALL HAVE LUNCHEON TOGETHER I AM COMING WITH SERGEI HOPE YOU ARE NOT TIRED FONDEST LOVE TENDEREST KISSES – NICKY

Nicky, Diary – 10 October – Livadia
At 9.30 I set out with Uncle Sergei for Alushta, where we arrived at one o'clock in the afternoon. Ten minutes later my beloved Alix arrived from Simferopol with Ella. After luncheon I got into the carriage with Alix and we drove together to Livadia.
   My God! What a joy to meet her here at home and to have her near to me – half my cares and worries have been lifted from my shoulders. I was overcome with emotion when we went in to the dear Parents. Papa was weaker today, and Alix's arrival, together with his talk with Father Ioann, have worn him out!

15 October [in Alix's hand] *Sweet Child, pray to God, he will comfort you don't feel too low, he will help you in your trouble, Your Sunny is praying for you and the beloved patient. Darling Boysy, me loves you, oh so very tenderly and deep. Be firm and make the Drs Leyden or the other Z[akharin] come alone to you every day and tell you how they find him, and exactly, what they wish him to do, so that you are always the first to know. You can help persuading him then too, to do what is right. And if the Dr has any wishes or needs anything, make him come direct to you. Don't let others be put first and you left out. You are Father dear's son and must be told all and be asked about everything. Show your own mind and don't let others forget who you are. Forgive me lovy.*

17 October In the morning Papa took communion with Father

Ioann. He felt weak from the emotion, besides which he had hardly slept at night. The day was wonderful and warm. It was already dark when we returned home. Sergei went with Alexei [uncles] by train to Vienna; the poor thing has developed consumption! After dinner, spent the evening with Papa – he is being tormented by a throat cough. Sat as always with my sweet, dear, darling Alix! [in Alix's hand] *Tell me everything, dushka, you can fully trust me, look upon me as a bit of yourself. Let your joys and sorrows be mine, so that we may be ever drawn nearer together. My sweet One, how I love you, darling treasure, my very own One.*

Dushka, when you feel low and sad, come to Sunny and she will try to comfort you and like her namesake warm you with her rays, God helping.

Only yours, quite your very own little spitzbub. Pussy mine!

Nicky, Diary – 20 October – Livadia

My God, my God, what a day! The Lord has called unto Him our adored, dearly beloved Papa.

My head is going round, I cannot believe it – it seems inconceivable, a terrible reality. We spent the whole morning upstairs with him! His breathing was laboured, he had to be given oxygen the whole time. At about 3.30 he took communion; then he started to have light convulsions – and the end came quickly! Father Ioann stood by him for over an hour, holding his head.

It was the death of a Saint! Lord, help us in these terrible days! Poor, dear Mama! In the evening, at 9.30 we held Prayers for the Dead – in the same bedroom! I felt as if I were dead also. The pains in Alix's legs have returned! In the evening I went to confession.

Sandro, Memoirs – 20 October

Nicky and I stood on the veranda of the beautiful palace in Livadia armed with bags of oxygen and watching the end of the Colossus. He died as he lived, a bitter enemy of resounding phrases, a confirmed hater of melodrama. Just muttered a short prayer and kissed his wife.

Everyone in the crowd of relatives, physicians, courtiers, and servants gathered around his now lifeless body realized that our country had lost the only support which kept it from falling down a precipice. Nobody understood it clearer than Nicky. For the first and last time in my life I saw tears in his blue eyes. He took me by the arm and led me downstairs into his room. We embraced and cried and cried together.

He could not collect his thoughts. He knew he was the Emperor now, and the weight of this terrifying fact crushed him.

'Sandro, what am I going to do,' he exclaimed pathetically. 'What is going to happen to me, to you, to Xenia, to Alix, to mother, to all of Russia? I am not prepared to be a Tsar. I never wanted to become one. I know nothing of the business of ruling. I have no idea of even how to talk to the ministers.'

Nicky, Diary – 21 October – Livadia
In the midst of our deep sorrow, the Lord has sent us a quiet and radiant joy: at 10 o'clock in the presence of the family my dear darling Alix was *anointed with the holy oils* and after the service we took communion together, with dear Mama and Ella. Alix repeated her responses and prayers wonderfully well and distinctly!

After luncheon we held Prayers for the Dead and again at 9 o'clock in the evening. The expression on Papa's face was wonderful, smiling as if he were about to laugh! Spent the whole day answering telegrams with Alix, and attending to the papers brought by the last courier. Even the weather has changed: it was cold with a gale blowing at sea!

22 October   Last night we had to carry dear Papa's body downstairs, as unfortunately it has rapidly begun to decompose. For this reason morning and evening prayers were held in the little church. Thank God, dear Mama is completely calm and is bearing her sorrow in a truly heroic way! I did nothing but answer the pile of telegrams.

There was a good deal of mental ferment about the question of where to arrange my wedding; Mama, myself and a few others considered it would be best to hold it quietly here while dear Papa is still under the same roof; but all the uncles are against this, saying I should be married in Petersburg after the funeral. To me this seems quite unfitting! In the afternoon we went down to the sea – the swell was enormous.

24 October   The day was grey – as it was in our hearts! In the morning I walked a little with dear Alix, then did some reading and writing. I still cannot bring myself to go into the corner room where dear Papa's body is lying – he is so changed since being embalmed, I cannot bear to dispel the wonderful impression of the first day!

27 October   Luckily the weather was good and the sea calm. At 8.30

we left our house, which stood sad and abandoned, and went to the church. The service was just ending. The coffin was carried out and entrusted to the cossacks, who took turns with the gunners and oarsmen from His Majesty's cutter to carry it to the pier at Yalta. Mama and all of us followed the coffin on foot. After the service we boarded the *Memory of Mercury* where the coffin was laid out on the quarterdeck under a canopy. A full guard stood around it. A wonderful, beautiful but tragic sight. As we approached Sebastopol it got rough.

Kaiser Wilhelm II to Nicky[37]**– 27 October – Neues Palais, Potsdam**
My dear Nicky

The heavy and responsible task for which Providence had destined you has come upon you with the suddenness of a surprise, through the so unexpected and untimely death of your dear lamented father. These lines are to express my fullest and warmest sympathy with you and your Alix and your poor distressed mother. I can well understand the feelings which must have agitated your heart in witnessing the ebbing away of the life of your father, as his illness and sudden passing away was so very like my own dear Papa's, with whose character and kind geniality the late Tsar had so many likenesses. My prayers to God for you and your happiness are unceasing. May Heaven comfort you in your grief and give you strength for your heavy duties, and may a long and peaceful reign give you the opportunity of looking after the welfare of your subjects. The sympathy and real grief at the so untimely end of your lamented father in my country will have shown you how strong the monarchical instinct is and how Germany feels for you and your subjects. As for me you will always find me the same in undiminished friendship and love to you.

What our political ideas are, we both know perfectly and I have nothing to add to our last conversation in Berlin, I only can repeat the expression of absolute trust in you and the assurance that I shall always cultivate the old relations of mutual friendship with your House, in which I was reared by my Grandfather, and some examples of which I was so glad to be able to give to your dear Papa in these last six months of his reign and which I am happy to hear were fully appreciated by him. I would have come myself to pray with you at the funeral, but I have so much to do with administration at home, that it is impossible.

Now, dearest Nicky, goodbye, God bless you and protect you and

---

[37] They wrote to each other in English.

dear Alix and give you happiness in your new married life, that is the warm wish of your most affectionate and devoted friend and cousin William.

Nicky, Diary – 28 October – Livadia
The day of dear Papa and Mama's wedding anniversary! What terrible suffering for her! Help us, Lord!

Queen Victoria to Nicky – 28 October – Balmoral Castle
Dearest Nicky,

I can hardly find words to express all my feelings in writing to you my dearest (future) grandson. The best I can find are comprised in 'God bless you.' May He indeed bless, protect, and guide you in your very responsible and very high position in which it has pleased Him to place you when still so young! May our two Countries ever be friends, and may you be as great a lover of Peace as your dear Father was!

What terribly sad scenes you must have gone through, loving your Father as I know you did! I am thankful darling Alicky was with you through this trying time of sorrow, tho' I can't help fearing she will feel the reaction afterwards. Your poor dear Mama how my heart bleeds for her! I know but too well *what* she suffers – What the lonely anguish she must be going through, and did go through! But she *is* blest in her Children, and you are such a dear, good son.

What a terribly long and trying journey you must be taking! You *will* understand I am sure, how very much disappointed and distressed I am not to see beloved Alicky, who is like my own child, *once* more before she marries, but I feel it *could not* be otherwise; and I hope and trust we may meet next year – and that you will not find England much further than Copenhagen. Once more God bless and protect you beloved Nicky.

Ever your devoted (future) Grandmama, VRI

KR, Diary – 29 October – St Petersburg
We received a visit from Nikolai Mikhailovich [Sandro's brother], who was in the Crimea during the last days of the late Emperor and was present at his death. We listened to him eagerly as he was the first eyewitness of those last events to tell us about Livadia; until now we had only received scraps of written news. He calls the dowager

Empress, the young Emperor and his brothers and sisters a holy family. Never before have I seen Nikolai, who is often dry and sardonic, so touched and moved.

I was most struck by what he said about Vladimir and Sergei supposedly trying to influence the young Tsar and bend him to their will. Nikolai thinks that they might just achieve their aim. But I think that Nikolai could be wrong. While I hope that the young Emperor will not succumb to anyone's influence, I fear that my wish will not be realized. Nikolai has warned me that the Emperor will want to use me. Others are also predicting a prominent post for me. I myself have a vague inner feeling. But I am also afraid; I am certainly not going to push myself forward.

Nicky, Diary – 29 October – in the train to Moscow
For me, the presence of my beloved Alix on the train is an enormous comfort and support! Sat with her the whole day.

30 October – Kremlin, Moscow   At 9.30 we got into the funeral train for our arrival in Moscow. On the platform we were met by Uncle Sergei, Ella and Uncle Misha. We carried out the coffin and placed it in a carriage. The streets were lined with troops and thousands of people – the order was remarkable. How many happy memories here in the Kremlin – and what a burden to have to carry out everything myself, instead of dear Papa! I read, received, and in between sat with my dear Alix.

Nicky to Queen Victoria – 30 October – Moscow
My darling Grandmama,

I must write to you a few lines, as the messenger leaves tomorrow. I cannot tell you what awful and trying days we are living through now! Your dear kind telegrams touched us all, more than words can say!

Ten days have already passed since that terrible event happened – it seems to be a nightmare – I cannot yet believe that my deeply passionately adored and beloved Father has been taken away from us! Though I knew how seriously ill he was, still the blow was a frightful one to poor dear Mama especially! Sweet darling Alicky's presence is such a comfort to me – I don't know how I would have stood it else! Dear aunt Alix and uncle Bertie being here – help also dearest Mama in her pain, which I am afraid will be still worse when we reach Petersburg, where we have never been alone – without beloved Papa!

The sympathy shown to us from everywhere and even from abroad – is marvellous and is most touching! Dearest Grandmama I am deeply grieved, that it is impossible for Alicky to come and say good-bye, before our wedding, to you – but, as Mama is probably going south soon the marriage has to be hastened with! But be sure that as soon as we can find any possibility of crossing over to England to see you – we shall do it. God grant that day may come very soon.

Forgive this hurried letter but I have so much to do that all my time is taken up! The one great comfort I have got in my utter mis-ery – is my darling Alicky's deep love, that I return her fully.

Now I must end.

With many kind messages from Mama and with my fondest love, believe me, dearest Grandmama, ever your most loving and devoted (future) grandson

Nicky

Nicky, Diary – 1 November – St Petersburg

We got into the funeral train at the station of Obukhovo and arrived in Petersburg at 10 o'clock. A bitter reunion with the remaining rel-atives. The procession from the station to the fort took four hours. After a requiem service we arrived at the Anichkov. How empty it seems! This was the moment I feared most for dear Mama. Aunt Alix and Uncle Bertie are downstairs. My Alix is for the moment with Ella. Dear Alix spent part of the evening with me – how strange to see her here – it reminds me of 1889.

KR, Diary – 1 November – St Petersburg

Yesterday I saw Nicky for the first time since he ascended the throne. This was at Nikolaevsky station at 10 o'clock in the morning, where we met the funeral train bearing the coffin of the late Emperor. The Empress came by the same train with her children, as well as Alexei, Sandro, the Waleses and Olia.[38] Sergei arrived a short time before with Ella and Uncle Misha.

After greeting me, he [Nicky] gave me a deep expressive look with his lovely, thoughtful and now sad eyes, and kissed me. The funeral procession moved off. We walked behind the coffin along the Nevsky and Admiralty Prospects, past the Synod and the Senate, along the English embankment, over the Nikolaevsky Bridge, along the

---

[38] Queen of Greece, KR's sister Olga.

embankment of Vassilievsky Island over Mitninski Bridge and through Alexander Park. Prayers were said by the Metropolitan in front of Kazan Cathedral.

The Emperor went in to kiss the icon. The day was warm, sombre and cloudy. Inside the fortress, when they opened the coffin I saw the face of the late Emperor in death; the familiar features were little changed; they looked peaceful, as if he were asleep.

Nicky, Diary – 2 November – St Petersburg

Slept well: but the moment I came to myself the memory of what has happened and the terrible feeling of oppression invaded of my soul with renewed vigour! Poor Mama again felt unwell and during the afternoon she fainted.

At 12 o'clock I received the full Council of State – I again had to make a speech! My dear Alix came to luncheon – it's sad to see her only at intervals! Alix, Uncle Bertie, Georgie [Duke of York] and I dined together at 9 o'clock. She sat with me in the evening.

KR, Diary – 2 November – St Petersburg

The young Tsar is the admiration of everyone, wherever His words are heard, either directly or in writing. I hear that the short speech He made in the Kremlin palace to the Moscow nobility was delivered in a loud, clear, assured voice. Yesterday, when receiving the Council of State, He addressed them most beautifully. I watched Him during the requiem service: the calm kind face, the thoughtful, deeply sad eyes, often half-closed. He is weighed down by his exalted rank. His modesty suffers from having to be everywhere and always the first.

The Empress was not at the requiem, she is not well, she has lumbago and fainted; this happens to her, her heart is not strong.

Nicky, Diary – 3 November – St Petersburg

It's a bore to see so little of Alix – I can't wait to be married – then there will be no more goodbyes!

KR, Diary – 3 November – St Petersburg

I have not yet talked to the Emperor's bride; but she smiles so sweetly whenever you greet her.

In the evening they covered the Emperor's body in the coffin with a pall up to his chest, in order to hide the hands which are beginning to turn black. The head is already looking quite black.

Nicky, Diary – 4 November – St Petersburg
My dear Alix came at four o'clock. It's the only time, before and after tea, that I can see her alone!

KR, Diary – 5 November – St Petersburg
At 11 o'clock the Danish king arrived with his son Valdemar and we were ordered to send a guard of honour to Warsaw Station. Before the train arrived the Emperor went out to greet the guard; he walked along the line of soldiers like a real Tsar. Olia told us that she asked the Emperor if he intended to retain the rank of colonel, bestowed on him by the late Emperor. The Emperor replied that was correct.[39] Splendid. At His command, Vladimir went to the station to meet the French extraordinary mission.

Nicky, Diary – 6 November – St Petersburg
At 11 o'clock we went to a service at the fortress. The King of Serbia arrived straight from the station. We lunched at home at one. Then I had to receive a mass of deputations: four German ones, two Austrian, a Danish and a Belgian – I had to talk to all of them! Went for a short walk in the garden – my head was spinning. The King of Serbia paid me a visit, then Ferdinand of Romania – they deprived me of those few free moments in the day when I am able to see Alix.

She came to tea with Ernie. At 7.30 I went to the Winter Palace to fetch Xenia for a requiem service. My dear darling Alix sat with me.

7 November We again had to relive those hours of grief and woe which were our lot on October 20th. At 10.30 the episcopal service began, then the funeral service and burial of our dear unforgettable Papa! It is painful and sad to write these words – it still seems as if we are living in a dream and that suddenly he will appear among us again!

On returning to the Anichkov, I lunched upstairs with dear Mama, she has remarkable self-control, and keeps her spirits up. Sat with my Alix.

---

[39] Nicky remained a colonel till the end.

KR, Diary – 7 November – St Petersburg

I stood to the right during both the liturgy and the burial service; a few steps behind me stood the Empress, the Emperor, all the family and foreign guests, but I did not see them, as I was trying not to move; except to cross myself. I was afraid I might feel faint, but it was all right. What a service it was, and what singing! The court singers surpassed themselves. When the time came for the last kiss, I could not bear it and started to cry.

It was impossible to watch without tears as our dear Empress quietly, meekly and submissively bent for the last time over the ashes of her beloved deceased. I did not see a single tear in the eyes of the Emperor. His grief is too deep. He cried himself out on the day of his father's death, and since then can no longer weep. He indicated to me with his eyes that I should go up to pay my last respects; but I chose not to understand until Vladimir conveyed to me verbally His permission to leave my place. After sheathing my sword, I went up to the coffin. I placed a small icon on the deceased. The whole church wept when the coffin was lowered into the grave next to the tomb of Empress Maria Alexandrovna.[40] I stayed behind in the cathedral while they finished closing the grave and celebrated a requiem.

Nicky, Diary – 8 November – St Petersburg

Returned home at 4.30 and only then saw my dear Alix. After tea I read in my room, while she worked. We dined at 8 and spent a quiet evening in the family circle. Two of the princes have already left: I wish the others would leave soon, too! It's easier to work without strangers in your way, their presence only increases my burden!

9 November My Alix came to me at four o'clock. We had tea upstairs. At 7 o'clock we all gathered in the Malachite room. There was a banquet for all the foreign princes in the Concert Hall. I nearly broke down as I sat at table – it is so painful to witness such an event, when your heart is like a stone.

Georgy [brother] to Nicky – 9 November – Abas Tuman

My dear Nicky

    Unfortunately you will not receive this letter in time for your

---

[40] Alexander II's wife, Alexander III's mother.

wedding, but nevertheless I congratulate you and Alix with all my heart; may you be happy and may God bless you. I am so sad not to be at your wedding; I am in despair that this is the second one in the family that is taking place without me. It's hard to always be away, and even more so to be completely alone. Although in the last three years I have become more accustomed to my solitude, it has become much harder to bear now, after the death of our dear Papa, after the terrible grief which has struck us. It's just so difficult to believe. It was such an unexpected and terrible blow. The whole visit to Livadia seems like a dream, which began pleasantly and well, but ended up as an awful nightmare.

Queen Victoria to Nicky – 10 November – Windsor Castle
Dearest Nicky,

I was so deeply touched by your dear kind letter and by all your Telegrams – and thank you warmly for them. These lines are to wish you every possible happiness that this World Alas! this sadly uncertain world ever can bestow and may a kind and merciful God bless and ever protect you.

You must have gone through such terribly trying and harrowing scenes! The various processions, the whole journey – and the last fearful ordeal!

How your poor dear Mama could go through it all is a marvel! All speak and write of your devotion to her, and of your kindness and goodness to all!

I need say nothing about your being a good Husband to my darling Alix. I know how safe she is with you and how you will watch over her!

My present is unfortunately not finished as I am having something purposely made for you. My present for Alicky is just finished in time.

I send you also the humble offering of my Munshi Abdul Karim for the Wedding. It is some very beautiful Indian embroidery.

I hear you are not going to leave St Petersburg, but going to the Anichkov Palace after the Wedding.

I fear it will be a sad Wedding and yet a happy one for yourselves!

God bless you, dearest Nicky.

Ever your devoted (future) Grandmama, VRI

KR, Diary – 10 November – St Petersburg
Olga told us how well the Emperor spoke when he sat next to her at

the dinner of the 9th: He does not wish to push anyone out; as Emperor he now wishes to investigate everything he did not agree with as Heir, to instigate changes slowly but persistently. Tomorrow he will be confronted by the first report from the Admiral-General,[41] with whom there may be disagreement on some points. He has said that it is better to sacrifice one man, even an uncle, than the good of the realm.

12 November   For my part, I place my brightest wishes and my most joyful hopes in the Successor. The young Tsar's wedding is fixed.

Nicky to Alix – 12 November – Tsarskoe Selo
My own precious little Sunny,

I awoke with your sweet name on my lips and prayed so deeply and fervently for your welfare, health and happiness. My own little one, my love for you is unspeakable – it fills me utterly and makes the darkness of these days bright.

God bless you, my Alicky, Nicky

Nicky, Diary – 13 November – Tsarskoe Selo
We walked in the garden and rode the bicycles – the sun came out for a bit, then it got colder. Saw dear Alix for tea – then took her back and said goodbye to her – we can't see each other again! I keep feeling as if it's someone else's wedding – it seems so strange to be thinking about my own wedding in such circumstances! Had dinner and spent the evening quietly – sat with Mama.

KR, Diary – 14 November – St Petersburg
Today is the Emperor's wedding. I very much miss the simple relations I previously enjoyed with Nicky. We used to see each other almost every day during the two years that he served with us. Now there can be nothing like that happy past. I would not call on him without an invitation, as this would be impolite and unseemly, while He has more than enough to do without me, but I am of course unhappy that I am not summoned. I say this sincerely.

It is said that the Emperor's uncles are trying to influence Him, that they do not hesitate to advise Him. But I think these rumours are

---

[41] Nicky's uncle, Grand Duke Alexei Alexandrovich.

fuelled by envy and are only empty gossip. I do know through Olia that Vladimir is importuning the Dowager Empress with various hints and suggestions, for instance he is insisting forcefully, but unsuccessfully, that the bride should be driven to the wedding in a golden coach, and that as future Empress certain diamonds should be presented to her.

Minnie [Empress Marie] is very aggrieved by all this. I also know that she never ceases praising the young Emperor, who surrounds her with the most solicitous affection and care. He is remarkably attentive to her.

Nicky, Diary – 14 November – St Petersburg

The day of my wedding! Everyone had coffee together, and then went off to dress: I put on the Hussar uniform and at 11.30 drove with Misha [brother] to the Winter Palace. The whole Nevsky was lined with troops waiting for Mama to drive past with Alix. While she was being dressed in the Malachite hall, we all waited in the Arabian room. At ten to one the procession set off for the big church, from where I returned a married man! My best men were: Misha, Georgie, Kyril and Sergei.[42] In the Malachite hall, we were presented with a huge silver swan from the family. After changing, Alix sat with me in a carriage harnessed in the Russian manner with a postilion, and we rode to the Kazan cathedral. There were so many people on the streets, it was almost impossible to pass!

On our arrival at the Anichkov we were met by a guard of honour. Mama was waiting for us in our rooms with the bread and salt. We sat the whole evening answering telegrams. We dined at 8 o'clock and went to bed early as she had a bad headache!

KR, Diary – 15 November

Yesterday at 10.30 in the morning, the whole of our family with the foreign princes gathered in the Arabian room of the Winter Palace. I came with Mama. After so many years she decided to take part in the Imperial procession, dressed in a Russian gown of silver brocade with pearls. The bridegroom-Tsar arrived a little before the Empress and the bride. He was wearing the uniform of the Hussars of the Life-Guard. If I had realized earlier that he wanted to dress up for the wed-

---

[42] Misha, Nicky's brother; Georgie, Prince of Greece; Kyril, Grand Duke Vladimir's son; Sergei, Grand Duke Sergei Mikhailovich, Sandro's brother.

ding, I would have said something, as I would like to see Him wearing our Preobrajensky uniform as often as possible. I presented the bride with a bouquet of white roses with red velvet ribbons, embroidered in gold with the cipher of Peter I. It was painful to watch the poor Empress. In a simple scalloped dress inset with white crepe, and pearls around her neck, she looked even paler and more delicate than usual, like a victim destined for sacrifice; it was an unbelievable effort for her to appear in view of a thousand eyes at such a difficult and desolate time.

While she and the Grand Duchesses attended the bride in the malachite room, where the ladies-in-waiting were arranging her hair and attaching the golden mantle lined with ermine to her dress, I saw the Tsar standing in the Arabian room. I stood in the corner by the entrance to the gallery; suddenly the Emperor came straight towards me, dragged me behind a column next to the wall and started to talk in a half-whisper.

The procession to the church was headed by the Empress with the king of Denmark; behind them came the Emperor and his bride. The halls were full. The poor Empress cried practically the whole time in church. The best men were: for the Emperor Misha, Georgie of Greece, Kyril and Sergei Mikhailovich; for the bride Boris, Mitia,[43] Nikolai Mikhailovich and Georgy Mikhailovich. It was strange and unaccustomed to hear Father Yanyshev read out: Praise to God's servant the Devout and Autocratic Great Tsar and Emperor Nicholas Alexandrovich. Father Ioann was also present in the Church, standing among the priests of the court.

The Emperor is just a little shorter than his bride, but not so much as to be noticeable. They both stood motionless under the crowns. I was able to see their faces as they circled round the lectern: their eyes were lowered, their expression concentrated. And then for the first time after the Emperor we heard the name of his bride: the Devout Tsarina and Empress Alexandra Feodorovna. When they left church she already walked in front, with the Dowager Empress and her father following.

Nicky, Diary – 15 November – Tsarskoe Selo
And so, I'm a married man! Happily, no one came to disturb us this morning – we answered our telegrams in peace! After coffee Mama came to visit us – she liked the decoration of our new rooms! We

---

[43] Boris, son of Grand Duke Vladimir; Mitia, brother of KR.

both prefer to sit in the corner one. We lunched at one. Went with Alix to the fortress, where we prayed at the tomb of dear unforgettable Papa; there were crowds of people! Rode my bicycle in the garden. At 5 o'clock the family came to visit us bringing presents for my Alix, and stayed for tea. She and I dined alone with Ernie, after which we accompanied him, Irène and Henry to the station. They left at 8.45. In the evening we sat upstairs reading letters from abroad until 11.

George, Duke of York to Queen Victoria – 16 November – Anichkov Palace

My dearest Grandmama

As Lord Carrington[44] starts tonight direct for England, I will take this opportunity of sending you a few lines. I know that both Papa and Lord Carrington have continually written to you and kept you informed of what has been going on here, and so I did not write to you. I have written to May each day and we have been so busy that there is not much time for writing and several days I had barely time to finish my one letter, so I hope you will forgive me for not having written before.

It has indeed been a terribly sad time here; but the Wedding came like a gleam of sunshine in the midst of the deep mourning. Poor Aunt Minnie has indeed been brave and has borne her terrible grief in a wonderful way, Mama has been of the greatest possible help and comfort to her, I don't know how she could have got on without her. Dear Alicky looked quite lovely at the Wedding, the Service was very fine and impressive and the singing quite beautiful, she went through it all with so much modesty but was so graceful and dignified at the same time, she certainly made a most excellent impression. I do think Nicky is a very lucky man to have got such a lovely and charming wife; and I must say I never saw two people more in love with each other or happier than they are. When they drove from the Winter Palace after the Wedding they got a tremendous reception and ovation from the large crowds in the streets, the cheering was most hearty and reminded me of England, an enormous crowd of several thousand people assembled in front of this Palace and cheered continuously from 3.0. till 8.0. The young couple showed themselves at the window several times.

Alicky got a great many lovely presents, I have never seen such

---

[44] Lord Chamberlain, sent by Queen Victoria to Russia.

jewellery, your charming locket was very much admired. Dear Nicky was most touched by your making him Col. in Chief of the Scots Greys, and it was the Regiment he admired more than any other, when he was at Aldershot this year, he is quite delighted about it. I know your giving him this Regiment has made a most excellent effect here.

The weather unfortunately has been bad, very cold with snow and rain alternately and no frost at all, I am disappointed as I wanted so much to see St Petersburg with snow and ice. I must say I have never been treated anywhere with so much kindness and civility as here from everyone I have met. This is the first time I have been to Russia, I certainly have got a most excellent impression of the people and the country. Uncle Alfred and Aunt Marie leave here tonight, the former for England and the latter for Coburg. Nicky has been kindness itself to me, he is the same dear boy he has always been to me, and talks to me quite openly on every subject. It is really quite touching to see the charming way he treats dear Aunt Minnie; and he does everything so quietly and nicely and naturally; everyone is struck by it, and he is very popular already. I am so glad that May, sisters and our Baby are with you at Windsor now, and that you are going to keep them with you till Papa and I arrive on the 6th.

I am so looking forward to seeing you and them all again. We leave next Sunday and shall spend one day with Aunt Vicky[45] in Berlin. God bless you dearest Grandmama with love to all and hoping to see you very soon.

I remain ever your most devoted and dutiful grandson Georgie

Alix to Queen Victoria – 16 November – Anichkov Palace
My darling Grandmama,

I am going to send You these lines through Lord Carrington who leaves tonight. How can I ever thank You enough for your sweet letter with good-wishes and blessings, for the lovely Presents. The pendant with Your dear portrait is *too* beautiful and I shall prize it very much – the lovely ring I wore for the Wedding and ever since, and when I look at it I have to think of the beloved giver. The stuffs, shawls and cape are charming and will be most useful – alas I shall long not be able to have the dresses made up. You can imagine what our feelings were at the Wedding – ten years ago at Ella's Wedding

---

[45] The Empress Frederick, Queen Victoria's eldest daughter, mother of Kaiser Wilhelm.

both our beloved Fathers were there – and now; poor Aunt Minnie all alone. She is an angel of kindness and is more touching and brave than I can say. Such a comfort her Father was here, so she had him to walk with. How I missed sweet Papa, is not to be said, and poor dear Nicky he felt the loss of his dear one quite terribly. But it is a comfort being married, I can be more with him and try and comfort and help him in all. He is so awfully good and dear to me, and my great love for him increases daily. We both are so intensely happy You gave him that splendid regiment and so deeply touched Your having thought of giving him that great pleasure. We have got such. nice little rooms here, as ours in the Winter Palace are not finished, and we did not wish to leave his dear Mother directly.

Darling Ernie, Irène and Henry left last night – alas they were but too short here – but he could not leave poor little Ducky so long alone. Uncle Alfred and Aunt Marie start tonight. I shall send You some of the myrtle and orange blossom I wore at the Wedding, and a bit of the dress as soon as I can.

The weather is most unpleasant, quite dark and a sort of rain.

It was really most kind of the Munshi sending those pretty stuffs.

Please forgive a short letter, as we have still any amount of telegrams to answer, and then perpetually Nicky has to be seeing people.

I received such lovely Presents, and I must describe them to You in my next letter.

Thanking You again for all the kindness you expressed in Your dear letter, and for the Presents, I remain, Beloved Grandmama dear, Your ever deeply devoted and dutiful, loving Child,

Alix

We were immensely touched that You gave a Dinner the day of our Wedding.

KR, Diary – 16 November – St Petersburg

I arrived for duty at the Anichkov at 11.30 and presented myself to the Emperor after the Minister of Justice had finished his report. I was invited to luncheon. At about one o'clock I was summoned by Minnie; there I found the Danish king [Christian IX], Willy [George I of Greece] and Olia, the Waleses and Uncle Misha. The newly-weds arrived. Nicky was wearing the Preobrajensky jacket (a short coat). At table I was seated at the place of the late Emperor, opposite Minnie.

It was the first time that, at Nicky's request, she had joined the others in the dining room, for she had previously been taking her meals alone; she was in tears, and when I saw this, I almost started to cry myself. When everyone left, she called me to her. She said she did not want to go anywhere, as there was no escape from her grief. She bears it with such resignation.

Nicky, Diary – 16 November – St Petersburg
We got up late as there was a mix up and they only woke us at 9 o'clock instead of 8. The day was full of hustle: Mouraviev came with a report and then I received people – so that I only managed to see dear Alix for one hour during the whole morning. We lunched together in the dining room, Mama also for the first time. At 3 o'clock went for a drive with Alix – it's strange to sit next to her in a carriage in Petersburg. Walked in the garden with Mama and Apapa. Had tea alone together. Wrote telegrams until dinner. Everyone came upstairs to us in the evening – to look at my wife's wedding presents!

17 November I am unbelievably happy with Alix, it's only a pity that my work takes up so much of the time that I would like to spend exclusively with her!

KR, Diary – 18 November
I did not see the Emperor or his wife at tea with the Empress. They came to dinner. He is so quiet, thoughtful, thin and pale; they are overloading him, he hardly goes into the air, and to stay without moving is bad for him. In the evening everyone went downstairs, to see the sumptuous presents He has given to his young wife. His study remains the same, the only addition being the writing table of the young Empress.

Nicky, Diary – 19 November – St Petersburg
All the Danish relatives came to lunch, to celebrate Aunt Alix's birthday – she has turned 50! Had tea at home and read together. We simply don't have the strength to leave each other!

Nicky to Georgy [brother] – 19 November – Anichkov Palace
First of all, Alix and I would like to send you our sincerest congratulations for your name day [26 November], we constantly pray God to send you a full and speedy recovery, and to comfort you, because it is so much more difficult to be alone after such great sorrow than it

is for us who are at least together! I was heart-broken for poor Mama, especially during the first days of our arrival at the Anichkov and the burial of our unforgettable Papa. Thank God, she bore and withstood these last ordeals heroically – there is no other word.

The day of the wedding was also absolute torture both for her and for me.

Throughout the whole ceremony, I could not get rid of the thought that beloved, unforgettable Papa was not among us, and that you were far away from the family and all alone; I had to summon up all my strength not to break down there in church – in front of everyone.

Now everything has calmed down a bit, and a completely new life has started for me. I cannot thank God enough for the treasure he has sent me in my wife. I am immeasurably happy with my darling Alix and feel that we will remain as happy together until the end of our lives. But the Lord has given me a heavy cross to bear; hope of His succour and the shining example of unforgettable Papa – these will help me serve and work for the interest of our beloved homeland! There is very little free time, there are always reports to be read and endless people to receive, but what can you do?

Alix to Queen Victoria – 24 November – Tsarskoe Selo
My darling Grandmama,

I am resting on the sopha [sic] after having been for a delightful walk with Nicky in the park. He is sitting near me and reading through his papers. We have come here for four days and enjoy the quiet and beautiful air – poor Nicky has so much to do, that this rest here is very good for him and having him all to myself is such utter happiness. I never can thank God enough for having given me such a husband – and his love to You touches me also so deeply, for have You not been as a Mother to me, since beloved Mama died.

It is so nice here and my room is full of plants and delicious smelling flowers, quite like at home.

Uncle Bertie will have told You all about the Wedding I hope. It was such a pity he and Georgie had to leave so soon.

I always wear Your pretty ring.

But now I must say goodbye, beloved Grandmama.

Kissing Your dear hand most tenderly,

I remain,

                                        Your very loving devoted Child, Alix
Nicky sends You his very best love.

Nicky, Diary – 25 November – Tsarskoe Selo
I was free, as practically nothing arrived for me to read. We lunched and dined alone. Words cannot express the bliss of living together in such a wonderful place as Tsarskoe!

26 November   Yesterday received a telegram from dear Mama saying that we can stay here one more day. My bliss is without bounds – it will be so sad to leave Tsarskoe, which has become such a dear place for us both; for the first time since our wedding we have been able to be alone and live truly soul-to-soul. [in Alix's hand] *Never did I believe there could be such utter happiness in this world, such a feeling of unity between two mortal beings. I love you – those three words have my life in them.*

27 November – St Petersburg   For the last time I strolled in the park with my darling wife. After taking tea, we left the Alexander Palace and set out for Petersburg; we arrived at the Anichkov about 6 o'clock. Mama and Aunt Alix were just finishing tea. [in Alix's hand] *No more separations. At last united, bound for life, and when this life is ended we meet again in the other world to remain together for all eternity. Yours, yours.*

3 December   Ella and Uncle Sergei came to luncheon, as well as Aunt Alix (as usual). At 3 o'clock went for a walk. A lot of snow has fallen, making a pathway for the sleigh. Skating has already been set up in the garden. Went with Alix to see Ella; we looked at several details of decoration for our rooms.

KR, Diary – 4 December – St Petersburg
After dinner Minnie invited me to have tea with her upstairs at 10.45. Here I heard from her something of the utmost significance: while Henry of Prussia was here, he told Nicky that his brother, the Emperor Wilhelm, was counting on Nicky visiting him in the summer for the opening of the new canal.

Nicky replied that he was not minded to make any visits while in deep mourning. Henry replied that his brother had come on a visit even though he had been in mourning for his father. Nicky then replied very firmly: 'Your brother is certainly not an example for me in this,' saying that his first trip abroad would be to Denmark to his grandfather. Minnie was highly pleased with this reply, and I was so delighted by her tale that I kissed her hand several times.

7 December   On returning from a reception in the formal rooms, the Emperor saw me by the doors to His study downstairs. He said how difficult His position was. I reminded Him of Tikhomirov's article, which talks of the difficult and important role of the Emperor Autocrat, adding, that as God chooses a Tsar, so He gives him strength.

I asked whether He had received any advice from his Father before the latter's death. Nicky replied that his Father had never once mentioned the responsibilities that awaited Him. During confession Father Yanyshev had asked the dying Emperor whether he had talked to his Heir. The Emperor had replied: No, he himself knows everything. Nicky added that even before, when sending Him abroad to foreign courts, his Father had never given Him any instructions and had left Him to act as He thought best. For this reason it was now both easier and more difficult for Him.

11 December   The young Empress again fell faint in church. If this is for the reason the whole of Russia longs for, then praise be to God!

George, Duke of York to Nicky – 13 December – Sandringham
My dear Nicky

I can't tell you, my dear Nicky, how pleased I was to see you these few days in Petersburg, although it was all so terribly sad: but you have always been so kind and dear to me, ever since we have known each other. I look upon you if I may do so, as one of my oldest and best friends. It was also nice the Club meeting once again. I wonder when we four will be altogether again, I hope soon.

Ever your very devoted Cousin and friend Georgie

Nicky, Diary – 14 December – Tsarskoe Selo
Today it is one month since we married – strange to say I am only just beginning to get used to the idea! My love for Alix keeps growing!

24 December   We had tea upstairs and at 6 o'clock went to church. Afterwards there was the Christmas tree in the blue drawing room, according to age-old custom! It was both joyful and sad – what a change from last year: dear Papa is no more, Xenia is married and so am I! Dear Mama showered us all with gifts as always! We dined at 8 o'clock. When we returned downstairs, Alix and I decorated our own Christmas tree!

31 December   [in Alix's hand] *The last day of the old year – what happiness to spend it together. Sweetest Angel, if little wify ever did anything that displeased you or unwillingly grieved and hurt you in the past year – forgive her duskhi! So deep and pure and strong my love has grown – it knows no bounds. God bless and keep you.*

Walked in the garden with Mama and Aunt Alix. The two of us had tea alone. Read until 7.30 and then went upstairs for the service. It was painful to stand in church and think of the terrible changes, which have happened this year. But putting faith in God I look forward to the next year without fear – because for me the worst has already happened, that which I feared all my life! But together with this irrevocable grief the Lord has rewarded me also with a happiness which I could never have imagined. He has given me Alix.

1895

Nicky – Emperor of Russia

Alix – his wife, Empress of Russia

Xenia - Grand Duchess, Nicky's sister, married to Sandro, Grand Duke Alexander Mikhailovich

Sandro – Grand Duke Alexander Mikhailovich, husband of Xenia

Georgy – Grand Duke Georgy, Nicky's brother

Ella – Grand Duchess, Alix's elder sister, married to Nicky's uncle, Grand Duke Sergei

Willy – Kaiser Wilhelm II of Germany, Nicky's cousin

1895

A DAUGHTER IS BORN

Nicky still grieves for his father – Alix is expecting a child
– Xenia and Sandro have a daughter, Irina – Georgy's
illness – Alix gives birth to a daughter, Olga – Family life.

Nicky, Diary – 1 January – St Petersburg
Today everything had a terribly different feel from other years! At 11
o'clock were present in church: Uncles Misha, Vladimir, Alexei and
Aunt Michen. Lunched with them and Aunt Alix. At 2 o'clock the
reception for the diplomatic corps began in the ball-room. It
reminded me so much of the reception there 10½ years ago – on the
day I took my oath of allegiance! On the other hand it is easier now,
because I am not alone – my dear Alix worked the ladies, while I took
care of the men. After receiving the son of the Emir of Bokhara, we
returned home at 3.30 – exhausted. Those wretched telegrams again
took up all day! Finished writing and did some reading. Boris and
Andrei[1] came for dinner. Went to bed early.

17 January An exhausting day. Went with Alix to the Winter
Palace. Lunched with Xenia and Sandro. I was in a terrible state
about having to go into the Nikolayevsky Hall and deliver a speech
to representatives of the nobility, the *zemstvos* [local councils] and
the town committees. Then there was a reception for each of the delegations in turn in the Concert hall. Returned home at 4 o'clock.
Strolled in the garden with Uncle Sergei.

---

[1] Sons of Grand Duke Vladimir.

From Nicky's speech to the representatives of all estates

I am aware that recently in some zemstvos *there have arisen the voices of people carried away by senseless dreams of taking part in the business of government.*

Let everyone know that I will retain the principles of autocracy as firmly and unbendingly as my unforgettable late father.

Nicky, Diary – 20 January

It is already three months that dear Papa is no longer with us, I still cannot believe that we will never see him again on this earth! It's too painful, too sad!

The whole family gathered in the fortress for a requiem service. On returning home I received Witte[2] and many others. We went skating, and then for a walk with Mama. After tea we said goodbye to Uncle Sergei. I finished reading *Le Journal de la Duchesse D'Angoulême* aloud to Mama.

22 January   At 2 o'clock in the Winter Palace the ladies' baise-main [kissing of the hand] took place – 550 ladies! My dear Alix looked remarkably beautiful in Russian costume. The whole ceremony lasted ¾ of an hour. On returning home we went skating. After tea I read aloud from a new book about Napoleon's life on the island of St Helena. Went for a drive with Alix after dinner. It was very windy.

Nicky to Georgy [brother] – 23 January – St Petersburg

I am up to my neck in work, but thank God I am able to deal with it fairly easily. There are receptions on Wednesdays and Fridays only – I am fed up with them! I remember how dear Papa could not bear them – how I understand him now!

Yes, it's hard to change yourself, when before all my thoughts were focused on military service, never mind the type of weapon; it was the one thing I adored and to it alone I was totally dedicated!

Apart from anything else, the knowledge that I am forever cut off from a life close to the armed forces – adds no little sorrow to my burden. But enough about this – I have no right to complain, rather I should thank God for the happiness which he has bestowed on the second half of my life, and for the treasure which I call my wife. She

---

[2] Count Sergei Witte, Finance Minister; later Prime Minister.

and Mama are my comfort, my hope, my peace. What would I do without Alix – It's too awful to contemplate!

Our future apartments are being prepared in the Winter Palace, Alix and I are taking an active part and are involved in every detail!

Nicky, Diary – 27 January – St Petersburg
My love for my darling wife grows ever deeper, ever more tender.

13 February This year there is no difference for us between Shrovetide and Lent, it's all just as quiet, only of course now we go to church twice. In such a mood you really want to pray, it's the obvious thing to do – the only and only great comfort on this earth is in the church and in prayer!

13 March – Tsarskoe Selo Alix did not feel too well all day, and lay on the sofa in her room. We drove together round the whole park. It was clear, but cold with a biting wind. After tea I wrote a letter to Mama, and then read for a long time. We dined at eight, and then sat in my study where I read aloud! I cannot express how much I enjoy these quiet evenings, alone with my sweet beloved wife! My heart turns to God with a prayer of thanks, for the gift of such complete and boundless happiness on this earth!

8 April – St Petersburg The anniversary of our engagement! I will never ever forget that day in Coburg – how happy I was then in every way. A wonderful, unforgettable day!

Nicky to Queen Victoria – 10 May – Tsarskoe Selo
Dearest Grandmama,

I thought so much of you, dearest Grandmama, when you sent us the sad news of the death of the poor Duchess of Roxburghe! It must be too hard for words, to lose one's best friends, like that, one after another – Sir H. Ponsonby, Sir J. Cowell and poor little Lord Drumlanrig. I know well what your feelings must be, having recently gone through one of the most fearful trials in this life – the loss of my dearly beloved Father!

In answer to your second letter mentioning the articles about England in the Russian papers, I must say that I cannot prevent people from putting their opinions openly in the newspapers. How often have I not been worried to read in English gazettes rather unjust statements in connexion with my country! Even books are being constantly sent to me from London, misinterpreting our actions in Asia, our interior politics, etc. I am sure there is as little hostility intended in these writings, as there is in the above mentioned ones. Nicky

Nicky, Diary – 14 May – St Petersburg
It poured with rain all night, and became noticeably cooler. Because of the damp, we did not go out for a walk. At 11 o'clock went to church.
[in Alix's hand] *A half a year now that we are married, how intensely happy you have made your Wify, you cannot think, God bless you, my own true, beloved husband – daily purer, stronger, deeper.*

19 May – Tsarskoe Selo   The weather was unsettled. In the morning we went for a walk. After the reports, I received visitors. We lunched alone. We looked over the upstairs rooms, over Alix's, which we are planning to arrange for a certain purpose![3]

25 May   Dear Alix is 23 years old! The first birthday that we are spending together, may God grant that we live many other such days together, in quiet joy and happiness!

Kaiser Wilhelm II to Nicky – 28 June – Sweden
Dearest Nicky
    Let me once more thank you with all my heart for the sending of those splendid ships of yours, which so ably and powerfully repre-sented the Russian navy at Kiel. Alexei was kindness and joviality itself and did everything in his power to make intercourse with our Russian comrades, everything that could be wished for.
    Goodbye, dearest Nicky, my best love to Alix and to you, with wishes for a quiet summer and a nice little boy to come. Believe me, dear Nicky, ever your most affectionate friend and cousin
                                                                        Willy

Nicky, Diary – 3 July – St Petersburg
I was working after tea when I was suddenly told that dear *Xenia has*

---
[3] Alix is pregnant.

had a daughter, Irina! Alix and I flew to the Farm. Thank God everything went all right. We saw Xenia and our little niece. Dined with
Misha. We went to say goodnight to Mama, who has calmed down
after her agitation!

Xenia to Nicky – 23 August – Bernsdorf
My dear darling Nicky

Here we are again in Denmark! But what a difference with our previous visits, how many changes since then! You cannot imagine how
difficult it is to be here without dear Papa, and how much we miss
him! In general it's not much fun here, which is understandable!

First we found poor Georgy in bed! Two days before our arrival he
started to cough up blood (and just when he was beginning to feel
better), and it happened again last night, but not as badly as the first
time. Of course this affects his nerves terribly and makes him very
upset!

Here all the girl cousins are learning to ride bicycles with great
enthusiasm, I shall also have to put myself to it, although it seems to
me I will never master how to do it.

I hope that dear Alix is in good health and feels quite well, and that
the children are not wearing her out too much with their endless
hopping! You have no idea how much I miss our delightful little
daughter! Of course she will be absolutely fine with you, but I feel
terribly sad without her!

Alix telegraphed me today to say that she [Irina] is quite well and
is growing every day. Everybody here is very interested in her, and
keeps asking me whom she looks like.

Sandro to Nicky – 6 September – steamship *Petersburg*
I had rather a boring time in Bernsdorf, and went to town in all three
times. Georgy spent most of the time lying down, and was ill at the
beginning ... our fears have been realized – Georgy's stay in Denmark
unfortunately did him harm. In my opinion there is absolutely no
need for Leyden. Chigayev is a wonderful doctor and should be given
complete charge of Georgy's treatment. We should not forget that
Leyden is a German, and on top of that a Jew, and that he does not
care at all what happens to Georgy. Besides which, Georgy needs to
be left in peace, so let him and the doctor decide what to do together,
without any outside pressure.

Xenia to Nicky – 11 September – Abas Tuman

Thank God that our little one is well, and thank you both for looking after her and showing so much interest, Alix was even there for her bath! In a few days you should be moving to Tsarskoe, there she will be nearer and it will be more convenient.

Georgy [brother] to Nicky – 11 September – Abas Tuman

The *Polar Star* was delayed, and at that moment I started this wretched spitting up of blood again and I had to take to bed; as it occurred several times I had to stay there for a full eight days. It was no fun at all, and to make matters worse I was forbidden to smoke. It was awful, but I managed for the whole eight days, after which I gradually began to smoke again. I felt fine as long as I was in bed, but for the first weeks of my stay there I had an almost constant fever, and I cannot say that I felt particularly well. Of course I was delighted to see the family after 4 years, but it did not really do me any good, as I lost even more than the 5 pounds which I had put on with such difficulty in May and June; I also get out of breath more easily. So these are the results of my trip. Very annoying.

Kaiser Wilhelm II to Nicky – 14 September – Jagdhaus Romingen

Dearest Nicky

God knows that I have done all in my power to preserve the European Peace, but if France goes on openly or secretly encouraged like this to violate all rules of international courtesy and Peace in peacetime, one fine day, my dearest Nicky, you will find yourself nolens-volens suddenly embroiled in the most horrible of wars Europe ever saw! Which will by the masses and by history perhaps be fixed on you as the cause of it. Pray don't be angry, if I perhaps hurt you quite unintentionally, but I think it my duty to our two countries and to you as my friend to write openly. As the seclusion and retirement the deep mourning has imposed upon you, debars you from seeing people and following in detail what is happening – behind the scenes. Think of the awful responsibility for the shaking bloodshed!

Now goodbye, dearest Nicky, best love to dear Alix and believe me ever your most devoted and faithful friend and cousin,

                                                                    Willy

Nicky, Diary – 28 September – Tsarskoe Selo
Happily Alix felt well and spent the whole day lying on the sofa in
the mauve room.

6 October From the evening Alix again started getting pains, which
she felt at night whenever she woke up. As they continued in the
morning, I decided not to go hunting and stayed at home. At about
10 o'clock Alix got up and spent the whole day on her feet as if nothing was the matter; and there was I thinking that these pains meant
the beginning of the end.

7 October My darling wife felt wonderful all day – things seem to
have come to a halt, and we were so hoping that by Sunday the great
event would have taken place!

Kaiser Wilhelm II to Nicky – 13 October – Neues Palais, Potsdam
Dearest Nicky
    That it is not the fact of a 'Rapport' or friendship between Russia
and France that make me uneasy – every sovereign is sole master of
his country's interests and he shapes his policy accordingly – but the
danger which is brought to our Principle of Monarchism through the
lifting up of the Republic on a pedestal by the form under which the
friendship is shown. The constant appearance of Princes,
Granddukes, statesmen, generals in 'full fig' at reviews, burials, dinners, races – with the head of the Republic or in his entourage makes
Republicans – as such – believe that they are quite honest excellent
people, with whom Princes can concoct and feel at home! Now what
is the consequence at home in our different countries? The
Republicans are Revolutionists de nature and treated – rightly too –
as people who must be shot or hung, they tell to our other loyal subjects: 'Oh, we are no dangered bad men, look at France! There you see
the Royalties hobnobbing with the Revolutionnaires! Why should
not it be the same with us?' The R[epublic] F[rançaise] is from the
source of the Great Revolution and propagate and is bound to do so,
the ideas of it. Don't forget, that Fauré – not his personal fault – sits
on the throne of the King and Queen of France 'by the grace of God'
whose heads Frenchmen Republicans cut off! The Blood of their
Majesties is still on that country!
    Look at it, has it since then ever been happy or quiet again? Has it
not staggered from bloodshed to bloodshed? And in its great
moments did it not go from war to war? Till it saused all Europe and

Russia in streams of blood? Till at last it had the Commune over
again? Nicky, take my word on it: the Curse of God has stricken that
People for ever! We, Christian Kings and Emperors have one holy
duty imposed on us by Heaven, that is to uphold the Principle 'von
Gottes Gnaden' [by the grace of God].

Your most devoted and affectionate friend and cousin,

Willy

Nicky, Diary – 21 October – Tsarskoe Selo

Again not a joyful day. It seems a pity and somehow shameful to take
off our mourning; it served as a visible link with a treasured past! The
only report was from the minister of war. The rest of the time I
answered telegrams. Lunched with Alix and Ella. The day was clear. I
met up with my little wife, as arranged, in the park. It was almost
dark when I returned home. Did some reading. The five of us dined
together again.

28 October The day was warm and quiet. The 29th wedding
anniversary of dear Mama and Papa! My heart aches at the thought
of how painful it must be for her. Help her, God!

3 November A day I will remember for ever, during which I suffered
a very very great deal. At about 2 o'clock dear Mama arrived from
Gatchina; she, Ella and I were with Alix the whole time. At exactly 9
o'clock a baby's cry was heard and we all breathed a sigh of relief!
With a prayer we named the daughter sent to us by God 'Olga'! When
all the anxiety was over, and the terrors had ceased, there was simply
a blessed feeling at what had come to pass! Thank God, Alix came
through the birth well, and felt quite alert in the evening. I ate late at
night with Mama, and when I went to bed, I fell asleep at once!

Xenia, Diary – 3 November – Tsarskoe Selo

The birth of a daughter (Olga) to Nicky and Alix! A great joy,
although it's a pity it's not a son! The birth pains began already last
night.

At 10 o'clock we went to Tsarskoe. Poor Nicky and Mama were
quite weak with exhaustion. The baby is huge – weighing ten pounds
– and had to be pulled out with forceps! A terrible thing to witness.
But thank God everything ended well. I saw dear Alix, she looks well;
little Olga lay next to her on the bed!

Nicky, Diary – 4 November – Tsarskoe Selo
Although Alix slept very little at night, she felt well. Of course I was present for our daughter's bath. She is a big baby weighing 10 pounds and measuring 55 centimetres. I can hardly believe it's really our child! God what happiness!!! At 12 o'clock the whole family arrived for a service of thanksgiving. Lunched alone with Mama. Alix spent the whole day lying in the mauve room, for a change of air. She felt well, so did the little darling. There was a mountain of telegrams.

Xenia, Diary – 5 November – Tsarskoe Selo
Alix started feeding herself. During dinner, the wet-nurse's son started *to take her breast*, and we all took turns to go in and watch the spectacle! The wet-nurse stood next to her, looking very satisfied!

Alix looks wonderful and is once more in good spirits. I saw Ott [doctor] – he is delighted that everything has turned out well. The little one has the longest black hair!

Nicky, Diary – 5 November – Tsarskoe Selo
A splendid night – no fever. After our daughter's bath I went for a walk. It was remarkably warm: 10°. Went to church with Mama. Alix again spent the day in the second room, with our little daughter lying next to her.

The first attempt at breast-feeding took place, and ended up with Alix successfully feeding the son of the wet nurse, while the latter gave milk to Olga! Very funny! Did some reading and writing. Mama, Xenia, Ella, Uncle Pavel and Sandro came to dinner. Spent a wonderful day!

6 November In the morning I admired our delightful little daughter: she does not look at all new-born, because she is such a big baby with a full head of hair. Went for a short walk alone. Returned to my darling wife at 3 o'clock. Thank God all is well; but the baby does not want to take her breast, so we had to call the wet-nurse again.

11 November Went for a walk with Mama until 4 o'clock. Had tea with Alix. The little one slept a lot and only woke up to feed. Xenia and Sandro came to dinner. Spent the evening, as always, with my darling in her room. Afterwards had tea with everyone in the mauve room.

Nicky to Queen Victoria – 12 November – Tsarskoe Selo
Darling Grandmama,

I thank you deeply for your kind letter which your special messenger just brought – and for the kind things you say. Dearest Alicky, who is lying near me in bed, begs to thank you most tenderly for your letter and good wishes. Thank God everything went off happily and both she and the little child are progressing most satisfactorily. She finds such a pleasure in nursing our sweet baby herself. For my part I consider it the most natural thing a mother can do and I think the example an excellent one!

We are both so pleased that you accepted to be Godmother of our first child, because I am sure it will prove a happiness to her after your constant signs of kindness and of motherly affection towards us. The name of Olga we chose as it has already been several times in our family and is an ancient Russian name.

You don't know, dearest Grandmama, the state of utter happiness I am in. It seems so strange to be a father!

Baby is going to be christened so early, so as that event can take place on our wedding-day and Mama's birthday. Dear Mama remained with us the whole time since the event and was such a comfort during the hours of expectation. We shall certainly send you some of baby's long hair; she is a wonderfully big child and promises to have large eyes. We both kiss you very tenderly and I remain ever your most loving and faithful grandson,

Nicky

Nicky to Georgy [brother] – 14 November – Tsarskoe Selo
It's so strange to think of myself as a 'father' now, as you might say a pater familias in the words of Kronstadt. At the same time you have also become the venerable uncle of two beautiful nieces.

You are surely aware that Alix is herself feeding our dear little daughter, and has turned herself into a veritable 'goat'. Feeding was quite difficult for the first few days, but now happily the baby has got used to it. Today she behaved herself perfectly at her christening, at least that is what I am told, for of course as the father, I was invited to leave the church during the ceremony, and returned only for the beginning of the mass – all together it lasted two hours.

Nicky, Diary – 14 November – Tsarskoe Selo
The morning was bright and suitably festive. At 10.45 our daughter

was taken in the golden carriage to the Great Palace. The procession to church began in the silver hall; I walked with Mama – Prince M. M. Golitsyn carried the baby. I sat alone in the room behind the church while the christening took place. Everything went well, and it seems that the darling little one behaved perfectly. The service finished at 1.30. After embracing Alix, I sat down to a family luncheon.

18 November Got up quite early. At 9.45 went to the station to meet Ernie and Ducky, whom I took straight to Alix. She hardly had time to dress. They hadn't seen each other for exactly a year, and now they were meeting again as parents! We put them in my old rooms.

27 November Our daughter keeps growing sweeter, today she smiled at us the whole time, what a delight!

17 December   Dear Alix was in a state, because the arrival of the new English nanny will entail some changes in our family life: our daughter will have to be moved upstairs, which is a pity and rather a bore!

18 December I myself washed our daughter in her bath.

Nicky to Georgy [brother] – 18 December – St Petersburg
What a bore to be near Princess Yurevskaya[4] she will undoubtedly do her best to drag you into her society. But at least you have one forcible excuse to refuse her invitations and visits – that you have come for peace and rest. I had a clash with her on paper last spring, about the marriage of her elder daughter, whose sponsor I should have been. Mama was in despair at the idea, so I very politely but firmly declined, and she was deeply offended!

By the way Yurevsky[5] is now in the cavalry school. He had no luck with the navy but managed to get into the cavalry. We'll wait and see what comes of it?

The little one is growing and getting heavier each day; she is now 12 pounds, which is very respectable for a six week old baby.

Yesterday a nanny arrived from England, whom we do not particularly like the look of – she has something hard and unpleasant in

---

[4] Princess Yurevskaya, born Princess Dolgorukaya, morganatic wife of Emperor Alexander II.
[5] Son of Princess Yurevskaya and Alexander II.

her face and looks like a stubborn woman. In general she's going to be a lot of trouble and I am ready to bet that things are not going to go smoothly. For instance, she has already decided that our daughter does not have enough rooms, and that, in her opinion, Alix pops into the nursery too often. How do you like that? It's all very boring, especially when the first apple turns out to be rotten.

Sandro and Xenia are very happy, they have an exceptional Englishwoman, who has already lived in Russia for 12 years!

Nicky, Diary – 19 December – Tsarskoe Selo
Today our daughter was moved upstairs to the nursery – May God bless her!

31 December – St Petersburg   We both slept wonderfully in our new home. The sun lit up my study most pleasantly as I was working in the morning. At 11 o'clock we went to church in the Anichkov; it was strange to feel like a guest there. After luncheon we went to our old rooms and collected the pictures, photographs and last things to take over to the Winter Palace. In the afternoon we sat at home and arranged everything.

Xenia brought Irina for our daughter's bath. At 7.30 we went back to church in the Anichkov and dined with Mama. The New Year is here! May God grant that it passes as peacefully, quietly and happily as the old, both for us and for mother Russia.

1896

Nicky – Emperor of Russia

Alix – Empress of Russia, Nicky's wife

Xenia – Grand Duchess, Nicky's sister, married to Sandro

Sandro – Grand Duke Alexander Mikhailovich, husband of Xenia

Ella – Grand Duchess Elizabeth, Alix's elder sister, married to Nicky's uncle, Grand Duke Sergei

Georgy – Nicky's brother who is ill with tuberculosis

Olga (sister) – Grand Duchess, Nicky's younger sister, also known as 'Baby'

Maria Pavlovna (the younger) – daughter of Nicky's uncle Grand Duke Pavel

KR – Grand Duke Konstantin Romanov (Kostia), Nicky's cousin and well-known poet

Georgie – George, Duke of York, later King George V of England

Willy – Kaiser Wilhelm II of Germany, Nicky's cousin

Prince Felix Yusupov

1896

THE CORONATION DISASTER

Nicky and Alix enjoy being parents – Foreign dignitaries flock to Moscow for the Coronation – The tragedy of the Khodinka stampede – The Montebello Ball – In the aftermath of the Khodinka disaster, a rift grows within the family – Nicky and Alix visit Paris – University disturbances in Moscow

Nicky, Diary – 1 January – St Petersburg
Slept well and woke up early. Enjoyed splashing in my bath, and after coffee sat down to the unbearable telegrams.

At 11 o'clock the ceremonial began. It was the first time we took part in the new year celebration together. Thank God, Alix coped marvellously not only with the church service and the ambassadors' reception, but also with receiving homage from the ladies, the Council of State, the Senate, the court and the suites! We inaugurated our dining room with a family luncheon. At 3 o'clock we went to pay a few visits to the family. We sat with dear Mama and had tea with her. On returning home I sat down to work. We dined alone and spent the evening hanging icons in the bedroom.

2 February Alix started to get ready for Uncle Vladimir and Aunt Michen's ball; she wore a beautiful crimson beret, like Tatiana in *Onegin*. The ball began with a mazurka performed by eight couples. It was a very lively ball. The ladies had their heads dressed in various ways.

We had supper with Aunt Michen. The dancing went on until 3.15. It was a joy to return home to our little bed.

21 February   At breakfast our little darling is brought to Alix; after she has been fed, she is placed on the sofa, and here she starts to exhibit a desire to speak, and makes all sorts of prolonged noises through her lips.

10 March   From today our daughter is being dressed in little short dresses!

Nicky to Empress Marie – 28 March, Easter – St Petersburg
Alix stood up wonderfully to the whole of the midnight service and liturgy; she rested only while I washed my face after the greeting ceremony.

This time, for the first three days, I had to kiss far more people than usual, as the Winter Palace was added to the rest. In all, judging by the number of eggs given away, it seems I have embraced 1600 people – a whole regiment! My cheeks are terribly sore after all this. I am longing to go to Tsarskoe, but at the same time I want to show Alix the breaking of the ice on the Neva, and indeed to see it myself, it should happen within the next few days.

Nicky, Diary – 29 March – St Petersburg
In the morning I did a lot of reading and received visitors after the reports. S. Dolgoruky and Meindorf came to luncheon. The new English ambassador O'Conor came to present his credentials. At 3 o'clock we went to the islands and went for a walk on Elagin. After dinner we went to the theatre. There was an excellent play called *Friends*. [in Alix's hand] *Sweet precious Nicky mine, no words can express how deeply I love you – more and more, day by day, deeper – truer. Lovy sweet do you believe it, do you feel hearty throb so quickly, and only for you, my husband.*

1 April   The weather was good but overcast. Xenia brought Irina to our little one's bath. She also weighs 20½ pounds, but our daughter is fatter!

Kaiser Wilhelm II to Nicky – 7 April – Coburg
Dearest Nicky,

The merry wedding which is taking place here and the faces of many of the guests remind me of two years ago when it was my good fortune to be able to help you to secure that charming and accomplished angel who is now your wife. The reminiscences of April 1894 were also felt by others and from that cause they agreed that we should send you the telegram you will have got. I venture to trust that I did not say or promise them anything that you have not afterwards found in your matrimonial life. May God's blessing be on you both especially in the next month when you are going to be crowned under admiring assistance of the world.[1]

Your affectionate cousin and friend,

Willy.

KR, Diary – 10 April – St Petersburg

At luncheon Vladimir sat next to my wife, having ceded to me the place next to the Empress. How sweet and friendly she is; it's only a pity that she finds it so difficult to overcome her shyness. Learned from her that she will have to stop feeding the baby before her departure for Moscow. At the moment she is feeding once a day, in the morning while she has coffee with the Emperor; I asked when exactly: before or after the coffee? She replied that the infant feeds while she is drinking her coffee. How delightful!

Ella to Nicky – 20 April – Moscow

Dearest Nicky,

At last the weather has changed and we have heat like in summer, so that I hope it will be *green* for the coronation. Please tell Alix: the furs I send tonight and have telegraphed to Ducky saying a Feldjäger will take it to Darmstadt.

I had a letter today from my old lady the Princess Golitsyn, in which she says that 'on avait sondé le terrain si le Prince serait à Moscou' [one had sounded out whether the Prince would be in Moscow] and that they said no, now somebody mentioned that the intention had been he should be attached to the Hessian court, of course such an honour would be an immense joy, so that I now ask you: did you have an idea of his coming for that reason? Was it for Ducky, if so, could you kindly telegraph you wish him to come or that all have already been chosen as I will let her know them directly. You see he would have to get his uniform in order as they always live in the country. What was so kind of you was placing Olsoufiev for

---

[1] The coronation of Nicholas as Tsar of all the Russias had been fixed for 14 May.

Ernie. His father was with the late Empress and he has a veneration for all the Hessian family.

I fear you must be overladen with work. Here the town is topsy-turvy with the preparations – dust, noise and Sergei[2] works hard daily with all the affairs.

I do hope you have quite good news about Georgy, now the winds, which come in spring, are so fearfully trying for those, whose lungs are delicate.

Tender kisses from Sergei to you three – from your loving Sister,

Ella

Nicky to Empress Marie – 27 April – Tsarskoe Selo
It seems to me that we should look upon all the difficult ceremonies in Moscow [the coronation] as a great trial sent to us by God, as at every step we will have to repeat what we did during those wonderful happy days thirteen years ago! The only thought that consoles me is that we will never have to perform the same rite again in our lives, and henceforth our existence will be smooth and even, I truly believe this. God will help us!

In general I am terribly fatigued, there are so many petty meaningless affairs before Moscow, it is as if my gentlemen ministers have decided to wear me out, they are so persistent and tiresome. I'm amazed my head hasn't burst with all the rubbish being stuffed into it. Alix and the baby are doing extremely well, thank God, and look wonderful: our little daughter gets rounder and chubbier.

Nicky, Diary – 29 April – Tsarskoe Selo
Today the unbearable English nanny left; what a relief to be rid of her at last!

7 May – Moscow   Woke up to the same depressing weather as yesterday. In the morning walked for a few minutes in the garden. Received the Emir of Bokhara and the Khan of Khiva and their suites. Ernie, Ducky, Victoria, Ludwig, Ella and Uncle Sergei lunched with us. We showed them our little daughter. Received Henry's huge suite; and the princes of Baden, Württemberg and Japan. In between all this I read.

Learned of the death of Arch-duke Karl Ludwig, who should have

---

[2] Grand Duke Sergei was Governor-General of Moscow.

come here. Because of this, the inspection of the camp and ceremonial reveille were cancelled. Uncle Freddie arrived to stay with us in Petrovskoe. We dined with him and the Connaughts. Spent a good evening with Georgie and Nicky [of Greece].

8 May At 4 o'clock we went to meet dear Mama, who arrived from Nice via Petersburg. They all look very brown. Had tea and dined en famille. At 9 o'clock the whole family, both from here and abroad, gathered to hear a serenade, beautifully sung by 1100 members of different choral groups.

KR, Diary – 8 May
At 9 o'clock I went to Petrovskoe, where the whole family had gathered round the Emperor, together with the foreign princes and princesses, to hear a serenade. It was performed in the courtyard of the palace by a thousand or more singers.

Every imaginable Moscow choir was there with its musicians; each singer carried a staff with a lantern – a sea of flickering lights; a huge number of people were crowded round the palace. We all listened from the balcony with their Majesties; after the first song, the Emperor said: Let's clap. A huge hourray rang out in answer to our applause; the night was quiet and softly luminous, a new moon shone in the sky.

9 May To describe today adequately would take a lot of talent. When we woke up this morning we were all delighted to see that the weather, which has been such a source of anxiety, had at last improved. It was calm and warm, the sun was shining joyfully as if wishing to join the Muscovites in greeting the Emperor as he entered his first city.

What exultation! A mass of people, the stands were crowded with spectators, the top rows taken up by thousands of *volost* [smallest administrative unit] representatives, the chime of bells filled the air. Then the first salute sounded, signifying that the Tsar had left Petrovskoe palace; the bells rang out even more joyfully; everyone removed their hats and crossed themselves. And then, through the Spassky gates, the head of the procession came into sight – the gendarmes; behind them His Majesty's own escort, then the sovereign's cossacks, behind them the Tsar's hunt, the court musicians and finally the golden coaches.

The procession stretched for a long, long way. Now there was a halt: the Emperor and Empresses had stopped to pray at the Iverskaya. The procession moved on again: the court liveries, the golden coaches and carriages, the embroidered uniforms, the horses covered with golden cloths. The Emperor appeared through the Spassky gates on a white horse, holding his hat in his hand. We also gave a huge cheer. The Tsar did not manage to salute the troops; without waiting for his greeting they welcomed him with an enormous roar. Before dismounting, he greeted only the 3rd and 4th companies.

A coach with a golden crown drew up; in it sat the Dowager Empress. The young Tsarina rode behind her in another coach without a crown. The Emperor walked between them into the Uspensky cathedral. I saw how they knelt together before the icons and the relics of the holy martyr Philip. From the Uspensky they proceeded to the Archangel cathedral, and from there past the cathedral of the Annunciation to the main steps, from the top of which the Tsar and the two Tsarinas bowed three times to the people. What a wonderful moment!

The Kremlin. The morning   I have written three pages about the solemn entrance, and seemingly not said anything. But then how to describe the atmosphere! They say that in the crowd many were praying, many made the sign of the cross as the Emperor passed. The Empress Marie cried the whole time in her golden carriage. It was too painful for her to remember how 13 years ago she had participated in the same celebrations with her beloved husband.

Some confusion arose at the moment of leaving the Uspensky cathedral for the Archangel: the priests who were walking in front of the Emperor made for the north gate, rather than the south. Vladimir (who is unable to speak quietly) shouted in a loud voice to the Metropolitan, who turned round and the procession then proceeded as it should. There were crowds of people on the streets. Our carriage had to go at a snail's pace. I did not notice a single drunk.

Nicky, Diary – 9 May – Moscow

The first difficult day for us – the day of our entrance into Moscow. The weather was magnificent. At 12 o'clock the whole throng of princes gathered and we sat down for luncheon. The procession started out at exactly 2.30. I rode on Norma. Mama sat in the first gold coach, Alix in the second – also alone. What can be said about the welcome, it was joyful and triumphant, as it can only be in Moscow!

KR, Diary – 13 May – Moscow

So the great day is at hand. The heart beats in anticipation of something out of the ordinary, significant, and full of deep meaning.

14 May – Coronation   That evening I felt as if I had woken up after a wondrous dream; it did not seem possible that everything I had seen, heard and experienced could have been real. By 7 o'clock I had already crossed the great rooms of the palace, which were full of people, and found myself on the main steps.

The Ivan the Great bell started to ring out, a salute was fired. There was not a single cloud in the sky, the cathedral square was flooded with bright sunshine. High up in the blue skies the swallows darted with shrill cries. It was already hot. The troops were forming up, the spectators taking their places in the stalls. At eight o'clock the family and foreign princes gathered in the great hall of the palace.

At 8.45 the doors opened and the Empress Marie appeared; our hearts bled when we saw her; she was wearing a crown and a heavy purple mantle, like a victim prepared for the sacrifice. Her face expressed suffering.

We all followed her into the Uspensky Cathedral. She was escorted by Alexei and the Danish crown prince. The procession was so long, due to the number of foreigners, that by the time she entered the cathedral, we had not even reached the main entrance. We heard the sound of cheers coming from far away on the square, greeting her appearance on the front steps. Inside the cathedral, the Grand Duchesses and Princesses stood to the right of the throne, a little below the dais; we men stood to the left. The Empress took her place on her throne, a little to the right of the thrones of the Emperor and young Tsarina. We took our places.

A roar from the square heralded their Majesties' procession. The priests went out to greet and asperse them with holy water. And then their Majesties entered and bowed to the cathedral icons. The Emperor was concentrated, his face had an expression of piety and supplication, his whole countenance emanated majesty. The young Tsarina is the embodiment of kindness and goodness. The Dowager Empress looked as young as she did 13 years ago, on the day of her own Coronation.

When the Emperor and his consort mounted their thrones, the dignitaries carrying their regalia and their assistants blocked my view, so that I could hardly see anything; I could only glimpse the Emperor with difficulty, but I could hear perfectly as he recited the Credo. His assistants were Vladimir and Misha. They helped him put on the purple mantle; at this point his large Andreevsky chain with the diamonds broke.

I could just see as he raised the crown onto his own head, and took the orb and sceptre; but I could not see anything of the Empress kneeling before him; I was only able to catch sight of him raising her to her feet and kissing her. I could hardly hear the speech of the Metropolitan Palady. In the same way I hardly heard the prayer read by the Emperor as he kneeled. It was only when everybody else fell to their knees and the Emperor alone remained standing, that I was able to gaze on him.

The Emperor embraced me; I nearly burst into tears and said: 'Christ be with you.'

15 May – Moscow The illuminations were magical – a sea of fire. We went to the palace: the Emperor was receiving congratulations from senior dignitaries and the nobility. A constant stream of costly dishes were offered along with the bread and salt; they arranged several big tables in the Andreevsky hall; what a useless expense! How much good could that amount of money have been put to!

17 May Yesterday there was a gala performance at the Bolshoi theatre. The Empress was in a silver brocade dress.

Nicky, Diary – 17 May – Moscow
The weather was wonderful all day. For the first time the morning was free! We went to visit Xenia and Sandro and then Ernie and Ducky. We had luncheon with Mama and then at 2 o'clock gathered upstairs for the ladies' congratulations. This began with the Grand Duchesses, then the ladies-in-waiting and after the ladies of society. It went on for an hour and a quarter. My legs started to ache. Later we drove to the Bolshoi theatre for a gala performance. As usual they were giving the 1st and last acts of *A Life for the Tsar* [Glinka] and a beautiful new ballet *The Pearl*.[3]

18 May Up until now, thank God, everything went perfectly, but today a great sin has taken place. The crowd spending the night on the Khodinka meadow, in anticipation of the distribution of the food and mugs, broke through the barrier and there was a terrible crush, during which it is terrible to say about 1300 people were trampled!!

---

[3] Danced by Matilda Kshessinskaya, against the wishes of the Dowager Empress.

The news left an ugly impression. We lunched at 12.30 and then Alix and I went to the Khodinka to be present at the unfortunate 'popular celebration'. There was nothing in particular to see; we looked out from the pavilion over the huge crowd surrounding the platform, where the orchestra kept on playing the national anthem and 'Be Glorified'.

We dined with Mama at 8 o'clock. We then went to the Montebello ball. It was very magnificently done, but the heat was unbearable. We left after supper at 2 o'clock.

KR, Diary – 18 May – Moscow
I heard from my people that apparently in the early morning, when they started to distribute gifts of tankards and china in the name of the Emperor on the Khodinka meadow, where a popular celebration had been planned for 2 o'clock, there was a terrible crush and up to 300 people were, it seems, trampled to death.

It was awful to have to go to the fete at 2 o'clock, knowing there had been such a misfortune before it had even started. Although I did not see anything, several people including Mitia,[4] told me that on the way they had met firemen with large waggons piled with the bodies of the unfortunate victims.

On the meadow, in front of the pavilion built for the Emperor on the model of Petrovskoe palace, thronged a crowd of seven hundred thousand, which is more people than Napoleon brought with him to Moscow. Here it was being said that nearer 1500 had died, rather than 300. When their Majesties appeared on the balcony of the pavilion, a huge cheer resounded. It was a solemn soul-stirring moment. In the evening we all went to a ball given by the French ambassador. The French government had lent magnificent furniture and Gobelin tapestries to adorn the house. I was told by Witte that the Treasury was going to release 300,000 roubles to help the families of the victims of the popular fete.

Xenia, Diary – 18 May – Moscow
A nightmare of a day! From yesterday evening a whole mass of people converged from all sides on the Khodinka – for today's popular celebration – and this morning the whole of this crowd rushed towards the distribution point of the gifts. A whole lot of people were

---

[4] Grand Duke Dmitri Konstaninovich, KR's brother.

suffocated and trampled to death by the pressure of the terrible crush – among them of course children. They say that by evening the number of dead had reached 1400, and although Nicky was told 360, in fact it's nearer 1000. Of course we talked and thought of nothing else all day. In the morning I sat for a while with Mama, at the time we still knew nothing, but before luncheon Uncle Sergei and the Chief of Police came to report to Nicky.

At 1.30 we went to Petrovskoe for the celebrations! What celebrations! The dust was appalling. There were a mass of people in the pavilion – the most august at the back!

Below was just one huge crowd, the orchestra and choir played the anthem and then 'Be glorified' endless times! It was painful and sad. While we were there, they were still carrying away bodies. Awful! All the same the 'Hourrah' was stupendous! At 10.15 we went to the Montebello ball. Of course we weren't at all in the mood! Nicky and Alix wanted to leave after half an hour, but the dear uncles (Sergei and Vladimir) begged them to stay, saying that it was sentimentality ('less sentimentality!') and would make a bad impression. What rubbish! Poor N and A were quite distressed, of course.

Sandro, Memoirs

My brothers could not control their indignation and we four demanded the immediate dismissal of Grand Duke Sergei [in charge of the event] and the calling off of all festivities. A painful scene ensued. The elder grand dukes rallied around Uncle Sergei.

'Don't you see, Nicky,' said Uncle Alexei, 'that the "Mikhailovichi" (the intimate name given to us, the sons of Grand Duke Mikhail) are inclined to play to the radical grandstand. They are openly siding with the revolution. They are trying to get the Moscow governorship for one of their own.'

My brother, Grand Duke Nikolai Mikhailovich, answered this infantile remark by a long, clear-cut speech. He explained all the horror of the situation. He evoked the shadows of the French sovereigns dancing in the Park of Versailles and ignoring the signs of the approaching storm. He appealed to the heart of the Emperor.

'Remember, Nicky,' he concluded, looking him straight in the eyes, 'the blood of those five thousand men, women and children will remain forever a blot on your reign. You cannot revive the dead but you must show your sympathy with their families. Do not let the enemies of the régime say that the young Tsar danced while his murdered subjects were taken to the Potter's Field.'

That night Nicky attended a big ball given by the French ambassador. The broad smile on the face of Grand Duke Sergei led the foreigners to believe that the Romanovs had lost their minds. We four left at the moment the dancing commenced, thus committing the gravest breach of etiquette and making Uncle Alexei exclaim with venom: 'There go the four imperial followers of Robespierre.'

Olga [sister], Memoirs

My blood froze. I felt sick. Yet I still stared on. Those carts carried the dead – mangled out of all recognition.

The catastrophe plunged Moscow into mourning. It had many repercussions. The enemies of the Crown used it for their propaganda. The police were blamed. So were the hospital authorities and the municipality. And it all brought to light many bitter family dissensions. The younger Grand Dukes, particularly Sandro, Xenia's husband, laid the tragedy at the door of Uncle Sergei, Governor of Moscow. I felt that my cousins were unjust to him. What is more, Uncle Sergei himself was in such despair and offered to resign at once. But Nicky did not accept it. By their efforts to throw the entire blame on one of their own kin, my cousins actually incriminated the entire family and that at a time when solidarity among them was so essential. When Nicky refused to dismiss Uncle Sergei they turned on him.

KR, Diary – 19 May – Moscow

It's painful to think that the sacred celebrations of the coronation have been marred by yesterday's terrible misfortune. More than a thousand people perished on the morning before the popular fete.

Added to that, there is no unity of opinion about the tragic event: it seems obvious that the main responsibility must lie with the governor-general, who should be stricken with guilt, and neither hide nor try to diminish what has happened, but should lay it open in all its horror. However it is not like that at all. Last night the Emperor heard that 300 people had died. He left for dinner in tears and deeply upset. I heard this from a witness – Sandro. The Emperor did not want to go to the French ball, but he was persuaded to go just for an hour; once there, Vladimir, Alexei and Sergei himself convinced the Emperor to stay for supper, on the grounds that leaving the ball would appear 'sentimental'.

So the Emperor left the ball after supper. One would have thought that Sergei would cancel the ball he was scheduled to give tomorrow, but he has not done so. And that, as soon as he heard of the disaster, he would have gone to the scene. I love him and it hurts that I am unable to disagree with the criticism of the Mikhailoviches. I share their opinion rather than the views of the Emperor's uncles.

Today their Majesties visited the wounded in hospital. At the Emperor's command, during the service in the church of the Birth of the Holy Virgin, 'the devoted servants of the Tsar who unwittingly gave their lives' were remembered. The Tsar has donated 1000 roubles for each of the families of the victims.

Xenia, Diary – 19 May – Moscow

Yesterday's misfortune keeps going round my head like a nightmare! In my opinion, Uncle Sergei's behaviour is beneath comment. He has washed his hands of everything, saying that it's nothing to do with him, and that Vorontsov is responsible for everything! Yesterday, he didn't even take the trouble to visit the scene of the disaster – it's out of his hands! We talked of nothing else while I sat with Mama in the morning.

I sat between Nicky and Georgy [the Greeks], and kept trying to tell Ella my opinions about everything that had happened! Her reply was: 'Dieu merci Sergei n'a rien à faire dans tout cela!' [Thank God Sergei has nothing to do with all this.]

Nicky and Alix came late straight from hospital. They only had time to visit one, where there were 160 wounded.

Nicky, Diary – 25 May – Moscow

The second birthday that my dear darling Alix is celebrating in Russia. May God grant us many other such days in our lifetime!

KR, Diary – 26 May – Moscow

The Tsar has left to spend two weeks with Sergei at Ilinskoe,[5] and the coronation celebration has come to an end.

Maria Pavlovna [the younger], Memoirs

The park was the chief charm of Ilinskoe. It bordered the river for some distance – cut by drives.

---

[5] A country residence of Ella and Sergei.

The place brought in nothing. Uncle Sergei spent, on the contrary, a great deal of money to maintain it. Each year there was a new caprice. He would have prize cattle brought in – a special breed of a bright beige colour, from Switzerland, I believe; at any rate, I have never seen them anywhere else. He liked fine horses, and organized an Ardenne stud, the only one in Russia. He was always having something built.

My uncle's suite and household were so numerous that each settling-down at Ilinskoe for the summer resembled the migration of an entire village. When we organized fêtes for the children of these people, we had always to plan for more than three hundred. My aunt had three women and one dressmaker, just for her personal service, without counting the maids.

The coffee finished, uncle took himself off to his rooms for a siesta; he took his nap stretched out in an arm-chair, his legs upon another chair covered with a newspaper so that it might not be soiled by his boots. My aunt went down to the garden and established herself within the shadows of a covered terrace where it was always cool. Here she would do a little painting, or have someone read to her aloud while she and the ladies did embroidery.

We sometimes drove to take tea and cakes with neighbours, especially with the Yusupovs, always great friends of our family. They had two sons, Nicholas and Felix, older than us by some years.

Felix Yusupov, Memoirs

The Grand Duke Sergei and the Grand Duchess Elizabeth [Ella] were among our most frequent guests and always came accompanied by their own gay and youthful entourage.

I adored the Grand Duchess but had little liking for the Grand Duke. His manners seemed strange to me and I hated the way he stared at me. He wore corsets, and when he was in his summer uniform the bones could be clearly seen through his white linen tunic. As a child, it always amused me to touch them, and this of course annoyed him intensely.

After supper the grown-ups played cards, and my brother and I had to go to bed. But nothing would have induced me to close my eyes until the Grand Duchess had come to say good night to me. She blessed me and kissed me and I was filled with a wonderful peace and went quietly to sleep.

KR, Diary – 26 May – Moscow

Everything that was light and joyful, all the impressive and moving experiences of the last three weeks, have been overshadowed and spoiled by the Khodinka catastrophe; but not so much by the catastrophe – which was the will of God – as by the attitude of those responsible.

Of course, Sergei is not personally responsible; although he is to blame for the lack of foresight; however, it is his fault that he is being showered with accusations. Had he gone to the scene of the incident, instead of welcoming the Emperor at the popular fete; had he put in an appearance at the funeral of the victims; had he told the Emperor that, as the person ultimately responsible, he no longer felt worthy of continuing as Governor General; had he himself requested the most thorough investigation – then no one would condemn him. On the contrary he would inspire general sympathy.

But instead of all this, what does he do? On the day of the catastrophe, he had arranged to have a group photograph taken in the courtyard with the Preobrajensky officers who were staying in his house. When they heard about the unfortunate event, the officers began to disperse, thinking that this was no time for photography. Sergei had them sent for, and the session went ahead. The Emperor, deeply distressed and in tears, does not want to go to the French ball. But Sergei himself, who should have been as upset as the Tsar, together with his brothers, persuades the Emperor to stay on at the ball for supper.

Finally, when the Emperor wants to instigate an extraordinary investigation, Sergei, instead of being pleased, makes it known to the Emperor through one of the ministers, that he will ask to be relieved of his post, if Pahlen is appointed as chairman of the investigating committee.

In a word, during the whole of this week Sergei has not acted in the way I consider that he should, rather to the contrary. All these days I have been suffering for Sergei. I love him dearly, we have been friends since childhood, and now I have to listen to condemnation of him from all sides; and yet I am not able to say one word in his defence; I am not able to talk to him: we would only argue, and that would serve no purpose.

Nicky, Diary – 26 May – Ilinskoe

Mama left for Gatchina and we immediately took the Moscow–Brest railway back as far as Odintsovo station, where we drove by carriage to Ilinskoe.

What indescribable joy to arrive in this lovely tranquil place! And the main thing is knowing that all those celebrations and ceremonies are over!

27 May Awoke with the wonderful realization that everything is over and that it is now possible to live for oneself, quietly and peacefully! It was sultry all day. After coffee I went for a walk and inspected all the surroundings of the house.

28 May We all had luncheon together, there were almost 30 people. Lay down and fell asleep for an hour and a half. At 5 o'clock the whole family drove in three carriages. We picked lilac and lily-of-the-valley.

KR, Diary – 29 May – St Petersburg
I have been tormented by doubts: should I tell Sergei about what I consider to have been his mistakes? I certainly don't want to talk to him: Sergei does not like anyone to disagree with him, he gets annoyed and loses his capacity to think coolly and logically. And there would be no use in writing to him. A quarrel could arise as a result of a letter.

Oh, if only the Emperor was more decisive! But he is surrounded by advisors. Vladimir is constantly giving him advice and even prompts him to revoke existing decisions, as for instance in the matter of Pahlen's appointment. The mandate was already prepared. Sergei, supported by Vladimir and Pavel – although none of them had read the script of the mandate – decided to ask to be relieved of his post – and so the Emperor never signed the mandate.

Nicky to Empress Marie – 31 May – Ilinskoe
For me, of course, the greatest joy is freedom, the absence of work (for the first time since our wedding). While out walking, I keep being surprised that I don't have to rush back for a reception or a report! I am delighted that Alix has taken up riding again, for the moment we go out alone together. I find it more pleasant than a whole cavalcade.

Nicky, Diary – 1 June – Ilinskoe
We dined at 7.30 as we had to go over to the [Yusupovs'] theatre at

Archangelskoe for 9 o'clock. The singers were Italians – they performed the opera *Lalla Ruk* with Arnoldson. After the performance
we walked back to their house, where we watched a very fine fire-
work display from the main terrace. Everything was remarkably
beautiful and well organized; the evening reminded me of previous
occasions, when the owners held feasts and festivities!

Maria Pavlovna [the younger], Memoirs

The coronation guests departed. We settled again at Ilinskoe into the
routine of country life. Dmitri and I always spent our summers there
with Uncle Sergei and Aunt Ella.

KR, Diary – 8 June – St Petersburg

In three days the Emperor has changed his mind as many times. At
first he agreed with the Minister of Justice, who, they say, wanted to
set up a commission in such a way as to exonerate both the Moscow
governor general and the Court ministry. Then Vorontsov suggested
the appointment of Pahlen. The Emperor readily agreed.

In the end, He went back on his decision, when Vladimir and his
brothers declared that, if Count Pahlen was appointed, they would
all resign from their posts. How outrageous can you get: to permit
yourself, in an autocratic state, to give an ultimatum to the Emperor,
to threaten and frighten!! Oh! If only the Emperor was sterner and
stronger!

2 July   It was painful for me to note that muted antagonism has broken out between Empress Marie and her daughter-in-law. I am even
more convinced than ever that the Emperor lacks resolve; he is too easily swayed in his opinion by whoever talked to him last. The Empress
is deeply perturbed, as are we all, that he signed Pahlen's mandate, and
then revoked it. It is all so unfortunate and embarrassing!

12 July   Sergei Mikhailovich[6] and I talked about the Emperor. Sergei
said that he had got to know him very well, while he was still heir,
and that he loved him very much. Sergei puts down his lack of resolve
and firmness to his upbringing; he also confirmed my opinion: that
no one, if you like, can have a constant influence on the Emperor;
unfortunately he is likely to be influenced by the last view expressed.

---

[6] Sandro's brother.

This tendency, to agree with the last opinion voiced, will probably get worse over the years. How painful, how sad, and how dangerous!

Xenia, Diary – 29 July – Mikhailovskoe
We had tea with Nicky and Alix. They only returned at about 6 o'clock. Nicky went duck shooting and killed 72 birds! We chatted a lot. Nicky clearly understands now about the uncles, and says that he won't try to keep them on, if they take it into their heads to resign!

Nicky to Georgy [brother] – 29 July – Peterhof
I don't want to talk about Moscow – it makes me sick to remember. It's not particularly comforting to think about the sad side of the coronation. This year seems to be a year of hard labour, with Alix and me as the martyrs: Moscow in the spring, and now soon all these intolerable foreign visits. First of all we are going to Austria, then Kiev, Germany, Denmark, England, France and finally Darmstadt; there at least we can hope for a complete rest. An attractive prospect, don't you think?

On top of it, we shall have to drag our poor little daughter with us, as all the relatives want to see her. I can imagine what the French will get up to in Paris – maybe they really will rename it Napoleondra, or something like it!

Georgy to Nicky – 5 August – Abas Tuman
I was very sad to hear about Sandro leaving the fleet. It is disgusting behaviour on the part of Uncle Alexei, as he put you in an untenable position with his stupid conditions.[7]

In general our dear uncles have behaved in a thoroughly improper manner recently. I am amazed at their effrontery, and even more by your patience.

Sandro, Memoirs
Nicky spent the first ten years of his reign sitting behind a massive desk in the palace and listening with near awe to the well-rehearsed bellowing of his towering uncles. He dreaded to be left alone with them.

---

[7] Sandro quarrelled with Grand Duke Alexei, who was the head of the Russian Navy.

Nicky to Queen Victoria – 10 October – Neues Palais, Darmstadt
Dearest Grandmama,

I am so sorry to have kept you waiting so long for my answer and not to have thanked you at once, for your two letters. Of course by this time you will have read all the details of our wonderful stay in France. The three days at Paris were very interesting but rather trying and I had hardly time enough to occupy myself with serious matters and even no real conversations with the principal men!

When I arrived here, there were four messengers waiting for me and it took me over a week to finish all that business. I am sorry not to be able to give you any answer whatever upon a certain question, which Lord Salisbury[8] and I had spoken about, but the thing is that I never had the occasion in Paris of discussing it.

As to Egypt, I must own, dearest Grandmama, the question is of a very serious character, as it does not only concern France alone, but the whole of Europe. It is of the highest interest for Russia to have her shortest communication sea route with East Siberia free and open. The British occupation of Egypt is a constant threat to our maritime route to the Far East, because it is clear that who so ever is the master of the valley of the Nile, the same holds possession of the Suez canal. This is the reason why Russia and France do not approve of England remaining in that part of the world and why the two countries want the real integrity of the Canal. Politics alas! are not the same as private or domestic affairs and they are not guided by personal or relationship feelings. History is one's real positive teacher in these matters and for me personally, except that, I have always got the sacred example of my beloved Father and also the result and proof of all His deeds!

Mr de Staal[9] would explain to you all these difficulties about Egypt very clearly if you once gave him the opportunity of speaking to you openly. But now enough of politics!

You may well imagine Alix's joy of being once more quietly at home. I am happy too to be here and rest for a short while, after having travelled for nearly six weeks without stopping. In the beginning the weather was lovely and we took long drives to the different pretty places about Darmstadt-Jugenheim, Wolfsgarten, etc. all so new to me. We go very often to the theatre, which is, I think, excellent and such a good way of occupying one's evenings. But unfortunately our stay here comes to an end in a week; I shall be just as sorry as Alix to leave this peaceful place.

---

[8] British Prime Minister.
[9] Ambassador to London.

Now goodbye, dearest Grandmama, with my best love to all, believe me your most loving and devoted grandson

Nicky

Ella to Queen Victoria – 3 November – Moscow
Dearest Grandmama,

Such loving thanks for your dear letter and charming presents. It was such a joy having news about you through Alix and Nicky. We thoroughly enjoyed ourselves together at Darmstadt and travelled most pleasantly together home. It must have been a great astonishment as people were saying we did not like each other etc. Well the abominable lies told about us to them are not edifying, the intrigues were simply disgusting but one day I trust all the truth will come out and the great thing is to have a clear conscience before God as who can change the unkindness of the world, in this case a set of jealous intriguers.

Our delightful journey freshened us both up, although poor Sergei looks very thin. People I suppose could not believe that we were harmless and happy, so began to prove the contrary.

Really we want nothing, we are very happy, we try to do our duty and I must say although it sounds vain people here like us and again proved their affection by receiving us most warmly when we arrived the other day here. Well in everything bad there is good and we have now our eyes open and some really true friends and after all few enemies.

We have lots to do here and every year like this place more and more. In every way I find it lucky we live in another town than Alix, for her sake chiefly, it makes her quite independent, later on when she is known as well as her opinions it won't matter as nobody can then say that whatever she does I have cancelled. She is already dearly loved in her new home and it is for me the greatest joy.

What I cannot understand is jealousy between Sisters or not liking the younger ones to be of a higher rank. I know that people watched at the Coronation to see would I kiss her hand, why it was a real joy a person one loves and she being so much younger than I has always been more like a child than a Sister. We used to laugh about our ranks at Darmstadt and how each of us has married, according to our ages always higher so that the eldest goes the last. May God grant we ten husbands and wives[10] may always love each other as we do and I am

---

[10] Ella, her sisters and brother and their spouses.

sure it is Papa and Mama's blessings and prayers which surround us and have made our family lives so happy. How sad you must feel without Liko[11] who was such a help to you, it is selfish, my speaking of our joys when so many others have such deep sorrows, poor Aunty do give her our love.

Tender kisses to you from Sergei and your loving Own Child,

Ella

Nicky to Sergei – 25 November – Tsarskoe Selo

Dear Uncle Sergei,

Thank you so much for your two detailed letters, which fully confirm the picture of the university disturbances. I approve absolutely of all your orders and the actions of the university authorities. Indeed, only decisive and consistent measures and a unified system 'without hesitation' can guarantee success.

As yet it is quiet at the University here, although Muravev predicts a possibility of the disturbances in Moscow being echoed here. I cannot help feeling regret and even envy, when I think of the wise system of higher education in England – stratas at universities, everyone studies as much as he needs, and most importantly, they constantly foster the physical development of the younger generation, and in so doing they are a thousand times right, because the country needs efficient, healthy workers, and not creatures with effete bodies and souls, torn away from their milieu and not knowing what to do with themselves. This is an extremely sore point for Russia, and which will require a lot of persistent work to resolve correctly and sensibly. This is the cause of the sad phenomenon of students letting themselves be enticed so easily along the wrong path, incited and led astray by a few dozen scoundrels and rascals!

As you already know, our daughter has not been very well; for no obvious reason she suddenly developed a fever, which lasted about a week but is now, thank God, over. We thought she was cutting her teeth, but nothing has happened yet.

Once a week we visit Gatchina. Mama is well and in excellent spirits. I have a lot of work to do, but I manage, with God's help and cannot complain; and as for family life – I wish everyone could have such utter happiness, serenity and bliss!

---

[11] Henry of Battenberg ('Liko'), husband of Victoria's daughter Beatrice, had recently died.

The new rooms here, in which you were the first to stay, now look habitable and cosy; they are eagerly awaiting you.

In the evening we are going to town, for the St George's Day celebrations, on which occasion I send you my most heartfelt greetings.

Alix and I embrace you and Ella fondly. God save you! Sincerely your

Nicky

Ella to Nicky – 22 December – Neskuchnoe

God bless you, dearest Nicky. I cannot find words to say how deeply you have touched us both and what a lovely mark of affection you have showed Sergei in sending him that touchingly hearty manifest. He could not read it without crying as every word went deep to our hearts and all you say about your dear Father – those words are a treasure and comfort, which have washed away all the sorrows of this year.

If you could only see how all his friends congratulated him with tears of joy in their eyes and when those kind words will be read everywhere all will see your trust in Sergei, what is written from the heart goes to the heart, however hard it may be, there always is a soft corner, which such words can penetrate to. No Xmas gift has been more welcomed with deep gratitude, than this paper, it will give him strength to enter the new year with courage and hope to merit your proof of confidence.

God bless you, dear Boy, God bless you, may He help you in your difficult task and give you strength and calm.

I hope you three are flourishing – to feel others happy to have such a great power in one's hands must give joy. Merry, merry Xmas and a very happy New Year from your loving old Sister and devoted subject

Ella

I hope my cross is a help and will keep far from you worries or pains.

1897–1898

Nicky – Emperor of Russia

Alix – Empress of Russia, Nicky's wife

Xenia – Grand Duchess, Nicky's sister, married to Sandro, Grand Duke Alexander Mikhailovich

Sandro – Grand Duke Alexander Mikhailovich, husband of Xenia

Georgy – Grand Duke Georgy Alexandrovich, Nicky's brother

KR – Grand Duke Konstantin Romanov, Nicky's cousin

Ella – Grand Duchess Elizabeth, Alix's elder sister

Willy – Kaiser Wilhelm II of Germany, Nicky's cousin

Georgie – George, Duke of York

1897

MARITAL BLISS I

Nicky's lack of character and resolve – Alix is expecting
another child – A row with Uncle Vladimir – A second
daughter, Tatiana, is born – Problems with Japan

KR, Diary – 8 January
Yesterday the Empress Marie came to visit Mama and told her in
secret something very interesting. Mama was lamenting the lack of
character and strength of will, the wavering and indecision shown by
Nicky in the spring following Khodinka and also in the story with
Sandro. Minnie replied that she was hoping that Nicky would gain in
resolve and little by little free himself from outside influences.

Nicky to Empress Marie – 9 January – Tsarskoe Selo
Yesterday Alix definitely felt some movement – hopping and kicking!
Please tell Xenia that if this goes on it will become quite indecent: only
lady elephants carry for 22 months (as Sandro knows). Not only will *she*
get worn out, but *we* will all be exhausted waiting, and then only for a
trunk to emerge from her? It's just not permissible!!![1]

KR, Diary – 20 January – St Petersburg
Misha[2] came to see us. He was sent for because of his father's illness
as it's impossible to know what the outcome will be. Misha has not

---

[1] Alix was three months' pregnant, and having to take things easy.
[2] Grand Duke Mikhail Mikhailovich, known as Miche-Miche, brother of Sandro.
Living in England, morganatically married to Pushkin's granddaughter, Countess
Sophie Merenberg.

been in Russia for 6 years, since 1891, when he got married without the consent or the knowledge of the Emperor, and went into voluntary exile; he was excluded from the service and is now in civilian clothes. He is older but no wiser. I have never felt well disposed towards him because of his stupidity and touchiness.

Nicky to Empress Marie – 22 January – Tsarskoe Selo
Today Alix at last got up. Ott wheeled her round the garden in her chair. Sitting up made her feel very dizzy; which is understandable after remaining lying down for seven weeks. But you can be quite confident, dear Mama, that we are more than careful about moving her, even when changing her position on the divan.

Nicky to Grand Duke Vladimir – 29 January – Tsarskoe Selo
Looking through the theatre repertoire, I notice that there will soon be another fancy-dress ball at the Marinsky Theatre. Therefore, in the event that we should wish to attend, I must warn you that I am completely against guests being in our box, or staying for supper in our room. My wife and I find it absolutely indecent and hope that such an incident will never recur either in this box or in any other!

I was especially hurt that you did it without any permission. Nothing of the kind ever happened in Papa's day, and you know how strictly I adhere to everything as it was then. It is also unfair to try and take advantage of the fact that I am young, and your nephew. Please bear in mind that I have become Head of the Family and I have no right to turn a blind eye to the actions of any member of the Family that I find wrong or inappropriate. More than ever our family needs to remain united and firm, in accordance with your grandfather's behests. And you ought to be the first to help me in this. In future, please spare me the necessity of writing such letters which make me feel abominable.

With sincere love,

your Nicky

KR, Diary – 4 February – St Petersburg
Empress Marie came to see Mama, who then told me all she had found out. Two weeks ago there was a masked ball at the Marinsky Theatre; Maria Pavlovna[3] appeared in the side upper imperial lodge

---

[3] Maria Pavlovna, wife of Grand Duke Vladimir, mother of Grand Dukes Kyril, Boris and Andrei. Known as Maria Pavlovna the elder.

with her usual coterie: the Naryshkins, the Ambassador Liechtenstein, Benckendorff, Ushakov and Khitrovo. This did not please people at all. When the Emperor heard about it, he wrote to Vladimir that as head of the family rather than as nephew, he could not allow outsiders to be admitted into the imperial lodge. Vladimir replied in a curt letter that he had never been subjected to such a sharp reprimand by either his father or his brother. Since then they have met and talked as if nothing had happened. May God grant that the Tsar continues to make his will known so decisively. But how could Vladimir permit himself to write to the Emperor in such terms! Minnie saw his letter and was appalled.

Sandro, Memoirs
The uncles always wanted something. Nikolai fancied himself a Great Warrior. Alexei[4] ruled the waves. Sergei tried to turn Moscow into his private domain. Vladimir advocated the cause of the Arts. They all had their favourite generals and admirals who were supposed to be promoted ahead of a long waiting list; their ballerinas desirous of organizing a 'Russian Season' in Paris; their wonderful preachers anxious to redeem the Emperor's soul; their miraculous physicians soliciting a court appointment; their clairvoyant peasants with a divine message.

Sandro to Nicky – 2 March
Forgive me for writing all this to you, but my heart aches, time is passing and we are standing still. No measures are being taken for a sizeable increase of our fleet. It would have been such a joy for me to work on a specific programme of ship-building to answer our needs *here*, in the Black Sea and in the East. It is shameful not to do anything, and to feel completely powerless to do anything for the fleet, even though I have the strong desire to work.

Nicky to Empress Marie – 20 March – Tsarskoe Selo
Yesterday our little daughter fell against a chair, and a large blue bump appeared on her forehead; she cried a little but then did not complain any more about her injury. Yesterday I went into town for a concert in aid of invalids, but I found it very boring as Alix was not

---

[4] Nicky's uncle, a brother of Vladimir and Sergei.

with me! Since your departure, I have continued taking a gun with me on my walk, and have killed 10 ravens.

Nicky to Georgy [brother] – 3 April – Tsarskoe Selo

The one happy and amusing event will be the meeting of the two daughters – Olga and Irina. I can just see them pulling each other's hair and quarrelling over the toys. I still can't believe that Xenia is the mother of two children! Her Andrusha is a big, healthy boy, but still very ugly;[5] please don't you tell her that. All parents always think that their children are the most beautiful in the world.

Nicky, Diary – 29 May – Tsarskoe Selo

The second bright happy day in our family life: at 10.40 in the morning the *Lord blessed us with a daughter – Tatiana*. Poor Alix suffered all night without shutting her eyes for a moment, and at 8 o'clock went downstairs to Amama's bedroom. Thank God this time it all went quickly and safely, and I did not feel nervously exhausted. Towards one o'clock the little one was bathed and Yanyshev read some prayers. Mama arrived with Xenia; we lunched together. At four o'clock there was a Te Deum. Tatiana weighs 8¾ pounds and is 54 centimetres long. Our eldest is very funny with her. Read and wrote telegrams.

KR, Diary – 29 May

Just before the officers' luncheon, I was informed by telephone from town that their Majesties had been blessed that morning with a daughter. The news soon spread, everyone was very disappointed as they had been hoping for a son.

2 June I heard from the Tsar that his daughters are called Olga and Tatiana like Pushkin's *Onegin*.

22 July The Empress Marie left already on the 19th for Denmark (to avoid meeting the Emperor Wilhelm, whom she does not greatly like).

I am not very fond of Michen [Maria Pavlovna] and avoid her whenever possible; I do not like the people she surrounds herself with, and I do not believe her sincerity.

---

[5] First son of Xenia.

Xenia to Nicky – 25 July – Abas Tuman
Thank God dear Georgy feels well and doesn't look too bad, although
he is of course very thin, but he seems contented and in better spirits than two years ago, when last I saw him.

Irina chatters without ceasing and is very sweet! She often talks
about 'Oksanka' and asks when 'Oksanka' is coming. At first she kept
wanting to go home to Oksanka. Isn't it touching! Well, and how are
things with you, all right I hope? I hope that Tatiana is taking her
mother's milk willingly, sorry I meant successfully.

Today is our wedding anniversary. Three years have already passed,
how time flies. I have been taking lots of photographs, and with
great success. I am sending you some taken by Sandro. Everyone
looks very good in them. Don't you think the children came out
well.

KR, Diary – 27 July [at the reception for Kaiser Wilhelm]
I was seated diagonally opposite the Tsar, who gave me several
friendly looks and signalled with his eyes as they started to play the
overture to *Lohengrin*.

30 July Three days ago in Moscow I had a long conversation with
Sergei over coffee; what didn't we talk about, and all in such an easy,
friendly manner. But not a word about Khodinka; this burning question, which stood between us for so long like some terrible phantom
of dissension, has been erased and forgotten.

Nicky to Empress Marie – 1 August – Peterhof
My dearest, darling Mama
In general – Wilhelm was courteous, calm and in extremely good
spirits, while she [Augusta Victoria] did her best to be pleasant but
looked awful in sumptuous gowns completely lacking in taste; in particular the hats she wore in the evening were frightful; heard here that
the Empress is completely under the influence of her court ladies.

13 September – Spala I found the saddest thing was going into
Papa's rooms, where all his things have remained in place; on the
table I found a letter from us children in 1886, when you were living
in the house for the first time and we had stayed behind in Peterhof!

The great dining room is also terribly reminiscent of former years,
with its smell – everything makes the heart ache so! The bedroom

made me think above all of the day when you had such a terrible back-ache, you had to lie motionless for twenty four hours!

Xenia to Nicky – 24 September – Ai-Todor

It was terribly painful to leave poor Georgy, he was so *sad* and upset he even *cried* as he said goodbye to us, which upset me so much that I howled for the whole of that day, and even afterwards it took me a long time to calm down. But now, thank God, he is no longer alone.

Today it was quite hot and we went to swim in the sea. It was 16 degrees in the water. We photographed each other in our bathing costumes, and I even snapped Sandro in the water in his birthday suit! Of course, this was not an entirely decent picture, so we developed and printed it ourselves!

10 October   We are flourishing here, in the full sense of the word.

The children are splendid and in great form. Andrusha had a slight sore throat, but is better now. He is so chubby you could eat him!!

Nicky to Empress Marie – 3 November, anniversary of father's death – Tsarskoe Selo

Our little daughters are growing, and turning into delightful happy little girls. Alix apologizes deeply for not having sent you the photographs she promised, but You will at last receive them with this letter. Olga talks the same in Russian and in English and adores her little sister. Tatiana seems to us, understandably, a very beautiful child, her eyes have become dark and large. She is *always* happy and only cries once a day without fail, after her bath when they feed her. The cossacks, soldiers and negroes are Olga's greatest friends, and she greets them as she goes down the corridor. Little Maria and Dmitri[6] often come to see us and romp around endlessly with Olga.

> Your Nicky, who loves you with all his heart.

Nicky to Georgy [brother] – 19 November – Tsarskoe Selo

I have now become such a keen hunter, that I rejoice at the cancellation of an audience, and use every free moment to fly to the woods, like a lazy schoolboy who enjoys skipping lessons!

---

[6] Maria Pavlovna the younger and Dmitri Pavlovich, the children of Nicky's uncle Pavel.

You probably remember that some nine years ago, Papa set free the bison from the menagerie in one of the woods near Gatchina. There they flourished and increased every year. But a few days ago the eldest and fiercest flew into a rage and killed two others; for this reason he has to be killed and I am allowing Misha [brother] to carry out the sentence with the help of Dietz. It should happen this week, and Misha is burning with impatience.

Nicky to Alix – November [no date] – Tsarskoe Selo
My Darling,
Come to me for a moment, I want to show you several beautiful things. Let me kiss your enchanting little face.
I love, love you madly.

KR, Diary – 6 December
After the parade, there was a large luncheon in the Nicholas Hall. The Empress Marie appeared here for the first time since the death of the Emperor; the two Empresses sat side by side.

Nicky to Georgy [brother] – 17 December – Tsarskoe Selo
The last two weeks have been very worrying for me, because of events in China – where the devil are the Germans? This was the reason we had to take Port Arthur, which will, with God's help, support our Siberian railway. Now the most important thing is that the Japanese should not move, pushed by the English – they are becoming very strong and dangerous in the East.

KR, Diary – 27 December
Sandro and Xenia had tea with us. I talked a lot with Sandro; he grieves, and not without reason, that the Emperor is so indecisive. In truth, he remains too often under the impression, and consequently under the influence, of the last words spoken to him. May God grant that time will develop his sense of independence, although it seems a lot to hope for. But he does have inestimable qualities: for instance calm, restraint, the absence of any impatience.

On the morning of the 29th, Sandro told me, although he could not vouch for it, that Alexei [Nicky's uncle] has apparently bought himself a house in Paris and stays there, rather than in a hotel, every time he travels. If it's true, one cannot but be amazed by such expenditure on the part of a Russian Grand Duke.

30 December   One would like to follow the example of Mitia [KR's brother], who always maintains the same way of life, whatever the circumstances, who is always balanced and true to himself. And with me it's always impulses, and inconstancy in everything. But I will soon be 40, and I fear it's too late to change.

1898

MARITAL BLISS II

Kaiser Wilhelm sends a New Year greeting – Sandro
desires to serve his country – Alix has measles – Nicky
returns to the Crimea for the first time since his father's
death – Nicky's grandmother, Queen Louise ('Amama')
dies and he goes to Denmark for the funeral – Alix is
expecting another child, but is not well

Kaiser Wilhelm II to Nicky – 4 January – Neues Palais, Potsdam
Dearest Nicky

The New Year has just opened and the old Year has closed. But I
cannot let it close without a glance at those lovely and brilliant days
of August, when I was able to embrace you and Alix, and without
thanking you for your kind, splendid, even lavish hospitality to
Victoria and me.

With deep feelings of gratitude do I remember the pleasant hours
I was able to spend with you, exchanging intercourse showing that
we were of one opinion in the principles we follow in the fulfilling
of the task, which has been set us by the Lord of all Lords. Each of us
tries to do his best for his country's development and welfare as is his
duty! But in community we seek to procure to our countries the
blessings of Peace!

Now good bye, dearest Nicky, best love to Alix and my most
respectful compliments to your dear Mama from your most devoted
and faithful friend and cousin,   Willy

KR, Diary – 18 January
Vladimir gave a ball. My wife was prevented from attending by a

cough, but I went along, greeted the host and hostess and quietly slipped out again. I was just going to get into my carriage, when the Emperor and Empress arrived; I hid in one of the adjoining rooms in order to avoid meeting them, otherwise it would have been awkward to leave. After waiting for them to pass, I returned home and finished writing the 1st scene of Act V.[1]

19 January   After luncheon the Tsar and Tsarina were in an affectionate mood, she sat on his knee, he caressed her and they kissed.

30 January   I do not really like the Emperor [Wilhelm], despite all his affection and kindness to me. Although he's a good fellow in many ways, and has much enthusiasm and strength of will, yet he is too much of a child and a buffoon. His familiarity is shocking.

Nicky to Georgy [brother] – 29 March – St Petersburg
We are expecting Mama home from Denmark on Good Thursday, and had thought of returning here from Tsarskoe, just before Easter, all because of the after-effects of Alix's rotten measles. Yesterday, for the first time after sitting at home for seven weeks, she went out for a walk in the garden!

For the same reason, she missed the whole season of Wagner operas, which were sung by the famous Reshke brothers; it's not just annoying, it really makes you mad. I am sure you were pleased by the 90 million roubles assigned for intensive shipbuilding for the new Pacific fleet. It's high time we became a force at sea, especially now when there's this kind of hunt and pursuit for Chinese ports. Thank God, we managed to occupy Port Arthur and Talianovan without blood, quietly and almost amicably! Of course, it was quite risky, but had we missed those docks now, it would be impossible later to kick out the English or the Japanese without a war. Yes, one has to look sharp; there on the Pacific ocean lies the whole future of the development of Russia and at last we have a fully open warm water port; while the railway will strengthen our position there still further.[2]

It's terrifying to think that Kyril,[3] who was on the *Rossiya* witnessed

---

[1] KR translated Shakespeare's play *Hamlet* into Russian.
[2] Russia was strengthening her position in the Pacific, having forced the Japanese to withdraw from Port Arthur. Russia had just signed a lease with the Chinese for the port.
[3] Grand Duke Kyril, the eldest son of Grand Duke Vladimir, was twenty-one.

and participated in everything that happened on the shores of the Yellow sea!

What did you think of the articles in the English papers? Greedy scoundrels! – they are never satisfied! The devil take them!

KR, Diary – 5 April

For the first time since 1894, the Empress Marie appeared for the procession, and walked in front with the Emperor, while the young Empress came behind with Misha, which was criticized by some people: they thought the first place belonged to Alexandra Feodorovna.

Xenia to Nicky – 26 April – Paris

I've gone mad about the shops. I am drawn to them and ruined as I can't stop buying!

Sandro, by the way, is exactly the same, *if not more so*, which does not stop him from getting cross with me! They do their best in these shops to get you to buy everything, and it's hard to refuse. I will be bringing hats and full suitcases back with me.

We sent Alix a small watch, hoping that it would reach her by the 23rd, unfortunately it did not arrive in time and I do not know whether she has received it.

We have been three times to Monte Carlo and had a good gamble. Sandro was very lucky, but the last time we both lost. It's a most amazing game. There were a lot of people, but few players as the season is over.

KR, Diary – 21 May

In the evening the Tsar and Tsarina sent me a delightful Fabergé thermometer as a present.

28 May Alix took me in her carriage [at Gatchina]; thus we spent more than half an hour face to face. We always speak in English together, which is quite difficult for me; added to this, she is not very talkative. She is terribly shy; the necessity of talking to a group of schoolgirls is a torture for her, she has difficulty in overcoming her fear in crowded gatherings. It's noticeable that she does not have her mother-in-law's charm, and still does not, therefore, inspire general adulation.

Sandro, Memoirs

The young Empress spoke Russian with difficulty. Her predecessors used to benefit by the lapse of time between their betrothals to the future Tsars and their ascension to the throne. The wife of Alexander III had lived in the country for seventeen consecutive years preceding her coronation, but Princess Alix was given exactly ninety-six hours to study the language and get acquainted with the national customs. Unable to grasp the relative standing of the innumerable courtiers she made errors, irrelevant in themselves but tantamount to formidable crimes in the eyes of St Petersburg society. It frightened her and created marked reserve in her treatment of visitors. This in turn gave circulation to the comparisons between the friendliness of the Dowager-Empress and the 'snobbish coolness' of the young Tsarina. Nicholas II resented this malicious matching of his mother against his wife, and very soon the relations between court and society became antagonistic.

KR, Diary – 15 June

The Tsar sent me as a present a magnificent Bokhara carpet, eleven feet long and 4 feet wide. Their Majesties took tea with Mama in the Gonzaga gallery. The Empress looked remarkably beautiful. She brought a camera with her and took several pictures of us all.

13 August – Moscow They say that I might be named as the next head of the military training schools. I myself would not be against such an appointment, as long as I was able to retain command of the regiment. But I do not think the Emperor will choose me: I think they make me out to be a man of the liberal tendency, almost a red, and that he will come to the opinion that it is better not to appoint me to a post, where I would be responsible either for educating the people or for bringing up the young.

Xenia to Nicky – 18 August – Abas Tuman

Dear Nicky!

We have a great request to you. I hope you won't think it too impertinent! Would you be good enough to send us the *Standart* [royal yacht] to Batum? (If you don't need it, of course) – for the crossing from Batum to Yalta.

Nicky to Empress Marie – 28 August – Livadia

I cannot describe to you what I felt, when for the first time since then [father's death], we entered Your house and then went into the bedroom!! It was as if that terrible event had *only just happened*, that it was *only yesterday* we lived through those torments of hope, doubt and inconsolable sorrow!!! *Everything* has remained exactly as it was. It is surprising when you think that now, four years later, we are living here with our children.

KR, Diary – 30 August

The papers brought the terrible news of the assassination of the Empress of Austria,[4] who was stabbed in the heart by some Italian anarchist. What a tragic fate for the poor Emperor!

Alix to Nicky – 20 September – Livadia

My own precious beloved Darling

You will read these lines when the horrid train will be carrying you always further and further away from poor Wify.

Our first separation since the marriage – I am frightened of it, I cannot bear the idea of your going away so far without me. But I must not grumble Motherdear is in great sorrow[5] and needs your comfort and your presence is also wished for by poor Apapa – what a joy still to think that you can be of use and help to others in grief. My thoughts will not forsake you for one instant and my tender prayers will surround. God bless and protect you, my own treasure, my lovy dear, and may He watch over you with his Angels.

I cannot bear to think what will become of me without you – you who are my one and all, who make up all my life. I shall write to you every day, so as that you can sometimes have a word from me when you are with all the others. It will seem to you like bygone years, only two beloved Ones are no more – how you will miss poor Amama – God help and comfort you! If they only do not keep you too long, tho' I understand poor Motherdear longing to have you near and to be able to pour out her heart to you. Kiss her fondly from me.

How horrid all will seem, so empty and sad – the nights all alone – send me a blessing before you sleep, I shall always do so for you –

---

[4] Elisabeth (Sisi), wife of Emperor Franz-Josef of Austria.
[5] Nicky's grandmother, the Queen of Denmark, had died aged eighty-one, and Nicky was going to the funeral in Copenhagen.

the winds will bring it you. Take care of yourself lovy sweet and come back well and strong to me.

Oh my 'dushka', to see your dear big sad eyes makes me wretched – ach, why cannot I go with you – but [what] was I to do with Irène [sister] who had made that long journey on purpose so as to see me before her great voyage. My absence won't be regretted there by any of the rest, as I am still somewhat a stranger amongst them all – and now they want to have only those there whom they were accustomed to see around poor Amama. Goodbye now my angel, my own true love, my joy, my Nicky, I kiss you and kiss you, your own Wify for ever and ever.

Nicky to Alix – 22–24 September – in the train from Livadia to Libau

My own beloved sweet Wify,

I cannot thank you enough for your tender dear long letter which you left me in the train. I read it after I lost sight of the launch that was taking you away on board the yacht. That was a horrid moment. Did you see me wave my cap out of the window? I followed you until you got into the boat but after that I lost sight of you in the dark. I stood there at the window until we passed Inkerman, where the bells were ringing. The moon shone beautifully and the harbour looked too lovely with the lit up ships – especially the *Standart*. I just got your first dear telegram from Livadia, it is comforting to know you safely at home!

God grant I may meet you there as quickly as possible. After all it is a long journey. How sad I am not to see your sweet beloved face – I cannot tell you. It is true, we are so accustomed to being constantly together, that now we are separated, I feel lost.

24 September   We have just arrived at Libau – it is fine but cold and rather windy; but what does it all matter since my sweety is not with me. I am writing to you now in my cabin on board the dear *Polar Star* – the two little inscriptions on the windows have remained as they were. My darling – I miss you so dreadfully and I am so jealous of the Feldjäger who is bringing this letter – that he will see you, my adored Wify!

Please excuse this stupid letter of mine, my darling, but as it was begun three days ago it is difficult to continue in the same swing.

I love you, I love you, pray for you and think of you night and day. I kiss you and Olga and Tatiana tenderly. Give my love to Irène and my compliments to everyone.

> Ever your own truly loving Huzy Nicky

God bless you and the children!

26–27 September – Copenhagen   Here I am, arrived at last after that endless voyage by rail and sea, sitting at the same table as two years ago, in the big middle room, which was our sitting room then in 1896. This is my room now, Aunt Thyra[6] is my neighbour to the right (Mama's old room) and Aunt Alix is to left in *our* bedroom! Everything reminds me so painfully of my sweet little Wify, that I could cry, knowing you to be so far away.

The yacht anchored at a place near Copenhagen called 'Bellevue' – a small pier and a few houses. My astonishment was great when on landing I was met by dear Apapa, Mama and the whole family. They all looked more cheery and less worn out than I imagined. As soon as we drove up to the house, they led me into the bedroom where stands the coffin, shut up, and surrounded by masses of flowers and wreaths which looks very pretty. Still I must say it seems sad to me to think that the body does not remain in a church near by – I think it would be preferable in every respect. Poor Apapa looks remarkably fresh, he goes into that room constantly and then takes long long walks – to which of course the family accompanies him.

The reason of the delay of the funeral is that everything concerning the burial, black cloth garments, catafalque etc. have been lost in a fire that occurred some 12 years ago and the ceremonials have disappeared! Apapa wants the funeral to be a state ceremony and they therefore need such a long time to get these preparations ready. When I come back I shall tell all I have heard from Mama and the others about poor Amama's last days – touchingly sad!!

My sweet darling I love you too madly and deeply for words.

> Nicky

28 September   When I see all the other young couples together I feel so forlorn and out of place. But I am quite sure that not one of those husbands loves his wife so strongly and devotedly as I love *my Alix*!

Your name is continually used here (Aunt Alix and little Alix of

---

[6] Nicky's aunt, wife of Ernest August II, Crown Prince of Hanover, Duke of Cumberland.

Cumberland[7]) and that makes me start up every time and gives me a shock. Fancy Boysy is so sad that he is alone, that it has made me forget about his very existence. He sends his respects to lady.

The Cumberland cousins are very nice and all three are such tall handsome charming girls. Misha [brother], that sinner, gets on perfectly well with them; during the walks two of them always hang on his arms!

Aunt Swan looks more hideous and repulsive than ever, her hair in a straight grey line hanging over her eyes, some teeth fallen out oh! simply awful the poor thing! Your friend the fat boy has become a sort of prized fat pig, in the literal sense of the word. I would not believe my eyes when I saw him in a sailor suit with a plainclothe's hat on with a bulging stomach and enormous bottom and legs! You can imagine how he gets teased, because except all that, he has got a nasty character, therefore it is too inviting not to tease him!

I never cease praying for you and our sweet little daughters and every night in my bed I send you three of my fondest kisses and blessings.

Ever your own truly loving and passionately devoted old *lausbub* and Huzy

Nicky

1 October   Georgie [Duke of York] is sitting and reading in my room, he writes daily to May. Is not that good? But now, my darling, I must close, as the others are going out for a walk. God bless you, my own Alix; a tender kiss to you, Olga and Tatiana.

Ever your very own

Nicky

George, Duke of York to Nicky – 11 October – Bernsdorf, Denmark

My dear Nicky,

I miss you, dear Nicky, very much here and our nice talks and smokes and was so pleased to see you again after so long. It was so kind of you letting me sit in your room and dress for dinner. I have now got your room and I am writing at your table and whenever I write to May (which I do every day) I think of you writing to Alicky.

---

[7] Aunt Alix: Alexandra, Princess of Wales, sister of Nicky's mother. Little Alix of Cumberland: daughter of Aunt Thyra.

At last the Turkish troops are leaving Crete, so I hope that difficult question will soon be settled and Georgie [of Greece] will go there as governor general.

Ever your devoted cousin and friend

Georgie

Nicky to Empress Marie – 21 November – Livadia
Alix is expecting another child and is not feeling well.

In the evenings she lies in bed and I read to her, we have already finished *War and Peace* and have just started Schilder's history of Emperor Alexander I, which Nikolai is so carried away with.

Twice a week couriers bring me a mountain of papers, and on those days I am in a bad mood!

KR, Diary – 17 December – St Petersburg
This morning their Majesties arrived at Tsarskoe; a third addition to the family is expected (probably in June). The Empress is in need of complete rest, which is why they are spending the winter in the country, rather than in town.

1899

Nicky – Emperor of Russia

Alix – Empress of Russia, Nicky's wife

Empress Marie – Nicky's mother

Xenia – Grand Duchess, Nicky's sister, married to Sandro

Sandro – Grand Duke Alexander Mikhailovich

KR – Grand Duke Konstantin Romanov, Nicky's cousin

Georgy – Grand Duke, Nicky's brother

Queen Victoria – of England

1899

DEATH OF A BROTHER

KR stages *Hamlet* – Queen Victoria and Nicky correspond
about Kaiser Wilhelm II – Alix is confined to a wheelchair
– Student unrest – A third daughter, Maria, is born –
Georgy dies of tuberculosis – Xenia's support for the Boers
– Nicky's indecisiveness.

Sandro to Nicky – 8 January
Autocracy, as I and all its true adherents understand it, cannot tolerate any compromises. Each compromise leads to a gradual erosion of
the principles of autocracy, and consequently, of power. Many
people, unfortunately, believe that you are inclined to reforms,
which would lead to a widening of public self-government.

KR, Diary – 28 January – St Petersburg
I started to read last year's article by Count L. N. Tolstoy 'What is Art'
in the journal 'Questions of Psychology and Philosophy'. An amazing mixture of sensible and absurd notions.

13 February   I wrote to the Tsar in Mama's name, inviting them to
a performance of *Hamlet* on the afternoon of the 16th. But he replied
that the Empress was in bed with influenza, and that they could not
come earlier than the end of next week.[1]

---

[1] KR later reports that they attended and were very pleased. Nicky asked for the
whole of *Hamlet* to be put on in the Hermitage theatre the following winter.

Queen Victoria to Nicky – 1 March – Windsor Castle
Dearest Nicky,

It is ages since you wrote to me and I to you, but I am sure you have not forgotten your old Grandmama who wishes much we could see each other again. I long to see darling Alicky so much.

But I feel now there is *something* that I *must* tell you, which you *ought* to know and which perhaps you do *not*.

It is, I am very sorry to say, that William [Kaiser Wilhelm, her eldest grandson] takes *every* opportunity of impressing before Sir F. Lascelles[2] that Russia is doing all in her power to work *against us* saying that she offers Alliances to other Powers and has made one with the Amir of Afghanistan against us! I need not say that I do *not* believe a word of this, neither do Lord Salisbury and Sir F. Lascelles.

With many loves to dear Alicky and kisses to the little girls believe me always your devoted Grandmama

VRI

Nicky to Queen Victoria – 13 March – St Petersburg
Dearest Grandmama,

I thank you from all my heart for your kind letter which touched me deeply. Count Vorontsov will be the bearer of this letter; he came with us to Balmoral.

I feel quite ashamed at not having written to you for such a long time and beg you to excuse me.

I am so happy you told me in that open way about William [Kaiser]. Now I fully understand what he is up to – it is a dangerous double game he is playing at. I heard very much the same from Count Osten-Sacken[3] from Berlin about the English policy, as what you and Lord Salisbury must have learnt from Sir F. Lascelles about us.

I am very glad you did not believe the story of the alleged alliance between us and the Amir of Afghanistan, for there is not a syllable of truth in it.

As you know dearest Grandmama all I am striving at now is for the longest possible prolongation of peace in this world. The latest events in China must have clearly proved this. I mean the new arrangement about railway-building. All that Russia wants is to be left quiet and to develop her position in the sphere of interest which

---

[2] British Ambassador to Berlin.
[3] Russian Ambassador to Berlin.

concerns her being so close to Siberia. Our possession of Port Arthur and the Manchurian railway are of vital importance to us and can in no way affect any other European power's interest. Neither is it endangering to China's independency. The idea alone of a collapse of that country – and of the possibility of its partition between the different powers – is frightening and I look upon it as the greatest calamity that might befall us!

I hope that the beautiful climate of the Riviera will be profitable to you.

If all is well we would so much like to pay you a private visit at Balmoral with our babies this autumn; we hope this plan will suit you.

Alix sends you her tenderest love and so does your ever devoted and loving grandson

Nicky

KR, Diary – 18 March – St Petersburg
In the highest circles I am considered a liberal, a dreamer, a fantasist, and am presented as such to the Tsar. And he, I think, holds just about the same opinion of me. He does not see me in the light of public opinion, the opinion of the non-ruling classes; the Tsar, it seems to me, does not quite trust me; at least, during the four and a half years of his reign, he has done nothing to demonstrate his trust to me. I have not received a single substantial appointment, except perhaps the Pushkin Commission.

Nicky to Empress Marie – 20 March – Tsarskoe Selo
The sleigh path is excellent, we go out together every day in the hunting sleigh and I drive – which is a great pleasure. Alix feels well in general, but cannot walk as she immediately feels pain; she goes about the rooms in a wheelchair.

I hope that because of the strong measures [in the universities] peace will at last be restored for this year! It's intolerable!

27 March The weather has become warmer and the snow is melting quickly. A mass of spring birds are singing in the woods; it's such a pleasure to walk, I simply don't want to go back home to the tedious reports. Here I spend 3 hours out of doors and feel much stronger – I am clearing the paths of snow.

KR, Diary – 21 April – St Petersburg
Xenia came to see Mama and told her that the Emperor is very distressed and perturbed by the measures taken against the students, but as always cannot bring himself to admit that he could put a stop to it all. In Xenia's words, Nicky's attitude to all this is that of a spectator!! If only he had more strength and self-confidence!

Nicky to Queen Victoria – 11 May – Peterhof
My dearest Grandmama,
   Today being the eve of your birthday I feel I must write to you. I am sorry these lines will reach you a few days later than I had intended, but let me still wish you much happiness for your dear birthday which we are so sorry not to have been able to spend together! How nice Ernie and Ducky are with you this year.
   We came over here two days ago and were sorry to leave Tsarskoe, but had to do it on account of the approaching event.[4] We have had summer weather until yesterday when it suddenly changed and became very cold, I hope though it will not last long. We love this place and especially our house, which is built quite on the border of the sea.
   The children are flourishing and have grown very much. Alix is feeling on the whole better and likes being rolled all over the place in her armchair, which is done by her husband!
   I was greatly shocked to see in the papers about the sad end of Lord Strafford and deeply sympathize with you in this loss of an old trusted servant.
   With renewed good wishes and Alix's best love I remain, dearest Grandmama, your truly loving grandson
                                                                                    Nicky

KR, Diary – 12 June – Strelna
I sent this sonnet, as well as the dedication to *Hamlet* to the Emperor, and received the following reply:
   '12 June 1899. My dear Kostia, it was with emotion that I read your touching dedication to the memory of my dear Father. Do of course print it at the beginning of your edition. The second sonnet also touched my heart: it would be difficult to capture the essence of military duty more succinctly or expressively.'

---

[4] Alix's delivery.

13 June The Tsar was very complimentary about my new verses, saying that Pushkin could hardly have done better.

Nicky, Diary – 14 June – Peterhof

A happy day: the Lord sent us a third daughter – *Maria*, who was safely born at 12.10! Alix hardly slept all night, and towards morning the pains got stronger. Thank God it was all over quite quickly! My darling felt well all day and fed the baby herself. Mama arrived from Gatchina at 4 o'clock. The immediate family gathered in church for a Te Deum. Had tea with Mama; wrote telegrams and went through the unbearable papers. I only managed to get out into the fresh air after dinner – the evening was marvellous.

Xenia, Diary – 14 June – On the yacht *Tsarevna*

What a joy that everything has ended safely, and the anxiety of waiting is over at last, but what a disappointment that it isn't a son. Poor Alix! We, of course, are delighted either way – whether it's a son or a daughter!

KR, Diary – 14 June

At 2 o'clock I received a telegram: THE GRAND DUCHESS MARIA NICOLAEVNA. And so, there's no Heir. The whole of Russia will be disappointed by this news.

Georgy [brother] to Nicky – 15 June – Abas Tuman

My dear Nicky

I congratulate you and Alix with all my heart on this new happiness for your family – the birth of your third daughter. I had been waiting for this news for over two weeks and was surprised at such a delay. I hope that Alix is well and that everything is fine. I am terribly sad and upset that I have not yet been able to see your daughters and get to know them; but what can I do! It means it's not my fate, and everything is the will of God. But life here is pleasant and I cannot complain of my fate; this autumn I will have been here eight years, and despite myself I have grown used to the life and the place. I simply cannot believe that I have already lived here so many years. It seems such a short time ago that we were sailing together on the *Azov*, but it is already eight years. I regret my navy service, which I so loved then, but I have already long since mentally said goodbye to it, unfortunately I am no longer fit for any kind of service. I am no longer able to walk at all, for instance, because of shortness of breath, and this is a great privation for me, as you yourself know how much I always loved walking and working.

[This was Georgy's last letter to his brother.]

KR, Diary – 28 June – Strelna
We heard that news had arrived of the death of the Heir, the Tsarevich Georgy. Pavel told us that the Emperor and his mother had each received two telegrams: one said that the Tsarevich had gone to Abas Tuman on his bicycle, after which he started coughing up blood; he was brought home in a hopeless condition; the second already told of his death. Many of us were disturbed by the fact that the consumptive Tsarevich was not prevented from exercising on a bicycle. It is said to be even less understandable, as the Tsarevich had been worse for the last few weeks; neither the Emperor, nor the Dowager Empress were aware of this deterioration, as all their enquiries received the answer that the patient was in excellent condition. Everyone was struck, as if by lightning, by this sad and unexpected news. But it seems to me that it is more a question of surprise than grief: the deceased was seldom seen and little known; he lived until the age of 27 far away, a stranger to everyone. It's impossible not to feel deeply sorry for [Empress] Marie, for whom this is a terrible blow. They say she weeps inconsolably, that she even fainted. The Tsar, the poor new Heir Misha, and their sister stood at the service for the dead with eyes red from tears.

Queen Victoria to Nicky – 2 July – Windsor Castle
Dearest Nicky,
Pray accept the expression of my sincerest sympathy in this great sorrow, for I know the affection you had for your poor brother Georgy whose life was so sad and lonely.
You will have felt sad at not having seen him for so long. Was it very sudden and what brought on this fatal haemorrhage?
I am so thankful that dear Alicky has recovered so well, but I regret the 3rd girl for the country.
Let me thank you also very much for your last kind letter for my birthday and the lovely and so very useful earrings your dear Alicky so kindly gave me.

Believe me always your devoted Grandmama

VRI

P.S. Since writing the above I have heard from Aunt Alix the very distressing sad circumstances of your dear Brother's death which must greatly add to your dear Mama's grief. Surely it was not prudent to let him bicycle?

Xenia, Diary – 2 July – Peterhof
In the evening Sandro asked Nicky about Misha, and it turns out he will not be called Heir and Tsarevich – the manifesto only says he is *next in line to the throne.* This is only a play on words and will, of course, give rise to all kinds of talk and misunderstandings – It's a great pity, although I am glad for Misha!

Empress Marie to Nicky – 4 July – On the train
My dear Nicky!

About our last conversation, I have thought more on it and consider it essential to clarify the question as soon as possible, because it could cause confusion. In all the churches they *have already prayed for* Misha as Heir and Grand Duke Mikhail Alexandrovich (but *not Tsarevich*) which is completely correct. Uncle Alexei was at the Alexander-Nevsky monastery yesterday and heard it for himself.

It is essential that it *immediately* be made known everywhere, that he is to be called Heir until a son is born to you.

Once again I embrace you with all my heart and thank you, my dear Nicky, for the comfort of your care and affection during this sad and terrible time. May God bless you!

Your deeply loving Mama

KR, Diary – 4 July – Strelna
We accompanied Empress Marie to Peterhof station. She was going to Batum to meet her son's coffin; with her were travelling: Alexei, Misha, Xenia (in her third month of pregnancy), Sandro and Olga.

Nicky to Alix – 10 July – Peterhof
My own sweet little Wify dear,

It seems strange to write to you, while I'm sitting downstairs in my room and I know that you are quietly on your balcony. But tomorrow I shall be far away and I do not want to let a day pass without your hearing from your husband, either from his lips or on paper – how he loves you and the three little ones! My darling, our separation this time is not long, so be cheery and try and have the babies as much as possible.

In the evening you will see Valdemar and have a tête-à-tête dinner. Please invite my old dog for your meals and do not forget to feed our dickies [birds] outside! I rather dread the meeting in Moscow; after four years of separation to see one's brother arrive in a coffin is a horrid idea. I'm afraid it will all so upset poor Mama! Well! There's nothing to be done, we must as usual take courage and carry our cross patiently, as Jesus Christ bids us. But sometimes it is overwhelmingly hard!

I dare complain the least, having *such happiness* on earth, having a treasure like you my beloved Alix, and already the three little cherubs. From the depth of my heart do I thank God for all His blessings, in giving me you He gave me paradise and has made my life an easy and happy one. Labour and passing troubles are nothing to me once I have got you by my side. Perhaps my expression does not show it, but I feel it deeply. Our prayers will meet in the evening, (only two nights) especially tomorrow, Olga's namesday.

You cannot imagine, my sweet darling, what a strange feeling it is, to be sitting near you and to be writing to you at the same time. I confessed I fibbed in telling you that I was going to write to Victoria, but I think you are none the worse sweetie-dear. It is a pity we could not go out in the launch, but I think it is safer we did not, on account of the wind and rather fresh air, and also it gave us a few hours more which we spend together. I write very badly, I do not know whether I am to write in the past or in the present.

God bless you, my own beloved wife! Be sure that my prayers and thoughts are constantly around you. I must end as we both wanted to play bezique. Goodnight my sweet darling Alix, my own wife, my joy, my happiness, my one and all! God bless you and the dear little daughters!

Ever your own truly devoted and deeply loving husband,

Nicky

Xenia, Diary – 14 July – Peterhof
A nightmare – the day of the funeral of our dear, wonderful Georgy.
The service began at 11 o'clock. Mama did not sit down once, but

stood there quite composed, without crying, but with an expression of profound suffering on her face. When they started to lower the coffin into the tomb, Mama, who had been holding me tightly by the hand, suddenly staggered, collapsed onto me (with wide open eyes, yet seeing nothing) and said loudly – 'Home, let's go home, I can't stand any more' and then tore herself away from me!

Nicky took hold of her from one side, but she kept pushing forward, trying at all costs to get past the tomb to go out, but it wasn't possible just then, as the tomb was open and there was no way past. Sandro was standing there, and supported Mama.

After a short while they brought a plank for us to walk over. Mama walked so quickly we could hardly keep up with her! It was such a nightmare, it will remain with me for ever!

I had a *terrible fright* (as did all those present). I kept thinking she was going to faint, but thank God, it didn't happen. None of us even had time to throw flowers into the grave of our Georjik!

In the carriage, Mama cried terribly, and kept pressing to her breast Georgy's hat, which she had snatched from the top of the coffin! It was terribly hard and painful for us to watch, while being unable to do anything to alleviate her suffering!

We drove straight to the landing stage, boarded the *Alexandria*, and went immediately to Peterhof. Nicky, Olga and I rode with Mama in the carriage and on the yacht. Once on the yacht, Mama started to regain herself and became calmer. I sat next to her the whole time, while the others had lunch below, they also brought us something, but Mama was unable to eat. The tears were beneficial to her, and little by little her nerves subsided.

23 July   I saw Aprak.[5] We had a long chat. She is horrified (as she told me) by what is being said, and in general by the speculation aroused by the manifesto! God alone knows what is being said, and poor Alix is being accused of not wanting Misha to be made, or called, the Heir.

KR, Diary – 12 August – Pavlovsk
I have been appointed head of the military training institutions, with effect in three months' time, that is on November 14. And so, in three months I shall have to give up the regiment. My heart aches at the thought.

---

[5] Princess Alexandra Alexandrevna Obolenskaya, Empress Marie's maid-of-honour, Xenia's friend.

Xenia to Nicky – 11 October – Ai-Todor

We are terribly interested in the war in the Transvaal, and are right behind the Boers and wish them every success in the war. I think there *can be no one* (except the English!) who isn't on their side!

Nicky to Empress Marie – 17 October, anniversary of father's death – Wolfsgarten

What I want with all my heart, is to continue what was begun by dear Papa, for the good and greater glory of our beloved Russia.

Nicky to Xenia – 21 October – Wolfsgarten

My dear Xenia!

Alix and I are enjoying ourselves here in every way with our children. The quiet life here has completely cured her of her pains, thank God! As long as they don't start again in the winter from standing at various occasions and receptions.

Like you and Sandro, I am completely absorbed by England's war with the Transvaal, each day I read every detail in the English papers, from the first to the last line, and then discuss my impressions with the others at table. I am glad that Alix thinks about everything as I do; she is, of course, appalled at the loss of English officers – but what can you do, it has always been like that in their wars!

Now I must end. Goodbye my dear Xenia. I embrace you warmly, also Sandro and the dear children, and the future fourth also! When do you think you will be in Petersburg?

Christ be with you.

Your very loving old Nicky

KR, Diary – 24 October – St Petersburg

I saw Sergei [Mikhailovich]. We deplored the indecisiveness of the Emperor, who has such a clear and correct view of things, and yet so easily falls prey to outside influences.

Nicky to Queen Victoria – 5 November – Wolfsgarten

My dearest Grandmama,

I am sorry not to have answered your dear letter before now and I thank you for it deeply. Also for your kindness you showed my brother Misha, who I hear returned to Denmark perfectly enchanted with his stay in Scotland.

I cannot tell you how much my thoughts are with you as I know how distressed you must be about the war in the Transvaal and the terrible losses already sustained by your troops. God grant it may come to a speedy conclusion!

Our stay here has been most enjoyable the weather favouring us quite particularly. Ernie and Ducky are looking *so happy* and well!

Last week we paid a visit to the Grand Duke and Grand Duchess of Baden who received us most amiably and kindly. It was for the first time that we have been at that place and we thought it very pretty.

Unluckily we must leave dear Wolfsgarten in two days and on our way home shall stop for some hours to see William at Potsdam. Then we go on to a shooting-place – Skernewitze – in Poland, intending to remain there for a week and hope to be home at Tsarskoe Selo on 16th November.

Alix and I we send you our fondest love. Believe me dearest Grandmama ever your most loving and devoted grandson

Nicky

Xenia to Nicky – 9 November – Ai-Todor

It's so good to know that *we all* share the same opinion about the Transvaal! May God grant the Boers success until the end, only it will be hard for them, poor things, when the English ask for reinforcements.

I am very glad you all enjoyed yourselves abroad and rested completely, and that Alix is feeling well. She needs to be very careful now and try to avoid getting tired, most of all not to stand for too long, so that the terrible pains don't return. And it's just now the most tiring time – parades, receptions etc, what a bore!

KR, Diary – 21 December – St Petersburg

Yesterday was New Year abroad, and *by order* of the Emperor of Germany, the beginning of the 20th century.

Although it would seem more correct to count its beginning as from January 1st 1901.

1900–1903

Nicky – Emperor of Russia

Alix – Empress of Russia

Empress Marie – Nicky's mother

Xenia – Grand Duchess, Nicky's sister

Sandro – Grand Duke Alexander Mikhailovich, Xenia's husband

Ella – Grand Duchess Elizabeth, Alix's elder sister

Olga (sister) – Grand Duchess, Nicky's younger sister, also known as 'Baby'

KR – Grand Duke Konstantin Romanov, Nicky's cousin

Anastasia – fourth daughter of Nicky and Alix

Georgie – George, Duke of York

Willy – Kaiser Wilhelm II of Germany, Nicky's cousin

Prince Felix Yusupov

The Spanish Infanta Eulalia

Count Witte – Minister of Finance

Cavalry Captain Garardi – on duty at Sarov

Aprak – Princess Alexandra Alexandrevna Obolenskaya, Empress Marie's maid-of-honour, Xenia's friend

1900

WAITING FOR A MIRACLE

Nicky congratulates KR on his new appointment – Nicky and Alix spend Holy Week in Moscow – Aunt Michen (Maria Pavlovna) is trying to find a husband for her daughter Helena [Elena] – Alix is expecting her fourth child – In the Crimea, Nicky falls ill with typhoid

Nicky to KR – 4 March – St Petersburg
Dear Kostia

In accordance with my promise, I would like to let you know that tomorrow, Sunday, your appointment will be confirmed. Believe me, that no one sympathizes, or shares your secret grief at having to leave the beloved regiment, as much as I do. May God send you every success in your new position. You can always count in all things on your truly devoted Nicky.

Nicky to Empress Marie – 5 April – Moscow
My dear darling Mama

Forgive me, dear Mama, that I didn't send You anything for Easter, but Fabergé sent your present here, thinking that you would return to Gatchina!

With all my heart Christ is Risen! I embrace you and the whole family

Your Nicky, who loves you deeply with all his heart

Nicky to Xenia – 5 April – Kremlin, Moscow
My dear Xenia!

I cannot describe to you the feelings I have experienced here since the beginning of Holy week, but I can assure you it is only now I have realized what it really means to *fast*. Alix shares my feelings completely, which is a great joy to me. We go morning and evening to various churches within the towers; the services in these ancient churches produce a feeling of enchantment.

We particularly like one tiny one – the church of the Exaltation of the Cross, the favourite of Tsar Alexei Mikhailovich. All the icons are covered with glass, because they were embroidered in silk by his daughters. We go there alone each evening with Ella and Uncle Sergei, there isn't room for anyone else; the singers stand outside.

Yesterday we walked along the Kremlin walls and went into the ancient church of the Annunciation, in the tower opposite our windows. We took turns to kiss the miraculous icon, which is surrounded by a mass of lamps and, as Ella bent towards it, the top of her hat got caught on one of the lamps. She turned her head in all directions, but there was nothing she could do. She blushed, we were bursting with laughter, but were unable to help, as the priest was standing between her and us, babbling on about the church. At last, after much effort, Trepov[1] managed to free her, and more importantly to steady the lamp, which was in danger of spilling on to her. She emerged from the church with us, all red and with her hair in a mess. Everyone smiled and bowed.

And now goodbye, my dear Xenia. I embrace you, Sandro and the dear children. Christ is Risen! Your deeply loving old brother,

Nicky

Kaiser Wilhelm II to Nicky – 24 April – Berlin

Dearest Nicky

In haste I just manage to write these few lines to thank you from the depth of my heart for your kind and dear letter you so kindly sent me through Kostia.

Indeed I do so well remember the events of your coming of age and the ceremonies which accompanied it! How bravely you spoke your oath and how deeply moved your dear father was when he embraced you afterwards! How time has gone by! Now you too are ruler of a Great Empire and have children and I have a grown up son!

Ever your most affectionate cousin and friend,

Willy

---

[1] Chief of Moscow Police.

Nicky to Queen Victoria – 7 May – Gatchina
Dearest Grandmama,

I cannot tell you how touched I was to receive your dear kind letter on the eve of my birthday. I thank you from the depth of my heart for all the love and great kindness you show me. Let me also wish you every possible happiness and good health for your dear birthday. I am afraid that this letter may not reach you in time, but until now I have not had one free moment to write.

Alix and I were both so glad that your visit to Ireland had been such a great success. I only hope it did not tire you too much!

We were also both enchanted with our stay in Moscow, those three weeks we spent there seem now a delightful dream and everything went off so well.

It was a joy to have seen Sergei and Ella there, who generally we meet only twice a year and then for a short time only.

I do hope you have got less worries now about the war. The Scots Greys telegraphed on my birthday from Kronstadt, which astonished me and at the same time gave me great pleasure.

You mentioned in your letter about the possibility of our meeting this year. That is our constant wish to come over to England and see you. This summer and autumn I am afraid will be taken up by the tiresome Shah of Persia and manoeuvres in different parts of Russia. But if there were a possibility of coming and seeing you we would be happy of doing so.

With renewed thanks and birthday good wishes believe me dearest Grandmama, ever your most loving grandson

Nicky

KR, Diary – 24 May – St Petersburg
I heard from Minnie [Empress Marie] about Maria Pavlovna's efforts to marry off her daughter Elena.[2] After the failure with Max [of Baden], they are desperate to find another husband. Their choice fell on Albert of Belgium, but he did not seem particularly keen. M.P. then wrote to the Emperor, asking him to invite the King of Belgium to Peterhof for the summer, while Elena wrote to the young Empress, declaring her whole future depended on this invitation. At this point Albert of Belgium announced his engagement to a Bavarian princess,

---

[2] Elena (or Helena) eventually married Nicholas, the third son of King George of Greece (Georgie) and Olga of Russia. Their youngest daughter, Marina, married George (later Duke of Kent), a son of King George V.

and Michen telegraphed the Emperor that there was no longer any need to invite the King.

Alix to Nicky – 23 June – Peterhof
My own precious Darling,

I must send you a letter today, already. It was horrid having to let you go off all alone and driving away from the station I felt a nasty lump in my throat and a suspicious moisture in the eyes. So I went straight off to the little church, and felt much calmer after praying for my darling. The service only lasted ¾ of an hour.

Had you been with me, I think we should have died as there were only three men to sing, I think a gardener and lamp-lighter. Each sang for himself and in another key. It was cruel to the ears; and the deacon from here has an impossible voice, so that I did not understand a word of the bible except, 'Martha ...' The priest's robes were much too short and immense black boots protruded from underneath – but it did not make me laugh. I felt too earnest and prayed for you with all my heart.

Coming home I met the children, so I walked home with them. Oh, my Sweet One, how I miss you, those orbs, lakes, where are they to gaze into? 'I love you, I love you, 'tis all that I can say,' and to be without you is really awful, my Nicky love! Our precious little girlies are my only comfort.

Every word from you is such a comfort to a lonely heart. I have grown so accustomed to have my Huzy near me that I can't bear being without him. If you could have seen my tea table! A wee table with a glass of milk, strawberries and a few biscuits.

I went to your room to see if any papers had come and found the door locked, but the key was there. It looked beastly dreary. I told them to bring any papers sorted there and am going to lay them carefully on the chair next to your writing table. Is that right? With great difficulty and many tears I got the children out of the room, as they wished to see the dentist work on my teeth, and Olga wished to sleep with me. But I must lay my pen down and be off. Goodnight, my precious, sweetest husband. God bless and protect you, and may holy angels watch over you and guard you – I cover your sweet face with kisses; forehead, eyes and mouth, and remain ever your tenderly loving little Wify

Alix

Nicky to Alix – 24 June – Cholm

My own beloved Sweety-dear,

I cannot believe that we are separated and I have caught myself several times going into your compartment to see what you are doing? My darling, how I love you!

How awfully I miss you and long to see your beloved face and cover it with kisses.

In two days God grant we may be able to clasp our arms round each other. I am eagerly awaiting a letter from you, as you wired that you were writing daily.

KR, Diary – 7 August – St Petersburg

Nicky [of Greece] went for a long ride with Elena, whom he likes, as she does him, but Maria Pavlovna rebuked her daughter for this, and told Georgy that Nicky could not expect to marry Elena, being neither a future King, nor having any fortune. She and Nicky, however, go together perfectly. I heard that Michen dreams of marrying her daughter to the Heir, Elena's first cousin, imagining that this would be permitted.

Nicky to Empress Marie – 10 October – Livadia

The children have very much grown, and the little baby is walking well, but falls often because her elder sisters knock into her and generally push her around, if one does not watch them. In the nursery, everything is going smoothly with the nanny and nursery maids – it's peace compared to the unfortunate past.

Xenia, Diary – 26 October – Ai-Todor

At around 2.30 I went to Livadia. Sandro came with me as far as Oreanda to see Witte and got out there.

When I arrived, I was amazed to learn that Nicky was in bed. He has a chill – yesterday evening his temperature was 38.8, this morning 38.2 and while I was there 37. Alix was lying on the bed in a dressing gown, as she feels sick all the time. I saw Girsh [royal physician], who said there is nothing on the lungs, but the spleen is enlarged. Nicky is complaining of pain in the thighs, besides which his head is throbbing. I sat with them and chatted. It was very funny to see them both in bed!

Count Witte, Memoirs

His Majesty the Emperor fell ill with typhoid in Yalta from 1st–28th November. During the Emperor's illness, which caused much alarm among his entourage, the following incident occurred.

One day, when according to his doctors, the Emperor was extremely unwell, I received a telephone call in the morning from the Minister of the Interior Sipiagin. As soon as I arrived, the question was raised of what to do if disaster struck and the Emperor died. What to do in such an event about the Heir to the throne?

I was very much surprised by the question, and replied, that in my opinion there could be no doubt, as the Grand Duke Mikhail had already been proclaimed Heir, and would thus immediately accede to the throne.

At this point I was given to understand that the Empress might be pregnant, and consequently a son could be born who would have a claim to the throne. To this I replied that the laws governing the succession do not allow for such a circumstance, and indeed how could they, because even if the Empress were pregnant, there was no way of knowing what the final outcome would be. According to the strict letter of the law, the Grand Duke Mikhail would immediately accede to the throne.

Then the old Grand Duke Mikhail Nikolaevich asked me: 'Well, and what would happen if then after a few months her Majesty gave birth to a son?'

I replied that it seemed to me, insofar as I knew Grand Duke Mikhail, that he was such an honest and noble man in the highest sense of the word, that he would himself renounce the throne in favour of his nephew, if he considered it useful and just. In the end, everyone agreed with me and it was decided that her Majesty should be informed privately of our meeting.

A few days later General Kuropatkin came to lunch with me, as he was leaving Livadia palace. Thus, after lunch, once we were alone, General Kuropatkin said to me: 'Tell me please, about the meeting you held?'

I told him.

Striking a tragic pose he jumped up and beat his breast, saying in a loud voice: 'I will stand by my Empress!'

Xenia, Diary – 27 October – Ai-Todor

Poor Nicky is lying in bed, he didn't sleep at all at night because of terrible pains in his back. In the morning his temperature was 38.2 –

during the day 38.7. His eyes are tired and pale! Girsh says that it's influenza! Thank God there's nothing in the lungs, or in general anywhere else. Poor Alix – she looks very tired.

29 October Later on I drove to Livadia and looked in on Nicky for a minute. The back of his neck hurts terribly, and he doesn't know where to turn his head. All the pain from his back and legs has gone upwards, and he is suffering terribly. Poor Alix has to some extent forgotten about her own sickness and is moving around more. Girsh is adamant, that it isn't typhoid (we asked him).

Girsh asked Nicky to call someone else, to put everyone's mind at rest – it was decided to call for [doctor] Tikhonov.

31 October We immediately went to Livadia. Along the way we met Tikhonov, who told us that several symptoms of typhoid had developed, and that they were almost sure that it was typhoid! At Livadia we immediately questioned Girsh. It's astounding that influenza should suddenly turn into typhoid! With Alix's permission Professor Popov was sent for; we had lunch alone together downstairs; a little later [Count] Fredericks arrived, tearing his hair and saying that he was in a terrible position, that everyone wanted news, while he was not allowed to tell anyone anything. He asked us to persuade Alix to allow a bulletin to be published, which we were able to do. She agreed that there is nothing worse than trying to conceal things!

We telegraphed poor Mama. Thank God Alix is calm. We sat with her for a while. We saw Nicky for a moment – but it was so dark in the rooms that I could hardly make him out. His voice was fine.

8 November Nicky slept badly again and is feeling out of sorts, the weakness has increased and he is beginning to get irritable. His temperature was 38.1 in the morning, 38.5 in the afternoon; poor Nicky – it's the beginning of the worst time now.

13 November Tikhonov talked with Sandro by telephone from Livadia at about 6 o'clock. They are not happy that Nicky's temperature is so low 36°, but the pulse is good at 66. They are afraid of a *haemorrhage*, God preserve us! *It's so terrifying*, help us God, save our Nicky!

Nicky to Empress Marie – 24 November – Livadia
About my little wife I can only say that she was my guardian angel, and looked after me better than any sister of mercy!

Ella to Nicky – 2 December – Moscow – Postcard
Most loving hearty wishes from Sergei and me to you Darling Nicky.
God bless this new year and give you health and joy.

KR, Diary – 18 December – St Petersburg
I had the unexpected pleasure of a letter from the Tsar in Livadia. He
says that the Empress, who looked after him like a Sister of Mercy
during his illness, feels wonderful and that he himself is much better
after his typhoid.

31 December   It will soon be midnight. The beginning of a new year
and a new century. I thank God for the past. Send me, Lord, reason
and strength for the future!

1901

DEATH OF GRANNY, BIRTH OF ANASTASIA

Queen Victoria dies – Nicky writes to Edward VII about
the Boer War – A fourth daughter, Anastasia, is born –
Nicky and Alix fall under the influence of Monsieur
Philippe – Nicky inspects the German fleet – Ernie and
'Ducky' are to divorce.

Xenia, Diary – 9 January – St Petersburg
The poor Queen died today [22 January in England] at 7 o'clock in
the evening! What a sorrow for the whole of England and the poor
family, particularly for Aunt Alix and Uncle Bertie!

The Queen was everything that was best about England, she was so
much loved, and exuded such enormous charm! Mama received two
telegrams from Aunt Alix, one after the other; the first one said she
seemed a little better, the second informed us of her death. Poor Aunt
Alix is in despair!

I feel terribly sorry for poor Alix. She did so love her grandmother!

**Nicky to King Edward VII – 16 January – Winter Palace, St
Petersburg**
Dearest Uncle Bertie,

I cannot let Misha go to London without writing a few lines to you
so as to express once more how deeply we all feel with you the terrible loss you have sustained. My thoughts are much with you and
dear Aunt Alix now, I can so well understand how hard this change
in your life must be, having undergone the same six years ago. I shall

never forget your kindness and tender compassion you showed Mama and me then during your stay here.

It is difficult to realize that beloved Grandmama has been taken away from this world. She was so remarkably kind and touching towards me since the first time I ever saw her, when I came to England for George's and May's wedding.

I felt quite like at home when I lived at Windsor and later in Scotland near her and I need not say that I shall forever cherish her memory. I am quite sure that with your help, dear Bertie, the friendly relations between our two countries shall become still closer than in the past, notwithstanding the occasional slight frictions in the Far East. May the new century bring England and Russia together for their mutual interests and for the general peace of the world. Please give my tender love to dear Aunt Alix and the cousins and believe me dearest Bertie ever your devoted nephew and friend,

Nicky

KR, Diary – 23 February

I was invited to stay for lunch; the reception dragged on and the Empress had to wait 20 minutes for the Emperor. She is looking very beautiful and despite her pregnancy, feels wonderful, unlike the other occasions; for this reason, everyone is anxiously hoping that this time it will be a son.

Nicky to King Edward VII – 22 May – Peterhof
Private

My dearest Uncle Bertie,

Let me once more express my joy at your lucky escape during the trials with the *Shamrock*. Having read the details in the papers one cannot but wonder that nobody on board was hurt. Pray forgive me for writing to you upon a very delicate subject, which I have been thinking over for months, but my conscience obliges me at last to speak openly. It is about the South African war and what I say is only said as by your loving nephew.

You remember of course at the time when war broke out what a strong feeling of animosity against England arose throughout the world. In Russia the indignation of the people was similar to that of the other countries. I received addresses, letters, telegrams, etc. in masses begging me to interfere, even by adopting strong measures. But my principle is not to meddle in other people's affairs; especially as it did not concern my country.

Nevertheless all this weighed morally upon me. I often wanted to write to dear Grandmama to ask her quite privately whether there was any possibility of stopping the war in South Africa. Yet I never wrote to her fearing to hurt her and always hoping that it would soon cease.

When Misha went to England this winter I thought of giving him a letter to you upon the same subject; but I found it better to wait and not to trouble you in those days of great sorrow. In a few months it will be two years that fighting continues in South Africa – and with what results?

A small people are desperately defending their country, a part of their land is devastated, their families flocked together in camps, their farms burnt. Of course in war such things have always happened and will happen; but in this case, forgive the expression, it looks more like a war of extermination. So sad to think that it is Christians fighting against each other!

How many thousands of gallant young Englishmen have already perished out there! Does not your kind heart yearn to put an end to this bloodshed? Such an act would universally be hailed with joy.

I hope you won't mind my having broached such a delicate question, dear Uncle Bertie, but you may be quite sure that I was guided by a feeling of deep friendship and devotion in writing thus.

I follow Georgie's journey with the greatest interest and am so glad that he has been on board my cruiser.

Thank God our little Olga's illness is taking a normal course.

With Alix's and my best love I remain dear Uncle your affectionate nephew,

Nicky

Olga [sister], Memoirs

I can still remember Uncle Bertie sitting unperturbed in front of his hotel, puffing a cigar while hordes of Germans stood outside staring at him with awe and curiosity.

'How can you stand it, Uncle Bertie?' I asked him one day.

'Why, it's as much entertainment for me to stare at them as it is for them to stare at me,' the King replied.

Nicky, Diary – 5 June – Peterhof

At about 3 o'clock in the morning, Alix started to have strong pains. At 4 o'clock I got up, went to my room and dressed. At exactly 6

o'clock in the morning *a little daughter – Anastasia – was born*.
Everything went off splendidly, quite quickly and thank God without any complications! Thanks to the fact that it all began and ended
while everyone was still asleep, we both had a feeling of calm and
solitude! After that I sat down to write telegrams to relatives and
friends in various parts of the world. At 11 o'clock Yanyshev said
prayers. At 3 o'clock there was a Te Deum at our church. Mama
arrived from Gatchina. Went for a short walk. After tea, Mama left.
Luckily Alix felt quite cheerful. The little one weighs 11½ pounds and
measures 55 centimetres. Went to bed early.

Xenia, Diary – 5 June – Sebastopol, on the yacht *Tamara*
Alix feels splendid – but my God! What a disappointment! ... a fourth
girl! They have named her Anastasia. Mama sent me a telegram about
it, and writes 'Alix has again given birth to a daughter!'

KR, Diary – 6 June – Strelna
The new born Grand Duchess Anastasia entered this world at 6 in the
morning, the birth was normal and lasted three hours, the baby is
quite big. Forgive us Lord, if we all felt disappointment instead of joy;
we were so hoping for a boy, and it's a fourth daughter.

Nicky, Diary – 10 July – Tsarskoe Selo
Returned from Peterhof at 12 o'clock. We lunched and dined alone.
In the afternoon I went to see Mama. Played [cards]. We spent the
whole evening at Renella, M. Philippe[1] talked and instructed us.
What a wonderful few hours.

11 July All the immediate family came to lunch at the farm. During
that time, 'our friend' [Philippe] was sitting with Alix and talking
with her. We showed him our daughters and prayed together with
him in the bedroom!
   Went with Alix to see Mama, who was making her first visit to the
garden. After that I played tennis.

---

[1] A Frenchman from Lyons, he was reputed to cure nervous diseases by hypnosis. He was subsequently to have an enormous influence on Alix. He died in 1905.

Felix Yusupov, Memoirs
The King of Montenegro's two daughters, the Grand Duchess Militsa and her sister the Grand Duchess Stana, played leading parts at the Court of Russia during this period. The first married the Grand Duke Pyotr Nikolaevich, the second married Prince Leuchtenberg and afterwards the Grand Duke Nikolai Nikolaevich. In St Petersburg, these two princesses were called 'the black peril'. They were much interested in occultism and lived surrounded by soothsayers and questionable prophets. It was through them that a French charlatan named Philippe, and later Rasputin, had access to the Imperial Court. Their palace, Znamenka,[2] was the central point of the powers of evil.

One day as my father was walking by the seaside in the Crimea, he met the Grand Duchess Militsa driving with a stranger. My father bowed, but she did not respond. Meeting her by chance a few days later, he asked her why she had cut him. 'You couldn't have seen me,' said the Grand Duchess, 'for I was with Doctor Philippe, and when he wears a hat he is invisible and so are those who are with him.'

One of the Grand Duchess's sisters told me that as a child she had once hidden behind a curtain and seen Philippe enter the room; to her astonishment, all those present knelt and kissed his hand.

Nicky, Diary – 13 July – Peterhof
A heavenly warm day. Had a small reception – 11 people. We lunched alone together. At 2.30 we went to Znamenka and sat in the garden until 5 o'clock. 'Our friend' [Philippe] was with us. On returning home we immediately went to have tea with Mama. Swam in the sea. After dinner we again spent the evening all together at Znamenka.

17 July – St Petersburg   The weather was wonderful with a pleasant breeze. At 9 o'clock the general parade began, the troops were in their shirts, we in jackets; it all looked very smart. The ceremonial march past ended at 11.30. 'Our friend' was present. After dinner we spent the whole evening at Znamenka.

19 July   Immediately after dinner, we hurried over to Znamenka. We sat upstairs, as Militsa was feeling unwell. We listened to 'our friend' all evening. It was a wonderful moonlit night as we returned home; and quite fresh.

---

[2] Home of Grand Duke Pyotr, a nephew of Tsar Alexander II and a grandson of Tsar Nicholas I, and his wife Princess Militsa of Montenegro.

20 July A wonderful day. The prophet Ilia did not visit us today in the guise of a thunderstorm! Alix came after me to the farm. Soon everyone from Znamenka arrived, together with 'our friend'. We had tea and walked in the park. We returned home at 6.15. Went for a swim in the sea. After dinner we went to Znamenka and spent a last evening with 'our friend'. We all prayed together.

21 July Wonderful weather again. We went to Znamenka and spent a last hour with 'our friend'. We said goodbye to him with great sadness. At 5 o'clock he left for Lyons.

Alix to Nicky – 27 August – Tsarskoe Selo

My own precious One,

I want you to find these lines when we are separated so as that you may feel Wify is near to you. My thoughts and earnest prayers will follow you all the time. Mr P [Philippe]'s too I know and that *is one* comfort *to me*, as otherwise our parting would be too awful.

The idea of having to part makes me wretched, but God grant we shall soon be together again – your sweet kisses – how I shall yearn for them. We have been so lucky that we are always together, only it makes every separation harder to bear.

Don't forget Saturday evening towards 10.30 – *all our thoughts* will fly to Lyons then. How rich life is since we know him and everything seems easier to bear.

Give my love to Uncles Alexei, Willy and Henry[3] please. Sweet precious Nicky, how I love you, there are *no* words to say *how* much. Thank you sweet angel for all the love you show me. I shall look well after our four tinies, they will be my comforters, I am better off than you in this case. I love you, love you and cover your precious face with tenderest burning kisses. God bless and protect you and keep you from all harm. Oh, how hard to part – fare well, sweety, my Nicky, my very own Boy, to whom I cling with every fibre. I kiss you, kiss you ever your own old

Wify

---

[3] Grand Duke Alexei Alexandrovich; George I, King of Greece (Uncle Willy); Henry, Prince of Prussia.

Officer in charge of special assignment for the Minister of the Interior
Report No. 257, Paris – To His Excellency, The Director of the Department of Police
I have the honour of sending your Excellency the article from the newspaper *Le Temps* about Doctor Philippe:

...The shutters are closed, and Philippe makes his entry, shrouded in shadow. I can vaguely make out a large man, with a long, hard figure. He goes round the room, and says to each person, taking their hand in his:

'I do not have a lot of time to give you, my friend, but believe and you will be cured.' The women then whisper in his ear, as if making an amorous confession. He looks at them, smiles at them, and they seem to rise towards him, as if he were lifting them, making them leave the ground. When a child is presented to him, he taps it gently on the cheek.

Then the great moment arrives! Philippe gives a talk. He says the world used to be a globe of fire! Then he adds some very inconvenient things about the cause of all humanity's ills. This lesson must be very instructive for the children present! Then he talks about magnetism, like someone who doesn't really understand what it is, and in very bad French. He talks about the existence of God, because he says he is acting in the name of God, and from time to time asks: 'Are you all listening to me?'

At which point the assembly reply in one voice: 'We all hear you, O master.'

'I,' says Philippe, 'am nothing in myself.'

The assembly utters a moan of denial.

Philippe goes on: 'I am nothing I tell you, nothing more than –' He looks around him, and seems to notice an old lady, who has been referred to as the 'marquise', and cries out in a harsh voice: 'Nothing more than that animal over there!'

The old lady replies politely: 'You are far more, O master!'

Nicky to Empress Marie – 2 September – Danzig
We Russians were all struck by what we saw.[4] The Emperor [Wilhelm] was in good spirits, calm and very pleasant.

---

[4] On a cruise from Copenhagen to Danzig, where Nicky inspects the German fleet.

27 October – Skernewitze   Dearest, darling Mama,

I want to warn you of a terrible and unexpected event. Can you imagine, Ernie and Ducky want to divorce. *Yes, divorce.* We learnt of this three days before our departure from Spala. Victoria wrote a long letter to Irène and Alix, with extracts from Aunt Marie's [Ducky's mother] letter to her. In it, she explains that in her view, Ernie and Ducky's relationship has not worked, that they were drifting further and further apart, and that in the end divorce was the only solution. The whole thing has been decided, and all that remains is for it to be formalized officially between the Darmstadt and Coburg ministers. It's all so sad and awful. I cannot say how much I pity and suffer for my poor Alix; she is trying not to let her grief show. In such a case, the loss of someone close is better than their disgrace – divorce. It's painful to think about the future for both of them, the poor little one, the whole country! I enclose Aunt Marie's letter to Alix. She recognizes that it was she who rushed to arrange their marriage, and that it has been a complete disaster.

Xenia to Nicky – 31 October – Ai-Todor

They have again approached us about the railway, it's a terrible bore, but Sandro has told them categorically that we *don't want it going through our* estate! (Just what we needed!) Let them do what they want somewhere else! Sandro has written to you in detail and I *terribly* hope that you will *forbid* them once and for all to even think about a railway. Let them build themselves an electric tram line, or something like that, only not a railway!

Empress Marie to Nicky – 5 November – Copenhagen

My dear sweet Nicky

I thank you with all my heart for your dear long letter from Skernewitze, which made me rejoice as always, although the contents were so terribly sad. Everything that you write about Ernie and Ducky upset me *so much*, that I was even unable to *sleep*. It's simply awful, and terrible to think about both their futures and the poor little one! I also feel *so* sorry for poor Alix, knowing how much she loves Ernie and how difficult and unpleasant it must be for her in every way. Yesterday I also received a very sad letter from Aunt Marie, who is, of course, in despair – but she says that they have not understood each other for a long time, and that the only way out is – divorce! I completely agree with what you say in this instance, that the loss of someone near is preferable to the public disgrace of – a divorce. I am always with you in my thoughts, and hope to hear today that you have safely returned to Tsarskoe.

Now it is time to end. I embrace you all tenderly, my dear children. Christ be with you!

Your deeply loving Mama

Alix to Xenia – 7 November – Tsarskoe Selo
Darling Chicken,

It is with a very heavy heart that I write to you today. Yes dear, it is true, Ducky wishes to be divorced and in a few days all will be finally settled. It nearly broke my heart when I got the news, it was so quite unexpected, I always hoped that in time things would come right. It is too long and too painful to write about. They have parted friends and each wrote to me saying of the other that they were the truest of friends and would always remain so. Only with her character married life thus was impossible to continue. It is not for *us to judge* tho' it is an awful step they are taking – when we meet again it will be easier to talk about than write. Only one thing I entreat of you, darling Xenia, whenever you hear nasty gossip, at once put a stop to it, for their sakes and ours. They parted as their characters could impossibly get on together, that is enough for the public.

She will not be missed in the country, as she never made herself beloved nor showed any liking for the country, alas! Poor girl, she is utterly miserable now without a home, tho' he leaves her the sweet Child. His home is desolate and everything will remind him of her whom he still cares for.

But I cannot write any more about it; you can think how we sisters who adore him and are very fond of her, have suffered. But we must believe that always all is for the best. You will not judge them harshly dear, my poor unhappy ones. It is doubly hard beginning 'society' life again when all know that one's brother and sister in law have gone asunder. All one's pride is crushed out of one.

A good kiss from your old Hen

George, Duke of York to Nicky – 21 December – Sandringham
My dear Nicky,

How very sad it is about Ernie and Ducky, when I saw them last year, I did not think they were at all happy together, but I never thought it would come to this; I am very sorry as I like them both.

You and I, thank God, are both so happy with our wives and children, that we can't understand this sort of thing.

Ever, dear Nicky, your devoted cousin

Georgie

1902

UNDER THE INFLUENCE – M. PHILIPPE

Nicky of Greece and Aunt Michen's daughter Helena are engaged – Ella is concerned about the influence of M. Philippe – Alix has a phantom pregnancy – KR meets M. Philippe – Uncle Pavel marries Mme Pistolkors to the horror of the family – Grand Duke Sergei is appointed guardian of Pavel's children, Maria Pavlovna and Dmitri Pavlovich

KR, Diary – 4 January – St Petersburg
For New Year there was a great procession at the Winter Palace. The Emperor, dressed in the uniform of the cavalry, led the Dowager Empress on his arm; she was wearing a lilac velvet gown, embroidered with silver. The young Empress, in pink brocade, walked with the Siamese crown prince, while his brother Chakrodon acted as her page. Maria Pavlovna was in orange and silver, Xenia in white and gold, Elena in a pink brocade dress; I walked with the latter. After mass, the reception for the diplomatic corps in the Georgevsky hall went on for a whole hour. Only the Emperor and the two Empresses talked to the diplomats, while we watched and waited.

6 January I led Xenia into church; she was wearing pinky-crimson velvet, embroidered with silver, copied in the style of Louis XV from a portrait at Gatchina. The Dowager Empress had a dress the colour of amethyst, richly embroidered in gold; the young Empress was in silvery-red brocade.

Nicky to George, Duke of York – 31 January – St Petersburg
My dearest Georgie,

Accept my belated but fondest thanks for your dear letter and for the delightful walking stick that you and dear May sent me for Xmas.

How happy you must be to be back home again after your long long voyage and also after your recent visit to Berlin. I thought of you two very often while on your trip. What a happiness it must be to see all the sweet children round one, after such a long separation!

We are here in the midst of a boisterous season. The duchesses of Sutherland and of Marlborough have spent over a fortnight in Petersburg appearing at all the balls and parties we gave. I greatly admire the former of them and have had long and interesting conversations with her.

The winter is cold and clear this year with any amount of snow, I assure you in the country it is a fathom deep. We had some excellent sport at our two places in Poland last autumn, I shot 20 heavy stags. It would be so nice if you both might have come to stay there with us some day, like Henry and Irène did. The archduke Franz-Ferdinand is here now, he is a most pleasant man and takes interest in everything. He leaves tomorrow. Please give my tender love to your dear wife and believe me, dearest Georgie, ever your loving and truly devoted cousin and friend

Nicky

George, Duke of York to Nicky – 2 March – York House, St James's
My dearest Nicky,

I was so delighted to get your dear letter, which the Duchess of Sutherland brought from Petersburg. I went to see her the other day and she talked of nothing but your great kindness to her and how much she had enjoyed her stay in Petersburg. I am glad you liked her, she is clever and very pretty. You seem to be having a very boisterous season with no end of balls and parties. I am glad you had such good sport in Poland and got so many fine stags. I should much like to see your charming places there. It is, alas, a long time since we met. Perhaps May and I may be going to Denmark next month for dear Apapa's birthday, how nice if you and Alicky could have come too, but I suppose it is so difficult for you to leave Russia at this time of year.

I am so sorry to see the Students have again been kicking up a row in the different Universities, as I know it must all be a great worry to you.

May and I are pretty busy now and we have a lot of tiresome functions to do, we go tomorrow to Bristol for one and next week to

Manchester. The children are still at Sandringham with Mama and Toria.[1] They are much happier in the country, as we still have fogs here in London. I am glad the archduke Franz-Ferdinand's visit went off so well, I only know him very slightly.

Please give my best love to your dear wife, who I hope is very well and all your sweet children. Ever, dearest Nicky, your loving and truly devoted cousin and friend

Georgie

Ella to Nicky – 3 April – Moscow

Darling Boy – dearest child – let me call you so and let an *old heart* pour out all its *prayers* before you – you *allowed* me to say all that *worries* me and I once wrote to you, you remember. You gave me my cross back this time, a *feeling of anguish* came over me and as if the whole time and in the train I heard a voice saying it is *too early, too early* he wants it still – and you with your perfect delicacy feared depriving me of a relic I cherish – here I send it back again and *wear it as long as you can* – I feel calmer when you have it and now you are in sore need in this time of hideous anguish.

Sergei does not know of this letter, it will probably be unlogical and overfeminine, but I have *picked other brains* and kept my *ears open* and as we hear much and through deeply clever devoted people with experience and love for *their sovereign* and country I thought who knows *even a woman* can be of use in heavy times.

Nicky dear, for heaven's sake be energetic now, more deaths may be in store ... put an end to this time of terror – forgive if I write *straight out* without phrases and look as if I were dictating, I don't expect your doing what I say. I only put it so in case these ideas might be of use to you.

Trepov was shot at and shortly after you change your excellent *firm decision* of Siberia – let all Russia know that *such crimes* are punished by *death* – if one wants no death as punishment let the assassins begin by not killing 'plus d'arret de mort, bien alors que les assassins commencent' – why could you not talk with men of brains and true servants of yours, Pleve,[2] Mouraviev, Zenger, Pobedonostsev,[3] Vladimir etc, in case you think Sergei might be a help, perhaps one might write to him.

---

[1] Victoria, daughter of Edward VII.
[2] V. K. Pleve, Minister of the Interior.
[3] Head of the Synod.

Xenia to Nicky – 4 April – Ai-Todor

It's sad that you don't have a friend or someone close, who would always be there to give good advice and generally be helpful, and in whom you could have complete trust.

Please don't be angry with me if I write openly, but I never manage to talk to you (anyway we see each other so seldom!) so I am taking this opportunity to speak out at last. You talk to Mama so seldom, I know it upsets her. It seems to her that you avoid all conversation with her, so what happens is that she remains silent and takes everything, until finally she can't stand it any more and she tells you everything she has had on her chest for a long time – she's in such a rush she doesn't manage to say everything. This does not satisfy her, so she waits for the next time. What I want to say is that you should talk to her yourself more often, and in that way relieve both her and yourself. The only place you can see more of each other is Peterhof, but it always seems to happen that you seldom see Mama alone – by the time you arrive everyone is already sitting down and there can be no conversation.

Once again I ask you not to be cross, everything that I have written comes straight from my heart and I only wish you well!

27 May   As for Sandro, I have to admit that it's very hard for me to be separated from him, I can never get used to it.

We spent the whole day in the fresh air and caught a lot of fish. I chatted with Klopov for a long time and he told me a lot of interest. You know him, he's a man who gets carried away, but who is alive, clever and good. He loves you terribly and suffers for you, as he knows how difficult and painful it is for you, but says that you are being undermined at every step, and that your good intentions are not fulfilled as they should be. Your name is misused, everywhere and in every way ... of course right behind your back ...

KR, Diary – 19 June

Mitia [KR's brother] returned with the unexpected and joyful news of the engagement of Nicky of Greece to Elena Vladimirovna. Two years ago, when Elena caught Nicky's eye, her mother Maria Pavlovna made sure he was told not to count on Elena because, as the third son of a king, he was not a suitable match for her. Now Maria Pavlovna has had to change her mind, as her search for other suitors for her daughter has been in vain.

Sandro to Nicky – 16 July – Sebastopol
Dear Nicky
    I thank You with all my heart for your frank letter. It upset and greatly saddened me.
    In 1899 You appointed me to the post of Chairman of the Council for Merchant Shipping, and from last year I have been Chairman of the Committee for Port Administration. Both these departments regulate extremely important matters, on which depend the prosperity of our marine trade and the development of our national fleet, which is so important for the correct economic development of Russia.
    This is how I understood my new appointment, but now it turns out my first duty is – service in the fleet, so I no longer understand about the other, how can it not count as a duty at all? How is it I have worked for the second winter from morning to night for three months, if this isn't service but some form of pastime.
    When I submitted to You my project for the main administration, I never expected that You would accept it and was prepared to have it rejected, in which case I would have resigned from my posts in the Ministry of Finance. I was even quite happy at the prospect. I could even have acted more plainly – and asked to be relieved of my duties without presenting any project at all, but I did not do this, considering it dishonest. I always remember the words You said to me immediately after the death of Your father in Livadia. Kissing me, You said: 'I hope you will always be there to help me.' For the past eight years I have tried in every way I could to fulfil the hope You expressed at that tragic and unforgettable time.
    With this as my guide, I acted according to my conscience, but now it turns out I have mixed my own personal ambitions with government affairs and am fishing for a higher position.
    Believe me, if You were to relieve me of everything tomorrow and leave me in the navy, I would be a happy man, but do I have the right to request this, it would be selfishness on my part. But I repeat, I cannot serve under Witte, it's only too clear to me what he is aiming for, and I cannot seem to condone his policies by my presence in his Ministry. I prefer navy service to anything else, I have given seventeen years of service and will always try to do everything in my power for the fleet. The navy staff knows and understands this, which is a great satisfaction to me.
    You write that You are surprised I consider serving in the navy less important than what I am doing at present in the Ministry of Finance. I repeat that is correct, if you compare my responsibilities in the fleet with my responsibilities at the Ministry. We obviously have a discrep-

ancy of viewpoint, navy service is a duty – the other position is a duty – but which is the most important – that is the question. I considered it to be the second, because it carries more responsibility. You consider it to be the first.

In that case, it would be better not to appoint me anywhere else and simply leave me in the navy, if this is Your opinion.

If this is so, You have not understood me, my best impulses have been misinterpreted and I regret having brought the question up, I should simply have asked to be dismissed from the Ministry of Finance.

I am grieved that I cannot command Your confidence, You may not say it, yet it comes through in the tone of Your letter.

Forgive this letter, I have poured my soul out, it really is too sad. The worst part is being misunderstood, when your best intentions are interpreted in a different light.

Goodbye. I embrace you and Alix fondly.

May the Lord keep You.

Ever your devoted

Sandro

Alix to Nicky – 22 July – Peterhof
My own beloved One,

Your dear old man will give you these lines before you go to bed. It is terrible to have to let you go off all *alone*, knowing that worries are awaiting you. But our dear Friend [Philippe] will be near you and help you answering William [Kaiser Wilhelm]'s questions. Be friendly and severe, that *he* realizes *he* dare not joke with you and that he learns to *respect* you and be afraid of you – that is the *Chief* thing. *How* I wish I were with you.

23 July
My own sweet One,

It was horrid letting you go off alone – from my balcony I watched the *Alexandria*. The music had stopped and the public gone when I returned. I went straight to bed – did not cry, as I promised to be good, but scarcely shut my eye the whole night and in consequence my headache continues. We 3 breakfasted in my sitting room, then Sergei went to Aunt Marie and Ella and I sat together until we went to the cottage. Your poor Mama turned up with a colossal pile of unanswered telegrams.

We drove round the Alexander Park, and during that time Ella assailed me about our Friend. I remained very quiet and gave dull answers, especially after she said *she* wanted to get to the bottom of it. She has heard many very unfavourable things about Him and that He is not to be trusted. I did not ask what one said – I explained that all came from jealousy and inquisitiveness. She said such secrecy had been spun around it. I said no, that we did everything openly and that in our positions there never can be anything hidden, as we live under the eyes of the whole world. That their whole house knows him, he eats with all, is not hidden. Did we see him often? Yes, several times. I stuck to the story of the remedy.

She finds it funny a foreigner doing such a thing. About 'Nikolasha' [husband of Anastasia of Montenegro] – I said that in bygone days spiritism interested him, that he has dropped it a long time ago – so that the conversation never took that turn, which might have been more difficult to explain to her. She thinks Militsa and Stana made too much of a secret – that he had been sent for in winter (I think then) – from a sure, trustworthy, source, I never asked who – and that one had tried to hush it up.

I am sure my answers are most unsatisfactory to her – let's hope that she won't begin again. Now Baby Bee is with her. I shall ask him whether anything was in the papers about the Canonization of F[ather] Serafim – if not, he is to write to Pobedonostsev and tell him that you wished it to be printed, as you had said.

Warm day, already one shower, sure to have more. I shall continue my letter later, sweetest love.

Xenia to Aprak – 19 August – Alexandria

Dear Aprak,

We have all felt so terribly disappointed since yesterday. Can you imagine anything so awful, it seems poor A. F. [Alix] isn't pregnant after all – for 9 months she had nothing, then suddenly it came, but completely normally, without any pain. The day before yesterday, Ott [Doctor] saw her for the first time and confirmed that there was no pregnancy, but that luckily everything internally was all right. He says that such cases do happen, and are caused by anaemia. It's so awful, we can't think about anything else, how terrible for them, painful and sad. All that long, tiresome waiting has ended in nothing!

I can just imagine what they will start saying, when it becomes known, and in order to avoid all the false rumours, I decided to write to you so that you should know the truth. She informed Mama herself and cried terribly. I did not see her yesterday all day, as I was lying with my leg up. I was stupid, or rather, clumsy enough, to trip on the stairs at Tsarskoe Selo on the day of the wedding. Today it's better and I can get about again. After breakfast I went with Mama to see the poor thing, and found her in a very sad mood, although she talks about it with great acceptance. Apart from the personal sorrow and disappointment, what a blow it must have been to their pride! Mama used the opportunity to speak frankly to Nicky about Ph.[ilippe] – she told him everything she had on her heart, but unfortunately only received rather vague explanations, although he said all the rumours were very much exaggerated, and so on. I am glad for Mama that she at last spoke out, but the result of their conversation was not satisfactory!

Please write to me. I embrace you warmly and send my best wishes. I hope you are feeling better now?

Love

                                                                    Xenia

KR, Diary – 20 August

An event ... I don't remember if I already noted this in the diary, but from the 8 August we have been waiting every day for confirmation of the Empress's pregnancy. Now we have suddenly learnt that she is not pregnant, indeed that there never was any pregnancy, and that the symptoms that led one to suppose it were in fact only anaemia!

What a disappointment for the Tsar and Tsarina! Poor things! Alix sent news of the sad discovery to Mama and my wife. Alix cried a lot when doctors Ott and Girsh, who were at last admitted to see her, determined that not only was there no pregnancy, but there never had been.

There has been a lot of talk in the family. All summer it was being said that their Majesties have become very close to Militsa. It was said that they spent almost every evening at Znamenka staying until late at night, and that at the same time the Empress avoided going out, on the pretext that the Dowager Empress was suffering from fatigue. It is said that at Militsa's their Majesties made the acquaintance of a certain Filipov [sic], who is neither a doctor nor a scientist, but who knows how to inoculate or cure certain illnesses, including syphilis.

It is surmised – on what grounds, I don't know – that this Filipov has influenced the Empress in order for her to produce a son rather than a daughter. Sergei Mikhailovich told me, that politically unfavourable reports on Filipov were obtained from Paris by our main secret police agent, and that the Emperor ordered the dismissal of this agent within 24 hours, which put the whole *Okhrana* [secret police] in a very difficult position, as this agent was apparently in possession of all the information on political criminals.

I can see and I know that the Dowager Empress and all those near to her, are very angry with Militsa and her sister Stana. Stana herself was my neighbour at dinner yesterday, and complained to me that she and Militsa are being wrongly accused of plotting and intrigues.

Xenia to Aprak – 20 August – Alexandria

Just a few words, dear Aprak, in addition to yesterday. This morning A. F. [Alix] had a minor miscarriage – if it could be called a miscarriage at all! – that is to say a tiny ovule came out! Yesterday evening she had pains, and at night too, by morning it was all over when this event happened! Now at last it will be possible to make an announcement and tomorrow a bulletin will be published in the papers – with information about what happened. At last a natural way out of this unfortunate situation has been found. She is in bed – as a precaution, as there can sometimes be bleeding in such cases. Thank God so far she is in good health. Mama and I talked to them both today about Ph.[ilippe], I felt very much relieved but unfortunately they once again failed to explain anything and were only surprised that everyone seems to think they are trying to conceal their friendship with Ph.[ilippe], when they never had any intention of keeping it a secret. Nevertheless the mystery remains – we still haven't found out exactly what he is! They said he is a very modest man and that it is pleasant to talk to him as he has such understanding and says 'things which do one good'! All the same it's good at least that *la glace est rompue*! [the ice is broken]

Mama is preparing to go to Denmark on Sunday, and I am leaving on the 22nd. The weather is impossible, 8°, and pouring, pouring without ceasing. With this I am ending.

Xenia

KR, Diary – 22 August

The doctor or scientist I mentioned on 19 August is not Filipov but Philippe, a Frenchman, and the name of the dismissed secret police agent is Rachkovsky!

Yesterday the following bulletin appeared in the newspapers, signed by the royal accoucheur Professor Ott and the royal surgeon Girsh. 'A few months ago, the state of Her Imperial Majesty the

Empress Alexandra Feodorovna underwent changes, which pointed to a pregnancy. At the present time, thanks to a departure from the normal course, the interrupted pregnancy has resulted in a miscarriage, which occurred without any danger, the temperature and pulse remaining normal. Peterhof, 20 August 1902.' The text of the bulletin has been criticized, particularly the use of the words 'thanks to'.

25 August   Elena[4] told me that her brother Yury, who has also fallen under the influence of Militsa, Philippe and their circle, talked to her for two whole hours about the sacred joy experienced by members of that circle, and reproached her for not visiting it. He begged her to attend their meetings in the name of their late mother.

He also said that Philippe's mission is drawing to a close, that soon he will die and will reappear afterwards to the circle of friends in the guise of another man. What nonsense!

We went to Znamenka for the dance-class. They had the famous Philippe there; after the dance-class we had tea with Militsa and saw him. He is a man of about fifty, small, with black hair and a black moustache, very unsightly in appearance, with an ugly southern-French accent. He talked about the decline of religion in France and in the West in general.

When I said goodbye to him he wanted to kiss my hand, and I only managed to pull it away with difficulty.

Sergei called me out on to the balcony and confessed his great anxiety over the frequent visits made by the Emperor and young Empress to Znamenka over the past year, where at Militsa's they have succumbed to the influence of Philippe; he, according to Sergei, is some kind of mystic.

Sergei maintains that their Majesties have fallen into a mystical frame of mind, that at Znamenka they pray with Philippe, that they can't wait to go there, and spend long evenings there, from which they return in an exalted state, as if in ecstasy, with radiant faces and shining eyes.

My personal opinion is that if their Majesties really have got carried away with mysticism or mystical states, it's really more funny than dangerous; what is bad, however, is that they shroud their visits to Znamenka in mystery. There is no way they can hide – the cossacks and the secret police are everywhere – and you cannot suppress or conceal what has been seen by many. They are only giving fuel to the gossip and rumours, which increase and spread the whole time.

---

[4] Daughter of Peter I, King of Serbia (from 1903); Yury is her brother George.

26 August   Ella, understandably, cannot approve of the secrecy with which her sister the Empress and the Emperor surround their acquaintance with Philippe, and blames Militsa for her pernicious influence.

Nicky to Alix – 29 August – Rishkovo
My own beloved Wify,

I begin this letter a few hours before Kursk, so as to finish it this evening. The train shakes a little so you must excuse my bad writing!

Sweet lovy-mine, how sad and how hard it was saying goodbye yesterday, I felt I could not speak to you during the last moments, for fear of bursting into tears.

Knowing that I was leaving you all alone (except the children) after such trying circumstances and with Ella too, made me more miserable than ever – I mean this separation is the most painful one we have had. But there is nothing to be done, God knows what is good for us, we must bow down our heads and repeat the sacred words 'Thy will be done.'

I don't know but I feel so quiet before arriving today there, that is the fulfilment of 'our Friend's' promise.

I tried to pray very fervently last night and this morning and that has also brought comfort to the soul.

After dinner it rained yesterday, but now it is lovely, quite warm and sunny. If it is so for the manoeuvres it will be simply delicious. There has been no talk yet. I sat much with Misha [brother] or read in my cabin. We walked at several stations.

It is 11 o'clock of the evening – the first part of the programme is finished. The first speech went off very well, but in the beginning one I stuck and could not for the life remember what I wanted to say. But in the end after a desperate attempt to speak, I succeeded in producing the second half of my speech, which was perhaps enough after all. The heat in the room was terrific.

Now it is late, my sweet Sunny, I must finish my letter by pressing you tenderly to my heart. God bless *you*, my darling and our sweet children. Misha kisses you very lovingly. I shall write every day.

Ever your own loving and devoted

Nicky

Alix to Nicky – 31 August – Peterhof
My own beloved one,

With what intense joy I received your precious letter this morning.

Thank you for it with all my heart. Yes, indeed, sweetie, this parting has been one of the hardest, but every day brings us nearer to our meeting again. How anguishing the moment of the speeches must have been.

Your precious letter and telegrams I've put on our bed so that when I wake up in the night I can touch something of yours. Fancy an old married woman speaking so – 'old fashioned' many would say. But what would life be without love – what would have become of Wify without you? You, my beloved treasure, the joy of my heart. To keep the children quiet, I made them think of things and then guess them. Olga always thinks of the sun, clouds, sky, rain or something belonging to the heavens, explaining to me that it makes her so happy to think of that.

Now, my pet, goodbye, God bless and keep you. A hearty kiss, sweet one, from your tenderly loving and devoted Wify,

Alix

Xenia to Aprak – 31 August – Sebastopol
Dear Aprak,

I am so glad for Mama that she is in Denmark, but she must constantly worry and be in a state of anxiety.

I am no longer in any doubt that what happened to A. F. [Alix] was suggestion, although they themselves are unaware of it. However she did admit to her sister that she prayed with Ph.[ilippe] on one occasion. It's all so strange and frightening, God knows how it will all end! I'm afraid that their friendship and association with these people will continue – everything will remain as before and we will look like fools. However we are not going to remain silent any longer, although we have to go about it in the right way, which is not easy – they have completely fallen under his influence. There are many things I could tell, only I don't want to write about it.

The wind is terribly strong today, dry and hot like a Sirocco, with dust blowing from Sebastopol.

Goodbye my dear Aprak. I embrace you warmly. My husband sends his regards.

Your Xenia

Nicky to Alix – 1 September – Rishkovo
There were any amount of ladies, some were rather good looking with fatal eyes and they kept looking steadily at Misha and me,

smiling sweetly, when we turned our heads in their direction. At the end of our tea, there stood such a wall of them around us, that we could not bear it any longer and got up.

M. Bariatinskaya asked very much about you. Our last visit was to the governor's house, where I spoke again. This time it was to the peasants. That went off well because it is much easier to talk to simple people. Sergei came from his bivouac and left immediately after. He wants to come to Peterhof to fetch Ella.

Now goodbye and God bless you, my sweet little Wify. I kiss you tenderly and all the children. I love you and want you, Oh! So naughty!!

Ever your loving and devoted

Nicky

Alix to Nicky – 3 September – St Petersburg
Sweetest lovey mine,

Tenderest thanks for your interesting letter all about your visit to Kursk. I followed the detailed description also in the papers. The image of the Virgin is the one Serafim loved and which cured him as a boy.

I can see you drinking tea, surrounded by a band of languishing ladies, and I know the adorable expression of shyness which creeps over you and makes your sweet eyes all the more dangerous. I am sure many hearts have beaten faster ever since then, you old sinner. I shall make you wear blue spectacles to frighten gay butterflies off from my too dangerous husband.

Rain, rain, water very high, but a little warmer today.

What an imposing and emotional sight the attack of those 80 battalions must have been, and then, that colossal luncheon on the meadow.

I must be off to bed. Good night, and God bless and keep you. A tender kiss my beloved Huzy from your very own wife,

Alix

KR, Diary – 19 September
How happy I was to free my conscience from the heavy burden of sin, which I accumulated during my trip down the Volga, when instead of thanking God for my recovery, I wilfully transgressed. I have again firmly resolved to liberate myself from my main sin.

19 October   Pavel has married O. V. Pistolkors, after she managed to obtain a divorce. The marriage took place in Livorno.[5] The affair is made more complicated by the fact that, as I have heard from two different sides, Pavel had given his word, through Vladimir, to the Emperor that he would not marry Olga Pistolkors.

The Emperor's position is very difficult: to be consistent and strictly fair, he should take the same line with Pavel as was taken in 1891 with Misha, when he married without royal permission.[6]

Nicky to Empress Marie – 20 October – Livadia

My dear darling Mama

Forgive me for not answering your last letter for so long. But it coincided with two events which, as you know, upset me very much. The first of course – was the marriage of Uncle Pavel. I heard about it from Pleve in Petersburg; he was informed by Mme Pistolkors' mother. Despite the source of the news, I wanted to verify it, and sent a coded telegram to Uncle Pavel.

The next day I received an answer from him, saying that the wedding had taken place at the beginning of September in the Greek church at Livorno, and that he was writing to me. The letter arrived ten days later. As probably in his letter to you, he did not say anything new. Filosofov told me that, on the day of his departure abroad, Uncle Pavel ordered him to bring him 3 million roubles to the train from his office, which was of course done.

From this it is quite clear that Uncle Pavel had decided in advance to put his wishes into action, and was preparing for a lengthy stay abroad. Already in the spring, I had a frank discussion with him, and finished by warning him of all the consequences which awaited him if he married. To everyone's distress, nothing helped. Bearing in mind the example of how unforgettable Papa dealt with Misha, it wasn't difficult to decide what to do with Uncle Pavel.

The closer the relative who refuses to submit to our family rules, the more severe his punishment should be. Don't you agree, dear Mama? Uncle Sergei asked to be appointed guardian to the poor children and their inheritance, which has already been done. Their affairs are in good order. The question that still remains open in this

---

[5] Grand Duke Pavel, Tsar Alexander III's youngest brother. His first wife, Alexandra of Greece, died in 1891, as a result of premature labour. The baby, who was named Dmitri, survived. Olga Pistolkors later became Princess Paley.

[6] Grand Duke Mikhail Mikhailovich (Miche-Miche), brother of Sandro, had lived in England following a morganatic marriage.

whole sad story, is whether the marriage will be recognized as legitimate, or not. The statutes on the imperial family say that morganatic
marriages are forbidden and that no marriage contracted WITHOUT
PERMISSION is considered real.

What guarantee is there that Kyril won't do the same thing tomorrow, or that Boris or Sergei Mikhailovich won't do it the day after
that? A whole colony of the imperial family will be living in Paris with
their semi-legal or illegal wives. God only knows what times these are,
when egoism rules alone over all other feelings: conscience, duty and
decency! The most painful thing is to think that a brother of our
adored Papa could behave so badly. Can the saintly example of his
life, and the constant striving of his reign to bring decency to Russia
and to the family, can all this have been for nothing?

It is from this point of view that I look at the question, and why,
dear Mama, I am so deeply upset by his action and do not feel any
pity for him!

My other sorrow, a completely personal one, was the loss of good
old Iman, which happened at the beginning of October, almost on
the same day as poor Raven [a horse]. He had been ill since the summer. He was such a good, clever, devoted dog!

I love you with all my heart and will remain devoted until my last
breath.

                                                                   Nicky

**Empress Marie to Nicky – 23 October – Amalienborg Palace,
Copenhagen**
My dear sweet Nicky

It seems so long since I had any news from you, I am waiting to
receive some at last, although I know how little free time you have,
especially now with various unpleasant matters. Uncle Pavel's wedding is a terribly sad affair! I kept hoping that it wasn't true, that he
wouldn't actually marry, that his love for his children would prevail,
but unfortunately he has forgotten everything, all his fundamental
obligations, his children, country, service, honour, everything, he
has sacrificed everything for that stupid woman, who is not worthy
of it. One can only pity him, the poor thing, as he is completely
blind and believes he has acted honourably in marrying her, forgetting all the rest. How could he do it, after everything he was told –
by each of his brothers and all of us. What will become of him, the
unfortunate? I am overwhelmed, particularly when I think of his
poor little children, for whom he was everything in life, and whom

he has abandoned. I hope it can be hidden from them for as long as possible, it's so cruel and sad! As for the scandal, I'm quite simply ashamed and have told no one – although it will soon get out and everyone will know! He's simply throwing dirt at our family! Awful, awful! And what a painful and disagreeable position he has put you in, my poor Nicky, you will be obliged to punish him, for such an act cannot go unpunished, on top of everything he's gone and married a divorced woman! No comparison with Mikhail M. [Miche-Miche].

I hope that you are all well, my dear children and grandchildren, and that you are enjoying the fine weather.

I kiss you tenderly, my dear Nicky. May the Lord bless you.

Your Mama

KR, Diary – 29 October

E. F. Djunkovskaya[7] came to see us. She told us that Pavel had written himself to his children, informing them of his marriage. It came as a great shock to the children, but they were more affected by the news that their father was unable to return to Russia; they are so attached to him, there can be no question of them rejecting him or that their love could in any way be diminished.

Felix Yusupov, Memoirs

I was still a child when I met the Grand Duke Dmitri Pavlovich and his sister the Grand Duchess Maria Pavlovna, both of whom lived with their uncle and aunt. Their mother, Princess Alexandra of Greece, had died in their infancy and their father, the Grand Duke Pavel Alexandrovich, had been obliged to leave Russia after his morganatic marriage to Madame Pistolkors, later Princess Paley.

George, Duke of York to Nicky – 17 December – Sandringham

My dear old Nicky,

How did you get on with William [Kaiser] when you met him this summer? He made himself most agreeable when he came here and I think he was pleased with his visit. May is making a capital recovery, fancy we have now got four sons, I wish one of them was yours.

Ever, dear old Nicky, your most devoted cousin and friend

Georgie

---

[7] Governess to Pavel's children, Dmitri and Maria.

1903

BATHING AT SAROV

The last great Imperial ball – Alix and Nicky go to Sarov
for the canonization of Father Serafim – They bathe in
the pool – Olga witnesses a miracle – Ernie and Ducky's
daughter dies – KR's moral struggle – Nicky's brother
Misha is in love with his English cousin Beatrice

Sandro, Memoirs
On January 22, 1903, 'all' St Petersburg danced in the Winter Palace.
I remember the date as it was to be the last spectacular ball in the history of the empire.

Almost a quarter of a century had passed since the night Nicky and
I watched the Tsar-Liberator appear with Princess Yurevskaya on his
arm in these high-ceilinged halls that reflected in their mirrors seven
generations of the Romanovs.

The uniforms of the Chevalier Guards remained the same but the
rest of the empire had undergone a terrific change. A new and a hostile Russia glared through the large windows of the palace. I smiled
sadly on reading the text of the invitation which demanded that all
guests wear the costumes of the seventeenth century: for at least one
night Nicky wanted to be back in the glorious past of our family.

Xenia wore a very becoming costume of a *boyarina*, richly embroidered and covered with glittering jewels. For myself I had chosen the
costume of a court falconer, consisting of a white-and-gold long coat,
– with golden eagles embroidered on the breast and on the back, – a
pink silk shirt, blue silk trousers and yellow leather boots. All other
guests followed their fancy, always remaining within the limits of the
seventeenth century. Nicky and Alix appeared dressed as the first Tsar
and the first Tsarina of the house of the Romanovs. Alix looked stun-

ning, but Nicky was obviously not sufficiently tall to do justice to his magnificent garb. The chief honours of the night were disputed between Ella and Princess Zinaida Yusupov.[1] My heart ached a bit at the sight of these two 'mad devotions' of my early youth. I danced every dance with Princess Yusupov, until it came to the famous Russian dance. She did it better than any ballerina but I limited my participation to hand-clapping and silent admiration.

The ball was pronounced a huge success. This magnificent pageant of the seventeenth century must have made a strange impression on the foreign ambassadors; while we danced, the workers were striking and the clouds in the Far East were hanging dangerously low.

Felix Yusupov, Memoirs

My mother was lovely. She was slim and had wonderful poise; she had very black hair, a soft olive complexion and deep blue eyes as bright as stars; she was clever, cultured and artistic, and above all she had an exquisitely kind heart. No one could resist her charm, and far from being vain and proud of her exceptional gifts she was modesty and simplicity itself.

Wherever my mother appeared she brought a delightful feeling of light and well-being. Her eyes shone with kindliness and sweetness. She dressed with quiet elegance, was not fond of jewellery.

The Spanish Infanta Eulalia,[2] Memoirs

Princess Yusupov was a most lovely woman, whose marvellous beauty stands out as typical of a period. She lived in extraordinary luxury, in a setting of unsurpassed splendour, surrounded by works of art of the purest Byzantine style, in a great palace the windows of which gave on to the city of a thousand cupolas. The magnificence and luxury of Russia, blended with the refinement and distinction of France, reached its culminating point in the Yusupov palace. Tall, exquisitely beautiful, she wore a *kokoshnik* [court tiara] set with enormous pearls and equally large diamonds, worth a fortune. A dazzling array of fantastic jewels from the East and West completed her costume: ropes of pearls, massive gold bracelets of ancient design, pendants of turquoises and pearls, multicoloured, glittering rings. All these gave to Princess Yusupov the majestic splendour of a Byzantine Empress.

---

[1] Felix Yusupov's mother.
[2] The daughter of Queen Isabella II of Spain, wife of Anthony of Orléans.

Olga [sister], Memoirs

All of us appeared in seventeenth-century court dress. Nicky wore the dress of Alexis, the second Romanov Tsar, all raspberry, gold, and silver, and some of the things were brought specially from the Kremlin. Alicky was just stunning. She was Tsarina Maria Miloslavskaya, Alexis's first wife. She wore a sarafan of gold brocade trimmed with emeralds and silver thread, and her ear-rings were so heavy that she could not bend her head.

Xenia, Diary – 8 July – Alexandria

We went to Mama's and I sat with her until 12 o'clock. Putiatin[3] was there and told us in detail about Serafim of Sarov, from where he has just returned – it was very interesting. Mama is going there on the 15th, with N and A and everyone else – We should also be going, but I will be indisposed on those dates, besides which there is no room for us on the train – they would need a second one for us.

Felix Yusupov, Memoirs

Father Serafim was born at Kursk in 1759; he came of a merchant family named Mochine. His parents were pious, honest folk and he himself was extremely religious from early infancy, spending hours in prayer before the ikons.

One day his mother took him to the top of a bell-tower which was under construction. The child slipped and fell a hundred and fifty feet to the cobblestones below. His distracted mother rushed down expecting to see his mangled body, but, to her astonishment and joy, he was standing up apparently unhurt. The news of this miracle spread throughout the town, and the Mochines' house was filled with people who came to see the child. Later in life he was several times in mortal danger and each time was saved by a miracle.

He entered the monastery of Sarov at the age of eighteen, but as he grew older he found monastic life too easy and retired to a hermitage in the forest of Sarov. He lived there for fifteen years, fasting and praying. People from neighbouring villages brought him food, but he gave most of it to the birds and wild animals, who were his great friends. The Mother Superior of a neighbouring convent went to visit him one day and was terrified to find a huge bear lying across his threshold. Father Serafim assured her that the bear was harmless, that he was a

---

[3] A court official.

most friendly animal and brought him honey every day from the forest. In order to convince her the hermit sent the bear to fetch some. The animal returned a few moments later, holding a honeycomb between his paws; this the Father gave to the astonished nun.

It is said that he spent a hundred days and nights standing on a rock, his arms raised to heaven, crying: 'Lord, have mercy upon us miserable sinners.'

Then one night some unknown men broke into his hermitage and demanded money. When he replied that he had none, they struck him on the head and left him for dead. Next morning he was found unconscious, covered with blood, with a fractured skull and several broken ribs. For a week he was critically ill but refused all medical assistance. On the ninth day he had a vision of the Blessed Virgin; he immediately began to mend and was soon completely cured. He then returned to his monastery and, taking a five years' vow of silence, shut himself up in his cell. At the end of the five years, overflowing with Divine grace, he devoted himself to the welfare of his fellow-men. Thousands of pilgrims came from all over Russia to beg for his help and his prayers. He welcomed them all with the same ardent charity, consoling, advising and curing.

Xenia, Diary – 10 July – Alexandria
Kyril arrived with a languid expression of persecuted innocence! He brought a letter from Aunt Maria to Mama and Nicky, asking permission for them to be married in secret.[4] What unbelievable stupidity, and all thought up to enable him to come out clean from the whole story.

Mama came later from her walk. We talked about K[yril]. In fact, the only honourable thing for him to do – is to marry her and take the corresponding punishment, but he doesn't want that!

Nicky, Diary – 17 July – on the road to Sarov[5]
At 11 o'clock we arrived in Arzamas. We were welcomed in a marquee on the platform by the nobility, the *zemstvo*, the towns and peasants

---

[4] He wished to marry Ducky, daughter of the Duke and Duchess [Aunt Marie] of Edinburgh, who had previously been married to Alix's brother Ernie. The Duchess of Edinburgh was a sister of Alexander III.

[5] A year before Philippe had so worked upon the imagination of the Empress that she and all around her were convinced that she was with child – until the illusion was exposed by the Empress's doctors.

Philippe explained what had occurred by her lack of faith and falling into a of Nizhegorodsky province. We got into carriages and set off along a good, dusty road. We went through large villages, where we were greeted by peasants outside the buildings along the road. We had tea in a marquee some 40 miles from Arzamas. At 6 o'clock we arrived at the Sarov monastery. There was something very special about going into the cathedral of the Assumption and then into the church of St Zosima and St Savvaty, where we were able to pray to the relics of the holy father Serafim. At 6.30 we went back to our house. Mama is staying opposite. A huge crowd of pilgrims thronged in the courtyard. At 8.15 the whole family had dinner at Mama's. In the evening we were given confession in the cell of saint Serafim, inside the new church, by the monk Simon, a former officer. Then we brought Mama to him. We went to bed feeling contented and not at all tired.

Olga [sister], Memoirs
Once Nicky was so hungry that he opened his cross and ate the contents – relic and all. Later he felt very ashamed of himself, but admitted that it had tasted 'immorally good'. I was the only one who knew about it. Nicky would not even tell George and Xenia. Our parents would have been shocked beyond words. I just laughed, and later whenever we had something nice to eat we would whisper to each other, 'It's immorally good,' and nobody knew our secret.

Anastasia to Nicky – 18 July – Postcard
To His Imperial Majesty, The Emperor, Sarov
                              Dear darling Papa
                              I kiss your hand
                              Anastasia [aged 2]

---

trance prophesied anew that the wish of the Empress to have a son would be gratified if she asked for the protection of St Serafim of Sarov. The saint was unknown in the Orthodox calendar, but on enquiries being made it was discovered that in the monastery of Sarov there had been a monk of the name of Serafim, whose life had been a model of virtue and who had the repute of performing miracles. The Emperor ordered the Holy Synod to canonize Serafim without delay. Pobedonostsev, the Head of the Synod, tried to explain that a man could not be proclaimed a saint by Imperial order, but he was told by the Empress Alexandra herself: 'The Emperor can do anything.' Serafim was canonized at Sarov with great pomp in the presence of Nicholas and Alexandra. By the order of Philippe, the Empress bathed at the dead of night in the spring, which was said to have been blessed by the saint. The promised miracle had been performed. [From V. Poliakov's biography of Empress Marie]

Nicky, Diary – 18 July – Sarov

We got up at 5.30 and went to early service with Mama. We took communion. The service ended at 7 o'clock.

From 9 to 10.30 we visited the churches and went into the caves under the hill. At 11.15 we went to the cathedral of the Assumption for the last solemn requiem for *staretz* [holy man] Serafim. Then we had lunch with Mama. At the hottest time of the day, Uncle Sergei, Nikolasha, Petiusha, Yuri and I set off for the hermitage by foot, along the Sarovka. Mama, Alix and the others went by carriage. The path through the woods was amazingly beautiful. We also returned home on foot; the crowd was touching and was remarkably orderly. At 6.30 the service began. During the procession, when the relics were brought out of the church of Sts Zosima and Savvaty, we carried the coffin on a litter. It was an incredible spectacle, to see how the crowd and especially the invalids, cripples and unfortunates reacted to the holy procession. It was a very solemn moment when the glorification began and then the kissing of the casket. We left the church at this time, having stood for three hours. We had a light meal with Mama, thinking that we would return for the end of the service, but the crowd had rushed back into the cathedral without waiting for the end of the service, and it was already impossible to get through.

19 July   We got up at 7.30 and went over to Mama and then to church, together with the Te Deum, the service lasted from 9 o'clock to 12.30. The holy procession was as moving as yesterday, this time the relics were exposed. One felt an enormous lift, both from the event itself and the extraordinary mood of the crowd. We had some *zakuski* with Mama and then lunch at 2.30 in the refectory.

We rested for about an hour. The heat was great, also the dust from the mass of pilgrims. At 4.30 we went to the pavilion of the Tambov nobility, who entertained us to tea. At 7.30 we dined with Mama.

Then we went in twos and threes down to the source, where we bathed with a particular emotion in the stream of icy water. We got back safely, in the darkness no one recognized us. We heard of many people being cured today and yesterday. Another cure happened in the cathedral, while the holy relics were being carried round the altar. God is miraculous through his saints. Great is his mercy towards dear Russia; there is inexpressible comfort in the evidence of this new manifestation of the Lord's grace towards us all; let us put our hope in the Lord for ever and ever. Amen!

Olga [sister], Memoirs
It was from the banks of the little river that I saw the first miracle. The waters of the Sarovka were considered healing because Serafim had often bathed there. I saw a peasant mother carry her wholly paralysed little daughter and dip her into the river. A little later the child was walking up the meadow, and there were doctors at Sarov to testify to the reality of the paralysis and the cure.

Cavalry Captain Garardi to the Director of the Department of Police
Deciphered coded telegram from Sarov – 19 July, 11.35pm
The day went off satisfactorily; the relics were brought into the cathedral for the last time and laid to rest in the shrine. At 2 o'clock Their Majesties partook of the monastery's table, at five o'clock they visited the pavilion of the Tambov nobility, at 10 o'clock at night Their Majesties went alone to the source, where they bathed; the police were not informed of this, only we were on guard. About ten thousand more people arrived.

Nicky to Empress Marie – 3 September – Manoeuvres near Brest
We had to walk the whole way on foot – the better to see the tens of thousands of shouting, smiling faces. My heart was pounding and something like tears welled up in my throat!

KR, Diary – 5 September
After dinner, I talked with Nikolai [Sandro's brother, the historian], who has arrived from the Caucasus because of his uncle's illness. He always has rather a sombre view of life; he considers the present situation in Russia to be fatal, he is expecting extraordinary events in the very near future. I cannot but agree with him, that the reason for our mood is the weakness of the Emperor, who is unconsciously influenced by other opinions, first one, then the other; the last one expressed is always right.

Nicky to Empress Marie – 22 September – Darmstadt
We had to climb up a lot of hills, but I like that. We were all amazed by the Emperor [Franz-Josef], who is 73 years old. He climbed for almost two hours without stopping, and was not at all out of breath.

Incredible! Apart from the Emperor, Archduke Franz-Ferdinand was with us the whole time. I was touched by the warmth and kindness with which they both treated me.

Kaiser Wilhelm to Nicky – 7 November – Neues Palais, Potsdam

Dearest Nicky

It is impossible for me to pass over the sudden and tragic death of that sweet little sunshine, without sending you just a word to tell you, how deeply I feel for you all in this sad affair. It is really very difficult to realize the facts, that darling child is no more among us![6] How joyous and merry she was that day at Wolfsgarten, when I was there, so full of life and fun and health, and to think that one shall never see her again in this world! What a terrible heartrending blow for poor Ernie, who doted and adored that little enchantress! May Heaven give him power to bear up under such a blow!

I am still under the charm of the 2 days I was able to spend with you and they remain a delightful souvenir for me.

With best love for Alix I remain ever your true and devoted friend and cousin

Willy

KR, Diary – 19 November

[I have been called] 'the best man in Russia'. But I know what this 'best man' is really like. How appalled all those people, who love and respect me, would be if they knew of my depravity! I am deeply dissatisfied with myself.

24 November   I again feel a surge of renewed strength and am ready to do battle with my passions. It's always like this after I have fallen; but this time I think I have more determination than I did for instance 10 years ago, exactly at the same date, i.e. 22nd November.

Xenia, Diary – 28 November – Gatchina

At 12.30 I went with Mama to Tsarskoe – straight to lunch. Poor Alix does not look at all well, I was quite horrified. She has become terribly thin and has an air of suffering, her temperature keeps rising every day (37.2; 37.3) and she is very weak. She stays in bed all day,

---

[6] Elizabeth, the daughter of Ernie and Ducky.

hardly eats anything, and is so sad that it's simply awful and too painful to see! Olga and Tatiana had lunch with us. Afterwards the little ones joined us and they all had a good romp with Nicky.

9 December I played at four hands on the piano with Misha [brother] upstairs in Olga's room. He is terribly keen on music at the moment, which is a good thing as it distracts him! Thank goodness he is generally in better spirits now. It turned out that he wrote to B[eatrice],[7] while still in Denmark, that they had to stop corresponding in that form, that is pouring out their feelings to each other etc; and since then their hearts have felt easier! Poor thing!

KR, Diary – 15 December

I have been reading through my diaries for the past 10 and 20 years. I am not pleased with myself. Ten years ago, I started out on the right path, I began to struggle earnestly with my main vice, and did not sin for seven years, or more correctly, only sinned in my thoughts. In 1900, already after my appointment as head of the military training institutions, I went astray during the summer in Strelna.

Then it was better for two years, but in 1902, after my illness, I sinned a lot during my trip on the Volga. Finally this year, 1903, I have gone completely astray and have lived in a constant state of war with my conscience.

The trip to Moscow and Tver seemed to have distracted me from unclean thoughts and desires, but now they have taken me over again. I keep struggling, telling myself that God has given me the heart, intellect and strength to fight successfully.

The misfortune is that even though I could fight, I don't want to, I weaken, forget my fear of God and fall; I know that the longer it goes on, the more ingrained the habit becomes and the more difficult and painful is the struggle. I almost gave in again, but this time resisted. But for how long? Help me, Lord! The Lord may help, but I myself reject his aid.

21 December Bad thoughts keep coming into my head; they bother me particularly in church. I'm ashamed to admit it, but it's true. It's never been so bad as during the last six months.

---

[7] Beatrice was Ducky's sister.

Xenia, Diary – 21 December – Gatchina

I received a *terrible* letter from Ducky about Misha and Beatrice. She is trying to show that he behaved in an ugly and dishonourable way towards her. And all this after one letter from Denmark, in which he wrote that, as they could not marry, it would be better to stop writing such letters to each other, and that he hoped they could remain on good terms etc.

Lord preserve us from the storm this provoked on their side, it turns out Beatrice is quite ill and has been sent to Egypt, where she cries and grows thinner. Most importantly, Ducky insists that her sister never even dreamt of being able to marry him (which is patently untrue) and indeed never imagined anything, which is why Misha's letter offended her so much. It seems Aunt Marie is dreadfully cross with Mama over this, all in all God knows what happened. One thing though is clear, that they had set their sights on marriage.

KR, Diary – 28 December

My life flows on happily, I am truly 'favoured by fate', I am loved, respected, appreciated, I am lucky and successful in everything that I do, but I lack the one essential thing: inner peace.

I am completely possessed by my secret vice. For quite a long time, I had almost succeeded in overcoming it, from the end of 1893 until 1900. But since then, and particularly since April of this year (just before the birth of our delightful Georgy) I again slipped up and started to roll, and am still rolling as if down an incline, lower and lower all the time.

And yet I, who stand in charge of the education of a large number of children and youths, should be well acquainted with the standards of morality.

Finally, I am no longer young, I am married, I have 7 children and old age is not so far away. But I am just like a weather-vane: sometimes I make a firm resolution, I pray devoutly, I stand for the whole of the service immersed in fervent prayers, and yet – immediately afterwards, with the return of impure thoughts everything is forgotten, and I surrender to the power of sin.

Is a change for the better really so unrealizable? Must I continue wallowing in sin?

1904

Nicky – Emperor of Russia

Alix – Empress of Russia

Xenia – Grand Duchess, Nicky's sister

Olga – Grand Duchess, Nicky's younger sister, also known as 'Baby'

KR – Grand Duke Konstantin Romanov, Nicky's cousin

Maria Pavlovna (the younger) – daughter of Nicky's uncle Grand Duke Pavel

Olga – eldest daughter of Nicky and Alix

Willy – Kaiser Wilhelm II of Germany, Nicky's cousin

1904

THE TURNING POINT

War breaks out between Russia and Japan – KR's moral
struggle continues – Alix's young nephew dies from
haemophilia – A son, Alexei, is born to Nicky and Alix –
Kaiser Wilhelm is to be godfather – Alexei starts to bleed
from the navel – KR bemoans Nicky's lack of resolve –
Port Arthur falls to the Japanese

KR, Diary – 1 January
The great procession took place in the Winter Palace. The Tsar
appeared in the uniform of the cavalry guard. The young Empress
has influenza and was not present. The Empress Maria Feodorovna
wore a Russian-style dress of amethyst velvet, richly embroidered
with gold, Maria Pavlovna was in orange, my wife in silver (her wedding dress), while Xenia and Olga were in white, embroidered with
gold.

Xenia, Diary – 1 January – St Petersburg
May the Lord bless the coming year, and all of us, and preserve the
peace. That's the most important!
    The procession took place at 11 o'clock. I walked with Kyril. The
service lasted quite a long time, then there was an endless reception
for the diplomatic corps (about an hour). Everyone looked on with
interest as Nicky talked to the Japanese!
    Afterwards Nicky told us, that he had said to the Japanese, that
Russia wasn't just a country – but a part of the world, and that in
order to avoid a war, it was better not to try her patience, or else it
could end badly.

KR, Diary – 9 January

For two weeks I have been in harmony with my conscience. It is always like this after I have sinned. At first after transgressing, the sin seems revolting, the heart is full of contrition and repentance, the imagination is clear and impure thoughts no longer invade the mind.

But as time passes, the depraved passion, at first unnoticeable and barely smouldering, gradually flares up into a conflagration, which envelops the mind and soul; seductive thoughts become more invasive, I cannot pray, and feel that I am sinking deeper and lower into the mire of vice.

At the moment for instance, after two weeks in a clear and pious mood, that which I thought I could resist has begun to acquire a seductive charm. Now is the time to be on guard, and to control the imagination, not letting it become a prey to impure thoughts. Will the Lord not help me in my struggle?

Of course He will help, I am deeply convinced of this. But my mind has been spoilt, I cannot direct my thoughts as I wish, and give in to my vice almost without resisting. It has been thus since the spring, and all summer and autumn of this last year. And yet before, there were those happy years, when I emerged victorious from the struggle. How to repeat those blessed years from 1893 to 1899?

Xenia, Diary – 14 January – Cannes

At Nice we went straight from the train to Aunt Marie's [Duchess of Edinburgh] for lunch. She is living at her villa with Ducky. We were so glad to see the youngest, she was pitiful to look at, she has grown so thin and looks so unwell, poor thing. After lunch we went into the garden among the orange trees, where Maria herself brought up the subject of Misha and Beatrice.

I could only tell her that Misha cannot marry, for Nicky has told him that definitely, and that he has submitted and looks upon it now as an impossibility. Then she left me with Ducky and went over to Sandro, and he explained everything to her in the right way – Misha's action etc. He came away with the impression that she hopes and wishes for the marriage to come off.

Ducky says that baby B. was in such a terrible state they feared she would lose her mind. They were terribly offended with Mama, and Ducky says she couldn't bear it any longer and wrote that letter to me, in the hope that I would help.

KR, Diary – 20 January

I lived in peace with my conscience from December 27th, but for the last few days seductive thoughts kept coming into my mind.

As I was coming home, I ordered my coachman to turn right along the Moika channel; before reaching the Nevsky I got out, let Foma [coachman] go, and continued on foot past the bath-house.

I intended to walk straight on – there were some people who recognized me by the doors to the bath-house. But without reaching the Pevchesky bridge, I turned back and went in. I took a cubicle.

And so I have surrendered again, without much struggle, to my depraved inclinations; I have again become inexpressibly disgusting and revolting to myself. Will I never be free of this?

Xenia, Diary – 25 January – Cannes

War has been declared!![1] May the Lord help us! It's so terrible, you simply don't want to believe it, or what it will bring with it. Mama telegraphed: 'greatly saddened by the news from the Far East, but the responsibility for this lies with them'. In one telegram it says that Kurito, the Japanese ambassador, was recalled from Petersburg before Russia's answer was received.

27 January We received the following telegram from Mama. [General] Alexeev reports that, at around midnight on the night of 26–27 January, the Japanese carried out a surprise attack on the squadron anchored by the outside road of Port Arthur fortress. Several of our warships received holes, the extent of the damage is being assessed. So everything has begun. Our poor sailors! God help them, but how terrible to be taken by surprise!

13 February – St Petersburg Nicky and Alix came to church – also Sandro. Alix was in tears, having just received the news of the death of her little nephew, Irène's youngest son. He had the terrible illness of the English family.[2] Not long ago the poor little thing fell and bumped his head, from that time on he was ill the whole time, and

---

[1] Russo–Japanese war, 1904–5.

[2] Haemophilia within the royal families of Europe can be traced through the descendants of Queen Victoria. Irène was married to Henry of Prussia (brother of Kaiser Wilhelm II). Their third son, Henry, suffered from haemophilia and died after an accident, aged four.

from the beginning there was no hope of him recovering. It's *simply awful*, and the poor parents.

KR, Diary – 14 February
I am fasting, trying to attain the remission of my sins, or rather of my main, mortal sin, and hope that I will be successful.

It torments me to think that: I sin, I become worse the whole time, I deserve God's wrath, but instead receive only God's favours. My sin is known to no one, I am loved, praised and promoted beyond what I deserve, my life is happy, I have a beautiful wife, who is appreciated and respected by all; delightful children; and finally I have received a special mark of favour from the throne – a mandate recognizing my services; a girls' gymnasium has been named after me. How is it I can't deal with it?

26 February   Witte was talking about Vladimir and Alexei. He considers both to be true Grand Dukes, incapable of intrigue or murky deeds. He has a sterner view of Sandro, and discerns in him, as in his brothers, a tendency towards intrigue and a lack of true grand ducal quality.

Witte considers Sandro's influence on the Emperor – which is indisputable – to be harmful. He holds a very high opinion of the Heir [Misha]. The Heir is not well known or appreciated by society; Witte sees in him a clear mind, an unshakable conviction in his opinions and a crystalline moral purity. Misha keeps away from affairs of state, does not offer his opinions and, perhaps, hides behind the perception of him as a good-natured, unremarkable boy.

Xenia, Diary – 13 March – St Petersburg
It has been revealed (Mama revealed it!) that Alix is expecting! It is becoming more noticeable now, but she, poor thing, has been hiding it for the moment, as she is probably afraid and does not want anyone to know about it too soon! She feels very well with it.

KR, Diary – 23 March
My spiritual state is bad. From the day of my departure from Niszny [Novgorod], on the 11th, I have been overwhelmed by impure thoughts, which unceasingly pursue me with enticing scenes, compiled by my depraved imagination from former memories.

I nearly succumbed to temptation in Moscow, but by some happy occurrence I was able to be firm and resist. Even now I am not at peace with my conscience, I try to bargain and – oh horror! – say to myself that once Easter is over, I will be able to give in to sin again.

28 March In church I was worried that my wife might feel faint, but luckily nothing happened. One was worried for the Empress for the same reason: by all the signs she is already about 6 months' pregnant, but has become, at the same time, much thinner in the face and is wonderfully beautiful.

She stood courageously for the whole service and then exchanged Easter greetings with everyone.

Xenia, Diary – 31 March – St Petersburg

A nightmarish day – the worst since war was declared. The *Petropavlovsk*, together with Makarov,[3] have been blown up by a mine with all their crew, everyone was killed, except Kyril and 6 officers as well as around 40 lower ranks!! Makarov put to sea early in the morning with the rest of the fleet, and on sighting the enemy began to pursue them, but when the number of enemy units increased to 30, they returned to harbour, at which point the battle ship *Petropavlovsk* ran into a mine, which destroyed it.

Poor Vladimir, he was terribly distressed, and kept repeating that it was a miracle Kyril was alive – and how! Aunt Michen was found in tears, she is calmer now, but the first shock was terrible because it was so unexpected.

The whole family started to arrive later, and at 2 o'clock there was a Te Deum. (From there I wrote a note to Mama, informing her of the Te Deum, it was the first she knew of anything, she was of course terribly upset and shocked, and it was just before a reception!) Nikolai[4] also came, Uncle Vladimir was terribly touched, and embraced him and wept (thank God that's all finished!)

We returned home for lunch. Sandro is in such a state, he looks awful, thinner and older, after today I think we all must do. God grant us never to live through another such day!

Sandro went home, leaving me at the Winter palace. Poor Alix is in bed – probably influenza! I found Mama there, she and Nicky are terribly upset and depressed!

[3] Commander of the Russian fleet.
[4] Grand Duke Nikolai Nikolaevich, the Emperor's cousin, known as Nikolasha or Nic-Nic to the family.

KR, Diary – 19 April

My mind is in a bad way again, I am again pursued by sinful thoughts, recollections and desires. I dream of going along to the bath-house on the Moika or to have the baths heated up at home, I can picture the familiar attendants, Alexei, Frolov and particularly Sergei Syroezkin. My predilection has always been for simple men; I have neither sought, nor found, partners in sin outside their circle. When passion speaks, the arguments of conscience, virtue and reason are silenced.

23 April   There was a family lunch in the Alexander Palace. The Empress – whose name day it was – is unmistakably pregnant; it is now very noticeable. The new addition to the family is apparently expected in July or August.

15 May   As a result of recollecting former years, I have once more fallen under the influence of impure thoughts, enticing dreams and imaginings. My way lay past the baths. I was sure that if I saw one of the attendants at the doors – I would not be able to resist and would go in. I was extremely agitated, all thoughts of virtue were stifled, I had almost lost the capacity of thinking sanely, and was ready to give in to temptation without much struggle. The doors to the bath-house were open, but there were no attendants in sight. By some miracle I refrained and drove past.

Now, you would think that this victory over myself would be a cause of joy, but no, quite the contrary, I was furious with myself for a long while afterwards, for not making the most of a convenient opportunity and going in.

21 May   I was overwhelmed by sinful thoughts during the committee meeting. I dismissed my coachman on the Morskaya, before reaching the corner with the Nevsky, and continued on foot.

I walked up and down twice past the bath-house doors; on the third time, I went in. And so, I have once again sinned in the same way. My mood is absolutely foul.

4 June   For my own part, I do not suppose that I will ever be in full agreement with Sandro. He is often mistaken about people, falls under their influence, then becomes disenchanted with them and seeks other counsellors; he has, it seems to me, a certain mercantile streak and is inclined towards personal gain.

17 June   In the morning, I used the baths at home. And so failed once more to keep up the fight.

23 June   I again renounced the struggle with my desires; it's not that I couldn't, I just didn't want to fight. In the evening they heated up our bath-house for me. The attendant Sergei Syroezkin was busy, so he brought along his brother, twenty-year-old Kondraty, who works as an attendant in the Usachevikh baths.

And I led the lad astray. Perhaps I caused him to sin for the first time, but it was already too late when I remembered the awesome words: Woe to him who leads even one of these young astray.

24 July   Since the 15 July we have been impatiently awaiting an addition to the Emperor's family.

26 July   In the morning, the bath-house. And once again I find myself, like a squirrel on a wheel, in exactly the same place.

The notebook of Empress Alexandra Feodorovna – 30 July 1904
Weight 4660; length 58. Measurement of the head 38; chest 39

The Heir Tsarevich Alexei Nikolaevich was born on Friday 30 July 1904 at 1.15 in the afternoon.

Nicky, Diary – 30 July – Peterhof
A great and unforgettable day for us, during which we were clearly visited by the grace of God. At 1.15 in the afternoon Alix gave birth to a son, whom we named Alexei as we prayed. Everything happened remarkably quickly – at least for me. In the morning I went to visit Mama as usual, after which I went to find Alix for lunch. She was already upstairs, and half an hour afterwards the happy event occurred. There are no words to thank God enough for sending us this comfort in a time of sore trials!

Dear Alix felt very well. Mama arrived at 2 o'clock and sat with me for a long time before her first meeting with her new grandson. At five o'clock I took the children to a Te Deum, with all the family present. Wrote a mass of telegrams. Misha came from the camp; he said he was now 'in retirement'. Dined in the bedroom.

KR, Diary – 30 July
Newspaper cutting: 'By the manifesto of 28th June 1899 We named

as Our successor Our beloved brother the Grand Duke Mikhail Alexandrovich, until such time as a son was born to Us. From now on, in accordance with the fundamental laws of the Empire, the Imperial title of Heir Tsarevich, and all the rights pertaining to it, belong to Our Son Alexei.'

God has sent their Majesties a son. What a joy! Russia has waited 10 years for an Heir, and now it has happened. Soon we heard the cannons begin firing from the fort – a 301 gun salute. The Heir has been named Alexei. The Te Deum had just finished when we reached the gothic church. The Tsar emerged from inside and, together with his mother and his elder daughters Olga, Tatiana and Maria, started to go round the assembly receiving congratulations. The whole family were there, as well as the closest of the courtiers, the general staff and the officers of the combined guards regiment and His Majesty's cavalry. They say that the labour lasted only two hours and that everything went well, the baby measures 58 centimetres and weighs 11 pounds.

Olga [sister], Memoirs
It happened during the war with Japan. The nation was really in the depths of depression because of all the disasters in Manchuria. All the same, I remember how happy the people looked when the news was announced.

You know that my sister-in-law had never quite given up hope that she would have a son born to her, and I am sure it was Serafim who brought it about.

KR, Diary – 2 August
At five o'clock my wife and I went to see the Dowager Empress and had tea with her. She, who had been so full of joy at the birth of the Tsarevich, was again preoccupied and aggrieved by news of our fleet.

The former Heir Misha was there, he is radiant with happiness at no longer being Heir.

Maria Pavlovna [the younger], Memoirs
We accompanied my uncle and aunt [Sergei, Ella] to Peterhof to attend the little Tsarevich's baptism. A gilded coach followed by a cavalry troop bore the newly born son to the church. He was accompanied by his nurse and the Mistress of the Robes. Since dawn regiments had been drawn up along the route the cortège would take, with its numerous gala carriages drawn by horses gay with plumes.

At eleven o'clock in the morning the imperial family and the court were ready, the men in their full-dress uniforms, the ladies adorned with jewels in gowns of gold and silver cloth with long trains. The Emperor, the Grand Dukes and Duchesses, the ambassadors, and the high dignitaries formed in procession; they reached the palace church by crossing halls filled with guests.

The little Tsarevich was carried at the head of the procession on a cushion of silver cloth by the Mistress of the Robes. The church glistened with light. At the entrance numerous members of the clergy, presided over by the Archbishop of St Petersburg, greeted the Emperor. The religious service ended, the child was brought back to the house with the same ceremonial. Felicitations and a banquet brought the day to an end.

In honour of the Army, then fighting on the distant plains of Manchuria, all the combatants were inscribed as godfathers to the young prince.

KR, Diary – 11 August

I took Olia to the christening at Peterhof. As soon as the procession set off, my wife went to town; it was better, as a precaution, that she did not participate in the ceremonial: there can be no doubt of her pregnancy.

Tatiana walked in the procession next to little Maria Pavlovna, behind Ella. I led Stana. The little girls were delightful in their sarafans: the two imperial daughters in blue, Marie and Irina also, and Marina, Elena in yellow. Little Johan and Gavril walked behind Sandro. The Emperor wore the Ataman uniform. The christening ceremony was performed by Father Yanyshev, while the service was taken by the Metropolitan Antony.

Alix to Nicky – 15 August – Peterhof

I am sure you miss Baby love, he is too sweet. Indeed one understands why God has just sent him *this* year to us and he has come as a real Sunbeam. God never forgets one, that is true.

And now you have him to work for and to bring up to your ideas, so as that he can help you when he is a big boy. I assure you one sees him daily grow.

Xenia, Diary – 16 August – Alexandria

We went to see Alix. And were present for the little one's bath. He's an amazingly hefty baby, with a chest like a barrel and generally has the air of a warrior knight.

Olga [daughter] to Nicky – 16 August – Peterhof
Dear Papa

Today there is a strong rain and we are sitting at home. Maria went to sleep in the afternoon, and Anastasia crept under the mattress and slept there with Maria on top of her.

When she got up we all laughed, and so did she. We are all waiting for you to return here. Is the weather good where you are?

I have not seen Mama and our brother, I hope I will see them this evening before bath time. I send you a big kiss dear papa.

Olga [aged 9]

Alix to Nicky – [no date] August – Peterhof
My own beloved sweet Angel,

Once more you leave your old Wify, but this time with a precious little son in her arms, who must comfort her heavy heart.

It is hard to part again, but thank God not for long – how happy the Cossacks will be to see you, more so than ever, as now our precious tiny is a new link between their former Ataman and themselves. I am sure Moscow will be excited when you pass. The nights will be so long and dreary.

I love to look at you when I cannot sleep and the room begins to get light. I am sure you will feel sad leaving your little family and new born son – we shall count the hours till you return. I'll try to be brave, but my stupid nerves are still so weak that it's more than I can do to keep those old tears back. Oh, how I love you!!! God alone knows *how* much.

I hope and trust that no bad news from the east will come whilst we are separated – and don't like your hearing all when I am not with you. Oh God is indeed good having sent in this sunbeam now, when we all need it so much, may He give us the force to bring Baby up well – and to be a real help and comrade to you when he is big.

Sweet One, goodbye and God bless and keep you and bring you quickly and safely back to me again. My earnest prayers and thoughts will never leave you. I cover your sweet face with loving tender kisses – Ever your Wify,

Alix

Kaiser Wilhelm II to Nicky – 16 August – Schloss Wilhelmshöhe
Dearest Nicky,

What a very kind thought that was of yours to ask me to be Godfather to your little boy! You can well imagine what our joy was when we read your telegram announcing his birth! 'Was longe währt, wird gut'[5] says an old German proverb, so may it be with this little dear one! May he grow to be a brave soldier and a wise and powerful statesman; and may God's blessing always rest on him and preserve him from all harm of body and soul. May he always be as a ray of sunshine to you both during your life, as he is now in the time of trial!

Henry is the bearer of these lines and of my sincerest and heartfelt wishes for you, Alix and the Boy! Accompanied by the gift of a Goblet for my little Godchild, which he will, I hope, begin to use, when he will think, that a man's thirst cannot be quenched by milk only! Perhaps he may then find out for himself one day, that 'Ein gut Glas Branntwein soll Mitternacht nicht schädlich sein'[6] is not only 'truism', but that often 'Im Wein ist Wahrheit nur allein'[7] as the butler sings in *Undina*, to be wound up by the classical words of our great Reformer Dr Martin Luther: 'Wer nicht liebt Wein, Weib und Gesang, der bleibt ein Narr sein Lebenslang.'[8] These would be the maxims I would try to see my Godchild educated up to!! There is great sense in them and nothing can be said against them!

The course of the war has been most trying to your army and navy and I deeply grieve for the loss of so many brave officers and men who fell or were drowned in doing their duty, loyally fulfilling the oath they swore to their Emperor.

There is no doubt to me that you will and must win in the long run but it will cost both money and many men, as the army is brave and well led can only be beaten by overwhelming numbers and time and patience.

I wonder what I am going to hear from Uncle Bertie at Kiel at all events and I shall keep you informed. Now goodbye dearest Nicky, with best love to Alix and the 'Sunray' [*sic*].

I remain ever your most devoted and affectionate friend and cousin

Willy

---

[5] 'Long waiting brings good results.'
[6] 'A good glass of spirits is no harm at midnight.'
[7] 'In vino veritas.'
[8] 'Who doesn't love wine, women and song stays a fool all his life.'

Nicky, Diary – 8 September – Peterhof
At 11 o'clock I took the children to church. We lunched alone. Alix
and I were very worried because little Alexei started bleeding from
the navel, and it continued on and off until the evening! We had to
send for Korovin and the surgeon Fedorov; at about 7 o'clock they
applied a bandage. The little one was remarkably calm and gay! How
painful it is to live through such moments of anxiety!

9 September In the morning there was blood on the bandage; from
12 o'clock until the evening there was nothing. The little one had a
peaceful day and hardly cried at all, and we felt reassured by his
healthy appearance!

10 September Alexei did not have a show of blood all day; I felt
relieved of a painful anxiety. I had three reports and a reception.
After lunch Nikolasha came to see me. We went for a walk together;
a wind was blowing, whipping up the water in the sea. In the
evening I read aloud.

11 September Thank God, dear Alexei has had no more bleeding
now for 48 hours! How much lighter my heart feels! The day was
calm and quite warm. Spent the evening in the bedroom.

Maria Pavlovna [the younger], Memoirs
Even in our house a certain melancholy reigned. My uncle and aunt
undoubtedly knew already that the child was born suffering and that
from his birth he carried in him the seeds of an incurable illness,
haemophilia – a tendency to bleed easily, an inability of the blood to
clot quickly. There is no doubt that the parents were quickly advised
as to the nature of their son's illness. Nobody ever knew what emotions were aroused in them by this horrible certainty, but from that
moment, troubled and apprehensive, the Empress's character underwent a change, and her health, physical as well as moral, altered.

KR, Diary – 12 September
I sent for Yatsko and he came to see me this morning. I easily persuaded him to be candid. It was strange for me to hear him describe
the familiar characteristics: he has never felt drawn to a woman, and
has been infatuated with men several times. I did not confess to him
that I knew these feelings from my own personal experience. Yatsko
and I talked for a long time.

Before leaving he kissed my face and hands; I should not have allowed this, and should have pushed him away, however I was punished afterwards by vague feelings of shame and remorse. He told me that, ever since the first time we met, his soul has been filled with rapturous feelings towards me, which grow all the time. How this reminds me of my own youth.

15 September   I heard from Xenia and Sandro, who were coming to see us and whom I met on the way, that the Empress Marie begged the Emperor not to appoint Nikolai,[9] which elicited surprise and the answer that there was never any question of it. The leader of the Moscow nobility, Prince Trubetskoi, wrote to Count Vorontsov saying that rumours of Nikolai's appointment were causing great concern among Moscow society, who, like the whole of Russia, have faith in Kuropatkin. This letter will be shown to the Emperor.

I returned by the road along which Yatsko would come in the carriage sent to fetch him. I called for him in order to fulfil his wish to visit me once more and say goodbye before his departure for Vilnius. I admit I was looking forward to seeing him, while at the same time dreading another meeting.

Now I know that his tendencies are the same as mine, I must be wary. Last time I restrained myself, but who can guarantee the future. He confessed his sins to me with even greater candour; he feels depressed, disgusted with himself, and suffers from pangs of conscience. I tried to cheer him up, certainly I did not reject him and I think I made him feel better, telling him that one has to forget the past and start to live afresh. And he was afraid that I might despise him.

He told me the names of people I had vaguely suspected of unnatural tendencies; Yatsko has sinned with several of them, but has now, it seems, firmly decided to give it all up. May God help him.

Alix to Nicky – 15 September – Peterhof
Sweetest One,

You have left and we have had luncheon and the Feldjäger comes soon. It was horrid seeing you drive off and I know what it costs you leaving our treasure – but thank God it was not last week, which would have been unbearable. My food stuck half in my throat, but I

---

[9] Nikolasha was appointed to the Far East instead of Kuropatkin, the previous Commander-in-Chief.

swallowed it down, for his little sake, and for him too I shall be brave, I must not give him bad milk and make him restless. Of course you had no time for writing, with all your receptions today ... baby dear's shoe and glove are to give you a nice warm feeling in your heart when you go to bed. Your beloved big sad eyes, I see them always before me. Our dear Friend I am sure is watching over you, as He did over Tiny last week – oh, what anguish it was, and not to let others see the knife digging in one. Thank God he is so well now! Sweet, beloved Angel, Goodbye and God bless and protect you. The Children kiss you 100 times and I cover your adorable face with kisses without end and remain for ever and ever your very own old Wify.

Sunny

Nicky to Alix – 16 September – on a train
My own beloved Sunny,

What joy your sweet letter gave me. My 'old man' put it on the table in my cabin where I found it after luncheon, and also in the evening before going to bed, that lovely surprise to get from our 'little one'. The tiny shoe and glove smelled so good of him: and the photo, which I never saw, is charming and very like. Thank you ever so many times, darling, for the kind forethoughts that touched me so. Only Wify could have such ideas to give pleasure to Huzy when he is away. Your telegrams are a great comfort, one feels nearer hearing twice a day. It was hard leaving yesterday. I had to gather all my will. I was so astonished and touched by Olga's behaviour, never for a moment did I think it was on account of me that she cried, until you told me the reason. I begin to feel more lonely now without the children than before – an experienced old Papa, that's what it is!!!

The night was extremely cold and we all felt it in the train. The day is bright and warm, quite the same fine weather as we had at home. I'm so glad it continues so and hope it will keep until my return. We are passing pretty woods in a very swampy country.

Your having shown our 'little one' to the [officer] produced a great effect, not only upon him, but on those he saw after that. I must say, it is after all a rest to be travelling in a comfortable train and not seeing people the whole day. If only we were together it would have been happiness and rest both, but alas not. Duty, duty, there is nothing to be done. Now goodbye, and bless you my sunshine and love, and our sweet children. Kiss my son very tenderly for me. Your own Huzy,

Nicky

Alix to Nicky – 18 September – Peterhof
Darling Nicky dear,

I am writing to you in pencil as I am still in bed. Baby Sweet is lying across my knees, awake and listening to his musical box. He slept very long this night after I had nursed him. Whilst drinking before he was smiling, and cooing away. You would have loved him so.

Fondest kisses from your own Sunny,

Alix

Nicky to Empress Marie – 22 September – Peterhof
Darling Mama

At times I suffer from terrible pangs of conscience that I am sitting here, instead of being over there to share the sufferings, privations and difficulties of the campaign with the army. Yesterday I asked Uncle Alexei what he thought? He answered that he did not feel my presence was necessary in *this* war. But to stay behind at such a time is, for me, far more difficult!

KR, Diary – 2 October
I am very upset by the failure of my sonnet. The news of our defeat made a painful impression.

18 November The present mood in society is far too like that of the end of the 70s, in 1880 or 1881. At that time the government had lost its way, but the presence of authority was still felt. Now, however, authority is shaky, and all our misfortunes stem from the Emperor's lack of will. Nothing is definite, the same matter will be viewed in one way today, and in quite another tomorrow.

The disturbance is increasing, and one senses ahead something unknown, but inescapable and terrible. On the 6th, 7th and 8th of November meetings took place of the members of the council of *zemstvo* workers; they discussed what general conditions were necessary for the smooth working and progress of social and political life. Instead of concerning themselves with their own rural affairs, they drew up their conclusions in eleven articles.

4 December It is as if the dam has been broken: in the space of two or three months Russia has been seized with a thirst for change. It is talked about loudly. The Dumas of Kaluga, Moscow and now Petersburg have unanimously adopted motions in which they respectfully ask for every freedom. Revolution is banging on the door. A constitution is being almost openly discussed. How shameful and how terrifying.

21 December   What terrible news! I have just read a report in *New Times*, compiled it must be said from foreign sources, about the fall of Port Arthur [to the Japanese]. The paper says that they surrendered, that Stessel agreed to the honourable conditions offered by the Japanese. But the word 'surrendered' tortures me; 'fell' perhaps, but 'surrendered'! Do Russians surrender?

23 December   I have been struck, as if by lightning, by the news of the fall of Port Arthur. The defenders had run out of ammunition, they were all suffering from scurvy and typhoid, there were endless wounded, the Japanese shells kept falling on the hospital and wounding those who were already injured. We blew up the forts and the ships in the port. It's another Sebastopol, exactly 50 years later.

28 December   I was plagued all day by bad thoughts. In the evening I felt like going to the bath-house, but for some reason did not. Now it is nearly 11 o'clock. Why didn't I go?

I am afraid of sin, afraid of going against my conscience, and yet I still want to sin. This struggle is exhausting.

29 December   Yet another day spoiled by bad thoughts. It must be physiological; it can't just be a question of decadence and lack of will. Some days when these thoughts occur, it is easy to banish them; at other times I am totally besieged by them. I mustn't give in, I must bear it until I feel better again.

So, I have resisted for another day. But I don't feel like praying.

30 December   The bad thoughts hounded me less today. Conscience and reason tell me I should forsake the path of indulgence once and for all, that is to say no longer to go to the bath-house, either at home or outside.

But my feelings and my will rebel – I want to see Sergei Syroezkin, whom I should not lead into temptation, since he is the first to wish it. That is the struggle. Lord help me.

Will I free myself from sin, will I conquer myself, or will sin overcome me?

What will the new year bring us?

May the Lord's name be blessed now and forever.

1905

Nicky – Emperor of Russia

Alix – Empress of Russia

Xenia – Grand Duchess, Nicky's sister, married to Sandro

Sandro – Grand Duke Alexander Mikhailovich, husband of Xenia

Ella – Grand Duchess Elizabeth, elder sister of Alix, married to Grand Duke Sergei

Olga – Grand Duchess, Nicky's younger sister, also known as 'Baby'

KR – Grand Duke Konstantin Romanov, Nicky's cousin

Grand Duke Pavel – Nicky's uncle, married to Olga Pistolkors, later Princess Paley

Maria Pavlovna (the younger) – daughter of Grand Duke Pavel

Willy – Kaiser Wilhelm II of Germany

Bernhard von Bülow – Prime Minister and President of Prussia

Pierre Gilliard – Swiss tutor of Nicky and Alix's children

V. F. Djunkovsky – aide-de-camp to Grand Duke Sergei

Boris Savinkov – a terrorist

Ivan Kalyaev – assassin of Grand Duke Sergei

Grigory Rasputin – a Siberian holy man

1905

THE TERROR

Strikes and disturbances in St Petersburg – 'Bloody Sunday' – Grand Duke Sergei is assassinated by Kalyaev – KR goes to Moscow – Ella visits Kalyaev in prison – Kalyaev is tried and executed – Ella assumes custody of Maria Pavlovna and Dmitri Pavlovich – Mutiny on the battleship *Potemkin* – Nicky signs a Manifesto – Peace is made with Japan – Pierre Gilliard becomes tutor to the Imperial children – Scandal over Kyril's marriage – Opening of the Duma – Alix and Nicky meet Rasputin – KR is being blackmailed

Ella to Nicky – [no date] January – Moscow
God bless you dear Nicky ever so many hearty wishes – peace – joy, all that is best
 Your loving Sister

Ella

Alix to Olga [daughter]
Beloved child,
 Mama kisses her girly tenderly and prays that God may help her to be *always* a good loving Christian child. Show kindness to all, be gentle and loving, then all will love you.
 God bless you.

Mama+

Nicky, Diary – 8 January – St Petersburg
A bright frosty day. A lot of work and reports. Fredericks [Minister of the Court] was there for lunch. Walked for a long time. Since yester-

day all the factories and works in Petersburg have been on strike.
Troops have been called up from the surrounding areas to reinforce
the garrison. Up until now the workers have remained calm. They
number 120,000 people. There is some priest at the head of the
workers union – the socialist Gapon. Mirsky[1] came in the evening to
report on the measures taken.

9 January ['Bloody Sunday']   A terrible day! There were serious disturbances in Petersburg as a result of the workers wishing to reach
the Winter Palace. The troops were forced to open fire in several parts
of the town, there were many killed and wounded.[2] Lord, how
painful and how sad! Mama arrived from town straight to church.
Lunched with everyone. Went for a walk with Misha. Mama stayed
with us for the night.

Alix to Olga [daughter]
Sweet child,
   I kiss you and thank you tenderly for your little notes. I'm sorry I
could not see you alone, but it's difficult these days. Soon I shall be
freer, and then you can tell us all, and everything that interests you.
You see, I am generally very tired and therefore often don't keep you
all for a very long time with us, and often very sad and don't want
you to see my gloomy face.

KR, Diary – 9 January
The rumours that have been going round town, to the effect that on
the 9th the striking workers intended to gather in Palace Square to
present a petition to the Emperor, have been proved true. Measures
were taken: both infantry and cavalry guarded the approaches to the
palace. After midday, dense crowds of people surged towards the
palace; the troops held them back, and in some places salvos were
fired.

11 January   The disturbances in the streets, the violence of the
crowd, who smash the street lamps and shop windows, looting the
goods, and the necessity of bloodshed make a depressing impression.

---

[1] Prince P. D. Svyatopolk-Mirsky, Minister of the Interior.
[2] Imperial troops opened fire on a peaceful demonstration of St Petersburg workers with a petition. More than 1,000 were killed, and 2,000 wounded in front of
the Winter Palace.

12 January What does the Emperor think? I heard that shortly before the 9th, when the disturbances were in preparation, he was not inclined to take them seriously and thought that they had been greatly exaggerated.

Boris Savinkov,[3] Memoirs

At the beginning of November 1904, Kalyaev again entered Russia illegally, this time to Moscow for Grand Duke Sergei. The gloomy days of surveillance began again. He bought a horse and a sleigh and became a Moscow 'cabbie', a driver, spending freezing nights on the Tverskaya.[4]

The Grand Duke was expecting an attempt on his life. He was running scared, changing palaces, trying to avoid a death that was already inescapable, already creeping up on him.

One night in December he moved from the Governor General's house to Nieskuchnoe, only to change his residence again a few days later. Now he took refuge in a palace in the Kremlin, behind its triple defences and guarded by the soldiers' bayonets. This was a serious obstacle to the surveillance.

But Ivan Kalyaev was indefatigable. He could hardly stand on his feet from exhaustion, could hardly manage to fix the harness, barely had the strength to sit on the coach box for days and nights on end, but nevertheless he stalked the grand duke like a shadow, invisible yet, like fate, inevitable. By the end of January he had already learnt all the Grand Duke's habits. The information was checked and completed by the whole surveillance team and the assassination planned for 2 February.

Maria Pavlovna [the younger], Memoirs

Moscow was torn with turmoil and uncertainty, but within the walls of the Kremlin, our life was peaceful. My aunt and uncle rarely went out, and at home received only their closest friends.

However, we all went to the Moscow Opera House to attend a war benefit. The big, old-fashioned closed carriage, cushioned inside in white silk, carried us to the theatre. It was not until some days later that we learnt how close we were to death.

---

[3] A famous terrorist, member of the Socialist Revolutionary Party.
[4] The main street of Moscow where Sergei was living in the Governor-General's Palace.

A band of terrorists who followed all my uncle's movements had been warned of our going out and knew the route we would take. One of the group, armed with bombs, was posted to destroy us, at a signal from an accomplice. But when this man saw that Dmitri and I were in the carriage he had not the courage to wave his handkerchief, the signal agreed upon.

It was all a matter of a second; the carriage passed.

The performance that evening was magnificent; one of the artists was Chaliapin, already at the height of his glory. The hall glittered with jewels and uniforms, and there was no thought of any such catastrophe as the one that we had just escaped.

Boris Savinkov, Memoirs
On the evening of Wednesday 2 February, the Grand Duke was to attend a performance at the Bolshoi theatre, in aid of the Grand Duchess Elizabeth [Ella]'s charity fund. Voskresensky square had been designated as the place of assassination. Two bomb throwers waited from 8 in the evening for the Grand Duke's carriage.

Ivan Kalyaev was waiting by the Duma. The final decision to attack rested with him. There could be no doubt of success. It was decided to wait until the end of the performance. He wandered around the square until late at night with the bomb in his frozen hands. It was windy, freezing and snowing.

Just after eight, the Grand Duke's carriage, resplendent with its characteristic bright white lamps, drew level with Kalyaev. Dressed in a peasant's coat, he ran up to the carriage, raised his arm, and immediately let it drop again.

Sitting in the carriage, apart from Grand Duke Sergei, were a woman and two children, as it turned out later Grand Duchess Elizabeth and the children of Grand Duke Pavel – Dmitri and Maria Pavlovna. By dropping his arm, he not only put himself at risk. He was risking that, which was infinitely dearer to him than life – the Organization, the work, his comrades and last of all the very possibility of success. But could he kill a woman?

Kalyaev returned his bomb and went off to bed. Where? At that late hour he could go neither to an inn, nor a hotel. He spent the night on the deserted streets of Moscow, warming himself by the bonfires and in the tea houses that remained open at night.

On Friday, 4 February, the Grand Duke was expected to spend the afternoon in his chancellery, in the Governor General's house on the Tverskaya. From 2 o'clock onwards Kalyaev was by the monument to

Alexander II in the Kremlin, with the bomb wrapped in a sheet of paper.

'Why won't you believe me? I tell you, I can manage alone.'

I knew Kalyaev. I knew that none of us could fend for himself as reliably as he could. I knew that he would throw the bomb, only when he was right up beside the carriage and not before, and that he would retain his sang-froid. But I was afraid of chance. I said: 'Listen, Ivan, it would still be better with two, than alone ... suppose you fail. Then what?'

He replied: 'I cannot fail.'

His confidence made me hesitate. He went on: 'If the Grand Duke comes, I will kill him. Rest assured.'

At that moment Moiseyenko [the coachman] turned to us from the coach-box: 'Make up your minds quickly. It's time.'

I made the decision: Kalyaev would go after the Grand Duke alone.

We got out of the sleigh and walked together towards Red Square. As we reached Gostinny Dvor, the clock on top of the Kremlin tower struck two. Kaliayev stopped.

'Goodbye Ivan.'

'Goodbye.'

He kissed me and turned to the right towards the Nikolsky gate. I went past the Spassky tower into the Kremlin, and stopped by the monument to Alexander II. From this spot the grand duke's palace was visible. A carriage stood by the gate. I recognized the coachman Rudinkin. I realized that the Grand Duke would soon be leaving for his chancellery.

As agreed, after leaving me, Kalyaev went to the ikon of the Iverskaya Mother of God. He had already long since noticed that, in the corner, a rough woodcut depicting a patriotic scene had been hung in a glass frame. And that the glass of this frame reflected, as in a mirror, the distance between the Nikolsky gates and the ikon. In this way, by standing with your back to the Kremlin looking at the picture, it was possible to observe the Grand Duke's entrance. It had been agreed that, after standing there, Kalyaev, dressed as a peasant as on February 2nd, would slowly walk into the Kremlin towards the Grand Duke. But here he obviously saw what I did, that is, the carriage in readiness at the entrance with the coachman Rudinkin. Judging by the time, he was still able to go back to the Iverskaya icon, and return again past the historical museum, through the Nikolsky gates into the Kremlin as far as the court house. At the court house he met the Grand Duke.

Ivan Kalyaev – 4 February – from prison

Contrary to all my expectations I came out alive on February 4th.

I threw from a distance of four feet, not more, the impact was such that I was sucked into the vortex of the explosion and saw the carriage disintegrate. After the cloud dispersed I found myself by the remains of the rear wheels. I remember I reeked of smoke, I had splinters in my face and my hat had been blown off. I did not fall, merely turned my face away.

Then I saw, about five feet away, near the gates, a heap of the grand duke's clothes and a bared torso. My hat was lying some 10 feet away from the carriage and I walked over and picked it up. I looked round. My coat was splintered with pieces of wood, hanging in shreds and singed all over. My face was pouring with blood and I understood that there was no escape, even though for several long moments there was no one around. I started to walk.

At that moment I heard a shout behind me, I was almost hit by a police sleigh and someone's hands grabbed me. I did not resist. A policeman, a passer-by, and an unpleasant detective bustled around me. 'Look, this must be a revolutionary, ah, thank God it didn't kill me, after all we were just there' muttered this captor, trembling. I regretted not being able to fire a bullet into this lowly coward. Why are you holding me, I won't run away, I've done my duty, I said.

From the Official Report – 4 February

The body of the Grand Duke was mutilated, with the head, the upper part of the chest and the left shoulder and arm being blown off and completely destroyed, while the left leg was broken, the thigh crushed, with the lower part, the shank and foot, becoming detached. The force of the blast created by the criminal shattered the body of the carriage in which the Grand Duke was travelling, besides breaking the glass of the outside window frames of those parts of the court buildings nearest to the Nikolsky gates, as well as of the arsenal building opposite.

V. F. Djunkovsky,[5] Memoirs

That day I did not see the Grand Duke, I went as usual to my office in the chancellery of the Trust for National Sobriety. Suddenly the telephone rang, I picked up the receiver and heard: 'The Grand Duke has just been killed.'

---

[5] Grand Duke Sergei's ADC.

I rushed into the chancellery, managed to impart the news to the staff and, hailing the first cab, drove to the Kremlin. It's hard to describe the pitiful scene that greeted my eyes: complete silence all around, very few people, some soldiers and officers carrying something covered with a soldier's coat, with the calm-faced Grand Duchess holding on. There were a few people from the suite and some passers-by.

I ran up, took the Grand Duchess's hand, kissed it and went with them, holding on to the stretcher. We carried it into the palace and straight to the Chudov monastery, where we set it down by the shrine of Bishop Alexei, and where the first requiem was immediately celebrated.

KR, Diary – 4 February

I was intending to go to Tsarskoe again for a family dinner. But at 5 I was informed that the dinner had been cancelled: I did not know why. At 6, as usual, I went upstairs; there I was told there was bad news from Moscow ... that an attempt had been made on Sergei ... that he had been killed by two hand-thrown bombs.

As if struck by lightning, for the first minute I could not take anything in. I went to say goodbye to Mama. She is never told any bad news. It was only as I was leaving her that I realised what I had lost, and burst into tears. I must prepare my wife – she loved Sergei so much.

Both my wife and I share the same feeling, that I must go to Moscow, to the body of my poor friend, to poor Ella, who has none of her relatives near her.

I went with my wife and Mitia [KR's brother] to see Vladimir. Vladimir himself cannot go to Moscow, as he is responsible for the security of the capital. To my question, shouldn't I go, he said: 'Si tu ne crains pas de t'exposer.' ['If you are not afraid of being exposed.']

Misha supported him, he considers that as the intention is to exterminate the whole ruling house, it is better not to expose oneself to danger. But I could not agree with them. And my wife also thought that I should go, even though she was afraid for me. She would go herself, were she not in the last month of her pregnancy.

When I got home, I sent a telegram to the Emperor, requesting a decision on whether I should go to Moscow. It was only half an hour before my departure that I received a telegram with a positive answer from the Emperor.

Nicky, Diary – 4 February – St Petersburg

A terrible crime was perpetrated in Moscow: Uncle Sergei was killed at the Nikolsky gates by a bomb thrown at him as he was driving in his carriage, his coachman was fatally wounded.

Poor Ella, bless her and help her, Lord!

Bernhard Von Bülow, Memoirs

When the Grand Duke Sergei, the Tsar's uncle and brother-in-law, was killed, Prince Friedrich-Leopold of Prussia was at the Russian court.

On his return, the Prince told me, that news of the crime committed in Moscow, reached Peterhof, where the Tsar was staying, some two hours before dinner. The Prince made enquiries as to whether dinner was still on, or whether, after being dealt such a blow by fate, the Emperor wanted to be alone. The Prince received the reply, that he could come to dinner without any problem.

The Empress, it's true, did not appear, but the Emperor, and his brother-in-law the Grand Duke Alexander Mikhailovich [Sandro], who was there at the time, were both in a splendid mood. There was no mention of the murder of the grand duke. After dinner, the Emperor and his brother-in-law, to the amazement of their German guest, amused themselves by trying to push each other off the long, narrow sofa.

Xenia, Diary – 4 February – St Petersburg

They killed poor Uncle Sergei in Moscow this afternoon! It's simply *appalling, appalling*, terrible, sad and shameful. He was out in his carriage, when some swine threw a bomb, and he was killed outright and blown to bits!

No, it's *simply not possible*! Poor Ella, how terribly sorry I feel for her – what unimaginable grief, and she is *all alone* there. I wish I could go to her, and be with her, the poor thing – these are terrible times in Moscow.

At 5.30 we went to Tsarskoe, where we found everyone together. Alix, of course, wants to go. Mama too, but they were advised against it – it's too risky. Although it's terrible to leave poor Ella alone – it's too painful to contemplate!

Maria Pavlovna [the younger], Memoirs

A beautiful winter's day was ending; everything was calm, and the noises of the city came to us muffled by the snow. Suddenly a frightful detonation shook the air and rattled the window-panes.

The silence that followed was so crushing that for some seconds we did not stir or look at each other. Fräulein Hase was the first to recover. She dashed to the window ... and I followed. Quick! quick! my thoughts buzzed.

One of the old towers of the Kremlin collapsed? Dmitri came running from his own study. We looked at each other, not daring to express our thoughts.

A flock of crows, frightened by the explosion, wheeled madly around the steeple and disappeared. The square began to show signs of life. People came running, all from the same direction.

Now the square was filled with people. My aunt ran out of the house, a cloak thrown over her shoulders, loosely. She was followed by Mlle Hélène[6] in a man's overcoat. Both were without hats. They clambered into the sleigh, which started immediately, at top speed, and was lost to our sight behind the angle of the square.

My aunt had hurried, as we had seen, to the corpse in the snow. She had gathered together the fragments of mangled flesh and placed them on an ordinary army stretcher, hastily brought from her workshop nearby. Soldiers from the barracks opposite had covered the body with their coats; then, hoisting the litter to their shoulders, they had carried the body to the shelter of the Monastery of the Miracle, and placed it in the church, directly next door to the palace in which we were staying.

It was only when this had been done that we were fetched. We went down to the first floor and by a little corridor gained the inside door which led to the monastery. The church was thronged; all were kneeling; many were weeping. Close to the altar steps, low on the stones, the stretcher had been placed. It could not have contained very much, for the coats covering it formed only a very small pile. At one end a boot protruded casually from the coverings. Drops of blood fell on the floor, slowly forming a small dark pool.

My aunt was on her knees beside the litter. Her bright dress shone forth grotesquely amid the humble garments surrounding her. I did not dare look at her.

Her face was white, her features terrible in their stricken rigidity. She did not weep, but the expression of her eyes made an impression on me I will never forget as long as I live.

Leaning on the arm of the Governor of the city, my aunt drew near

---

[6] Hélène Djunkovskaya was the sister of ADC Djunkovsky and a governess to Maria Pavlovna, the younger, and Dmitri Pavlovich who were in the custody of their Uncle Sergei since the morganatic marriage of their father, Grand Duke Pavel.

the door slowly, and when she perceived us she stretched out her arms to us. We ran to her.

'He loved you so, he loved you,' she repeated endlessly, pressing our heads against her. I noticed that, low on her right arm the sleeve of her gay blue dress was stained with blood. There was blood on her hand, too, and under the nails of her fingers, in which she gripped tightly the medals that my uncle always wore on a chain at his neck.

Dmitri and I succeeded in leading her back towards her rooms. She let herself fall weakly into an arm-chair. Her eyes dry and with the same peculiar fixity of gaze, she looked straight into space, and said nothing.

My aunt had several times demanded news of my uncle's coachman. He lay in the hospital, his life despaired of, his body torn by the same bomb that had killed my uncle. Towards six in the evening Aunt Ella went herself to visit the wounded man; and, in order not to dismay him by signs of mourning, she wore to the hospital the same gay blue dress she had worn all afternoon.

She went farther! When the coachman asked news of my uncle she had the courage to reply to him with a smile that it was the Grand Duke himself who had sent her to him. The poor man died peacefully during the night.

Aunt Ella did not eat, but she entered the room before the end of the repast and sat with us at the table. She still wore the same blue dress. Facing her white, worn face, we were ashamed to eat.

She said that she wanted to spend the night in my room; she did not want to be alone in her apartment on the first floor. Before sending Dmitri to bed, she had asked us to say our prayers before her, and we knelt down together, all three.

KR, Diary – 5 February

They say that Sergei did not live for a minute; death followed instantaneously, there was almost nothing left of the body, the remains were gathered up in a coffin which is now in the Chudov monastery; Ella is amazingly self-possessed, in the evening she visited the coachman in hospital, he received 79 wounds, but is not yet dead. Sergei had been living with Ella and Pavel's children in Nieskuchnoe, but moved to the Nikolski palace at the beginning of January. When I arrived at the Nikolski Palace, Ella and the children were by the coffin at a requiem service in the Chudov monastery, which is linked to the palace by a covered passage. I walked over. The coffin is of oak, with golden eagles. Kneeling before it were Ella, Maria and Dmitri, all in white.

Ella told me that on the previous morning Sergei had been extremely happy, as he had received from the Emperor a miniature portrait of Alexander III without diamonds, surrounded by a laurel wreath of gold. After lunch she heard a loud noise from inside the rooms, as when snow falls from the roof, only louder, and she immediately thought that something terrible must have happened: it flashed through her mind that Sergei could have met with an accident.

All morning she had felt a vague unease; first of all, she had persuaded Sergei against a trip to Petersburg, pointing out the possibility of an attack. She could see people running on to the square. She was told Sergei had just driven out in his carriage. Ella quickly put on her hat and coat and set off in the direction of the noise.

On Senate square, before the Nikolski gates, there was already a crowd of people. They did not want to let her pass, but she pushed through to the place where the remains of poor Sergei were lying – part of the torso and a leg, a blown off hand, pieces of the body and clothes.

She fell on his right hand and took off the rings. Her face was covered with the blood of the victim. They found pieces of the gold chain, on which his cross and medallions had hung. She rummaged around in the snow, which for a long time afterwards continued to give up small bones and bits of cartilage, pieces of the body and splinters from the carriage.

Ella herself arranged for a stretcher from her Red Cross organisation, on which the remains were placed and covered with a soldier's coat. All this was done in front of her. She ordered the stretcher to be taken to the Chudov monastery.

Her calmness, her goodness, her submission to the will of God, and her lack of anger are striking and deeply moving. How glad I am to be with her, the only one of the whole family.

Maria Pavlovna [the younger], Memoirs
Uncle Sergei and Aunt Ella had never had any children of their own. Their relations towards each other were distinguished by a strained fondness that rested on my aunt's serene acceptance of my uncle's decision in all matters great and small. Proud and timid, both of them, they seldom showed their true feelings and never offered confidences.

Converted to the Orthodox religion, my aunt had become each year more devoutly attached to its forms and practices. Although himself pious and scrupulous in observance of all the rites of Orthodoxy, Uncle Sergei regarded with anxiety his wife's increasing absorption in things spiritual, and ended by regarding it as immoderate.

He treated her rather as if she were a child. I believe that she was hurt by his attitude and longed to be better understood, but it was as if she were being driven deeper and deeper within herself for refuge. She and my uncle seemed never very intimate. They met for the most part only at meals and by day avoided being alone together. They slept, however, up to the last year of their life together, in the same great bed.

My uncle, the Grand Duke Sergei, was possessed of a unique personality and of a character that remained to me, to the very day of his dreadful death, incomprehensible. The fourth son of the Emperor Alexander II, he was in 1891 appointed by his brother, Alexander III, as Governor-General of Moscow, and he continued in this post under the new reign. It was a position of great power and consequence, and his devotion to his duty was absolute. Even in the country, when he was supposed to be resting, he was constantly receiving couriers from Moscow and giving audiences.

From their early youth Uncle Sergei and my father [Pavel] had been devoted to each other, and my uncle was also profoundly attached to my mother. The early death which came to her, as I have said, at Ilinskoe, left him with a sense of bereavement for which he could never be consoled. He ordered the rooms in which she had spent her last hours to be kept intact, exactly as they were when she died there. He had these rooms locked, and throughout the remainder of his life himself guarded the key, allowing no one else to enter.

He was as tall as my father. Like my father he had broad shoulders above a body excessively thin. He wore a small beard, closely trimmed. His hair, which was thick, was cut short and so brushed as to stand up briskly all over his head. In characteristic posture he stood erect, head up, chest out; his elbows would be drawn closely in towards his sides, and with the fingers of one hand he toyed with a jewelled ring that he habitually wore on the little finger of the other.

When he was vexed or surly, his lips would be compressed to one crisp straight line and his eyes became little hard points of light. Cold, inflexible, the world called him, and not without cause, but towards Dmitri and me he displayed a tenderness almost feminine. Despite which he demanded of us, as of all his household or following, exact and immediate obedience. The house, the farms, all business affairs, and the least personal detail of our separate lives he felt it incumbent upon him to direct himself, and to his least decision would permit not the slightest contradiction. Introspective, essentially diffident, his true spirit imprisoned within him, he hid private impulses of exceeding sensitiveness, and acted according to rigid conventions and to convictions altogether royalistic. Those few who knew him well were deeply devoted to him, but even his intimates feared him, and Dmitri and I feared him too.

In his fashion he loved us deeply. He liked to have us near him, and gave us a good deal of his time. But he was always jealous of us. If he had known the full extent of our devotion to our father it would have maddened him.

Aunt Ella was one of the most beautiful women I have ever seen in my life. She was tall and slight, of blonde colouring, with features of extraordinary fineness and purity. She had eyes of a grey-blue, on one of which was a spot of brown, and the effect of her glance was unusual.

Even when in the country my aunt gave a great deal of time and attention to her appearance. She designed most of her dresses herself, sketching and painting them in water-colours, planning them with care, and wearing them with art and distinction. My uncle, who had a passion for jewels, gave her many – so that she had a different set to harmonize with almost every costume that she wore.

Throughout our early childhood – throughout, indeed, our uncle's lifetime – Aunt Ella showed no interest in us or in anything that concerned us, and she saw as little of us as she could. She appeared to resent our presence in the household, and our uncle's evident affection for us. At times she said things to me that wounded me.

I recall one such time when she had dressed for an outing and seemed to me particularly beautiful. It was a simple dress of white muslin but she had her hair fixed a new way – gathered, unbound, at the back of her neck by a bow of black silk – and the effect was enchanting. I exclaimed: 'Oh! Auntie, you look like the picture of a little page in a fairy story.'

She turned to my nurse without smiling and spoke in a dry, sharp tone: 'Fry, you really must teach her not to make personal remarks.'

She swept away.

Of dressing for dinner she made a veritable ceremony and one that required much time. The maids, the mistress of the wardrobe, all were assembled. Cambric linen bordered with lace was made ready in a basket lined in rose satin. Wash basins were filled with hot water perfumed with verbena. Rose petals were floated in the bath.

Commercial cosmetics scarcely existed in Russia at the time. I believe that my aunt had never in her life seen rouge, and she used powder very rarely. Painting the face was an art almost unknown to Russian ladies of that day, and to princesses unknown entirely. Aunt Ella made her own face lotion, a mixture of cucumber juice and sour cream. She never permitted the summer sun to touch her skin, guarding it whenever she went out with a silk veil of thick mesh and a silk parasol lined in green.

After the maids and other attendants had taken off her outer dress of the afternoon, my aunt would shut herself in her dressing-room alone. With the chosen stockings, shoes, petticoats, and all the other complicated apparel of the period arrayed in orderly piles around them, the retinue waited. From the neighbouring room could be heard the splashing of water. Only when my aunt had bathed and put on her corset did she open the door. Then the maids would step briskly forward, each with her special task to perform.

While they were dressing her, my aunt would regard herself attentively, usually with pleasure, in a high triple mirror, so arranged that she saw herself from all sides. The final adjustments she made with her own hands. If the costume did not satisfy her in every particular, she had it taken off and demanded another which she adjusted with the same care and patience.

One of the maids dressed her hair. She did her nails herself. They were curiously shaped, very flat and thin, curving forward over the ends of the fingers.

Manicuring accomplished, the dress of the evening donned – now came my part in the rites. My aunt would tell me the jewels she intended to wear, and I would go to her jewel cabinets – an array comparable almost to the show cases at a jeweller's – and bring her her choice.

Soon my uncle, with habitual exactitude, would knock at the door to say that dinner was ready. Both of them would kiss me, then disappear; and Dmitri and I, having supped early, would be sent to bed.

One evening I remember, in those early days, I saw my aunt in court dress – majestic with her sweeping train of brocade, ablaze with jewels, and resplendently beautiful. Mute before the spectacle, I raised myself to the tips of my toes and placed a kiss full of devotion on the back of her white neck, directly underneath a magnificent necklace heavy with sapphires. She said nothing, but I could see her eyes, and the cold, hard look in them chilled me to the heart.

Xenia, Diary – 5 February – Tsarskoe Selo
Lord, the thought of *Moscow* is just too terrible. Poor Ella! Zinaida

[Yusupov] telegraphed that she 'is bearing her terrible grief like a saint'!

Nicky has forbidden the family to go to Moscow. It's terrible to think that she, poor thing, is *alone*, and that we are unable to see her although we are so near. The murderer is a man of about 30, he hasn't said who he is, but he's very pleased with what he has done!

Sandro, Memoirs

Uncle Sergei, Grand Duke Sergei Alexandrovich, played a fatal part in the downfall of the empire, having been partially responsible for the Khodinka catastrophe during the coronation of the year 1896.

Try as I will, I cannot find a single redeeming feature in his character. A very poor officer, he commanded the Preobrajensky Regiment, the crack regiment of the Imperial Guard. A complete ignoramus in administrative affairs, he held fast to the general governorship of the Moscow area, which should have been entrusted to a statesman of exceptionally seasoned experience.

Obstinate, arrogant, disagreeable, he flaunted his many peculiarities in the face of the entire nation, providing the enemies of the regime with inexhaustible material for calumnies and libels. The generals visiting the messroom of the Preobrajensky Regiment listened with stupefaction to the chorus of officers singing a favourite song of Grand Duke Sergei, with its refrain consisting of the words – 'and peace, and love, and bliss'. The august commander himself illustrated those not very soldier-like words by throwing his body back and registering a tortured rapture in his features.

The Tsar should never have allowed Uncle Sergei to retain his post in Moscow after the storm of indignation caused by the Khodinka catastrophe. As though to accentuate his repugnant personality on a background of virtue, he married Grand Duchess Elizabeth. No two human beings could have offered such a contrast.

Ravishing beauty, rare intelligence, delightful sense of humour, infinite patience, hospitality of thought, generous heart, all gifts were hers. It was cruel and unjust that a woman of her calibre should have tied up her existence to a man like Uncle Sergei. Everybody fell in love with 'Aunt Ella' the very first moment she arrived in St Petersburg from her native Hesse-Darmstadt. One evening in her company, and the memory of her eyes, her skin, her laughter, her genius for putting one at ease, threw us all into the depths of despair at the realization of her approaching betrothal.

I would have given ten years of my life to stop her from entering the church on the arm of haughty Sergei. I liked to think of myself as her 'cavaliere servente', and I despised the condescending grimace of her husband when exaggerating his St Petersburg drawl he would address 'Aunt Ella' as 'my child'. Too proud to complain she stayed by his side for nearly twenty years, her loyalty undiminished by the passing of time and her sorrow adding a spiritual halo to her beauty.

V. F. Djunkovsky, Memoirs

Grand Duke Konstantin Konstanovich [KR] arrived, representing the Emperor. They say that at first, the Emperor wanted to go to Moscow to be present at his uncle's funeral, but thanks to the influence of Trepov, decided not to. The same thing happened with Vladimir Alexandrovich, Sergei Alexandrovich's elder brother, who, they say, begged the Emperor to let him go with tears in his eyes, but the Emperor would not permit it. And yet, I think that if the Emperor had not listened to Trepov, and had come to Moscow – it would have made a colossal impression and would have increased the Tsar's standing with his people.

The sister of the Grand Duke – the Grand Duchess Marie [Duchess of Edinburgh], came from abroad for the funeral with her daughter Princess Beatrice, as did the Grand Duke Pavel, the Duke of Mecklenburg-Strelitz, the Grand Duke of Hesse [Ernie], brother of the Grand Duchess, with his [new] wife the Duchess Eleonora, as well as the Grand Duchess's sister Princess Victoria Battenberg.

As well as these exalted personages, many private individuals and deputations came as well. There were so many wreaths the coffin was drowned in greenery, every day the people were allowed in to pay their respects at specific hours; a hundred people were let in at a time. Services were held from morning to night, without interruption. The Grand Duchess did not wish the people to be constrained in any way, and they were allowed free access to the Kremlin.

KR, Diary – 6 February

Here in Moscow, the absence of close relatives creates a strange and painful impression. One can allow that Vladimir has a heavy burden – he is responsible for the security of the capital. But Alexei? They say he is coming, but he is not here yet. Pavel's title of lieutenant-general has been restored, and he is expected here. They say that it is dangerous for their Majesties to leave Tsarskoe. If it were not for me, poor Ella would have to appear at the official requiem service alone.

9 February I went downstairs in time for Pavel's arrival. We went over together to see the coffin. I cried bitterly at the sight of Pavel beside his brother's coffin. Then we prayed next to the holy relics. Pavel recounted that he had been at Tsarskoe yesterday, and that the Tsar and the two Empresses are all inconsolable, because they cannot pay their last respects to the deceased: it is too dangerous for them to leave Tsarskoe.

All the Grand Dukes have been informed by letter, that not only can they not go to Moscow, but they are also forbidden to attend the requiem services at either the Kazan or the Isaac cathedral. Trepov informed the Emperor about this, that is the danger to us all, after which the order was issued. Nevertheless, Alexei [Pavel's brother] wanted to go to Moscow at all costs. The Emperor asked Pavel to persuade Alexei not to go to Moscow; he cannot, or rather does not want, to forbid him, as he is so much older and could be the Emperor's father. The Emperor talked of having irrefutable proof that Alexei is being tracked like a wild beast, in order to be killed. Pavel managed to persuade Alexei not to go. Alexei sobbed like a child, crying: 'What a disgrace!'

Now that Pavel is here, and Ella's brother is arriving tomorrow, I am no longer needed and can go home.

Pavel brought with him a package that was handed to him by Sergei 13 years ago, with instructions for it to be opened in the event of his death. In it, he asked to be buried in the Preobrajensky uniform. But on the day of his death, Sergei was wearing the coat of the Kiev regiment. There is no possibility of changing him into that of the Preobrajensky, because of the disfiguration of the body.

We carried the firmly sealed coffin through the west door and into the small Andreev church, where it will lie until it is decided where it will be buried.

At Ella's request, her sister Victoria told me that Ella had gone to visit Sergei's murderer. She talked with the wretch for a long time, and gave him an icon. I had heard about this visit the day before from A. P. Ignatieva, the general's wife, and told Pavel, Marie, Victoria and Beatrice about what I had heard. They were not aware that Ella had been to see the murderer, they did not believe it and even laughed. And indeed, such courage, such greatness of spirit are simply unbelievable. She is a saint.

Maria Pavlovna [the younger], Memoirs

Two days after the murder, [Ella] drove off in a carriage draped with black cloth and crape, and remained away a long time. She had gone to the prison to see the murderer! This struck the administration into utter confusion; nothing like it had ever happened before. No one knows to this day exactly what passed between my aunt and her husband's assassin. She insisted on speaking with the prisoner alone.

Ivan Kalyaev to his comrades – from prison

My meeting with the Grand Duchess took place on the evening of 7th February, in the offices of the police station of the Piatnitsky district, where I had been specially brought. I was not warned of the meeting, nor had I asked for the Grand Duchess. When she came in towards me, all in black, with the weary step of someone overcome with grief, and tears in her eyes, I did not recognize her, and at first supposed that one of the detainees had come to identify me. 'I'm his wife,' whispered the Grand Duchess, drawing near me. I did not rise to meet her, and she slumped helplessly onto the chair next to mine, lowered her head into her hands and continued crying.

'Princess,' I said, 'don't cry. It had to be so. Why do they talk to me only after I have committed a murder,' I thought out loud.

'You must have suffered a lot, to take this decision,' she said, but here I interrupted her and jumped up, very much agitated by her tears: 'What does it matter whether I suffered, or not. Yes I suffered, but I join my suffering to that of a million others. Too much blood is being spilt around us, yet we have no other form of protest against a cruel government and a terrible war. But why do they talk to me only after I have committed murder?' I repeated, interrupting my own musings.

'Yes, it's a great pity that you did not come to see us, and that we did not know you earlier.' The Grand Duchess pronounced these words without, I think, any ulterior thought.

'Surely you know what they did to the workers on 9th January, when they went to see the Tsar? Did you really think that this could go unpunished? There's a terrible war of hatred being waged against the people. You declared war on the people, we took up the challenge. I would give my life a thousand times, not just once. Russia must be free.'

'But honour, the honour of our country,' she said.

I was, I repeat, in a state of great agitation, and did not really let her speak. 'The honour of our country,' I replied sarcastically.

'Do you really imagine that we don't suffer? Do you think we don't wish the good of the people?'

'Yes, you are suffering *now*,' I said, 'and as for the good ... let's leave the good aside.'

We both fell silent and I sat down. The Grand Duchess was also somewhat calmer and started talking about the Grand Duke: that he had been expecting death, which is why he had left the post of Governor-General, that he was such a good man. Here I again interrupted the Grand Duchess and, to spare her feelings, said: 'Let's not talk about the Grand Duke. I don't want to discuss him with you. I'll tell everything at the trial. You know that I carried this out completely consciously. The Grand Duke assumed a specific political role. He knew what he wanted.'

'Yes, I can't enter into political discussions with you. I only wanted you to know, that the Grand Duke forgives you, and that I will pray for you.'

I will not conceal that we looked at each other with a kind of mystical feeling, like two condemned men who have been spared. I – by chance; she – by the will of the Organization, by my will, as both the Organization and I consciously strove to avoid unnecessary bloodshed.

And looking at the Grand Duchess, I could not help noticing on her face an expression of gratitude, if not towards me, then at least to fate, for not letting her perish.

'I beg you to accept this icon in memory of me. I will pray for you.' And I took the icon.

For me, this was a symbol of her recognition of my victory, a symbol of her gratitude to fate for preserving her life, and her repentance for the crimes of the Grand Duke. The Grand Duchess rose to leave. I also got up.

V. F. Djunkovsky, Memoirs

Nobody knows how the conversation between the Grand Duchess and Kalyaev went, and there were no witnesses. From the few comments by the Grand Duchess it is only possible to conclude, that this interview satisfied the Grand Duchess's christian sentiments, and that Kalyaev's heart was touched: he took an icon from her and kissed her hand. A few days later, when the first impression had faded and Kalyaev's reason had taken over again from his heart, he felt guilty towards his own party for his weakness, and wrote the Grand Duchess a letter full of disrespect and reproaches. Many, at that time, criticized the Grand Duchess for taking such a step, but those who knew the Grand Duchess, understood that she was incapable of acting in any other way. With her all-forgiving character, she felt the need to offer a word of solace even to Kalyaev, who had so inhumanely deprived her of a husband and a friend.

Ivan Kalyaev, from Prison – February 1905 – a poem

A woman like shadow, a ghost with no life
Sat next to me clasping my hand
She looked, and she whispered to me: 'I'm his wife'
And wept and shed tears with no end.

Her frock was so black and it smelled of the grave,
But her tears... – They just told everything
So I didn't reject her, I spared woman-slave
From the camp of the Enemy King

Then she nervously murmured: 'I'm praying for you ...'
Translated by A. Maylunas

Boris Savinkov, Memoirs

Subsequently this conversation was reported in the press, in an incorrect and tendentious version which caused Kalyaev many painful moments.

Ivan Kalyaev to Ella – [no date] – from prison

I did not know you, you came to me of your own accord: therefore, the responsibility for the consequences of our meeting lies solely with you.

Our meeting took place, to all outward appearances, in circumstances of intimacy. What passed between us was not meant for publication but concerned us alone. We met on neutral ground, at your own direction, tête à tête, and were thus entitled to the same right of incognito. How to explain your selfless christian feeling otherwise?

I trusted your nobility, supposing that your exalted official position and your personal merit would provide sufficient guarantee against the kind of malicious intrigue, in which even you have been to some extent implicated. But you were not afraid to be seen to be involved: my trust in you has not been justified.

There is a malicious intrigue and a tendentious version of our private meeting. The question arises: could either have happened without your participation, albeit passive in the form of non-resistance, when your honour dictated the opposite course of action. The answer is contained in the question itself, and I protest vigorously against a political interpretation of my decent feelings of sympathy for you in your grief. My convictions and my attitude to the Imperial House remain unchanged.

I fully recognize my own mistake: I should have reacted to you impassively and not entered into any conversation. But I was gentle with you, and during our meeting I suppressed that feeling of hatred, which I in reality feel for you.

You know now what motives guided me. But you proved unworthy of my magnanimity. Because for me there is no doubt, that you are the source of all the stories about me, for who would have dared to reveal the substance of our conversation without first asking your permission (the newspaper version is distorted: I never admitted to being a believer, I never expressed the slightest repentance).

The fact that you remained alive is also my victory, and one which made me rejoice doubly when the Grand Duke had been killed.

KR, Diary – 19 February

On the ninth day after Sergei's death, Maria [Duchess of Edinburgh] and Pavel left Moscow for Tsarskoe, Maria will stay there for some time, while Pavel went on to Paris. His wife [Olga Pistolkors], who received the title of Countess Hohenfelsen from the Regent of Bavaria, accompanied Pavel until Verjbolovo and waited for him there.

He is permitted to return to Russia from time to time, even with his wife, but not to live here. Maria and Dmitri [the children] will remain with Ella, Pavel does not want to take them from her. The Emperor has made her their guardian.

Maria Pavlovna [the younger], Memoirs

During all these sad days my aunt gave proof of an almost incomprehensible heroism; no one could understand whence came the strength so to bear her misfortune. Always shut up in herself, she became more so. Only her eyes and sometimes the beaten look on her face betrayed her suffering; and with an energy that, following long years of almost complete passivity, was astonishing, she took charge herself of all the grisly details.

Ella to Nicky – 26 February – Moscow
Let me tenderly thank you for all your delicate kindness, which gives
me such great comfort.

May God guide and help us to bring up Maria and Dmitri as well
as Sergei had begun. I will do my very best and knowing his ideas and
principles, only need try and follow what has always been before my
eyes and warm up those tender little hearts as true christians and real
Russians, founding all on faith and duty.

That I may live in this house during my life is an intense comfort
and I find such immense strength and peace being near St Alexe's
relics and my darling in the peaceful little chapel.

May I have the furniture, which is partly historical and all taken out
and stored away with the catalogue in the Kremlin, so that after my
death all will be put back as it was?

I am looking for Sergei's testament, until now I have found no
paper – it is awfully painful, but I can't bear the idea, anybody touching his precious papers and things. He loved order so that for his sake
I work away.

KR, Diary – 28 February
And so, for the last six months I have not sinned as before, that is today
with someone else; but it's true that I sinned with myself three times.

12 March   We went to an exhibition of portraits from the time of
Peter I to our day, organized by Grand Duke Nikolai Mikhailovich.
We were shown round by Diaghilev. It is unpleasant for me to meet
him, also though he does not suspect this, unpleasant because I
know something about him from Yatsko.

V. F. Djunkovsky, Memoirs
The president of the court, an aged senator, took the proceedings
nervously, without restraint, got into dispute with Kalyaev over his
comments, and generally conducted himself in a way lacking by far
the necessary dignity.

By his own comments he provoked Kalyaev into impudence, as a
result of which Kalyaev was removed from the courtroom. At this, his
defence lawyer M. L. Mandelstam, became extremely agitated.

The prosecution, Shcheglovitov[7] was also far from being up to the

---

[7] Later (1906) Minister of Justice.

task; his characteristic was to hold forth when it wasn't necessary, for the facts spoke for themselves and the shorter his speech, the more effective it would have been, yet he dragged out his prosecuting statement, making it long and boring, although quite smooth; however, when he had finished, it was impossible to conclude what he wanted – did he want the ultimate punishment for the criminal or was he asking for mercy.

All in all, his speech lacked quality. It made a depressing impression on me, the more so because it gave Kalyaev an opportunity for making jibes: he very easily picked up on the less successful parts of the speech and said, that the speech would be forgivable, if it were made by a police sergeant, but that it was somewhat surprising to hear it from the lips of an educated man with a 'star' on his chest.

I left the courtroom with a very bad impresssion.

KR, Diary – 28 March

No parade in the Imperial presence has been arranged – there can be no question at the moment of their Majesties being able to leave Tsarskoe.

Although the secret police recently managed to catch 12 revolutionaries with documents and a cache of explosives, the danger of assassination has not been eradicated for those in high places. Vladimir is also unable to appear anywhere, if his presence is known in advance.

Maria Pavlovna [the younger], Memoirs

And so the winter passed, and at the first breath of spring we went to Tsarskoe Selo to spend the Easter holidays. There, too, the atmosphere was far from joyous. The imperial family lived in the shadow of threatened death and political upheaval. The war with Japan continued, unpromisingly; the situation at home became more and more complicated and acute. Weak, indecisive, timorous, the government, unable to agree upon any energetic action, stood shakily aloof and let events precipitate themselves. The reign of assassinations and assaults had begun.

Established now completely at Tsarskoe Selo, the sovereigns since the war lived in comparative retirement made sadder by anxiety. The dangers that threatened the Emperor had led to the organization of a curiously complicated system of spying and tattling; spies were set to watch spies; the air was filled with whisperings, cross-currents of fear and mistrust.

On the eve of Easter, while we were still at Tsarskoe, a serious conspiracy came to light. Two members of the terrorist organization made themselves up as singers, intending to enter as such into the choir that sang in religious services at the court. They planned, apparently, to bring in bombs under their vestments, and to hurl those bombs in the church as they chanted during Easter mass. The Emperor, although knowing of the plot, went to church with his family as usual. A number of persons were arrested that day. Nothing further happened; but that mass was the saddest that I have ever attended.

Pavel to Nicky – 12 April – Paris
Dear Nicky!

I have just received a telegram from Alexei [Pavel's brother], saying you wish me to come alone. I am really astonished by this, as you yourself gave me permission to bring my wife with me. Quite apart from the pain of being separated from her, I am in the silliest position in relation to the embassy and the French, as encouraged by your promise, I informed them my wife would be coming with me. I beg you to change your decision. After all, no one except her children will see her, and she poor thing was so overjoyed at the thought of seeing them, most of all because her son will be promoted to officer at the end of April and she would so like to be able to congratulate him on that day. I beg you, by all that is dear to you, not to deny me this request. I will be eagerly awaiting your telegram.

I embrace you all fondly,

Your Pavel

Xenia, Diary – 22 April – Tsarskoe Selo
Uncle Pavel arrived at 2 o'clock straight from Paris, but only for four days! He wanted to come with his wife, but he was not permitted. He is offended with Nicky for the letter he wrote to him (it seems fairly sharp!), and is generally not in a good mood. He is also, for some reason, cold and unaffectionate with the children, and they are visibly shy of him!

Sandro, Memoirs
Uncle Pavel was the nicest of the four uncles of the Tsar, although he too possessed an inclination for 'mounting the high horse', which

trait he owed to his close friendship with his brother Sergei. He danced well, he was greatly admired by women, and he looked quite attractive in his dark-green-and-silver dolman, raspberry tight breeches and low boots of a Grodno Hussar. Satisfied with the care-free life of a brilliant officer, he never occupied a position of respon-sibility. His first wife, a Princess of Greece, died when he was still very young, and he married for the second time the divorced wife of a colonel, thus committing a double breach of the regulations prevail-ing in the imperial family, no grand duke being permitted to marry a commoner and no divorced woman being received at court. He had to leave Russia for an indefinite stay in Paris. I believe he benefited considerably by his forced exile through meeting people of intelli-gence and importance. It changed his character, bringing out human traits formerly hidden under a mask of nonsensical haughtiness.

Xenia, Diary – 24 April – Tsarskoe Selo

Uncle Pitz [Pavel] was in a good mood after his interview, and his relations with the children have been restored. They won't let go of him, while on the first day he was terribly cold towards them.

25 April   Ella says, that Uncle Pavel is calming down. Now the one thing he wants is to adopt the youngest Pistolkors (his own son in fact), who is now living with them. He is eight years old.

Maria Pavlovna [the younger], Memoirs

Our apartments at Tsarskoe Selo were in the Great Palace of Catherine II. The Empress would have us come often to the Alexander Palace to play with her daughters. Their nursery apart-ments occupied an entire wing on the second floor of the Alexander Palace. These rooms, light and spacious, were hung with flowered cretonne and furnished throughout with polished lemonwood. The effect was luxurious, yet peaceful and comfortable. Through the win-dows you could see the palace gardens and guardhouses and a little beyond, through the grille of a high iron gate, a street corner.

The Emperor's daughters were governed as we were, by an English head nurse assisted by innumerable Russian nurses and chamber-maids, and their nursery staff was uniformed as ours was, all in white, with small nurse-caps of white tulle. With this exception: two of their Russian nurses were peasants and wore the magnificent native peasant costumes.

Dmitri and I spent hours examining our young cousins' toys; one could never tire of them, they were so fine. Especially enchanting to me was the French President's gift to Olga at the time when she was taken with her parents on their first visit to France. In a trunk covered with soft leather was a doll with a complete trousseau: dresses, lingerie, hats, slippers, the entire equipment of a dressing-table, all reproduced with remarkable art and fidelity.

Secret Petition: Ministry of Interior to Prince Hilkov[8] – 7 May

Dear Prince Mikhail Ivanovich

The sentence of the Special Session of the Governing Senate, by which the murderer of grand duke Sergei Alexandrovich, Ivan Kalyaev, is sentenced to death by hanging, is to be carried out on the 10th May within the walls of Schlisselburg prison, to which place the prisoner will be brought on the morning of the 9th May, on a boat belonging to the Petersburg river police.

In order to transport the prisoner, and also to convey the executioner to the place of execution, a second boat is needed, which the Governor of St Petersburg does not possess.

Consequently, I have the honour of humbly asking your Highness not to refuse to put at the disposal of the Chief of the St Petersburg river police, during the night of the 8th to 9th May, one of the river boats of the Ministry of Communications, which should be at the Police pier, opposite the Summer gardens, at 3 o'clock in the morning.

Boulygin

Execution of Kalyaev as recounted in 1920 by Nicolas Fedorov, an emigré in Paris who witnessed the execution at Schlisselburg

At two o'clock in the morning, as the first lights of dawn colour the sky, four jailers come to fetch the prisoner in his cell and lead him, handcuffed, into the courtyard of the fortress.

The executioner Philipiev takes hold of Kalyaev and binds his shoulders and arms tightly, making him look even punier than before.

Lifting his red bonnet and bowing, with a bestial smile on his coarse face, the executioner invites Kalyaev with a theatrical gesture to mount the scaffold. Without the slightest hesitation, the

---

[8] Minister of Transport.

condemned man climbs the steps and turns to face us. Not a muscle of his face moves, but he stares with a sad and vacant look into the beyond. For a moment a tear seems to brush his eyes, as if his thoughts were flying one last time towards those dear to him.

A deathly silence hangs over those present. Suddenly Philipiev's hoarse voice rings out, asking his victim melodramatically if he wishes to address a last prayer to God. Kalyaev replies: 'I have already settled all my accounts with life; but I would like to repeat, on this very scaffold, that I am happy to die for the cause of the Revolution.'

A clerk reads out the interminable sentence. When he has accomplished his task, we can quite distinctly hear Kalyaev saying: 'I am happy to have retained my composure right until the end.'

The executioner envelops him in a large white shroud, which covers his head. Then he orders: 'Get up onto the block.' Kalyaev objects: 'How can you expect me to get up onto the block. You have covered my head, I can't see anything.' Philipiev immediately grabs tightly hold of him, and having lifted him up onto the bench, hastily passes the rope round his neck: then with a sudden blow he knocks the block away.

But the rope is too long; the feet hit the floor. The hanged man convulses hideously. Cries of horror rise up from the little troop around the scaffold. Calling two assistants to help him, the executioner rushes back to the gallows and the three of them pull on the rope to finish off the execution.

Xenia, Diary – 12 May – Gatchina

Olga [sister] is terribly upset about Misha and Dina.[9] He, poor thing, fell in love with her, while she, unfortunately, from the beginning did nothing to stop it, rather she let herself be carried away by the same feeling!

This has caused so many complications, everyone has begun to notice their relationship. Olga wanted to bring her here to live, now that she is alone after the departure of her brother, but to *bring them together purposely* – is stupid. All this is extremely tiresome.

KR, Diary – 18 May

We returned home for dinner. In the meantime a newspaper had arrived with the terrible news of the loss of the great part of our fleet.

---

[9] The Tsar's brother, now twenty-six, and Dina Kossikovskaya, a lady-in-waiting.

Roszdestvensky[10] was injured at the the very beginning of the battle, and taken on to one of the other ships, but we don't yet know which one. The Japanese apparently captured several of our ships, we had if not 3 thousand men, then certainly 2 thousand taken prisoner.

How terrible, what a disgrace and how much sorrow!

Xenia, Diary – 3 June – Gatchina
Mama has not been to Petersburg since January 9th! Misha tried in vain to dissuade her from going, but thank God everything went all right. It makes you sick to think about all the outrages.

7 June Yesterday, the 6th, Nicky received a deputation of seven town and country representatives, headed by S. Trubetskoi (professor in ordinary). He gave a long speech, and began by thanking N for receiving them. Nicky said the following to them: 'I have been happy to listen to you. I do not doubt, gentlemen, that you were guided by a feeling of burning love for the motherland, in your direct attitude to me. With all my heart, I grieve with you and my people over the misfortunes, such as war, which Russia has suffered – and which must still be expected, as well as all our interior disorders. Discard your doubts. My will is the Tsar's will.'

9 June I found Mama with Nicky and Alix in the garden. Nicky is pleased at having received those gentlemen – it's a load off his mind! The thing is, he is now in their hands and has to be terribly careful.

15 June The most unbelievable news has arrived, simply disgraceful, it makes you feel ashamed! You want to go and hide from yourself!! There has been a mutiny on the *Potemkin*, the commander and several officers have been killed! They arrived in Odessa yesterday evening, and this morning the body of a sailor was brought ashore, with a placard on his chest, saying that he had been killed by the officers for complaining about the bad food. They informed the authorities that if the body was touched, they would begin bombarding the town! Armed cutters are sailing along the shore, while the sailors incite the people, who are joining them and issuing proclamations. Looting has started in the port, God knows what's happening and there is nothing to be done! It's terrible, terrible what we have lived to see! A squadron has left Sebastopol. This news has

---

[10] Commander of the Russian fleet against the Japanese.

simply killed us, we have been wandering around in a daze all day –
what a nightmare, it's too awful.

18 June There was no news all day. At last in the evening, a telegram arrived from Chukhnin, saying that yesterday all the officers of
the *St George the Victorious* had been taken ashore, and that today as
she left for port (Odessa) she ran onto a sand bank, while the
Potemkin has put to sea! There is no news at all of the squadron, you
can think what you will! When the squadron arrived yesterday, the
Potemkin went out to meet them ready for battle, broke through their
lines, and as she sailed past the *St George* the crew gave her an ovation, shouted 'hourrah' and made a commotion. Krieger then gave
the signal to return to Sebastopol, but at that moment on the *St
George*, the crew rushed on to the bridge and prevented this, after
which they put the officers aboard the cutter and the mineship, and
towed them ashore. Chukhnin is afraid there may be mutiny on
other ships. Lord! How terrible, what a nightmare! What is this?
Why, why are we being punished so by God?! I am walking as if in a
dream, unable to understand anything!

20 June The *Potemkin* put into port, demanded provisions and coal,
but the authorities refused and took the strongest measures. They
were told that those who came ashore would be treated as deserters.
   The ringleaders are only 12 men in all, a small number of the crew
joined them, the rest are nothing but a herd of sheep. The crew of
the *Prut* also mutinied, beat up the master of the watch, and arrested
the commander. They then went to Odessa, but when they didn't
find the *Potemkin* there, they turned back to Sebastopol and gave
themselves up! God alone knows! The crew of the *St George* gave the
ringleaders up to the authorities. The officers returned, having been
begged by the crew to come back aboard!

KR, Diary – 20 June
What is happening to Russia? What disorganization, what disinte-
gration; just like a piece of clothing that is beginning to rip and tear
along the seams, and fall open. There is actual mutiny on the Black
Sea Fleet warship *Potemkin Tavrichesky*, the crew revolted and killed
the commander. Odessa, Lodz and Sebastopol have been placed
under martial law.

22 June Terrible, unbelievable news from Odessa. It's complete revolution. The unprecedented, shameful incident on the battleship

Potemkin, where the crew revolted and killed the commander – my own dear friend Jenia Golikov – and nearly all the officers, would also be incredible, if it were not a real occurrence.

Xenia, Diary – 25 June – Gatchina
I feel so depressed, it's impossible. It's terrible what's happening – strikes, murders, discontent, a general lack of authority! I read a memorandum issued by the nobility – it's strong and cruel, but unfortunately true.

The *Potemkin* put in at Costanta and gave itself up. The ringleaders will probably all disappear and only the sheep will suffer. They are being treated as if they were the villains.

Alix to Olga [daughter] – 4 August – Near Pskov
Darling little Olga,

Papa and Auntie Olga [Nicky's sister] have gone for a walk in the lovely woods; my old legs hurt too much to walk, so I remained at home. Now the train has at last stopped. We got quite soaked this morning; my new waterproof cape was wet through. We saw lots of soldiers; cavalry, infantry, and artillery. The country is very pretty.

Whilst we were standing about in a village, the peasants came round us and began talking. One woman asked me how you four were and where I had left you. Was it not kind of her? Others gave us bread and salt and picked the nicest flowers they could find in their gardens. I am sewing away hard for the bazaar. Lots of trains pass us, all very long. An old lady of 98 came to see us this morning, and brought bread, salt – she lives close by and we want to pay her a visit if we have time. Aunt Olga has painted a very pretty postcard of Sarov and is going to have it printed.

I wonder how you all are. I feel so sad without my sweet little girlies. Be sure to be very good and remember, elbows off the table, sit straight and eat your meat nicely. I kiss you all very tenderly, and Sofia[11] too. Goodbye, darling child, and God bless you. Ever your loving old,

Mama +

Xenia, Diary – 6 August – Alexandria
A great day – terrible. The manifesto about the Duma has been published at last! May God grant that it's in time!

---

[11] Sofia Ivanovna Tiutcheva, the governess of the Tsar's children.

Kaiser Wilhelm to Nicky – 9 August – Schloss Wilhelmshöhe
Dearest Nicky,

Your manifesto directing the formation of the Duma made an excellent impression in Europe – especially in my country and I beg you to receive my warmest congratulations. It is a great step forward for the Political development of your country and gives the People an opening by which they will be able to bring before you their hopes and wishes and enable a communal work of master and country for the nation's welfare. You will be able to keep in touch with all sorts and conditions of men and infuse into them directly your spirit and your ideas, which are formerly hindered by the great bulky wall of the 'Tchin'[12] bureaucracy regarded with much suspicion by your subjects.

Your most devoted and affectionate friend and cousin

Willy

Xenia, Diary – 12 August – Alexandria
Misha fell asleep in his chair. He's bored without Dina!

Olga [sister], Memoirs
Poor Misha had an unfortunate habit of falling asleep at the wheel. That evening he was driving very fast – we were terrified of being late – and then quite suddenly he nodded, the car left the road and turned a complete somersault. We were both thrown out – miraculously unhurt. The car was not damaged. We just pushed it back on the road and drove on.

Xenia, Diary – 13 August
We had dinner at the Cottage with Nicky, Alix, Misha and Christo.[13] Nicky talked about the peace talks, which will seemingly not lead to anything, and about the mediation of President Roosevelt, who wrote to him quite bluntly, that we should not forget the Japanese are the victors and be prepared to make concessions. He wants to get us to make peace at all costs!

KR, Diary – 17 August
Today's papers brought news of the peace that has been agreed by

---

[12] Rank. The Kaiser was talking of the civil service promotion system.
[13] Prince Christopher of Greece.

representatives of Russia and Japan in Portsmouth, North America. We have conceded the southern part of Sakhalin, but refused to pay a single penny. Witte achieved a considerable diplomatic victory. Nevertheless, there is nothing joyful about this peace, crowning, as it does, such an unfortunate war for our forces. Not only does the peace bring no joy, it is even rather frightening.

Xenia, Diary – 17 August – Alexandria

I almost fainted from surprise this morning when I opened the papers and read that it's peace! Yesterday it hadn't even crossed our minds! It appears the Japanese have given in on every point, there will be no reparations to them, although we are ceding the lower part of Sakhalin. Of course, it's long since been time to end this terrible war, but not now and not in this way! The war started without reason, continued that way and ended even more stupidly! They imposed it on us, in the same way they have now imposed the peace, because that's what America and England want – I don't know who else, but Russia has practically not been consulted!! We were so longing to end the war after Mukden – and before and after Tsusima, but now it's simply shameful! – and offensive, although it has to be said that the Japanese have been modest in their demands!

18 August   We were at Mama's. Nicky, Petia[14] and Olga also. Mama asked Nicky to cheer up and at least look as if he considered the peace a necessity – he replied, 'Yes, faire bonne mine a mauvais jeu'! ['Putting a good face on it.']

Today I have begun to take stock of my feelings, and have come to the conclusion that *it's necessary and better this way*. But the feeling of resentment remains somewhere in the depths of my soul, and will *always be there*. This wasn't what we expected! Praise be to God for the saving of so many lives! But how will the army take this news!? No one can understand why there should be peace *now*?

KR, Diary – 22 August

Olia [KR's sister] told me, that when the Emperor sent Witte to America for the peace talks with the Japanese plenipotentiaries, he was so convinced that our conditions would be unacceptable, that he did not even entertain the possibility of peace. But when Japan

---

[14] Peter, Prince of Oldenburg, Olga's husband.

accepted our terms, there was no alternative but to conclude peace. And so the Emperor was caught out unexpectedly and has, in the words of Olia, who saw him and the Empress at Peterhof, been dropped in at the deep end.

Xenia, Diary – 23 August – Alexandria
The peace is signed thank God, it's one nightmare less, but all the same I can't quite believe it and it's not what was wanted!

Pierre Gilliard, Memoirs
It was first suggested I should teach French to the Grand-Duchesses Olga and Tatiana. For my first lesson a royal carriage came to take me to Alexandria Cottage where the Tsar and his family were residing. I was taken up to a small room, soberly furnished in the English style, on the second storey. The door opened and the Tsarina came in, holding Olga and Tatiana by the hand. After a few pleasant remarks she sat down at the table and invited me to take a place opposite her. The children sat at each end.

The Tsarina was still a beautiful woman at that time. She was tall and slender and carried herself superbly. But all this ceased to count the moment one looked into her eyes – those speaking, grey-soul eyes which mirrored the emotions of a sensitive soul.

Olga, the eldest of the Grand-Duchesses, was a girl of ten, very fair, and with sparkling, mischievous eyes and a slightly *retroussé* nose. She examined me with a look which seemed from the first moment to be searching for the weak point in my armour, but there was something so pure and frank about the child that one liked her straight off.

Tatiana was eight and a half. She had auburn hair and was prettier than her sister, but gave one the impression of being less transparent, and spontaneous.

The lesson began.

KR, Diary – 28 September
The newspapers are full of terrible news! It's still no better in the Caucasus, the killings go on, as do the bombings, they are firing into the streets from the houses, the armenians and the tartars continue cutting each other up. In Moscow the bakers are on strike, as are the plumbers, the locksmiths, the tram conductors and the print work-

ers, the newspapers do not come out. The historical exhibition in the Tauride palace has been closed and the palace is being prepared for the meeting of the State Duma. What will we see this winter? There's no way of avoiding bloodshed.

1 October   I heard from Kyril that he is a married man [to Ducky] having deliberately broken the Imperial prohibition, he then hurried to confess (the wedding took place in Bavaria on the 25th September). But the Emperor did not wish to receive him and instructed the Court Minister Baron Fredericks to inform Kyril that he is stripped of the title of Grand Duke, as well as his revenues from the Appanages, and excluded from the services.

Kyril should have realized all this before, as the Emperor had warned him on several occasions of such a punishment should he marry Ducky, his first cousin. Despite this Kyril is deeply offended that the Emperor refused to receive him and conveyed his displeasure through a third party.

It seems to me that Kyril is only reaping the fruits of his own behaviour: instead of avoiding meeting the woman he loved, but whom he had neither the right nor the permission to marry, he was constantly with her for more than a year.

3 October   In the order concerning the fleet it was announced that Kyril is excluded from the services, but there was no mention of him losing his grand ducal title.

Xenia, Diary – 3 October – Ai-Todor
Nikolai telegraphed (in code) that Kyril was married on the 25th and that he arrived in Petersburg on Saturday, but was not received and ordered to return back. His title and monies are all forfeited. Uncle Vladimir [Kyril's father] asked for him to retain his title, but in vain, and so decided to resign from all his own administrative duties. A terrible *péché* [sin], so unsuitable, and only to the advantage of certain persons!

Nicky to Empress Marie – 5 October – Peterhof
Dear sweet Mama
    This week there has been a drama in the family over Kyril's unfortunate marriage. I learned from Nicky [Sandro's brother], that he was married on 25th September in Tegernsee. On Friday during the hunt,

Nicky told me that Kyril was arriving the next day! I have to say that such impudence made me very cross – impudence because he knew very well that he had no right to come *after the wedding*. Wishing to prevent the possibility of Kyril turning up at our house, I sent for Fredericks and told him to go to Tsarskoe Selo and inform Kyril of the four points, as well as of my displeasure at his arrival, and to order him to return abroad immediately.

Nevertheless I was having doubts about punishing a man publicly several times over, and at the present time; when people are generally ill-disposed towards the family. After much reflection, which finally ended in giving me a headache, I decided to use the occasion of your little grandson's nameday, and telegraphed Uncle Vladimir, saying that I was restoring Kyril's title. The other forms of punishment will, of course, remain in force. According to those whose opinion I have sought, these three penalties are sufficient, as long as they remain for a long time!

Ouf! What tiresome, unpleasant days these have been. Now that the whole thing has been decided, it's a weight off my shoulders! It would be interesting to know what Aunt Michen[15] thinks? How she must have hated us!

Goodbye, my dear sweet Mama. I am always with you in my thoughts. I embrace you fondly, also dear Apapa. Christ be with you!

Your Nicky, who loves you deeply with all his heart

KR, Diary – 8 October

Yesterday's Imperial manifesto arrived by telegraph: it guarantees freedom of speech, conscience and association; the right of election to the State Duma is extended to those not included under the manifesto of 6th August. Count Witte is appointed chairman of the Council of Ministers. Laws will be considered as effective only with the approval of the State Duma.

This important news produced a painful impression. It's the end of Russian autocracy. These new freedoms are not an expression of the free will of the sovereign power, but rather concessions wrenched from this power by force.

Xenia, Diary – 14 October – Ai-Todor

All over Russia there are disturbances, strikes, meetings etc.; it's a sor-

---

[15] Maria Pavlovna, Kyril's mother, wife of Grand Duke Vladimir, Nicky's uncle.

row and a disgrace! The mood is oppressive, besides which I feel terribly depressed! In Petersburg, the strongest measures are being taken. Trepov has been appointed, and all the armed forces are under his control. It has been announced that, in the event of street disturbances, the troops will open fire without mercy.

KR, Diary – [no date]

Shortly before 17 October, Nikolasha was summoned to Peterhof, consultations were held, Nikolasha met with a representative of the workers, a certain Ushakov, and became convinced that it was necessary to abandon the autocracy. Count Ignatiev, Goremykin and Court Minister Fredericks tried to convince the Emperor not to give in. Richter pointed to Count Witte as the only man capable of dealing with present situation. On the morning of the 17th, Nikolasha and Fredericks were summoned to Peterhof, together with Count Witte, who presented a draft of the manifesto. The Emperor crossed himself and signed.[16]

Olga [sister], Memoirs

There was such gloom at Tsarskoe Selo. I did not understand anything about politics. I just felt that everything was going wrong with the country and all of us. The October Constitution did not seem to satisfy anyone. I went with my mother to the solemn Te Deum which marked the opening of the first Duma. I remember the large group of deputies from among the peasants and factory people. The peasants looked sullen. But the workmen were worse: they looked as though they hated us. I remember the distress in Alicky's eyes.

Xenia, Diary – 19 October – Abas Tuman

In Petersburg yesterday there were disturbances and even clashes with the troops – there were some victims. Sandro has resigned, that is, has left the post of commander-in-chief, as it would be awkward to stay on now. There have been more demonstrations in Yalta – both good and bad.

There is move towards attacking the Jews, and they say that today many Jews have moved to America. We have been asked not to use

---

[16] The manifesto of 17 October granted liberty of conscience, freedom of the press and of assemblies, and gave legislative rights to the Duma.

the high road (how stupid). Nicky writes: 'Now things have become much easier!' Poor thing, what must he have felt and gone through!

21 October   The railway strikes are continuing. Telegrams are arriving from all over Russia about attacks on the Jews – it's simply terrible, how will it all end.

KR, Diary – 22 October – Tashkent
The railway strikes continue, we haven't been able to leave for five days, and are sitting in Tashkent like captives.

26 October   A certain degree of calm is noticeable, if not in the borderlands, then in the native Russian towns. My companions and I support the autocratic principle, and entertain the hope that, if a large number of peasant representatives are returned to the State Duma, then it may still be possible to return to the autocratic model, which undoubtedly has the support of our peasant masses. This would be quite unheard of in the history of counter-revolution. But one very much wants to believe it could happen.

Rasputin to the Emperor Nicholas II – Telegram
LITTLE FATHER TSAR!
HAVING ARRIVED IN TOWN FROM SIBERIA, I WOULD LIKE TO BRING YOU AN ICON OF THE BLESSED ST SIMON VERKHOTURSKY THE MIRACLE-WORKER, WHO IS SO REVERED AMONG US; WITH FAITH THAT THE HOLY SAINT WILL PRESERVE YOU FOR ALL THE DAYS OF YOUR LIFE AND HELP YOU IN YOUR SERVICE FOR THE GOOD AND HAPPINESS OF YOUR DEVOTED SONS.

Nicky, Diary – 1 November – Peterhof
At four o'clock we went to Sergevka. We had tea with Militsa and Stana. We made the acquaintance of a man of God – Grigory,[17] from the Tobolsk region.

KR, Diary – 3 November
Rebellion is gaining the whole of Russia; and even if some measure of calm is gradually being restored, the times remain very worrying!

---

[17] The first reference to Rasputin in Nicky's diary.

2 December   There is a mood of alarm throughout Russia; the atmosphere is heavy and stifling, as if before a storm. The Duma keeps being postponed, yet everyone looks to it for salvation. But might the storm not break sooner than expected? And from which cloud? Will there be a revolt, or will it be forestalled by a dictatorship? It's terrifying.

8 December   The revolutionaries have discarded their masks and are openly calling for revolt. In Moscow they have published a manifesto and declared a general strike.

Xenia, Diary – 10 December – Ai-Todor
Something terrible is about to happen in Moscow, there are barricades on the streets, and clashes between armed units and the troops. All the railroads in Moscow are on strike!

KR, Diary – 11 December
In Moscow there is an armed struggle, barricades, the revolutionaries are supported by armed brigades, the government by the troops. Surely the climax must be near?

14 December   In Moscow the troops are doggedly fighting the revolutionaries, who keep building barricades first in one place, then another. They are trying to annihilate them with machine guns and artillery.

17 December   In Moscow calm has not yet been completely restored, but the troops appear to have gained the upper hand over the insurgents.

22 December   I was very disturbed by a letter from Captain Sosnitsky, who embezzled up to 3 thousand roubles from a military school fund, and having not returned the money, was dismissed from the service.

In justification, he writes that no one is free from sin 'even you yourself'; he continues that once during the summer of 1903 I arrived at the camp in the evening during his tour of duty, and from there went to the Krasnoe Selo baths. 'What happened there, you will of course remember,' writes Sosnitsky.

The next day, coming off duty, he went to the baths, and heard from the attendant who looked after me, that we did something together and that I gave him 20 roubles. Sosnitsky says he will keep it a secret for the time being, but if it should ever appear in print, it would hardly be proper for me to remain in my post. The incident in the baths that Sosnitsky alludes to is not true.

I remember that evening very well – I did indeed go to the baths, but never gave 20 roubles to the attendant, indeed there was no cause. However it's only untrue in relation to the occasion in question. What's frightening is that there were other occasions.

I did not receive Sosnitsky yesterday, nor will I receive him; I will not take any precautions, what will be will be. Do I not deserve to be punished?

Xenia, Diary – 31 December – Ai-Todor
What will the New Year bring us? May God bless it, send us peace and help poor Russia, and let us hold on to our happiness!

1906–1907

Nicky – Emperor of Russia

Alix – Empress of Russia

Xenia – Grand Duchess, Nicky's sister, married to Sandro

KR – Grand Duke Konstantin Romanov, Nicky's cousin

Maria Pavlovna (the younger) – daughter of Nicky's uncle, Grand Duke Pavel

Georgie – George, Duke of York

Willy – Kaiser Wilhelm II of Germany, Nicky's cousin

Pierre Gilliard – Swiss tutor of Nicky and Alix's children

Tatiana– second daughter of Nicky and Alix

Grand Duke Pavel – Nicky's uncle, morganatically married to Olga Pistolkors, later Princess Paley

Ania Vyrubova, lady-in-waiting and intimate friend of Alix

1906

FIGHTING THE DUMA

The Heir meets his tutor – Nicky opens the Duma and makes a conciliatory speech – The Duma is seen as a nest of revolution – KR's baby is christened – An attempt on the life of Prime Minister Stolypin – Fears of assassination abound – Nicky asks Stolypin to receive Rasputin – The family are horrified at the news that Stana and Nikolasha are to marry

Tatiana to Alix – Tsarskoe Selo
My Darling Mama!
  I thank you 100 times for your dear letter which I was very pleased to get it. How funny it is that Olga and Anastasia lunch in your bedroom. Now we will go to bed and rest a little bit. I kiss you and Papa 100000000 times but I can't count it myself.

                                                                                        Tatiana

Pierre Gilliard, Memoirs
The Imperial family used regularly to spend the winter at Tsarskoe Selo, a pretty little country town some thirteen miles south of St Petersburg. It stands on a hill at the top of which is the Great Palace, a favourite residence of Catherine II. Not far away is a much more modest building, the Alexander Palace, half hidden in trees of a park studded with little artificial lakes. The Tsar Nicholas II had made it one of his regular residences ever since the tragic events of January, 1905.
  The Tsar and Tsarina occupied the ground floor of one wing and

their children the floor above. The central block comprised state apartments and the other wing was occupied by certain members of the suite.

It was there that I saw the Tsarevich, Alexei Nikolaevich, then a baby of eighteen months old, for the first time, and under the following circumstances. As usual, I had gone that day to the Alexander Palace, where my duties called me several times a week. I was just finishing my lesson with Olga Nicolaevna when the Tsarina entered the room, carrying the son and heir. She came towards us, and evidently wished to show the one member of the family I did not yet know. I could see she was transfused by the delirious joy of a mother who at last has seen her dearest wish fulfilled. She was proud and happy in the beauty of her child. The Tsarevich was certainly one of the handsomest babies one could imagine, with his lovely fair curls and his great blue-grey eyes under their fringe of long curling lashes. He had the fresh pink colour of a healthy child, and when he smiled there were two little dimples in his chubby cheeks. When I went near him a solemn, frightened look came into his eyes, and it took a great deal to induce him to hold out a tiny hand.

At that first meeting I saw the Tsarina press the little boy to her with the convulsive movement of a mother who always seems in fear of her child's life. Yet with her the caress and the look which accompanied it revealed a secret apprehension so marked and poignant that I was struck at once. I had not very long to wait to know its meaning.

Xenia, Diary – 30 January – St Petersburg

Aprak came, we chatted a lot, she was glad to see me, as I was her. God only knows what happened, what we have lived through during the past five months, what haven't we seen. I told her everything that happened here, what they are saying – it's terrible how little confidence there is in Witte!

We went to have tea with Nicky and Alix. Little Alexei has grown remarkably, is running around and very sweet. Alix needled me about the Crimea and the so-called panic we had, when we were ready to flee abroad on the yacht! When I talked of all the horrors we have lived through, she said: 'Only those who were there, really know what it was ...' After that I was silent and my head started to ache.

29 March   Nicky and Alix came to tea with all the children. The little one is delightful. He occasionally says: hourrah!

5 April Misha is looking sombre, while Mama keeps scolding him about not doing enough and letting himself go in Tsarskoe, despite everything that has been said!!

KR, Diary – 19 April
The Emperor is to read a speech from the throne. Alix has said that, in planning the ceremonial, she has tried to avoid imitating western models, and to remain in keeping with Russian customs, but I very much doubt whether she is that familiar with these customs, and anyway how to adapt them to a parliament?

21 April When planning the ceremonial for the opening of the Duma, the Empress wanted to arrive by yacht right up to the Winter Palace. But this was discarded because of the possibility of bad weather, which would be very awkward for the ladies in Russian costume.

   Then the question arose of how the Emperor should appear at the opening, should he wear the crown and purple mantle? Fredericks[1] was proposing to see Count Pahlen after me, to consult with him.

Xenia, Diary – 24 April – Gatchina
We had a chat with Misha. In general, his mood is depressed, he never talks to us about anything other than the question that interests him, or something similar, otherwise he is not interested.

26 April Sandro and I went to town. Mama wanted to come tomorrow by train, but later Misha telephoned to say that Trepov had begged Mama (a bit late!) to come to Peterhof, in order to go with Nicky and Alix by sea, and to return the same way. Mama is presumably not very pleased (and with reason – it was very late to ask such a thing!) but will probably comply, which is of course sensible.

27 April – St Petersburg A day full of emotions!! And hopes for a better future!! Thank God, everything went off splendidly and with great solemnity – just as it should.

   Mama got dressed upstairs, while Olga sat with us. Then we went to Nicky and Alix. The family were waiting in her rooms. The procession began at a quarter to two. Nicky walked alone, the crown and

---

[1] Minister of Court.

regalia were carried in front of him. In the armoury hall there were many society ladies and a large crowd of other people. From there the grand duchesses went through the Romanov gallery into the St George hall, where we took our places on a platform to the right of the throne. We were joined by the ladies-in-waiting, Mama, Alix and the duty guard. The Te Deum had already begun.

Directly opposite us were the members of the Council of State and high officials, to the left the members of the Duma, who included several men with repulsive faces and insolent disdainful expressions! They neither crossed themselves nor bowed, but stood with their hands behind their backs or in their pockets, looking sombrely at everyone and everything.

But among the peasants there were such wonderful faces, as well as several soldiers from the St George cavalry, the cossacks etc. After the Te Deum (celebrated by Antony, the choice of reading for the Lesson was very tendentious for such an occasion – the words of the Saviour: Ask and ye shall be given! etc) Mama and Alix stood in front of us on the platform, with the grand dukes next to us on the steps of the throne – then Nicky mounted the steps and sat on the throne.

He did this with such simplicity, yet at the same time it was such a solemn moment! After this Fredericks handed him the speech, which he read standing, in a loud steady voice. Every word penetrated the soul – tears welled up in the throat.

We all experienced an indescribable emotion, it's difficult to convey what we felt. It was a great historic moment, unforgettable for those who witnessed it. He spoke so well, saying just what was needed, asking everyone to come to his aid. When he finished, a cheer broke out, which was taken up by everyone including in the other halls – it sounded magnificent. The choir sang the anthem (it was all terribly emotional!)

Mama and Alix were crying and poor Nicky was standing there in tears – his self control finally overcome, he could not hold back his tears!

We returned with Nicky and Alix to Peterhof. The public gave us a warm welcome as we walked along the embankment with Nicky, Mama, and Alix to get into our carriages. There was a huge cheer. Some man, standing on a pedestal, shouted in a loud voice: 'Thank you, your Majesty.' Children and adults were standing on the balconies and at the windows of the Winter palace, also cheering, waving their handkerchiefs, greeting us!

We sat upstairs having tea, exchanging impressions and rejoicing that everything went off so well, and most of all that the day was over! Nicky was delighted that he would at last be able to sleep properly – last night he couldn't sleep – he kept lying there, waking every few minutes with a feeling of sadness and melancholy in his heart!

28 April   Yesterday's ceremony made a huge impression on many people – they were not expecting such majesty. Nicky spoke so well, his firm voice and his control impressed everyone, at last they feel that *he is someone!*

30 April   The Duma is such filth, such a nest of revolutionaries, that it's disgusting and shaming for the rest of Russia in front of the whole world!

Nicky, Diary – 30 April
It became cold. At 11 o'clock we went to church. At 1.30 we went to Tsarskoe with the four girls, Maria and Dmitri. From the station we went to Pavlovsk to the christening of little Vera Konstantinova [KR's daughter]. After the service there was a magnificent tea, which the family threw themselves upon hungrily. At 5 o'clock we arrived at the Alexander Palace, changed and went to the children's island. We picked a mass of lily of the valley.

KR, Diary – 5 May
The Duma's answer to the throne speech is – filth. The Duma is a hearth of revolution.

Maria Pavlovna [the younger], Memoirs
About three miles from Tsarskoe Selo was Pavlovsk, the seat of the Grand Duke Konstantin [KR]. No unfortunate improvements had marred this eighteenth-century masterpiece and it remained exactly as it had been when it belonged to Tsar Paul I.

The Grand Duke was a most cultured man, a musician, a poet and an actor. Many people still remember his talented performance in one of his own dramas, *The King of Judea*.

Xenia, Diary – 22 May – St Petersburg
On Saturday Gurko[2] spoke in the Duma on the agrarian question, he

---

[2] The First Deputy of the Minister of the Interior.

spoke well and calmly, but was received coldly. When he had finished, they called on Gertzenstein – a Jew! – to answer! How sad, that among all those deputies, they couldn't find anyone else but a Jew to answer.

28 May   Sandro and I sat at home, and then with Mama – we talked the whole time about Misha! Mama is more against it than ever.

KR, Diary – 28 July
People of a particularly monarchist inclination are awaiting the dissolution of the Duma, dictatorship, severe measures, executions, violence, terror in answer to terror. Others, and I count myself among them, consider that it's better not to touch the Duma and to let it discredit itself in public opinion.

Xenia, Diary – 12 August – Gatchina
There has been a nightmarish attempt on the life of poor Stolypin[3] – but neither he, nor his wife, were hurt. Some men in policemen's uniforms came to his villa during a reception. It appears one of them got inside the house and there was immediately a terrible explosion. Part of the ground and first floor collapsed and were blown to splinters, and all the people in the front hall were killed or wounded. His children, his fourteen-year-old daughter and three-year-old son, who were upstairs, fell as the floor collapsed, both her legs were broken and her life is in danger, the boy has a fractured hip! Poor children – what for? About 60 people were killed or wounded. Many of the injured died soon afterwards. Among the dead are: General Zamiatin, who served various ministers of the Interior over many years, and Governor Khvostov, the husband of Unkovskaya, who has an enormous family! The poor old doorman was killed. What a horror!

Nicky, Diary – 12 August
Heard about the explosion in Stolypin's house, thank God he was not hurt, but his son and daughter have been injured. A lot of people killed and wounded, half the house destroyed.

---

[3] Both Prime Minister and Minister of Interior (1906–11).

Xenia to Nicky – 4 September – Gatchina

There is so much I would like to tell you, but I can't write everything. How many terrible events have happened since we last saw each other, how much has poor Russia had to live through, as have we all – it's simply not bearable! And the future seems so cheerless! But one mustn't lose heart – one wants to believe that the Lord will not abandon us!

Xenia, Diary – 5 September

Nikolai [Mikhailovich] told us by telephone that the cavalry parade did not take place. The regiment was already getting impatient, and when they learnt that Nicky was not coming it was too late to change plans. It seems Stolypin telegraphed Nicky, begging him not to come, as they had uncovered a hellish plot. Three cars were to have driven up during the parade and thrown bombs! You can't even comprehend such a nightmare. Of course, they have all disappeared, and until now no trace of them has been found. Aren't our police wonderful!

Nicky to Stolypin – 16 October – Peterhof

Pyotr Arkadievich!

A few days ago I received a peasant from the Tobolsk district, Grigory Rasputin, who brought me an icon of St Simon Verkhotursky. He made a remarkably strong impression both on her Majesty and on myself, so that instead of five minutes our conversation went on for more than an hour. He will soon be returning home. He has a strong desire to see you and to bless your injured daughter with an icon. I very much hope that you will find a minute to receive him this week.

This is his address: St Petersburg 2, Roszdestvenskaya, 4. He is staying with the priest Yaroslav Medved.

Xenia, Diary – 3 November – Biarritz

Nikolai [Mikhailovich] told us the most unbelievable news, that Yury and Stana are to divorce, and that she wants to marry Nikolasha.[4] He saw Yury in Paris, who told him himself. How awful, what disgusting nonsense!

---

[4] Nic-Nic, Grand Duke Nikolai Nikolaevich.

KR, Diary – 6 November
I learned with horror from my wife, who was at the Hussar celebration, that Stana is divorcing Yury and is going to marry Nikolasha!!! Authorization of this marriage can only be seen as connivance, due to Nikolasha's closeness to the Emperor, and that of Stana to the young Empress; it breaks all church convention, which forbids first cousins to marry. Kyril was not allowed to marry Ducky, because they were first cousins, nor was Misha allowed to marry Beatrice. Stana is Nikolasha's first cousin, if not by birth, then by virtue of her first marriage. In these dark times, divorce in the family is something inauspicious and deplorable.

10 November   According to Andrusha,[5] Nikolasha is declaring that he hasn't lifted a finger to bring about his marriage, that it was inspired from above, that it would have been impossible without Philippe's influence from beyond the grave. Andrusha has heard from Stana's step-son Sandro, that apparently neither she, nor Nikolasha are particularly drawn to each other. Others maintain that she is deeply in love.

Kaiser Wilhelm II to Nicky – 18 November
Dearest Nicky,
   We had capital sport today. We killed 4600 pheasants and I brought down 1001! With 1184 shots! Best love to Alix and the boy.
                                                                Willy

Nicky, Diary – 19 December – Tsarskoe Selo
Read until 8. Stana and Militsa came to dinner, and spent the whole evening telling us about Grigory [Rasputin].

---

[5] Grand Duke Andrei Vladimirovich.

1907

NOTHING BUT TROUBLES

Misha still hopes to marry Dina – Ania Taneeva marries
Vyrubov – The second Duma – Demonstrations in the
streets – Maria Pavlovna (the younger) is to marry
Swedish Prince Wilhelm – Grand Duke Pavel refuses to
come to the wedding without his wife – The second
Duma is dissolved – Misha and Dina are prevented from
marrying – Kyril's marriage is recognized – The third
Duma opens

Nicky, Diary – 4 February – Tsarskoe Selo
Ania Taneeva presented her future husband – Vyrubov.[1] Was success-
ful in my reading, in that I finished everything that had piled up.
Went for a drive after dinner and played billiards.

Ania Vyrubova, Memoirs
It was about a month before my marriage in 1907 that the Empress
asked Militsa, Grand Duchess Pyotr, to make me acquainted with
Rasputin. I had heard that the Grand Duchess was very clever and
well read, and I was glad of the opportunity of meeting her in her
palace on the English Quay in Petrograd. Interesting as I found her,
I was nevertheless thrilled with excitement when a servant
announced the arrival of Rasputin. Before his entrance the Grand
Duchess said to me: 'Do not be astonished if I greet him peasant fash-

---

[1] Ania Taneeva, lady-in-waiting to Alix, and an intimate friend, who would be an
intermediary with Rasputin. Her father was a director of the Imperial Chancery, her
husband a naval officer, Boris Vyrubov.

ion,' that is, with three kisses on the cheek. She did so greet him and then she presented us to each other. I saw an elderly peasant, thin, with a pale face, long hair, an uncared-for beard, and the most extraordinary eyes, large, light, brilliant, and apparently capable of seeing into the very mind and soul of the person with whom he held converse. He wore a long peasant coat, black and rather shabby from hard wear and much travel. We talked and the Grand Duchess, speaking in French, bade me ask him to pray for some special desire of mine. Timidly I begged him to pray that God would permit me to spend my whole life serving their Majesties. To this he replied: 'Your whole life will be thus spent.'

KR, Diary – 21 February
On the streets near the Tauride palace [where the Duma resided] there were throngs of people, walking up and down with red flags and singing revolutionary songs, but they were soon dispersed. In general, the opening of the second Duma has gone off more quietly than was expected.

Xenia, Diary – 21 April – Gatchina
The children were romping around downstairs during tea. Little Alexei is remarkably sweet, but spoilt.

29 April The wedding of Nikolasha and Stana takes place today in Livadia. They even found somewhere to get married! Sandro absolutely refused to send a telegram.

Nicky, Diary – 30 April – Tsarskoe Selo
At night it rained, there was a storm all day. We left for the palace before 3 o'clock. Ania [Vyrubova] was upstairs dressing for her wedding. We blessed her and then went to the church. After the ceremony everyone congratulated the newly-weds in the church hall. We returned home at 4.30. I ran into the garden. Ania and her husband had tea with us. Received Stolypin. Played billiards with Dmitri.

Xenia, Diary – 30 April – St Petersburg
Yesterday's wedding took place in the little Livadia church, and was attended by a large number of guests and officials, afterwards there

was a huge lunch! Mama is beside herself – and so upset that she had to take tranquillizing drops.

She even wrote a letter to Nicky, and got it all off her chest by expressing her displeasure and her surprise!

Pavel to Nicky – 12 May – Paris
Dear Nicky,

I am answering your second telegram by letter. Your words that a conversation on a matter that concerns me personally will take place 'only after Maria's marriage' – force me to inform you at once that I cannot come. Let everyone know why, for what reason the father will not be present at either the engagement or the wedding of his daughter.[2] I was willing to be understanding at the beginning and patiently endured everything, but after five years of exemplary family life I have the right to expect a different attitude towards us both.

Could you really think that I would leave my wife alone, she whom everyone here loves and respects, may God grant to everyone a position such as hers, while I myself participate in the wedding celebrations? I did not make the break and sacrifice everything to let her then be humiliated and insulted without reason. If she cannot take the place which belongs to her by virtue of our morganatic marriage, a marriage recognized by you in decrees to the Senate and the Minister of Court, then I can also not be present – this is my unshakeable decision. Can you only tell me why she may not come to Russia and what Maria's marriage has to do with it?

If it's because she has been divorced, or rather she divorced because of me, then Nikolasha's recent marriage, to which you gave your permission and blessing, has once and for all broken all the existing impediments in this respect. I know in your heart you are just and kind and that you realize I am right.

Furthermore, this is not the only reason I am denied the possibility of giving my blessing to my daughter Maria. I cannot attend the wedding as long as this shameful wardship is in force. To be officially on the side lines in the presence of all the foreign princes who will be coming to my daughter's wedding – the very idea is unbearable.

As for the Swedish prince, what can I say about him? I do not know him. As the children are wards, the father doesn't have the opportunity of either meeting the fiancé or pronouncing himself for or

---

[2] Maria Pavlovna (the younger), Pavel's daughter, had announced her engagement to Wilhelm, second son of Gustav, King of Sweden.

against, or expressing his opinion that a girl of seventeen is too young to be given away in marriage. The wardship has decided so many questions without me that in reality the children have been distanced from me to the utmost possible degree. And all this because of the severe attitude you and Alix have towards me. I have suffered greatly, yet continued to hope that in the end, seeing how we live, you would understand and forgive me. Alas! I was bitterly mistaken. It's terribly painful to write all this to you, whom I love as fondly as before, but you will feel the truth echoed in my every word! May God keep you in these grave and turbulent times!

Your sincerely devoted

Pavel

Nicky, Diary – 22 May – Tsarskoe Selo

At 9 o'clock went riding with Dmitri. It was raining at first, then the weather improved and it became hot.

Returned home at 1 o'clock and learned at lunch that poor Anastasia has diphtheria. It was immediately decided that I would move to the farm with the other children, while Alix would stay with her. What a time to be separated, during such worrying days!

The move was completed quite quickly, and the children were in bed on time. I settled into my former dressing room, next to them upstairs. In the evening Alix arrived with reassuring news. The first inoculation was carried out at one in the afternoon.

In the evening I walked with her back to our house, and returned to the farm at 11 o'clock.

27 May A wonderful hot day. In the morning I saw Anastasia through the window. After church, the second son of Gustav of Sweden arrived – Wilhelm, the future husband of Maria Pavlovna. He lunched with us. I took him to the Gothic house, where he is staying.

Strolled and sat with Alix, saw Ania Vyrubova. Then Ella and Victoria brought the young Swede to see Alix. They had tea with us at the farm, and there was a thunderstorm. Received Stolypin. We dined together on the balcony.

KR, Diary – 28 May

Tatiana [KR's daughter] came running to me, very agitated and with tears in her eyes, and whispered in my ear, so her brothers wouldn't hear, that her friend and contemporary Maria P[avlovna] is engaged. Maria wrote to her from Peterhof that her fiancé is the Swedish prince, the second son of the Heir, so Maria, who is three months younger than our Tatiana, is going to be married. The wedding will only take place in a year's time. Let it now be our daughter's turn. But I somehow wouldn't want to let her go abroad. What about Misha?!

Xenia, Diary – 2 June

Uncle Pavel has been absent the whole time. At first, he intended to come for his daughter's engagement – but he put the condition that he would not come without his wife – which was refused; then he wrote that he was not coming, and sent an official reply to the groom's letter, asking for his daughter's hand, saying that as she had a guardian (appointed without his knowledge or consent) he was not in a position to say anything, and signed the letter Grand Duke Paul!

What incredible heartlessness! I feel so sorry for poor Maria – he's spoilt everything for her!

KR, Diary – 3 June

This afternoon they published the manifesto about the dissolution of the Duma and the convening of a new one on the 1st November this year, and most importantly about the changing of the voting laws.

So – it's a coup-d'état. In truth the Russian people can now breathe more easily.

Nicky, Diary – 3 June – Tsarskoe Selo

The weather was wonderful. Our mood was just as luminous following the dissolution of the Duma. Spent the morning with Alix. Went to church, then we lunched to music. At 2.15 went with the children to the landing stage, where we boarded the *Tsarevna* with Victoria, Maria, Dmitri and Wilhelm, to watch the motor launch races.

We returned to the farm at 6 o'clock, having stopped off at our house to talk to Alix. We played tennis. In the evening I strolled with Alix.

4 June Another wonderful day. Sat with Alix in the morning. Thank God, it's already the second day after the dissolution of the Duma, and it's completely calm everywhere.

KR, Diary – 10 June
Nikolasha's marriage gives no peace to Sandro and Georgy, who are staying with Empress Marie. We do not, of course, approve of the marriage, although we have long since resigned ourselves to it.

Olia [KR's sister] found out that, at the Emperor's command, Nikolasha's income, as an Emperor's grandson, has been raised to that of an Emperor's son. Now what was the reason, and is it fair?

Alix to Nicky – 17 July – Peterhof
My own beloved One,

You will find this note when you are on your way already. God bless and keep you, my own sweetest Treasure and bring you safely back to me and your little Ones. I know how deeply you will feel the separation from baby sweet – and he too will be lonely without his darling Papa.

It's not easy letting you go – I do not like bidding you goodbye, my Own One tho' distance makes nothing really, when one loves. The souls and hearts are together and nothing can part them ever. I am glad you have those nice boys on board to remind you of last year – to see fresh faces and hear others talk will rest you, I have no doubt. I so hope everything will go smoothly and with no hitches or unpleasant talks – Gr[igory] watches over this journey and all will be well.

So sad that we were not together alone today – my stupid neck and then people. Lovy mine I shall look after your Sunbeam and guard him for you carefully.

Goodbye my husband, my One and all. Holy Angels hover around you. God's blessing be upon you. Tenderly and fondly with an aching heart – I kiss you – every sweet little spot I love so passionately. For ever your very own

Wify

Nicky to Alix – 20 July – Royal yacht *Standart*
My own beloved Darling,

I thank you from all my heart for your sweet letter. It touched me deeply, I read it before going to bed and it did me such good. I feel quite lonely by myself down in the cabins. The doors to yours are open and I look into them often, always thinking I will find my Wify. I miss you and the children frightfully, so do all the officers!

Yesterday the weather was lovely till the night, the sea was a looking-glass ... about 2 in the night we came into the Baltic and then we rolled rather strongly. I could not get to sleep for a long time, it reminded me so of that night in the North Sea before Dunkirk. Those hours I was pleased you were not on board. We slackened speed until the morning when it became quieter – then we again went quicker. When I came on deck I saw that all my gentlemen were gay and well.

After luncheon it began again to be rough, but now everyone is accustomed to the rolling. Lots of the young sailors were sick, but not the singer boys. I walk much on deck and have long talks with each separately. At table, Fredericks sits at your place and Izvolsky[3] on my left. The latter tells me lots of interesting things. I send occasional winks to the boys at the other end and see broad smiles in answer. The sky is grey over the sea with its white crested waves. I do hope the weather will get fine for the meeting. This afternoon's colder than it was in our home waters.

Sweetie, dear, how I miss you and the children!

KR, Diary – 23 July – Gatchina

I was in town and saw Olia, who came back from Gatchina at one o'clock and returned there again in the evening. Her presence was needed there in view of the dramas going on in the family. It seems that Misha (the former Heir) has been in love for two years with his sister Olga's lady-in-waiting Dina Kossikovskaya (the daughter of the one who played the queen with me in *Hamlet* at the Hermitage theatre; Dina herself and her late sister played court ladies). This love is mutual. Petia and Olga only noticed it too late and were not able to discern when friendship turned into love. Now they are afraid that Misha has decided to get married.

He is being sent to Karlsbad and is leaving on 28th July. Olia learned that on the evening of the 22nd, Misha was at Gatchina at the Warsaw road station, where he saw Kossikovskaya, who was leaving the country. We are afraid that Misha has arranged to get married somewhere abroad on the 30th or 31st. What harm our family does to itself, and how it undermines the Emperor and the ruling house! The further we go, the worse it gets.

On the 15th July, 'acceding to the request of Vladimir', as it was put in the Senate *ukaz*, the Emperor recognized Kyril's wedding; his wife [Ducky] is to be known as the Grand Duchess Victoria, and their daughter recognized as a princess of the imperial blood.

---

[3] Minister of Foreign Affairs (1906–10).

How strange it all is! What does it have to do with Vladimir's request? How can that request legitimize that, which is not legal? After all, Kyril married his first cousin, which is not allowed by the church. It's even stranger since before, Kyril's wife was known as the Princess Kyrillovsky, signifying that she was a person, with whom Kyril had entered into a morganatic marriage. Kyril refused that title and insisted on his own. His wife is now a grand duchess.

Where do we have a strong authority, acting with reflection and continuity? One becomes more and more fearful for the future. Everywhere is arbitrary rule, indulgence, weakness.

Xenia, Diary – 14 August – Gatchina

At around 5 o'clock we went to see Alix. She was alone at home, we had tea together (she had not gone to Kronstadt because of a heavy cold). The children were romping around energetically, little Alexei was playing up, getting cross with his sisters, but they were also partly to blame!

Pavel to Nicky – 27 October – Paris

Dear Nicky,

Yesterday Alexei informed me about your gracious permission for me to come to Petersburg together with my wife, for which I beg you to accept my most heartfelt gratitude. As Alexei has already written to you, please, could you kindly arrange that by November 10, my children arrive from Moscow to Tsarskoe, where I shall be coming to visit them from Petersburg.

Again I thank you fervently and remain faithfully yours,

Pavel

George, Duke of York to Nicky – 15 December – Sandringham

My dear Nicky,

I trust now that your new Duma will work better than the last two and that the country will gradually quiet down and give you less trouble and anxiety than it has during these last few years.

What do you say to Georgie [of Greece] at last being married,[4] now all the members of *the* Club are married. Your devoted cousin and friend

Georgie

---

[4] To Marie Bonaparte. Their son Andrew was the father of Prince Philip, husband to Queen Elizabeth II.

Alix to Tatiana [daughter] – 30 December – Tsarskoe Selo
My darling Tatiana,

Very tender thanks for your dear little letter. Yes, I am sorry to say that there were terrible mistakes in this letter, yet more than in others. Try to be more attentive and think nicely before spelling a word.

Such a joy to know that you have all normal temp: I have 36.7 last night 37.5 and a headache. I hear Papa walking upstairs – it is lucky he can see you and give me news of you all. I have got such a collection of letters from you all now. Shall give Ania your kisses. She has gone to town for church and lunches with her Parents.

Doctor just made an injection again – today in the right leg. Today it is the 49th day that I am ill, tomorrow begins the 8th week.

Tell Baby sweet that Mama kisses him very, very tenderly and wants him to get quickly well again. It is so sad seeing none of you dears, tho' today Anastasia may come down.

Dear Children,

Two big kisses for your very nice letter – Olga is reading it now and laughing over it. I lay in the dark a long time – then Auntie came. Papa has returned. Glad you had tea together.

Alix to Maria [daughter] – 30 December
My darling little cherie,

I hope you will be able to read this letter all alone, tho' it is in English. Many thanks for your nice letter.

I am delighted that you are all so much better. God grant I shall soon see you all again. I am going to have quite a party in my bedroom for luncheon – Papa, Olga and Anastasia. Is it not grand?

My headache has quite passed, but the head still feels rather tired. Now I must read the Bible and prayers as I do not go to Church. I hope you and Tatiana do so too.

Very fondest kisses my little girly dear, from your loving old Mama. God bless you.

1908–1909

Nicky – Emperor of Russia

Alix – Empress of Russia

Xenia – Grand Duchess, Nicky's sister, married to Sandro

Sandro – Grand Duke Alexander Mikhailovich, husband of Xenia

KR – Grand Duke Konstantin Romanov, Nicky's cousin

Olga (sister) – Grand Duchess, Nicky's younger sister

Olga – eldest daughter of Nicky and Alix, aged thirteen

Tatiana – second daughter of Nicky and Alix, aged eleven

Prince Felix Yusupov

Pierre Gilliard – Swiss tutor of Nicky and Alix's children

Grigory Rasputin – a Siberian holy man

N. P. Sabline – officer on imperial yacht *Standart*

1908

FAMILY LIFE I

Sandro's brother Mikhail has written a book – Xenia is in France – F. is in love with her; Sandro is very taken with F.'s wife – On the train they confess to each other – Back in Russia, there are rumours they are to divorce – Alix and Nicky often see Grigory Rasputin – Grand Duke Alexei dies

Xenia, Diary – 3 May – Biarritz
I read Misha's idiotic book *Never Say Die.*[1] It's unbelievable and disgusting how he describes his life before his marriage!

Sandro, Memoirs
My second brother, Mikhail Mikhailovich, had none of Nikolai Mikhailovich's talents. He adored the military service and enjoyed himself immensely in the Egersky Regiment of the Guards. His good looks, generous heart and dancing ability endeared him to St Petersburg society, and very soon 'Miche-Miche' became a recognized favourite in the capital. Unfortunately he was a marrying man. At the age of twenty, immediately after coming into possession of his money, he started building a luxurious palace. 'We must have a decent place to live in,' he told his architects. 'We' meant him and his future wife. He did not know as yet whom he was going to marry but he wanted to marry someone as soon as possible.

In constant search for the 'girl of his dreams' he made several

---

[1] The book Grand Duke Mikhail Mikhailovich [Miche-Miche] wrote in England about his exile and his love story.

attempts at marrying outside of the ranks of royalty. It created painful scenes between him and our parents and it led nowhere. Finally he concluded a morganatic marriage with a daughter of the Duke of Nassau whose maternal grandfather was the celebrated Russian poet Pushkin. That put an end to Miche-Miche's elaborate plans of lavish entertainments in the beautiful brand-new palace. He was asked to leave Russia and remained the rest of his life in London.

Xenia, Diary – 15 June – Paris
I drove to Fontainebleau with F.[2] We went by another road part of the way – and had tea in a little restaurant in the forest, I can't remember the name, but it was very clean and simple. We had such a good nice heart-to-heart talk I feel so terribly sorry for him – he loves me so much, it will be so painful for him to part from me. I'm so sad that it all happened, so sad for him. He keeps saying: 'You are the love of my life', and I feel that it's true!

16 June   There was so much we wanted to say to each other, but we were unable to speak, it was all so sad! Our train was leaving at 1.50 and we arrived with 5 minutes to spare. I drove with F. again, Sandro with her[3] – and we said goodbye in the motor. They did not come to see us off – we had all decided that it was better that way – it was terrible. It was so terribly sad, there simply aren't words. We managed to control ourselves.

In the compartment, we gave vent to our feelings and both cried! It was terribly sad! We talked openly and admitted everything to each other – my dear little husband forgave me everything, but confessed his own feelings for her. It's all so complicated, she and I were such friends, and yet we really loved each other.

Felix Yusupov, Memoirs
The Grand Duke Alexander was 'tall, dark and handsome', with a strong personality. His marriage to the Grand Duchess Xenia, the Tsar's eldest sister, was a departure from the time-honoured tradition by which members of the imperial Family married foreigners.

---

[2] F. – Xenia's admirer, possibly a Russian prince.
[3] The wife of 'F'.

Sandro, Memoirs

I knew my new attitude toward life was bound to disturb my happiness but I did not care. Nothing made any difference so long as Russia and ourselves seemed to be going to the devil.

Xenia, Diary – 24 June – Gatchina

Here they have decided that Sandro and I are divorcing! When I asked what it was all about, I was told that it was nothing, but there had been rumours from abroad – *ce soit de son flirt avec F.* ['to do with the flirtation with F']. Olga had also heard something.

Nicky, Diary – 4 August – Peterhof

Arrived at Peterhof at 6.30. At that time Alix was talking to Grigory [Rasputin], whom I also saw for half an hour!

Xenia, Diary – 7 September

... Afterwards we went to see Nicky and Alix. Alix was in the garden, quite far from the house, with Olga, Tatiana and the unchanging A. Vyrubova! She spends the whole day there, lying on a mattress on the ground! She was in good spirits, saying she was sleeping quite well, and looks better than last time. She complained of pains inside her back and legs, occasionally winced and moved slightly, then at other times seemed to forget everything and climbed without difficulty up to the bench on the hill.

She plays an increasingly important role in everything.

Nicky passed by and we all returned to the house and had tea on the balcony downstairs. Nicky is happy and contented.

Rasputin to Maria [Nicky and Alix's daughter] – Telegram

MY DEAR PEARL M! TELL ME HOW YOU TALKED WITH THE SEA, WITH NATURE! I MISS YOUR SIMPLE SOUL. WE WILL SEE EACH OTHER SOON! A BIG KISS.

MY DEAR M! MY LITTLE FRIEND! MAY THE LORD HELP YOU TO CARRY YOUR CROSS WITH WISDOM AND JOY IN CHRIST. THIS WORLD IS LIKE THE DAY, LOOK IT'S ALREADY EVENING. SO IT IS WITH THE CARES OF THE WORLD.

Pierre Gilliard, Memoirs

Maria was a fine girl, tall for her age, and a picture of glowing health and colour. She had large and beautiful grey eyes. Her tastes were very simple, and with her warm heart she was kindness itself. Her sisters took advantage somewhat of her good nature, and called her 'fat little bow-wow'. She certainly had the benevolent and somewhat *gauche* devotion of a dog.

Nicky, Diary – 1 November – Tsarskoe Selo
In the morning received the sad news from Paris of dear uncle Alexei's death, from lobar pneumonia, which lasted 6 days. My favourite uncle is dead, a noble, honourable, courageous soul! May the Kingdom of Heaven be his!

Sandro, Memoirs
Uncle Alexei, Grand Duke Alexei Alexandrovich, was admitted to be the best-looking man in the imperial family, although I am afraid his tremendous weight would have handicapped him with the modern girls. A man of the world to his finger tips, a Beau Brummell and a bon vivant hopelessly spoiled by women, particularly by those of Washington, D.C., he travelled a great deal. The necessity of spending a year away from Paris would have caused him to resign his post. He had a post. Strange as it may seem, he was the grand admiral of the Russian Navy. His knowledge of naval affairs could not have been more limited. The very mention of pending naval reforms brought a hostile frown on his handsome face. [He was] not interested in anything that did not pertain to love-making, food and liquor.

Nicky, Diary – 6 November – Tsarskoe Selo
We went for a drive and dropped in on Ania V[yrubova]. We saw Grigory [Rasputin] and talked for a long time.

7 November At 10.30 Kyril presented himself, I permitted him to return for the funeral, and gave him back his navy and suite uniforms.

N. P. Sabline,[4] Memoirs
I think it was in 1908, during a cruise on the yacht *Standart* that I

---

[4] Officer on imperial yacht *Standart*.

became closer to the imperial family. In our conversation the Empress started to hint that she knew Rasputin. She started saying that there are people, whose prayers have a particular force because of their ascetic way of life, and at last declared that in Russia there was such a man, that it was Rasputin, and suggested that I should meet him. I ascribe her blind faith in Rasputin, as indeed the Emperor's, to their boundless love for the Heir, who was suffering from an illness pronounced incurable by the doctors.

Like a drowning man clutching at straws, they held on to the belief that, if the Heir was alive, it was only due to the prayers of Rasputin. I absolutely refute the possibility of any kind of physical intimacy between Rasputin and either the Empress or Vyrubova.

Olga [sister], Memoirs

When I saw him [Rasputin] I felt that gentleness and warmth radiated from him. All the children seemed to like him. They were completely at their ease with him. I still remember their laughter as little Alexis, deciding he was a rabbit, jumped up and down the room. And then, quite suddenly, Rasputin caught the child's hand and led him to his bedroom, and we three followed.

There was something like a hush as though we had found ourselves in church. In Alexei's bedroom no lamps were lit; the only light came from the candles burning in front of some beautiful icons. The child stood very still by the side of that giant, whose head was bowed. I knew he was praying. It was all most impressive. I also knew that my little nephew had joined him in prayer. I really cannot describe it – but I was then conscious of the man's utter sincerity.

I realized that both Nicky and Alicky were hoping that I would come to like Rasputin. I was certainly impressed by the scene in the nursery and I allowed the man his sincerity. But, unfortunately, I could never bring myself to like him.

It was his curiosity – unbridled and embarrassing. In Alicky's boudoir, having talked to her and Nicky for a few minutes, Rasputin waited for the servants to get the table for the evening tea and then began plying me with most impertinent questions. Was I happy? Did I love my husband? Why didn't I have any children? He had no right to ask such questions, nor did I answer them. I am afraid Nicky and Alicky looked rather uncomfortable. I do remember I was relieved at leaving the palace that evening and saying, 'Thank God he hasn't followed me to the station,' as I boarded my private coach in the train for St Petersburg.

Olga [daughter] to Alix – 4 December – Tsarskoe Selo
With all my heart I thank you sweetest Mama dear for your dear little note and kiss you tenderly for it and will never through it away
from me. I will trie to do what you wrote to me in the little note. So
sorry that never see you alone Mama dear, can not talk so should trie
to write to you what could of course better say, but what is to be done
if there is no time, and neighter can I hear the dear words which
sweet Mama could tell me. Good-bye.

God bless you. Kisses from your very own devoted daughter

Olga

Nicky, Diary – 27 December – Tsarskoe Selo
We went to Ania V's, where we saw Grigory. We lit her Christmas tree
together. It was very pleasant – we returned at 12.15.

31 December May the Lord bless the coming year, and send dear
Russia peace, happiness and tranquillity; and us patience, strength,
and the ability to fulfil our duty and obligations towards our
country!

1909

FAMILY LIFE II

Rumours spread about Alexei's health – Grand Duke
Vladimir dies.

KR, Diary – 1 January
For the New Year their Majesties had a service in the church of the
great Palace of Tsarskoe Selo; we didn't stand with the choir but
downstairs. The Dowager Empress came from Gatchina. Their
Majesties brought their two eldest daughters, Olga and Tatiana, with
them into the church. The younger ones were upstairs in the gallery.

I don't know whether the Heir was there with them: he has a bad
leg, they say it's an inflammation of the knee joint, but I don't know
for sure. At the end of the service, the Emperor kissed the cross first,
then the Dowager Empress and Empress Alexandra afterwards. The
latter is still feeling weak, avoids getting tired and is being careful. For
this reason, the Emperor received the congratulations of the diplomatic corps without her.

Alix to Olga [daughter] – 1 January – Tsarskoe Selo
My sweet little Olga,

May the new year 1909 bring you much happiness and rich blessings. Try to be an example of what a good little obedient girlie ought
to be. You are the eldest and must show the others how to behave.
Learn to make others happy, think of yourself last of all. Be gentle
and kind, never rough nor rude. In manners as well as in speech be
a real lady. Be patient and polite, try to help sisters in every possible
way.

When you see somebody sad, try to cheer them up and show them a bright sunny smile. You know so well to be sweet and gentle with me, be so towards sisters too. Show a loving heart. Above all, learn to love God with all the force of your soul and He will ever be near you. Pray to Him with all your heart. Remember He sees and hears everything. He loves His children dearly, but they must learn to do His will.

I kiss you very tenderly, sweet child and bless you lovingly. +

God be with you and the Holy Virgin watch over you.

Your old Mama

11 January
Olga dear,

You want me to write a letter. Girlie mine, you must remember that one of the first things is to be polite and not rude, neither in manners nor in words. Rude words in the mouth of little children is more than not nice. Be always thoughtful and frank. Listen to those who are older than you. Remember above all to always be a good example to the little ones, only then our Friend will be contented with you.

They are small and don't understand things so well, and will always imitate the big ones. Therefore you must think of every word you say and what you do.

Be particularly polite to all the servants and nurses. They look after you so well. Think of Mary, how she has nursed you all, how she does her very best for you, and when tired and feels not well you must not add by making her nervous. Listen to her, be obedient and always kind. I have made her your nurse and you must always be good with her and also S.I.[1] You are big enough to understand what I mean.

Be good and listen to your mother. Read this to Tatiana. Always beg pardon when you have been rude or disobedient. Now try your best, and I shall be happy.

A loving kiss from your old Mama+

KR, Diary – 14 January
I asked the Emperor about putting on *The Bride* [*of Messina*] at the Tsarskoe Selo Chinese theatre.

The Tsar said that the Empress is very unwilling to receive, and is fearful of people, especially in crowds, and that we would hardly want to perform in front of their Majesties in an empty theatre.

---

[1] Sofia Ivanovna Tiutcheva, governess.

Pierre Gilliard, Memoirs

In spite of all her efforts, she [the Empress] never succeeded in being merely amiable and acquiring the art which consists of flitting gracefully but superficially over all manner of subjects.

The fact is that the Tsarina was nothing if not sincere. Every word from her lips was the true expression of her real feelings. Finding herself misunderstood, she quickly drew back into her shell.

Her natural pride was wounded. She appeared less and less at the ceremonies and receptions she regarded as an intolerable nuisance. She adopted a habit of distant reserve which was taken for haughtiness and contempt.

But those who came in contact with her in moments of distress knew what a sensitive spirit, what a longing for affection, was concealed behind that apparent coldness.

She had accepted her new religion with entire sincerity, and found it a great source of comfort in hours of trouble and anguish; but above all, it was the affection of her family which nourished her love, and she was never really happy except when she was with them.

Tatiana to Alix – 17 January – Tsarskoe Selo

My darling Mama!

I hope you wont be today very tied and that you can get up to dinner. I am always so awfuy sorry when you are tied and when you cant get up. I will pray for you my darling Mama in church. I hope that we can go some day to Annias [Vyrubova] little house with you. Please sleep well and dont get tied.

Perhaps I have lots of folts but please forgive me. It is very nice that you didnt go to church yesterday els I am shore you would be much more tied. Was it nice to [dine] yeasterday with Ania in your little room.

I try to listen what Mary says now as much as I kan. Did you see without us at Annias brother! I find him very nice, and how do you! Many, Many kisses to my beloved Mama. Sleep well and I hope that you wont be tied. Your loving dauther

Tatiana

I will pray for you in church.

Nicky, Diary – 4 February – Tsarskoe Selo

At 6 o'clock the Archimandrite Theophane and Grigory came to see us. He also saw the children. Just at that time we were informed by telephone of the sudden death of dear uncle Vladimir.

Sandro, Memoirs
Grand Duke Vladimir Alexandrovich possessed a hidden talent for all arts. He painted well, he was a patron of the ballet and the original financial backer of Sergei Diaghilev, he collected ancient icons, he visited Paris twice a year, and he adored giving elaborate parties at his splendid palace in Tsarskoe Selo.

A kind-hearted man, he fell victim to his eccentricities. A stranger meeting Grand Duke Vladimir Alexandrovich was certain to be taken aback by the roughness and by the shouting voice of this grand seigneur of Russia. He treated the younger grand dukes with a maximum of contempt.

None of us could have engaged him in conversation unless prepared to discuss subjects of art or the finesses of French cooking. His visits to Paris meant a red-letter day for the chefs and maîtres-d'hotel of the Ville Lumière, for after making a terrific row about the 'inadequacy' of the menu he would invariably finish the evening by putting a lavish tip in every hand.

Nicky, Diary – 7 February – Tsarskoe Selo
At 4 o'clock received Friedrich Leopold, who has been sent by Wilhelm [Kaiser] for the funeral. We talked until 5 o'clock. Read after tea. Played billiards with Dmitri in the evening. Went to bed early.

Rasputin to the imperial children – February – Telegram
DEAR LITTLE CHILDREN! THANK YOU FOR REMEMBERING ME, FOR YOUR SWEET WORDS, FOR YOUR PURE HEART AND YOUR LOVE FOR THE PEOPLE OF GOD. LOVE THE WHOLE OF GOD'S NATURE, THE WHOLE OF HIS CREATION IN PARTICULAR THIS EARTH. THE MOTHER OF GOD WAS ALWAYS OCCUPIED WITH FLOWERS AND NEEDLEWORK.

Nicky, Diary – 29 March, The Holy Resurrection of Christ – Tsarskoe Selo
After lunch I went for a walk with Dmitri. There was a frost and a lot of snow. It looked quite wintery. After tea, we sat upstairs in the nursery with Grigory, who arrived unexpectedly.

26 April From 6 to 7.30 we saw Grigory, together with Olga. After dinner I had a go at billiards with Dmitri and in the evening sat for a while again with Grigory in the nursery.

23 June   Went for a walk and sailed in the kayak. After tea we were visited by: Theophane, Grigory and Makary. At 7 o'clock we went to Gatchina. We dined with Maria, Xenia, Sandro and Olga [sister]. Returned home at 11 o'clock.

Alix to Nicky – 24 June – Tsarskoe Selo
My own precious one,

You will read these lines when the train will already be carrying you far away from Wify and children. It is very hard letting you go all alone – the first journey in the country since all the troubles – but I know you are safe in God's hands.

You will think of me tonight. We confess after 9 at Ania's parents' house and take Holy Communion tomorrow morning. We shall go to vigil tonight, then from the station we shall go to the Lancer's church so as to have had services before that great moment for which I am so little prepared. It will be a great comfort in our separation, but I feel so unworthy of that blessing, so unready for it – one never is enough prepared.

From all my heart, Sweetie One, do I pray for your forgiveness if in any way I hurt or displeased you – you know it never has been intentionally done – I love you far too much for that.

Our love is so one with our life – we are so completely united, that one never can doubt one's love and unity – nothing can come between us or lessen it.

Nobody has such a husband, so pure and unselfish, trusting and kind – never a word of rebuke if I am naughty, always serene, no matter what battle may be going on inside. God bless you over and over again for all your love and everything and may He richly reward you for all. It is so, so difficult to part. We have so rarely been separated – but souls and hearts are yet together. I shall wire daily.

Goodbye my treasure, I bless and kiss you over and over again and hold you tight in my arms. Forever and ever your *very* own true old,

Wify

Nicky, Diary – 15 August – Peterhof
I wanted to go riding, but it started to rain, so I stayed at home. Went for a walk just before tea. Read until dinner. In the evening had a long talk with Grigory.

1910

Nicky – Emperor of Russia

Alix – Empress of Russia

Xenia – Grand Duchess, Nicky's sister, married to Sandro

Sandro – Grand Duke Alexander Mikhailovich, husband of Xenia

Misha – Grand Duke Mikhail, Nicky's brother

KR – Grand Duke Konstantin Romanov, Nicky's cousin

Tatiana – second daughter of Nicky and Alix, aged thirteen

Maria – third daughter of Nicky and Alix, aged eleven

Alexei – Heir and Tsarevich, son of Nicky and Alix, aged six

Georgie – George, Duke of York, first cousin of both Nicky and Alix

Prince Felix Yusupov

S. I. Tiutcheva – governess of the Imperial children

1910

EVENINGS WITH GRIGORY

Alix is not well – Nicky and Alix continue to see Rasputin – The family are worried about his influence – Misha's mistress Natalia Wulfert (Brassova) is expecting his child, and Misha asks for Nicky's help in speeding up her divorce – KR sees Ella for the first time as a nun

Xenia, Diary – 1 January – St Petersburg
Sergei [Sandro's brother] came this afternoon and complained about everything. It's so sad and incomprehensible, one feels so sorry for Nicky.

Sandro, Memoirs
As inspector-general of the Russian Artillery [Sergei] did all in his power to impress upon the sluggish minds of the Imperial Government the inevitability of war with Germany. His advice was ignored but later on he was pointed out to the opposition party in parliament as 'the man responsible for our unpreparedness.' Early in life his habit of looking perennially hurt earned him the nickname 'Monsieur Tant Pis' (so much the worse). He was a close friend of Nicky's for forty years. He never married, although his faithful companion was none other than the ballet dancer Matilda Kshessinskaya, Nicky's old flame.

Nicky, Diary – 3 January – Tsarskoe Selo
After dinner we did a puzzle for a bit; then had a game of billiards. We saw Grigory between 7 and 8 o'clock.

6 January   Went for a good walk with Dmitri [Pavlovich]. Played billiards with him before dinner. At 9.30 he went into town. After this
Grigory came to see Alix, we sat with him for a long time and talked.

10 January   Saw Grigory for a short while.

Xenia, Diary – 11 January – St Petersburg
Sergei [Mikhailovich] arrived straight from Tsarskoe. He took me off
with him, and I sat while he had dinner. He recounted his conversation with Nicky: he told him everything, about everything that was
happening, about how he was being misled over military affairs and
deceived etc.

He tried to show him that his mistake was in not listening to those
close to him, besides which poor Nicky is preoccupied and upset by
Alix's health. She has again had severe pains in the heart and is very
much weaker. They say it's on the nerve lining – the nerves or the
heart valves. Evidently it's much more serious than was thought.

Nicky, Diary – 12 January – Tsarskoe Selo
At 6 o'clock Izvolsky came to see me. After dinner I read. We saw
Grigory.

14 January   After tea I read. At 7.30 there was a German dinner in
Prussian uniforms with Kostia and Nikolasha's families. Read. We saw
Grigory.

KR, Diary – 17 January
The most reverend Vladimir wanted to speak with me. The bishop
talked about some God's fool, Grigory, a simple peasant, who was
introduced to the Empress Alexandra by Militsa, and who apparently
has great influence over the Tsarina's household.

I was somewhat unpleasantly surprised that the bishop should
touch on a subject completely foreign to us, and in which it is
extremely difficult to distinguish where the truth ends and the
rumours begin.

Sandro, Memoirs
Militsa and her sister Stana [Nikolasha's wife] exercised an excep-

tionally bad influence on the young Tsarina. Superstitious, gullible, excitable, these two Montenegran grand duchesses fell an easy prey to native and foreign adventurers.

Each time they ran across a 'remarkable' man (as Monsieur Philippe and Rasputin), they dragged him to the Imperial palace.

Nicky, Diary – 21 January – Tsarskoe Selo
In the evening we saw Grigory and talked for a long time with him.

George, Duke of York to Nicky – 24 January – Marlborough House, London
My dear Nicky,

Our general elections have just come to an end and Mr Asquith's party has again been returned but with a very reduced majority, in fact there are about the same number of Unionists as Liberals. I should not be at all surprised if we do not have another general election before the year is over. I am glad to see that the Duma is getting on much better now and I hope in time that it will cease to give you trouble or anxiety.

Affairs in Greece look very bad and I am very sorry for poor uncle Willy[1] who has indeed been abominably treated by his ungrateful people, it looks almost impossible if he would be able to remain there. And I fear the Cretan question will continue to give the 4 Protecting Powers a great deal of trouble.

Ever, my dear Nicky, your very devoted cousin and friend

Georgie

Nicky, Diary – 27 January – Tsarskoe Selo
After dinner I saw Grigory for half an hour.

3 February   At 7.30 there was a big dinner for the Emir of Bokhara. Returned at 9.15. We talked for a long time with Grigory.

8 February   We saw Grigory.

12 February   After dinner we saw Grigory. In the evening I received Stolypin.

---

[1] William, King George I of Greece, was a brother of the mothers of both Nicky and George.

14 February   I saw Grigory; we said goodbye to him.

Tatiana to Alix – 8 March – Tsarskoe Selo
My sweet own darling Mama,
   Please forgive me that I have not did what I would last day. I am so sad that I did that, what I knew you would not like. Please forgive me I did not want to do it really Mama dear. I never, never wont do something I know you don't like and I wont do it without asking you my sweet Mama. How is your head?
   I am so afread that S.I. can speak to Maria about our friend some thing bad. I hope our nurse will be nice to our friend now.[2]
   Please tell Papa that I also ask him my pardon. I am so sad I made that what you and Papa don't like. Sleep well my own sweet Mama darling and I hope that tomorrow your poor head wont each any more. God bless you sweet darling. Many loving kisses to all from all. Your ever loving own daughter

                                                              Tatiana

Alix to Maria [daughter] – 11 March – Tsarskoe Selo
My darling little Maria,
   Your letter made me quite sad. Sweet child you must promise me never again to think that nobody loves you. *How* did such an extraordinary idea get into your little head? Get it quickly out again.
   We all love you *very tenderly*, only when too wild and naughty and won't listen, then must be scolded; but to scold, does not mean that one does not love, on the contrary, one does it so as that you may cure your faults and improve.
   You generally keep away from the others, think that you are in the way, and remain alone with Irina [Xenia's daughter] instead of being with them. They imagine then that you do not want to be with them; now you are getting a big girl it is good that you should be more with them.
   Now do not think any more about it, and remember that you are *just* as precious and dear as the other 4 and that we love you with all our heart. God bless you Darling Child. I kiss you ever so tenderly.

                                                   Your loving old Mama+

---

   [2] Sofia Ivanovna Tiutcheva, the governess, was eventually dismissed after criticizing Rasputin's visits to the nursery.

Xenia, Diary – 15 March – St Petersburg

I sat for a long time with S.D.[3] She is still under the shock of a conversation with S. I. Tiutcheva in Tsarskoe yesterday, and everything that is going on there: the attitude of Alix and the children to that sinister Grigory (whom they consider to be almost a saint, when in fact he's only a *khlyst!*[4]).

He's always there, goes into the nursery, visits Olga and Tatiana while they are getting ready for bed, sits there talking to them and *caressing* them. They are careful to hide him from Sofia Ivanovna, and the children don't dare talk to her about him. It's quite unbelievable and beyond understanding.

They are all under his influence and pray to him. I was simply crushed by this conversation.

Olga and I had dinner at the Anichkov. As I only had one thing on my mind, it was all I could talk about. But who can help? It's very difficult and 'ticklish' for the family. There are the most terrible rumours about him!

The Provisional Government's Extraordinary Commission of Enquiry, Petrograd, 1917

In 1910, on the advice of the former Empress, the nanny [Vishniakova] of the imperial children went for three weeks' 'rest' to Pokrovskoe, with Rasputin. One night in the village of Pokrovskoe, Rasputin crept into Vishniakova's room and seduced her.

On returning to Petrograd Vishniakova rushed to tell the Empress about this, and about how, once at night on the way back, she had seen Rasputin lying in the couchette with Zinaida Mandshtet, wearing only his underwear.

S. I. Tiutcheva – Testimony to the Extraordinary Commission of Enquiry

'On hearing my story, the Empress informed [me] she did not believe such slanders, and saw in them the work of dark forces, wishing to ruin Rasputin, and forbade me to mention it to the Emperor. The same day a courier arrived with an order for me to appear before the Emperor in his study at 6.30 in the evening. When I walked into the Emperor's study at the appointed time, he asked me:

---

[3] Alix's lady-in-waiting, S. D. Samarina.

[4] A member of an exotic sect who used flagellation and sex.

'"Sofia Ivanovna, you will already have guessed why I have sent for you. What is going on in the nursery?" I then told him everything that had happened. "So you also do not believe in the sanctity of Grigory?" asked the Emperor. I answered negatively and the Emperor said "And what if I told you that all these difficult years I have survived only because of his prayers?"

'"You have survived them because of the prayers of the whole of Russia, Your Majesty," I replied. The Emperor started to say that he was convinced it was all a lie, that he did not believe these stories about R, that the pure always attracts everything dirty.'[5]

Misha [brother] to Nicky – 29 March – Orel, Russia
Dear Nicky,

If you want to make me happy and reassured, then please fulfil my request. As I already told you the last time I saw you, Natalia Wulfert[6] is expecting my child in July, which is why I must already take steps to ensure that her divorce is finalised by that time, as I cannot countenance that her husband – Lieutenant V – should have any rights over my child.

In order to avoid disturbing you, I was going to write myself to the head of the ecclesiastical court to expedite the divorce, but decided against doing so without your permission. Be so kind, dear Nicky, tell me what to do to speed up Natalia's divorce, should I write to the head of the consistory myself, or will you instruct Fredericks to do so, in which case I will also write to him myself. I ask you please to let me know what you decide.

Let me repeat that I am concerned with Natalia's divorce only for the sake of the child, as I have already told you.

I have no intention of marrying her, of that I give you my word. I would so like to have some good news to reassure her with, otherwise she worries and gets upset the whole time, poor thing, so much so that recently her health has greatly suffered.

Once more, my dear Nicky, I very, very much ask you to help in this matter.

I embrace you warmly. May the Lord keep you.

Your loving Misha

---

[5] The result of this conversation was Tiutcheva's dismissal.

[6] The daughter of a Moscow lawyer. Her mother was Polish. After a brief marriage to a Moscow merchant she divorced him and married Captain Wulfert of the Cuirassier Regiment. Misha was the officer commanding and she soon became his mistress.

Nicky to King George V – 25 April – Tsarskoe Selo
Dearest Georgie,

Just a few lines to tell you how *deeply* I feel for you the terrible loss you and England have sustained.[7] I know alas! by experience what it costs one. There you are with your heart bleeding and aching, but at the same time duty imposes itself and people and affairs come up and tear you away from your sorrow.

It is difficult to realize that your beloved Father has been taken away. The awful rapidity with which it all happened! How I would have liked to have come now and be near you!

I beg you dearest Georgie to continue our old friendship and to show my country the same interest as your dear Father did from the day he came to the throne. No one did so much in trying to bring our two countries closer together than Him. The first steps have brought good results, let us strive and work in the same direction. From our talks in days past and from your letters I remember your opinion was the same.

I assure you that the sad death of your Father has provoked throughout the whole of Russia a feeling of sincere grief and of warmest sympathy towards your people. God bless you my dear old Georgie! My thoughts are always near you.

With much love to you and dearest May, ever your devoted friend
Nicky

KR, Diary – 6 May – Pavlovsk
Ella appeared, for the first time since her consecration as Mother Superior of the Order she created, all in white, her head and forehead covered by a wimple, over which was a white veil, with a pectoral cross and a rosary.

Felix Yusupov, Memoirs
She [Ella] built the Convent of Martha and Mary of which she became the Mother Superior.

With a last touch of worldliness, for she had been a woman of extreme elegance and great taste, she had the dress of her Order designed by Nesterov, a Muscovite painter, a long pearl-grey robe of fine wool, a lawn wimple which framed the face, and a white woollen veil that fell into long classical folds.

The nuns were not cloistered, but dedicated their lives to visiting

---

[7] King Edward VII, Uncle Bertie, had died aged sixty-nine (6 May in England).

the poor and caring for the sick. They also travelled through the provinces, founding new centres. The institution developed rapidly; in a few years all large Russian cities had similar establishments. The Ordinka Convent had to be enlarged: a church, a hospital, workshops and schools were added.

The Mother Superior lived in a small, simply furnished three-room house; her wooden bed had no mattress and her pillow was stuffed with hay. The Grand Duchess slept little, a few hours at most, when she was not spending the whole night by a sick bed, or praying over a coffin in the chapel. Hospitals and nursing homes sent her their worst cases, and she nursed them herself.

King George V to Nicky – 14 May – Marlborough House, London
My dearest Nicky,

These last three weeks have been terrible, my heart has been nearly breaking and at the same time I have had to carry on all my duties and bear my new responsibilities and see so many people to arrange about the last sad ceremonies and entertain William, 7 Kings and numerous Princes and Representatives from practically all the countries of the world.

I saw Sir Arthur Nicholson today and he told me of all your kindness and sympathy which has touched me deeply and all the sorrow which has been expressed in Russia.

Everyone loved and respected beloved Papa and they knew that his great object was Peace. I can't yet realize that I shall never see his dear face again or hear his dear voice, his illness was so sudden and the end came so quickly, but it was quite peaceful without a struggle.

Yes, dearest Nicky, I hope we shall always continue our old friendship to one another, you know I never change and I have always been very fond of you.

Yes, indeed I know how from the first my dear Father tried to do all he could to bring our two countries together and you may be sure that I shall show the same interest in Russia that He did.

And I know you will do the same and I feel certain that when our two peoples know each other better and understand each other, that our endeavours will be crowned with success. We are now working splendidly together in Persia, there may be difficulties with Germany, but I think they can be overcome. If only England, Russia and France stick together the peace in Europe is assured.

Ever your devoted friend,

Georgie

Maria [daughter] to Alix – 17 May – Peterhof
My dear Mama!

How are you feeling. I wanted to tell you that Olga would very much like to have her own room in Peterhof, because she and Tatiana have too many things and too little room. Mama at what age did you have your own room?

Please tell me if it's possible to arrange. Mama at what age did you start wearing long dresses? Don't you think Olga would also like to let down her dresses. Mama why don't you move them both or just Olga. I think they would be comfortable where you slept when Anastasia had diphtheria.

I kiss you

Maria

P.S. It was my idea to write to you.

Nicky to Empress Marie – 4 October
My dear darling Mama

I thank you with all my heart for your kind letter. You and I must have been thinking and feeling the same thing at the same time, because a little more than three weeks ago, I wrote to Misha about that very thing. Starting with the fact that nowadays it is impossible to remain incognito anywhere, I told him what an awful impression it would make, if people knew who he was travelling with.

I am not ordering, but advising him not to travel in the train with her [Natalia Wulfert] and not to stay together in the same hotel. At the end I added that I was sure she would agree with me, if she loves him as much as he thinks, and that she would want to cause him as little harm and detriment as possible. I wrote the letter as kindly as possible, and received a telegram from him in answer, saying that he was very grateful. I hope he follows my advice. It's all more than painful and sad, and I don't like to bring up this unpleasant matter with you too often, as I know how much suffering it causes you.

Olga [sister] wrote to me in the same terms as you.

I don't know where Xenia is now? Has she not returned to Russia!

Everything here is going well. There has been a whole kaleidoscope of relatives, as you might say, passing through. Now it's time for me to end. Goodbye, my dear darling Mama. I embrace you fondly. May the Lord keep you.

From your old Nicky,
who loves you with all his heart.

Alexei to Nicky – 22 October – Tsarskoe Selo
Dear Papa
   Forgive me for writing so messily. I hope that you will soon come.
A very big kiss.

Alexei

Alix to Nicky – 22 October – Tsarskoe Selo
My beloved darling,
   It is so sad and empty in the little house without you, I miss you
quite too terribly. After you left I remained in your room a little trying to be brave, though not succeeding. After my bath I prayed long
and read the whole Akathist to the Kazan Mother of God and then
got calmer. It took ages before I got to sleep. Baby Sweet came in his
dressing gown to wake me and drew up the curtains.
   Had the masseuse, the head is better, but the whole body aches
very much – the weather has also to do with it. So sad you are not
here, not to hear your men's voices is also melancholy.
   Such a storm this night, and heavy showers from time to time. I
hope you have it finer for the shooting. Ella sent me a kind, affectionate little letter, knowing I would feel lonely this morning. The
doctor comes, so must stop and finish after.
   Very tenderest kisses from your very own little,

Wify

KR, Diary – 27 November
In the train on the way to Pavlovsk, I learnt from the Court Minister
Baron Fredericks that Misha is at present in Florence, with Madame
Wulfert, the divorced wife of his Majesty's cuirassier, with whom he
has a liaison. They have a three-month-old child, who has been
given her brother's surname.[8] According to Fredericks, Misha has
given his word to the Emperor not to marry her, but has said he will
not give her up.

King George V to Nicky – 7 December – Buckingham Palace
My dearest Nicky,
   I am glad you have been able to get a few days shooting since you
came home and that you got two fine elks the day you wrote to me.

---

[8] She and her son later took the name Brassov.

I shoot as often as I can and have had some very good days, but our weather has been very wet and stormy. I have been and still am very much bothered and worried by our political affairs, the elections have taken place but the state of the parties is exactly the same.

May and I with the 3 eldest boys who have just come home for their holidays return to Mama and Toria at Sandringham on the 22nd where we spend Christmas together, but it will be alas a very sad one for us all without beloved Papa.

Ever, dearest Nicky, your most devoted old cousin and *friend*

Georgie

1911

Nicky – Emperor of Russia

Alix – Empress of Russia

Xenia – Grand Duchess, Nicky's sister, married to Sandro

KR – Grand Duke Konstantin Romanov, Nicky's cousin

Tatiana – second daughter of Nicky and Alix, aged fourteen

Maria – third daughter of Nicky and Alix, aged twelve

Georgie – King George V of England, first cousin of both Nicky and Alix

Maurice Paléologue – French Ambassador in St Petersburg

M. P. Bok – daughter of Prime Minister Stolypin

1911

DEATH OF THE PRIME MINISTER

Chaliapin performs *Boris Godunov* – Nicky and Georgie correspond about maintaining peace in Europe – Empress Marie is distressed about Rasputin's role in Alix's household – Xenia is still seeing F. – Misha is under surveillance – Prime Minister Stolypin is assassinated – Tatiana apologizes to her mother

KR, Diary – [no date] January
Almost the whole family gathered in the two boxes of the Marinsky theatre for Chaliapin in Mussorgsky's *Boris Godunov*, the Emperor was there with Olga Nicolaevna [daughter] and the Empress Mother. I was fortunate enough to sit next to the Emperor. Chaliapin is without compare as an actor.

After the scene with Boris and the children, the curtain unexpectedly opened: the choir were on stage, with Chaliapin among them on his knees, singing the anthem.

We did not immediately understand what was going on. Realizing that they went on to 'God save the Tsar' I jumped up ... then the Empress, my wife, little Olga, Irina and Xenia stood up too, as did the Emperor himself. The orchestra took up the anthem, the hall was filled with cheering and clapping. The anthem was repeated three times. The Empress pushed forward the Emperor, who was standing in the corner, hidden from the public by the curtain, and he bowed to the actors and the audience. I had not experienced a moment of such intensity for a long time, and was unable to hold back my tears.

Nicky to King George V – 10 January – Tsarskoe Selo
My dearest Georgie,

I was very pleased to have made the acquaintance of Lord Revelstoke, who kindly offered to be the bearer of my letter.

He told me so much about you and of your beloved Father and that he had seen me in 1893 at your wedding.

I thank you once more for your kind letter in which you speak about your intended visit to India. I think it a grand idea. You will be the first British sovereign who sets his foot on Indian soil. May your visit bring you and England all the benefit you expect of it. I do not doubt that it will produce a tremendous impression in the whole world!

Luckily Alix feels much better and stronger again. Our children caught chicken pox after Xmas and have been laid up for a fortnight with the exception of Olga. Now they have nearly recovered.

Both my sisters have gone mad about the skating-rink, which lies quite near to your embassy. Olga daily goes there and meets many of its members and spends gay mornings with them. That sport has become a mania among the Petersburg society; I think it a pity, because out of door exercise is infinitely more healthy.

From Jan. 1 there is no more elk shooting till the month of August, but I hope to be able to go for some small game. Our winter is a mild one and there is not much snow.

I hope that dear May and the children are quite well. With fondest love from Alix and me to you both, ever dearest Georgie your loving and devoted old cousin and friend

Nicky

Nicky, Diary – 12 February – Tsarskoe Selo
After dinner I read, then we went to Ania's where we talked for a long time with Grigory.

King George V to Nicky – 2 March – Buckingham Palace
PRIVATE
My dearest Nicky,

No doubt you may have seen in the newspapers that I have invited William [Kaiser Wilhelm] and his Wife to come over to England for the unveiling of Grandmama's statue on May 16th.

Papa had always intended to invite William for that ceremony and he I know was very anxious to be present at it. His visit of course will be an absolutely private one, and it has no political significance whatever, he is coming as one of the family and the eldest grandson of Grandmama. I wished to tell you this in case the newspapers should invent a lot of rubbish about his visit.

I trust that the negotiations between Russia and Germany may soon be brought to a satisfactory conclusion. You may be sure dear Nicky that your Government will be kept informed as to the course of any discussions which may take place between England and Turkey or Germany in regard to the Baghdad railway and other cognate questions.

I feel convinced that if Russia, England and France have mutual understandings that the Peace of Europe will not be disturbed, but of course that will not prevent either of us having friendly relations with the other Powers, it is only right that we should.

I rather fear at the present moment that Germany is trying to isolate France, I may be wrong, but that is what I think. No doubt Germany rather resents the friendly understandings which exist between England, Russia and France, but they have not been come to in any way against her but for the benefit of peace and civilization. I know you don't mind my writing to you quite frankly what I think, as we have always been such good friends, I like to tell you everything.

Ever, dearest Nicky, your devoted and loving old cousin and *friend*

Georgie

Tatiana to Alix – 20 April – Tsarskoe Selo
Mama my darling,

How about tomorrow? Must I lie in bed or no (ah of course no) I had a little as I walked but my head does not hurt as I lay and now it passed. Can you write deary I would like to know. I would like so much to go to the review of the second division as I am also the second daughter and Olga was at the first so now it is my turn. What will you about that??

Ah!!!????!!!! Maria asks when must we have Delacroix for the hair as we did not have him for such a long time. Yes Mama and at the second division I will see whom I *must* see ....
.... you know whom .... !!!!??!?!

Now goodbye. God bless you two angels. God be with you always and every where you are.

Many kisses from your loving, devoted, thankful true daughter

Tatiana

P.S. Kiss Ania very much.

KR, Diary – 20 May
I talked for an hour with Minnie [Empress Marie] both before and after lunch. She spoke openly. It is sad to see that if her relations with the Empress are not exactly bad, they are not quite right either.

She criticised the cold and constant draught in her daughter-in-law's rooms, blaming this for the latter's continual ill health. [Minnie] catches cold at Tsarskoe because of it.

She is distressed that they continue to receive in secret some God's fool, Grisha, who orders the Empress A. and the children to keep it secret and not to say that they have seen him. It can hardly be beneficial to accustom the children to such dissimulation. Stolypin[1] reported at some point to the Emperor that this Grisha is a rogue, but was told in reply to leave Grisha alone.

22 May I presented myself to the Emperor. I asked about the Empress's health. She is still unwell, sometimes better, then worse again. The Emperor is so patient, and doesn't complain, but he admits it is tiresome and depressing.

Nicky, Diary – 4 June – Tsarskoe Selo
After dinner we had the joy of seeing Grigory, after his return from Jerusalem and Athens.

Xenia, Diary – 20 July – Paris
At lunch I quarrelled with F. and we both got offended over absolutely nothing! As a result, he did not come to me afterwards, as he always does!

At four o'clock I went into the garden and he followed me there. We had tea and read. We went for a short walk, but were both extremely tense and weak. The children are now at Merran. Sandro is at Interlaken and they see each other every day.

Nicky, Diary – 4 August – Tsarskoe Selo
Aunt Olga [Queen of Greece] and Mitia [KR's brother] came to dinner. They left at 10 o'clock. Then Grigory arrived and sat with us until 11.30.

---

[1] Pyotr Arkadievich Stolypin, who in 1906 had succeeded Count Witte as the Tsar's Prime Minister.

KR, Diary – 3 September – Belgorod
We learnt with horror, that the evening before last in Kiev, the prime minister Stolypin was wounded by several revolver shots. His condition is serious, but not without hope.

The Ministry of Foreign Affairs of Russia to All Russian Embassies – 6 September
TOP SECRET
The bearer hereof, Major-General of the Gendarme Corps Alexander Vasilevich Gerasimov, is commissioned by His Imperial Majesty abroad and is charged with the task of taking all reasonable measures to prevent the marriage of Madame Brassova [Wulfert] to Grand Duke Mikhail abroad.

For the purpose of executing His Imperial Majesty's order, all Russian Embassies, Missions and Consulates abroad shall render Major-General Gerasimov every reasonable assistance that he might need to accomplish the task and, should necessity arise, put under arrest any persons at the discretion of Major-General Gerasimov.

Acting Chief of the Ministry of Foreign Affairs A. Neratov

Nicky to Empress Marie – 10 September – Sebastopol
Dear sweet Mama

At last I have found the time to write to you about our journey, which has been filled with the most varied impressions, both joyful and sad.

I was getting quite tired, but everything had gone so well and smoothly and our spirits were high, when on the evening of the 1st the filthy assassination of Stolypin took place. Olga and Tatiana were with me, and we had just left our box during the second interval, as it was very hot in the theatre. At that moment we heard two noises, like the sound of an object falling, and, thinking that a pair of binoculars must have fallen on someone's head from above, I ran back into the box.

To the right I saw a group of officers and others dragging someone, a few ladies were screaming, and there right opposite me stood Stolypin. He turned slowly to face me, and made the sign of the cross in the air with his left hand. It was only then that I noticed he was very pale and that he had blood on the right arm of his jacket. He sat down quietly and started to unbutton his jacket. Fredericks and Prof. Rein helped him.

Olga and Tatiana had followed me back into the box and saw everything that happened. While Stolypin was being helped out of the theatre, there was a commotion in the corridor next to our box, where they wanted to lynch the assassin, but, unfortunately in my view, the police managed to rescue him from the crowd and took him away to another building for a first interrogation. Nevertheless he was pretty beaten up, with two broken teeth. Then the theatre filled up again, quietened down and I left with the girls at 11 o'clock. You can imagine with what feelings? Alix had not heard anything and I told her about what had happened. She took the news quite calmly. It had made a great impression on Tatiana, who cried a lot, and they both slept badly. Poor Stolypin suffered a lot that night and had to be given morphine.

I returned to Kiev at 9 in the morning. Here I learnt at the landing stage from Kokovtsev that Stolypin had died. I went straight there, and there was a special requiem in my presence. The poor widow stood there, unable even to cry; her brothers are with her.

Christ be with you! I embrace you warmly, my dear Mama. Greetings to everyone.

Your very loving Nicky

M. P. Bok [Stolypin's daughter], Memoirs

On the first of September there was a performance at the theatre in the imperial presence, which was, of course, only by special invitation. My father was sitting in the first row of the stalls, not far from the imperial box, where the Emperor and the Grand Duchesses were sitting.

The second interval. Papa got up and, leaning on the balustrade of the orchestra pit, turned with his back to the stage to talk to the court minister baron Fredericks. He was in a white, summer jacket, the same as I saw him in his coffin.

His tall, stately figure could easily be seen from the furthest corners of the theatre, now half empty because of the interval. The majority of the audience were in the foyer.

Suddenly a figure in a tail coat advanced straight towards my father from the centre entrance. Here, where almost everyone was in uniform, the sight of that figure in black tails conveyed an impression of malevolence. But before anyone had time to realize what was happening, the man in tails had gone up to my father and fired at him twice at point blank range.

Momentarily numbed by shock, those who were present saw how

Papa remained standing for a few more seconds. Then, slowly turning towards the imperial box and carefully making the sign of the cross, he fell heavily onto the nearest seat. Bright spots of blood appeared on the white material of his jacket.

At that time the crowd fell on the assassin, who was trying to slip away. People in the auditorium, or who ran in from the foyer, grabbed hold of him and tried to tear him to pieces.

Xenia, Diary – 13 November – Ai-Todor
I feel depressed and I'm very annoyed. F. says that it's time for him to go, he hates it here, that he's sick of the whole set up and everything. I understand. But we are also leaving at the end of next week, and I'm trying to persuade him to leave with us.

They have already begun to talk about us. He senses this, although I have said nothing to him. It's such a pity that he came this year, when everyone is staying here! The fault is ours, but on the other hand, why may we not have whom we choose?

Tatiana to Alix – 26 November – Livadia
My sweet, darling, own Mama dear,

I beg your pardon that I don't listen to you and that I contradict you, that I am disobedient. At once I never feel anything but afterwards I feel so sad and miserable that I made you tired of telling me always to do that and so on.

Please forgive me my own precious Mama darling. Really now I'll try and be as good and as kind as I can be, else I know how disagreeable it is to you when one of your daughters don't listen to you and behaves bad.

I know it is very bad of me to be so horrid with you my dear Mama, but really, really my sweet one I *will* try and be as good as I can and never tire you and always listen [to] every word you will tell me.

Forgive me deary. Write to me please a word only that you forgive me and then I can go and sleep with a clear conscience. God bless you always and wherever you go – show this letter to nobody.

Kisses from your own loving, devoted, thankful and true daughter,

Tatiana

Xenia, Diary – 29 November
He went off to pack and at 11 o'clock left for good. It's sad, but most

Nicky

Papa

Mama

Kaiser Willy

Ella

Xenia

Sandro

Misha

Olga

Georgie (detail)

Felix

(right) Zinaida

(left) Alix   Rasputin

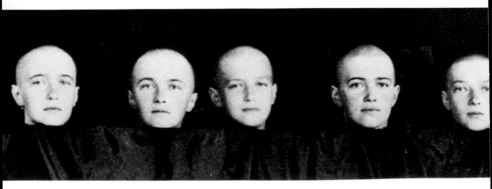

(top) Olga, Tatiana, Maria, Anastasia

(above) The five children, 1917

(left) Alexei

of all I don't know when we'll see each other again! We were together for over six months!

30 November   It's terrible how much I miss F.!

1912

Nicky – Emperor of Russia

Alix – Empress of Russia

Xenia – Grand Duchess, Nicky's sister, married to Sandro

Sandro – Grand Duke Alexander Mikhailovich, husband of Xenia

Empress Marie – Nicky's mother

KR – Grand Duke Konstantin Romanov, Nicky's cousin

Olga (sister) – Grand Duchess, Nicky's younger sister

Misha – Grand Duke Mikhail, Nicky's brother

Olga – eldest daughter of Nicky and Alix, aged seventeen

Tatiana – second daughter of Nicky and Alix, aged fifteen

Maria – third daughter of Nicky and Alix, aged thirteen

Georgie – King George V of England, first cousin of both Nicky and Alix

Prince Felix Yusupov

Ania Vyrubova – lady-in-waiting and close friend of Alix

Pierre Gilliard – Swiss tutor of Nicky and Alix's children

Maurice Paléologue – French Ambassador in St Petersburg

Mikhail Rodzianko – Chairman of the Duma

A. Krasilnikov – a police agent

1912

INHERITED CURSE

The Rasputin scandal grows – Alexei has a brush with
death – Misha marries Natalia Wulfert secretly in Vienna
– The family reacts with horror

Xenia, Diary – 25 January – St Petersburg
I went to see Alix, whom I found in bed, in her large room. We talked
about Hermogene, Iliodor [bishops] and most importantly, Gr.
Rasputin. The papers are forbidden to write about him – but a few
days ago his name was again mentioned in several of them, and
those issues confiscated.

Everybody already knows and talks about him, it's terrible the
things they say about him, about Alix, and everything that goes on
at Tsarskoe. The Yusupovs came to tea – always the same conversation – and at the Anichkov in the evening and over dinner I
recounted all I had heard. How will it all end? It's terrible.

26 January A motion was tabled in the Duma, and adopted unanimously, on the question of the confiscation of certain newspapers
because of Rasputin; the unfortunate ministers now have to answer?
It's all simply terrible.

Nicky, Diary – 11 February – Tsarskoe Selo
At four o'clock Grigory arrived, we received him in my new study
with all the children. It was a great comfort to see him and listen to
him talk.

Mikhail Rodzianko, Memoirs
The Dowager Empress said to me: 'I have heard that you intend to speak to the Emperor about Rasputin. Don't do it. Unfortunately he will not believe you, besides it will distress him greatly. He is so pure in heart that he does not believe in evil.'

To this I replied to the Empress that, unfortunately, I was not able to remain silent during my audience about such an important matter. I was obliged to speak, obliged to inform my tsar. The matter was too serious and the potential consequences too dangerous.

'Has it really gone that far?'

'Your Majesty, it's a question of the dynasty. And we monarchists can no longer remain silent. I am happy, your Majesty, that you granted me the honour of seeing you and talking to you openly on this matter. As you can see, I am extremely affected by the responsibility that lies with me. I most humbly allow myself to ask for your blessing.' She looked at me with her kind eyes and said with emotion, putting her hand on mine: 'May the Lord bless you.'

I was already on my way out, when she came forward a few steps and said: 'But don't hurt him too much.'

Subsequently I heard from Prince Yusupov, that after my audience with the Emperor, the Empress Marie went to him and declared: 'It's either me or Rasputin,' saying that she would leave, if Rasputin remained.

Nicky, Diary – 15 February – Tsarskoe Selo
Mama came to tea; we had a conversation with her about Grigory.

Xenia, Diary – 16 February – St Petersburg
Mama talked about her conversation yesterday. She's so pleased that she spoke out. Now they have heard and know what is being said, though Alix defended Rasputin, saying that he's an exceptional man and that Mama should get to know him etc.; Mama's only advice was to send him away now, when the Duma are waiting for an answer, to which Nicky said that he couldn't see how he could do it, while she declared that they couldn't give in.

In general everything she said was besides the point, and there is obviously a lot she doesn't understand – she castigated society (dirty-minded gossips), Tiutcheva [ex-governess] for talking too much and lying, and the ministers 'all cowards'.

But nevertheless they were both grateful to Mama for talking so candidly, and she even kissed Mama's hand!

10 March   In the train, Olga [sister] told us about her conversation with [Alix]. For the first time she admitted that the poor little one has that terrible illness[1] and that she herself has become ill because of this and will never fully recover.

As far as Grigory is concerned, she said how can she not believe in him, when she can see that the boy feels better the moment he is near him, or prays for him.

It seems that in the Crimea, after our departure, Alexei had a haemorrhage in the kidneys (how appalling!), and they sent for Grigory. Everything stopped when he arrived! My God, how terrible, how sorry I feel for them!

Ania V[yrubova] came to see Olga today, and also talked about G[rigory], about how she met him (through Stana) at a difficult moment of her life (during her divorce) and how much he helped her etc.

I'm appalled by all the stories and sublimations – I talked about the bath-house, about how they say that she lives with him! How everything is falling on her shoulders now!

16 March   Princess Yusupov came to tea. She stayed for a long time and talked a lot. She recounted her conversation with Alix about Grigory and *everything*. He has gone to Siberia, and not at all to the Crimea. Someone sent him an anonymous message by telegraph, for him to leave there. Alix did not know anything about it, but was overjoyed and immediately said: 'He always senses when I need him!'

---

[1] Haemophilia. Pierre Gilliard, Alexei's tutor, wrote this description after talking to Dr Derevenko, one of the many doctors who treated the Tsarevich. 'He told me that the heir was a prey to haemophilia, a hereditary disease which in certain families is transmitted from generation to generation *by the women* to their male children. Only males are affected. He told me that the slightest wound might cause the boy's death, for the blood of a bleeder had not the power of coagulating like that of a normal individual. Further, the tissue of the arteries and veins is so frail that any blow or shock may rupture the blood-vessel and bring on a fatal haemorrhage.

'Such was the terrible disease from which Alexei was suffering, such the perpetual menace to his life. A fall, nose-bleeding, a simple cut – things which were a trifle to any other child – might prove fatal to him. All that could be done was to watch over him closely day and night, especially in his early years, and by extreme vigilance try to prevent accidents. Hence the fact that at the suggestions of the doctors he had been given two ex-sailors of the Imperial yacht, Derevenko and his assistant Nagorny, as his personal attendants and bodyguard. They looked after him in rotation.'

KR, Diary – 18 March – Pavlovsk
Recently, on the 14th, my wife had lunch with their Majesties, and
was embarrassed by the behaviour of the Heir, who is almost two
years older than Vera. He wouldn't sit up, ate badly, licked his plate
and teased the others. The Emperor often turned away, perhaps to
avoid having to say anything, while the Empress rebuked her elder
daughter Olga, who was next to her brother, for not restraining him.
But Olga cannot deal with him.

Maria [daughter] to Alix
Mama darling,
   I hope you did not forget that at Easter in Russia one must give the
'three kisses' to the people. Anastasia kisses you and Papa. I kiss you
all too. Your loving,

                                                                                                          Maria

Tatiana to Alix
My sweet darling dear beloved own dearest Mama,
   I am so awfully sorry that you wont come with us. I hope that you
will feel better tomorrow when we come. Fancy it will be the first
time that we will sleep on the *Standart* it is awfully sad Mama dearest. I hope that Ania will be nice with you and wont tire you and spe-
cialy wont come in to you to disturb when you lie or when you want
to be alone. Such I petty I could not stay with you Mama dear. It
would be such a pleasure to me. I do hope you wont feel too tired.
Please Mama darling dont run about the rooms to see how they are.
Send Ania or els you will be very tired to receive Auntie and Uncle.
   I will try and be as good as I can on board with the officers.
   Goodbye till tomorrow. Dont worry sweety about baby I will look
after him and all will be alright. God bless you my sweet own darling.
   Many many kisses to you angel from your own loving devoted and
true daughter

                                                                                                          Tatiana

Nicky, Diary – 21 June – Port-Baltic
Got up early to a wonderful, clear morning. At 9.30 we saw the
German ships. At exactly 10 o'clock the *Hohenzollern* dropped anchor
between us and the *Polar*, and its cruiser *Moltke* in among our ships.
I went over to Wilhelm and at 11 o'clock returned to the yacht. Then
he and his son Adalbert came over to us and stayed for lunch.

22 June   At 5 o'clock I went aboard the cruiser *Moltke*, which I inspected together with Wilhelm. At 8 o'clock the whole family, with the exception of Alix, went over to the *Hohenzollern*. He gave us presents. We dined, listened to some beautiful music and then saw a film in the dining room, and returned back.

Felix Yusupov, Memoirs

[During] the summer of 1912 the Tsar went to Port-Baltic to meet the Emperor of Germany. This was not a pleasure trip, as neither the Tsar nor the Tsarina like the Kaiser.

'He thinks he is a superman,' the Tsarina once said in my hearing, 'and he's really nothing but a clown. He has no real worth. His only virtues are his strict morals and his conjugal fidelity. His reported love-affairs are a myth.'

Nicky to KR – 14 September – Bielovejie

Dear Kostia

I have been meaning to write to you ever since I read aloud to Alix your play *King of Judea*.

It made the deepest impression on me – more than once my eyes filled with tears and I had a lump in my throat. I am certain that to see your play on stage and to hear the beautiful paraphrasing of what each of us knows from the Gospels, all this could but produce the most profound effect on the spectator!

It is for this reason that I share the opinion of the Holy Synod that it cannot be publicly staged. However, the Chinese theatre of the Hermitage could be made available for it, as well as the singers who participate in the 'Ismailovsky celebrations'.

I told your wife in conversation that, as well as the lofty sentiments which it inspired in me, I was also fired by a hatred of the Jews, who crucified Christ. I think the common Russian man would feel the same thing, if he saw it on stage, and from there it would not be far to the possibility of a pogrom. These are the impressions evoked by the dramatic strength of your latest work.

You will, of course, have heard from your two eldest sons about the celebrations at Borodino and in Moscow.[2] It reminded me of the Poltava days in 1909. Only this time the atmosphere was even more exalted. The tour of the Borodino field made an indelible impression

---

[2] The hundredth anniversary of the battle of Borodino against Napoleon.

on me, especially the thought that every clod of earth under our feet had been washed in the blood of one of 58,000 of our heroes, both dead and wounded, during those two days! And then to meet and talk with a *survivor of the battle* – a 122-year-old former sergeant major! I felt as I would in the presence of the greatest relics! In Moscow everything went well and successfully, but for me at least, Borodino was far greater and more intense!

I wish you, dear Kostia, a safe journey and a full recovery in Egypt. I kiss your wife and sister. Alix sends you her warmest regards

With all my heart your Nicky

King George V to Nicky – 23 September – Balmoral Castle
Dearest Nicky,

I am so pleased all the ceremonies and festivities at Moscow for the 100th anniversary of your war with Napoleon went off so success-fully and that the weather was fine.

As to our friend, that good fool of a Michel,[3] who I am sure bores you with his many grievances as he does me. He has lived here in England many years and dear Papa was always most kind and friendly to him and I have invariably tried to be the same. Of course I do not know what he may have said to you at Moscow with regard to his wife being given a title by me, to the acceptance of which you gave your consent.

Unfortunately however I have not the power to grant a title in England to a foreign subject and still more impossible in the case of the wife of a Russian Grand Duke. I expect as soon as I get to London he will come and see me and I do not look forward to our interview with any pleasure as I fear I have no alternative but to refuse his request. Sorry to have bothered you with this long story, but thought it better to explain my position fully, in case he troubles you again on the subject. He has never mentioned the subject to me yet and your letter was the first I had heard of it.

Ever, dearest Nicky, your devoted friend and cousin

Georgie

Pierre Gilliard, Memoirs
I gave Alexei the first lesson in the presence of his mother. The child

---

[3] Miche-Miche, Sandro's brother. His wife lost her title because of her morganatic marriage, but was subsequently given the title Countess Torby.

was then eight and a half. He did not know a word of French, and at first I had a good deal of difficulty. My lessons were soon interrupted, as the boy, who had looked to me ill from the outset, soon had to take to his bed.

Both my colleague and myself had been struck by his lack of colour and the fact that he was carried as if he could not walk. The disease from which he was suffering had evidently taken a turn for the worse.

Ania Vyrubova, Memoirs

One day the Empress took the child for a drive and before we had gone very far we saw that indeed he was very ill. He cried out with pain in his back and stomach, and the Empress, terribly frightened, gave the order to return to the palace. That return drive stands out in my mind as an experience of horror. Every movement of the carriage, every rough place in the road, caused the child the most exquisite torture, and by the time we reached home he was almost unconscious with pain.

The next weeks were endless torment to the boy and to all of us who had to listen to his constant cries of pain. For fully eleven days these dreadful sounds filled the corridors outside his room, and those of us who were obliged to approach had often to stop our ears with our hands in order to go about our duties.

During the entire time the Empress never undressed, never went to bed, rarely even lay down for an hour's rest. Hour after hour she sat beside the bed where the half-conscious child lay huddled on one side, his left leg drawn up so sharply that for nearly a year afterwards he could not straighten it out.

His face was absolutely bloodless, drawn and seamed with suffering, while his almost expressionless eyes rolled back in his head. Once when the Emperor came into the room, seeing his boy in this agony and hearing his faint screams of pain, the poor father's courage completely gave way and he rushed, weeping bitterly, to his study. Both parents believed the child dying, and Alexei himself, in one of his rare moments of consciousness, said to his mother: 'When I am dead build me a little monument of stones in the wood.'

The family's most trusted physicians, Dr Raukhfus and Professor Fedorov and his assistant Dr Derevenko, were in charge of the case and after the first consultations declared the Tsarevich's condition hopeless. The haemorrhage of the stomach from which he was suffering seemed liable at any moment to turn into an abscess which could at any moment prove fatal.

One day at luncheon a note was brought from the Empress to the Emperor who, pale but collected, made a sign for the physicians to leave the table. Alexei, the Empress had written, was suffering so terribly that she feared the worst was about to happen. This crisis, however, was averted.

On the second occasion, on an evening after dinner when we were sitting very quietly in the Empress's boudoir, Princess Henry of Prussia,[4] who had come to be with her sister in her trouble, appeared in the doorway very white and agitated and begged the members of the suite to retire as the child's condition was desperate.

At eleven o'clock the Emperor and Empress entered the room, despair written on their faces. Still the Empress declared that she could not believe that God had abandoned them and she asked me to telegraph Rasputin for his prayers.

His reply came quickly. 'The little one will not die,' it said. 'Do not allow the doctors to bother him too much.' As a matter of fact the turning point came a few days later, the pain subsided, and the boy lay wasted and utterly spent, but alive.

Pierre Gilliard, Memoirs
One evening after dinner the Grand Duchesses Maria and Anastasia gave two short scenes from the *Bourgeois Gentilhomme* in the dining-room before Their Majesties, the suite, and several guests. I was the prompter, concealed behind a screen which did duty for the wings. By craning my neck a little I could see the Tsarina in the front row of the audience smiling and talking gaily to her neighbours.

When the play was over I went out by the service door and found myself in the corridor opposite Alexei's room, from which a moaning sound came distinctly to my ears. I suddenly noticed the Tsarina running up, holding her long and awkward train in her two hands. I shrank back against the wall, and she passed me without observing my presence.

There was a distracted and terror-stricken look on her face. I returned to the dining-room. The scene was of the most animated description. Footmen in livery were handing round refreshments on salvers. Everyone was laughing and exchanging jokes. The evening was at its height.

A few minutes later the Tsarina came back. She had resumed the

---

[4] Her sister Irène, whose son Henry had died from the same disease a few years earlier.

mask and forced herself to smile pleasantly at the guests who crowded round her. But I had noticed that the Tsar, even while engaged in conversation, had taken up a position from which he could watch the door, and I caught the despairing glances which the Tsarina threw him as she came in. An hour later I returned to my room, still thoroughly upset at the scene which had suddenly brought home to me the tragedy of this double life.

Yet, although the invalid's condition was still worse, life had apparently undergone no change. All that happened was that we saw less and less of the Tsarina. The Tsar controlled his anxiety and continued his shooting-parties, while the usual crowd of guests appeared at dinner every evening.

Nicky, Diary – 5 October – Spala

We did not spend a happy name day today, as for the last few days Alexei has been suffering from a second internal haemorrhage. Professor Fedorov arrived yesterday. Thank God he found a certain improvement today. There was a service and a lunch with the house suite. The weather was warm and grey.

Pierre Gilliard, Memoirs

On October 4th the fever was worse, reaching 102.5° in the morning and 103.3° in the evening. During dinner the Tsarina had Professor Fedorov fetched. On Sunday, October 7th, the patient's condition was still worse. There were, however, a few guests at luncheon. The next day, as the Tsarevich's temperature went up to 105° and the heart was very feeble, Count Fredericks asked the Tsar's permission to publish bulletins. The first was sent to St Petersburg the same evening.

Thus the intervention of the highest official at Court had been necessary before the decision to admit the gravity of the Tsarevich's condition was taken.

Why did the Tsar and Tsarina subject themselves to this dreadful ordeal? Why, when their one desire in life was to be with their suffering son, did they force themselves to appear among their guests with a smile on their lips? The reason was that they did not wish the world to know the nature of the Heir's illness, and, as I knew myself, regarded it in the light of a state secret.

On the morning of October 10th the child's temperature was 103.5°. About midday, however, the pains gradually subsided, and the doctors could proceed to a more thorough examination of the invalid, who had hitherto refused to allow it on account of his terrible sufferings.

At three o'clock in the afternoon there was a religious service in the forest. It was attended by a large number of peasants from the surrounding districts.

Beginning on the previous day, prayers for the recovery of the Heir were said twice a day. As there was no church at Spala, a tent with a small portable altar had been erected in the park as soon as we arrived. The priest officiated there morning and night.

KR, Diary – 9 October
There was a bulletin in the *Evening Times* about the illness of the Tsarevich. He is the Emperor's only son! May God protect him!

Nicky, Diary – 9 October – Spala
I stayed in Alexei's room until 2 o'clock, when he began to quieten down and fall asleep. He had quite a good day in general, and slept frequently, his temperature was back to 39.5. Went for a short walk in the morning with the girls. Played some tennis after lunch. The weather was warm. Took turns with Alix to sit with Alexei.

10 October   Today, thank God, saw an improvement in dear Alexei's condition, his temperature went down to 38.2.

After serving mass, the children's religious instructor father Vasilev brought the chalice to Alexei and gave him communion. What a comfort it was for us. After this Alexei was quite quiet and cheerful for the rest of the day.

Everyone felt in better spirits. In the afternoon I went for a good walk with Irène and all the girls. After tea I answered the many telegrams of sympathy.

12 October   Thanks to God dear Alexei is much better, during the day his temperature went down to 37.9. He was carried over onto the sofa, where he had an excellent nap. Outside it was cold, nearly 0. Went for a walk with Olga and Tatiana.

13 October   There was a frost at night and the day was very cold. Alexei slept well; his temperature was 38.1.

Nicky to Empress Marie – 20 October – Spala
Dearest darling Mama!

I am writing to you with a heart filled with gratitude to the Lord God, for his compassion in granting us dear Alexei's recovery!

After my last letter from Bielovejie his leg was hurting for a few days, as we now know from an awkward movement he made while jumping into the boat. [Dr] Botkin discovered he had a bruise and a small swelling below his abdomen, right at the beginning of the left leg. As the swelling subsided during the following week and Alexei felt well, I did not bother to write to you about it. On 2nd October he started to complain of great pain in the same place, and from then on his temperature started to go up every day. Botkin pronounced that Alexei had a serious haemorrhage on the left side and that he needed complete quiet. We immediately sent for the wonderful surgeon Fedorov, whom we have known for a long time and who has made a special study of this type of case, as well as dear Raukhfus. Our paediatrician Ostrogorsky had already arrived. I have to say that the sight of so many doctors is always depressing, but they were all so good, so kind and touching in their treatment of Alexei, that I will always remember them with gratitude.

The days from 6th–10th October were the worst. The poor little mite suffered terribly, the pains gripped him in spasms, which re-occurred practically every quarter of an hour. He was delirious day and night from the fever, and used to sit up in bed, a movement which immediately brought on the pain again.

He was practically unable to sleep, or even cry, and simply moaned and repeated 'Lord have mercy on us!'

I could hardly bear to stay in the room, but I had to relieve Alix, as she was understandably exhausted from spending days at a time at his bedside. She withstood it all better than I did while Alexei was so bad, but now that the danger has, thank God, passed, she is feeling the consequences of what she went through. It has taken its toll on her poor heart. However she is taking greater care of herself and spends the days lying on the couch in Alexei's room.

On 10th October we decided to give him communion, and he *immediately* felt better, his temperature dropped from 39.5 to 38.2, the pains almost ceased and he fell into a peaceful sleep for the first time.

All our people, the cossacks, the soldiers and others were so touching; from the first days of Alexei's illness, they asked the priest Alexander Vasilev, the children's religious instructor, to celebrate a Te Deum for his recovery in the open air. They asked him to do so every day until Alexei was better. A mass of Polish peasants also came and cried while he delivered them a sermon!

We have received so many telegrams, letters and icons, with wishes for the little one's speedy recovery.

I continue to receive documents twice a week as before, and between that and sitting at his bedside – my whole time has been taken up and I simply haven't able to write to you, dear Mama. Now I am completely myself again, and have been hunting quite often, which calms the nerves, otherwise I was afraid of turning into an old woman.

From your old Nicky, who loves you with all his heart.

Misha to Empress Marie – 31 October – Hotel Du Parc, Cannes
My dear Mama

If only you knew how painful and distressing it is for me to upset you, yet I know my letter will bring you great sorrow, and I ask you in advance to hear me out and forgive me.

I so much want you to believe me, when I say it's more than painful for me to distress you, dear Mama, but I am obliged to inform you that on the 16/29 October, that is two weeks ago, I was married to Natalia Sergeyevna Brassova.

I have suffered greatly over this last period, but was unable through force of circumstances to talk to you of that, which has been the main focus of my life for all these years, moreover you yourself evidently never wished it.

It is already five years since I met Natalia and I love and respect her more each year. But morally it was always very hard on me, and in particular the last year in Petersburg convinced me that the only way out of this painful and false situation was marriage. But I never wanted to distress you, and might never have decided on this step, were it not for little Alexei's illness, and the thought that as Heir I could be separated from Natalia, but now that can no longer happen.

Let me say again, that more than anything I am tortured by the fact of distressing you and Nicky so terribly, but to go on living as before was simply not bearable. And so I beg you, my dear Mama, to forgive and understand me as a mother, whom I love deeply with all my heart,
Your Misha

Misha to Nicky – 1 November – Hotel Du Parc, Cannes
Dear Nicky

I know that my letter will cause you a lot of sorrow, and I ask you in advance, as your brother, to listen and understand me. I am even more sorry to distress you, when you are already so preoccupied by Alexei's illness, but it was precisely this circumstance, and the thought that I could be separated from Natalia Brassova, that prompted me to marry her.

I have already loved her for five years, and can no longer say that on my side it was only a distraction. On the contrary, with each year I have become more deeply attached to her, and the thought that I could be deprived of her and our child – was simply unbearable.

At first I did not consider the possibility of marrying her, but the last five years, and particularly the past one in Petersburg, changed my intentions. You should know that, even during the two difficult years living apart (when I was in Orel), we were always a family, and I always looked on Natalia as my wife and always honoured her, which is why the humiliations and insults which she inevitably had to bear in Petersburg because of her position, were so terribly painful for me.

I give you my word that I did not act under pressure from anyone. Natalia never talked to me about it or demanded it, I myself came to the conclusion that to live in this way was dishonourable and that I had to escape from a false position. All this prompted me to take the decision and get married to Natalia.

Our wedding took place at the Serbian church of St Savva in Vienna on 16/29 October. I know that punishment awaits me for this act, and am ready to bear it.

Maurice Paléologue, Memoirs

[In a bookshop] I saw a slender young woman of about thirty come in and take a seat at a table on which an album of prints was laid out.

She was quite a delight to watch. Her whole style revealed a quiet, personal and refined taste. Her chinchilla coat, open at the neck, gave a glimpse of a dress of silver grey taffeta, with trimmings of lace. A light fur cap blended with her glistening fair hair.

Her pure and aristocratic face is charmingly modelled, and she has light, velvety eyes. Round her neck a string of superb pearls sparkled in the light, which had just been turned up.

She gave each print the most careful scrutiny, which occasionally made her blink and bend her neck. Every now and then she turned to a stool on her right, on which another album had been placed. There was a dignified, sinuous and soft gracefulness about her every movement. As I came out in the street I saw another elegant car behind mine. My footman asks me 'Your excellency, don't you know who this lady is?' 'No, who is it?' 'It is Countess Brassova, wife of Grand Duke Mikhail.'[5]

Empress Marie to Nicky – 4 November – Hvidore

My dear sweet Nicky! I cannot tell you how much your dear letter touched me and moved me to the depths of my soul. It's terrible to think what you must have lived through during this painful time and what torments you have had to bear, watching the suffering of your dear beloved little Alexei. I give thanks to God that things are improving now, that he is no longer in pain and is sleeping well. I hope the journey will not do him any harm, nor the cold and bad weather. I was sure, that the doctors would advise taking him to the south, although I understand how difficult it would have been for you to take that decision. I am not sure that everything can and should be sacrificed for the sake of his health?

I fully understand your feelings of gratitude when, after taking communion, he began to feel better, also seeing so much sympathy around must have been of some comfort to you both in those moments of despair. I am happy for you that the last weeks have been calmer, and that you have been able to go hunting.

Now I must tell you of a *terrible cruel new blow*!

I have just received a letter from Misha, in which he informs me of *his marriage*! I simply can't believe it, and can hardly understand what I am writing, it's so unspeakably awful in every way, and has *completely killed me*!

I only ask that it should remain a secret, so there shouldn't be *another scandal*, there have been other marriages in *secret*, which everyone *pretended not to know about*. I think it's really the only thing that can be done now, otherwise I won't be able to show myself any more, it's such a *shame and a disgrace*!

May God forgive him, I can only pity him. But my God! What a sorrow and how hard it is to bear such blows! Thank God, dear Xenia is with me, she is supporting me, it's a great comfort to talk to her. But now I must end, I'm not in a state to write about it any more, it's too painful.

May the Lord keep you and bless you, my dears. I embrace you fondly, especially dear Alexei, please tell him how touched his grand-

---

[5] This conversation took place later, when Natalia was granted the title Countess Brassova.

mother is that he remembered her. Once again I thank you, my dear Nicky, for your dear letter.

Your deeply loving Mama

Nicky to Empress Marie – 7 November – Tsarskoe Selo

My dear sweet Mama!

I thank you with all my heart for your kind words. I was also going to write to you about this new sorrow, which has befallen our family, but you had already heard the disgusting news.

I enclose the letter I received in the train on the way here. Read it and see for yourself, can he really, after everything he has written, remain in the service and in command of your cavalry?

Yes, dear Mama, I say as you do – may the Lord forgive him! Unfortunately everything is over between him and me now, because he has broken his word.

How many times did he tell me, without my asking, *he himself gave* his word that he would not marry her. And I believed him implicitly! What upsets me particularly – is that he refers to Alexei's illness as having forced him to rush into this ill-considered step! He doesn't seem concerned with either your distress, or our distress, or the scandal this event will cause in Russia. And at such a time, when everyone is talking of war, and just a few months before the Jubilee of the Romanov dynasty!!! It's shameful and awful!

My first thought was also to keep the news quiet, but on reading his letter two or three times I realized that it's impossible for him to return to Russia now. Sooner or later everyone here will find out, and will be surprised if nothing has happened to him, as the others were dealt with very severely.

About two months ago, Fredericks learnt from Vrangel that Misha had requested a large sum of money from his office, and that apparently he even bought an estate in France.

Now all is clear. I cannot find words to express, dear Mama, how I feel about what you must be suffering. May the Merciful Lord give you strength! What luck that dear Xenia is with you at the moment, to share the torments of your heart.

Alix and I both embrace you tenderly. Alexei sends you a big kiss and thanks you. Thank God he is cheerful and happy. Christ be with you.

Your old Nicky, who loves you with all his heart.

Olga [sister], Memoirs

Misha was [Nicky's] only remaining brother. He could have given Nicky so much help. I tell you again that all of us were to blame. Of the three sons of Uncle Vladimir one was banished, another, Boris, was living quite openly with a mistress, and the third, Andrew, was never much use to my brother. Yet those three were the sons of the senior Grand Duke and, after Alexei and Mikhail, stood next in succession. Nicky had not a single member of the family to turn to, except, perhaps, Sandro, my brother-in-law, but even there things got difficult in time when we heard of Sandro and Xenia having serious disagreements! What example could we give to the nation? Little wonder that poor Nicky, lacking support on all sides, became a fatalist. He would often put his arm round me and say, 'I was born on Job's day – I am ready to accept my fate.'

Nicky to Empress Marie – 21 November – Tsarskoe Selo

Dear sweet Mama

Poor Misha is evidently not responsible for his own actions at the moment; he thinks and reasons as she tells him, and it's utterly useless to argue with him. Mordvinov [Misha's former ADC] has very much asked us NOT TO WRITE to him AT ALL, as she not only reads any telegrams, letters and notes, but takes copies which she shows to her people and then keeps in the bank together with the money. She's such a cunning, wicked beast that it's disgusting to even talk about her.

Until we meet very soon, dear Mama, Christ be with you! I embrace you lovingly

Your Nicky, who loves you with all his heart

Misha to Empress Marie – 7 December – Cannes

My dear Mama,

I await stern punishment for my act, which was dictated to me solely by my conscience. I am ready to bear all the punishments and deprivations, I do not fear them, the only thing which is very painful is the distress, which I have unintentionally caused you. Dear Mama, surely I have only acted as befits any honourable man – in that my conscience is clear. With all my heart I beg you not to judge me harshly, but to give me your blessing, as a mother whom I love deeply. May the Lord keep you, my dear Mama. I embrace you warmly. I love you with all my heart.   Misha

Maria [daughter] to Alix – 14 December – Tsarskoe Selo

My Mama darling,

I thank you so *very* much for your dear letter. I am so sorry that your heart is still No. 2. I hope your cold is better. My temperature now is 37.1 and my throat acks less than yesterday. Am so sorry not to see you today, but sertenly its better for you to rest. 1000 kisses from your own loving

Maria

King George V to Nicky – 16 December – Sandringham

My dearest Nicky,

I can't tell you how much I have felt for you and dear Alicky in all your anxiety during your dear little boy's illness. I trust he is really better now and does not suffer any more pain. Are you going to send him to the South during the winter?

I have also felt for you so much on account of dear Misha. I am so fond of him, that I am in despair that he should have done this foolish thing and I know how miserable you must be about it. What a lot of worries and anxieties there are in this world.

Ever, dearest Nicky, your very devoted cousin and old friend

Georgie

Much love from May and the children.

Report of Police Agent Krasilnikov on the marriage of Grand Duke Mikhail Alexandrovich

ABSOLUTELY CONFIDENTIAL

Your Excellency Sir Stepan Petrovich[6]

In my telegram of November 21 (Russian style), No 382, I humbly reported to Your Excellency that, according to the information received, the marriage of His Imperial Highness Grand Duke Mikhail to Mme Wulfert was contracted in Vienna, allegedly, in the summer of the current year.

However, Grand Duke Mikhail spent all last summer in Russia, as far as I know, staying mostly in Gatchina, and he left abroad only in September, surveillance having been established since the very arrival of His Imperial Highness in Berlin, and so it seemed that the

---

[6] S. P. Beletskiy, Director of the Police Department.

guards might not have missed the journey of His Imperial Highness to Vienna.

Having carried out a most discreet, confidential inquiry of the matter in Kissingen, as well as in Berlin and Vienna, I am now able to humbly inform Your Excellency about the circumstances and the exact time of His Imperial Highness' marriage.

Having left Russia abroad on September 12/25, the Grand Duke stopped at the Esplanade Hotel in Berlin and stayed there together with Mme Wulfert until September 24 (Russian style), and then [he] went to Kissingen where Mme Wulfert received treatment at Dr Apolant's sanatorium.

In late October, as Mme Wulfert's course of treatment was completed, the Grand Duke decided to leave Kissingen for Cannes. On October 27 (Russian style) the Grand Duke wired from Kissingen to the Esplanade Hotel asking if they could book tickets for him in a sleeping-car from Frankfort-on-the-Main to Paris. Having received a positive answer from the hotel, the Grand Duke wired them to book 4 tickets in a sleeper and 4 1st-class tickets to Paris for October 29. Next day, His Imperial Highness wired to the Esplanade Hotel informing that he did not need the tickets.

Having suddenly changed his mind, on September 29 the Grand Duke must have declared to their companions that he and Mme Wulfert were leaving that day in a motor-car via Switzerland and Italy to Cannes, and the children, the persons accompanying them, and the servants were supposed to travel by rail from Paris to Cannes.

The same day, the Grand Duke and Mme Wulfert drove in the automobile only to Würzburg where they took the train via Munich and Salzburg to Vienna, which His Imperial Highness reached in the morning of October 30 and stopped at the Tegethof Hotel. At 4 p.m. of the same day the Grand Duke and Mme Wulfert drove to the Serbian Church of St Savva (No 3 Weitgasse) where they were married.

The entry made was as follows, 'Mikhail Alexandrovich, Russian Grand Duke, b. on 22nd November, 1878, in St Petersburg, and noblewoman Natalia Brassova, b. on 7th June, 1880, in Pezowa, near Moscow'.

On October 31, His Imperial Highness and Mme Wulfert travelled from Vienna, via Munich where they stopped for one day, to Cannes where they arrived in the morning of November 3.

As the guard did not follow the Grand Duke in an automobile, they could not know anything, the itinerary and the aim of the trip having been kept secret even from the persons close to them.

Begging Your Excellency to accept the assurance of my deep respect and sincere devotion.

A Krasilnikov
Agent No 1638
Paris
December 17 (30), 1912

Maurice Paléologue, Memoirs
In their gilded exile the young couple enjoyed a very pleasant existence, dividing their time between Paris, London, the Engadine and Cannes. Thus everything turned out as Natalia desired.

Olga [sister], Memoirs
Neither the Emperor nor either of the two Empresses ever received Misha's wife.

1913

Nicky – Emperor of Russia

Xenia – Grand Duchess, Nicky's sister, married to Sandro

Sandro – Grand Duke Alexander Mikhailovich, husband of Xenia

Olga (sister) – Grand Duchess, Nicky's younger sister

Ella – Grand Duchess Elizabeth, elder sister of Alix, now a nun

Grand Duke Pavel – Nicky's uncle

Olga – eldest daughter of Nicky and Alix, aged eighteen

Tatiana – second daughter of Nicky and Alix, aged sixteen

Maria – third daughter of Nicky and Alix, aged fourteen

Anastasia – fourth daughter of Nicky and Alix, aged twelve

Alexei – Heir and Tsarevich, son of Nicky and Alix, aged nine

Willy – Kaiser Wilhelm II of Germany, Nicky's cousin

Prince Felix Yusupov

Ania Vyrubova – lady-in-waiting and close friend of Alix

Pierre Gilliard – Swiss tutor of Nicky and Alix's children

A. A. Mosolov – a court official

1913

IRINA AND FELIX

The police are watching Rasputin – Xenia goes to Paris
and meets her brother Misha – The three hundredth
anniversary of the Romanov dynasty – Continuing
worries over Alexei's health – Xenia and Sandro arrange
for Misha to meet Empress Marie in England – Sandro
goes to America – Felix Yusupov becomes engaged to
Irina, daughter of Xenia and Sandro

A. A. Mosolov, Memoirs
[The Education of the Imperial Children]
At that time, Olga was at seventeen already quite a young lady, but
she still behaved like a girl. She had beautiful light hair, her face – a
wide oval – was purely Russian, not particularly regular, but her
remarkably delicate colouring and her pretty smile, which disclosed
remarkably even, white teeth, gave her a great freshness.

Tatiana (fifteen) was a little taller, more delicate and slender, her
face was rather longer and her whole appearance was more aristocratic and well-bred, her hair was darker than her older sister's, but
she did not smile as often. She was, to my mind, the most beautiful
of the sisters.

Maria (thirteen) at this time was a young girl with a happy Russian
face and unusual strength.

The youngest – Anastasia (eleven) was still a child. When she was
very small, she promised to turn into quite a beauty – but this was
not realized. Her face was less regular than that of her sisters, but very
lively. If you happened to be sitting next to her at table, you had constantly to be ready for some unexpected question. She was bolder
than her sisters and very witty.

Olga's character was even, good, with an almost angelic kindness. Tatiana, on the other hand, had a difficult character, more reserved, but with perhaps deeper spiritual qualities than her sister. Maria was kind, though not without a certain obstinacy, but less able than her two elder sisters. Anastasia, whose character was not yet formed, of course, would certainly be very capable, but was the only one of the grand duchesses who was capricious.

The girls were beautifully dressed, and if sometimes the severest arbiters of fashion criticized the taste of the Empress in her own clothes, apart from her formal attire, as far as the children were concerned, all were agreed that they could not be better dressed. And despite the fact that they were usually dressed alike, each had her own personal touch, particular to her style, a certain sort of ribbon or an imperceptible variation in cut. The Empress and the girls were dressed for the most part by the dressmaker Lamanova of Moscow.

All the children loved the *Standart*. Of course the grand duchesses had a very gay time on board, all the young men courted them, each one had her flirt. Of course it has to be said that these officers were remarkably schooled by one of the elder officers, who was considered the flirt of the Empress herself.

When the Tsarevich was in good health, the Empress looked better also, she became more animated on the *Standart* and willingly talked with the officers.

Apart from the suite, the only people to come into close contact with the grand duchesses were their closest relatives, the children of Grand Duchess Xenia. They saw the grand duchesses often, and were usually invited for afternoon tea and tennis. Xenia had only one daughter, Irina, and six sons.

I honestly do not think that it ever entered the children's heads that one could live in any other way. They were not demanding. One film show on Saturdays gave them a topic of conversation for the whole week.

Various attempts were made to find playmates for the heir. First they chose the children of sailors, then the children or nephews of the Tsarevich's nurse [Nanny] Derevenko,[1] then they decided not to have anyone at all.

Without any ulterior thought, I became close to the tutor Gilliard, an extremely clever and educated man, and in my opinion, a first class pedagogue. The difficulty in teaching the Tsarevich lay in the

---

[1] Alexei's nurse was a sailor, Derevenko; his doctor, by coincidence, was also Derevenko.

fact that, as soon as his education and instruction were going well, the Heir fell ill – his haemophilia causing terrible sufferings in the case of internal bleeding. Of course, after the sleepless nights and unbearable pain, the child was completely nervously exhausted, although little by little the tutor had to bring his pupil up again to a certain level of knowledge and behaviour. In Gilliard's words, Alexei's main fault was inattention.

Pierre Gilliard, Memoirs

The Grand Duchesses were charming – the picture of freshness and health. It would have been difficult to find four sisters with characters more dissimilar and yet so perfectly blended in an affection which did not exclude personal independence, and, in spite of contrasting temperaments, kept them a most united family. With the initials of their Christian names they had formed a composite Christian name, Otma, and under this common signature they frequently gave their presents or sent letters written by one of them on behalf of them all.

I am sure I shall be forgiven for allowing myself the pleasure of recording some personal memories here – memories which will enable me to recall these girls in all the bloom and spontaneous enthusiasm of their youth. I might almost say their childhood. For these were girls who fell victims to a dreadful fate at a time when others were blossoming into womanhood.

Their relations with the Tsar were delightful. He was Emperor, father, and friend in one. Their feelings for him were dictated by circumstances, passing from religious veneration to utter frankness and the warmest affection. Was it not he before whom the ministers, the highest dignitaries of the Church, the grand dukes, and even their mother bowed in reverence, he whose fatherly heart opened so willingly to their sorrows, he who joined so merrily in their youthful amusements, far from the eyes of the indiscreet?

In short, the whole charm, difficult though it was to define, of these four sisters was their extreme simplicity, candour, freshness, and instinctive kindness of heart.

Their mother, whom they adored, was, so to speak, infallible in their eyes.

Her Majesty talked English with them, the Emperor Russian only. The Tsarina talked English or French with the members of her suite. She never spoke Russian (though she spoke it pretty well ultimately) except to those who knew no other language. During the whole period of my residence with the Imperial family I never heard one of them utter a word of German, except when it was inevitable, as at receptions, etc.

Maria [daughter] to Alix

My dear darling Mama,

You don't know how sorry I am that you feel bad. It is so awful to see how you suffer. You are [so] patient that I cannot understand. Anastasia kiss you and is sad that you can't come down, and wishes you good night. God bless you.

Maria

Note from Anastasia

(Madam dearest, I am afraid to go home [to bedroom] in the dark so I sat down on the W.C. picking my toe in the dark.)

I hope you're well soon. Go to bed and be quiet. Good night. Sleep well.

Olga [sister], Memoirs

[on Anastasia] My favourite god-daughter she was indeed! I liked her fearlessness. She never whimpered or cried, even when hurt. She was a fearful tomboy. Goodness only knows which of the young cousins had taught her how to climb trees, but climb them she did, even when she was quite small. It was not generally known that she had a weak back and the doctors ordered massage. Anastasia hated what she labelled 'fuss'. A hospital nurse, Tatiana Gromova, used to come to the palace twice a week and my naughty little niece would hide in a cupboard or under her bed, just to put off the massage by another five minutes or so. I suppose the doctors were right about the defective muscle, but nobody seeing Anastasia at play would have believed it, so quick and energetic she was. And what a bundle of mischief!

Pierre Gilliard, Memoirs

[on Anastasia] ... extremely idle, though with the idleness of a gifted child. Her French accent was excellent, and she acted scenes from comedy with remarkable talent. She was so lively, and her gaiety so infectious, that several members of the suite had fallen into the way of calling her 'Sunshine', the nickname her mother had been given at the English Court.

Nicky, Diary – 2 January – Tsarskoe Selo
Today turned out to be a holiday for me, as it was the anniversary of the death of the reverend Serafim of Sarov.

I went with Olga [sister] and the girls to a mass. Returned at 12.15. Xenia came to lunch. Alix continued to have pain in her face and head. Went for a good walk with Olga, the girls and Irina [Xenia and Sandro's daughter] in the park and around the big lake.

3 January Alix stayed in bed until tea-time. After lunch, I went with the girls to slide down the steep bank of the narrow pond. It was unbelievably slippery; we fell as we climbed back up, but we kept on doing it all the same.

4 January Lunched with the girls. Olga and Tatiana went to town. Went for a walk with Maria and Anastasia. The elder daughters returned at 7.30. After dinner I read aloud 'Chopping wood'.

The surveillance of Rasputin – a Police Department Report – 18 February
1) Surveillance of the well-known *staretz* and peasant from Pokrovskoe, Tiumen district, Tobolsk province, Grigory Efimovich RASPUTIN-NOVY, 41 years old, was carried out according to the order of the late Chairman of the Council of Ministers State Secretary Stolypin, in 1910. At that time Rasputin was only under observation for a few days, after which the surveillance ceased.

2) Surveillance of him was ordered again by the former Minister of the Interior Senator Makarov from 23 January 1912, and during the period from that date until 16 January 1913 the aforesaid surveillance discovered the following:

Rasputin did not often go out alone, but when he did, he usually made his way to the Nevsky prospect or other streets where there are prostitutes, and accosted them, then took one of them and went with her to a hotel or the baths.

During Rasputin's first trip in 1912, surveillance of him revealed six such incidents, whose particular characteristics are as follows:

On 4th February, on leaving the prostitutes Botvinkina and Kozlova/ house no.11, Sviechny alley/ Rasputin went straight to the Golovins' in the company of some others. He left there after two hours and went to the Nevsky prospect, where he again picked up a prostitute and went with her to the baths on Koniushennaya street.

On 6th February, Rasputin left Zinaida Mandshtet, with whom he spent an hour and a half, and went straight to the Nevsky prospect, where he picked up the prostitute Petrova and went with her to the baths at house no.26 on the Moika.

During Rasputin's second and third visits to Petersburg/ from 29th June to 9th August and from 19th–23rd September 1912/ the surveillance only noted that he was visited by Zinaida Mandshtet and Maria Sazonova, his other female admirers being absent from Petersburg at that time, as well as two of the usual incidents of meetings between Rasputin and prostitutes.

On the 21st November Rasputin was visited by Maria Sazonova, together with another unknown lady and a young girl, and she stayed with him for two hours. After this Rasputin came out with Sazonova, from whom he rapidly parted. In the Stoliazny alley he picked up a prostitute and went with her to a flat on Kaznacheisky street. He soon came out of there, and found another prostitute on Sennaya square, with whom he spent 45 minutes in the hotel.

It turns out, according to the first prostitute, that Rasputin bought her two bottles of beer, although he did not drink himself, asked her to undress, looked at her body, then paid her two roubles and left.

On 22nd November, as he was walking along the streets, Rasputin accosted several women with lewd suggestions, to which they responded with threats, and some even spat on him.

If, as described, during Rasputin's first visits to Petersburg he displayed a certain care in his meetings with prostitutes, looking behind him, going into dark alleys etc, then during his last visit in January of this year, he conducted these meetings quite openly, besides which Rasputin was not afraid to appear on the street in a drunken state on one occasion, while on another he committed an act of sacrilege in relation to an Orthodox church.

On 13th January 1913, Rasputin left his house with Sazonova, parted from her quite soon, and went to the Nikolaevsky station, where he walked up and down for ten minutes, looking at women. Then he went into the pastry restaurant on Znamenskaya street, and on emerging from there, stopped to answer a call of nature on the porch of the church. After that he went to the hotel at no.14 Suvorovsky prospect, where soon afterwards they brought him a prostitute from the restaurant. After half an hour Rasputin came out and returned home.

Ella, from her Deposition

When rumours started to reach me about how Rasputin was not as he seemed, and that in his private life he conducted himself in quite another way than with the imperial family, I warned my sister, but she told me that she did not believe these rumours, that she considered them slanders, of the sort that generally pursue people of a saintly life.

Nicky, Diary – 18 January – Tsarskoe Selo
At 4 o'clock we received good old Grigory, who stayed with us for an hour and a quarter.

Pierre Gilliard, Memoirs
It became more and more usual to see him [Rasputin] with Madame Vyrubova, who had a little house quite near to the Alexander Palace.

Ania Vyrubova, Memoirs
The Emperor and Empress used to call Rasputin simply 'Grigory' and he called them 'Papa' and 'Mama'. They used to kiss when they met, but neither the Emperor nor the Empress ever kissed his hands.

Olga [sister], Memoirs
Rasputin was there [at Vyrubova's] and he seemed very pleased to meet me again, and when the hostess with Nicky and Alicky left the drawing-room for a few moments, Rasputin got up, put his arm about my shoulders, and began stroking my arm. I moved away at once, saying nothing. I just got up and joined the others. I'd had more than enough of the man. I disliked him more than ever. Believe it or not, on my return to St Petersburg I did a strange thing – I sought my husband [Prince of Oldenburg] out in the study, and told him all that had happened at Ania Vyrubova's cottage. He heard me out and with a grave face he suggested that I should avoid meeting Rasputin in the future. For the first and only time I knew my husband was right.

Xenia, Diary – 4 March – St Petersburg
Misha telegraphed from Paris, for us to come next week 'if you want to see me', saying he will be staying two weeks. Not a single word of encouragement or greeting!

Kaiser Wilhelm II to Nicky – 5 March – Berlin
Dearest Nicky,

May I inform you that we now have definitely fixed the date for the wedding of our dear Sissy[2] for the 24th of May.

The main object of my lines is to convey to you and Alix our most cordial invitation to the wedding ceremonies. We both would only be too delighted if you could give us the pleasure of your presence and I fervently hope that you will be able to leave Russia for a few days to meet many of your relatives; as we have asked your dear Mama, Aunt Alix, Georgie and May, Valdemar etc. to enable all the 'Geschwister' to meet each other as well as Aunt Thyra.

With best love from Victoria and me to Alix and all the children believe me ever your most devoted cousin and friend

Willy

Xenia, Diary – 15 March – St Petersburg
We talked a lot about Misha. Nicky has said and repeated to him, that he can come to Russia whenever he *wants* – but she is forbidden.

19 March – Paris I left St Petersburg and arrived here, exhausted both mentally and physically. The parting with Mama was very painful – For the whole journey, I could not think of her without tears, then my meeting and conversation with Misha finally finished me off.

But now that I have told him *everything* and got it all off my chest after three months, I feel somewhat better. He sat with me for two hours and we talked the whole time. As I told him about Mama, the terrible winter, and her health and state of mind, I was unable to hold back my tears – nor was he. We cried on each other's shoulders.

Poor Mishkin, he is suffering so much. I told him about Alexei's illness, and about Nicky; here he was more attentive, and occasionally made a remark or asked a question. He says that he was unable to do otherwise, that he suffers for Mama and regrets having to break his word to Nicky, but that he was obliged to act in this way. Of course, there were many things I didn't touch on, there was no time. In the train as I was leaving, I received a telegram from F. saying that he was leaving for England, that he was just dead! I should think so! I miss him terribly here!

---

[2] Kaiser Wilhelm's daughter Victoria Louise (Sissy) married Ernest August, Duke of Brunswick-Lüneburg, in 1913.

Felix Yusupov, Memoirs

The most delightful of all was the Grand Duchess Xenia. Her chief attraction lay not in her beauty but in the rare, delicate charm which she had inherited from her mother, the Empress.

Her wonderful grey eyes seemed to penetrate one's innermost soul, and everyone who came near her fell a slave to her grace, modesty and kindness of heart. From early childhood I looked forward to her visits and, when she left, I would wander about the rooms, rapturously sniffing a delicious odour of lilies of the valley which still lingered in the air.

Xenia, Diary – 22 March – Paris

It was *so sad* saying goodbye to Misha, when will we meet again? He was so sweet and touching, and kept thanking me the whole time for coming, my poor little boy! It's hurtful and sad that he has slipped away from us again!

Tatiana to Alix – 26 March – Tsarskoe Selo

My dear darling Mama,

I just had a bath and before that a chair, so today I had two chairs. I hope you will sleep well my darling angel and that I will see you not in bed with a bad heart, but feeling well and in your sitting room.

Then I'll come tomorrow at nine to say good morning before my lesson which I have together with Olga. God bless you my own beloved Mama deary. Sleep nicely and be well to-morrow. 100000000000000000000000000000000000000   x 100000000000000000000000000000 so many times I kiss you.

Your own loving devoted true and thankful for all daughter

Tatiana

Kiss Papa dear.

Xenia, Diary – 11 April – St Petersburg

During our absence (as I already knew) Irina and Felix had seen each other several times, and that they like each other, the stupid children! I even talked about it to Mama. She is not quite sure whether it would be a good thing!

Felix Yusupov, Memoirs

Having been told of the disagreeable rumours that were being circulated about me, the Dowager Empress expressed the wish to see me. Irina was her favourite grandchild, and all her thoughts were for her happiness. I knew that our fate was in her hands.

Nicky, Diary – 18 April – Tsarskoe Selo
After tea we sat for a long time with Grigory.

Alexei to Nicky – 8 May – Tsarskoe Selo
Dear Papa
   I think of you every moment. I know where you are going now. Keep well. May God protect you!

                                                                 Alexei

Anastasia to Nicky – 8 May – Tsarskoe Selo
My darling sweet dear Papa!!!
   I want to see you so much. I have just finished my arithmetic lesson, I think I did quite well. We are going to nurses' school. I am very glad. Today it is rainy and very damp. I am in Tatiana's room, Tatiana and Olga are here. When you see Boba, tell him I'm going to beat him again and that my hands are itching.
   I'm trying very hard to breed worms, but Olga says I stink, which isn't true. When you come I am going to bathe in your bath. I hope you haven't forgotten the story I told you during our walk.
   I am sitting picking my nose with my left hand. Olga wanted to biff me one, but I escaped her swinish hand. When you come I will meet you at the station. Be happy and healthy.
   A big squeeze to your hand and face. Thinking of you. Love you always, everywhere

                                                                 Anastasia

Nicky, Diary – 20 May – Moscow
Woke up to a heavenly morning. At 10 o'clock we arrived at the landing stage at Kostroma and drove to the cathedral, which was surrounded by lines of troops. I inspected them, then we went inside the cathedral and soon joined the holy procession to the foundation site of the large memorial to the 300th anniversary of the Romanov dynasty. Each of us put a stone with his name. After the foundation ceremony, the troops performed a ceremonial march-past.

Xenia, Diary – 24 May – Moscow
At a quarter to four we all gathered at the railway to meet Nicky and
Alix, everyone – ministers, suite, high officials, court ladies etc; the
solemn procession started out from the station – Nicky and the men
on horseback, we in carriages. It was magnificent, a mass of people,
and everything, thank God, went off splendidly. At the Spassky gates,
everyone dismounted and proceeded in procession on foot to the
Archangel cathedral. During the service, Nicky lit a lamp at the tomb
of M.F.[3]

Rasputin was standing by the entrance, everyone saw him, except
for me! Rasputin is once again in evidence all over the place, there is
such discontent and protest among the clergy! They say Maklakov[4] is
preparing a report for Nicky! How unfortunate it all is – certainly if
he were a minister, he would not dare show himself.

6 June   Alix looks better. We talked with Nicky and Alix about Irina
and Felix. They had already heard something, and in principle have
nothing against it, except that Alix says that he used to have a bad
reputation. I know from people who know him well, that this is a lie.

And even if there was something, then it's all past. We said goodbye to them also, probably for a long time.

Ania Vyrubova to Rasputin – 9 June – Telegram
MAMA [ALIX] DELIGHTED BY TELEGRAM. THE LITTLE ONE'S LEG HURTS. WE
ARE LEAVING. I MISS YOU. I BELIEVE YOU CONTINUE TO PRAY FOR YOUR
OWN.

Pierre Gilliard, Memoirs
The Tsarevich was in the schoolroom standing on a chair, when he
slipped, and in falling hit his right knee against the corner of some
piece of furniture. The next day he could not walk.

The Tsarina was at her son's side from the first onset of the attack.
She watched over him surrounding him with her tender love and
care and trying by a thousand attentions to alleviate his sufferings.
The Tsar came the moment he was free. He tried to comfort and
amuse the boy, but the pain was stronger than his mother's caresses
or his father's stories, and the moans and tears began once more.

---

[3] Mikhail Feodorovich, the first Romanov (1613–45).
[4] Minister of the Interior and Chief of the Gendarmerie.

Every now and then the door opened and one of the Grand Duchesses came in on tip-toe and kissed her little brother, bringing a gust of sweetness into the room. For a moment the boy would open his great eyes, round which the malady had already painted black rings, and then almost immediately close them again.

One morning I found the mother at her son's bedside. He had had a very bad night. Dr Derevenko was anxious, as the haemorrhage had not been stopped and his temperature was rising. The inflammation had spread further and the pain was even worse than the day before. The Tsarevich lay in bed groaning piteously.

His head rested on his mother's arm, and his small, deathly-white face was unrecognizable. At times the groans ceased and he murmured the one word 'Mummy!' in which he expressed all his sufferings and distress.

His mother kissed him on the hair, forehead, and eyes, as if the touch of her lips could have relieved his pain and restored some of the life which was leaving him.

Think of the tortures of that mother, an impotent witness of her son's martyrdom in those hours of mortal anguish – a mother who knew that *she herself* was the cause of his sufferings, that *she* had transmitted to him the terrible disease against which human science was powerless! *Now* I understood the secret tragedy of her life!

Ania Vyrubova to Rasputin
I am sending you, dear father Grigory, a letter from the eldest. Our little one is still very ill, they say that an inner vessel has burst because of the fever and cough, there is haemorrhaging, swelling on the side, pain and fever. The others have all been slightly ill. Pray for us.

Your Anna

Xenia, Diary – 12 June – Paris
Nikolai [Sandro's brother] came this morning, bringing a confidential letter from Misha complaining about us all, that we don't write, that we don't care about him, don't do anything that he asks etc.; I was completely destroyed for the whole day – the whole thing is untrue!

17 June Both Nikolai and I received long letters from Misha – he's still complaining about everyone! Mama telegraphed today [from

London], hoping that he might come to England. But how to arrange it? I wrote and telegraphed him about it.

23 June   I sat with Mama talking about Misha, she was crying. She so wants to see him! Sandro sent him a telegram, saying that he *must* come.

11 July – London   Prince F. met me at the station and said that he had seen Misha – with her – and that he looked rather embarrassed for her!

Mama feels better, but was very agitated at the prospect of seeing him. At last he arrived, and they disappeared into the next room for a minute, but returned looking quite calm! Thank God it went all right! I was so anxious for Mama.

12 July   Mama was very happy to see him! She was completely unable to sleep – she was so excited and upset. Misha arrived at around 12 and we walked together as far as Piccadilly.

In the evening they had a good quiet talk, thank God, and he was happy to be able to speak. She saw his wife and told her a few home truths in front of Misha, which she also repeated to me in front of him. She is so sad and upset. In general it's terribly *pénible* [unpleasant] on all sides.

Nicky, Diary – 16 July – Peterhof

In the evening Alexei's right elbow began to hurt, from waving his arms about too much while playing. He could not sleep for a long time and was in great pain, poor thing!

17 July   At 7 o'clock Grigory arrived, and spent a short while with Alix and Alexei; he talked with me and the girls and then left.

Soon after his departure the pain in Alexei's arm started to go away, he himself became calmer and began to fall asleep. Spent the evening sticking photographs into my album.

Pierre Gilliard, Memoirs

The months passed, the expected miracle did not happen, and the cruel ruthless attacks followed hard on each other's heels. The most fervent prayers had not brought the divine revelation so passionately implored. The last hope had failed. A sense of endless despair filled the Tsarina's soul: it seemed as if the whole world were deserting her.

Rasputin said: 'Believe in the power of my prayers; believe in my help and your son will live!'

The mother clung to the hope he gave her as a drowning man seizes an outstretched hand. She believed in him with all the strength that was in her. As a matter of fact, she had been convinced for a long time that the saviour of Russia and the dynasty would come from the people, and she thought that this humble *moujik* had been sent by God to save him who was the hope of the nation. The intensity of her faith did the rest, and by a simple process of auto-suggestion, which was helped by certain perfectly casual coincidences, she persuaded herself that her son's life was in this man's hands.

Rasputin had realised the state of mind of the despairing mother who was broken down by the strain of her struggle and seemed to have touched the limit of human suffering. He knew how to extract the fullest advantage from it, and with a diabolical cunning he succeeded in associating his own life, so to speak, with that of the child.

Sandro, Memoirs
In the summer of 1913, I felt bored with our annual programme. Xenia and the children stayed in the grand hotel at Treport, while I went to America.

Xenia, Diary – 24 July – Treport
Sandro is going to America on Saturday. He thinks that M.I.[5] won't even want to see him!

4 August Today articles appeared in the *Herald* and the *Daily Mail* about Sandro's arrival in America, and how he will be the guest of Mr and Mrs V![6] I can imagine their rage. Indeed, nothing could be more stupid! Now they have spoilt all his enjoyment, and we had so successfully kept it all a secret, no one here knew anything.

5 August Sandro telegraphed that he will be staying on there – M.I. is only coming in November. How stupid! Now what?!

19 August I received a letter from Sandro – which bothered and

---

[5] The wife of Xenia's Prince F.
[6] Almost certainly Mr and Mrs Vanderbilt.

upset me – saying that he is really resting, that he is happy to be with M.I. He is thinking of returning towards the 30th, and going to Petersburg with the children. He asks what my plans are – do I want to go to the Crimea and return to Paris in November, when M.I. will be there. It's all very vague and funny. F. is such a comfort in moments of sadness and melancholy.

21 August   Sandro is leaving on Saturday. He is now in Newport, and is going to New York in a few days. M.I. is at her mother's.

26 September – Ai-Todor   Dined en famille with Irina at Livadia. Alix is still the same – she dined with us. We chatted a lot. Sandro told us all about America.

Talked with Alix about Felix. Everyone kept asking whether we are sure about him – which I cannot say, unfortunately, that we are.

Felix Yusupov, Memoirs
Before my engagement to Irina had been officially announced, Dmitri [son of Grand Duke Pavel] came to see me to ask whether there was any truth in the rumour that I was to marry his cousin. I replied that there was some question of it but that nothing, so far, had been settled. 'Because,' he went on, 'I too intend to marry her.' I thought at first that he was joking, but not at all; he assured me that he had never been more serious in his life. Princess Irina would have to choose between us. We made a mutual promise not to say or do anything that might influence her. But, when I repeated this conversation to Irina, she said that she had made up her mind to marry me and that nothing and no one would induce her to change her mind.

Dmitri bowed before a decision which he realised was final, but our friendship was to suffer and our relations were never the same afterwards.

Xenia, Diary – 1 October – Ai-Todor
[Princess] Zinaida Yusupov and Felix came for tea. The three of us talked a lot about her. At last we cleared up everything. We decided not to announce anything before the winter, when everyone will be gathered together, and with Mama.

Olga [sister], Memoirs
I still remember their drawing-rooms and tables crammed with

crystal bowls filled with uncut sapphires, emeralds, and opals – all used as decorations. I think that all that fabulous wealth never spoiled Princess Yusupov. She was kindly and generous and she could be a loyal friend. But, alas, she was a tragic mother – she spoiled her children far too much.

Felix Yusupov, Memoirs

I was never parted from my dog: he went everywhere with me and slept on a cushion by my bed. When Serov, the well-known artist, painted my portrait, he insisted that Gugusse should be in the picture, saying that the dog was his best model.

Xenia, Diary – 3 October – Ai-Todor

Afterwards, Sandro, Felix, Irina and I went to the pine grove to see Krasnov [an architect]. He wants to build a little house rather like a bungalow. We chose a place near to us, leaving the previously cleared site for a large house in the future. Krasnov is very amusing and stutters terribly.

Felix Yusupov, Memoirs

The Grand Duke Alexander Mikhailovich [Sandro]'s estate, Ai-Todor, was near ours, and the memories it evokes are particularly dear. The old house was smothered in flowers, its walls were covered with roses and wisteria; everything about the place was infinitely pleasing.

Xenia, Diary – 4 October – Ai-Todor

At four o'clock we went to see the Yusupovs. They were waiting at the old house by the church. We looked over it – and admired the view from the balcony. The Yusupovs are suggesting they live in it temporarily, but for that it would have to be completely rebuilt.

We had tea with them – it was so cold, it was awful. We decided to bless them tomorrow, so that among ourselves, at least, everything should be clear and decided!

5 October Just after 5 the Yusupovs arrived with Felix and we blessed the children. May the Lord bless them and may He send them happiness! It was very emotional. We all kissed and shed tears. We showed them the new house.

7 October   A wonderful morning. I wrote on the balcony. I went with Krasnov to the suite's house, and they showed me where the bathrooms will be – three downstairs and one upstairs.

Nicky, Diary – 8 October – Livadia
The sun was very hot. Played tennis in the afternoon. Xenia, Sandro and Irina came for tea.

Xenia, Diary – 8 October – Ai-Todor
We had tea at Livadia. We told them about Irina. They heard that the engagement would be announced in a few days' time. Alix said she would never let a daughter of hers marry him.

9 October   Irina and Felix appeared. They lunched with us. In the afternoon we went with Irina and Felix to see Krasnov. He showed us the plans for the little house on Irina's plot. Rather in the Italian style. He stuttered in the most impossible way.

Nicky, Diary – 9 October – Livadia
The officers stayed for lunch and presented themselves to Alix upstairs. We played tennis. Dined with Olga and Tatiana at Ai-Todor. There I saw Felix, Irina's fiancé.

Xenia, Diary – 19 October – Ai-Todor
Wonderful weather. At 11.30 we set out at great speed with the Yusupovs, Minnie, Irina, our Nikolaevs, Bernov and Krasnov. We left Ai-Petri. A heavenly place. I travelled with Zinaida in a covered motor as we both had bad colds! We drove for an hour and a half. We went into a little house: one large room with a little bedroom off it. Eight *versts* on there is a place with an amazing view over the whole Kokoz valley (you can see their house), and the mountains, you can even see the sea, but there was a haze. Driving through a beech wood you come out onto a plateau – so beautiful!

Yusupov has given this delightful place and the little house to Irina! It's so terribly touching, the princess and I were quite overcome, he loves her so much. Irina quite lost her head, she couldn't even thank him properly. In the end I got her to kiss him!

Pavel to Nicky – 21 October – Boulogne-sur-Seine
Dear Nicky,

Please find enclosed the letter from the King of Sweden which I have answered, refuting all unfair attacks against Maria.[7]

If only you could see what the poor girl was looking like when she arrived to us!

She was fainting every minute, she was white as a sheet, she could not eat or sleep, she was coughing dreadfully, and she still complains about her kidneys. She is only beginning to recover under the influence of our love and caress.

It is *unthinkable* that she should return to Sweden, and I beg your permission for us to begin negotiating a divorce. At any rate, it is better than her life there and the harassment of the impudent old mesmerizer Munthe. All this is sad and painful.

Today we expect that a consultation from a doctor for renal diseases will tell us what to do further on.

I shall be informing you as to how the circumstances will develop, about everything concerning Maria, for I know about your kind and cordial attitude to my children.

Embracing you fondly and kissing Alix's hands,

Your Pavel

Xenia, Diary – 31 October – St Petersburg
Felix came to lunch. The children romped around with him. Sandro has heard various things about him in Paris and is terribly upset and has upset me also.

Felix Yusupov, Memoirs
We must have been twelve or thirteen when one evening during our parents' absence we suddenly thought of going out disguised as women. My mother's wardrobe supplied us with all we needed for this fine scheme. Once dressed, made up, adorned with jewellery and muffled in fur-lined velvet pelisses that were much too long for us, we slipped out by a secret staircase and sallied forth to wake up my mother's hairdresser. As we said we were going to a fancy-dress ball, he agreed to lend us wigs.

Thus attired, we prowled around the city. We soon attracted the attention of passers-by on the Nevsky Prospect, which was the hunt-

---

[7] Maria Pavlovna (the younger), married to Swedish Prince Wilhelm.

ing-ground of all the St Petersburg prostitutes. To get rid of the men who accosted us, we replied in French: 'We are already engaged,' and pursued our dignified way. We hoped to escape them for good and all by entering The Bear, a fashionable restaurant. Forgetting to leave our pelisses in the cloakroom, we took a table and ordered supper. It was atrociously hot in the restaurant, and we were stifled in our furs. Everyone stared at us with great curiosity; some officers sent us a note, inviting us to have supper with them in a private room. The champagne began to go to my head: removing a long string of pearls, I made it into a lasso and amused myself by aiming it at the heads of people seated at a neighbouring table. Naturally, the string broke, and the pearls scattered all over the floor, to the joy of those present. Finding ourselves the cynosure of all eyes, we became uneasy and thought it would be prudent to slip away. We had found most of the pearls, and were on our way to the door when the head waiter came with the bill. As we had not a penny, we were obliged to see the manager and confess. The good man proved most indulgent, was very much amused by our adventure, and even lent us the money to take a carriage home. On arriving at the Moika, we found every door closed; I called outside my faithful Ivan's window, and he was convulsed with laughter to see us in our ridiculous get-up.

But the next day things took a bad turn. The manager of The Bear sent my father the missing pearls and the supper bill.

Xenia, Diary – 4 November – Paris
At last we have arrived.

Sandro had a talk with Felix. That is to say he himself began. As soon as he arrived, Mordvinov and Dmitri warned him, what was being said about him. He told Sandro, that even if a quarter of what was being said about him was true, he would not consider he had the right to marry. I believe him completely, and in his sincerity, so does Sandro, but it's all extremely unpleasant.

Felix Yusupov, Memoirs
I was a difficult child. I still think remorsefully of all those who wore themselves out in an effort to bring me up properly. First on the list was a German nanny who had been with my brothers, and who went off her head. This was partly due to her unrequited passion for my father's secretary, and partly no doubt to my bad temper. My parents had to send her to a mental home.

After a drunken German who went to bed every night with a bottle of champagne, there followed a succession of Russian, French, English, Swiss and German tutors, to say nothing of a Roman Catholic priest who afterwards taught the Queen of Rumania's children. Many years later, the Queen told me that the memory of me was still a nightmare to the wretched priest, and she wanted to know if what he had told her about me was true. I had to admit that nothing could be truer! I still remember my music teacher whose finger I bit so savagely that the poor woman was unable to play the piano for a year.

Xenia, Diary – 6 November
In the morning we went with Felix and Irina to choose Irina a present: there was a most beautiful thing – a diamond chain with a pink pearl at the end, and also – a diamond brooch. They chose the first.

Sandro to Xenia – 9 November – Paris
My dear Xenia!

I have been very upset all this time by the rumours about Felix's reputation, but it's impossible to ignore it. I shall have to talk to him, and in any case there's no need to hurry with the wedding, we need to put him to the test and if his behaviour is satisfactory, then the wedding can go ahead! But if we start hearing things about him again, the wedding might have to be cancelled. I will tell you everything I have heard: at one point I thought he should not be allowed to see Irina at all here, but now I think they can come and talk. Previously I did not believe anything that was being said, now I don't want to believe, but there must be something, opinion about him is too steadfast. It's very sad.

Nicky, Diary – 11 November – Livadia
Today Count Sumarokov [Felix Yusupov], a young student, took part in the tennis – he is the best player in Russia. He can really teach one something. He also had tea with the officers.

Xenia, Diary – 22 December – St Petersburg
A very emotional day.

At 4 o'clock we all went to a Te Deum for the engagement – the

Yusupovs, Olga, Tatiana, Ducky, Kyril, Olga, Petia, the Kutuzovs.
Luckily Feodor [Xenia's son] did come. I was so afraid he wouldn't
show up! (but what an expression on his face, it made me want to
cry). All our people were in church, it went very well. May God
send them happiness and love. I can't believe that Irina is getting
married!

Nicky, Diary – 24 December – Tsarskoe Selo

After tea, I went to town with the girls, to the Anichkov. We went to
church with Xenia and all the children. There was a family Xmas tree
in the blue drawing room, then a noisy meal in Papa's study. We
returned home at 10.30. Then Alix and I had our own tree.

1914

Nicky – Emperor of Russia

Alix – Empress of Russia

Xenia – Grand Duchess, Nicky's sister, married to Sandro

Sandro – Grand Duke Alexander Mikhailovich, husband of Xenia

Empress Marie – Nicky's mother

Olga (sister) – Grand Duchess, Nicky's younger sister

Misha – Grand Duke Mikhail Nicky's brother

Olga – eldest daughter of Nicky and Alix, aged nineteen

Tatiana – second daughter of Nicky and Alix, aged seventeen

Maria – third daughter of Nicky and Alix, aged fifteen

Anastasia – fourth daughter of Nicky and Alix, aged fourteen

Alexei – Heir and Tsarevich, Nicky and Alix's son, aged ten

Georgie – King George V of England, first cousin of both Nicky and Alix

Prince Felix Yusupov – engaged to Irina, daughter of Xenia and Sandro

Ania Vyrubova – lady-in-waiting and close friend of Alix

Maurice Paléologue – French Ambassador in St Petersburg

Sir George Buchanan – British Ambassador in St Petersburg

Pierre Gilliard – Swiss tutor of Nicky and Alix's children

1914

THE GREAT WAR

Irina marries Felix Yusupov – Alix is upset with Ania
Vyrubova, who is infatuated with Nicky – President
Poincaré of France visits St Petersburg – The Great War
breaks out – Nicky leaves for the front – Rasputin returns
from Siberia and his influence grows – Alix sets up
hospitals, where she, Ania and the two elder girls work as
nurses – Alix is accused of pro-German sentiments

Xenia, Diary – 11 January – St Petersburg
Felix arrived with Krasnov [the architect]. We talked about the house
they are going to build on Irina's plot, then I had a talk with him
about electric lighting at Ai-Todor.

Nicky, Diary – 16 January – Tsarskoe Selo
We had breakfast. Xenia, Sandro, Irina, Felix and Bagration (on
duty).[1] Walked with Marie. It has begun to thaw again. Read until 8
o'clock. For dinner: Ella and Bagration. We spent the time doing puzzles out of little wooden pieces.

Xenia, Diary – 4 February – St Petersburg
Mama arrived and gave Irina a wonderful diamond and pearl brooch.
We then also gave Irina our presents – a sapphire necklace, my own
emerald brooch with diamonds and rubies and three pearl sprays,

---

[1] Prince K. A. Bagration-Mukhranski, an aide-de-camp to the Emperor and KR's
son-in-law.

and a little diamond necklace. I am also going to give Irina a few emeralds for the diadem which Felix is having made.

5 February Went to tea at Tsarskoe with Sandro and Irina. The whole family were gathered and they were very kind! Alix gave Baby Rina [Irina] two strings of pearls and she's thrilled – it's just what she wanted, but was afraid she would not get!

7 February What a terribly tiring day – so much to do and think about, and my heart is so heavy! Irina and Felix took communion.

9 February, the wedding – St Petersburg Our darling has gone – what joy, yet my God! How empty the house feels (and my *heart*!) after all the excitement and bustle of the last days. May the Lord only bless their happiness and life. It's the most important – the rest is nothing.

She did not come with us to early service, she overslept as she could not get to sleep last night – she was crying, the poor thing! We lunched alone. It took a long time to get her ready. A lot of people gathered to see her – all the old spinsters. We blessed her in our bedroom and set out. They gave us a state coach. Everyone was already waiting. Mama and Nicky were her sponsors. We passed down the hall. Vasia walked in front with an icon (what a dear!), Nicky led Irina, I walked behind him with Mama, who was led by Sandro.

We mounted the church steps. Mama and Alix went up and joined them at the top. What I went through, what an effort I had to make to conduct myself properly. I was glad when it was all over. They both looked so lovely, so young, happy and she – so lovely in the little diadem which he gave her, and my veil. Nicky said he had never seen her so beautiful! Then there was a reception in the winter garden. Mama stood near the entrance to the hall, the young couple a little further on, and we – next to them. Champagne was served the whole time. It took about an hour. A mass, mass of people. Many strangers.

The young couple were radiant, it's the only thing that kept me going.

Towards six o'clock we left. Irina and Felix passed by to see his parents. We went home, to welcome them with the bread and salt! They were photographed again in the hall.

After changing we had tea – for the last time all together, and at seven o'clock we went to accompany them to the station. All the children, the Yusupovs, their friends, all of us. We went into the carriage and said goodbye there. They continued to look radiant, but my soul was dark as *night*. May God grant them a safe arrival, and every, every good thing ... my God. What emptiness in the house. Dinner went off in silence, everyone kept wiping tears and sniffing. It's painful to realize she's never coming back to *our* house. Terrible!

Nicky, Diary – 9 February – Tsarskoe Selo

Alix and I went to town with the children, to the Anichkov for the wedding of Irina and Felix Yusupov. Everything went off very well. There were a lot of people. Everyone filed through the winter garden past Mama and the newly-weds, to congratulate them.

Felix Yusupov, Memoirs

The Tsar inquired through my future father-in-law what I would like for a wedding present. He thought of offering me an office at Court, but I replied that His Majesty would gratify my wishes to the full by granting me the privilege of using the Imperial box at the theatre. On receiving my reply, Nicholas II laughingly agreed.

We were overwhelmed with gifts: the most gorgeous jewels as well as the simplest and most touching presents from our peasants.

Irina's wedding-dress was magnificent; it was of white satin embroidered in silver, with a long train. Her lace veil, which had belonged to Marie-Antoinette, was held by a tiara of rock-crystal and diamonds.

The question of what I should wear gave rise to lively discussion. I firmly refused to appear in a tail-coat in the daytime, but all the suggestions made raised a storm of protest. Finally the uniform of the nobility – a black frock-coat with collar and lapels embroidered in gold, and white broadcloth trousers – was decided on.

Alix to Nicky – 28 April – Livadia

My sweetest treasure, my very Own one,

You will read these lines when you get into your bed in a strange place and unknown house. God grant that the journey may be a pleasant and interesting one, and not too tiring nor too dusty. I am so glad to have the map, as then can follow you hourly. I shall miss you *horribly*, but I am glad for you that you will be away for 2 days and get new impressions and hear nothing of Ania's stories.

My heart is heavy and sore – must one's kindness and love always be repaid thus? The black family[2] and now she?

One is always told one can never love enough – here we gave our hearts our home to her, our private life even – and this is what we have gained! It is difficult not to become bitter – it seems so cruelly unjust.

... cannot get accustomed for ever so short, not to have you in the house, tho' I have our 5 treasures. Well my Sunshine, my own precious One & thousand tender kisses from your own old Wify. God bless & keep you.

King George V to Nicky – 16 June – Windsor Castle
My dearest Nicky,

I confess that I feel so anxious upon this subject [the peace of Europe] that I write this private letter to explain what is causing me this anxiety. It is the present unsatisfactory state of affairs in Persia.

It is my great desire to see a friendly feeling towards Russia preserved in British public opinion and in both political parties, the Conservative as well as the Liberal, that makes me most anxious that our two Governments should have a frank and friendly exchange of views on the whole situation in Persia. It would be most regrettable if any divergence of views were to arise between our two Governments, or any impression were to gain ground that the Anglo–Russian agreement about Persia was working to the advantage of one country and the disadvantage of the other.

I know my dear Nicky that I can count upon your friendship of so many years, to do all you can to remove any difficulties or misunderstandings which may now exist between our two Countries with regard to Persian affairs.

I hope you spent a pleasant time at Livadia and that dear Alicky is much better now and stronger from her stay there. Aunt Minnie [Empress Marie] is very well, she and Mama are so happy to be together again. May joins me in sending you and Alicky our best love.

I remain always your devoted old friend and cousin

Georgie

Nicky, Diary – 7 July – St Petersburg
I spent the whole morning receiving. At exactly two o'clock the

---

[2] Stana and Militsa, the Montenegran grand duchesses.

French squadron put into port. At 7.30 there was an official dinner
with speeches. After the talks, we bid goodbye to the kind president
[Poincaré] and returned home at 10 o'clock.

Maurice Paléologue, Memoirs – 7 July

I kept an eye on the Tsarina Alexandra opposite whom I was sitting.
Although long ceremonies are a very great trial to her she was anxious to be present this evening to do honour to the President of the
allied Republic.

She was a beautiful sight with her low brocade gown and diamond
tiara on her head. Her forty-two years have left her face and figure still
pleasant to look upon. After the first course she entered into conversation with Poincaré who was on her right.

Before long however her smile became set and the veins stood out
in her cheeks. She bit her lips every minute. Her laboured breathing
made the network of diamonds sparkle on her bosom. Until the end
of dinner, which was very long, the poor woman was obviously
struggling with hysteria. Her features suddenly relaxed when the Tsar
rose to propose his toast.

When I returned to St Petersburg by rail at a quarter to one in the
morning, I heard that this afternoon the principal factories went on
strike – for no reason and on a signal from no one knows where.

8 July The President of the Republic has spent today visiting St
Petersburg.

Felix Yusupov, Memoirs

St Petersburg, called the 'Venice of the North' because of its situation
on the Neva estuary, was one of the finest capitals in Europe. It is difficult to imagine the beauty of the Neva River with its quays of pink
granite and the splendid palaces that bordered it. The genius of Peter
the Great and Catherine II was apparent everywhere, in the beautiful
monuments, wide avenues and lovely buildings.

The railings of the garden in front of the Winter Palace were
designed for the Empress Alexandra by a German architect. The
palace, built at the beginning of the eighteenth century by the
Empress Elizabeth, is the masterpiece of the famous architect
Rastrelli. The railings are hideous, but no matter what was done to
disfigure the Winter Palace, it always retained its majestic dignity.

St Petersburg was not entirely Russian; a European influence was introduced by the Empresses and Grand Duchesses who, for nearly two hundred years, were foreign princesses – most often German – and also by the presence of the diplomatic corps. With the exception of a few families that kept up the traditions of old Russia, most of the aristocracy who lived there were very cosmopolitan. They had a snobbish infatuation for foreign countries, and loved to visit them. It was considered good form to have one's laundering done in London or Paris. Most of my mother's contemporaries affected to speak French only, and spoke Russian with a foreign accent.

Sandro, Memoirs

A stranger visiting St Petersburg during the last year of the lull that preceded the suicide committed by Europe on August 1, 1914, felt an irrepressible desire to settle down permanently in the brilliant capital which combined the classical beauty of arrow-like avenues with a passionate undertone of life, cosmopolitan in its leanings but thoroughly Russian in its recklessness. The coloured barman of the Hotel d'Europe hailed from Kentucky; the actresses of the Mikhailovsky Theatre rattled off their lines in French; the majestic columns of the imperial palaces bore witness to the genius of Italian architects; but important Government officials spent from three to four hours over a luncheon table, and in the month of June the pale rays of the midnight sun penetrating into the shady corners of the parks found long-haired students heatedly discussing with pink-cheeked girls the transcendental values of German philosophy. No mistake could have been made as to the ultimate nationality of the city that ordered its champagne by the magnum, never by the quart.

And then, there was Peter the Great. Moulded in bronze by the deft hands of Falconet, the Emperor stood in the centre of the Plaza of the Senate, observing from his rearing mount the stern blocks formed by clearly cut streets. He succeeded in building this miracle-town of the North on the treacherous foundation of the Finnish marshes at the cost of one hundred and twenty-five thousand lives sacrificed to yellow fever for the sake of a Greater Russia, and an arrogant smile was now lighting his demoniac face.

Everything was beautiful. Everything suggested an imperial town.

The golden needle of the building of the admiralty stood visible for miles around; the immense windows of the grand ducal palaces were burning with the flames of the sunset; a clear echo repeated the hoof-beats of the trotters against the wooden pavement of the wide thoroughfares; the yellow and blue Cuirassier Guards going for an afternoon stroll glared into the oddly shaped eyes of the stately women piercing through a thin net of laced veils; the decorous footmen seated behind the costly carriages waited in front of the shop-windows, which were crowded with rows of pink pearls and green emeralds; the red-bricked chimneys of mammoth factories towered over a shining river chained by numerous bridges; and the human swans of the imperial ballet glided each night to the accompaniment of the best orchestra in the world.

Maurice Paléologue, Memoirs – 8 July

The time for departure was approaching. The Tsar told Poincaré he would like to continue the discussion a few minutes longer.

'Suppose we go on the bridge, Monsieur le President? It will be quieter.'

Thus I found myself alone with the Tsarina who asked me to take a chair on her left. The poor lady seemed worn out. With a forced smile she said in a tired tone: 'I'm glad I came tonight ... I was afraid there would be a storm ... The decorations on the boat are magnificent. The President will have lovely weather for his voyage.'

But suddenly she put her hands to her ears. Then with a pained and pleading glance she timidly pointed to the ship's band quite near to us which had just started on a furious allegro with a full battery of brass and big drums.

'Couldn't you? ...' she murmured ...

Olga [sister], Memoirs

I spoke to Nicky and he replied that Willy [Kaiser Wilhelm] was a bore and an exhibitionist, but he would never start a war. And somehow I thought of my father and Uncle Bertie. Both hated war, and so did Nicky. Both were strong, and I wondered if Nicky was. Both were feared by Willy – but did *he* fear Nicky or Georgie? I did not think so.

Nicky, Diary – 19 July – St Petersburg

The usual reports in the morning.

After lunch I summoned Nikolasha and informed him of his appointment as commander-in-chief until such time as I joined the army.

Went for a walk with the children. At 6.30 we went to church. On our return we learnt that *Germany* has declared war on us. Olga [sister], Dmitri and Ioann [son of KR] were there for dinner. During the evening, the English Ambassador Buchanan arrived with a telegram from Georgie. Spent a long time with him composing a reply. Then I saw Nikolasha and Fredericks. Had tea at 12.15.

Sir George Buchanan[3] to King George V – July 20/2 August – St Petersburg – Telegram
Your telegram No. 423.
AT AUDIENCE WHICH I HAD WITH EMPEROR AT 11.0 O'CLOCK LAST NIGHT, HIS MAJESTY WROTE FOLLOWING MESSAGE WHICH HE DESIRED ME TO TELE-GRAPH TO THE KING:
MESSAGE BEGINS:
I WOULD GLADLY HAVE ACCEPTED YOUR PROPOSALS HAD NOT GERMAN AMBASSADOR THIS AFTERNOON PRESENTED A NOTE TO MY GOVERNMENT DECLARING WAR. EVER SINCE PRESENTATION OF THE ULTIMATUM AT BELGRADE, RUSSIA HAS DEVOTED ALL HER EFFORTS TO FINDING SOME PACIFIC SOLUTION OF THE QUESTION RAISED BY AUSTRIA'S ACTION. OBJECT OF THAT ACTION WAS TO CRUSH SERBIA AND MAKE HER A VASSAL OF AUSTRIA. EFFECT OF THIS WOULD HAVE BEEN TO UPSET BALANCE OF POWER IN BALKANS WHICH IS OF SUCH A VITAL INTEREST TO MY EMPIRE AS WELL AS TO THOSE POWERS WHO DESIRE MAINTAINANCE OF BALANCE OF POWER IN EUROPE. EVERY PROPOSAL, INCLUDING THAT OF YOUR GOVERNMENT, WAS REJECTED BY GERMANY AND AUSTRIA, AND IT WAS ONLY WHEN FAVOURABLE MOMENT FOR BRINGING PRESSURE TO BEAR ON AUSTRIA HAD PASSED THAT GERMANY SHOWED ANY DISPOSITION TO MEDIATE. EVEN THEN SHE DID NOT PUT FORWARD ANY PRECISE PROPOSAL. AUSTRIA'S DECLARATION OF WAR ON SERBIA FORCED ME TO ORDER A PARTIAL MOBILIZATION, THOUGH, IN VIEW OF THREATENING SITUATION, MY MILITARY ADVISERS STRONGLY ADVISED A GENERAL MOBILIZATION OWING TO QUICKNESS WITH WHICH GERMANY CAN MOBILIZE IN COMPARISON WITH RUSSIA. I WAS EVENTUALLY COM-PELLED TO TAKE THIS COURSE IN CONSEQUENCE OF COMPLETE AUSTRIAN MOBILIZATION, OF THE BOMBARDMENT OF BELGRADE, OF CONCENTRATION OF AUSTRIAN TROOPS IN GALICIA, AND OF SECRET MILITARY PREPARATIONS BEING MADE IN GERMANY. THAT I WAS JUSTIFIED IN DOING SO PROVED BY GERMANY'S SUDDEN DECLARATION OF WAR, WHICH WAS QUITE UNEX-PECTED BY ME AS I HAD GIVEN MOST CATEGORICAL ASSURANCES TO THE EMPEROR WILLIAM THAT MY TROOPS WOULD NOT MOVE SO LONG AS MEDI-ATION NEGOTIATIONS CONTINUED.
IN THIS SOLEMN HOUR I WISH TO ASSURE YOU ONCE MORE THAT I HAVE

---

[3] British Ambassador to Russia 1910–17.

DONE ALL IN MY POWER TO AVERT WAR. NOW THAT IT HAS BEEN FORCED ON
ME, I TRUST YOUR COUNTRY WILL NOT FAIL TO SUPPORT FRANCE AND
RUSSIA IN FIGHTING TO MAINTAIN BALANCE OF POWER IN EUROPE. GOD
BLESS AND PROTECT YOU.

[SIGNED] NICKY

MESSAGE ENDS.

EMPEROR SAID THAT HE HAD NO OBJECTION TO ABOVE BEING PUBLISHED
WITH OTHER PAPERS.

IN COURSE OF CONVERSATION HIS MAJESTY OBSERVED THAT MOBILIZA-
TION DID NOT NECESSARILY ENTAIL WAR, AND THAT THERE HAD BEEN FRE-
QUENT CASES IN HISTORY WHERE IT HAD BEEN FOLLOWED BY
DEMOBILIZATION. GERMAN EMPEROR KNEW PERFECTLY WELL THAT RUSSIA
WANTED PEACE AND THAT HER MOBILIZATION COULD NOT BE COMPLETED
FOR ANOTHER FORTNIGHT AT LEAST BUT HE HAD DECLARED WAR WITH
SUCH HASTE AS TO RENDER ALL FURTHER DISCUSSION IMPOSSIBLE AND AS
TO THROW DOUBT ON GERMANY'S GOOD FAITH THROUGHOUT.

GERMAN STATEMENT ENTIRELY MISREPRESENTS CASE AND ITS EVIDENT
OBJECT IS TO PERSUADE HIS MAJESTY'S GOVERNMENT THAT RESPONSIBILITY
FOR WAR RESTS WITH RUSSIA IN THE HOPE OF INDUCING THEM TO REMAIN
NEUTRAL. I WOULD VENTURE TO SUBMIT WITH ALL RESPECT THAT IF WE DO
NOT RESPOND TO EMPEROR'S APPEAL FOR OUR SUPPORT, WE SHALL AT END OF
THE WAR WHATEVER BE ITS ISSUE, FIND OURSELVES WITHOUT A FRIEND IN
EUROPE, WHILE OUR INDIAN EMPIRE WILL NO LONGER BE SECURE FROM
ATTACK FROM RUSSIA. IF WE DEFER INTERVENTION TILL FRANCE IS IN DANGER
OF BEING CRUSHED SACRIFICES WE SHALL THEN BE CALLED UPON TO MAKE
WILL BE MUCH GREATER WHILE WE MAY ... [remainder of telegram not
received]

Ania Vyrubova, Memoirs

It was not true, she [Alix] exclaimed. Certainly armies were moving,
but only on the Austrian frontiers. She hurried from the room and I
heard her enter the Emperor's study. For half an hour the sound of
their excited voices reached my ears. Returning, the Empress dropped
on her couch as one overcome by desperate finding. 'War!' she murmured breathlessly. 'And I knew nothing of it. This is the end of
everything.' I could say nothing. I understood as little as she the
incomprehensible silence of the Emperor at such an hour, and as
always, whatever hurt her hurt me. We sat in silence until eleven
when, as usual, the Emperor came in to tea, but he was distraught
and gloomy and the tea hour passed in almost complete silence.

Nicky to Maurice Paléologue [during an audience] – from Paléologue's Memoirs

The Kaiser was never sincere, not for a moment! In the end he was hopelessly entangled in a net of his own perfidy and lies. Have you ever been able to account for the telegram he sent me six hours after giving me his declaration of war? It's utterly impossible to explain what happened. It was half-past one in the morning of July 19. I had just received your English colleague who had brought me a telegram from King George begging me to do everything possible to save peace. I had drafted, with Sir George Buchanan's help, the telegram with which you are familiar, which ended with an appeal for England's help in arms as the war was forced on us by Germany.

The moment Buchanan had left I went to the Empress's rooms, as she was already in bed, to show her King George's telegram and have a cup of tea with her before retiring myself. I stayed with her until two in the morning. Then I wanted to have a bath, as I was very tired. I was just getting in when my servant knocked at the door saying he had a telegram for me.

'A very important telegram, very important indeed ... a telegram from His Majesty the Emperor William!' I read the telegram, read it again and then repeated it aloud ... but I couldn't understand a word. What on earth does William mean, I thought, pretending that it still depends on me whether war is averted or not! He implores me not to let my troops cross the frontier! Have I suddenly gone mad? Didn't the Minister of the Court, my trusted Fredericks, at least six hours ago bring me the declaration of war the German Ambassador had just handed to Sazonov [Minister of Foreign Affairs]?

I returned to the Empress's room and read her William's telegram. She had to read it herself to bring herself to believe it. She said to me immediately: 'You're not going to answer it, are you?' 'Certainly not!'

Pierre Gilliard, Memoirs

I had met the Tsar in Alexandria church a few hours before, and I was struck by the air of weary exhaustion he wore. The pouches which always appeared under his eyes when he was tired seemed to be markedly larger. He was now praying with all the fervour of nature that God would avert the war which he felt was imminent and all but inevitable.

Later the same day, the Tsar appeared, looking very pale, and told them that war was declared, in a voice which betrayed his agitation, notwithstanding all his efforts. On learning the news the Tsarina began to weep, and the Grand Duchesses likewise dissolved into tears on seeing their mother's distress.

I did not see the Tsar again until after lunch. He looked even worse than on the previous evening, and his eyes sparkled as if he had the fever. He told me he had just heard that the Germans had entered Luxembourg and attacked French customs houses before war was declared on France.

Nicky, Diary – 20 July – Peterhof

A good day, particularly from the point of view of morale. Went with Maria and Anastasia to church. We lunched alone. At 2.15 we took the *Alexandrie* to St Petersburg and then went by carriage straight to the Winter Palace.

I signed the manifesto of the declaration of war. From the Malachite room we went to the Nikolaevsky hall, where the manifesto was read out and a Te Deum celebrated. The whole hall sang 'Save us, Lord' and 'Many years'.

I said a few words. On our return the ladies rushed to kiss our hands and jostled Alix and myself slightly. Then we went onto the balcony over Alexander Square and bowed to a huge mass of people. At about 6 o'clock we went out onto the embankment and made our way back to the cutter through a large crowd of officers and public. We returned to Peterhof. Spent the evening quietly.

Ania Vyrubova, Memoirs

At this time a telegram arrived from Rasputin in Siberia, which plainly irritated the Emperor. Rasputin strongly opposed the war, and predicted that it would result in the destruction of the Empire. But the Emperor refused to believe it and resented what was really an almost unprecedented interference in affairs of state on the part of Rasputin.

Nicky, Diary – 23 July – Peterhof

In the morning we heard the good news: *England has declared war on Germany*, because the latter has attacked France and violated the neutrality of Luxembourg and Belgium in the most shameless way.

The campaign could not have started in a better way for us on the external side. Received all morning and in the afternoon until 4 o'clock. My last interview was with Paléologue, who came to inform me officially of the rift between France and Germany. Went for a walk with the children. Mordvinov (on duty) was there for lunch and dinner. The evening was free.

24 July *Today, Austria finally declared war on us.* Now the situation has become quite clear. At 11.30 I held a meeting of the council of ministers at the farm. Alix went into town in the morning and returned with Victoria and Ella. As well as them, Kostia [KR] and Mavra[4] came to lunch: they have just returned from Germany and had difficulty crossing the frontier. A warm rain fell all day. Victoria and Ella came to dinner.

King George V to Nicky – 31 July – Buckingham Palace
Dearest Nicky,

Both you & I did all in our power to prevent war, but alas we were frustrated and this terrible war which we have all dreaded for so many years has come upon us. Anyhow Russia, England and France have clean consciences and are fighting for justice and right. I feel sure D.V. that we shall be victorious in the end, for the right spirit exists in all our troops and Navies. I deeply sympathize with you in these anxious days and I trust that your troops will soon be able to move, ours will shortly be in France cooperating with the French. I trust for all our sakes that this horrible war will soon be over and peace once more exist in Europe. God bless and protect you my dear Nicky. With best love from May and myself to dear Alix.

Ever your very devoted cousin and friend

Georgie

Pierre Gilliard, Memoirs
Dr Derevenko entered the room. In his hand he held an evening paper announcing the violation of Swiss neutrality by Germany.[5]

'Again! They must be crazy, mad!' cried the Tsarina. 'They have absolutely lost their heads!'

Realizing she could not keep me now, she abandoned her resistance and began to speak kindly of my relations, who will be without news of me for some considerable time.

'I myself have no news of my brother [Ernie],' she added. 'Where is he? In Belgium or on the French front? I shiver to think that the

---

[4] The family nickname for KR's wife.
[5] Gilliard was Swiss.

Emperor William may avenge himself against me by sending him to the Russian front. He is quite capable of such monstrous behaviour! What a horrible war this is! What evil and suffering it means! What will become of Germany? What humiliation, what a downfall is in store for her? And all for the sins of the Hohenzollerns – their idiotic pride and insatiable ambition. Whatever has happened to the Germany of my childhood? I have such happy and poetic memories of my early years in Darmstadt and the good friends I had there. But on my later visits Germany seemed to me a changed country – a country I did not know and had never known. I had no community of thought or feeling with anyone except the old friends of days gone by. Prussia has meant Germany's ruin. The German people have been deceived. Feelings of hatred and revenge which are quite foreign to their nature have been instilled into them. It will be a terrible, monstrous struggle, and humanity is about to pass through ghastly sufferings ...'

5 August   When Alexei found he could not walk this morning he was in a terrible state. Their Majesties have decided that he shall be present at the ceremony all the same. He will be carried by one of the Tsar's cossacks. But it is a dreadful disappointment to the parents, who do not wish the idea to gain ground among the people that the Heir to the Throne is an invalid.

Maurice Paléologue, Memoirs – 5 August

At the end of the nave opposite the iconostasis the three Metropolitans of Russia and twelve archbishops stood in line. In the aisles on their left was a group of one hundred and ten bishops, archimandrites and abbots. A fabulous, indescribable wealth of diamonds, sapphires, rubies and amethysts sparkled on the brocade of their mitres and chasubles. At times the church glowed with a supernatural light.

Buchanan and I were on the Tsar's left, in front of the court.

Towards the end of the long service the Metropolitan brought their Majesties a crucifix containing a portion of the true cross which they reverently kissed. Then through a cloud of incense the imperial family walked round the cathedral to kneel at the world-famed relics and the tombs of the patriarchs.

During this procession I was admiring the bearing and the attitudes of the Grand Duchess Elizabeth [Ella], particularly when she bowed or knelt. Although she is approaching fifty she has kept her slim figure and her old grace. Under her loose white woollen hood she was as elegant and attractive as in the old days before her widowhood, when she still inspired profane passions. To kiss the figure of the Virgin of Vladimir which is set in the iconostasis she had to place her knee on a rather high marble seat. The Tsarina and the young grand duchesses who preceded her had to make two attempts – and clumsy attempts – before reaching the celebrated icon. She managed it in one supple, easy and queenly movement.

The service was now over.

'What a comforting sight for your Majesty! How splendid it is to see all these people swept by patriotic exaltation and fervour for their rulers!'

Her answer was almost inaudible but her strained smile and the strange spell of her rapt gaze, magnetic and inspired, revealed her inward intoxication.

The Grand Duchess Elizabeth joined in our conversation. Her face in the frame of her long white woollen veil was alive with spirituality. Her delicate features and white skin, the deep, far-away look in her eyes, the low, soft tone of her voice and the luminous glow round her brow all betrayed a being in close contact with the ineffable and divine.

'What do you expect, Monsieur l'Ambassadeur? We are Russians and therefore superstitious. Anyhow, isn't it obvious that the Tsar is pre-destined to disasters?'

Lowering his voice and fixing me with his sharp, yellow eyes in which dull flames glowed from time to time, he gave me a list of the incredible series of accidents, miscalculations, reverses and disasters which has marked the reign of Nicholas II in the last nineteen years.

The series opens with the coronation when two thousand *moujiks* were crushed to death in a stampede in Khodinka meadow, near Moscow. A few weeks later the Tsar went to Kiev and saw a steamer with three hundred spectators founder in the Dnieper under his eyes. After a further few weeks he saw his favourite minister, Lobanov, die in his train quite suddenly. Living as he did in constant peril of the bombs of anarchists his whole soul was longing for a son, a Tsarevich. Four girls were successively born to him and when God at last gave him an heir the child bore the germ of an incurable disease. As he has no taste for either pomp or company all he desires is to forget the responsibilities of power in the tranquil delights of family life. His wife is an unhappy neurotic who carries an atmosphere of unrest and worry about with her.

But that's not all. The Tsar had dreamed of the ultimate reign of

peace on earth but was dragged by a few schemers at his court into
the war in the Far East. His armies were beaten, one after another, in
Manchuria. His fleets were sunk, one after another, in the Chinese
seas. Then a fierce tempest of revolution swept across Russia. Risings
and massacres followed each other in uninterrupted succession. The
murder of Grand Duke Sergei opened the era of political assassinations. And just when the hurricane had begun to die down Stolypin,
the President of the Council who was hailed as the saviour of Russia,
fell one evening under the revolver of a member of the Secret Police
right in front of the imperial box in Kiev theatre.

Empress Marie to Nikolai Mikhailovich [Sandro's brother] – 7 September – St Petersburg

They are such *monsters*, that they have no equal in history and
inspire only horror and revulsion. The Japanese behave quite differently towards their prisoners, like gentlemen, while the Germans are
worse than *wild* beasts. For fifty years I have detested the Prussians,
but now I feel towards them an implacable hatred.

Nicky, Diary – 14 September – Tsarskoe Selo

Dmitri lunched with us, he has just come from the army with a message from Nikolasha. In the evening we waited a long while for
Grigory to arrive. Then we sat for a long time with him.

Alix to Nicky – 19 September – Tsarskoe Selo

My own, my very own sweet One,
    Looking after the wounded is my consolation, and that is why the last
morning I even want to go there whilst you were receiving, so as to keep
my spirits up and not break down before you. To lessen their suffering,
even in a small way, helps the aching heart. Except all I go through with
you and our beloved country and men, I suffer and for my 'small old
home' and her troops and Ernie [her brother] and Irène [her sister] and
many a friend in sorrow there – but how many go through the same?
    And then the shame, the humiliation to think that Germans
would behave as they do! One longs to sink to the ground. But none
of such conversation in this letter. I must rejoice with you that you
are going and I do – but yet egoistically I suffer horribly to be separated – we are not accustomed to it and I do so endlessly love my very
own precious Boysy dear.

Soon 20 years I belong to you – and what bliss it has been to be your very own little Wify. How nice if you see dear Olga, it will cheer her up and do you good. I shall give you a letter and things for the wounded for her.

I love you, as man was rarely loved before, and kiss you, and press you tenderly to my old heart. Forever your very own old,

Wify

Maria to Nicky – 21 September – Tsarskoe Selo

I congratulate you, my darling Papa, with victory. Today the four of us went to church with Mama. We had lunch alone and then went in the train with the wounded. We went to see Ania and had tea with her.

From there we went to the large palace infirmary. Mama, Olga and Tatiana went to do the bandaging. Alexei and I went through all the wards and talked to almost every soldier. Then Mama, Alexei and I went home, as Mama had a reception for the sisters of mercy who are leaving for the front. Then we went to the small infirmary, where Your gunner is a patient. There Mama and our sisters again did the bandaging, while Alexei and I went to see the officers.

The four of us had dinner with Mama. Alexei, thank God, is all right. I send you a big kiss, my own darling. I love you terribly.

Your own Maria

You have to take me with you next time, or else I will jump onto the train myself, because I miss you. Sleep well.

Alexei to Nicky – 22 September – Tsarskoe Selo

My Darling Papa,

I am delighted by the victory. I'm better. I am still in bed. Anastasia was trying to strangle M. Gilliard. We are all waiting for you.

Your loving Alexei

Maria to Nicky – 22 September – Tsarskoe Selo

My dear Papa!

I thank you most awfully for your telegram. I have just been to Aleksei's to pray, but as it turned out Anastasia managed to pray right in front of my nose. What a gaffe! I have a cold sore on my lip.

Your Maria

Anastasia to Nicky – 23 September – Tsarskoe Selo
My brilliant Papa!

I am writing again, while Shura brushes my hair for the night. Olga is having a meeting, Tatiana is also there. Ania had dinner with us, now she is on the couch, Maria is writing to you, and Mama went to see Alexei. Today we studied, then all four of us went to the store, we worked a lot plus it was rather jolly.

I don't want to go to bed, bah! I want to be there with you, wherever you are, as I don't know where it is. Alexei is better, he's in bed and in very good spirits. Pyotr Vasilievich [Russian teacher] and M. Gilliard read to him and play at various games. I'm so sorry I'm writing so badly, but my hand won't write.

I have to go to sleep. I kiss you 1 000 000 times, your hands and feet. I salute you.

Your devoted 13-year-old lass called Nastasia

Sleep sweetly and see me in your dreams, and I shall dream of you, which means we'll be quits.

Pierre Gilliard, Memoirs
When war broke out in 1914, Olga was nineteen and Tatiana had just had her seventeenth birthday. They had never been to a ball. The only parties at which they had appeared were one or two given by their aunt, the Grand Duchess Olga. After hostilities one thought, and one thought alone, inspired them – to relieve the cares and anxieties of their parents by surrounding them with a love which revealed itself in the most touching and delicate attentions.

If only the world had known what an example the Imperial family were setting with their tender and intimate association! But how few ever suspected it! For it was too indifferent to public opinion and avoided the public gaze.

Alix to Nicky – 24 September – Tsarskoe Selo
Sweetheart, I hope you sleep better now, I cannot say that of myself, the brain seems to be working all the time and never wanting the rest. Hundreds of ideas and combinations come bothering one and then we are never alone together.

But now I must try and get to sleep, so as to feel stronger tomorrow and be of more use – I thought I should do so much when you

were away, and Becker [period] spoilt all my plans and good intentions. Sleep well wee One, holy Angels guard your slumber and
Wify's prayers and love surround you with deep devotion and love.

25 September Good morning my treasure. Today the Feldjäger
fetches the letter later so I can write still a little.

There are so many spies everywhere that it may be true, but it
would be very sad, as there are still many very loyal subjects in the
Baltic provinces. This miserable war, when will it ever end. [Kaiser]
William, I feel sure must at times pass through hideous moments of
despair, when he grasps that it was he, and especially his anti-Russian
set, which began the war and is dragging his country into ruin. All
those little states, for years they will continue suffering from the
aftereffects.

It makes my heart bleed when I think how hard Papa and Ernie
struggled to bring our little country to its present state of prosperity
in every sense. With God's help here all will go well and end glori-
ously, and it has lifted up spirits, cleansed the many stagnant minds,
brought unity in feelings and is a 'healthy war' in the moral sense.

Only one thing I long that our troops should behave exemplarily
in every sense, and not rob and pillage – leave that horror to the
Prussian troops. It is demoralizing, and then one loses the real control over the men – they fight for personal gain and not for the country's glory, when they reach the stage of high-way robbers – No
reason to follow bad examples – There are always ugly sides and
beautiful ones to everything, and so is it here. Such a war ought to
cleanse the spirits and not defile them, is it not so? – Some regiments
are very severe I know and try to keep order – but a word from above
would do no harm, this is my very own idea, Darling: because I want
the name of our Russian troops to be remembered hereafter in the
countries with awe and respect – and admiration.

Here people do not ever quite grasp the idea that other people's
property is sacred, and not to be touched – victory does not mean pillage. Let the priests in the regiments say a word to the men too on
this topic.

Now I am bothering you with things that do not concern me, but
only out of love for your soldiers and their reputation.

Sweetest treasure, I must be ending now, and get up. All my prayers
and tenderest thoughts follow you; may God give you courage,
strength, and patience. And our Friend helps you carry your heavy
cross and great responsibilities – and all will come right, as the right
is on our side. I bless you, kiss your precious face, sweet neck and

dear loving handies with all the fervour of a great loving heart. How lovely to have you soon back again. Your very own old

                                                                                      Wify

20 October   My love of loves, my very own One

Oh, how I shall miss you – I feel so low these days already and the heart so heavy – it's a shame as hundreds are rejoicing to see you soon – but when one loves as I do – one cannot but yearn for one's Treasure.

Twenty years tomorrow that you reign and that I became Orthodox! How the years have flown, how much we have lived through together. Forgive me writing in pencil, but I am on the sofa and you are confessing still.

Without end I kiss you and press you to my heart with boundless love & fondness. Ever, Nicky, mine, your very own little

                                                                                      Wify

22 October

My own beloved One,

Mme Becker [period] is a bore, should be much freer without her. How vile one having thrown bombs from aeroplane on to King Albert's [of Belgium] Villa in which he just now lives – thank God no harm was done but I have never known one trying to kill a sovereign because he is one's enemy during the war!

I gave my good night kiss to your cushion and longed to have you near me – in thoughts I see you lying in your compartment, bend over you, bless you and gently kiss your sweet face all over. Oh, my Darling, how intensely dear you are to me; could I but help you carrying your heavy burdens, there are so many that weigh upon you.

Goodbye Sweetheart, I bless and kiss you Your very own

                                                                                      Wify

27 October

My own sweetest Nicky dear,

I have come earlier to bed, as am very tired – it was a busy day, and when the girls went to bed at 11.

I also said goodnight to Ania, her humour towards me has been not too amiable this morning – what one could call rude and this evening she came lots later than she had asked to come and was queer with me. She flirts hard with the young Ukrainian – misses and longs for you – at times is colossally gay; she went with a whole party of our wounded to town (by chance), and amused herself immensely on the train – she must play a part and speak afterwards of herself the whole time and their remarks about her. At the beginning she was daily asking for more operations, and now they bore her, as they take her away from her young friend, tho' she goes to him every afternoon and evening again.

It's naughty my grumbling about her, but you know how aggravating she can be. You will see when we return how she will tell you how terribly she suffered without you, tho' she thoroughly enjoys being alone with her friend, turning his head. Be nice and firm when you return and don't allow her foot-game etc. Otherwise she gets worse after – she always needs cooling down.

Ever your very own old

Sunny

Pierre Gilliard, Memoirs

Relations between Her Majesty and Madame Vyrubova were very intimate, and hardly a day passed without her visiting her Imperial mistress. The friendship had lasted many years. Madame Vyrubova had married very young. Her husband was a degenerate and an inveterate drunkard, and succeeded in inspiring his young wife with a deep hatred of him. They separated, and Madame Vyrubova endeavoured to find relief and consolation in religion. Her misfortunes were a link with the Tsarina, who had suffered so much herself, and yearned to comfort her. The young woman who had had to go through so much won her pity. She became the Tsarina's confidante, and the kindness the Tsarina showed her made her her lifelong slave.

Madame Vyrubova's temperament was sentimental and mystical, and her boundless affection for the Tsarina was a positive danger, because it was uncritical and divorced from all sense of reality.

The Tsarina could not resist so fiery and sincere a devotion. Imperious as she was, she wanted her friends to be hers, and hers alone. She only entertained friendships in which she was quite sure of being the dominating partner. Her confidence had to be rewarded by complete self-abandonment. She did not realize that it was rather unwise to encourage demonstrations of that fanatical loyalty.

Madame Vyrubova had the mind of a child, and her unhappy experiences had sharpened her sensibilities without maturing her judgement. Lacking in intellect and discrimination, she was the prey of her impulses. Her opinions on men and affairs were unconsidered but none the less sweeping. A single impression was enough to convince her limited and puerile understanding. She at once classified people, according to the impression they made upon her, as 'good' or 'bad,' – in other words, 'friends' or 'enemies'.

It was with no eye to personal advantage, but out of a pure affection for the Imperial family and her desire to help them, that Madame Vyrubova tried to keep the Tsarina posted as to what was going on, to make her share her likes and dislikes, and through her to influence the course of affairs at Court. But in reality she was the docile and unconscious, but none the less mischievous, tool of a group of unscrupulous individuals who used her in their intrigues. She was incapable either of a political policy or considered aims, and could not even guess what was the game of those who used her in their own interests. Without any strength of will, she was absolutely under the influence of Rasputin and had become his most fervent adherent at court.

Anastasia to Nicky – 28 October – Tsarskoe Selo
My golden, good, darling Papa!

We have just finished dinner. So I am sending you my nice card. I'm sure you will be pleased. Today I sat with our soldier and helped him to read, which I enjoyed very much. He has begun to learn to read and write here. Two more poor things died, we sat with them only yesterday.

Olga is hitting Maria, and Maria is shouting like an idiot. A dragoon and a big idiot. Olga sends you another big kiss. I have already washed and must now go to bed. Tomorrow I will finish this letter.

Greetings Your Imperial Majesty! Good morning! I am going to have my tea. I slept well, without Mama and my sisters. I have my Russian lesson now. Pyotr Vasilievich is reading Turgenev's *Hunter's Notebook*. It's very interesting.

I wish you all the best. 1 000 000 big kisses.

Your devoted and truly loving daughter, 13-year-old servant of God

Nastasia

May God protect you.

Tatiana to Alix – 29 October – Tsarskoe Selo
My sweet darling angel, Mama dear,

I do so hope that you all sleep well and won't feel so tired tomorrow as you will probably do so much the whole day.

Please forgive me, my Mama Sweet, if I ever hurt you involuntarily by saying something about your former home, but really if I do say something, it is always without thinking that I can hurt you, or something like that, because really, when I think of you I only think that you are our angel, Mama dear – a Russian, and always forget that it was not always so, and that you had another home before you came to Papa here.

Do forgive me deary. Now goodbye. I pray God give you a good sleep and that you'll be well and happy tomorrow.

1000 kisses to my own darling, sweet, precious Mama, from her ever-loving, thankful and true daughter,

Tatiana

Alix to Tatiana – 29 October – Tsarskoe Selo

Thank you, sweetheart, for your loving words. You do not hurt me my little girlies, but those who are older might sometimes think but its all quite natural.

I perfectly understand all Russians' feelings, and *cannot* approve our enemies' actions. They are *too* terrible, and therefore their cruel behaviour hurts me greatly – also what I have to hear out there. I am *quite* Russian, as you say but I can't forget my old home.

1000 kisses

Mama+

Pierre Gilliard, Memoirs

Tatiana was rather reserved, essentially well balanced, and had a will of her own, though she was less frank and spontaneous than her elder sister. She was not so gifted, either, but this inferiority was compensated by more perseverance and balance. She was pretty, though she had not quite Olga Nikolaevna's charm.

If the Tsarina made any difference between her children, Tatiana Nikolaevna was her favourite. It was not that her sisters loved their mother any less, but Tatiana knew how to surround her with unwearying attentions and she never gave way to her own capricious impulses. Through her good looks and her art of self-assertion she put her sister Olga in the shade in public, as the latter, thoughtless about herself, seemed to take a back seat. Yet the two sisters were passionately devoted to each other. There was only eighteen months between them, and that in itself was a bond of union.

Alexei to Nicky – 30 October – Tsarskoe Selo
Darling Papa,

We keep having damp weather but the air is clear. We made a bonfire today and I smeared my face with soot.

God keep you!

Your loving Alexei

Alix to Alexei – 31 October – Tsarskoe Selo
My very own boy!

I am terribly sad because you are not with me, but I know that Papa is
anxiously awaiting us. My prayers and all my thoughts will be with you
all the time. Study well, eat quickly and a lot – do not run too much.

You may pray with your sisters in the evening – and at that time I
shall think about you. I hope to see you on Sunday evening.

Send news by telegrams, I shall be waiting for them anxiously. I don't
like to stay away long from my little one I shall long much for him.

Be good my joy and obedient.

Farewell my Sunshine. May God protect you. I bless you and kiss
you tenderly. Your very own

Mama

Sleep well. We shall return soon.

**Nicky to Maurice Paléologue [during an audience] – from
Paléologue's Memoirs**
'What we must keep before us as our first objective is the destruction
of German militarism, the end of the nightmare from which
Germany has been made to suffer for more than forty years. We must
make it impossible for the German people even to think of revenge.
If we let ourselves be swayed by sentiment there will be a fresh war
within a very short time. As for the precise terms of peace I must tell
you at once that I accept here and now any conditions France and
England think it their duty to put forward in their own interest.'

Alix to Olga – 13 November – Tsarskoe Selo
My Olga child,

Thank you, Sweetheart, for your loving note. It is your Christening
day too tomorrow. Fancy, already 19 years have passed since then.
Sleep well and God bless you. 1000 kisses from your own old

Mama+

Pierre Gilliard, Memoirs

[Olga] picked up everything extremely quickly, and always managed to give an original turn to what she learnt. I well remember how, in one of our first grammar lessons, when I was explaining the formation of verbs and the use of the auxiliaries, she suddenly interrupted me with: 'I see, monsieur. The auxiliaries are the servants of the verbs. It's only poor "avoir" which has to shift for itself.'

Misha to Nicky – 15 November – St Petersburg

Dear Nicky

As I am leaving for the war, from which I may not return, I want to ask you for one request, in which I hope you will not refuse me and which depends entirely on you. It is very hard for me to go away, leaving my family in such an ambiguous position. I wish for my only beloved son to be accepted by society as my son, and not as the son of an unknown father, as he is registered on his birth certificate. It hurts me to think about it, I am possessed by this thought at a time when my soul is full of longing and readiness to serve our beloved country.

Remove from me the burden of the worry that, if something were to happen to me, my son would have to grow up with the stigma of illegitimacy (of being born out of wedlock).

Where other people are concerned, the question of legitimizing children born before marriage is easily decided by the court, but in the case of my son the court is powerless! You alone can do this, as it is your right. I beg you to use your prerogative and give the order for my son Georgy, born to Natalia before our marriage, to be recognized as our legitimate son. Spare him in this way from the difficult position I have outlined in the future. At the moment he is not aware of the situation, but in the future he will feel it very much.

And after all, he is not to blame! Take pity on him, and on me as a father! This is perhaps my last personal request. To expedite the matter, I enclose the certificate of birth and baptism of my son Georgy.[6]

I embrace you warmly, dear Nicky, your very loving

Misha

Alix to Nicky – 17 November – Tsarskoe Selo

My own beloved One,

Let's hope she [Ania Vyrubova] will hold herself in hand. I take all

---

[6] Georgy was legitimized in March 1915.

much cooler now and don't worry over her rudenesses and moods like formerly – a break came through her behaviour and words in the Crimea – we are friends and I am very fond of her and always shall be, but something has gone, a link broken by her behaviour towards us both – she can never be as near to me as she was. One tries to hide one's sorrow and not pride with it – after all it's harder for me than her, tho' she does not agree – as you are all to her and I have the children – but she has me whom she says she loves. It's not worth while speaking about this, and it is not interesting to you at all.

I bless you, kiss you all over and gently press you to my deeply loving old heart.

Ever, Nicky my Own, your very own

Wify

Nicky to Alix – 18 November – in the train

My own beloved Sunny + darling Wify,

We have finished luncheon and I have read through your sweet tender letter – with moist eyes. This time I managed to keep myself in hand the moment of parting, but it was a hard struggle.

Lovy mine, I miss you horribly, much more than my tongue could tell it you.

Every day a messenger will leave with papers from town; I shall try and write often, as to my surprise I can write while the train is moving!

My hanging bar proved to be very practical and useful! I hung on it and climbed lots before eating. It is really good for one in the train and shakes the blood and the whole system up!

I love the pretty frame you gave me, it lies before me on the table, for safety sake, else a sharp knock might break the nice stone.

All the miniatures are good except Maria's. I am sure that everybody will appreciate it.

It is such joy and comfort to see you well and doing so much work for the wounded. As our Friend said, it is God's mercy, that at such a time you should be able to do and to stand such a lot. Believe me, my sweet love, do not fear, but be more *sure* of yourself, when you are alone, and everything will go off smoothly and successfully. Now God bless you + my very own Wify-dear. I kiss you and the children tenderly. Sleep well and try not to think you are lonely! Ever your own Huzy

Nicky

Alix to Nicky – 21 November – Tsarskoe Selo
My Lovebird,
I don't want the Feldjäger to leave tomorrow without a letter from me. This is the wire I just received from our Friend: 'When you comfort the wounded, God makes his name famous through your gentleness and glorious work.' So touching and must give me strength to get over my shyness. It's sad leaving the wee ones!
Now Light of my life, farewell. God bless and protect you and keep you from all harm. I do not know when and where this letter will reach you. Blessings without end and fondest kisses from us all. Your very own

Sunny

Alexei to Nicky – 24 November – Tsarskoe Selo
Dear Papa
Yesterday we played at war. I took the enemy trench in one moment but was immediately thrown back and taken prisoner. But at that very second I broke away and scrammed! My fortifications remained. I feel well. How is your health? Write to me! A big kiss. May God protect you!

Your loving Alexei

Nicky to Alix – 25 November – in the train
My beloved Sunny-darling,
The train shakes abominably, so excuse my writing.
Splendid rich country that of the cossacks, lots of fruit gardens, they are becoming prosperous and above all that tremendous *inconceivable* quantity of tiny children, babies, future subjects! All that makes one overjoyed and with faith in God's mercy I may trust and look with calm to what is in store for Russia!
This second a telegram from our Friend was brought me at a small station where I took a run. I think it a most comforting one!
Now, lovy-mine, I must end. I kiss you and the dear children fondly and tenderly. Me longs for you and wants you so!! God bless & protect you +!

Nicky

Alix to Nicky – 28 November – Tsarskoe Selo
My very own precious One,
To my horror I saw the announcement in the papers, that in all the restaurants and cabarets (of bad reputation) *drinks* would be sold for

the profit of her *branch store* (my name in big letters) till 3 in the
morning (now all restaurants are closed at 12) and that Tango and
other dances would be danced for her profit. It made a shocking
impression – you forbid (thank Heaven) wine – and I, so to speak,
encourage it for the store, horrid and with right all furious, the
wounded too. And the ministers' aides de camp were to collect
money. There was no possibility any more to stop it – so we asked
Obolensky to order the rest to be closed at 12 except the decent ones.

Our love to N.P. [N.P. Sabline, Nicky's aide-de-camp] Glad, you two
sinners had pretty faces to look at – I see more other parts of the
body, less ideal ones!!

Wify

Alexei to Nicky – 28 November – Tsarskoe Selo
My dear Papa!

They have made me a soldier's coat, and I stood guard in it today.
Today P.V.P. [Pyotr Vasilievich, Russian teacher] brought me from
Petrograd three entrenching spades in leather cases. It has been raining for three days, which stops us playing. I am studying all right and
feel well.

Write to me! May the Lord keep you! A big kiss,

Alexei

Pierre Gilliard, Memoirs
Alexei was the centre of this united family, the focus of all its hopes
and affections. His sisters worshipped him and he was his parents'
pride and joy. When he was well the palace was, as it were, transformed. Everyone and everything seemed bathed in sunshine.
Endowed with a naturally happy disposition, he would have developed quite regularly and successfully had he not been kept back by
his infirmity. Each of his crises meant weeks and sometimes months
of the closest attention, and when the haemorrhage had been heavy
it was followed by a condition of general anaemia which made all
hard work impossible for him, sometimes for a considerable period.

Alexei to Nicky – 29 November – Tsarskoe Selo
Dear darling Papa

Tomorrow I shall have some money. Derevenko is giving me his
yellow boots. Today I shall blacken them. The weather is nothing

special, a slight frost, but no snow. I worked quite well all this week. Today there will be a cinema. I feel lonely the whole time without you. I hope to see you soon. Keep well. Write to me! May God protect you! A big kiss.

Your loving Alexei

Alix to Nicky – 1 December – Tsarskoe Selo
Our Friend wired: 'Be crowned with earthly happiness, the heavenly wreaths follow you.'

17 December   This morning our Friend told her [Ania] by telephone that He is a little more quiet about the news.

I kiss you ever so tenderly and bless you. Ever my Nicky your very own tenderly loving

Sunny

Maurice Paléologue, Memoirs – 25 December – St Petersburg
I have heard the Empress charged with having retained sympathies, preferences and a warm corner in her heart for Germany. The unfortunate woman in no way deserves these strictures; she knows all about them and they give her great pain.

Alexandra is German neither in mind nor spirit and has never been so. Of course, she is German by birth, at least on the paternal side. But she is English through her mother. In 1878, at the age of six, she lost her mother and thenceforward resided habitually at the court of England. Her upbringing, education and mental and moral development were thus quite English. She is still English in her outward appearance, her deportment, a certain strain of inflexibility and Puritanism, the uncompromising and militant austerity of her conscience.

In her inmost being she has become entirely Russian. I have no doubt of her patriotism. Her love for Russia is deep and true. And why should she not be devoted to her adopted country which stands for everything dear to her as a woman, wife, sovereign and mother? When she ascended the throne in 1894 she knew already that she did not like Germany, and particularly Prussia. In recent years she has taken a personal dislike to the Emperor William and he it is whom she holds exclusively responsible for the war, this 'wicked war which makes Christ's heart bleed every day.'

But her moral naturalisation has gone even further. By a curious process of mental contagion she has gradually absorbed the most ancient and characteristic elements of the Russian soul, all those obscure, emotional and visionary elements which find their highest expression in religious mysticism.

Her morbid proclivities she inherits from her mother's side ... [they] betray themselves in her sister Elizabeth [Ella] as a kind of charitable exaltation ... These hereditary tendencies which would have been more or less checked if she had continued to live in the practical and balanced West, have found in Russia the atmosphere most favourable to the perfect development. Are not all those symptoms – moral unrest, chronic melancholy, vague sorrows, the see-saw between elation and despondency, the haunting obsession of the invisible and the life beyond, and superstitious credulity – which are outstanding features of the Empress's personality, tradition and endemic in the Russian people?

Alexandra's submissive acceptance of Rasputin's ascendancy is no less significant. She is behaving exactly like one of the old Tsarinas of Moscow when she sees in Rasputin a *Bojy tchelloviek* 'a man of God', 'a saint persecuted – as Christ was – by the Pharisees' or when she endows him with the gifts of prophecy, miracle-working and exorcisms, or allows the success of a political step or a military operation to depend upon his blessing.

1915

Nicky – Emperor of Russia

Alix – Empress of Russia

Misha – Grand Duke Mikhail, Nicky's brother, married to Natalia Wulfert (Brassova)

Olga (sister) – Grand Duchess, Nicky's younger sister

Olga – eldest daughter of Nicky and Alix, aged twenty

Tatiana – second daughter of Nicky and Alix, aged eighteen

Maria – third daughter of Nicky and Alix, aged sixteen

Anastasia – fourth daughter of Nicky and Alix, aged fourteen

Alexei – Heir and Tsarevich, son of Nicky and Alix, aged eleven

KR – Grand Duke Konstantin Romanov, Nicky's cousin

Grand Duke Andrei – son of Grand Duke Vladimir and Maria Pavlovna the elder

Georgie – King George V of England, first cousin of both Nicky and Alix

Prince Felix Yusupov – married to Irina, daughter of Xenia and Sandro

Maria Pavlovna (the younger) – daughter of Nicky's uncle Grand Duke Pavel, sister of Dmitri Pavlovich

Ania Vyrubova – lady-in-waiting and close friend of Alix

Pierre Gilliard – Swiss tutor of Nicky and Alix's children

Maurice Paléologue – French Ambassador in St Petersburg

V. A. Jukovskaya – one of Rasputin's circle

1915

LOVE LETTERS

Ania Vyrubova critically wounded in a train crash – The
Yusupovs have a daughter, Irina – Alix starts to insist to
Nicky that he replace his uncle Nikolai Nikolaevich
(Nikolasha) as commander-in-chief of the army – The
21st anniversary of Nicky and Alix's engagement – Death
of KR – Alix begins increasingly to interfere in politics
and becomes nervous of her sister Ella and the Moscow
clique she believes are against her – Misha writes to his
wife Natalia from the front line – Rasputin is attacked in
the press – Russian troops sustain heavy losses – Nicky
assumes high command of the army – Alexei accompanies his father to the front – He has another haemorrhage
and Nicky has to bring him back to Tsarskoe

Pierre Gilliard, Memoirs
Another result of the war, as agreeable as unexpected, was that
Rasputin had retired into the background. At the end of September
he had returned from Siberia completely recovered from the terrible
wound which had all but ended his days. But everything pointed to
the fact that since his return he was being more or less neglected. In
any case, his visits were more and more infrequent. It was true that
as Alexei had been so much better during the winter there had been
no need to resort to his intervention, so that he had found himself
deprived of what had been his great stand-by.

But when all is said, his power remained quite formidable. I had
proof of the fact a short time after, when Madame Vyrubova was all
but killed in a terrible railway accident. She was nearly dead when
she was dragged from under the fragments of the shattered carriage,

and had been brought to Tsarskoe Selo in a condition which seemed desperate.

Nicky, Diary – 2 January – Tsarskoe Selo
Received all morning until 1.15. At 2 o'clock went with the children to the manège, for the Christmas tree for the wounded. Went for a walk. Learnt from Voeikov[1] that there had been a train collision at 6 o'clock between Tsarskoe Selo and the town. Among others, poor Ania was severely wounded, and was brought here to the palace infirmary. Went there at 11 o'clock. Her parents were with her. Grigory came later.

3 January In the morning we heard that Ania was a little better. Alix went to an operation and stayed until almost one.

Before the reports I walked for twenty minutes. Sabline[2] was there for lunch and dinner (on duty). Went with the children to the Christmas tree in the manège, and then to the infirmary to see Ania. Sat with her; also looked in on three wounded men from Nizhnynovgorod.

We all returned together for tea. Read until dinner.

4 January Went to church with the children. There was the last Christmas tree in the manège, with a *lezghinka* [dance] at the end.

We visited Ania in the infirmary; thank God she is better, although she is in pain all over her body. Walked in the darkness before tea. At 6 o'clock received Trepov. Read the whole evening.

Maurice Paléologue, Memoirs – 6 January
He gave her a resounding kiss on the hand. It was Rasputin.

With a swift glance at me he enquired: 'Who is it?'

Madame O— introduced me. He continued: 'Oh, yes; the French Ambassador! I'm pleased to meet him. He's the very man I want to see.'

He began to rattle along, so much so that Madame O—, who acted as interpreter, had not even time to translate.

Thus I had a chance of taking stock of him. Dark, long, and ill-

---

[1] Major-General V. N. Voeikov, commandant of the Alexander Palace in Tsarskoe Selo, 1913–17, and son-in-law of the Court Minister Count Fredericks.
[2] N. P. Sabline, Nicky's aide-de-camp.

kempt hair; stiff black beard; high forehead; broad, aquiline nose. But the whole expression of the face was concentrated in the eyes – light-blue eyes with a curious sparkle, depth, and fascination. His gaze was at once penetrating and caressing, naive and cunning, direct and yet remote. When he was excited it seemed as if his pupils became magnetic.

In short, jerky phrases and with a wealth of gesticulation, he gave me a pathetic picture of the sufferings inflicted on the Russian people by the war:

'There are too many dead and wounded, too many widows and orphans, nothing but ruin and tears! Think of all the poor fellows who'll never come back, and remember that each of them has left behind him five, six ... ten persons who can only weep!! I know of villages where everybody's in mourning ... And what about those who do come back! What are they like! Legless, armless, blind! ... It's terrible! For more than twenty years we shall harvest nothing but sorrow on Russian soil!'

'Yes, indeed, it's terrible enough,' I said; 'but it would be far worse if all these sacrifices were to be in vain. A peace that was no peace, a peace which was the result of war-weariness would be not merely a crime against our dead: it would bring with it internal crises from which our countries might never recover.'

'You're right. We must fight on to victory.'

V. A. Jukovskaya [a member of Rasputin's circle], Memoirs

I remember that strange man, with his quiet, hoarse voice, the enigmatic smile of the thin pale lips, the magnetic look that flared momentarily in the clear eyes, which looked not simply with the pupil, but with the whole eye, from behind whose unassuming iris, someone at times looked out, someone terrible, powerful, enticing you into an impenetrable labyrinth, where he will gladly lead you, as long as you can find your own way back.

I remember his strange ability to transform himself instantaneously, like a magician of old: strike the ground and up jumps a grey wolf, roll over and up flies a black raven, fall like a stone to the ground – and away creeps a green wood goblin. So it was here: one moment a simple, illiterate peasant was sitting there, rough, scratching himself from time to time, his tongue moves clumsily and the words slip out awkwardly, like a badly fastened load, then suddenly he is transformed into an inspired prophet – the guardian of a secret known to him alone – and beckons you to follow him into the heights of spiritual discovery, into a realm until now unknown, when sin and truth are harmoniously blended into one, but then the changeling turns again, the white teeth are gritted in a wild animal sensuality, from behind the heavy veil of wrinkles someone shamelessly beckons, someone rapacious, unbridled, like a young beast, who caresses like a beast with a secret thirst for destruction.

The unseen were-wolf strikes the ground for the last time, and in place of the ungirdled mischief-maker, there sits a grey siberian wanderer, who for thirty years has sought God on this earth, talking with quiet gentleness about the blue lakes, the endless forests, of a mossy bed, his words are simple and guileless, he himself is guileless – but for how long?

Felix Yusupov, Memoirs
There is no doubt that the *staretz* [Rasputin] had hypnotic powers.

Alix to Nicky – 27 January – Tsarskoe Selo
My own beloved Nicky,

We had an operation this morning – rather long but went off well. Ania gets on all right tho' her right leg aches, but the temp. is nearly normal in the evening. Only speaks again of getting into her house. I foresee my life then! Yesterday evening I went as an exception to her, and so as to sit with the officers a tiny bit afterwards, as I never have a chance.

She is full of how thin she has grown, tho' I find her stomach and legs colossal (and most unappetizing) – her face is rosy, but the cheeks less fat and shades under her eyes.

She has lots of guests: but dear me – how far away she has slipped from me since her hideous behaviour, especially autumn, winter, spring of 1914 – things never can be the same to me again – she broke that intimate link gently during the last four years – cannot be at my ease with her as before – tho' she says she loves me so, I know it's much less than before and all is consecrated in her own self – and you.

Let us be careful when you return. How I wish one could sink that odious little Breslau!

Must end now, Treasure, my Sunshine, my Life, my love I kiss and bless you. Ever your very own

Sunny

Felix Yusupov, Memoirs
There was a dance every Saturday at the Taneevs. These parties were
large and very gay. Anna, the eldest Taneev girl, was tall and stout
with a puffy, shiny face, and no charm whatever. Although she was
not at all intelligent, she was extremely crafty and rather sly. It was
quite a problem to find partners for her. No one could have foreseen
that this unattractive girl would one day become the intimate friend
and evil genius of the Tsarina. It was largely due to her that Rasputin
owed his amazing rise to favour.

Alexei to Alix – 25 February – Tsarskoe Selo
Forgive me I am very tired, and ask you to allow me not to go to
church.

Alix to Nicky – 27 February – Tsarskoe Selo
My very own deeply beloved One,
   Our Friend's blessing and prayers will help.
   Such a comfort for me that you saw and were blessed by him this
evening.
   I press you tenderly to my old loving heart and remain your very
own

                                                                   Wify

Maurice Paléologue, Memoirs
What a curious person Madame Vyrubova is! ... She is the daughter
of Taneev, Director of the Emperor's Privy Seal office, and has practically no money. It is all that the Empress can do to get her occasionally to accept some cheap jewel, or a dress or cloak.
   Physically she is coarse and heavily-built, with a round head,
fleshy lips, limpid eyes devoid of expression, a full figure and a high
colour. She is thirty-two years of age. She dresses with a thoroughly
provincial plainness and is very devout, but unintelligent. I have met
her twice at the house of her mother, Madame Taneev (née Tolstoy),
who, by contrast, is well-informed and distinguished. We had a long
talk together. Vyrubova struck me as unattractive and very dull-wit-
ted. As a girl she was maid-of-honour to the Empress who arranged
her marriage with a naval officer, Lieutenant Vyrubov. After a few
days of married life came divorce.
   At the present time Madame Vyrubova lives at Tsarskoe Selo in a

very modest villa at the corner of the Srednaya and the Zerkovnaya, 200 metres from the Imperial Palace. In spite of all the decrees of etiquette the Empress frequently pays prolonged calls on her friend; she has even reserved a room for her in the palace itself.

The result is that the two women are nearly always together. In any case Madame Vyrubova regularly spends the evening with the sovereigns and their children. No one else ever enters the family circle. They play draughts and patience, do puzzles; occasionally a little music. Highly proper novels, English novels for preference, are read aloud. When the children have gone to bed Madame Vyrubova stays with the sovereigns until midnight and thus takes part in all their conversation, always on Alexandra's side. As the Emperor never ventures to decide anything without his wife's opinion, or rather approval, the net result is that it is the Empress and Madame Vyrubova who really govern Russia! ...

Vyrubova cuts a very poor figure. To account for her position and importance in the imperial palace perhaps it is enough to refer to her personal devotion to the Empress, the devotion of a servile and inferior being loyal to a lady who is always ailing, weighed down by her own power, a lady who is prey to all sorts of terrors and feels that some horrible fate is for ever hanging over her.

Nicky to Alix – 28 February
My own beloved Darling,

Though very sad of course at leaving you and the dear children – this time I start with *such* peace in the soul, which even astonishes me. Does it come from having talked with our Friend last evening, or is it the paper that Buchanan gave me, Witte's death[3] or perhaps a feeling of something good going to happen at the war – I cannot say, but a real Easter comfort is rooted in my heart!

I wish I could have left it to you. I was so happy to have spent two days at home – perhaps you saw it, but I am stupid and never say what I feel. Such a nuisance to be always so occupied and never to sit quietly together and talk! In the afternoon I can never remain at home, such a yearning of getting into the fresh air – and so all the free hours pass and the old couple is very rarely together.

Especially now when A[nia] is not well and cannot come to our house.

Do not overtire yourself, my Love, think of your health, make the

---

[3] Witte had died aged 77.

girlies work for you sometimes. God bless you and them! With tenderest love and kisses ever your endlessly loving old Huzy

Nicky

I will always let you know where I am going.

Alix to Nicky – 1 March – Tsarskoe Selo
My very own Huzy dear,
   Baby madly enjoyed your bath, and made us all come and look on at his pranks in the water. All the daughters beg too for the same treat some evening – may they? – Then we went to Ania, I worked, Olga glued her album, Tatiana worked. I went into the room where the *Strannitza* [wanderer] was with her lantern – we talked together and then she said her prayer. Ever, my Treasure, your very own

Wify

Alexei to Nicky – 2 March – Tsarskoe Selo
Darling Papa,
   It was wonderful in your bathtub. Mama and the girls were there too.
   God bless you!

Alexei

Alix to Nicky – 4 March – Tsarskoe Selo
My own beloved Darling,
   I shall tell the children to fetch your paper and send it with this letter – Baby has written in French, I told him to do so and he writes more naturally than with Peter Vas[ilievich, Russian tutor]. His leg is almost all right, does not limp – the right hand is bandaged and rather swollen, so won't be able to write probably for a few days. But he goes out twice daily. The four girls are going to town.
   Ever your very own Wife,

Sunny

7 March   100 times I told Ania about you too, who you are, and that an E[mperor] never goes daily to a sick person – what would one think otherwise, and that you have your country first of all to think of, and then get tired from work, and need air and it's good you should be with Baby out, etc.

Sunny

Anastasia to Nicky – 7 March – Tsarskoe Selo
My dear darling golden Papa!
I thank you so much for letting us use your bath. We bathed in it yesterday, it was such a delight. I went first, there was lots of water. I was able to swim all round it and then jumped in from the side, it was lovely. Fantastic! Then I splashed around some more with Maria, then it was unfortunately time for me to get out. Ortino was there barking the whole time. Then Olga and Tatiana had their bath and really enjoyed themselves!!! It was awfully good.
I am waiting for you! 1000000000000 big kisses. Your loving and *truly devoted* daughter

Nastanka
May God keep you.

Alexei to Nicky – 7 March – Tsarskoe Selo
My dear Papa!
Today there is a strong frost! Lots of snow, the tower is frozen.
Yesterday I was at Pavlovsk, the locomotive there flattened one of my pennies. The day before yesterday I saw at the farm, how they prepare milk and cream and make butter. It looks very appetizing. I feel well. I am studying satisfactorily. Keep well. May the Lord keep you!

A big kiss, Alexei

Pierre Gilliard, Memoirs – Spring
Alexei, playing in the park in Tsarskoe Selo, slipped behind his youngest sister, who had not seen him coming, and threw a huge snowball at her. His father had witnessed the act. He called the boy to him and talked to him severely. 'You ought to be ashamed of yourself, Alexei! You're behaving like a German, to attack anyone from behind when they can't defend themselves. It's horrid and cowardly. Leave that sort of behaviour to the Germans!'

Nicky, Diary – 28 March – Tsarskoe Selo
Walked for half an hour. At 2.15 we went to town to the Yusupovs', for the christening of their grand-daughter Irina.[4] Mama and I were

---

[4] Daughter of Irina and Felix.

her godparents. The priest almost drowned the little mite. We had a magnificent tea with chocolate. Returned to Tsarskoe Selo at 5.30.

Alix to Nicky – 4 April – Tsarskoe Selo
My very own Treasure,

Forgive me, precious One, but you know you are too kind and gentle – sometimes a good loud voice can do wonders, and a severe look – do my love, be more decided and sure of yourself – you know perfectly well what is right, and when you do not agree and are right, bring your opinion to the front and let it weigh against the rest. They must remember more who you are and that first they must turn to you.

Your being charms every single one, but I want you to hold them by your brain and experience. Though *Nikolasha*[5] is so highly placed, yet you are above him. The same thing shocked our Friend, as me too, that Nikolasha words his telegrams, answers to governors, etc. in your style – his ought to be more simple and humble and other things. You think me a meddlesome bore, but a woman feels and sees things sometimes clearer than my too humble sweetheart. Humility is God's greatest gift – but a Sovereign needs to show his will more often. Be more sure of yourself and go ahead – never fear, you won't say too much.

Goodbye and God bless you Lovy my very Own dear One – I press you tenderly to my heart and kiss you all over and hold you tight, oh so tight.

5 April   Tatiana and Anastasia were there in the day and found our Friend with her. He said the old story that she cries and sorrows as gets so few caresses. So Tatiana was much surprised and He answered that she receives many, only to her they seem few. Her humour seems not famous (the chief mourner) and notes cold, so mine too.

I send you your Image from our Friend of St John the Warrior, which I forgot to give yesterday morning.

I have been rereading what our Friend wrote when he was at Constantinople, it is doubly interesting now – quite short impressions. Oh, what a day when mass will again be served at St Sophie.

---

[5] Relations between Nicky, and particularly Alix, and Grand Duke Nikolai Nikolaevich [Nikolasha] had been bad for some time. The main reason was the pressure brought to bear on Nicky by the Grand Duke in 1905, influencing Nicky to sign the manifesto of 17 October granting wider civil liberties.

Only give orders that nothing should be destroyed or spoiled belonging to the Mahomedans, they can use all again for their religion, as we are Christians and not barbarians, thank God!

What a lot of prisoners we have taken again! Now this must go. Goodbye, Nicky love, I bless and kiss you over and over again with all the tenderness of which I am capable.

6 April

My own beloved Darling,

Well, I shall ask our Friend to quite particularly pray for you there – but, forgive my saying so – it's not for N[ikolasha] to accompany you – you must be the chief one, the first time you go. You find me an old goose, no doubt, but if others won't think of such things, I must.

Au fond, our Friend would have found it better you had gone after the war to the conquered country, I only just mention this like that. Ever your very own

Sunny

Nicky to Alix – 8 April – Mogilev [Stavka, military GHQ]

My own precious Darling,

Fondest loving thanks for your dear letter so full of sweet words and for two telegrams. Have not I also thought of you and of this day 21 years ago? I wish you health and everything a deeply loving heart can wish and thank you on my knees for all your love, affection, friendship and patience you have shown these long years of our married life!

The weather today reminds me of that day at Coburg. It is sad not to be together! Nobody knew it was our engagement day – curious how people quickly forget – tho! it means nothing to them.

It was simply extraordinarily warm and lovely the smell in the pinewood – one felt soft and weak etc!

I send you Ella's telegram to decipher – cannot imagine what she wants?

God bless my precious Sunny. I kiss you and children very very tenderly! Ever your very own Huzy,

Nicky

Alix to Nicky – 8 April – Tsarskoe Selo

My very own beloved Husband,

Tenderly do my prayers and grateful thoughts full of very deepest love linger around you this dear anniversary! How the years go by! 21 years already! You know I have kept the grey princess dress I wore that morning? And shall wear your dear brooch. Dear me, how much we have lived through in these years – heavy trials everywhere, but at home in our nest, bright sunshine!

I am finishing my letter to you on the sofa. The big girls are in town, the little ones walked, then went to their hospital and now have lessons, Baby is in the garden. I lay for ¾ of an hour on the balcony – quite strange to be out, as it happens so rarely I get into the fresh air. The little birdies were singing away – all nature awakening and praising the Lord! Doubly it makes one feel the misery of war and bloodshed – but as after winter cometh summer, so after suffering and strife, may peace and consolation find their place in this world and all hatred cease and our beloved country develop into beauty in every sense of the word.

I wear your cross on my grey teagown and it looks too lovely – your dear brooch of 21 years ago I have also got on. Sweet treasure I must end now.

9 April

My own Sweetheart,

There is an English lady who does wonders in Belgium in her war kit and short skirts – rides and picks up wounded, flies about to get vehicles to transport them to the nearest hospital, binds up their wounds – and once even read the prayers over the grave of a young English officer who died in a garret in a Belgium town taken by the Germans, and one dared not have a regular funeral. Our women are less well educated and have no discipline so I don't know how they will manage 'en masse' – wonder who allows them to form themselves.

4 May

My own sweetest of Sweets,

Be firm, Lovy mine, show your own mind, let others feel you know what you wish. Remember you are the Emperor, and that others dare not take so much upon themselves – beginning by a mere detail, as the Nostitz story – he is in your suite and therefore Nikolasha has absolutely no right to give orders without asking your permission first.

If you did such a thing with one of his aide de camps without warning him, would he not set up a row and play the offended, etc. and without being sure, one cannot ruin a man's career like that.

I meddle in things not concerning me – but it's only a hint – (and it's your own regiment, so you can order whom you wish there).

See that the stories of the Jews is [*sic*] carefully done, without unnecessary rows, not to provoke disturbances over the country.

Wify

Anastasia to Alix – 7 May – Tsarskoe Selo
My darling Mama dear

I hope that you are not too tired, we will try not to quarrel, argue or fight, so sleep well. May God keep you. Your loving daughter

Nastanka

KR, Diary – 12 May
I have been feeling unwell. During the day I have had several attacks of spasmodic pain in the chest, which makes me feel very depressed. [This is the last entry in KR's diary.]

Nicky, Diary – 2 June – Tsarskoe Selo
The same sort of day, reminiscent of autumn. Went for a short stroll. Mordvinov was there for lunch (on duty). Went for a walk with Maria and Anastasia.

Went to see Mama at the Anichkov with Olga and Tatiana. Returned at 7 o'clock and received Sazonov. After his report little Georgy Konstantinovich came in and informed me of Kostia's [KR's] death. At 9.15 we went to Pavlovsk for the first requiem service. Aunt Olga, Mavra and Mitia were present; none of his grown-up sons were there.

Nicky to King George V – 3 June – Tsarskoe Selo – Telegram
TO: HIS MAJESTY THE KING, LONDON

ALIX AND I SEND YOU OUR WARMEST GOOD WISHES FOR YOUR BIRTHDAY. MAY GOD BLESS YOUR COUNTRY AND CROWN WITH SUCCESS OUR UNITED EFFORTS TO BRING ABOUT A SPEEDY AND VICTORIOUS END TO THIS TERRIBLE WAR. LOVE TO MAY

NICKY

Nicky, Diary – 8 June – Peterhof
At 10.30 I set out with Ella, Olga, Tatiana and Maria to town, straight

to the Petropavlovsk cathedral. The requiem service and funeral
lasted two and a half hours. It was sad to look at Aunt Olga, Mavra
and particularly poor Tatiana [KR's daughter] when they lowered
Kostia's body into the grave!

Lunched with Mama. Returned to Tsarskoe Selo at 4 o'clock. Went
out on the ponds with Alexei. The day was fine.

Alix to Nicky – 10 June – Tsarskoe Selo

My very own precious One,

It is with a heavy heart I let you leave this time – everything is so
serious and just now particularly painful and I long to be with you,
to share your worries and anxieties. You bear all so bravely and by
yourself – let me help you my Treasure. Surely there is some way in
which a woman can be of help and use.

I do so yearn to make it easier for you and the ministers all squab-
bling amongst each other at a time, when all ought to work together
and forget their personal offences – have as aim the welfare of their
Sovereign and Country – it makes me rage. In other words 'tis treachery, because people know it, they feel the government in discord and
then the left profit by it.

If you could only be severe, my Love, it is so necessary, they must
hear your voice and see displeasure in your eyes; they are too much
accustomed to your gentle, forgiving kindness.

At a time, such as we are now living through, one needs to hear
your voice uplifted in protest and reprimand when they continue
not obeying your orders, when they dawdle in carrying them out.

They must learn to tremble before you – you remember M. Philippe
and Grigory say the same thing too. You must simply order things to
be done, not asking if they are possible (you will never ask anything
unreasonable or a folly).Where there is a will there is a way and they
must all realize that you insist upon your wish being speedily fulfilled
only don't ask, but order straight off, be energetic for your country's
sake!

The same about the question which our Friend takes so to heart and
which is the most serious of all, for internal peace's sake – the not calling in the Second class – if the order has been given, you tell N[ikolasha]
that you insist on its counter-ordering – by your name to wait, the kind
act must come from you – don't listen to any excuses – (am sure it was
unintentionally done out of not having knowledge of the country).

Therefore our Friend dreads your being at the Headquarters as all
come round with their own explanations and involuntarily you give

in to them, when your own feeling has been the right one, but did not suit theirs. Remember you have reigned long, have far more experience than they – N. has only the army to think of and success – you carry the internal responsibilities on for years – if he makes faults (after the war he is nobody), but you have to set all straight.

No, harken unto our Friend, believe Him, He has your interest and Russians at heart – it is not for nothing God sent Him to us – only we must pay more attention to what He says – His words are not lightly spoken – and the gravity of having not only His prayers, but His advice – is great. The Ministers did not think of telling you, that this measure is a fatal one, but He did.

How hard it is not to be with you, to talk over all quietly and to help you being firm. Shall follow and be near you in thoughts and prayers all the time. May God bless and protect you, my brave, patient, humble one.

I cover your sweet face with endless, tender kisses – love you beyond words, my own, very own sunshine and joy. I bless you. Sad not to pray together, but Botkin finds wiser my remaining quiet, so as soon to be quite all right again.

Your own Wify

Our Maria will be 16 on the 14th, so give her diamond necklace from us, like the other two got.

12 June

My very Own,

God, what a hideous war! Sweet brave Soul how I wish one could rejoice your poor tortured heart with something bright and hopeful. I long to hold you tightly clasped in my arms, with your sweet head resting upon my shoulder – then I could cover Lovy's face and eyes with kisses and murmur soft words of love.

I kiss your cushion at nights, that's all I have – and bless it. Now I must go to sleep. Rest well, my treasure, I bless and kiss you ever so fondly and gently stroke your dear brow.

Forgive me, but I don't like the choice of Minister of war.

14 June

My own beloved Nicky,

I send you a stick (fish holding a bird), which was sent to Him [Rasputin] from New Athos to give to you – he used it first and now sends it to you as a blessing – if you can sometimes use it, would be nice and to have it in your compartment near the one Mr Ph[ilippe] touched.

Now goodbye my very own, longed for Treasure, my Sweetheart. I kiss you ever so fondly and pray God to bless, protect and guide you.

15 June
My own beloved One,

As though also Samarin instead of Sabler,[6] whom it is better not to change before one has a very good one to replace him, certainly Samarin would go against our Friend and stick up for the Bishops we dislike – he is so terribly Moscovite and narrowminded.

Yes, Lovy, about Samarin I am *much* more than sad, simply in *despair*, just one of Ella's not good, very bigoted clique, bosom friend of Sophie Iv. Tiutcheva [the ex-governess], that bishop Trifon I have *strong* reason to dislike, as he always spoke and now speaks in the army against our Friend – now we shall have stories against our Friend beginning and all will go badly. I hope heart and soul he won't accept – that means Ella's influence and worries from morn to night, and he against *us*, once against Grigory and so awfully narrowminded a real Moscow type – head without soul ...

Wify

Alexei to Nicky – 16 June – Tsarskoe Selo
Cher Papa,

Hier pour la première fois j'ai marché à pieds nus, c'était très amusant. Alexis et Serge ont couru avec moi dans le sable qui nous brûlait les pieds. Comme je suis content que tu reviennes bientôt. Je t'embrasse [Yesterday I walked barefoot for the first time, it was great fun. Alexei and Sergei ran with me in the sand, which burnt our feet. How happy I am that you are coming back soon. I embrace you.]

Alexei

Alix to Nicky – 16 June – Tsarskoe Selo
My beloved One,

I have absolutely no faith in Nikolasha – know him to be far from clever and having gone against a man of God's, his work can't be blessed, nor his advice be good.

When Grigory heard in town yesterday before He left, that

---

[6] Samarin was Procurator of the Holy Synod, July–September 1915; Sabler was Procurator of the Holy Synod, 1911–15.

Samarin was named, already then people knew it – He was in utter despair, as He, the last evening here, a week ago today, begged you not to change him Sabler just now, but that soon one might perhaps find the right man – and now the Moscow set will be like a spider's net around us, our Friend's enemies are *ours*, and Shcherbatov [Minister for Foreign Affairs] will make one with them. I feel sure.

I beg your pardon for writing all this, but I am so wretched ever since I heard it and can't get calm – I see now why Grigory did not wish you to go there – here I might have helped you. People are afraid of my influence.

Grigory said it (not to me) and Voeikov, because they know I have a strong will and sooner see through them and help you being firm. I should have left nothing untried to dissuade you, had you been here, and I think God would have helped me and you would have remembered our Friend's words. When He says not to do a thing and one does not listen, one sees one's fault always afterwards. Only if he does accept, Nikolasha will try and get round him too against our Friend that's Nikolasha's campaign.

I entreat you at the first talk with Samarin and when you see him, to speak very firmly – do my Love, for Russia's sake – Russia will not be blessed if her Sovereign lets a man of God's sent to help him – be persecuted, I am sure.

Tell him severely, with a strong and decided voice, that you forbid any intrigues against our Friend or talks about Him, or the slightest persecution, otherwise you will not keep him. That a true Servant dare not to go against a man his Sovereign respects and venerates.

You know the bad part Moscow plays, tell it him all, his bosom friend S. I. Tiutcheva spreads lies about the children, repeat this and that her poisonous untruths did much harm and you will not allow a repetition of it.

You know what this war is to me in every sense and that the man of God's who prays incessantly for you, might be in danger again of persecution – the God would not forgive our weakness and sin in not protecting him. You know Nikolasha's hatred for Grigory is intense. Sabler is a very conceited man, in summer I had occasion to see it, when I had that talk with him about the evacuation question. Rostovtsev [head of Alix's Chancellery] and I carried off a most unpleasant impression of his self-sufficiency – blind adoration of Moscow and looking down upon Petersburg. The tone in which he spoke shocked Rostovtsev greatly. That showed me him in another light, and I realized how unpleasant it would be to have to do with him. When one proposed him for Alexei before I unhesitatingly said no; for nothing such a narrowminded man. Our Church just needs the contrary – soul and not brain – God Almighty may He help put things aright, and hear our prayers and give you at last more confidence in your own wisdom, not listening to others, but to our Friend and your *soul*.

Nothing is trivial now – all is grave. I venerate and love old Goremykin [Prime Minister] had I seen him, I know how I should have spoken – he is so frank with our Friend and does not grasp, that Samarin is *your* enemy if he goes and speaks against Grigory. God wishes your poor Wify to be your help. Grigory always says so and Mr Ph[ilippe] too – and I might warn you in time if I knew things. Well, now I can only pray and suffer.

I am sure better, sunnier days will come. If they only knew how they harm instead of helping you, blind people with their hatred against Grigory! You remember dans *Les Amis de Dieux* it says, a country cannot be lost whose Sovereign is guided by a man of God's. Oh let Him guide you more.

Sunny

17 June Wify ought to send you bright and cheery letters, but it's difficult, as am feeling more than lowspirited and depressed these days – so many things worry me. Now the Duma is to come together in August, and our Friend begged you several times to do it as late as possible and not now, as they ought all to be working in their own place – and here they will try to mix in and speak about things that do not concern them.

Never forget that you are and must remain autocratic Emperor – we are not ready for a constitutional government ... Nobody knows who is the Emperor now – you have to run to the Headquarters and assemble your ministers there, as tho' you could not have them alone here like last Wednesday.

It is as tho' Nikolasha settles all, makes the choices and changes – it makes me utterly wretched. You are remaining still long away, Grigory begged not – once all goes against his wishes my heart bleeds in anguish and fright; Oh, to keep and protect you from more worries and miseries, one has enough more than the heart can bear – one longs to go to sleep for a long rest.

Grigory telegraphed to A[nia] from Viatka: 'travel quietly, sleep, God will help, kiss all.' Goodnight wee One, sleep peacefully – holy Angels guard your slumber and loving Wify's earnest prayers for her very own precious sunny, big-eyed Darling.

Goodbye and God bless you, beloved Sunshine, caress and kiss with unboundless love and tenderness. Ever, Nicky mine, your very own Wify

Sunny

22 June
My own beloved One,

You see how *he* turns your words and orders round – the slanderers were to be punished and not he – and that at the Headquarters one wants him to be got rid of (this I believe) – ah, it's so vile – always liars, enemies – I long knew Dzhunkovsky hates Grigory and that the Preobrajensky [regiment] clique therefore dislikes me, as through me and Ania he comes to the house.

If we let our Friend be persecuted we and our country shall suffer for it – once a year ago one tried to kill him and one has slandered him enough. As if they would not have called the police straight in to catch him in the act – such a horror! Speak, please to Voeikov about it.

Loman says they will, so as to force one to get rid of Grigory and Ania, I am so weary, such heartache and pain from all this – the idea of dirt being again spread about one we venerate is more than horrible.

If Dzhunkovsky is with you, call him, tell him you know (no names) he has shown that paper in town and that you order him to tear it up and not to dare to speak of Grigory as he does and that he acts as a traitor and not as a devoted subject, who ought to stand up for the Friends of the Sovereign, as one does in every other country.

25 June   Russia, thank God, is not a constitutional country, tho' those creatures try to play a part and meddle in affairs they dare not. Do not allow them to press upon you – it's fright if one gives in and their heads will go up.

I fear I anger and trouble you by my letters – but I am alone in my misery and anxiety and can't swallow what I think my honest duty to tell you.

Nikolasha knows my will, and fears my influence (guided by Grigory) upon you; it's all so clear.

Now goodbye, my very own tenderly beloved one. I cover you with kisses and ask God's blessing upon you. Ever your own old

Wify

Nicky to King George V – 25 June – Mogilev
My dear Georgie,

Many thanks for your kind letter that Capt. Kedroff brought me three weeks ago. I am sorry I did not answer you directly, but just then I was very busy about some changements among the ministers, which you have probably heard of. Now it is over a fortnight that I am here. We have lived through very anxious and difficult moments.

That retreat in Galicia under the enemy's pressure had to be effectuated to save our army – solely on account of the lack of ammunition and of rifles. And this reason is a most painful one.

But my country has well understood it and everywhere the people are setting to work for the needs of the army with redoubled energy and with an unanimous mighty wish to contribute in our final victory over our powerful enemy. And powerful they are – one cannot deny it them!

I am going home in a few days, as thank God, the news from the front is better. It will soon be a year that this terrible war is raging and goodness knows how long it may still last – but *we shall fight* to the end!

With my fond love to dear May. Ever my dear Georgie your devoted cousin and friend

Nicky

Misha to Natalia Brassova – 6 July – the front lines
My dearest darling Natasha,

The courier has just arrived bringing your dear letter, for which I kiss and embrace you tenderly, of course it's a pity it isn't longer, but no one is to blame for that. It's terrible how our separation affects the nerves, I get anxious and upset about every little thing. For some reason I can't write at all today, yet I so want to express all the feelings, which are pouring from my heart I so want to tell you of my boundless love and devotion. If only you knew, my dearest, how worn out I am by this life without you, without tenderness, without love!

May God grant that this nightmare of a time passes quickly, yet at the same time I feel ashamed to be complaining, as everyone is living these hard times and suffering terrible losses.

May the Lord keep and bless you, my dearest, tender angel. I embrace you with love, and caress you in my thoughts and bless you. Yours always,

Misha

King George V to Nicky – 8 August – Windsor Castle
My dear Nicky,

I feel most deeply for you in the very anxious days through which you are now passing, when your army has been compelled to retire on account of the lack of ammunition and rifles, in spite of the splendid and most gallant way are fighting against our most powerful enemy . . .

I can assure you that in England we are now straining every nerve to produce the required ammunition and guns and also rifles and are sending the troops of our new armies to the front as fast as we possibly can.

England has made up her mind to *fight this awful war out to an end*, whatever our sacrifices may be, our very existence is at stake. I am so glad to see by your letter that Russia also means to *fight* to the end and I know France is of the same opinion.

God bless you my dear Nicky. Ever your devoted cousin and friend

Georgie

Tatiana to Alix – 15 August – Tsarskoe Selo

Mama, darling angel mine!

I pray for you both dearies, the whole time, that God will help you now in this terrible time. I simply can't tell you how awfully sorry I am for you, my beloved ones. I am so sorry I can in no way help you or be useful.

In such moments I am sorry I'm not a man. Bless you my own beloved one. Sleep well. I kiss you and Papa dear awfully much. Your own loving and true daughter,

Tatiana

Maurice Paléologue, Memoirs – 16 August

For the first time Rasputin has been attacked by the press. Hitherto the censorship and the police had protected him against newspaper criticism. It is the *Bourse Gazette* which has opened the campaign.

The man's whole past, his ignoble beginnings, thefts, drunken bouts, debaucheries and intrigues, the scandal of his relations with high society, officials and clergy, are ruthlessly exposed. But, cleverly enough, no allusion is made to his intimacy with the Emperor and the Empress.

'How is it possible?' writes the author of these articles. 'How has an abject adventurer like this been able to make a mockery of Russia for so long? Is it not astounding to think that the official Church, the Holy Synod, the aristocracy, ministers, the Senate, and the numerous members of the Council of Empire and the Duma have demeaned themselves before this low hound? Is it not the most terrible charge we can level against the regime? Only yesterday the political and social scandals which the name of Rasputin conjures up seemed perfectly natural. Today Russia means to put an end to all this ... '

Maria Pavlovna [the younger], Memoirs – 20 August

All their thoughts and methods had become shadowy and indirect. The Empress, for instance, wished to know the opinion of Paléologue, the French ambassador, as to her project of sending her husband to the front. She knew that my father and his wife were on friendly terms with Paléologue; so she asked them to give a dinner for him, and sent to that dinner Madame Vyrubova, her bourgeois counsellor, with instructions to find out Paléologue's attitude.

Madame Vyrubova was, in her own way, sincerely and altogether disinterestedly devoted to the Empress, but because of her shallowness in general and her blind worship of Rasputin in particular she did not command respect.

M. Paléologue was dumbfounded at the thought of so important a mission being entrusted to such a clod. He told her, diplomatically, that it seemed too late for an outside and contrary opinion to be of any avail. Stammering, she repeated, one by one, his polished phrases, and said she would try to repeat to the Empress all that he had said.

Nicky, Diary – 22 August – Tsarskoe Selo

At 10.30 the three of us went into town – to the Winter Palace, where I held the first meeting of the committee for the provision of military supplies and equipment to the army. Afterwards, I was talking with the members of the committee, when Alix came in with Alexei and also went round with them. Returned to Tsarskoe Selo before one o'clock. The weather was wonderful. Went for a good walk in Babolovo. After tea I received Polivanov and then went to church. Ania and N.P. [Sabline] were there for dinner. At ten o'clock I said goodbye to dear Alix and the children, and set off. May God bless my journey and my decision![7]

---

[7] To remove Grand Duke Nikolai Nikolaevich (Nikolasha) and assume command of the Russian forces himself.

Alix to Nicky – 22 August – Tsarskoe Selo

My very own beloved One,

Your faith has been tried – your trust – and you remained firm as a rock, for that you will be blessed. God anointed you at your coronation, he placed you where you stand and you have *done your duty*, be *sure*, quite *sure* of this and he forsaketh not His anointed. Our Friend's prayers arise night and day for you to Heaven and God will hear them.

I do hope Goremykin will agree to your choice of Khvostov[8] – you need an energetic minister of the interior – should he be the wrong man, he can later be changed – no harm in that, at such times – but if energetic he may help splendidly and then the old man does not matter.

Too kind, don't be. All is for the good, as our Friend says, the worst is over. God is with you and our Friend for you – all is well later all will thank you for having saved your country.

I give no other as that carried my blessing and you have Grigory's St Nikolas to guard and guide you.

I kiss you without end and bless you. Holy Angels guard your slumber – I am near and with you for ever and none shall separate us. Your very own wife

Sunny

23 August All my thoughts and prayers surround you in tenderest love. Such calm filled my soul (tho' terribly sad) when I saw you leave in peace and serene. Your face had such a lovely expression, like when our Friend left. God verily will bless you and your undertakings after this moral victory. Wonder how you slept – I went straight to bed, deadbeat and very lonely.

I copy out 2 telegrams from our Friend. If you have an occasion, show them to N.P. [Sabline] one must keep him up more about our Friend, as in town he hears too much against him, begins to heed less to His telegrams. Goremykin asked whether you would be back this week (to disperse the Duma then) I said you could not possibly yet tell.

The children and I went to Znamenia at 3¼ and I placed a very big candle, which will burn very long and carry my prayers to God's throne for you and before the Virgin and St Nikolas. Now, my love I must end. God bless and protect and help you and all you undertake. Kisses without end on all dear places, for ever your very own trusting proud Wify

---

[8] Minister of the Interior 1916.

Ania Vyrubova, Memoirs

The Empress Dowager, whom the Emperor visited immediately after the ministerial conference, was by this time thoroughly imbued with the German-spy mania in which the Empress and Rasputin, not to mention myself, were involved. She believed the whole preposterous tissue of lies which had been built up and with all her might she struggled against the Emperor's decision to assume supreme command of the army. For over two hours a painful scene was enacted in the Empress Dowager's gardens, he trying to show her that utter disaster threatened the army and the Empire under existing conditions, and she repeating over and over again the wicked slanders of German plots which she insisted that he was furthering. In the end the Emperor left, terribly shaken, but with his resolution as strong as ever.

Nicky, Diary – 23 August – Mogilev

Slept well. The morning was rainy: after midday the weather cleared up and it became quite warm. At 3.30 arrived at *my headquarters*, one *verst* from the town of Mogilev. Nikolasha was waiting for me. After talking with him, received General Alekseyev with his first report.[9] It all went well! After having tea, went to look at the surrounding area. The train is standing in a small, thick wood. We dined at 7.30. Afterwards went for another walk. The evening was splendid.

Nicky to King George V – 24 August – Petrograd

To His Majesty the King,

I have heard with much pleasure that the British submarine E-8 has joined My Naval Forces and wish to express to You My cordial thanks. The Baltic Sea represents a most favourable field of operations for submarine activity and the presence of British boats of that type will render a most important service to our general cause. I am sure that E-8 will perform deeds as brilliant and successful as E-1 quite lately again.

I beg You to accept my deepest sympathy for the sad and heroic loss of submarine E-13.

NICHOLAS

---

[9] Removing Nikolai Nikolaevich (Nikolasha) as supreme commander and assuming his position himself proved to be the most unwise and unpopular decision Nicky was to make during the war.

Nicky, Diary – 24 August – Mogilev

Woke around 9 o'clock. The morning was so beautiful in the woods. After tea went to Mogilev to the cathedral, and from there to the governor's offices, which are being used to house General Alexeev [chief of staff], and well as the staff and administration of general headquarters. After the report we went over to the governor's residence, where Nikolasha is staying. I signed the mandate for him and the army order concerning my assumption of the high command from yesterday's date.

Lord, help and guide me! Returned to headquarters just before lunch. In the afternoon went for a walk beyond the Dnieper along the Gomelsky road and in a nice wood. Towards evening it started to rain. Lost at dice.

Alix to Nicky – 24 August – Tsarskoe Selo

My own beloved One,

Baby dear's left arm hurts and is very swollen, hurt from time to time in the night and today – the old thing, but he has not had it for very long, thank God. Mr Gilliard read aloud and then showed us the magic lantern.

We all send our love to N.P.

God bless and protect you my Treasure – miss you very, very much. As you know cannot be otherwise; press you tenderly to my heart and cover you with caresses and kisses. I bless you and pray for God's help. Ever your old

Wify

Ella's prayers are with you – she is going for these last days to Optin convent.

Nicky to Alix – 25 August – Mogilev

My own beloved darling Sunny,

Thank God it is all over and here I am with this *new*, heavy responsibility on my shoulders! But God's will fulfilled – I feel so calm, a sort of feeling after the Holy Communion!

The whole morning of the memorable day August 23, while coming here, I prayed much and read your first letter over and over again. The nearer the moment of our meeting approached the more peaceful felt my soul.

Nikolasha came in with a good cheery smile and simply asked for my order when he was to leave. I answered, in the same way, that he could remain for two days; then we spoke about questions concerning the military operations, about some generals etc. and that was *all!*

The following days at luncheon and dinner he was talkative and of a good humour that we all have rarely seen him in for many a month! Petia[10] also, but his adcs were black in their expressions – it was even funny.

I must do justice to my gentlemen beginning by old Friend – they behaved well and I did not hear any discordant note, not one word to snap at.

Of course while Nikolasha was here I asked him to be present both mornings at the report. Alexeev does it so well. He was most touched by the little image and blessing you sent through me. Nikolasha repeated to me that he leaves this place with a quiet feeling knowing I have such a help as Alexeev under me.

We spoke much about the Caucasus, he likes it and interests himself in the people and fine nature, but he begs not to remain long after the end of the war.

He put on at once a fine old circassian sword a present Shervashidze had given him years ago and is going to wear it the whole time. He thinks he will remain at Pershino about 12 days and then start straight for Tiflis meeting the old count W. at Rostov on the Don. The whole collection of black women[11] join him from Kiev at his estate and start altogether!

Now begins a new clean page and what will be written on it only God Almighty knows?

I signed my first *prikaz* [order] and added a few words with rather a trembling hand!

We have just finished our evening meal and after that I had a long talk with Lagiche and then with gen[eral] Williams.

Georgie and the King of the Belgians have both answered my telegrams in which I announced this change with us – so quick!

I am delighted you spoke and soothed dear old Gor[emykin]. Please tell him next time that as soon as Government Council and Duma have finished their work – they must be closed, quite the same whether I am back or still here!

Why not see Kroupensky, he is a trustworthy man and can tell you perhaps things worth hearing.

Fancy, my Wify, helping Huzy when away! What a pity you did not perform that duty long ago, or at least now during this war!

---

[10] Grand Duke Pyotr Nikolaevich, Nikolasha's brother.
[11] Militsa and Stana, the Montenegran grand duchesses.

Nothing gives me more pleasure than to feel proud of you, as I have all these last months when you worried me thoroughly to be firm and stick to my opinion.

We just finished playing domino when I got a telegram through Alexeev from Ivanov, who announced that today our 11th army (Sherbachev) in Galicia attacked two German divisions (the 3rd guard and 48th infantry) with the result that over 150 officers and 7000 men, 30 guns and many machine-guns were taken!

And that happened directly after our troops had heard about my taking over the leadership. That is really God's mercy and such a quick one!

Now I must end, it is late and I must go to bed!

God bless you, my beloved treasure, my Sunbeam. I kiss you and dear children very tenderly. Ever your own old Huzy

Nicky

Give Ania my fond love.

Anastasia to Nicky – 26 August – Tsarskoe Selo
My dear sweet darling Papa!

I am sitting on the sofa next to Alexei having dinner with M. Gilliard, while Maria is running round like a fiend. I am already allowed to go to the infirmaries again, but the weather is so foul and cold that I am not going out.

[Dr] Ostrogorsky came to see me this morning, but Maria and I were still in bed, so Maria hid under the blanket when he came to examine me, and when he had finished I quietly drew back the blanket and Maria had to crawl out, which made her very embarrassed. But as soon as he shut the door I was tipped out onto the floor. We haven't done anything very interesting during the day.

May the Lord be with you. I kiss you 10000000000 times. Your loving and truly devoted daughter

Caspian Nastaska

Alix to Nicky – 2 September – Tsarskoe Selo
My own beloved One,

Such a glorious sunny morning, both windows were wide open all the night and now too. I have new ink now, it seems the other is at an end now, it was not Russian.

It always grieves me to see how bad things one makes here, all comes from abroad, the very simplest things, as nails for instance,

wool for knitting, knitting needles in metal and any amount of necessary things. God grant, that after this terrible war is ended, one can
get the fabrics to make leather things, and prepare the fur themselves
– such an immense country dependent on others.

Now goodbye, Lovy mine, the man must leave. God bless you and
protect you I kiss every dear spot over and over again and hold you
tight in my arms. Ever your own very own Wify

Alice

6 September
Beloved Nicky dear,

Every morning and evening I bless and then kiss your cushion and
one of your images. I always bless you whilst you sleep and I get up
to draw open the curtains. Wify sleeps all alone down here, and the
wind is howling melancholy tonight. How lonely you must feel, wee
One. Are your rooms at least not too hideous?

So many yellow and copper leaves, and alas also many are beginning to fall – sad autumn has already set in.

God bless help, strengthen, comfort, guard and guide. Ever your
very own

Wify

Andrei Vladimirovich, Diary – 6 September – St Petersburg
A few days ago Alix came to have tea with Mama [Maria Pavlovna the
elder] at Tsarskoe Selo, with her two eldest daughters. It should be
noted that this is the first time in twenty years that Alix has been to
visit Mama without Nicky.

But the most interesting was the ensuing conversation. Alix complained bitterly that whatever she did, she was criticized, particularly
in Moscow and Petrograd. Everyone was against her, and therefore
her hands were tied.

'Some sisters of mercy have just arrived from Germany, and for the
sake of our work I should receive them, but I can't do it, because it
will be used against me.'

Mama asked her whether it was true that she and the whole Court
were moving to Moscow? 'Ah, so you've heard that too! No, I am not
moving, nor will I be doing so, but it's what "they" would like me to
do, so they can move here themselves (here she gave a clear hint that
'they' were Nikolai Nikolaevich and the Montenegrans), luckily we
heard about it in time and measures were taken. "He" is now leaving
for the Caucasus. It wasn't possible to put up with it any longer. Nicky

wasn't aware of anything that was going on in the war; "he" never wrote to him, or told him anything. From all sides they have been trying to wrench Nicky's power away from him. They snatched as much as they could. It's not admissible at a time when what is needed, is a firm and unshakeable power in the midst of this collapse of authority. I begged Nicky not to dismiss Goremykin at such a time. You can't just send away people who are devoted. Who will he have left?'

Mama, recounting this conversation to me, said that Alix gave the definite impression of being sincerely distressed by the turn of events. Her displeasure with the Montenegrans and their schemes was striking; although she did not say what, it was clear that she had learnt of something grave, that threatened not just her personally, but also Nicky. This is the key to her enigmatic behaviour, as it then seemed, at Aunt Minnie's [Empress Marie's], when she was talking to Xenia. Mama repeated several times that Alix had made a profound impression on her. Here was very real despair; Alix looked at things exactly as we do, and everything that she said was clear, affirmative and true.

This episode in our family life is important, in that it gave us the possibility of understanding Alix. Almost the whole of her life in our country has been veiled in a shadowy incomprehensible aura. Nobody really knew her, in fact, or understood her, and the guesses or suppositions that were made, became in time an array of the most varied legends. It was difficult to know, where the truth was. This was a great pity. The figure of the Empress should shine out over the whole of Russia, should be seen and understood, otherwise the role gets pushed into the background, and the figure loses its essential popularity.

Of course, the conversation between Alix and Mama described above, cannot restore everything that has been lost over the past twenty years, but for us in any case that conversation was very important. We saw her in a new light, and realized that many of the legends are false, and that she is on the right path. And if she didn't say more than she did, she obviously had a reason. It was evident that she had a lot on her heart, and her visit to Mama was prompted by the need to pour out at least part of it.

Nicky to Alix – 9 September – Mogilev
My beloved dearest Sunny,

So many many thanks for your sweet long letters, which come now more regularly about 9.30 of the evening.

You write quite as you talk. The behaviour of some ministers continues to astonish me! After all I have told them at the famous evening sitting, I thought they might have understood me and that I meant seriously what I said.

Well, so much the worse for them! They were afraid of shutting up the Duma – it has been done! I left for here and changed Nikolasha against their advice; the people have taken this step naturally and have understood – as ourselves. The proof – lots of telegrams I get from different parts and in most touching expressions. All this shows us clearly one thing – that the ministers living always in *town* know extremely little of what goes on in the whole country. Here *I can judge* rightly of the real proof among the different classes of people: everything must be done to carry on the war to a victorious end and no doubt is expressed about it. *This* all the deputations I received the other day told me officially – and so it is everywhere in Russia.

The only two exceptions are Petrograd and Moscow – two needledots on the map of our country!

Misha has wired to ask if he may come for the end of the week. I am very glad to see him here. Well, my precious Love-bird, I must end. God bless you and the children +. Me loves you so and prays for you fervently daily. I send two telegrams from our Friend – so his son has been taken![12]

Bless you and kiss you tenderly.

Nicky

Alix to Nicky – 15 September – Tsarskoe Selo
Remember to keep the Image in your hand again and several times to comb your hair with His comb before the sitting of the ministers.

Goodbye, dear Beloved, my own sweet husband, joy of my heart – I cover you with tender longing kisses.

17 September The Duma exist – there is nothing to be done, and with such a hard worker, the old man would get on all right. Excellent you did not see Rodzianko [Chairman of the Duma], at once their noses went down – you shut the Duma which they thought you would not dare to – all quite right.

Really, my Treasure, I think he is the man our Friend hinted to Ania in his wire; I am always careful in my choice.

---

[12] Into the army, despite Rasputin's request.

I bless you my Angel, God bless you and the holy Virgin.
Cover you with longing, loving tender kisses.

Sunny

Nicky to Alix – 18 September – Mogilev
My precious beloved Sunny,
   Strange how accurately our Friend foresaw the time I would be away – 'one month you will be there, and after that you will return'!
   And now me must end. God bless you, my beloved precious Love-bird + I kiss you and the children passionately and tenderly. Thank Ania for her letter. Ever your own old Huzy

Nicky

I let Dmitri go to his father [Pavel].

Pierre Gilliard, Memoirs – September
The Tsar returned to Tsarskoe Selo for a few days, and it was decided that Alexei should go back with him to GHQ, for he was most anxious to show the Heir to the troops. The Tsarina bowed to this necessity. She realized how greatly the Tsar suffered from loneliness, for at one of the most tragic hours of his life he was deprived of the presence of his family, his greatest consolation. She knew what a comfort it would be to have his son with him. Yet her heart bled at the thought of Alexei leaving her. It was the first time she had been separated from him, and one can imagine what a sacrifice it meant to the mother, who never left her child, even for a few minutes, without wondering anxiously whether she would ever see him alive again.

Alix to Nicky – 3 October – Tsarskoe Selo
My Own beloved Darling,
   In the evening we see our Friend at Ania's to bid goodbye. He begs you very much to send a telegram to the King of Serbia, as he is very anxious that Bulgaria will finish them off – so I enclose the paper again for you to use it for your telegram – the sense in your words and shorter of course reminding them of their Saints and so on. Make Baby show you Pyotr Vasilievich envelope, it's sweet. I shall also address my letter separately to him, he will feel prouder. Derevenko has got our presents for him and can arrange them in the bedroom.

I kiss you without end and hold you tightly clasped to my old heart which yearns for you ever, Nicky sweet, your very own Wify

Alix

6 October I am sending you a very fat letter from the Cow [Vyrubova], the lovesick creature could not wait any longer, she must pour out her love otherwise she bursts.

God bless and protect you and keep you from all harm. A thousand kisses from your own old

Wify

Nicky to Alix – 6 October – Mogilev

My own precious Love-bird,

So many tender thanks for your loving letters. I am in despair that I have not written once since we left, but truly I am occupied here every moment except from 2.30 till 6. And having Tiny of course also takes a part of the time, which I certainly do not regret. His presence brings light and life to us all – the foreigners included!

It is awfully cosy sleeping near each other; I pray with him every evening since the train, he says the prayers much too quick and it is difficult to stop him. He enjoyed the review enormously, followed me and stood the whole time during the march past, which was excellent. That review I shall never forget.

The weather was perfect and the whole impression remarkable. The life here is the same as usual. Only the first day Alexei lunched with Mr Gilliard in my room; but then he begged very much to lunch with everybody – sits on my left and behaves well, but is sometimes inclined to be rather gay and noisy, especially while I am talking to others in the saloon. In any case it makes them smile and pleased.

We motor out in the afternoons (in the mornings he plays in the garden) either in the wood or to river bank, where we make a bonfire and I take my walk round about.

I am astonished how much he can and wants to walk and does not complain of being tired on returning home! He sleeps quietly, I too notwithstanding the strong light of his icon-lamp. In the morning he awakes early, between 7 and 8, sits up in bed and begins a gentle talk with me. I answer him half sleeping and then he lies down and remains quiet till they come in to awake us.

Pavel is very nice and modest, we have had a good talk. He knew about his wife's letter and is not pleased with it.

God bless you, my Sunny, my beloved Wify. I kiss you and the girlies tenderly. A[nia] too.

Ever your own

Nicky

Alix to Nicky – 10 October – Tsarskoe Selo
My own beloved Darling,

Our Friend, whom we saw last night, is otherwise quiet about the war, now another subject worries him very much and he spoke scarcely about anything else for two hours. It is this that you must give an order that waggons with flour, butter and sugar should be obliged to pass. He saw the whole thing in the night like a vision, all the towns, railway lines etc. It's difficult to give over from his words, but he says it is very serious and that then we shall have no strikes.

Very tender kisses, Sweetheart from your own deeply endlessly loving old

Wify

1 November Our Friend was always against this war, saying the Balkans were not worth the world to fight about and that Serbia would be as ungrateful as Bulgaria proved itself.

12 November
My own beloved Nicky, dear,

In case therefore if we do not see each other the 14th, I send you my very, very tenderest loving thoughts and wishes and endless thanks for the intense happiness and love you have given me these 21 years – oh, Darling, it is difficult to be happier than we have been and it has given one strength to bear much sorrow. May our children be as richly blessed – with anguish I think of their future – so unknown!

Well, all must be placed into God's hands with trust and faith. Life is a riddle, the future hidden behind a curtain, and when I look at our big Olga, my heart fills with emotions and wondering as to what is in store for her – what will her lot be.

Now my sweetest love, I must end my scrawl. Let me know about when to expect you. God bless and protect, guard and guide you.

I kiss you with deepest tenderness and boundless love and devotion, and long to rest my weary head upon your breast. Ever, Huzy mine, your very own old

Sunny

Maria Pavlovna [the younger], Memoirs

Towards the close of 1915, early in December, I took two weeks off and visited my father at Tsarskoe Selo and my aunt Ella at Moscow.

My aunt had greatly changed during the last few years. In spite of the fact that she was living in a nunnery, she came now into contact with a greater number and variety of people. This had broadened her outlook, made her softer, more human. Not only did she come face to face with phases of life of which previously she had known nothing, but she had now to take into account opinions and viewpoints entirely at variance with her own. She remained, however, always a little puzzled, never quite able to attain a complete balance. Seeking in Orthodoxy to build her life and by Orthodoxy to establish a religious order firmly founded upon ancient Russian precepts and customs, she still remained a foreigner in her psychology, and her attempts seemed often naive and uncoordinated.

But the atmosphere that she had created around herself revealed so clearly and so charmingly her inner self, that in spite of all my love for life, I was attracted.

Nicky, Diary – 3 December – Mogilev

Alexei started a cold yesterday, and this morning had a slight nose bleed after sneezing. We left Mogilev in order to visit the guard. But since the blood, although intermittent, did not get any less, I decided, on the advice of [Dr] Fedorov, to return to headquarters.

4 December Alexei slept fitfully. In the morning his temperature had gone up to 39, but by midday it had dropped to 37.5. Blood was still seeping from his left nostril, although less profusely. In general he was coughing less and was in better spirits. We arrived in Mogilev at 12.15, after exactly twenty four hours. Invited my staff to lunch. Walked up and down the platform. Received a report from Alexeev. At four o'clock we set out north. Sat a lot with Alexei; also read a lot.

5 December At last at 11 o'clock we arrived at Tsarskoe Selo. Alix and our daughters met us. We brought Alexei home in the motor and straight upstairs to his room – the corner one. There was a doctors' conference; Poliakov cauterized his left nostril and then left him alone without a swab in the nose.

There was no fever, he was in excellent spirits. I went for a walk alone before lunch, then with Maria and Anastasia in the afternoon.

It was thawing, there was a mass of snow. At 6.30 we went to church. We dined alone; I received my presents upstairs in Alexei's room.

Ania Vyrubova, Memoirs
I was with the Empress when the telegram came announcing the return of the Emperor and the boy to Tsarskoe Selo, and I can never forget the anguish of mind with which the poor mother awaited the arrival of her sick, perhaps her dying child. Nor can I ever forget the waxen, grave-like pallor of the little pointed face as the boy with infinite care was borne into the palace and laid on his little white bed.

Above the blood-soaked bandages his large blue eyes gazed at us with pathos unspeakable, and it seemed to all around the bed that the last hour of the unhappy child was at hand. The physicians kept up their ministrations, exhausting every means known to science to stop the incessant bleeding.

In despair the Empress sent for Rasputin. He came into the room, made the sign of the cross over the bed and, looking intently at the almost moribund child, said quietly to the kneeling parents: 'Don't be alarmed. Nothing will happen.' Then he walked out of the room and out of the palace.

That was all. The child fell asleep, and the next day was so well that the Emperor left for his interrupted visit.

Nicky, Diary – 6 December – Tsarskoe Selo
It was strange and pleasant to spend my nameday at home! Went to church. All the family came to lunch; we sat in the small library at three tables. Then we went to sit with Alexei. He was feeling well; his temperature was 37.3, he had a slight cough but the bleeding stopped after a second cauterization.

Went for a walk with Tatiana, Maria and Anastasia. The weather was pleasant, snow was falling softly. Answered telegrams. Mama came to tea. After dinner Grigory arrived; we sat together at Alexei's bedside.

Ania Vyrubova, Memoirs
I know of many cases of illness where the prayers of Rasputin were asked, and had he been so minded he might have demanded and been given vast sums of money. But the fact is he often showed himself extremely reluctant to exert whatever strange power he possessed. In some instances where sick children were involved he

would even object, saying: 'If God takes him now it is perhaps to save him from future sins.'

Alexei to Nicky – 16 December – Tsarskoe Selo
Dear Papa

Now I am better and I feel well. This morning I got up late. I have a diet! Yesterday evening Aunt Ella came. While they were having dinner I started to knit a scarf from different coloured wool.

Doctor Poliakov came this morning and poked around in the nose and ears, but not in his, in mine! In the morning my temperature was 36.1 and on the street there were 26 degrees of frost. Send my greetings to Golan and Mordvinov, also to the others. It's such a pity I am not with you!!!

May God protect you!! I kiss you.

Your loving Alexei

18 December
Dear Papa

Today I got dressed for the first time. In this whole time I have only lost one pound. There are 8 degrees of frost outside. In a quarter of an hour the doctors will be here, probably to poke around again. I miss you. Coming for the Christmas tree?

I don't know what to write, everything is the same as always.

Give my greetings to all who remember me.

May the Lord God keep you! A big kiss,

Alexei

19 December
Cher Papa,

Hier j'ai déjeuné en bas, j'étais très content. Hier Maman avait mal aux dents, mais maintenant elle n'a plus mal. J'ai commencé avec Gilliard deux grandes forteresses, j'éspère que dans quelques jours nous ferons la bataille. Ce matin dehors il y a trois degrés de froid, je sortirai demain, je suis très content !!!!!

Salue grassouillet (belge) et tout nu!!! et tout le monde. Je t'embrasse,

ton Alexei[13]

---

[13] Dear Papa, Yesterday I had breakfast downstairs, I was very happy. Yesterday Mama had toothache, but now she doesn't have it any longer. I started two large fortresses with Gilliard, I hope we can have a battle in a few days. This morning it is three degrees of frost outside, I shall go out tomorrow, I am very happy!!!!!

Say hello to pudgy (Belgian) and all naked [sic] and everyone. I hug you.

Your Alexei

Maurice Paléologue, Memoirs – 27 December
A curious sign of the favourite preoccupations of the Russian mind is
the pleasure taken by Russian authors in describing life in prison,
penal settlements and exile. It is a familiar theme with all their nov-
elists; each of them seems to think himself under an obligation to
make the sinister *milieu* of a goal or Siberian penitentiary the scene
of some moving incident.

Dostoievsky began it when he incorporated his personal recollections in the book which I consider his masterpiece, the *Memories of the
House of the Dead*. Tolstoy, in *Resurrection*, introduces us with his ruthless realism to the minutest details, material, administrative and
moral, of solitary confinement and transportation. Korolenko, Gorky,
Tchekov, Veressaiev, Andreiev, Dymov, etc., have also made their contribution to this gallery of horrors, where the background of every picture is the Fortress of SS. Peter and Paul, the citadel of Schlüsselburg,
the sepulchural solitudes of Turuchansk and Yakutsk, or the frozen
shores of Saghalien. It is probable that the majority of their readers say
to themselves: 'Perhaps I shall go there myself one day.'

King George V to Nicky – 27 December – Buckingham Palace
Emperor of Russia: On the occasion of our New Year, when our two
Armies are fighting against a Common Enemy, I am anxious to
appoint you a Field Marshal in my Army as a mark of my affection
for you.

If you accept, it will be a great pleasure to me, and an honour to
the British Army.

Nicky to King George V – 29 December – Mogilev
Deeply grateful for the great honour you do me in appointing me a
Field Marshal of the British Army. I accept this high distinction with
much pleasure.

Nicky

Nicky, Diary – 31 December – Mogilev
I arrived in Mogilev and went straight to headquarters. Worked until
3 o'clock and then went for a walk in the garden. Afterwards I wrote
to Alix and read a book. At 11.45 I went to the New Year service. I
prayed fervently that the Lord would bless Russia with a definitive
victory and fortify our faith and patience!

1916

Nicky – Emperor of Russia

Alix – Empress of Russia

Sandro – Grand Duke Alexander Mikhailovich, husband of Xenia

Ella – Grand Duchess Elizabeth, elder sister of Alix, now a nun

Olga (sister) – Grand Duchess, Nicky's younger sister

Maria Pavlovna (the younger) – daughter of Nicky's uncle Grand Duke Pavel, sister of Dmitri Pavlovich

Andrei Vladimirovich – son of Grand Duke Vladimir and Maria Pavlovna (the elder)

Grand Duke Nikolai Mikhailovich – a brother of Sandro

Olga – eldest daughter of Nicky and Alix, aged twenty-one

Alexei – Heir and Tsarevich, son of Nicky and Alix, aged twelve

Georgie – King George V of England, first cousin of both Nicky and Alix

Prince Felix Yusupov – married to Irina, daughter of Xenia and Sandro

Ania Vyrubova – lady-in-waiting and close friend of Alix

Pierre Gilliard – Swiss tutor of Nicky and Alix's children

Maurice Paléologue – French Ambassador in Petersburg

Grigory Rasputin

V. A. Jukovskaya – one of Rasputin's circle

A. A. Mordvinov – ADC to Grand Duke Mikhail

V. V. Shulgin – a deputy in second, third and fourth Duma

V. M. Purishkevich – leader of the right-wing faction in the Duma

1916

THE MURDER OF GRIGORY

Rasputin's influence continues to grow – He describes how
he seduces women – Alix is losing her mental equilibrium
– The Empress is increasingly unpopular – Ania Vyrubova
and Rasputin are blamed for their pernicious influence –
Olga, Nicky's sister, wants to divorce Prince Peter
Oldenburg and marry Colonel Kulikovsky – Alix
continues to interfere in affairs of state – Yusupov,
Purishkevich and Grand Duke Dmitri Pavlovich murder
Rasputin – Yusupov and Dmitri Pavlovich are banished –
The family try to intercede on Dmitri's behalf

Alix to Nicky – 1 January – Tsarskoe Selo
My own beloved Angel,
    The children are lunching next door and making wonderful noises.
'Engineer-Mechanic' [period] has arrived unexpectedly and so pre-
vents med[icine] which is a bore.
    This instant, quite unexpectedly your sweetest letter was brought –
oh thank you Lovy mine, thank you tenderly for your sweet words
which warmed up my aching heart – the best gift for the beginning
of the new year. Oh Lovy mine, what good it does a tender word like
that! you don't know, how much it means to me, nor how terribly I
miss you – I yearn for your kisses, for your arms, shy Childy only
gives them me in the dark and Wify lives by them.
    I hate begging for them like Ania, but when I get them, they are
my life, and when you are away, I recall all your sweet looks and
every word and caress.
    Goodbye my Angel Dear, I bless and kiss you over and over again.

2 January Oh, to have wings and fly over every evening to cheer you up with my love. Long to hold you in my arms, to cover you with kisses and feel that you are my very Own, whoever dares call you 'my own', – you nevertheless are mine, my own treasure, my Life, my Sun, my Heart! 32 years ago my child's heart already went out to you.

I reread your letter and love it.

Wify

Nicky, Diary – 2 January – Mogilev

Slept splendidly as usual in Mogilev [Stavka, military GHQ]. The report was not long. Read after lunch. Went for a walk from 3 to 4. Wrote to Alix. Answered the last new year telegrams. After dinner played dominoes.

Nicky to Alix – 4 January – Mogilev

My darling Sunny,

So many thanks for your dear letter of last evening, which came after mine had left.

Sweet One, me wants you and your good kisses and caresses! Just *here*, without reach of ministers and others, we would have plenty of time of talking quietly upon different matters and of spending cosily some hours!

But – what is to be done; as you rightly said, not long ago, in a letter, that our separation is *our own* personal sacrifice for our country in this serious time and this thought makes it much easier to bear.

Now my sweet little girl, I must end as the messenger has to leave. God bless you and the dear children. I kiss you passionately and them tenderly! Ever your own old Huzy

Nicky

Alix to Nicky – 7 January – Tsarskoe Selo

My very own beloved Darling,

Such a craving for your caresses, yearning to hold you in my arms and rest my head upon your shoulder, as in bed and to cuddle up close and lie quite still upon your heart and feel peaceful and at rest. So much sorrow and pain, worries and trials – one gets so tired and one must keep up and be strong to face everything. I should have liked to see our Friend, only never ask Him to the house when you are not there, as people are so nasty.

28 January   Oh, could but our children be equally blessed in their married lives – the idea of Boris[1] is too unsympathetic and the child would, I feel convinced, never agree to marry him and I should perfectly well understand her. Only never let Michen guess other thoughts have filled the child's head and heart – those are a young girl's holy secrets which others must not know of, it would terribly hurt Olga, who is so susceptible. That conversation has made me feel far from cheery, and as it is I feel very low at your going and my old heart cramps itself in pain – cannot get accustomed to our separations. Here, Baby's note will amuse you ...

My Own, my light, my love, sleep well and peacefully, feel my tender arms encircling you, and your dear sweet head rest it in thoughts upon my breast, (not upon the high cushion you dislike).

Goodbye, my Treasure, my Husband, Sunshine beloved, God bless and keep you, holy Angels guard you and the force of my intense love. Oh my Boy, how I love you! Words cannot express it, but you can read it in my eyes.

Oh, the lonely night.

5 February
My own Sweetheart,

Zero this morning, windy, snowing hard. Thank God Baby's night was on the whole good – woke up several times, but not for long and did not complain. His both arms are bandaged and the right ached rather yesterday – but our Friend says it will pass in two days.

The last nights his sleep was restless, tho' painless and he did not complain about his arm, tho' could not bend it. Probably hurt himself holding on to the cord of the sledge when several are tied together. But Derevenko says he is quite cheery, so don't worry, Lovebird. We dined upstairs, so as that he should be in bed and move less. The quieter he keeps, the better.

I got to sleep after 4 – scarcely swollen, but felt it still and the head whole time strange and jaw too – more like a chill in the head, without a cold and difficult to open the mouth again in the jaw. Heart aches all these days and don't feel nice – do hope that Alexei and I shall be decent for your return ...

Yes, I too admire those men who go on working at these vile gases and risking their lives. Oh, to think that humanity should have stooped so low.

---

[1] Son of Grand Duke Vladimir and Maria Pavlovna.

Alexei to Nicky – 10 February – Tsarskoe Selo
Dear Papa
I shall miss you a lot and hope that you will soon come back. I will be good while you are gone and will study well. I hope you sleep soundly and have good dreams (for instance, about me!) May God protect you!

Your devoted Son

Alix to Nicky – 11 February – Tsarskoe Selo
My very own precious one,
You generally have some painful impressions here. Tuesday brought splendid good – and then that wretched story about our Friend. She [Ania] will try her best with him – tho' in his present humour he screams at her and is so awfully nervous. But it's sunny weather and so, I hope, he will have changed again into what he always was. He is frightened to leave, says one will kill him – well, we shall see how God turns all!
All this gave you pain and worry and you could not get any joy out of your visit, beloved Sunshine – but you warmed up old Sunny and she feels your last kiss still upon her lips! Your visit was like a dream – so empty now again! I have nothing to tell you yet today.

Wify

Olga [sister], Memoirs
It is important to remember that Nicky and Alix were fully aware of Rasputin's past. After Rasputin had been to the palace a few times, wildly exaggerated reports about his influence at court made many people try to turn him into a tool to further their own ambitions. Rasputin was besieged with petitions and presents were showered on him, but he never kept anything for his own use. I know he helped the poor of St Petersburg and elsewhere.
And not once did I hear him beg for any favours from Nicky and Alicky. I often heard him make requests for others. I am sure that his attachment to my brother and his wife was utterly devoid of self-interest. He might so easily have amassed a fortune, but he died owning a Bible, some clothes, and a few things given him by the Empress for his personal use. Even the furniture in his flat in Gorokhovaya Street in St Petersburg did not belong to him.
It is true that he received large sums of money, but all of it was given away. Rasputin kept just enough to provide food and clothing

for his family in Siberia. And if, at the very end, he became conscious of the political power he could exert, it was only because some ruthless and unscrupulous people forced him.

Felix Yusupov, Memoirs

Rasputin burst into cynical laughter; he was tipsy and in a confidential mood. 'And that's that, my dear fellow,' he continued, smiling strangely. 'Women are worse than men and have to be dealt with first. Yes, this is how I proceed: I take all the ladies to the public baths. I just say: "And now undress and wash the *moujik*." If they put on airs, I have a good way of convincing them and ... they soon swallow their pride.'

V. A. Jukovskaya, Memoirs

I got up and started to say goodbye. R[asputin] quickly jumped up: 'Let's go to my little place, my honey bee, sit with me and let's talk for a while. You're in such a hurry, where are you rushing off to?'

Going up to the bedroom, I noticed on the bedside table a large basket of lily of the valley, and next to it a large desk top portrait of the Tsarina, taken in profile, with, in the corner written in her hand, 'Alexandra'. Noticing my glance, R. carelessly scratched under his arms and said: 'The Tsarina sent them!'

'They're very beautiful,' I said, admiring the flowers.

Glancing at the flowers R. said indifferently: 'What good are they in winter? It's good when they flower in the woods in spring, then, my honey bee, the scent from them is some kind of woodland blessing! In the winter there's only one distraction,' and he went on scratching.

'Don't you ever get tired of all this?' I asked.

'And what is there to get tired of?' he retorted. 'You probably think that I sleep with everyone who comes to me? Well, if you want to know, since the autumn there have been no more than fourteen women, who ... they can say what they want, the imps all lie, that I sleep with the Tsarina, but what the imps and idolaters don't know is that my affection is far more than just that (he made a gesture).

'Do you want to know about the Tsarina? Do I ever see her alone? The children are there, or Annushka [Ania], or the nannies, do you really think that's what she seeks from me? What the devil does she need me for. She can get as much of that as she wants. But she doesn't believe them, she believes in me and loves my affection. But I always tell the whole truth.

'If you could see their life now, even if they are tsars, you wouldn't want to live like that! He is alone and she is alone, there is no one they can trust, everyone is willing to sell them out, but I caress her and comfort her, and she becomes calm. Is my affection disinterested? My affection is like no one else's, it's such as they have never known, nor ever will again. Do you understand, darling?

' ... Do you want me to show you how I caress ... Remember always,' he continued sitting closer, 'that it is through the body that you get to know the spirit. It's nothing if you stray a little, only you mustn't let the sin torture you, you mustn't think about the sin or turn away from good works. This, you understand, is what you must do: sin and forget about it, but if, say, I sinned with you and then could think about nothing but you afterwards – then the sin would be irredeemable.'

'You mean one can do anything, as long as one doesn't think about it?' I said.

'Quite so, my honey bee, the thoughts should be holy, and through that I will make you holy. And afterwards we will go to church and pray together, then you will forget your sin and feel joy.'

'But if it's considered a sin, why do it?' I asked.

R. frowned: 'But repentance, and prayer – they cannot be attained without sin,' he said quickly. 'How can you make the thoughts holy without sin, they won't be holy!'

'And are yours holy?'

'Well, of course, I am holy,' said R. simply, leaning closer, looking in my eyes. 'It's necessary to sin! Without that you cannot know...'

Bending lower and lower, screwing up his body and wringing his hands, R was in a frenzy. It seemed to me that at such moments he was oblivious to everything except his wild desire, that it was possible to pierce or cut him and that he wouldn't even notice. Once I pricked him in the hand with a thick needle, and on removing it noticed that it hadn't drawn blood, and he hadn't even felt it. It was the same on this occasion.

The brutalized face drew nearer, became flatter, the wet hair stuck to it like braids of wool, through which the narrow, burning eyes looked like glass ... I broke free and went over to the wall, thinking he would come after me. But he came slowly towards me, swaying, and whispered hoarsely: 'Let us pray!'

Taking me by the shoulder he led me over to the window, where there hung an icon of St Simon Verkhotursky, pushed the velvety lilac wood rosary into my hands and flung me onto my knees, while he himself started to bow down to the ground, at first silently, then repeating:

'Blessed Simon Verkhotursky, have mercy on me, a sinner!' After a few minutes he asked me in a hollow voice: 'What is your name?' and when I replied, he started to bow again, repeating his name and mine. After doing this some five or ten times, he got up and turned towards me, he was ashen, sweat was pouring down his face, but he was breathing quite easily and his eyes looked gently and kindly.

'So now, honey bee, do you understand what the spirit is? Let me kiss you,' and he gave me a dispassionate, monastic kiss ...

Alix to Nicky – 2 March – Tsarskoe Selo
My own Sweetheart,

Dear me, how weary one is! Your beloved presence and tender caresses soothe me and I dread your departure.

Do remember to keep our Friend's Image near you as a blessing for the coming 'move forwards' – oh how I wish we were always together, to share all, see all. Such an anxious time is ahead! And when we shall meet again – is a vague thing. All my prayers will incessantly follow you, sweetest love. God bless you and your work and every undertaking and crown it with success.

The good will come and you are patient and will be blessed, I feel so sure, only much to be gone through still. When I know what the 'losses' of lives mean to your heart – I can imagine Ernie's suffering now. Oh this hideously bloody war!

Excuse bad writing, but head and eyes ache and heart feels weak after all this pain.

Oh Lovy mine, beloved, precious Sunshine – it's so depressing when you go – you are yet far more lonely, so I ought not to complain – but to feel your sweet being near me is such a consolation and calm.

Wify

3 March
My very own Sweetheart,

Oh it's lonely without you and I miss you awfully. So sad to wake up and find an empty place beside me. Thanks tenderly for your evening's telegram. Such sorrow without you, every moment one expects you to be looking in. I slept well, the effect of the medicine still acts, and I feel my heart not nice in consequence. Vladimir Mikhailovich [*sic*, Dr Derevenko] continues electrifying the face. The pains only come from time to time, but I feel rather giddy and nasty and have to eat carefully, not to bring on the pains in my jaw. Olga and Anastasia have Becker [period]. Ania coughs worse, so remains home and will only come in the afternoon, which is much wiser.

I see your beloved, sad eyes still before me, when you left, it's an awful wrench each time. O Lovy, thanks again and again for all your tender caresses which warmed me up and were such a consolation.

The heart is so heavy and sad and when physically run down, one gets yet more depressed. I try not to show it to others.

Very mild today again.

Ania is sad she never had an occasion to see you alone, personally I think she gets calmer and more normal, less aggressive when she has less chance, because the more one has, the more one wants, if you need talks, then of course it's another thing. But she gets over those things much better now, you have trained her and in consequence her temper is calmer and we have no stories. She was killing about telephones and visits and stories about our Friend, flinging her stick about the room and laughing – Oh how I long for you!!!

                                                                    Sunny

4 March
My very own Sweetheart,

I am really anxious about Ania; once a man was capable to try and buy others to kill our Friend he is capable of revenging himself upon her. She had an awful row by telephone with Grigory for not having gone today, but I entreated her not to – besides she has a terrible cough and Mme B[ecker]. Then the woman came and made a scene to her for not going to town and he sort of predicts something is going to happen to her which certainly makes her yet more nervous.

One gets so bitterly disappointed in Russian people, they are so far behind still we know such masses and yet when one has to choose a minister, none is capable to hold such a post.

                                                                    Wify

Olga [sister], Memoirs
Alicky was indeed a sick woman. Her breath often came in quick, obviously painful gasps. I often saw her lips turn blue. Constant worry over Alexei had completely undermined her health.

Maria Pavlovna [the younger], Memoirs
At that period of her life an almost fanatical absorption in home

affairs left her no affection or consideration to expend elsewhere. For years before the war she had shut herself within her family circle; and, since the birth of the heir to the throne, had devoted herself wholly to his care.

His health, from the first precarious, had not improved with the years; there were days when it seemed that all hope must be abandoned. Watching the course of the terrible disease in her son, this poor mother became more and more distracted, and lost in a measure, I think it may be said, her mental equilibrium.

Only the most official ceremonies, those which it was impossible to avoid, now took place at the court; and these ceremonies were now the only connection of the imperial couple with the outside world. They lived in such seclusion that word to them or from them had to be passed through people often ignorant and sometimes unworthy.

Nicky to Alix – 9 March – Mogilev
My beloved Sunny,

Tenderest thanks for your dear letter and for all your love in each line!

I drink them and savour every word you write and often bury my nose and press my lips to the paper you have touched.

Fancy the weather with you having suddenly again changed to hard frost! Here it is thawing rapidly – which is the great reason why our attacks are beginning these days. If we wait a week longer in many parts of our fronts the trenches will be swamped with water and the troops would have to be brought very far back.

And then they would have to remain for a month or six weeks without any possibility of moving forward until the roads and country get dry. Then most certainly the Germans would attack us with masses of heavy artillery – like last summer. Therefore it was decided to take the initiative into our own hands, profiting by their onslaughts at Verdun. God bless and protect our gallant troops! Please do not speak about this to *any* one.

Yesterday I went to the cinematograph. They showed us two amusing pictures with Max Linder playing the principal part, which I am sure the children would enjoy.

I am glad you have found a new book for us to read aloud – have not those two of Marston arrived from England?

Till now I had no time to read for my own pleasure – though I play domino every second evening.

Well I think I must end my letter. God bless you, my own darling

Wify, and our children. Tenderest kisses and love to you all! From your own Huzy

Nicky

Alix to Nicky – 10 March – Tsarskoe Selo
My own Sweetheart,

Dear me, how much we have seen and lived through in these 21½ years of married life.

One just brought me your beloved letter for which very tenderest thanks. So, my angel also kisses my letters as I always do yours, every page and more than once. Today it smells of cigarettes.

[Dr] Belarminov says I need stronger specs to read with, eyes over-tired and the aching comes also from gout – the same as my face nerve pains too – but he is contented with the eyes themselves and says they are very good, only I overtask them.

I am glad to have seen him, as the pain is often very strong and that acts on my head, and I see worse for reading. (I personally know they get bad from much crying and from many unshed tears too, which fill the eyes and that must drink themselves up again – this all I did not tell him.) Then he gives me an ointment to rub in exteriorly if they ache much.

13 March
My very Own,

So anxious for news. The children were all in Church and are now going out, hot sun, wind, frost in the shade, last night rain. You cannot imagine how terribly I miss you – such utter loneliness – the children with all their love still have other ideas and rarely understand my way of looking at things the smallest even – they are always right and when I say how I was brought up and how one must be, they can't understand, find it dull. Only when I quietly speak with T[atiana] she grasps it. Olga is always most unamiable about every proposition, tho' may end by doing what I wish. And when I am severe – sulks me.

Am so weary and yearn for you. There are also many things which A[nia], with her bringing up and being out of another set, does not understand and many a worry I would never share with her. I used to do it with N.P. [Sabline] because he, as a man with inborn tact, understood me. We all have our ways and thoughts and I feel so horribly old at times and low spirited – pain pulls one down and perpetual anxiety and worry since the war goes on. Your precious calming presence gives me strength and consolation.

I take things too deeply to heart – try to master it – but, I suppose, God gave me such a heart which fills up my whole being. Forgive my writing all this and pay no attention to it, I am only a bit down. Oh, I must be off to Vladimir Nikolaevich to electrify myself.

I bless you, kiss you over and over again and press you to my yearning heart, Sweet Angel, Treasure, Beloved! Ever your very own weary old

Sunny

14 March

My own sweet Treasure,

I send you an apple and flower from our Friend – we all had fruit as a goodbye gift. He left this evening – quietly, saying better times are coming and that he leaves spring-time with us. He told her [Ania] He finds Ivanov would be good as Minister of War on account of his great popularity not only in the army, but all over the country.

In that He is certainly right – but you will do what you think best. I only asked He should pray for success in your choice, and He gave this answer.

Ever your very Own

Nicky to Alix – 14 March – Mogilev

My beloved Wify,

How distressing about your pain in the face and in the eye. Is it really nerves? I am so sorry for you, my darling, not to be near you and try and comfort you while you suffer.

At the front things go very slowly, in some places our losses are heavy and many generals commit bad blunders. That is the worst part of it all that we have so few good generals – it seems to me that after the long winter rest they have forgotten all experience they acquired last year!

Dear me, I begin to complain, but that one *ought* not to do! I feel well and perfectly confident in the ultimate success. God bless you, my One and All, my Treasure, my Lovebird. Many, many tenderest kisses to you and our children. My love to A[nia]. Ever your own old Huzy

Nicky

Alix to Nicky – 17 March – Tsarskoe Selo

My beloved,

For Baby's sake we must be firm as otherwise his inheritance will be awful, as with his character he won't bow down to others but be his own master, as one must in Russia whilst people are still so uneducated – Mr Philippe and Grigory said so too.

Sister Olga arrives on Sunday, to everybody's great surprise. I fear she comes to speak about her wishes for the future – what am I to say about your thoughts on that subject. The moment when all minds are so unpatriotic and against the family it's hard she should think of such things and his part is unpardonable, and personally I fear Sandro is egging her on – I may be wrong – but that story worries me very much and I don't find she ought to have brought up this theme now. Perhaps she wants to follow him to the Caucasus as one says his regiment goes off there – that would be more than unwise and give occasion for much talk and ugly talk.[2]

I am so glad to hear that people are contented at Shuvaiev's nomination – God grant him success.

Now my Darling I must close my letter. All the children fondly kiss you and I cover you with tender, gentle kisses and deep love, sweet Huzy mine. Ever your old

Wify

Olga [sister], Memoirs
Poor Alicky was all agony and dejection. Of course, I never told her about all the fantastic rumours. She told me how she missed Nicky. We both cried at parting. Yet the visit I had most dreaded was to my mother. I had to tell her of my decision to marry the man I loved. I had been prepared for a terrible scene, but my mother remained quite calm and said that she understood. And that was something of a shock in its own way.

Alix to Nicky – 26 March – Tsarskoe Selo
My very own precious Love,

Once more the train will be carrying you off from us, when you read my letter. This week has flown; it was an unexpected joy you came. I am glad Dmitri accompanies you now, it will make the journey brighter and less lonely. The idea of you going off all alone again,

---

[2] Olga, Nicky's younger sister, had divorced Peter of Oldenburg and wished to marry Nikolai Kulikovsky, Peter's aide-de-camp, who had been her lover for many years.

is great pain. If I feel this terrible loneliness every time, tho' have the dear children, what must your sensations be all alone at the Headquarters! And Passion-week and Easter approaching, those lovely services, you will be sad standing all by yourself in Church. God help you, my own Lovebird.

You never can come here without there being some story to pain you or make you anxious and give worry. Now poor Olga's intentions and plans for the future have assailed us and I cannot tell you the bitter pain it causes me for you. Your own sweet sister doing such a thing!

I understand all and don't and can't grudge her longing first for liberty and then happiness, but she forces you to go against the family laws. When it touches one's own nearest, it's far worse.

She, an Emperor's daughter and sister! Before the country, at such a time when the dynasty is going through heavy trials and many counter-currents are at work, is sad. The society's morals are falling to pieces and our family, Paul, Misha and Olga show the example, not speaking of the yet worse behaviour of Boris, Andrei and Sergei.

How shall we ever stop the rest from similar marriages? It's wrong she puts you into this false position and it hurts me it's through her this new sorrow has been inflicted upon you. What would your Father have said to all this? We have been far too weak and kind to the family and ought many a time to have thundered at the young ones. Do, if only possible, find an occasion of speaking to Dmitri about his goings on in town, and at such a time. I, wickedly perhaps, did hope Petia [Prince of Oldenburg] would not give the divorce. It may seem cruel and I don't mean to be so, because I tenderly love Olga, but I think of you first and that she makes you act wrongly. Nice sunshine, I hope it will shine upon your way too.

Passionately I press you to my heart and kiss you with infinite tenderness, eyes, lips, forehead, chest, hands, every tenderly loved place which belongs to me.

Alix

Alexei to Nicky – 30 March – Tsarskoe Selo
Mon cher Papa

Aujourd'hui un monsieur français m'a apporté un cinématographe. Il m'a montré comment il faut le faire marcher, c'est très amusant. Il y avait un homme qui fumait sa pipe dans le nez de son voisin et chassait tout le monde du banc.

Je t'écris à la machine parce que cela m'amuse.

Salue tout le monde. Je t'embrasse,

ton Alexis[3]

Alix to Nicky – 2 April – Tsarskoe Selo
My own beloved Sweetheart,

Oh, what an unexpected joy it was when Madeleine brought me your precious letter, I never thought you would find time to write. How dead tired you must have been yesterday after that endless war-council. I hope you were contented with all the plans. As you liked that sweet English book, I am sending you another by the same author, which we also like. It is also charming and interesting; tho' not as sweet as the Boy. Yes Lovy, it reminds me of 22 years ago, and I would give much to be alone with you in such a garden, it's so true; every woman has in her the feeling of a mother too towards the man she loves, it's her nature, when it's all deep love!

I love those pretty words and how he sits at her feet under the tree and he has such a lovely, sunny soul, 'my little boy blue'.

We all of us read the story with wet eyes.

Pavel comes to us to tea today, I suppose Dmitri will turn up tomorrow, if it does not bore him.

I lay out on the balcony yesterday and Ania read to me, today I'll sit near the children while they work.

Maria is in a grumpy mood and grumbles all the time and bellows at one, she and Olga have B[ecker] – Olga has become better humoured I find, it shows she is feeling stronger.

I long to hold you tightly in my arms and let your head rest upon my breast like in bed and feel your sweet loving presence, and to cover you with kisses. Ever Huzy mine, your very own old

Wify

Nicky to Alix – 3 April – Mogilev
My own beloved One

Fondest thanks for your dear letters; now I don't see any troops they are my only comfort.

---

[3] My dear Papa,

Today a French gentleman brought me a cinematograph. He showed me how to make it work, it was very funny. There was a man who smoked his pipe in his neighbour's nose and chased everyone off the bench.

I'm typing this for you because it amuses me.

Greetings to everyone. I embrace you

your Alexis

Thanks also for the little image – I have put it on my chain!
Now I will wear *something* from you!

Here are three flowers I found yesterday during the walk. Again no
time to write, always people who want to see me and make endless
reports. I hope that during Passion week they will leave me quiet.

Thank you so for the new book you sent me. Lovy-mine, me loves
you so, really more than ever and miss you so these days especially.
I must finish already. God bless you + and the children. I kiss you and
them tenderly. Ever, my beloved Wify, your own old Huzy

Nicky

Alix to Nicky – 5 April – Tsarskoe Selo
My own sweet Treasure,

During the evening Bible I thought so much of our Friend, how the
bookworms and pharisees persecute Christ, pretending to be such
perfections (and how far they are from it now). Yes, indeed, a
prophet is never acknowledged in his own country. And how much
we have to be grateful for, how many prayers of His were heard. And
where there is such a Servant of God, the evil crops up around Him
to try and do harm and drag him away. If they but knew the harm
they do, why He lives for His Sovereign and Russia and bears all slanders for our sakes.

Our Friend writes so sadly, that as He was driven away from
Petrograd there will be many hungry ones there this Easter. He gives
such a lot to the poor, every penny he receives goes to them and it
brings blessings too to those who brought him the money ...

... If Shav[elsky] speaks about Friend or the Metropolitan, be firm
and show that you appreciate them, and that when he hears stories
against our Friend, he is to stand up with energy against all and forbid their talks and they dare not say he has anything to do with the
Germans – and he is generous and kind to all, as Christ was, no matter what religion, as a real Christian should be. And once you find
His prayers help bear one's trials, and we have had enough examples
– they dare not speak against him, you be firm and stand up for our
Friend.

Olga [sister], Memoirs
I do remember hearing in St Petersburg that my sister-in-law poured
money like water on Rasputin. Once again there was not any foundation to it. Alicky was very careful, as you might say. It would have

been utterly out of character for her to throw money about. She gave him only shirts and a silk belt she had embroidered, and also a gold cross which he wore.

Alix to Nicky – 7 April – Tsarskoe Selo

I send you the petition of one of Aunt Olga's wounded men. He is a Jew. Has lived since 10 years in America. He was wounded and lost his left arm on the Carpathians. The wound had healed well, but he suffers fearfully morally as in August he must leave, and loses the right of living in either the capital or other big town. He is living in town only on the strength of a special permit, which a previous minister of the Interior gave him for one year. And he could find work in a big town.

His English is wonderfully good. I read a letter of his to little Vera's English governess and Aunt Olga says he is a man with good education, so to speak. 10 years ago he left for the United States to find the opportunity to become a useful member of human society to the fullest extent of his capabilities, as here it is difficult for a Jew who is always hampered by legislative restrictions. Tho' in America, he never forgot Russia and suffered much from homesickness and the moment war broke out he flew here to enlist as soldier to defend his country.

Now that he lost his arm serving in our army, got the St George medal, he longs to remain here and have the right to live wherever he pleases in Russia, a right the Jews don't possess. As soon as discharged from the army, as a cripple, he finds things have remained the same as before, and his headlong rush home to fight, and loss of his arm has brought him no gain. One sees the bitterness, and I fully grasp it – surely such a man ought to be treated the same as any other soldier who received such a wound. He was not obliged to fly over here at once. Tho' he is a Jew, one would like him to be justly treated and not different to the others with similar losses of limb.

With his knowledge of English and learning he could easier gain his bread in a big town of course; and one ought not to let him become more bitter and feel the cruelty of his old country. To me it seems hard upon all – it's so cruel to my mind. The bad ones can be severely punished. Can you tell me what decision you write on the petition; as Aunt Olga wanted to know.

Nicky to Alix – 7 April – Mogilev [NB: This date may be incorrect]

My own Lovebird,

Only a few lines, because me again has no time, the ministers having sent me hills of papers – probably before Easter.

I wrote on that petition of the wounded jew from America – to allow living in any place of Russia and sent it to Sturmer.[4]

Tenderest thanks for your dear letter and for the little eggs. I do hope Baby's arm won't hurt him long. I thought so much of you in our little church this morning – it was very nice and peaceful here, lots of officers of the staff and their families took the communion. The morning, when I can't get out it is always sunny, and when I drive out or row – it becomes cloudy – so me cannot get brown!

Tomorrow is the 8th – my prayers and thoughts will surround you, my girlie, my own Sunny. I did fight for you then and again yourself too!! Like little Boy Blue, but more tenacious.

God bless you and the children. I kiss you over and over and them too. Ever your own Nicky

8 April

My own precious Love,

I must begin my letter on this date in remembrance of what happened 22 years ago! I think there was a concert that evening at Coburg and a Bavarian band played; poor u[ncle] Alfred was rather tired from his dinner and kept dropping his stick with a crashing noise! Do you remember?

Last year too we were asunder this day – it was just before the journey to Galicia!! It is really trying to be far away from each other during Passion week and Easter. Of course I did not miss one service.

In your telegrams you asked me several times what you were to answer Ella? I simply looked through her paper of the drawings and had not the slightest idea what I was supposed to say – so I wrote that I thought the work very well done! But what work I meant I do not know. Ha! Ha! My sweet Love, I want you so! Please do not have M.B. [Mme Becker] when I come home! Now me must go to bed. Good night, my beloved Darling; sleep well and dream gently – not about Catholic priests!

April 9th. Ending this letter after lunch. Just got your dear one with the tiny eggs, as book marker, for which I thank you so fondly. The image and egg I will place in church opposite to where I stand. Today there were lots of people and children who took Holy Communion, the latter would stare at me and bow many times after, stumbling against each other!

Now me must end. God bless you, my precious Treasure and send

---

[4] Chairman of the Council of Ministers, and Minister of the Interior; from 1916, Minister of Foreign Affairs.

you a happy peaceful Easter. Many tender kisses to you and the dear
children from your ever loving and truly devoted Huzy

Nicky

Alix to Nicky – 10 April – Tsarskoe Selo
Christ has risen!
My own sweet One,
   I kissed your photo three times last night and this morning – the
big Image, on which you are three times. Your card lay on my breast
during the whole service – cannot tell you how unutterably sad I felt
the whole night, such pain in the heart and with difficulty kept back
my tears – your loneliness is too hard – God bless and richly recompense you for all your sacrifices.

Nicky to Alix – 27 April – Mogilev
My beloved Wify,
   Tenderest thanks for your dear letter together with one from Olga
and from Alexei. Tiny begins his like this – 'I count days, and you
know why!' Rather sweet!
   It rained till noon and became suddenly cold – only 10 – after the
heat on the previous days. The French ministers arrived with several
officers – they had long conference ... and dined, both being my
neighbours; in this way I escaped the necessity of a talk extra.
   The idea of making a new large loan in the country, what you write
about, I think a very good one.
   Before leaving, I told the ministers to work out a large plan for
years to come for a new railway building scheme – so this new idea
about the money – would just help the other to be brought into execution.
   Just now I got the following telegram: 'La centenaire met aux pieds
de Vos Majestés sa profonde reconnaissance et sa fidelité a un passé
toujours présent. Leonille Wittgenstein.' So prettily worded I find.
[The centenarian expresses to your Majesties her deep gratitude and
her devotion to a past that is always present. Leonille Wittgenstein.]
I enclose a letter from Olga, which please send me back. Poor girl, it
is natural, that she worries; so long she has kept her feelings back –
that she has to let them out and craves for real personal happiness,
which she has not had.

Alix to Nicky – 1 May – Tsarskoe Selo
My beloved precious One,

Excuse my bothering you with petitions, but our Friend sent them me.

Ania arrived last night at her destination.

I have nothing interesting to tell you, perhaps after Nikolai M[ikhailovich] has been – he asked to see me alone, cannot simply imagine why.

Wify

Alexei to Alix – 18 May – Mogilev
Dear Mama

Yesterday I missed you a lot. Together with Papa we sniffed the pillow and the curtain, you know why.

Yesterday V. Nikolaevich won a lot of money at nain jaune. Today Gilliard had a hair wash. He is as fluffy as a sheep. This ink is impossible.

In the evening I prayed for you (+ many times). It feels empty without you.

May God protect you.

Your Alexei

Ania Vyrubova, Memoirs
The Empress was never happy except in the few minutes each day when she was reading the child's daily letter. At nine o'clock at night she went up to his bedroom exactly as though he were there and she was listening.

Alix to Nicky – 23 May – Tsarskoe Selo
My sweetest Treasure,

Our Friend begs very much that you should not name Makarov as minister of the Interior – a party wants it, and you remember how he behaved during the stories of Iliodor and Hermogene [bishops] and never stood up for me – it would indeed be a great mistake to name him.

I spent yesterday evening in the hospital. Have Mlle Schneider with a report.

God bless you, my One and all – I cover you with kisses. Ever your own old

Sunny

Tomorrow I shall be 44.

Felix Yusupov, Memoirs

My mother had been among the first to protest against Rasputin. After a long conversation with the Tsarina, she thought she had succeeded in shaking her confidence in her 'miracle-worker'. But Rasputin's clique was on the watch. A thousand pretexts to keep my mother away were found very quickly. She had had no contact with the Empress for some time when, in the summer of 1916, she resolved to make a last attempt, and asked to be received at the Alexander Palace.

Her Majesty greeted her very coldly and, on hearing the object of her visit, requested her to leave. My mother said that she would not do so until she had spoken her mind. She talked at great length. When she had finished, the Empress, who had listened in silence, rose and dismissed her with the words: 'I hope I never see you again.'

Nicky to Alix – 2 June – Mogilev

My own Lovebird,

Ever so many thanks for your dear letter N 506 (fancy what a N). Every evening before praying with Sunbeam I tell I him what you have wired to me and then read to him all his letters. He listens lying in bed and kisses your signature.

He becomes talkative and asks many questions, because we are alone; sometimes if it is late, I have to hurry him to say his prayers. He sleeps very well and quietly and loves having the window open. The noise of the street does not disturb him.

I send you some of the latest photos – the first represent the arrival of the image and the last – the Te Deum under pouring rain. Choose which ever you like!

Yesterday I saw Bark;[5] he is working on that loan for the railways which interests you. He leaves in a week for England and France.

Now my sweetheart, I must end. God bless you+ and the girlies.

I kiss you all over your beloved face and loves so tenderly. Ever, Wify-mine, your own   Nicky

Nicky to King George V – 5 June – Mogilev

My dearest Georgie,

I entrust this letter to Mr Bark, who is going to England and France for a new financial conference.

---

[5] Peter Bark, Finance Minister, highly thought of in international financial circles. In 1915 he had attended an Allied financial conference in Paris where he had agreed substantial credits to Russia in exchange for shipments of Russian gold.

Words fail me to express my deep sorrow at Lord Kitchener's tragical end, as well as my innermost sympathy for you and for your whole country.[6] Indeed his disappearance at such a time is a hard blow of providence. Everybody in Russia admires the magnificent way in which the English ships fought and tackled the whole German fleet in the North Sea [the Battle of Jutland].

Everyone understood the first false news sent all over the world by the enemy in the right way and it was a relief when we heard the confirmation of what we had hoped – in the official announcement of the British Admiralty. Of course your casualties and losses are great, but how far heavier are those of the Germans! Probably they won't be able to go out to sea for some time and in this respect your gallant navy has rendered us a most important service in the Baltic Sea, for which we are deeply grateful.

Thank God our advance in Galicia and in our western provinces is developing successfully, but we had to begin earlier than the date fixed by all Allies, on account of those poor Italians. They sent us desperate telegrams insisting upon our immediate attack. Those were very trying days for the chief of my staff and for myself, as we were not quite ready yet!

I am so glad to hear that you are feeling quite well and strong again. Please give my very best love to dear May. More than ever do I trust that the Allies shall bring this war to ultimate victory.

God bless you, my dear Georgie. Believe me ever your most loving cousin and true friend

Nicky

Alix to Alexei – 21 June – Tsarskoe Selo
My dearest Alexei!

My tender thanks for your lovely card. I enclose your salary. It had slipped my mind; I had your money here. The weather is strange, hot, stuffy and the sky not very clear. I'm going for a drive with O[lga] and Tatiana, then will be at Ania's.

Nicky to Alix – 13 July – Mogilev
Lovy-mine,

Tenderest thanks for your two dear letters – the morning note from

---

[6] Lord Kitchener had embarked on a mission to encourage Russia to continue their resistance to the Germans. He was drowned when his ship, HMS *Hampshire*, hit a German mine and sank off the Orkney Islands.

the train, which I only read in the afternoon, and the goodbye letter, that Baby gave me during St[urmer]'s report. Thank God he is quite well, slept very soundly near his old father and is full of life and energy as usual.

It is for me to thank you, my Darling, for coming here all that way with our girlies and bringing here life and sunshine notwithstanding the rainy weather. I am afraid that you felt tired from the constant running up and down and to and fro.

Of course, as usual, I did not tell you half the things I had intended to say, because when we meet after a long separation, somehow I get stupidly shy and sit and gaze at you – which already is a joy for me!

I am looking so much forward to our meeting before A[lexei]'s birthday!

When we drove back from the station, Baby was thinking aloud and suddenly said: 'Once again alone!' Very short and clear!

Now we will steam up the river to his favourite beach with a comparatively small company.

The weather is calm and half cloudy – very mild.

God bless you + my beloved Sunny and the girlies! Ever so many tender kisses from your old loving, devoted and adoring old Huzy

Nicky

King George V to Nicky – 13 July – Buckingham Palace

My dearest Nicky,

W[illiam]'s speech at Kiel about the great Naval victory of the German fleet made me laugh.

I am quite convinced that they lost more ships and more men than we did and we drove them back into their ports. I trust that this action will help your fleet in the Baltic. I am overjoyed at the splendid advance your gallant troops are making in Galicia and in your Western Provinces, it is wonderful the number of prisoners they have taken (nearly 300,000), and many guns and machine guns. The advance of our troops and those of the French have been quite successful on the Somme so far, but our progress must be slow, between us we have taken over 21,000 prisoners and 100 guns. The Germans are very strong in front of us.

Ever your most devoted cousin and true friend

Georgie

Nicky to Alix – 3 August – Mogilev

My own beloved Angel,

How I do hate when you leave and to see the train taking you and the girlies away! I have *such calm* in the soul when you are near me, I want to send all worries and nuisances far away and enjoy your presence without speaking – of course when we are alone.

Thank you oh! so tenderly for having come and given me this treat and rest of the heart's yearning and craving for you.

Now I will be strong and calm till your next visit. Loving thanks also for your dearest letter which soothed a bit the pain of separation!

Baby went to dine with his two tiny friends and I received Count Bobrinksy who did not remain long and made a good impression upon me. We dined in the tent – it was rather cold and damp inside – I would prefer the balcony another time.

After praying with Baby I managed to finish all my papers, which gives me always some satisfaction! And took a delightful drive along the high road and round by the long bridge by a beautiful moonlight. The air was very cold; so good before going to bed.

Sleep well, my precious Sunny.

Alix to Nicky – 11 August – Tsarskoe Selo
My own Sweetheart,

Have not seen Dmitri, yes, I suppose his nerves are again, alas, good for nothing, it's indeed a great pity. Don't let him go to that lady so often – such society is his ruin – nothing but flattery and he likes it and then of course service becomes dull. You must keep him firmer and don't let him be too free with his tongue either.

Tender blessings and 1000 kisses from your old

                                                                  Wify

14 August   More than ever my thoughts are and will be with you these days, and I have asked our Friend to remember and pray much.

I send you my Image back again, I have had a little border and safe ring made to it. Also foggy, grey and rather cold, a September day.

Dmitri took tea with us yesterday – his heart is not in a good state, moves like mine also therefore of course has at times pains, feels weak, and gets out of breath. He ought to make a cure, as it is only beginning and then he can be quite cured.

Irina and Felix take tea.

I cover you with kisses and remain your deeply loving old

                                                                  Wify

Felix Yusupov, Memoirs

The Emperor and the Empress both loved Dmitri [the son of Grand Duke Pavel] and looked upon him as a son; he lived at the Alexander Palace and went everywhere with the Tsar. He spent all his free time with me; I saw him almost every day and we took long walks and rides together.

Dmitri was extremely attractive: tall, elegant, well-bred, with deep thoughtful eyes, he recalled the portraits of his ancestors. He was all impulses and contradictions; he was both romantic and mystical, and his mind was far from shallow. At the same time, he was very gay and always ready for the wildest escapades. His charm won the hearts of all, but the weakness of his character made him dangerously easy to influence. As I was a few years his senior, I had a certain prestige in his eyes. He was to a certain extent familiar with my 'scandalous' life and considered me interesting and a trifle mysterious. He trusted me and valued my opinion, and he not only confided his innermost thoughts to me but used to tell me about everything that was happening around him. I thus heard about many grave and even sad events that took place in the Alexander Palace.

The Tsar's preference for him aroused a good deal of jealousy and led to some intrigues. For a time, Dmitri's head was turned by success and he became terribly vain. As his senior, I had a good deal of influence over him and sometimes took advantage of this to express my opinion very bluntly. Almost every night we took a car and drove to St Petersburg to have a gay time at restaurants and night clubs and with the gypsies.

Nicky to Alix – 5 September – Mogilev

Good morning, my own Darling!

The sun is so bright and warm, but in the shade it is cold. And you, poor things, are rattling away towards the north, where is real autumn and the leaves are yellow and falling. Your beloved letter is a real comfort for me and I have often reread it and kissed the dear lines.

In Romania near the Danube their troops have behaved better and the general outlook is good.

At Salonica the Serbians are moving forward and have pushed the Bulgars away.

Now, Lovy-mine, I must end. God bless you + and the girlies! I kiss you all most tenderly and remain your own old

Nicky

9 September

My very own Lovebird,

Tenderest thanks for your dear long letter in which you give over some messages from our Friend. That Protopopov[7] is, I think, a good man, but he is much in affairs with fabrics etc. Rodzianko proposed him long ago as minister of Commerce instead of Shakhovsky. I must think that question over as it takes me quite unexpectedly. Our Friend's ideas about men are sometimes queer, as you know – so one must be careful especially in nominations of high people.

All these changes exhaust the head. I find they happen much too often. It is certainly not at all good for the interior of the country, because every new man brings changes also into the administration. I am sorry my letter has become so tiresome, but I had to answer your questions.

God bless you + the girlies! I kiss you all tenderly. Ever, my sweet Sunny, your own   old Nicky

Alexei to Alix – 9 September – Tsarskoe Selo

My dear Mama,

This is my first English letter to you.[8] Today I took my cat into the garden but she was very timid and ran on to the balcony. She is now asleep on the sofa and Joy [the spaniel] is under the table.

With much love to you and my sisters.

From Alexis

Alix to Nicky – 20 September – Tsarskoe Selo

My own sweet Angel,

You don't mind my coming with ideas, do you deary, but I assure you, tho' ill and with bad heart, I have more energy than the whole lot put together and I can't sit calmly by. Bobrinsky was glad to see me so and says I am therefore disliked, because one feels (the left set) I stand up for your cause, Baby's and Russia's.

Yes, I am more Russian than many another, and I won't keep quiet. I begged them to arrange (what Grigory said) that goods, flour, butter, bread, sugar should all be weighed out beforehand in the shops and then each buyer can get his parcel much quicker and there won't

---

[7] Nicknamed Kalinin, he was the Deputy-President of the Duma from 1914. On 18 September 1916 he became Minister of the Interior.

[8] All Alexei's previous letters had been in Russian and French.

be such endless tails – all agreed it's an excellent idea – now why did
not they think of it before.

Ever your own old Sunny
Does Mr Gibbes [English tutor to Alexei] read the English papers
first?

Pierre Gilliard, Memoirs
The Germans were the only people in Europe who knew Russia. Their
knowledge of it was fuller and more exact than that of the Russians
themselves. They had known for a long time that the Tsarist regime,
with all its faults, was the only one capable of prolonging the Russian
resistance. They knew that with the fall of the Tsar Russia would be
at their mercy. They stopped at nothing to procure its fall.

The Germans had adopted the classic procedure, so well known to
history, of striking the monarch in the person of his consort. It is, of
course, always easier to damage the reputation of a woman, especially when she is a foreigner. Realizing all the advantages to be
derived from the fact that the Tsarina was a German princess, they
had endeavoured to suggest very cunningly that she was a traitor to
Russia. It was the best method of compromising her in the eyes of the
nation. The accusation had been favourably received in certain quarters in Russia and had become a formidable weapon against the
dynasty.

The Tsarina knew all about the campaign in progress against her
and it pained her as a most profound injustice, for she had accepted
her new country, as she had adopted her new faith, with all the fervour of her nature. She was Russian by sentiment as she was
Orthodox by conviction.

Alexei to Alix – 20 September – Mogilev
My dear Mama,
Today I am glad to say that I am much better and able to go out
again. I am having my lessons as usual and am going to the cine-
matograph this evening.
With much love to you and my sisters.

From Alexei

22 September
My dearest darling Mama
I am writing you my letter. I send you countless kisses. There are

almost no yellow leaves, but it is cold (+3). If the weather is like this, you will enjoy it here.

Get ready as quickly as possible.

Come here, as soon as possible.

We await you with delight and with raspberry jam!!!

Yesterday we went over the new bridges. Dmitri and N.P. send a kiss to everyone. I am going for a drive now.

May the Lord God protect you all! I kiss you.

Alexei

King George V to Nicky – 22 September

My dearest Nicky

With regard to your answer to my telegram of last month, I can assure you that both I and my Government are most desirous that the recognition by the Allies, that Russia is fully entitled to the possession of Constantinople and the Straits, should be published as soon as possible in their respective Capitals. But the French Government is against this being done at the present moment, lest it might strengthen the Turkish Alliance, and encourage the Turks to fight to the bitter end. I know you will also appreciate the necessity for regarding the sentiment of my eighty million Moslem subjects in India and elsewhere. We must choose the right time as far as they are concerned to make the announcement, in order to reduce as much as possible the chance of any serious rising amongst them.

I have recently heard from our friend Mr Anderson, who says 'The Germans realise so far as England and France are concerned that it must be a fight to the finish, on the other hand they still have hopes of being able to detach Russia and are working hard to this end.' What nonsense, they little know you and your people if they think they can make a separate peace with Russia.

Goodbye and God bless you, my dearest Nicky.

Georgie

Maurice Paléologue, Memoirs

There has been no change in what the Emperor says; he still proclaims his determination to win and his absolute confidence in victory. But despondency, apathy and resignation can be seen in his actions, appearance, attitude and all the manifestations of the inner man.

Nicky to Alix – 23 September – Mogilev

My own beloved One,

Tenderly do I thank you for your dear long letter, explaining so well your conversation with P[rotopopov].[9] God grant, he may be a man we want just now! Fancy, Shakhovsky, who wanted to have to be in that place!

Yes, verily you ought to be my eye and my ear there – near the capital, while I have to stick here. That is just the part for you to keep the ministers going hand in hand and like this you are rendering me and our country enormous use. Oh! You, precious Sunny, I am so happy you have at last found the right work for yourself.

And at same time I have very much to do – scarcely any time to begin arranging the photos in my album.

Well, now I must end. God bless you +, my Angel, my Heart, Brain and Soul. Fondly do I kiss you and the girlies. Ever your own

Nicky

Alix to Nicky – 12 October – Tsarskoe Selo

My very own Sweetheart,

It's with a very heavy heart I leave you again – how I hate these goodbyes, they tear one to pieces. Thank God, Baby's nose is all right, so that is one consolation. Lovy mine, I do love you so beyond all words; 22 years have steadily increased this feeling and it's simply pain to go away.

You are so lonely amongst this crowd – so little warmth around. How I wish you could have come for 2 days only, just to have got our Friend's blessing, it would have given you new strength.

I know you are brave and patient – but human – and a touch of His on your chest would have soothed much pain and given you new wisdom and energy from Above – these are no idle words – but my firmest conviction. Alex[ei] can do without you for a few days.

Oh Manny man – stop that useless bloodshed – why do they go against a wall, one must wait for the good moment and not go on and on blindly. Forgive my saying so, but all feel it.

You need not receive anybody else, except Protopopov which would be a good thing, or send for him again, let him oftener speak to you, ask your council, tell you his intentions, it will help the man immensely. It's for your good and our dear countries I say all this, not from greed to see you (that wish you know will ever exist) but I too

---

[9] New Minister of the Interior.

well know and believe in the peace our Friend can give and you are
tired, morally, you can't deceive old Wify!

Nicky to Alix – 12 October – Mogilev

My own precious beloved One,

Again you leave us two to return to your work and tiresome worries! I thank you lovingly and deeply for having come here and for
all your love and caresses! How I will miss them!!

God grant, in two weeks and a half we may meet again. For the
nearest future I don't see any possibility of my leaving this place, alas!

I had hoped so we might have been allowed to go to the south and
spend a few days together in our train. Perhaps it may still happen.

I shall miss you especially in the evenings, which were ours!

God bless your journey and your coming home. Do take care of
yourself and don't overtire yourself.

I kiss your sweet face lovingly and tenderly, my own Sunny, my
Wify, my little girly of by gone days. Clasping you once more in my
loving arms – ever, my precious Darling

14 October

My own Treasure,

Yesterday the whole day Baby was looking pale and sad – I thought
he felt lonely. But in the afternoon he played gaily his usual game in
the same little wood of the old stavka. Only during his dinner he
complained about his head, so he was put to bed, which he did willingly. The temp[erature] rose rapidly and he was sick. Before 9.0 he
went to sleep and slept well, only awaking twice to have to run!

This morning the temp[erature] is normal and he is quite cheery –
but we have kept him in bed ... It must be still the consequence of
the first chill or having eaten something not very digestible. In any
case I hope it is the end now. Oh! How happy I am at the thought of
coming home for a few days and seeing you and the girlies!

Now, my beloved Sunny, I must end. God bless you all! Many tender kisses from your own

Nicky

Alexei to Alix – 15 October – Mogilev

Dearest darling Mama

Today I am quite better. T= 36.6. I'm going to have lunch with
everyone. I want to devour like 100 wolves!!!

The day has been wonderful since the morning. The sun is shining brightly, but it's cold (1½ degrees). We're going to see each other in 3 days. Hourrah!

God + protect you and my sisters! Greetings to all. I kiss and hug you. Your son and brother.

Nicky to Alix – 26 October – Mogilev

My own precious and beloved Darling,

I thank you from the depth of my old heart for your dear letter, you left on my table, in saying goodbye. We both felt so lonely and sad, when the train moved off and we saw you standing in front of the door. And directly after we caught a glimpse of your motor taking you all back to the house. Then Babykins went to his cabin to play and I received old Trepov all the time until we stopped at Tosno!

After praying with Alexei I had a little game at domino with Dmitri. All went to bed early and slept soundly! We get up late – Babykins even after 10 o'clock. The whole day I read a very interesting Engl[ish] book *The Man who dined with the Kaiser* newly appeared. When I have finished it I will send it to you.

Al[exei] played with his favourite nain jaune. Before arriving his nose bled, so Doctor Isakianz was sent for and burnt it – now it is all right. The same people met us and after a few words I dismissed them. I walked up and down the platform and thought so much of you and of the girls. The silence about the place is rather astonishing – I expected to hear wild shrieks of Anast[asia] or Maria tormenting Mordvinov. Instead Al[exei]'s cat ran away and hid under those big logs of timber; we put on our coats and went out to look for it. Nagorny at once discovered the cat with the aid of an electric lamp, but it took us a long time to make the brute come out – it would not listen. At last he caught it by the hind legs and pulled it through the narrow space.

Now everything is quiet in the train – I said goodnight to Alexei and many of the suite have gone to the cinema of course! I feel rather lonely, but am happy to be able to write to you; I imagine I am speaking very slowly.

Last evening I got the following telegram from Motherdear: Is it true that we'll see each other soon? I wonder to know when and how long? Because M[aria] P[avlovna] will be 26, could I put her off. I laughed when I read this and immediately wired to her the necessary details.

When you get this epistle, we will be in Kiev. I am sorry you won't get any letter from me these days, because I doubt my having any time to write. Anyhow this one may count for two.

Oh! My Treasure, my Love! How I miss you! It was such real happiness to be six days together at home. And the nights too!

God bless you + and the girlies. I kiss you ever so tenderly and nestle closely to you. I hug the children – A[nia] too. Ever, Sunny-mine, your very own old

Nicky

Alix to Nicky – 31 October – Tsarskoe Selo
My beloved Sweetheart,

I feel cruel worrying you, my sweet, patient Angel – but all my trust lies in our Friend, who only thinks of you, Baby and Russia. And guided by Him we shall get through this heavy time.

God bless and help you. Your own old

Wify

Nicky to Alix – 3 November – Mogilev
My own beloved Treasure,

Such fond thanks for your dear letter.

Tiny strained a sinew in the upper part of his right leg, it is a bit swollen, but not hurt really, only he often awoke this night and moaned in his sleep. Fedorov told him to remain quietly in bed. He is very gay and is surrounded by all the three masters, so there is a pretty row going on in the next room.

God bless you, my own Sunny, and our girlies. Tenderest kisses from your own old

Nicky

Alexei to Alix – 3 November – Mogilev
My darling Mama,

I was very happy to talk to you and my sisters on the telephone. It was difficult to hear because the line was steel and not copper!

It is real winter here. At 7 o'clock in the morning it was -6 degrees. There's lots of snow.

How is Olga's cat!?!

It's time to send my salary. Please !!!!!!!!!! =10!

Alexei Romanov

Ania Vyrubova, Memoirs
Entering the Empress's door one day, I found her in a passion of
indignation and grief. As soon as she could speak she told me that
the Emperor had sent her a letter from Nikolai Mikhailovich, in
which the Empress was specially charged with the most mischievous
political machinations.

'Unless this is stopped,' the letter concluded, 'murders will certainly begin.'

Sandro, Memoirs
My eldest brother, Nikolai Mikhailovich, was, no doubt, the most
'radical' and the most talented member of our family. Mother
mapped out a distinguished military career for him, and in order to
please her he graduated from the War College. His real interests lay
in the direction of pure historical research. He consented to serve in
the Chevalier Guards simply because of his friendship with the
Empress Marie (my mother-in-law), who was its Honorary
Commander.

His intellectual superiority over his fellow officers took all enjoyment out of his regimental contacts; gradually he drifted away from
his military environment toward the archives and the libraries of St
Petersburg and Paris. His monumental biography of Emperor
Alexander I, written after years of gathering material and verifying
data, remains unsurpassed in the historical literature of Russia.

No student of the first twenty-five years of the nineteenth century
could ignore the analysis of the events and the general survey of the
period given by Nikolai Mikhailovich. When translated into French
it created a stir among the Napoleonic experts, causing many a trea-
tise to be revised, changed or rewritten. The French Academy elected
him a member – an honour seldom, if ever, accorded to a foreigner.
He remained a bachelor and stayed alone in his very large palace,
surrounded by books, manuscripts and botanical collections.

Alix to Nicky – 4 November – Tsarskoe Selo
My own sweet Angel,
    Warmest thanks for your dear letter just received. I read Nikolai
[Mikhailovich]'s and am utterly disgusted. Had you stopped him in
the middle of his talk and told him that, if he only once more
touched that subject of me, you will send him to Siberia – as it
becomes next to high treason.

He has always hated and spoken badly of me since 22 years and in the club too (this same conversation I had with him this year). But during war and at such a time to crawl behind your Mama and Sister and not stick up bravely (agreeing or not) for his Emperor's Wife – is loathsome and treachery.

He feels people count with me, begin to understand me and ask for my opinion and that he can't bear. He is the incarnation of all that's evil, all devoted people loathe him, even those who do not much like us are disgusted with him and his talks. And Fred[ericks] old and no good and can't shut him up and wash his head and you my Love, far too good and kind and soft – such a man needs to be held in awe of you.

He and Nikolasha are my greatest enemies in the family, not counting the black women [Stana and Militsa] – and Sergei.[10] He simply could not bear Ania and me – but so much the cold rooms, I assure you. I don't care personal nastiness, but as your chosen wife – they dare not Sweety mine, you must back me up, for your and Baby's sake. Had we not got Him – all would long have been finished, of that I am utterly convinced.

Wify

Alexei to Alix – 4 November – Mogilev
My dearest darling Mama,

It's a terrible bore having to write in bed in such good weather. The muscle of my leg is hurting. S.P. [Sabline] won't let me walk.

A big kiss to you all. May God protect you!+

Yours

Nicky to Alix – 5 November – Mogilev
My own precious Darling,

Tender thanks for your dear letter. I am really sorry to have disturbed you and made you angry with N. [Mikhailovich]'s two letters, but in my continual hurry I did not read them, as he spoke so long and fully. But he omitted to speak about you, dwelling only on the stories about spies, fabrics, workmen, disorders, ministers and the general outlook inside the country! Had he said anything about you, do you doubt Huzy would have not upstood for you?

And I must add – he did not want to hand me his letters – I took

---

[10] Sergei Mikhailovich, another brother of Sandro.

them from him and he gave them rather unwillingly! Certainly I do not defend him, but explain facts as they were.

Babykin's leg is a little better, he slept very well and it hurt him for about a ¼ of an hour in the evening.

Yesterday I received that good gen[eral] Manikovski, the head of the artillery department and he told me many things concerning the workmen and the frightful propaganda among them with heaps of money being distributed among them to make strikes and that on the other side no resistance is offered against this, the police does nothing and no one seems to care what will happen! The ministers are as weak as usual – that is the result.

Now, my Lovebird, I must end.

God bless you + and the girlies! With fondest kisses ever your own old

Nicky

Maurice Paléologue, Memoirs – 6 November

During recent months the Emperor suffered from nervous maladies which betray themselves in unhealthy excitement, anxiety, loss of appetite, depression and insomnia.

The Empress would not rest until he had consulted the quack Badmaiev,[11] an ingenious disciple of the Mongol sorcerers. The charlatan soon discovered in his pharmacopoeia the remedy appropriate to the case of his august patient: it is an elixir compounded of 'Tibetan herbs' according to a magic formula and has to be prescribed very strictly.

Every time that the Tsar has used this drug, his baneful symptoms have vanished in a twinkling, he has not only recovered sleep and appetite, but experienced a general feeling of well-being, a delightful sense of increased vigour and a curious euphoria.

Judging by its effects, the elixir must be a mixture of henbane and hashish, and the Emperor should be careful not to take too much.

Nikolai Mikhailovich to Nicky

Dear Nicky

What can I say to you about the Frenchman Paléologue, the gentleman only causes confusion wherever he can, talks nonsense in various salons, and instead of being the effective representative of

---

[11] A doctor of Tibetan medicine and godson of Emperor Alexander III.

our friend France, only thinks about his career and his own skin, so one cannot trust him. Yours ever,

Nikolai Mikhailovich

Alexei to Alix – 6 November – Mogilev
My dear sweet darling Mama
  I slept well last night, but got to sleep late. The weather is wonderful. The sun is teasing me! The pains have got less. I can walk although I'm trying not to. I am having a happy day. I am playing a lot. My *salary? I am waiting*!!! A big kiss. May God+ protect you!!! Hourrah!

Your loving A. Vth [Fifth] Romanov

8 November
My darling, own, sweet dear Mama,
  It's warm. Tomorrow I will get up. My salary! I beg you!!!!! There's nothing to eattttt! I am also unlucky at nain jaune.
  So what!!! I shall soon start selling my clothes books and will finally die of hunger.
  We all kiss your hand!!
  I kiss you many times
  Greetings from Joy and Kotka, Toad and Zubrovka. May God keep you!!

Alexei

Nicky to Alix – 10 November – Mogilev
My own precious Sunny,
  Many thanks for your dear letter. When you get this one you will have heard from Sturmer about the changes which are absolutely necessary now. I am sorry about Protopopov, a good honest man, but he jumped from one idea to another and could not decide himself to stick to his opinion. I remarked that from the very beginning. People said he was not normal some years ago from a certain illness. It is risky leaving the Min. of Int. in such hands at such times!
  While these changes go on the Duma will be shut for 8 days, else they would say one does it under their pressure. In any case Trepov will try and do his best. He comes back, on Sunday I think, with a list of names, which we have spoken about with Mm. and him. Only please don't mix in our Friend!
  It is I who carry the responsibility and I want to be free to choose accordingly.

God bless you + my beloved darling. Oh! how happy I will be to rest in your dear arms. With tender kisses to you all ever your very own

Nicky

Alix to Nicky – 12 November – Tsarskoe Selo
My own beloved One,

I am writing to you in our hospital in one of the wards – was too dead tired last night to think of anything and had to put my things together and arrange your letters. My head goes round in a ring.

I assure you, but it's for your and Baby's sake, believe me. I don't care what bad one says of me, only when one tries to tear devoted, honest people, who care for me – away – it's horribly unfair.

I am but a woman fighting for her Master and Child, her two dearest ones on earth – and God will help me being your guardian angel, only don't pull the sticks away upon which I have found it possible to rest when also you were alone with us two against everybody, who promised revolution if you went. You stood up against all and God blessed your decision. I repeat again – it does not lie in the name of Protopopov but in your remaining firm and not giving in – the Tsar rules and not the Duma. Forgive my again writing, but I am fighting for your reign and Baby's future.

God will help, be firm don't listen to men, who are not from God but cowards. Your Wify, to whom you are ALL in ALL.

True unto death.

Rasputin to the Imperial family – 25 November – Telegram
BELIEVE, DO NOT BE AFRAID, BEQUEATH YOUR REALM TO YOUR LITTLE ONE IN ITS ENTIRETY, AS YOU RECEIVED IT FROM YOUR FATHER, AND AS HIS SON WILL RECEIVE IT ALSO.

Nicky, Diary – 2 December – Tsarskoe Selo
In the morning before my walk I received Voeikov. From 11 to one received Trepov, Bark, Polovstov and Shakhovsky [Nikolasha's adjutant]. Walked next to Alix's char-à-banc. Read. We spent the evening at Ania's talking to Grigory.

Felix Yusupov, Memoirs
Each of my visits to Rasputin convinced me more and more that he

was the cause of Russia's disasters, and that if he disappeared the diabolical spell cast over our Tsar and Tsarina would vanish with him.

Being convinced of the necessity for action, I discussed the matter
with Irina and found she agreed with me completely. I imagined that
it would be easy to find a few determined men ready to help me to
find a way of eliminating Rasputin.

-'What can one do when all the ministers and most of the people
in close contact with His Majesty are the tools of Rasputin? The only
solution is to kill the scoundrel, but there's not a man in Russia who
has the guts to do it. If I weren't so old, I would do it myself.'

These words of Rodzianko, head of the Duma, decide me; but how
can one deliberately prepare to murder a man in cold blood?

I have repeatedly stated that I am by nature a peaceful man. The
very idea of spilling blood fills me with horror. Yet the more I
thought about it the more convinced I was that I would have to conquer my personal feelings in this matter.

During Dmitri [Pavlovich]'s absence at Headquarters I saw a good
deal of a certain Captain Soukhotin who had been wounded and was
undergoing treatment in St Petersburg. I confided in this trusted
friend and asked if he would help me in my plan. He consented without a moment's hesitation.

Our conversation took place on the day of Dmitri's return, and I
saw him the day after: Dmitri made no secret of the fact that the idea
of killing Rasputin had haunted him for months, but he had not yet
found a way of doing it.

Ania Vyrubova, Memoirs

It was with feelings of unspeakable relief that we left the Stavka for
Tsarskoe Selo. In the Imperial train with us travelled young Grand
Duke Dmitri Pavlovich who even then was probably involved in a
deadly plot against their Majesties. Yet this young man was able to
keep up the pretence of friendship with the Empress, sitting beside
her couch and entertaining her by the hour with amusing gossip and
stories. Hearing the laughter the Emperor often opened his study
door to listen and join in the conversation. It was a merry journey
home, yet within a few days after we arrived troubles again began to
multiply.

Every move of Rasputin from the hour when he began to frequent
the palaces of the Grand Dukes, especially from the day he met the
Emperor and Empress in the drawing room of the Grand Duchess
Militsa, to the midnight when he met his death in the Yusupov

Palace on the Moika Canal in Petrograd, is a matter of the most minute police record.

The police know how many days of each year Rasputin spent in Petrograd and how much of his time was lived in Siberia. They know exactly how many times he called at the palace at Tsarskoe Selo, how long he stayed and who was present. They know when and under exactly the circumstances Rasputin came to my house, and who else came to the house at the same time. The police know more about Rasputin than all the journalists.

From a report by the Police Department on the surveillance of Rasputin, 1916

The surveillance of the peasant from Pokrovskoe village, Tiumen district, Tobolsk province, Grigory Efimovich RASPUTIN, living at no. 64 Gorokhovaya street, did not at first yield any significant results, as he was too careful, besides he was shielded by his acolytes, who tried to spirit him away; thus it went on for some time, until one of the persons in charge received an anonymous letter, threatening to kill Rasputin. Using this pretext, the Department of Security [Okhrana] suggested to Rasputin that they appoint two agents to guard him. He accepted the suggestion and agents Terekhov and Svistunov were put in place.

At the same time, the agents protecting Rasputin fulfilled a role for the Department of Police – to find out, as far as possible, who the people were who visited him, and which places he himself visited. Rasputin had complete faith in the agents, and often took them along with him, which made their work significantly easier.

Those people who often visited Rasputin, and whom the agents were not able to identify, became the subject of special police observation to establish their identity, using a local police observer.

When Rasputin travelled to the village of Pokrovskoe or to Moscow, the agents appointed to him accompanied him by order of the Police Department, and as they were on official business, communicated the information they had gathered on Rasputin to the Department of Security twice a week by registered letter, or if they journeyed elsewhere or returned to Petersburg, they telegraphed separately.

About a year ago, news of another supposed attempt on Rasputin's life was received, at which point it was ordered that more stringent measures to guard him be adopted, so 5 men were appointed to him in two shifts, as well as a chauffeur with a separate motor, in all the protection and surveillance of Rasputin took 11 men.

Each day Rasputin had between 80 and 100 visitors, excluding regulars. People who came with petitions were identified, and it was simply ascertained what matter this or that person had come about.

The results of the surveillance of Rasputin, with a note of the identified persons, were usually forwarded to the Police Department, while the draft copy remained with the Department of Security. In all, to keep Rasputin under observation, up to 5000 people were used. As well as establishing his contacts, the surveillance included inspecting his correspondence and each day a detailed diary of events was kept.

Rasputin often went to Tsarskoe Selo, to Vyrubova, to whose flat the Tsarina would then come, sometimes also the Tsar, and often their children.

During the past year Rasputin almost always went to Tsarskoe Selo by motor. Rasputin was seldom sober. Simanovich and the restaurant 'Villa Rodé' were his purveyors of wine, spirits, fruits etc.

Vyrubova visited Rasputin almost every day. Whenever Rasputin went to her house in Tsarskoe Selo, the Empress would arrive some 30 minutes later. The meeting would last about 1 hour 20 minutes. One day it happened thus: Rasputin came to Vyrubova's with Osinenko and Pahodze, about 20 minutes later Tsarina Alexandra arrived. About 15 minutes after her arrival Osinenko and Pahodze came out and walked around in the vicinity of the house for about 50 minutes, while Rasputin remained with the Empress. Then Osinenko and Pahodze returned into Vyrubova's house, stayed for 30 minutes and then they all returned to Petersburg.

Felix Yusupov, Memoirs

Purishkevich[12] was also of the opinion that Rasputin should be done away with secretly. At a meeting with Dmitri and Soukhotin, we decided that poison was the surest means of killing him without leaving any trace of murder.

Our house on the Moika was chosen as the place of execution; I was fitting up an apartment in the basement which lent itself admirably to the accomplishment of our scheme.

This decision at first gave me a feeling of disgust: the prospect of luring a man to my house to kill him horrified me. No matter what the man was, I could not bring myself to plan the murder of a guest.

---

[12] Member of the Duma, leader of right-wing party.

V. V. Shulgin,[13] Memoirs

I was leaving for Kiev. Purishkevich stopped me in the Catherine Hall of the Tauride palace. I replied:

'I'm leaving.'

'Well then, all the best.'

We parted, but then he stopped me again.

'Listen, Shulgin. You're leaving, but I want you to know ... Remember December 16th.'

I looked at him. He had the same look that I had already seen once, when he told me a particular secret.

'Remember December 16th ...'

'Why?'

'You'll see. Goodbye ...'

But he turned again.

'I'll tell you ... you I can ... on the 16th we're going to kill him.'

'Whom?'

'Grishka.' [Rasputin]

He hurriedly told me what would happen. Then:

'How do you feel about it?'

I knew he wouldn't listen to me. All the same I said:

'Don't do it.'

'What? Why?'

'I don't know ... It's disgusting ... '

'What a wimp you are, Shulgin.'

'Perhaps, but again perhaps not ... I don't believe in Rasputin's influence.'

'How's that?'

'Just like that ... It's all nonsense. All he does is to pray for the heir. He has no influence over the choice of ministers. He's a cunning peasant ...'

'So, according to you, Rasputin isn't doing any harm to the monarchy?'

'Not only is he harming it, he's killing it.'

'Then I don't understand you ...'

'But it's obvious. By killing him you won't help anything ... Look! There are two sides. The first – it's what you yourself called "ministers' leapfrog". The reshuffling occurs either because there is no one to appoint, or because whoever you appoint you can't please anyone, because the country has gone mad about the so-called "people of public confidence", while the Emperor has no faith in them at all ...

---

[13] Deputy in the second, third and fourth Dumas.

Rasputin has nothing to do with it. Even if you kill him – you won't change anything.'

'What do you mean, won't change anything?'

'No you won't ... Everything will still be the same ... the same "ministers' leapfrog". And the other side – that's how Rasputin is killing them: and you can't do away with that by killing him ... it's too late ...'

'What do you mean I can't! Excuse me, please ... so we're just supposed to sit there? That's a disgrace. Surely you understand what that means? One hardly dares say it. The monarchy is going to its ruin ... You know, I am not a coward ... I'm not easily intimidated ... Remember the second State Duma ... however bad things were then, I knew we would pull through ... But now I tell you the monarchy is collapsing, and with it all of us, and with us – Russia ... Do you know what is happening? The cinemas have been forbidden to show the film which shows the emperor putting on the St George cross. Why? Because as soon as the sequence starts, a voice pipes up from the darkness: "Little-father Tsar is with Georgie, little-mother with Grigory ... "'

I wanted to say something, but he wouldn't let me speak:

'Wait. I know what you're going to say ... You're going to say that it isn't true about the Tsarina and Rasputin ... I know ... I know ... I know ... It's all untrue, but what does it matter? I ask you. Go and prove it ... Who will believe you? You know, Julius was no fool when he said "no suspicion should fall on the wife of Caesar" ... And here we're not just talking about suspicion ... here ...'

He jumped up:

'We can't go on sitting here. What does it matter. We're coming to the end. It can't get worse. I'm going to kill him like a dog ... Farewell ...'

Felix Yusupov, Memoirs

My intimacy with Rasputin – so indispensable for our plan – increased each day. But what an effort it was!

Rasputin made me lie down on the sofa. Then, staring intently at me, he gently ran his hand over my chest, neck and head, after which he knelt down, laid both hands on my forehead and murmured a prayer. His face was so close to mine that I could see only his eyes. He remained in this position for some time, then rising brusquely he made mesmeric passes over my body.

Rasputin had tremendous hypnotic power. I felt as if some active energy were pouring heat, like a warm current, into my whole being. I fell into a torpor, and my body grew numb; I tried to speak, but my tongue no longer obeyed me and I gradually slipped into a drowsy state, as though a powerful narcotic had been administered to me. All I could see was Rasputin's glittering eyes: two phosphorescent beams of light melting into a great luminous ring which at times drew nearer and then moved farther away.

Alix to Nicky – 4 December – Tsarskoe Selo
My very precious One,

Goodbye, sweet Lovy!

It's great pain to let you go – worse than ever after the hard times we have been living and fighting through. But God who is all love and mercy has let the things take a change for the better, just a little more patience and deepest faith in the prayers and help of our Friend – then all will go well.

I am fully convinced that great and beautiful times are coming for your reign and Russia. Only keep up your spirits, let no talks or letters pull you down – let them pass by as something unclean and quickly to be forgotten.

Show to all, that you are the master and your will shall be obeyed – the time of great indulgence and gentleness is over – now comes your reign of will and power, and they shall be made to bow down before you and listen to your orders and all forgivingness.

Why do people hate me? Because they know I have a strong will and when am convinced of a thing being right (when besides blessed by Grigory), do not change my mind and that they can't bear. But it's the bad ones.

Remember Mr Philippe's words when he gave me the image with the bell. As you were so kind, trusting and gentle, I was to be your bell, those that came with wrong intentions would not be able to approach me and I would warn you. Those who are afraid of me don't look me in the eyes or are up to some wrong, never like me.

How will the lonely nights be? I cannot imagine it. The consolation to hold you tightly clasped in my arms – it lulled the pain of soul and heart and I tried to put all my endless love, prayers and faith and strength into my caresses. So inexpressibly dear you are to me, husband of my heart.

God bless you and my Baby treasure – I cover you with kisses; when sad, go to Baby's room and sit a bit quietly there with his nice people. Kiss the beloved child and you will feel warmed and calm. All my love I pour out to you, Sun of my life.

Sleep well, heart and soul with you, my prayers around you – God and the holy Virgin will never forsake you.

Ever your very very Own

Nicky to Alix – 4 December – In the train

My own deeply beloved darling Sunny,

I have not read your letter, as I like to do it in bed, before going to sleep. But I thank you before hand for all the love and sweet kindness you have written in it. I will deliver this letter at Tosno and hope it will reach you this evening. Yes, these days we spent together were indeed hard ones – but it is only thanks to you that I stood them more or less calmly.

You are so staunch and enduring – I admire you more than I can say! Forgive me if I have been cross or impatient, sometimes one's temper has to get through!

Of course it would have been bliss if we could have remained together the whole difficult time. But now I firmly believe that the greatest hardship is over – and it won't be as difficult as before. And then I intend becoming sharp and biting.

God grant our separation will not be a long one. I am the whole time in thoughts near you, never doubt that.

I bless you with all my loving heart and the girlies too. Keep well and strong, my own Lovebird, my One and All! Sleep well and gently!

Your very own old Huzy Nicky, true unto death

Give her my love.

Pierre Gilliard, Memoirs

Many attempts had been made, even by the Tsarina's greatest friends at Court, to open her eyes to the true character of Rasputin. They had all collapsed against the blind faith she had in him.

But in this tragic hour the Grand Duchess Elizabeth [Ella] wished to make one last effort to save her sister. She came from Moscow intending to spend a few days at Tsarskoe Selo with the relations she loved so dearly. She was nine years older than her sister, and felt an almost maternal tenderness for her. It was at her house, it will be remembered, that the young princess had stayed on her first visit to Russia. It was she who had helped the Empress with wise advice and surrounded her with every attention when she started her reign. She had often tried to open her sister's eyes before, but in vain. Yet this time she hoped that God would give her the powers of persuasion which had hitherto failed her, and enable her to avert the terrible catastrophe she felt was imminent.

As soon as she arrived at Tsarskoe Selo she spoke to the Tsarina, trying with all the love she bore her to convince her of her blindness, and pleading with her to listen to her warnings for the sake of her family and her country.

The Tsarina's confidence was not to be shaken. She realized the feelings which had impelled her sister to take this step, but she was terribly grieved to find her accepting the lying stories of those who desired to ruin the *staretz*, and she asked her never to mention the subject again. As the Grand Duchess persisted, the Tsarina broke off the conversation. The interview was then objectless.

A few hours later the Grand Duchess left for Moscow, death in her heart. The Tsarina and her daughters accompanied her to the station. The two sisters took leave of each other. The tender affection which had associated them since their childhood was still intact, but they realised that there was a broken something lying between them.[14]

Felix Yusupov, Memoirs
Later the Grand Duchess Elizabeth, who appeared very rarely at Tsarskoe Selo, made a last attempt to convince her sister. She promised to come and see us on leaving the Alexander Palace. We all waited eagerly for her arrival, anxious to hear the result of the interview. She entered the room trembling and in tears:

'She drove me away like a dog!' she cried. 'Poor Nicky, poor Russia!'

Ella, from her deposition
In December 1916 I had a final, decisive conversation with the Tsar and Tsarina on the subject of Rasputin. I pointed out that Rasputin rankled society, was compromising the imperial family and leading the dynasty to ruin. They replied that Rasputin was a great man of prayer, that all the rumours about him were slanders, and asked me not to touch on the question any further.

---

[14] This was the last meeting of Ella and Alix.

Alexei to Alix – 9 December – Mogilev
My dear Mama

Yesterday we again went into the forest and played at robbers, it was very jolly. As usual I had the pony. The snow is now very deep and the trees are quite covered too, so that we often get a shower of snow as we go under them. With much love from

Alexei

Alix to Nicky – 12 December – Tsarskoe Selo
Beloved Sweetheart,

For a precious letter and card my tenderest thanks. I am too happy you went to the dear Image – such peace there – one feels away from all worries that minute whilst pouring out one's heart and soul in prayer to her, to whom so many come with their sorrows ...

Then to the 'Dessiatinni' monastery – relics of St Barbara are kept there. Sat a moment at the Abbesses room and then I asked to be taken to the old woman Maria Mikhailovna ... and we went to her on foot through the wet snow.

She lay in bed in a small dark room, so they brought a candle for us to see each other. She is 107, wears irons (now they stay near her) – generally always works, goes about, sews for the convicts and soldiers without spectacles – never washes.

And of course no smell, or feeling of dirt, scraggy grey hair standing out, a sweet fine, oval face with lovely young, shining eyes and sweet smile. She blessed us and kissed us. To you she sends the apple (please eat it).

13 December
My own dearest Angel,

Tenderest thanks for Your dear card. Am so anxious (as you have no time to write) to know about your conversation with that horrible Trepov. I read in the paper that he told Rodzianko now, that the Duma will be shut about on the 17th till first half of Jan. Has he any right to say this, before the official announcement through the Senate is made.

My Angel, we dined yesterday at Ania's with our Friend. It was so nice, we told all about our journey and he said we ought to have gone straight to you as we would have brought you intense joy and blessing and I fear disturbing you!

He entreats you to be firm, to be the Master and not always to give in to Trepov – you know much better than that man (still let him lead you) – and why not our Friend who leads through God.

Remember why I am disliked – shows it right to be firm and feared and you be the same, you a man – only believe more in our Friend (instead of Trepov). He lives for you and Russia.

And we must give a strong country to Baby, and dare not be weak for his sake, else he will have a yet harder reign, setting our faults to right and drawing his reins in tightly which you let loose. You have to suffer for faults in the reigns of your predecessors. Let our legacy be a lighter one for Alexei. He has a strong will and mind of his own, don't let things slip through your fingers and make him have to build up all again.

Be firm. I your wall, am behind you and won't give way – I know He leads us right. It's all getting calmer and better, only one wants to feel Your Hand – how long, years, people have told me the same – 'Russia loves to feel the whip' – it's their nature – tender love and then the iron hand to punish and guide.

How I wish I could pour my will into your veins. The Virgin is above you, for you, with you, remember the miracle – our Friend's vision.

Oh, dear, I must get up. Been writing Xmas cards all the morning. Heart and soul burning with you – Love boundless, therefore seems harsh all I write – pardon, believe and understand. I love you too deeply and cry over your faults and rejoice over every right step

Wify

14 December   7 of frost and thick snow. Scarcely slept this night again, remaining till luncheon in bed as all aches still and have a slight chill. Such loving thanks for your dear letter.

Be Peter the Great, Ivan the Terrible, Emperor Paul – crush them all under you – now don't you laugh, naughty one.

I really cannot understand. I am but a woman, but my soul and brain tell me it would be the saving of Russia – they sin far worse than anything the Sukhomlinovs ever did. Forbid Brusilov etc. when they come to touch any political subjects, fool, who wants responsible cabinet.

Remember even M. Philippe said one dare not give constitution, as it would be your and Russia's ruin, and all true Russians say the same.

Months ago I told Sturmer about Shvedov to be a member of Council of the Empire to have them and good Maklokov in they will stand bravely for us. I know I worry you – ah, would I not far, far rather only write letters of love, tenderness and caresses of which my heart is so full – but my duty as wife and mother and Russia's mother obliges me to say all to you – blessed by our Friend.

Sweetheart, Sunshine of my life, if in battle you had to meet the enemy, you would never waver and go forth like a lion – be it now in the battle against the small handful of brutes and republicans.

Be the Master, and all will bow down to you. Do you think I should fear, ah no – today I have had an officer cleared out from Maria's and Anastasia's hospital, because he allowed himself to mock at our journey, pretending Protopopov brought the people to receive us so well; the Doctors who heard it raged – you see Sunny in her small things is energetic and in big ones as much as you wish – we have been placed by God on a throne and we must keep it firm and give it over to our son untouched – if you keep that in mind you will remember to be the Sovereign – and how much easier for an autocratic sovereign than one who has sworn the Constitution.

Beloved One, listen to me, yes, you know your old true girly. 'Do not fear,' the old woman said and therefore I write without fear to my agooweeone. Now the girlies want their tea, they came frozen back from their drive – I kiss you and hold you tightly clasped to my breast, caress you, love you, long for you, can't sleep without you – bless you. Ever your very Own

Wify

Maurice Paléologue, Memoirs

[From the conversation with the former Minister of Justice, Shcheglovitov] 'The Tsar is the Anointed of the Lord, sent by God to be the supreme guardian of the Church and the all-powerful ruler of the Empire.[15] In popular belief he is even the image of Christ upon earth.

As he receives his power from God it is to God alone that he must account for it. The essential divinity of his authority has the second result that autocracy and nationalism are inseparable. Then, down with the fools who dare to assail these dogmas! Constitutional liberalism is a heresy as well as a stupid chimera.

There is no national life except within the framework of autocracy and orthodoxy. If political reforms are necessary they must be carried out only in the spirit of autocracy and orthodoxy.'

---

[15] Paléologue added in a footnote: 'The Tsar is not, as is often said, the head of the Church. He is only its supreme guardian. From the religious point of view his only privilege is that in the communion service he has the right to take the cup and the bread from the altar himself.'

Alix to Nicky – 16 December – Tsarskoe Selo
My own beloved Treasure,

   Olga had a Committee yesterday evening, but it did not last long. Volodia Volkonski, who always has a smile or two for her – avoided her eyes and never once smiled – you see how our girlies have learned to watch people and their faces – they have developed much interiorly through all this suffering.

   They know all we go through, it's necessary and ripens them. They are happily at times great ladies – but have the insight and the feeling of the soul of much wiser beings. As our Friend says they have passed heavy *kursi* [schooling].

   Full of Petrograd horrors and rages that nobody defends me, that all may say, write, hint at bad things about their Empress and nobody stands up, reprimands, punishes, lavishes, fines those types.

   Yes, people are not to be admired, cowards. But many will be struck off future court lists, they shall learn to know in time of peace what it was in time of war not to stand up for one's Sovereign. Why have we got a ramolic rag as M[inister]. of the Court [Fredericks]? He ought to have brought all the names and proposed law to punish them for slandering your wife.

   A private husband would not one hour have stood these assaults upon his wife. Personally I do not care a straw – when I was young I suffered *horribly* through those injustices said about me (oh how often!) – but now the worldly things don't touch me deeply, I mean nastinesses – they will come round some day, only my Nicky ought really to stick up a bit for me, as many think that you don't care and hide behind me ...

Maurice Paléologue, Memoirs – 16 December
Countess R—, who has just spent three days in Moscow ordering clothes from the famous dressmaker, Lamanova, confirms what I have recently heard about the rage of the Muscovites against the imperial family: 'I dined in different circles each evening,' she said. 'Everywhere one hears the same indignant outcry. If the Emperor appeared on the Red Square today, he would be booed. The Empress would be torn to pieces. The kind, warm-hearted and pure-minded Grand Duchess Elizabeth [Ella] dare not leave her convent now. The workmen accuse her of starving the people. There seems to be a stir of revolution among all classes.'

Maria Pavlovna [the younger], Memoirs
My aunt Ella, the Empress's sister, was also under incessant attack.
During the anti-German demonstrations in Moscow a crowd had
gathered in front of her nunnery, shouting insults and threats.

Ania Vyrubova, Memoirs
On the afternoon of December 16, I was sent by the Empress on an
errand, entirely non-political, to Rasputin's lodgings. I went, as always,
reluctantly, because I knew the evil construction which would be
placed on my errand by any of the conspirators who happened to see
me. Yet, as in duty bound, I went. I stayed the shortest possible time,
but in that brief interval I heard Rasputin say that he expected a late
evening visit to the Yusupov palace to meet Grand Duchess Irina, wife
of Prince Felix Yusupov.

   Although I knew that Felix had often visited Rasputin it struck me
as odd that he should go to their house for the first time at such an
unseemly hour. But to my question Rasputin replied that Felix did
not wish his parents to know of his visit. As I was leaving the place
Rasputin said a strange thing to me. 'What more do you want?' he
asked in a low voice. 'Already you have received all.' All that his
prayers could give me? Did he mean that?

   That evening in the Empress's boudoir I mentioned this proposed
midnight visit, and the Empress said in some surprise: 'But there
must be some mistake. Irina is in the Crimea, and neither of the older
Yusupovs are in town.' Once again she repeated thoughtfully: 'There
is surely some mistake,' and then we began to talk of other things.

Alix to Nicky – 17 December – Tsarskoe Selo
My own beloved Sweetheart,
   You will finish the nice English novel in the train. Oh, the joy, the
consolation of having you home again. At such a time to be separated I assure you is at times absolutely exasperating and distracting
– how much easier to have shared all together and spoken over everything, instead of letters, which have less force alas, and often must
have aggravated you, my poor patient Angel.

   But I have to try to be the antidote to others' poison. Has Baby's
'worm' quite been got rid of. Then he will get fatter and less transparent – the precious Boy!

   We are sitting together – can imagine our feelings and thoughts –
our Friend has disappeared yesterday, A[nia] saw him and he said

Felix had asked him to come in the night, a motor would fetch him to see Irina. A motor fetched him (military one) with 2 civilians and he went away.

This night big scandal at Yusupov's house – big meeting, Dmitri, Purishkevich etc. all drunk. Police heard shots. Police searching and Justice entered now into Y[usupov]'s house did not dare before as Dmitri was there. Governor of the city has sent for Dmitri, Felix wished to leave tonight for Crimea, begged Kalinin [Protopopov] to stop him. Our Friend was in good spirits, but nervous these days and for A[nia] too.

Felix pretends He never came to the house and never asked him. I still trust in God's mercy that one has only driven Him off somewhere. Kalinin is doing all he can. Therefore I beg Voeikov, we women are alone with our weak hands. Shall keep her to live here as now they will set at her nest.

Cannot and *won't* believe He has been killed. God have mercy. Such utter anguish (am calm and can't believe it). Thanks dear letter. Come quickly – nobody will dare to touch her or do anything when you are here. Felix came often to Him lately.

Kisses, Sunny

Maurice Paléologue, Memoirs – 17 December

About seven o'clock this evening an excellent informer, who is at my service, told me that Rasputin was murdered this morning during a supper at the Yusupov palace. The murderers are said to be young Prince Felix Yusupov, (who married a niece of the Tsar in 1914) the Grand Duke Dmitri, son of the Grand Duke Paul, and Purishkevich, leader of the Extreme Right in the Duma. Two or three society women are supposed to have been present at supper. The news is still being kept a strict secret.

Before telegraphing to Paris, I tried to obtain some confirmation of what I have just heard. I immediately went to see Countess K—. She telephoned to Madame Golovin, a relation of hers and the great friend and protectoress of Rasputin. A weeping voice replied: 'Yes, the Father disappeared last night. No one knows what's become of him. It's a horrible disaster!'

The news was circulating in the Yacht Club by the evening. The Grand Duke Nikolai Mikhailovich refused to credit it: 'We've had Rasputin's death announced too often before. Each time he has come back to life, and more powerful than ever!'

However, he telephoned to Trepov, the President of the Council, who replied:

'All I know is that Rasputin has disappeared; I presume he has been murdered. I can't tell you any more: it's the Chief of the *Okhrana* who has the matter in hand.'

THE NIGHT BEFORE – 16–17 December

Purishkevich, Memoirs
Dr Lazavert is supposed to drive up to the Duma watch tower in an empty car, dressed as a chauffeur, and I am to get out and go to Yusupov's palace.

I feel completely calm and in control. In any case I have taken with me a steel knuckle-duster and my revolver, a wonderful thing, a *sauvage* model, who knows I might have to resort to either one or the other.

I don't know why, this verse from Horace's ode has been running through my head all day: 'Don't ask, don't try to guess, Leuconoe, it's not for us to know what end the gods have prepared for either you or I.'

Felix Yusupov, Memoirs
In the middle of the room stood the table at which Rasputin was to drink his last cup of tea.

My two servants, Gregory and Ivan, helped me to arrange the furniture. I asked them to prepare tea for six, to buy biscuits and cakes and to bring wine from the cellar. I told them that I was expecting some friends at eleven that evening, and that they could wait in the servants' hall until I rang for them.

When everything was settled, I went up to my room. By eleven o'clock everything was ready in the basement. Comfortably furnished and well lit, this underground room had lost its grim look. On the table the samovar smoked, surrounded by plates filled with the cakes and dainties that Rasputin liked so much. An array of bottles and glasses stood on a sideboard. Ancient lanterns of coloured glass lit the room from the ceiling; the heavy red damask portières were lowered. On the granite hearth, a log fire crackled and scattered sparks on the flag-stones. One felt isolated from the rest of the world and it seemed as though, no matter what happened, the events of that night would remain for ever buried in the silence of those thick walls.

The bell rang, announcing the arrival of Dmitri and my other friends. I showed them into the dining room and they stood for a little while, silently examining the spot where Rasputin was to meet his end.

Purishkevich We sat down at the round table and Yusupov invited us to have a glass of tea and try some of the cakes, before we laced them with the necessary ingredient.

Yusupov I took from the ebony cabinet a box containing the poison and laid it on the table. Doctor Lazavert put on rubber gloves and ground the cyanide of potassium crystals to powder. Then, lifting the top of each cake, he sprinkled the inside with a dose of poison which, according to him, was sufficient to kill several men instantly.

Purishkevich Choosing all the cakes with pink cream (there were two sorts, with pink or chocolate cream), Dr Lazavert took off the tops, spread each one thickly with poison, then replaced the tops so as to make them look normal.

Yusupov There was an impressive silence. We all followed the doctor's movements with emotion. There remained the glasses into which cyanide was to be poured. It was decided to do this at the last moment so that the poison should not evaporate and lose its potency.

Purishkevich We went upstairs to the drawing room. Yusupov took out from the writing desk two phials of potassium cyanide solution, which he gave to Dmitri Pavlovich and myself, and with which, twenty minutes after he left to fetch Rasputin, we were to half-fill two of the four goblets standing next to the bottles downstairs in the dining room.

Lazavert changed into his chauffeur's uniform. Yusupov put on a civilian overcoat, turned up the collar and saying goodbye, went out.

Yusupov When everything was ready, I put on an overcoat and drew a fur cap over my ears, completely concealing my face. Doctor Lazavert, in a chauffeur's uniform, started up the engine and we got into the car which was waiting in the courtyard by the side entrance. On reaching Rasputin's house, I had to parley with the janitor before he agreed to let me in. In accordance with Rasputin's instructions, I went up the back staircase; I had to grope my way up in the dark, and only with the greatest difficulty found the door. I rang the bell.

'Who's that?' called a voice from inside.

I began to tremble. 'It's I, Grigory Efimovich. I've come for you.'

I could hear Rasputin moving about the hall. The chain was unfastened, the heavy lock grated. I felt very ill at ease.

He opened the door and I went into the kitchen. It was dark. I imagined that someone was spying on me from the next room. Instinctively, I turned up my collar and pulled my cap down over my eyes.

'Why are you trying to hide?' asked Rasputin.

'Didn't we agree that no one was to know you were going out with me tonight?'

'True, true; I haven't said a word about it to anyone in the house, I'll go and dress.'

I accompanied him to his bedroom; it was lighted only by the little lamp burning before the ikons. Rasputin lit the candle; I noticed that his bed was crumpled. He had probably been resting. Near the bed were his overcoat and beaver cap, on the ground his high felt-lined galoshes.

Rasputin wore a silk blouse embroidered in cornflowers, with a thick raspberry-coloured cord as a belt. His velvet breeches and highly polished boots seemed brand new; he had brushed his hair and carefully combed his beard. As he came close to me, I smelt a strong odour of cheap soap which indicated he had taken pains with his appearance. I had never seen him look so clean and tidy.

'Well, it's time to go; it's past midnight.'

'What about the gypsies? Shall we pay them a visit?'

'I don't know; perhaps,' I answered.

'There will be no one at your house but us tonight?' he asked, with a note of anxiety in his voice.

I reassured him by saying that he would meet no one that he might not care to see, and that my mother was in the Crimea.

'I don't like your mother. I know she hates me; she's a friend of Elizabeth's [Ella]. Both of them plot against me and spread slander about me too. The Tsarina herself has often told me that they were my worst enemies. Why, no earlier than this evening, Protopopov came to see me and made me swear not to go out for the next few days. "They'll kill you," he declared. "Your enemies are bent on mischief!" But they'd just be wasting time and trouble; they won't succeed, they are not powerful enough ... But that's enough, come on, let's go.'

I picked up the overcoat and helped him on with it.

Suddenly, a feeling of great pity for the man swept over me. I was ashamed of the despicable deceit, the horrible trickery to which I was obliged to resort. At that moment I was filled with self-contempt, and wondered how I could even have thought of such a cowardly crime. I could not understand how I had brought myself to decide on it.

I looked at my victim with dread, as he stood before me, quiet and trusting. What had become of his second sight? What good did his gift of foretelling the future do him? Of what use was his faculty for reading the thoughts of others, if he was blind to the dreadful trap that was laid for him?

Purishkevich At a quarter to one, as had been agreed, the grand duke and I went downstairs to the dining room and poured the potassium cyanide into the two goblets, at which point Dmitri Pavlovich began to worry that, as he offered the cakes to Rasputin, Felix Yusupov might in haste eat a pink one, or pick up by mistake one of the goblets with the poison. 'It won't happen,' I assured the grand duke.

'As far as I can see, Yusupov's distinguishing characteristics are his self-control and sangfroid.' Having completed our task, we returned upstairs, straining to catch the slightest sound from the street.

'They're coming!' I whispered suddenly, moving away from the window. Lieutenant S rushed over to the gramophone, and a few moments later the sounds of the American march 'Yanky-Doodle' rang out, it still haunts me at times, even now. Holding our breath we went into the lobby and stood one behind the other at the top of the staircase leading down: I was nearest the stairs, my knuckle-duster in my hand, behind me the grand duke, then Lieutenant S, and lastly Dr Lazavert.

Yusupov As we entered the house, I could hear the gramophone played 'Yankee Doodle went to town.'

'What's all this?' asked Rasputin. 'Is someone giving a party here?'

'No, just my wife entertaining a few friends; they'll be going soon. Meanwhile, let's have a cup of tea in the dining room.'

I offered him wine and tea; to my great disappointment, he refused both. Had something made him suspicious? I was determined, come what may, that he should not leave the house alive.

We sat down at the table and began to talk. We reviewed our mutual acquaintances, not forgetting Ania Vyrubova and, naturally, touched on Tsarskoe Selo.

Rasputin asked for some tea. I immediately poured out a cup and handed him a plate of biscuits. Why was it I offered him the only biscuits that were not poisoned? I even hesitated before handing him the cakes sprinkled with cyanide.

He refused them at first: 'I don't want any, they're too sweet.' At last however, he took one, then another ... I watched him, horror-stricken. The poison should have acted immediately but, to my amazement, Rasputin went on talking quite calmly.

I then suggested he should sample our Crimean wines. He once more refused. Time was passing, I was becoming nervous; in spite of his refusal, I filled two glasses. But, as in the case of the biscuits – and just as inexplicably – I again avoided using a glass containing cyanide. Rasputin changed his mind and accepted the wine I handed him. He drank it with enjoyment, found it to his taste and asked whether we made a great deal of wine in the Crimea. He seemed surprised to hear that we had cellars full of it.

'Pour me out some Madeira,' he said. This time I wanted to give it to him in a glass containing cyanide, but he protested: 'I'll have it in the same glass.'

'You can't, Grigory Efimovich,' I replied, 'you can't mix two kinds of wines.'

'It doesn't matter, I'll use the same glass, I tell you ... '

I had to give in without pressing the point, but I managed, as if by mistake, to drop the glass from which he had drunk, and immediately poured the madeira into a glass containing cyanide. Rasputin did not see anything.

I stood watching him drink, expecting any moment to see him collapse.

But he continued slowly to sip his wine like a connoisseur. His face did not change, only from time to time he put his hand to his throat as though he had some difficulty in swallowing. He rose and took a few steps. When I asked him what was the matter, he answered: 'Why, nothing, just a tickling in my throat.'

'The Madeira's good,' he remarked, 'give me some more.'

Meanwhile, the poison continued to have no effect, and the *staretz* went on walking calmly about the room.

I picked up another glass containing cyanide, filled it with wine and handed it to Rasputin.

He drank it as he had the others, and still with no result.

There remained only one poisoned glass on the tray. Then, as I was feeling desperate, and must try to make him do as I did, I began drinking myself.

A silence fell upon us as we sat facing each other.

He looked at me; there was a malicious expression in his eyes, as if to say: 'Now, see, you're wasting your time, you can't do anything to me.'

Suddenly his expression changed to one of fierce anger; I had never seen him look so terrifying. He fixed his fiendish eyes on me, and at that moment I was filled with such hatred that I wanted to leap at him and strangle him with my bare hands.

The silence became ominous. I had the feeling that he knew why I had brought him to my house, and what I had set out to do. We seemed to be engaged in a strange and terrible struggle. Another moment and I would have been beaten, annihilated. Under Rasputin's heavy gaze, I felt all my self-possession leaving me; an indescribable numbness came over me, my head swam ...

When I came to myself, he was still seated in the same place, his head in his hands. I could not see his eyes. I had got back my self-control, and offered him another cup of tea.

'Pour me a cup,' he said in a muffled voice, 'I'm very thirsty.' He raised his head, his eyes were dull and I thought he avoided looking at me.

While I poured the tea, he rose and began walking up and down. Catching sight of my guitar which I had left lying on a chair, he said: 'Play something cheerful, I like listening to your singing.'

I found it difficult to sing anything at such a moment, especially anything cheerful. 'I really don't feel up to it,' I said. However, I took the guitar and sang a sad Russian ditty.

He sat down and at first listened attentively; then his head drooped and his eyes closed. I thought he was dozing. When I finished the song, he opened his eyes and looked gloomily at me: 'Sing another. I'm very fond of this kind of music and you put so much soul into it.'

I sang once more but did not recognize my own voice.

Time went by; the clock said two-thirty ... the nightmare had lasted two interminable hours. What would happen, I thought, if I had lost my nerve?

Upstairs my friends were evidently growing impatient, to judge by the racket they made. I was afraid that they might be unable to bear the suspense any longer and just come bursting in.

Rasputin raised his head: 'What's all that noise?'

'Probably the guests leaving,' I answered. 'I'll go and see what's up.'

In my study, Dmitri, Purishkevich and Soukhotin rushed at me, and plied me with questions.

'Well, have you done it? Is it over?'

Purishkevich   Yusupov silently entered the study, pale and upset. 'No,' he said, 'it's not possible. Can you imagine, he's had two goblets of poison, he's eaten several pink cakes, and as you can see nothing has happened, absolutely nothing, and at least fifteen minutes have gone by since then. He is now sitting on the sofa looking sombre, and as far as I can see the only effect the poison has had on him is to make him belch the whole time and dribble.

'Gentlemen, what do you advise me to do?'

'Well then,' replied the grand duke, 'let's leave it for today and let him go in peace, maybe we can get rid of him some other way, another time and in different circumstances.'

'Never!' I exclaimed. 'Can't you understand, your highness, that if we miss him today he will be out of our reach for ever, do you really think he'll come back to Yusupov tomorrow once he realizes he has been deceived today? Rasputin cannot and must not leave here alive,' I added in a half-whisper, emphasizing every word.

'But how?' asked Dmitri Pavlovich.

'If poison doesn't work,' I replied, 'we'll have to go for broke and show our hand, we can either all go down together, or let me do it alone, I'll either dispatch him with my *sauvage* or smash his skull in with my knuckle-duster. What do you say?'

'Well, yes,' replied Yusupov, 'if you put it that way then of course we will have to resort to one of those two methods.'

'Would you mind very much if I shot him, come what may? It will be quicker and easier.'

'By all means,' I replied. 'It's not a question of who kills him, but of making sure he's killed tonight.'

No sooner had I said these words, than Yusupov crossed over to his writing desk with a determined air and, taking out of the drawer a small format Browning, turned and went downstairs with a firm step.

Yusupov   I took Dmitri's revolver and went back to the basement.

Rasputin was where I had left him; his head drooping and his breathing laboured. I went up quietly and sat down by him, but he paid no attention to me. After a few minutes of horrible silence, he slowly lifted his head and turned vacant eyes in my direction.

'Are you feeling ill?' I asked.

'Yes, my head is heavy and I've a burning sensation in my stomach. Give me another little glass of wine. It'll do me good.'

I handed him some Madeira; he drank it at a gulp; it revived him and he recovered his spirits. I saw that he was himself again and that his brain was functioning quite normally. Suddenly he suggested that we should go to the gypsies together. I refused, giving the lateness of the hour as an excuse.

I turned my head and saw the crystal crucifix. I rose to look at it more closely.

'What are you staring at that crucifix for,' asked Rasputin.

'I like it,' I replied, 'it's so beautiful.'

Rasputin stood before me motionless, his head bent and his eyes on the crucifix. I slowly raised the revolver. Where should I aim, at the temple or at the heart?

A shudder swept over me; my arm grew rigid, I aimed at his heart and pulled the trigger. Rasputin gave a wild scream and crumpled up on the bearskin.

For a moment I was appalled to discover how easy it was to kill a man. A flick of the finger and what had been a living, breathing man only a second before, now lay on the floor like a broken doll.

On hearing the shot my friends rushed in, but in their frantic haste they brushed against the switch and turned out the light. Someone bumped into me and cried out; I stood motionless for fear of treading on the body. At last, someone turned the light on.

Purishkevich Without waiting a second, those of us who had been standing upstairs literally flew head over heels down the banisters, falling in our haste against the dining room door: it opened, but one of us must have pushed the electric switch, for the light in the room immediately went out.

Feeling along the wall by the entrance we put on the light and the following spectacle appeared before our eyes:

In front of the sofa in the seating area, on a white bear skin, lay the dying Grigory Rasputin, and over him, holding the revolver behind his back in his right hand, stood Yusupov, completely calm, looking into the face of the murdered *staretz* with an expression of indescribable loathing.

Yusupov Rasputin lay on his back. His features twitched in nervous spasms; his hands were clenched, his eyes closed. A bloodstain was spreading on his silk blouse. A few moments later all movement ceased. We bent over his body to examine it.

The doctor declared that the bullet had struck him in the region of the heart. There was no possibility of doubt: Rasputin was dead. Dmitri and Purishkevich lifted him from the bearskin and laid him on the flag-stones.

Purishkevich Dmitri Pavlovich took the victim by the shoulders, I lifted him by the legs, and we carefully laid him on the floor, his feet towards the outside windows and his head towards the stairs by which we had come in.

Now as I stood over the body, I was seized by the most powerful and diverse emotions: but the main one, as I remember now, was a feeling of the greatest amazement that such a seemingly ordinary and disgusting peasant, this Silenus or Satyr, could have such an influence on the fate of Russia and on the life of a great nation, whose country comprised a whole section of the globe, rather than a realm. How did you manage to bewitch both the Tsar and the Tsarina, you scoundrel? – I thought.

He was not yet dead: he was breathing, agonizing.

With his right hand, he had covered his eyes and half of his long, pitted nose; his left hand lay along his body; his chest rose occasionally and his body shuddered. He was stylishly dressed, peasant style, in magnificent boots, velvet breeches and a richly embroidered cream silk shirt, fastened with a thick, crimson, tassled silk belt. His long black beard was carefully brushed and seemed even to shine or gleam with some product.

I don't know how long I stood there: finally Yusupov's voice rang out. 'Well, gentlemen, let's go upstairs and finish what we have begun.' We left the dining room, putting off the light and pulling the door slightly to.

Yusupov Our hearts were full of hope, for we were convinced that what had just taken place would save Russia and the dynasty from ruin and dishonour.

As we talked I was suddenly filled with a vague misgiving; an irresistible impulse forced me to go down to the basement.

Rasputin lay exactly where we had left him. I felt his pulse: not a beat, he was dead.

Scarcely knowing what I was doing I seized the corpse by the arms and shook it violently. It leaned to one side and fell back. I was just about to go, when I suddenly noticed an almost imperceptible quivering of his left eyelid. I bent over and watched him closely; slight tremors contracted his face.

All of a sudden, I saw the left eye open ... A few seconds later his right eyelid began to quiver, then opened. I then saw both eyes – the green eyes of a viper – staring at me with an expression of diabolical hatred. The blood ran cold in my veins. My muscles turned to stone.

I wanted to run away, to call for help, but my legs refused to obey me and not a sound came from my throat.

Then a terrible thing happened: with a sudden violent effort Rasputin leapt to his feet, foaming at the mouth. A wild roar echoed through the vaulted rooms, and his hands convulsively thrashed the air. He rushed at me, trying to get at my throat, and sank his fingers into my shoulder like steel claws. His eyes were bursting from their sockets, blood oozed from his lips. And all the time he called me by name, in a low raucous voice.

No words can express the horror I felt. I tried to free myself but was powerless in his vice-like grip. A ferocious struggle began ...

This devil who was dying of poison, who had a bullet in his heart, must have been raised from the dead by the powers of evil. There was something appalling and monstrous in his diabolical refusal to die.

I realized now who Rasputin really was. It was the reincarnation of Satan himself who held me in his clutches and would never let me go till my dying day.

By a superhuman effort I succeeded in freeing myself from his grasp.

He fell on his back, gasping horribly and still holding in his hand the epaulette he had torn from my tunic during our struggle. For a while he lay motionless on the ground. Then after a few seconds, he moved. I rushed upstairs and called Purishkevich, who was in my study.

Purishkevich I heard someone's footsteps at the foot of the stairs, then the sound of the door opening to the dining room where Rasputin was lying, which evidently whoever came out did not close.

'Who on earth could that be?' I thought, but I hardly had time to think of an answer when a wild, inhuman shriek rang out, which seemed to me to be the voice of Yusupov. 'Purishkevich, shoot, shoot, he's alive! He's getting away!'

'A-a-h.' Yusupov appeared and rushed straight upstairs, still screaming; he looked simply ghastly; his handsome big blue eyes bulged and looked even larger than usual; he seemed to be only half-conscious, hardly seeing me, and with a mad look rushed to the door to the main corridor and ran to his parents' apartments.

There was not a moment to be lost and, without losing my composure, I took my *sauvage* out of my pocket, set it to 'fire' and ran downstairs.

What I saw downstairs could have been a dream, had it not been a terrible reality: Grigory Rasputin, whom I had seen half an hour ago breathing his last on the stone floor of the dining room, was running through the light snow of the palace courtyard along the railings leading to the street, falling from side to side, in the very same clothes I had seen him in almost lifeless.

For the first minute I could not believe my eyes, but his loud cries as he ran through the stillness of the night:

'Felix, Felix, I will tell everything to the tsarina! ...' convinced me that it really was him, Grigory Rasputin, that he could walk thanks to his phenomenal vitality, that in a few moments he would be through the gates into the street where, without giving away his identity, he could turn to the first passer-by and ask them to save him, as people were trying to kill him in that palace ... and all would be lost, we would be discovered. I rushed in pursuit and fired.

In the quiet of the night the deafening noise of my revolver carried through the air – missed.

Rasputin went faster; I fired a second time at a run – and again missed.

I cannot express the feeling of rage I felt against myself at that moment. The proficient marksman, who practised the whole time on Semenovsky parade ground with small targets, today seemed incapable of shooting a man at 20 paces. The moments passed ... Rasputin was already at the gates, when I stopped and bit myself hard on the left wrist, to force myself to concentrate, and this third time hit him in the back.

He stopped; carefully taking aim I fired a fourth time, apparently hitting him in the head, for he collapsed face down onto the ground in the snow, tearing at his head. I ran up to him and kicked him as hard as I could in the temple.

He was lying with his hands stretched out in front of him, clawing at the snow as if he wanted to crawl forward on his stomach; but he was already unable to move and just lay there grinding and gnashing his teeth.

I was certain now that his time was up, that he would not get to his feet again. I stood over him for a moment or two to satisfy myself there was no longer any point in guarding him, and then crossed quickly back into the palace through the same little door, but I remembered clearly that in the interval between the shots two men had passed along the pavement in the street, one of whom rushed over to the railings upon hearing gunfire.

'What to do? What to do?' I repeated to myself out loud, going into the drawing room. I'm alone. Yusupov is out of action; the servants have not been initiated into the affair, and the corpse is lying there by the gates ...

Once I had found out where Yusupov was, I went to try and calm
him down.

I found him in a brightly lit bathroom bending over the basin,
holding his head and retching.

'Dearest one! What is it, calm yourself, he is no more! I've finished
him off! Come with me, dear, let's go to your study.'

Visibly still feeling sick, Yusupov fixed me with a vacant look, but
obeyed, and taking him by the waist I carefully led him back to his
apartments. As he was walking he kept repeating: 'Felix, Felix, Felix,
Felix.'

It was obvious that something had happened between him and
Rasputin during those short moments when he had gone to the
apparently dead man in the dining room, and that something had
deeply affected his mind.

We passed through the lobby at the very moment when downstairs
Yusupov's soldiers were dragging the corpse into the hall by the
stairs.

Yusupov I felt very ill, my head swam and I could scarcely walk. I
rose with difficulty, automatically picked up my rubber club, and left
the study.

As I reached the top of the stairs, I saw Rasputin stretched out on
the landing, blood flowing from his many wounds. It was a loathsome sight. Suddenly, everything went black, I felt the ground slipping from under my feet ...

Purishkevich Slipping away from me, Yusupov dashed into the
study, snatched from the desk a rubber dumb-bell, and rushed back
downstairs towards Rasputin's body.

For having poisoned him and seen the poison have no effect, shot
him and seen the bullet did nothing – he obviously couldn't believe
that Rasputin was really dead, and now began to beat him around
the temples as hard as he could with the two-pound weight, in an
unbelievable state of frenzy and wild rage.

From my position at the top of the stairs, I did not at first understand and was even more dumbfounded when, to my greatest amazement, Rasputin still appeared, even now, to display signs of life.

Turned over face upwards, he was rasping, and I saw quite clearly
from upstairs how the pupil of his open right eye rolled as if looking
at me, uncomprehending yet terrifying (even now I can see that eye
before me).

Regaining my senses I shouted to the soldiers to pull Yusupov off the dying man, as he could splash himself and everything around with blood and in the case of an investigation the authorities would uncover the truth, even without police dogs, by the traces.

The soldiers obeyed, but it took an immense effort to drag off Yusupov, who was still beating Rasputin about the head, mechanically but with ever increasing ferocity. Finally they pulled the prince aside.

Together, the two soldiers led him upstairs by the arms and sat him down, covered in blood, on the deep leather sofa in the study. He was an appalling sight, not only was his exterior appearance terrible, but also his inner state, as he repeated inanely 'Felix, Felix, Felix, Felix' with a vacant stare and twitching face.

I ordered the soldiers to obtain some material quickly from somewhere and to wrap the corpse in it completely from head to toe and bind it tightly with rope.

The body was completely wrapped in some sort of blue material; it even seemed to me it might be a curtain, tightly bound with rope. The head was covered. Now I saw that Rasputin was indeed a corpse and could no longer come to life.

Five minutes later I heard a car, and the grand duke and his companions quickly came up the stairs from the courtyard.

Dmitri Pavlovich was in an almost light-hearted mood; but when he saw me he understood that something had happened.

'What's happened?' he asked, glancing around, and I explained the situation to them briefly, asking them to hurry, though this last request proved to be unnecessary: they themselves understood that there wasn't a moment to lose and leaving Yusupov in the care of one of his soldiers, we dragged Rasputin's body into the grand duke's car, where we added two two-pound weights and some chains I had brought that night to Yusupov's apartment and, getting in, we drove to the place we had chosen for drowning the corpse of the victim.

The grand duke was driving.

The car drove fairly slowly through the town. It was very late and the grand duke was obviously concerned about arousing the suspicions of the police by going too fast. The car windows were wound down. The clear, frosty air was vivifying. I was completely calm, despite everything I had been through.

I looked out of the window. We were already beyond the town, judging by the surrounding houses and the endless fences. The lighting was very dim. The road became worse, we went over potholes and each time the body at our feet jumped, despite being sat on by the soldier, and I experienced a nervous shiver at every bump as my knee touched the soft, repulsive corpse which was not yet quite cold despite the frost.

At last in the distance appeared the bridge from which we were to throw Rasputin's body under the ice.

Dmitri Pavlovich slowed down, drove onto the bridge from the left and stopped by the parapet.

For one moment the bright headlights shone onto the guard hut on the right side of the bridge, but the grand duke immediately extinguished them and the surroundings were in darkness. The car motor continued to throb on the bridge.

Opening the car door silently and as quickly as possible, I jumped out and went over to the parapet, followed by the soldier and Dr Lazavert; we were joined by lieutenant S who had been sitting next to the grand duke, and the four of us (Dmitri Pavlovich was standing guard by the car) dragged out Rasputin's body and threw it through the broken ice under the bridge: we had forgotten to attach the weights to the corpse with the chains, so we hurriedly threw them in too, while we stuffed the chains into the victim's coat and threw that into the same hole. Dr Lazavert felt round the car in the dark and found one of Rasputin's boots, which he also hurled from the bridge.

It all took only two or three minutes, after which Dr Lazavert, lieutenant S and the soldier got into the back, while I sat with Dmitri Pavlovich, we put on the headlights and drove on over the bridge.

That we weren't seen on the bridge seems to me to this day to be quite unbelievable. This was the sequence of events from the evening of the 16th December to the morning of the 17th.

It's getting light. I am writing these lines with the first rays of a dawning winter's day. It's still dark, though I feel the day is near. I cannot sleep.

*　*　*

Ania Vyrubova, Memoirs

The next morning soon after breakfast I was called on the telephone by one of the daughters of Rasputin, both of whom were being educated in Petrograd.

In some anxiety the young girl told me that her father had gone out the night before in the Yusupov motor car and had not returned. I was startled, of course, and even a little frightened, but I did not then guess the real significance of her news.

When I reached the palace I gave the message to the Empress, who listened with a grave face but with little comment. A few minutes later there came a telephone call from Protopopov in Petrograd.

The police, he said, had reported to him that some time after the last midnight a patrolman standing near the entrance of the Yusupov Palace had been startled by the report of a pistol. Ringing the door-bell, he was met by a Duma member named Purishkevich who appeared to be in an advanced state of intoxication.

In answer to the policeman's inquiry as to whether there was trouble in the house the drunken Purishkevich said in a jocular tone that it was nothing, nothing at all, only they had just killed Rasputin. The policeman, probably a none too intelligent specimen, took it as a casual joke of one of the high-born. They were always joking about Rasputin.

Later in the day, however, came a telephone message from Grand Duke Dmitri Pavlovich, asking to be allowed to take tea with the Empress that afternoon at five. The message was conveyed to the Empress, who, pale and reflective, answered formally that she did not care just then to receive his Highness.

Dmitri took the reply in bad grace, insisting that he must see the Empress as he had something special to tell her. Again the Empress refused, this time even more curtly.

Almost immediately afterwards, almost as if the two men were in the same room [they were], there came a telephone message from Felix Yusupov. Felix demanded an audience with the Empress that he might give her a true account of what had occurred. Her Majesty's reply was: 'If Felix has anything to say let him write to me.' Several times before the day ended telephone messages came from Felix to me, but none of these would the Empress allow me to answer.

Felix finally wrote a letter to the Empress. I cannot quote this letter verbatim, but I remember exactly its contents. By the honour of his house Prince Felix Yusupov swore to his Sovereign Empress that the rumour of Rasputin's visit to his home was without foundation whatever.

He had indeed seen Rasputin in the interests of Irina's health, but he had never decoyed the man to his palace, as charged. There had been a party there, on the night in question, just a few friends, including Dmitri, to celebrate the opening of Felix's new apartments. All, he confessed, became drunk, and some foolish and reckless things were said and done.

By chance, on leaving the house, one of the guests had shot a dog in the courtyard. That was absolutely all. This letter was not answered, but was turned over to the Minister of Justice.

Purishkevich – 17 December

S. relayed to me Dmitri Pavlovich's request to go immediately to his palace. I got into the car and we set off.

At the palace I found Yusupov as well as our host, both in a state of great agitation, drinking cup after cup of black coffee and cognac, as they explained they hadn't been to bed at all that night, and had spent a very tense day as the Empress already knew about the disappearance and possible death of Rasputin and was accusing us of his murder.

Fräulein Golovin, Rasputin's secretary, had revealed where Grigory went in the evening, and the whole of the police and special services had already been mobilized to find the body and unravel all the strands of the affair.

'Because of that monster,' remarked Yusupov, 'I had to shoot one of my best dogs and lay it out in the courtyard where the snow was stained by the blood of your murdered *staretz* ... I did it in case our Sherlock Holmeses find a first lead to Rasputin's disappearance and decide to analyse the blood or resort to police dogs. I spent the whole of the rest of the night with my soldiers tidying up the house,' he concluded, 'and now as you can see, Dmitri Pavlovich and I are composing a letter to the Empress which we hope to deliver to her today.'

I helped in the drafting of the letter, which we finished an hour and a half after my arrival.

When the letter was signed and sealed, Dmitri Pavlovich left the study to have it delivered, although we all three felt a certain degree of embarrassment as everything we had written in the letter was a skilful fabrication and cast us in the role of unfairly outraged virtue.

Taking advantage of his absence, I asked Yusupov: 'Tell me, prince, what happened between you and Rasputin in those few moments when you went down to the dining room for the last time, when as you remember we had seemingly left him at his last breath on the cold floor?'

Yusupov smiled hopelessly: 'What happened then I will never forget for the whole of my life. When I went in to the dining room, I found Rasputin in the same position, I took his hand to feel for a pulse. It seemed to me there was none and when I placed my hand on his heart that wasn't beating either. But then, imagine my horror, Rasputin suddenly opened up one of his satanic eyes, then the other, fixed me with a look of indescribable intensity and hatred, then with the words "Felix! Felix! Felix!" suddenly jumped up and tried to grab me, I quickly dodged out of the way as best I could and then – I don't remember any more.'

Sandro, Memoirs
I knew Alix would see in Rasputin's assassination a thrust at herself
and at her policies. Suspicious and hysterical, she would crave
revenge and would fight harder than ever for the ministers put in
their positions by the alleged 'saviour' of her son.

Felix and Grand Duke Dmitri showed themselves poor tacticians.
Too young to understand the soul of an offended woman, they had
played straight into the hands of the Rasputin crowd. Rasputin alive
was just a man, known to everybody as a drunken peasant reaching
for money. Rasputin dead stood a chance of becoming a slaughtered
prophet.

He had always threatened that the imperial family and Russia
would follow him to his grave, should anyone make an attempt
against his life. I laughed at his black-mailing prophecies but I
visualized the despair of superstitious Alix who took his words for
Gospel-truth.

I found my mother-in-law [Empress Marie] still in her bedroom
and was the first to tell her of the latest sensation.

She jumped up: 'No! No!'

Whenever she heard something alarming she expressed her
anguish and stupefaction in that half-interrogating, half-exclama-
tory 'No!'

Her reaction was similar to mine: the Lord be praised for taking
away Rasputin, but we were in for a much greater trouble. The idea
of her granddaughter's husband Felix and her nephew Dmitri stoop-
ing to murder caused her pain.

As an Empress she was horrified; as a Christian she was opposed to
the shedding of blood, no matter what noble considerations had
prompted the culprits. We agreed I should wire Nicky for permission
to go to St Petersburg. The affirmative answer arrived from Tsarskoe
Selo: Nicky had left the Stavka in the early morning, rushing to the
side of his wife.

Olga [sister], Memoirs
I never interfered, either with advice or criticism. I knew little or
nothing of purely political matters, and the rest was their own affair.
But look at the family!

My mother and Aunt Ella alone had Nicky's interests really at heart
– but neither my mother nor my aunt knew all the details as they
were. They, too, had based their judgements on rumours. Yet at least
they were quite sincerely anxious. All the others began coming to

Tsarskoe Selo to give uncalled-for advice, to utter violently worded warnings, even to make scenes.

Some even thought that Alicky should be sent to a convent. Nicky's young cousin, Dmitri, with some friends of his, gave full support to a vile conspiracy. There was just nothing heroic about Rasputin's murder ... Trotsky said [of] it – that it 'was carried out in the manner of a scenario designed for people of bad taste'. You could hardly call Trotsky a champion of the monarchy. It was a murder premeditated most vilely.

Just think of the two names most closely associated with it even to this day – a Grand Duke, one of the grandsons of the Tsar Liberator, and the scion of one of our great houses, whose wife was a Grand Duke's daughter. That proved how low we had fallen!

Pierre Gilliard, Memoirs

Suddenly the news of Rasputin's death fell like a thunder bolt. The same day we left for Tsarskoe Selo.

I shall never forget what I felt when I saw the Tsarina again. Her agonized features betrayed, in spite of all her efforts, how terribly she was suffering. Her grief was inconsolable. Her idol had been shattered. He who alone could save her son had been slain.

Now that he had gone, any misfortune, any catastrophe, was possible. The period of waiting began – the dreadful waiting for the disaster which there was no escaping.

A. A. Mordvinov, Memoirs

It is painful for me to remember that particular evening in the Alexander Palace, in December 1916, almost immediately after the murder of Rasputin, and which I spent on duty with the Grand Duchesses.

There upstairs, in one of their modest bedrooms, the four of them sat on the sofa, huddled up closely together.

They were cold and visibly terribly upset, but for the whole of that long evening, the name of Rasputin was never uttered in front of me.

They were in pain, because the man was no longer among the living, but also because they evidently sensed that, with his murder, something terrible and undeserved had started for their mother, their father and themselves, and that it was moving relentlessly towards them.

I tried as best I could to dispel their gloomy mood, but almost without success ... The stormy sea of political passions, calumnies, posturing and the most decisive threats, had now in reality come too close to this flowering, monastic little haven.

Maurice Paléologue, Memoirs – 18 December

Rasputin's corpse has not yet been found. The Empress is stricken with grief. She has begged the Emperor, who is at Mogilev, to return to her at once.

It is confirmed that the murderers are Prince Felix Yusupov, the Grand Duke Dmitri and Purishkevich. There was no lady present at supper. If so, how was Rasputin enticed to the Yusupov palace?

Judging by the little I know, it is the presence of Purishkevich which gives the drama its real meaning and high political interest. The Grand Duke Dmitri is a young man about town of twenty-five, active, a fervent patriot and capable of courage in the hour of battle, but flighty and impulsive; it seems to me he plunged blindly into this adventure. Prince Felix Yusupov is twenty-nine and gifted with quick wits and aesthetic tastes; but his dilettantism is rather too prone to perverse imaginings and literary representations of vice and death, so I am afraid that he has regarded the murder of Rasputin mainly as a scenario worthy of his favourite author, Oscar Wilde. In any case his instincts, countenance and manner make him much closer akin to the hero of Dorian Grey than to Brutus ...

On the other hand, Purishkevich, who is over fifty, is a man of doctrine and action. He has made himself the champion of orthodox absolutism; he brings equal vehemence and skill to his advocacy of the theory of the 'Tsar Autocrat, God's Emissary'.

In 1905 he was the president of the famous reactionary league, the Association of the Russian People, and he it was who inspired and directed the terrible pogroms against the Jews. His participation in the murder of Rasputin throws light on the whole attitude of the Extreme Right in the last few months; it means that the champions of autocracy, feeling themselves threatened by the Empress's madness, are determined to defend themselves in spite of the Emperor; and if necessary *against* him.

Andrei Vladimirovich, Diary – 19 December

Kyril, Gavril and I went to Dmitri, to tell him that, without going into details about whether or not he was guilty of the murder of Rasputin, we were all behind him and he could count on us.

Whatever happened – we would be for him. Dmitri was very touched and grateful for our moral support, however he solemnly declared that on the famous night he had not seen Rasputin, nor had he soiled his hands with his blood.

In order to demonstrate that he was not involved in the affair, he recounted the following: on December 16th he had supper with Felix Yusupov at his house, in the flat giving out onto the garden. At about 3 o'clock he left the house with two ladies, and in the yard he was set upon by a dog, which he shot with his browning. He accompanied the ladies back to Caravannaya street, and then returned home. He didn't know anything more about the matter.

Felix Yusupov said on the subject of his friendship with Rasputin, which was interesting from the point of view of studying his psychology, that after one recent conversation, during which he talked disrespectfully and vulgarly about Papa and Alix, he stopped going to see him.

After that, Dmitri told us what happened when he was arrested. On the morning of December 18th, he was telephoned by Adjutant-General Maximovich[16] who told him the following: 'Your Imperial Highness, what I am obliged to tell you will come as a great blow to you, for the moment I must ask you not to leave your house and to wait for me.' Then he arrived and informed Dmitri that he had received an order over the telephone from Alix to place him under house arrest.

Although, Maximovich admitted, he did not have the right to do so without an order from the Emperor, he nevertheless asked him to stay at home, for his own safety. So that, in fact, Dmitri was arrested by order of Alix.

Maurice Paléologue, Memoirs – 20 December

Rasputin's corpse was discovered yesterday in the ice of the little Nevka, alongside Krestovsky Island and near the Bielosselsky Palace.

Up to the last moment the Empress has been hoping that 'God would spare her her comforter and only friend.'

The police are not allowing any details of the drama to be published. Besides, the *Okhrana* is pursuing its enquiries in such secrecy that even this morning Trepov, the President of the Council, replied to the impatient questions of the Grand Duke Nikolai Mikhailovich:

'Monsieur, I swear to you that I have nothing whatever to do with what is going on, and know nothing of the enquiry.'

---

[16] Assistant-Commander at Headquarters.

There was great rejoicing among the public when it heard of the death of Rasputin the day before yesterday. People kissed each other in the streets and many went to burn candles in Our Lady of Kazan.

When it was known that the Grand Duke Dmitri was one of the assassins there was a crush to light candles before the ikons of Saint Dmitri.

The murder of Grigory is the sole topic of conversation among the unending queues of women who wait in the snow and wind at the doors of butchers and grocers to secure their share of meat, tea, sugar, etc. They are saying that Rasputin was thrown into the Nevka alive, and approvingly quoting the proverb:

'A dog's death for a dog!' They are also whispering that the Grand Duchess Tatiana, the Emperor's second daughter, witnessed the drama disguised as a lieutentant of the Chevaliers-Gardes, so that she could revenge herself on Rasputin who had tried to violate her.

And carrying the vindictive ferocity of the *moujik* into the world of the Court, they add that to satiate her thirst for vengeance the dying Grigory was castrated before her eyes.

Another popular story is this: 'Rasputin was still breathing when he was thrown under the ice of the Nevka. It is very important, for if so he will never become a saint.' It is a fact that the Russian masses believe that the drowned can never be canonized.

Nicky to Pavel – 20 December – Tsarskoe Selo
Dear Uncle Pavel

I am unfortunately unable to lift Dmitri's house arrest until the end of the preliminary investigation. I have ordered that this be hurried up, also that Dmitri should be looked after with care.

This is all so painful and sad, yet who is to blame if not he himself, for being imprudent enough to get into such a mess?

I pray God that Dmitri will emerge clean and unblemished by anything.

Sincerely yours,

Nicky

Maurice Paléologue, Memoirs – 20 December
As soon as Rasputin's body was taken from the Nevka it was conveyed with much mystery to the Tchesma Veterans' Home, five kilometres from Petrograd on the Tsarskoe Selo road.

After Professor Kossorotov had made an examination of the body and noted the marks of the wounds, Sister Akulina, the young nun whom Rasputin knew in the old days at the nunnery of Okhtai where he exorcized her, was brought into the room where the autopsy was performed. Armed with an order from the Empress she proceeded to lay out the body, assisted solely by a hospital orderly. No one else has been admitted to the presence of the dead man: his wife and daughters, and even his most fervent disciples, have pleaded in vain for permission to see him for the last time.

The pious Akulina, once possessed by the Evil One, spent half the night in washing the body, embalming its wounds, dressing it in new garments and laying it in the coffin. She ended up by placing a crucifix on the breast and putting a letter from the Empress into the dead man's hands. This is the wording of the letter, as reported to me by Madame T.

My dear martyr, give me thy blessing, that it may follow me always on the sad and dreary path I have yet to traverse here below. And remember us from on high in your holy prayers!

ALEXANDRA

The next morning, which was yesterday, the Empress and Madame Vyrubova came to pray over the corpse of their friend, which they smothered with flowers, ikons and tears.

Has the great dramatist of History conceived many episodes more pathetic than this baneful Tsarina and her pernicious companion, weeping over the swelling corpse of the lustful *moujik* whom they loved so madly and Russia will curse for centuries?

About midnight the coffin was conveyed to Tsarskoe Selo in charge of Madame Golovin and Colonel Loman, and then laid in a chapel of the imperial park.

Andrei Vladimirovich, Diary – 21 December
The following people met at my house: Mama [Maria Pavlovna, the elder], Uncle Pavel, Kyril, Boris and later Sandro.

We met at the suggestion of uncle Pavel, who wanted to inform us of the following: on 19th December he had been to see Nicky at 11 o'clock at night, and had asked by what right Alix had ordered Dmitri's arrest. Nicky replied that the order had been his, but here it is necessary to note some discrepency in the facts.

If the order had come from Nicky, he would have issued it directly to Maximovich. If Alix had received a telegram from Nicky, she would have said as much to Maximovich, and would not have asked him to do her a personal favour, as Maximovich pointed out to Prince Vassilchikov today.

This is the way Nicky covered up for Alix. On the question of releasing Dmitri, he said he was unable to give an answer at present, but would send one tomorrow morning. And indeed, the next morning uncle Pavel received the following letter from Nicky, which he read out to us:

'I am unable to lift Dmitri's house arrest until the end of the investigation. I pray God that Dmitri will emerge unblemished from an affair into which he has been dragged by his impetuosity.'

Then uncle Pavel recounted his meeting with Dmitri, and how he swore, both on an icon and on the portrait of his mother, that he had not sullied his hands with the blood of that man. The aim of the meeting, was to decide whether or not to send Nicky the reply he had prepared, and he read out a letter which we all approved.

Then Sandro arrived, and we discussed what we would do if Nicky did not have Dmitri released and pursued the inquiry until the end. We decided that uncle Pavel would then go to Nicky and show him the danger of the situation, which is as follows:

By the very fact of Dmitri's arrest, his participation in Rasputin's murder has been demonstrated for the whole of Russia to see. And the death of Rasputin has been welcomed throughout Russia, with the rejoicing going as far as hymns being sung in theatres, people kissing on the streets etc.

In fact the names of Yusupov and Dmitri are on everyone's lips and they are national heroes for having liberated Russia from a nightmare of filth. The more Dmitri is persecuted, the higher he will be elevated, and this will incite the whole of Russia against Tsarskoe Selo, including the army, who will be behind Dmitri to a man.

Maria Pavlovna [the younger], Memoirs

This uncertainty affected Dmitri quite differently than it did Yusupov. The popularity that his name enjoyed gave him no satisfaction; on the contrary, it frightened him; and he also was frightened by the gathering consequences of the murder, so entirely opposite to those he had expected.

Yusupov spoke at length, yet not without nervousness, of his absolute assurance that neither of them would be touched. He believed in his lucky star and counted upon the protection of public opinion.

Against that opinion, he held, the court would never proceed openly.

Ania Vyrubova, Memoirs

The coffin, accompanied by a kind-hearted sister of mercy, arrived at Tsarskoe. The same day the Emperor came home from the front, and in the presence of the Imperial Family and myself the briefest of services were held. On the dead man's breast had been laid an ikon from Novgorod, signed on the reverse by the Empress and her daughters as a last token of respect.

The coffin was not even buried in consecrated ground, but in a corner of the palace park, and as it was being lowered a few prayers were said by Father Alexander, priest of the Imperial chapel. This is a true account of the burial of Rasputin, about which so many fantastic tales have been embroidered.

The horror and shock caused by this lynching, for it can be called by no other name, completely shattered the nerves of the family.

The Emperor was affected less by the deed itself than by the fact that it was the work of members of his own family.

'Before all Russia,' he exclaimed, 'I am filled with shame that the hands of my kinsmen are stained with the blood of a simple peasant.'

Before this he had often shown disgust at the excesses of the Grand Dukes and their followers, but now he expressed himself as being entirely through with them all.

Nicky, Diary – 21 December – Tsarskoe Selo

At 9 o'clock the whole Family went out past the photography building and right into the field, where we witnessed a sad spectacle: the coffin with the body of unforgettable Grigory, who was killed by some scum on the night of Dec. 17th at Yusupov's house, which had already been lowered into the grave.

Father Alexander Vasilev read the liturgy, after which we returned home. The weather was grey with 12 degrees of frost. In the afternoon went for a walk until the reports. Received Shakhovsky and Ignatiev. In the afternoon went for a walk with the children.

Andrei Vladimirovich, Diary – 22 December

According to the rumours, Rasputin was buried yesterday night at 3 a.m. at Tsarskoe Selo, in the presence of Nicky, Alix, their daughters (except Olga), Protopopov, Pitirim and Ania Vyrubova, next to the shelter, where they are intending to erect a church over his grave.

It's so touching, further comment is superfluous.

Maurice Paléologue, Memoirs – 23 December

To throw public curiosity and surmise off the scent, the *Okhrana* is spreading a rumour that Rasputin's coffin has been conveyed to his native village of Pokrovskoe, near Tobolsk, or to a monastery in the Urals.

As a matter of fact, the obsequies were celebrated with the greatest secrecy at Tsarskoe Selo last night.

The coffin was buried in a plot of ground which Madame Vyrubova and two Moscow merchants bought recently on the edge of the imperial park, near Alexandrovka, with a view to building a chapel and almshouses upon it. About a month ago Monsignor Pitirim came to give this piece of land his official blessing.

The only persons present at the interment were the Emperor, the Empress, the four young Grand Duchesses, Protopopov, Madame Vyrubova, Colonels Loman and Maltzev and the officiating priest, Father Vasilev, arch-priest of the Court.

The Empress had secured possession of the blood-stained blouse of the 'martyr Grigoir' and is preserving it piously as a relic, a *palladium* on which the fate of her dynasty hangs.

Several Grand Dukes, among whom I am told are the three sons of the Grand Duchess Marie Pavlovna, Kyril, Boris and Andrei, are talking of nothing less than saving tsarism by a change of sovereign. With the help of four regiments of the guard, whose loyalty is said to be already shaken, there would be a night march on Tsarskoe Selo; the monarchs would be seized, the Emperor shown the necessity of abdicating and the Empress shut up in a nunnery. Then the accession of the Tsarevich Alexei would be proclaimed under the regency of the Grand Duke Nikolai Nikolaevich.

The promoters of this scheme think that the Grand Duke Dmitri, by his share in the murder of Rasputin, is marked out by fate to direct the plot and win over the troops. His cousins, Kyril and Andrei Vladimirovich, went to see him in his palace on the Nevsky Prospect and begged and prayed him to 'persevere relentlessly with his work of national salvation'. After a long mental conflict, Dmitri Pavlovich finally refused to 'lay his hands on the Emperor'; his last word was: 'I will not break my oath of fealty.'

Ania Vyrubova, Memoirs

Yusupov and the others were by no means through with the Rasputin affair. Now that they had murdered and were applauded for the deed by all society, it seemed to them that they were in a position to claim full legal immunity.

Grand Duke Alexander Mikhailovich [Sandro], the Emperor's brother-in-law, went to Dobrovolsky, Minister of Justice, and with a good deal of swagger told him that it was the will of the family – that is, of the Grand Dukes – that the whole matter should be quietly dropped.

The next day, December 21, Alexander Mikhailovich drove with his oldest son to Tsarskoe Selo and, without the slightest assumption of deference or respect, entered the Emperor's study, demanding, in the name of the family, that no further investigation of the manner of Rasputin's death be made. In a voice that could easily be heard in the corridor outside the Grand Duke shouted that should the Emperor refuse this demand the throne itself would fall.

Maria Pavlovna [the younger], Memoirs

Not knowing any of the details, my Aunt [Ella] sent Dmitri an enthusiastic and probably incautious wire which was brought to the attention of the Empress. As a result, she had been accused of complicity. And now, in spite of her devotion to her sister and of all her Christian feelings, my aunt's patience was at an end.

Ania Vyrubova, Memoirs

This was by no means the end of letters and telegrams seized by the police and brought to the palace. Many were written by relatives and close friends, people of the highest rank, and they all revealed a depth of callousness and treachery undreamed of before by the unhappy Sovereigns.

When the Empress read these communications and realized that her nearest and dearest connections were in the ranks of her enemies, her head sank on her breast, her eyes grew dark with sorrow, and her whole countenance seemed to wither and grow old.

A few days later the Grand Duchess [Ella] sent her sister several sacred ikons from the shrine of Saratov. The Empress, without even looking at them, ordered them sent back to the convent of the Grand Duchess in Moscow.

In the British Embassy, the Ambassador Sir George Buchanan was personally aiding the Grand Dukes to overthrow Nicholas II and to replace him by his cousin Grand Duke Kyril Vladimirovich. Sir George Buchanan's main purpose, it was said, was not so much to further the ambitions of the Grand Dukes as it was to weaken Russia as a factor in the future peace conference. Unable fully to believe that an ambassador of one of the Allied Powers would dare to meddle maliciously in the internal affairs of the Empire, the Tsar had nevertheless decided to communicate this information in a personal letter to his cousin King George of England. The Empress, deeply indignant, advised a demand on King George for the Ambassador's recall, but the Emperor replied that he dared not, at such a critical time, make public his distrust of an Ally's representative. Whether or not the Emperor ever wrote his letter to King George I never knew, but that his anxiety and depression of spirits persisted I can well testify.

Felix Yusupov, Memoirs

A plot was hatched by the Grand Dukes and several members of the aristocracy to remove the Tsarina from power and force her to retire to a convent. Everyone plotted, even the generals. As for the British Ambassador, Sir George Buchanan, his dealings with radical elements caused him to be accused by many Russians of secretly working for the Revolution.

Maria Pavlovna [the younger], Memoirs

That afternoon, around three o'clock, Laiming came to say that General Maximovich wanted to speak to Dmitri on the telephone. After a short conversation Dmitri returned, and told us that Maximovich asked him to come immediately as he had an important and urgent order to transmit.

We silently exchanged glances. The lightning had flashed. But we did not yet know where the bolt had struck.

Pale to the very lips, Dmitri ordered his car and left, accompanied by General Laiming. Yusupov and I remained alone. Our anxiety was so great that we could not even speak of it. Yusupov had now lost all his self-assurance. To still in a measure my own apprehensions I sat down at the piano and began to play the accompaniment of a gipsy song. Felix, leaning against the top of the instrument, sang in a low tone. My fingers shook.

Half an hour passed. Finally behind us the door flew open. I started and turned around. Dmitri stood on the threshold, grasping the

handle of the door. It seemed to me that his features had changed
almost beyond recognition. Felix and I looked at him in silence, not
daring to say a word. Dmitri, leaving the door, advanced into the room.

'I have received the order to leave for the Persian front, accompanied by the aide-de-camp of the Emperor appointed to watch me.
During the trip I will have no right to see or correspond with anyone.
My exact destination is not yet known,' he told us in an impassive
voice, making an effort to remain calm.

'You, Felix, are exiled to your estate in Kursk Province. The chief of
police will let us know later as to the time of departure of our trains.'

Dmitri threw his cap upon the divan and began pacing the room.
We were crestfallen. It was not the question of the punishment
which at first glance seemed very mild, as much as that of the influence which it might have upon the further course of events. All
Russia was watching to see what would be the reaction of the court
to the death of Rasputin, and its attitude towards his assassins.

The persecution of the assassins, although quite legal in its essence,
would nevertheless signify to the public the excessive devotion of the
Empress to the memory of Rasputin, confirming the worst rumours
of his influence, and demonstrate anew the helpless passivity of the
Emperor.

What, moreover, would become of Dmitri? His exile to the remote
Persian front carried with it an evident element of risk.

Felix put on his grey soldier's coat and bade us goodbye. We
embraced. Followed by his captain, Felix went down the stairs, and
the outside door shut behind him with a heavy slam.

Someone knocked at the door. It was my brother's valet with a
small, square box of unpainted wood.

'Your Highness, this has just been brought for you,' he said, as if
embarrassed.

'Give it to me; what is it?' said Dmitri.

'That's just it; I don't know what it is. I won't give it to you. I only
brought it to show you; there might be something dangerous in it ...'

'A bomb?' laughed Dmitri. 'Give it to me, I'll look.'

The valet cautiously handed him the box.

'Don't shake it, Your Highness, it might explode ... '

We examined it carefully on all sides. Dmitri took a pen-knife and
placed the blade under the top.

'No, no, Your Highness, don't do it yourself, in the name of God,'
the servant begged him fearfully. 'Let me open it.'

Dmitri shook the box at his ear and, ascertaining that it could contain nothing terrible, gave it back. The valet left and returned a few

minutes later still more embarrassed. The top had been taken off; on the bottom of the box, carefully packed with cotton-wool and tissue paper, gleamed the blue enamel of a Serbian order. This little incident distracted us for a while.

Ania Vyrubova, Memoirs

Into this troubled atmosphere a letter was brought to the Emperor by the Minister of the Interior, who had a right to seize suspicious mail matter. It was a letter written by the Princess Yusupov to the Grand Duchess Xenia, sister of the Tsar and mother of Felix Yusupov's wife.

It was a most indiscreet letter to be sent at such a time, for it was a clear admission of the guilt of all the plotters. Although as a mother (she wrote) she felt deeply her son's position, she congratulated the Grand Duchess Xenia on her husband's conduct in the affair.

Sandro, she said, had saved the whole situation, evidently meaning that his demand for the immunity for all concerned would have to be granted. *She was only sorry that the principals had not been able to bring their enterprise to the desired end.* However, there remained only the task of confining *Her.* Before the affair was finally concluded, she feared, they might send Nikolai Nikolaevich and Stana to their estates.

Sandro, Memoirs

The members of the imperial family asked me to defend Dmitri and Felix before the Emperor. I was going to do so anyway, although their ravings and cruelty nauseated me. They ran around, they conferred, they gossiped, and they wrote a silly letter to Nicky. It almost seemed that they expected the Tsar of Russia to decorate his two relatives for having committed a murder.

'You are strange, Sandro, you do not realize that Felix and Dmitri have saved Russia.'

They called me strange because I could not forget that Nicky in his quality of Supreme Protector of Justice was duty bound to punish the assassins, particularly as they happened to be members of his family.

I wished to God Nicky would greet me with severity!

Disappointment awaited me. He embraced me and talked to me with overemphasized kindness. He knew me too well not to understand that my real sympathies were entirely on his side and that only my fatherly devotion to Irina brought me to Tsarskoe Selo.

I delivered my speech for the defence, faking a tone of conviction.

I begged him not to treat Dmitri and Felix as common murderers but as misguided patriots inspired by a desire to help their country.

'A very nice speech, Sandro,' he said after a silence. 'Are you aware, however, that nobody has the right to kill, be it a grand duke or a peasant?'

Straight to the point! Nicky may not have been as much of an orator as some of his relatives but he certainly knew his A.B.C. of justice.

When I was leaving, he promised to be 'moderate' in the choice of a punishment for the two youngsters. As it happened, they were not punished at all. Dmitri was sent to the Persian front, Felix exiled to his comfortable country estate in the province of Kursk. Next day I left for Kiev travelling with Felix and Irina who had rushed from the Crimea to meet us on our way. While in their car, I learned the full and gruesome details of the crime. I wished then and I do now that Felix would some day repent and realize that no decorous explanations and no acclaim of the masses could justify a murder in the eyes of a true Christian.

King George V to Nicky – 28 December – Sandringham
My dearest Nicky,

I take this opportunity of writing to you by the Mission which I am sending to Russia. First let me offer you and Alix my loving good wishes for the New Year and I pray that it may bring us, the Allies, the blessings of a victorious peace. I know full well you will keep your promise to me to fight to the end, as we are prepared to do, whatever difficulties may confront us and whatever sacrifices it may entail ...

When the Spring comes we must attack the enemy with all our strength at the same time and I feel sure that he will not be able to resist us for long.

With best love from May. Ever my dear Nicky your most devoted cousin and friend,

Georgie

Andrei Vladimirovich, Diary – 29 December
At 2.30 the whole family gathered at Mama's to sign a collective letter to Nicky, asking that Dmitri be allowed to live in Usov or Ilinskoe instead of Persia, where any stay could prove fatal for his health because of the climate.

While everyone was talking, Ducky took me aside and asked me to tell Mama to be extremely careful with Aunt Mavra [KR's widow], who reports everything that goes on in the family to Alix, and has already more than once badly let down members of the family.

Among other things, it's her fault Nikolasha was banished to the Caucasus. Then Ducky started to recount part of her own conversation with Alix, concerning Nikolasha. Alix assured Ducky that she was in possession of documents, which proved that Nikolasha wanted the throne for himself, and that was why he had to be sent away.

Letter from the Grand Dukes to Nicholas II – 29 December
YOUR IMPERIAL MAJESTY

All of us, whose signature you will read at the end of this letter, earnestly and urgently beg you to moderate your stern decision concerning the fate of Grand Duke Dmitri Pavlovich. We know that he is physically ill and deeply shaken, as well as morally distressed. YOU, as his former Guardian and Senior Trustee, know that his heart has always been filled with the deepest love for YOU, THE EMPEROR, and for our Country. We beseech YOUR IMPERIAL MAJESTY, in view of the youth and truly weak health of Grand Duke Dmitri Pavlovich, to permit him to reside in either Usov or Ilinskoie.

YOUR IMPERIAL MAJESTY must be aware of the conditions, in which our troops in Persia find themselves; in view of the lack of accommodation, epidemics and other scourges of humanity, for the Grand Duke Dmitri Pavlovich to remain there would be equivalent to his complete demise, and in Your heart YOUR IMPERIAL MAJESTY will surely be moved with pity for a youth, whom you have loved, who since his youth has had the good fortune to spend much time with you, and for whom YOU have been as good as a father.

May the Lord Inspire YOUR IMPERIAL MAJESTY to change YOUR decision and replace anger with mercy.

> YOUR IMPERIAL MAJESTY'S
> deeply devoted and sincerely loving
>
> Olga. Maria. Kyril. Victoria. Boris. Andrei. Pavel.
> Maria. Elizaveta. Ioann. Elena. Gavril. Konstantin.
> Igor. Nikolai [Mikhailovich]. Sergei [Mikhailovich].

Hand-written note by Nicky on this letter
No one has the right to commit murder; I know that many are

troubled by their conscience, and that Dmitri Pavlovich is not the only one implicated in this. I am surprised by your request.

Nicholas

Nicky to Nikolai Mikhailovich – 31 December – Tsarskoe Selo
Obviously Count Fredericks made a mistake – he should have given you my order to leave the capital for Grushevka for two months. I ask you to do this and not to appear at tomorrow's reception.

There is no need to concern yourself further with the commission for peace negotiations.

Nicky, Diary – 31 December – Tsarskoe Selo
Received reports. Before lunch went upstairs to Alexei; his hand is quite better. Went for a walk. To church at 6 o'clock. Worked in the evening. At ten to midnight we went to the service. I prayed fervently that God will have mercy on Russia!

1917

Nicky – Emperor of Russia

Alix – Empress of Russia

Xenia – Grand Duchess, Nicky's sister, married to Sandro

Sandro – Grand Duke Alexander Mikhailovich, husband of Xenia

Misha – Grand Duke Mikhail, Nicky's brother

Empress Marie – mother of Nicky

Olga (sister) – Grand Duchess, Nicky's younger sister

Maria Pavlovna (the younger) – daughter of Nicky's uncle Grand Duke Pavel, sister of Dmitri Pavlovich

Grand Duke Andrei Vladimirovich – son of Grand Duke Vladimir and Maria Pavlovna (the elder)

Olga – eldest daughter of Nicky and Alix, aged twenty-two

Tatiana – second daughter of Nicky and Alix, aged twenty

Maria – third daughter of Nicky and Alix, aged eighteen

Anastasia – fourth daughter of Nicky and Alix, aged sixteen

Alexei – Heir and Tsarevich, son of Nicky and Alix, aged thirteen

Princess Olga Paley – wife of Grand Duke Pavel

Prince Felix Yusupov – married to Irina, daughter of Xenia and Sandro

Irina Yusupov – wife of Felix, daughter of Xenia and Sandro

Georgie – King George V of England, first cousin of both Nicky and Alix

Pierre Gilliard – Swiss tutor of Nicky and Alix's children

P. V. Petrov – Russian language tutor to the imperial children

Ania Vyrubova – lady-in-waiting and close friend of Alix

Lord Stamfordham – Private Secretary to King George V

A. J. Balfour – British Foreign Secretary

Maurice Paléologue – French Ambassador in St Petersburg

Count Paul Benckendorff – Grand Marshal of the Court

Mikhail Rodzianko – Chairman of the Duma

General M. V. Alexeev – chief of staff, army supreme command

Prince Valia Dolgorukov – a member of the imperial court

1917

THE BEGINNING OF THE END

Confidence in the government and the dynasty has been lost – Rasputin's murder investigated – The imperial children contract measles – The situation in Petrograd is critical: shortages of bread and other supplies have led to increasing disturbances, which the government cannot contain – Nicky decides to return to Tsarskoe, but his train is not allowed through – Under pressure from the army, the Duma and the Committee of Workers' and Soldiers' deputies, Nicky abdicates on 2 March, also on behalf of Alexei – Misha, who is offered the throne, abdicates in turn – Nicky returns to Tsarskoe and the family are held under arrest – Visits from Kerensky – A British invitation is withdrawn – The conditions under which the family are held deteriorate – Nicky's last meeting with his brother – The family are despatched to Tobolsk in Siberia – Alexei's health – Empress Marie, Xenia, Sandro, Olga are in the Crimea

Felix Yusupov to Xenia – 2 January – Rakitnoe
Dear Mamasha!

I thank you very much for your letter. I am forbidden to write, and could not do so earlier. I was afraid it would be seized on the way. I am tortured by the thought that you and the Empress Marie will think of the man, who did this, as a murderer and a criminal, and that this feeling will prevail over all others.

However much you may recognize the veracity of this act and the reasons which prompted its execution, in the depths of your heart you will always have the feeling 'But he's still a murderer!'

Knowing perfectly what that man felt before, during and after, and what he is still feeling now, I can say absolutely definitely that he is not a murderer, and was only the weapon of providence, which gave him that inexplicable, superhuman strength and peace of mind, which enabled him to carry out his duty to his country and the Tsar, by destroying that evil diabolic power, which was a disgrace to Russia and the whole world, and before which all had been powerless until now.

Irina looks on it the same way I do. It is a great comfort.

I send you many many kisses, also to all the children, Baby and Papochka [Sandro].

Felix

Andrei Vladimirovich, Diary – 4 January

All in all, we are living in strange times. The most mundane things get interpreted in the wrong way. We wrote to Nicky asking for a softening of Dmitri's lot, and this was seen as something like a family revolt. How this happened is quite inexplicable. Why is all this happening, whom does it benefit? They must have a reason for wanting the family to be at loggerheads, and more importantly, to quarrel with the Emperor.

It's all very serious and we shall have to take measures to ensure that the Emperor knows us, and how devoted we are to him.

Maurice Paléologue, Memoirs – 13 January

Old Prince Kurakin, a master of necromancy, has had the satisfaction of raising the ghost of Rasputin the last few nights.

He immediately sent for Protopopov, the Minister of the Interior, and Dobrovolsky, the Minister of Justice; they came at once. Since then, the three of them have been in secret conclave for hours every evening, listening to the dead man's solemn words.

What an extraordinary creature old Prince Kurakin is!

With his bowed frame, bald head, hook nose, pallid complexion, piercing and haggard eyes, hollow features, halting, sepulchral voice and sinister expression, he is the typical spiritualist.

At Count Witte's funeral two years ago, he was seen gazing fixedly for several minutes at the dead man's haughty features (the coffin being open in accordance with orthodox rites). Then the sepulchral voice was heard: 'We'll compel you to come to us tonight!'

14 January During the railway journey back to Petrograd I discussed what the Grand Duke [Nikolai Mikhailovich] had told me
with Madame P—.

'I'm even more pessimistic than he,' she exclaimed with flashing
eyes. 'The tragedy now on its way will be not only a dynastic crisis
but a terrible revolution; we can't escape it. Don't forget what I'm
foretelling; the disaster is at hand.'

I then quoted her the terrible prophecy which the blindness of
Louis XVI and Marie Antoinette wrung from the lips of Mirabeau in
September, 1789:

All is lost. The King and Queen will perish. The people will batter
their corpses!

Sandro, Memoirs
Back in Kiev I drafted a long letter to Nicky, stating my estimate of
the measures to be taken, if the army and the empire were to be saved
from a rapidly approaching upheaval. My six-day stay in the capital
left no doubts in my mind as to the fact that the outbreak of the revolution was to be expected not later than early spring.

The worst of what I saw and learnt dealt with the odd encouragement given to the plotters by the British ambassador, Sir George
Buchanan. He imagined he was protecting the interests of the Allies
and that a liberal government would be better capable of scoring vic-
tories. He discovered his mistake twenty-four hours after the triumph
of the revolution and wrote a dignified post-mortem several years
later.

**Sandro to Nicky – begins 25 December 1916 – ends 25 January
1917**
Dear Nicky!

It pleased you, on 22 December, to ask my opinion on a certain
subject, and in so doing I had to touch on almost all the matters
which preoccupy us, I asked your permission to speak openly, and
you granted it. After everything that I said, I feel obliged now to
speak further.

We are living the most dangerous moment in the history of Russia,
it is a question of whether Russia can be a great and free country,
capable of independent development and growth, or whether we are
to be dominated by the merciless German fist, everybody feels this,
either with their reason, or their heart or their soul, and this is why,

with the exception of cowards and enemies of the homeland, everyone is giving their lives and their property to achieve this aim. Yet at this sacred time, when each one of us is, as it were, standing the test as a man, in its highest sense as a Christian, there are forces within Russia which are dragging you, and consequently Russia, towards inescapable ruin. I say You and Russia quite deliberately, because Russia cannot exist without the Tsar, but it has to be understood that the Tsar cannot govern a country such as Russia alone, this has to be understood once and for all, and that it is consequently absolutely essential to have chambers and a ministry with one chief; I say chambers, because the mechanisms are far from perfected and are not accountable, although they must become so in order to assume the full burden of responsibility towards the people, the present situation is unthinkable, when all the responsibility rests with You, and on You alone.

Reasonable government should be made up of people who are first of all honest, liberal and devoted to the principle of monarchy, certainly not rightists or worse extreme rightists, because such people can only perceive power in terms of: governing with the aid of the police, resisting the free development of society and giving power to our generally useless clergy.

The chairman of the Council of Ministers must be someone in whom you have complete confidence, he chooses and is responsible for all the other ministers, they must all be of one mind, one persuasion, one will, carrying out one policy each in his own field, not each carrying out his own policy as we see now. The chairman and all the ministers should be chosen among people who enjoy the confidence of the country and whose achievements are well known, not excluding of course members of the Duma. Such a ministry would find sympathy in all right-minded circles, and should present to you a programme of measures, which should accord with the greatest task at present i.e. victory over the Germans, and include those reforms which could be introduced easily, without compromising the main aim, and which the country is waiting for.

The main condition for the programme not being changed once it has been established, and which the government must be sure of, is that no unfortunate influences can be brought to bear on you, and You will support your government with all your limitless power, for at the moment quite the opposite is true, and no minister can be sure of tomorrow, everything is uncoordinated, people from the sidelines are being appointed as ministers, they do not enjoy any confidence and are probably even surprised themselves at their promotion, but as there are in general few honest men, they lack the courage to admit to you that they are not qualified for the job, and that their appointment will only harm the common cause, and that their actions border on the criminal.

January [no date] – Kiev The appointments made recently show that you have definitively decided to follow an internal policy diametrically opposed to the wishes of Your devoted supporters, these policies will only play into the hands of the leftist elements as for them, the worse the situation is the better; for as discontent grows, so the very principle of monarchy is threatened, and those who stand for the idea, that Russia cannot exist without the Tsar, are left without any ground to stand on, as the facts of the collapse are plain to see. Such a situation cannot go on for long. I again repeat that you cannot govern a country without listening to the voice of the people, without meeting their needs, considering them incapable of having their own opinion, without wanting to admit that the people know their own needs.

When I think that, with a few words and a stroke of the pen, you could calm everything and give the country what it yearns for, that is a government of confidence and freedom to the forces of society, on the one firm condition that the Duma supported the Government to a man, and that there would then be a huge upsurge of national strength and consequently an assured victory, it is unbelievably painful that there is nobody you can trust, nobody who understands the situation instead of the sort who simply pander to something incomprehensible.

25 January As you can see a month has passed and I still haven't sent my letter, I kept hoping that you would take the path shown to you, not in fear but in conscience, by those who are true to you and who love Russia. But events have shown that Your advisors continue to lead You and Russia towards certain ruin, and in such circumstances it would be a crime to remain silent before both God, You, and Russia. Discontent is growing rapidly and the further it goes, the greater the gap between You and Your People.

You obviously think that the measures taken by the government will restore Russia to the right path, the path to victory and renaissance, and consider that all of us who hold the opposite view are mistaken, but as a test, look back and compare the state of Russia at the beginning of the War with today, can that comparison not convince you who is on the side of truth.

In conclusion I have to say that, however strange it may seem, the Government is today the organ that is preparing revolution, the people do not want it, but the Government is using all available means to create as many discontented people as possible, and is succeeding. We are witnessing the unheard of spectacle of a revolution from above, not below.

your devoted Sandro

Sandro, Memoirs
Once more I was in St Petersburg, fortunately for the last time in my life. On the day fixed for my talk with Alix a message came from Tsarskoe Selo informing me she did not feel well and could not receive me. I wrote her a strong letter imploring her to give me a chance to see her as I was staying in the capital for but a few days.

Nicky to King George V – 4 February – Tsarskoe Selo
My dearest Georgie,
   I thank you very much for your kind long letter. I entrust mine to the care of Lord Milner, whose acquaintance I was very pleased to make. Twice I had the occasion of seeing all the members of your mission. I hope they will return safely to England – the journey has become now still more risky since those d—d pirates sink every ship they can only get hold of. In a couple of days the work of the Conference will come to an end. May its results be fruitful and of useful consequences for both our countries and for all the Allies.
   The weak state of our railways has since long preoccupied me. The rolling stock has been and remains insufficient and we can hardly repair the worn out engines and cars, because nearly all the manufactories and fabrics of the country work for the army.
   That is why the question of transport of stores and food becomes acute, especially in winter, when the rivers and canals are frozen.
   Everything is being done to ameliorate this state of things which I hope will be overcome in April. But I never lose courage and egg on the ministers to make them and those under them work as hard as they can.
   But whatever the difficulties may be yet in store for us – we shall go on with this awful war to the end.
   Alix and I send May and your children our fond love.
   With my very best wishes for your welfare and happiness. Ever my dearest Georgie, your most devoted cousin and friend,

Nicky

Sandro, Memoirs

Then I received an invitation from Alix to be present at a luncheon in Tsarskoe Selo. Oh, those luncheons! It seems that forty years of my life were wasted in going to luncheons at Tsarskoe Selo. This was the last time I was to see the Tsar's children.

We took our coffee in the 'mauve salon', while Nicky went into the adjoining bedroom to announce my visit to Alix.

I walked in cheerfully. Alix lay in bed, dressed in a white negligee embroidered with lace, her beautiful face set in a serious expression which augured trouble for the determined intruder.

I kissed her hand, and her lips just skimmed my cheek, the coldest greeting given me by her since the first day we met in 1893. I took a chair and moved it close to her bed, facing a wall covered with innumerable ikons lit by two blue-and-pink church lamps.

'I have been your faithful friend, Alix, for twenty-four years. I am still your faithful friend, and as a friend I point out to you that all classes of the population are opposed to your policies. You have a beautiful family of children, why can you not concentrate on matters promising peace and harmony? Please, Alix, leave the cares of the state to your husband.'

She blushed. She looked at Nicky. He said nothing and continued to smoke. It is annoying that when talking of the last Tsar's behaviour in moments of distress, I am obliged to repeat that same silly phrase: 'he said nothing and continued to smoke'. But what can I do if any other description of his attitude would be likely to distort the truth?

I went on. 'Remember, Alix, I remained silent for thirty months! For thirty months I never said as much as a word to you about the disgraceful goings-on in our government, better to say *your* government! I realize that you are willing to perish and that your husband feels the same way, but what about us? Must we all suffer for your blind stubbornness? No, Alix, you have no right to drag your relatives with you down a precipice! You are incredibly selfish!'

'I refuse to continue this dispute,' she said coldly. 'You are exaggerating the danger. Some day, when you are less excited, you will admit that I knew better.'

I got up, kissed her hand, received no kiss at all in return, and left. I never saw Alix again.

Passing through the 'mauve salon' I saw the Tsar's aide-de-camp Linevich talking to Olga and Tatiana. His presence next to the Tsarina's bedroom surprised me.

Ania Vyrubova, Memoirs

Meanwhile the Grand Duke Alexander Mikhailovich [Sandro] persisted in his demand for an interview with the Empress, and as his letters to her failed of their object he began to write to the Grand Duchess Olga. The Empress, whose courage was great enough to enable her to ignore any possible danger to herself, decided to see the man and once and for all let him have his say.

In this decision the Emperor concurred, but he stipulated that he should be present in case the conversation should become unduly disagreeable. The Emperor's aide-de-camp for the day happened to be a spirited young officer, Lieutenant Linevich, who after luncheon on the day set for the audience, lingered in the palace, apparently occupied in an amusing puzzle game with Tatiana. Afterwards he told me that so well did he know the extent of the Grand Ducal cabal, and especially the character of Alexander Mikhailovich, that he had remained on purpose and that his sword had been ready at any moment to rescue the Empress from insult or from attempted assassination.

As we expected the Grand Duke had nothing new to say to the Empress, but merely reiterated in more than usually violent terms the demand for Protopopov's dismissal and for a constitutional form of government.

The Grand Duke, purple with anger, rushed out of the Empress's sitting room, but instead of leaving the palace, as he was expected to do, he entered the library, ordered pens and paper and began to write a letter to the Emperor's brother, Mikhail. No sooner had he begun his epistle than he perceived standing respectfully in the room the aide-de-camp. 'No, your Highness, I am on service today and as long as your Highness is here it is not permitted for me to leave.' In a fury Alexander Mikhailovich got up and left the palace.

Sandro to Nikolai Mikhailovich [his brother] – 14 February – on the train

Dear Nikolai!

On the road – I have just left Rakitnoe, where I spent a very pleasant twenty-four hours with Irina and Felix – I found both of them in good health, Irina has perhaps even put on a little weight, their mood was buoyant, but militant. I spent 6 days in Petrograd instead of four, the reason being my determination to see A[lix] at any cost, in fact as I was passing through Tsarskoe Selo, I left a letter for A. asking her in the kindest terms to accord me the time for a talk, and begging her not to rush me, as our conversation would be a long one; the next day I received an invitation to go to Tsarskoe at three o'clock, but thanks to our general confusion I was invited to a sitting of the conference at three hours' notice, and so through O.N. [Olga Nicolaevna] I asked to be excused and to come another day. I was told Thursday, but at the last moment was informed they were ill and could not receive me. That same day Georgy [brother of Sandro] was lunching with the Emperor, who told him that Alix could not receive me because of ill-health, and that I should return to Kiev. But as I am stubborn, I immediately wrote another letter to Alix, in which I tried to convince her to receive me, and assured her that it was more important for her to see me, than for me to return to Kiev.

As a result, in the morning, I was summoned through Tatiana at a quarter past two, and arrived at a quarter to, expecting to wait until the appointed time, but I was admitted straight away into the mauve room, where Nicky, the children and Aide-de-Camp Linevich were doing a puzzle. Nicky greeted me with great kindness and took me immediately to see Alix, who was lying in the bedroom. I was allowed to kiss her hand, though her expression was icy, and I was told that her heart has always been open to all, that it was I myself who did not want to talk to her, that I never visited her when I came to Petrograd, which it is true happened three times. I accepted the blame, but added that I always knew if someone wanted to talk to me or not. Then I asked her to permit me to speak openly and to believe that I spoke without any selfish motive, and that what I was going to say came from the depths of my heart, and that my only aim was to help her and Nicky.

Unfortunately, what I had planned to say was disrupted by Nicky's arrival, so that I had to leave aside the whole part of my speech about the soul, and how she must feel with her soul where the truth lies, and how I could tell from many things that she was not living through her soul; so I proceeded straightaway to an exposé of the present situation in Russia, and the measures which need to be taken to save both Russia and their throne.

I spoke for a long time, an hour and a half, and touched on absolutely all the issues, at each step coming up against her objections, which cannot tolerate even the slightest criticism; she is in a state of complete and incurable delusion, her main argument was that everyone needs to be brought to heel, and put in their place, instead of interfering in what does not concern them, that one needs patience to give the present government time, and more in the same vein.

I demonstrated to her that we have had more than enough

patience, that a government, which does not inspire confidence and is composed of persons who cannot meet the needs and aspirations of the people, can do nothing, that the mood is growing, the dissatisfaction increasing, that it's impossible to govern relying on the police alone etc; but nothing helped. I read aloud to them the letter I had wanted to send Nicky, but had given him directly, and after reading it supplemented my arguments with more proofs, assuring them that my letter reflected the views of the overwhelming majority, but all to no avail – Her face still bore the same expression of regret and certainty as to my delusion.

Nicky took an absolutely passive role in the conversation, occasionally adding his objections, but without conviction; she, on the other hand, talked the whole time, excitedly and hurriedly, however I did not leave a single of her objections without response.

Nicky was the third person, whose actions were being discussed in his presence, but he spent most of the time examining his circassian coat, adjusting its folds, and listening.

The bedroom, with three walls covered from ceiling to floor with icons, with its lamps and oratory, was like a heathen temple with all the attributes of Orthodoxy, but totally devoid of soul, and not once during our whole conversation was her face lit by the pleasant expression it sometimes wears, rather the whole time her lips remained tightly compressed and her expression angry.

After our conversation, and a parting so chilly as to be polar, I went with Nicky into the other room and talked with him for a further 20 minutes.

To sum up: One can expect no good from Tsarskoe and the question is therefore the following: either to sit back with folded arms and wait for the ruin and humiliation of Russia, or to save Russia by taking heroic measures. The situation is without issue, and such as Russia has never experienced before, and so people who love Russia find themselves at a cross roads and wonder how to act; for the first time in our lives, we have to ask how far we are bound by the oath given. In all, it's a nightmare, from which I can see no escape. As for D.P. [Dmitri Pavlovich] and F. [Felix], everything is going as I supposed, in a few days it will all be over and consigned to oblivion.

On the day of my departure I wrote A.[lix] a letter, in which I said that I was deeply upset that our conversation had resulted in absolutely nothing, and repeated that what I had said was not merely my own opinion but that of the overwhelming majority, that I had gone to her in the hope of finding an ally to help convince N to take the only possible and correct course, but she would not listen to my voice and that if it proved necessary I would continue to write to her.

What drives me completely to despair is the total absence of spiritual consciousness in either of them, and that being so one cannot expect them ever to perceive or understand the meaning of truth.

The problem of the railways has reached crisis point, we are on the verge of a catastrophe, there is no more coal or food, we are living from day to day, everything is in complete disarray, yet there is no leadership from above, it's enough to drive you mad, up there it's like water off a duck's back, all is blindness and submission to God, in such circumstances there has to be a power of evil, otherwise how can I explain to myself such total blindness and deafness.

I hope you are in good health, send me a few words back with the messenger.

Your Sandro

Felix Yusupov to Nikolai Mikhailovich – 14 February – Rakitnoe
Dear Uncle Bimbo!

I could not reply earlier, as Al. Mikh. [Sandro] is only just now returned to Kiev. Thank you very much for your letter, also for Stepanov's letter, which I have read. I received them the day the investigators arrived. It was very opportune. I did not expect such a swift change on the part of General Panov. As a clever and prudent man he understood where the strength lies.

The visit of the procurator and investigator to Rakitnoe was very amusing. It began with them having to walk two *versts* through an appalling snowstorm. By the time they reached our house they looked like icicles. They went about their business with great zeal, but received no less energetic a rebuff from the Maestro. He refused outright to go over again what he had already told them, and expressed his surprise at their arrival, insofar as he was at Rakitnoe and was therefore serving his punishment, furthermore he had received his sentence after he had signed a (detailed) protocol, which had then been submitted for His Majesty's consideration, consequently he found it utterly incomprehensible that he should be interrogated again as a witness, after the case had seemingly been closed at His Majesty's command.

As for general questions, he would be delighted to answer them. The official interrogation gradually turned into a friendly conversation which lasted 4½ hours in two sessions.

The result of this conversation was that, when the procurator and the investigator returned to their room, my valet, who had been instructed to spy on them, heard one say to the other: 'It now seems completely clear to me that the Prince is in no way implicated, and that the press had blown the whole thing up.'

After a very superficial interrogation of my valet Nefedov, we invited them to dinner and entertained them with the gramophone in the evening. The next day they returned home. It was very cold, and the procurator was given a reversible fur coat, which was very like the coat worn by a young man in R's apartment on that fatal night 'Exceedingly funny!' The latest news on the affair: the investigation will be closed in a few days' time, no culprits have been found, the evidence is insufficient.

Dmitri will not be interrogated. Purishkevich has already been questioned (on the eve of his interrogation he received a letter from the Maestro). You have probably read his answer in the newspapers. For the moment all is going well, let us hope that luck will not abandon us in the future. Today is the 14th. It's terrible to think what is happening in Petersburg. I very much hope the Duma will understand the government's challenge and will not become ensnared in the trap set for them by Protopopov. Al. Mikh. [Sandro] came to see us yesterday and is leaving for Kiev this evening. I think he is now convinced that nothing can be achieved through talk alone. You cannot reason with the insane.

How can they not see, that if they do not do what is necessary from above, then it will be done from below. How much innocent blood will be spilt. The Emperor it seems, will soon be going to the Stavka, Emp. Marie should use the opportunity to go there with people who will help and support her, together with Alexeev and Gurko,[1] and demand that Protopopov, Shcheglovitov [minister] and Ania be arrested and Al. Feod. [Alix] sent to Livadia. This measure alone can save us, if it's not already too late. I am convinced that the Emperor's passive reaction to everything that happens, is the result of Badmaev's medicines. There are such herbs, that act gradually and reduce a man to complete cretinism.

I must end my letter, Al. Mikh. is leaving.

Irina and I kiss you fondly and think of you constantly. Your sincerely devoted and loving

                                                                    Felix

---

[1] Generals Mikhail Vasilievich Alexeev and Vassily Gurko.

Irina Yusupov to Xenia – 16 February – Rakitnoe
Darling Mama

I would so like to go to Petrograd with you, but Felix won't allow it. He says it is dangerous for me to go there. You ask in your letter when we are expecting the investigators? They have already been!

Felix refused to repeat what he had already said to the inquiry in Petrograd, he only answered various new questions, which he had not been asked in Petrograd. He talked to them for more than two hours. It seems they spent less time questioning Felix, rather for the most part Felix questioned them about various matters.

In the afternoon, when they had written down everything Felix had told them, he saw them again, and questioned them once more about various things. After which the most amazing thing happened. He decided to invite them to dinner!

The whole thing was very funny. The procurator sat next to Felix's mama, and the investigator next to me. At dinner the investigator was very tactless: he told us how he had killed a 'dog' while out hunting, instead of a 'wolf'! When we asked the procurator whether he enjoyed hunting, he replied that he had never killed anything in his life and didn't even like such conversations. After dinner we put on the gramophone to entertain them. In all I had a very amusing time!

Empress Marie to Nicky – 17 February – Kiev
My dear darling Nicky

I have had no news of you for such a long time, that I miss you terribly and feel the need at least to talk to you by letter. So much has happened since we last saw each other, but my thoughts never leave you and I know how difficult these last months have been for you.

You know *how* dear you are to me, and how painful it is for me not to be able to help you. I can only pray for you and ask God to give you strength and inspire you to do all you can for the good of our dear Russia. I'm sure that you yourself realize how deeply your sharp reply offended the family, in making a terrible and undeserved accusation against them.

I hope also with all my heart that you will soften the lot of poor Dmitri P. and will not leave him in Persia, where the climate is so awful in summer that he will not be able to bear it with his bad health. Poor Uncle Pavel wrote to me in despair that he was not even able to take his leave of him or embrace him, as he was sent away in such a sudden way at night. It is not like you with your good heart to act in this way and it caused me a lot of pain.

I have had a little travelling church installed for the week next to the green study, to avoid having to go twice a day to the Ignatievs'. It's very agreeable and cosy, so nice and tranquil. I have invited the good old priest from the Sofiisky cathedral, and am delighted with the services, I feel calm and there is nothing to distract me, just what one wants for one's devotions. Unfortunately the weather has changed again, it is cold, 10 degrees after a real spring day yesterday. I had hoped that the winter was over. I hope you are all well. I embrace you all tenderly, my dears. May the Lord keep you, I wish you well, my dear Nicky. Your old Mama who loves you dearly, Baby Olga kisses you.

Tatiana to Alix – 18 February – Tsarskoe Selo
Mama darling, sweet one,

I was such a fool today! When you called me several times to come to you (whilst Ania was there in the afternoon), I wanted to so *awfully* much. But then I felt that if I'll come, I'll howl, and I didn't want to be such an idiot before Ania, but I so wanted to go to you and be caressed.

And then I never thanked you as I wanted to for the nice drive. I was so pleased, but by some stupid idea of mine, I did not want to show that I was pleased. When you asked me if I wanted to drive I said I did not know. It was not true – because I wanted to but I was afraid you would be tired of driving. I was so happy in the morning, that it was simply the devil which got into me and made me so beastly nasty. Please forgive me, my own precious Mama sweet. God bless you, my angel.

I kiss you 1000 times and still more, as I love you. Good night, deary, from your own loving – very, very much more than I can say in the world – child,

Tatiana

Alix to Nicky – 22 February – Tsarskoe Selo
My very Own precious One,

Verily God has sent you a terrible hard cross to bear and I do so long to help you carry the burden. You are brave and patient, but my very soul feels and suffers with you, *far* more than I can say.

I can do nothing but pray and pray and Our dear Friend does so in yonder world for you – there He is yet nearer to us – tho' one longs to hear His voice of comfort and encouragement. God will help, I feel

convinced and send yet the great recompense for all you go through
– but, how long to wait still.

It seems as tho' things were taking a better turn – only, my Love,
be firm, show the Master hand, it's that what the Russians need. Love
and kindnesses you have *never* failed to show – now let them feel
your fist at times. They ask for it themselves – how many have told
me – 'we want to feel the whip' – it's strange but such is the Slav
nature, *great* firmness, hardness even – and warm love. Since they
have now begun to 'feel' You and Kalinin they begin to quieten
down.

They must learn to fear you, love is not enough. A child that adores
its father, must still have fear to anger, displease or disobey him – one
must play with the reins, let them loose and draw them in, always let
the master-hand be felt; then they also far more value kindness –
only gentleness they do not understand.

Human hearts are strange and not tender or susceptible in the
higher classes, strange to say. They need decided treatment, especially now. I am sad that we cannot be alone for our last luncheon,
but they are your own who also want to see you. Poor little Xenia
with such boys and her daughter married into that wicked family –
and with such a false husband – I pity her deeply.

Feel my arms encircling you, feel my lips tenderly pressed upon
yours and always together never alone. Farewell – Lovy Sweet, come
soon back again to your own very own

Sunny

Nicky, Diary – 22 February – Tsarskoe Selo
Read, packed. Misha was there for lunch. Said goodbye to all my dear
family and went with Alix to Znamenia [church], and from there to
the station. At 2 o'clock left for the Stavka. The day was sunny and
frosty. Read, felt bored and rested.

Ania Vyrubova, Memoirs
I realized that I was becoming feverish and that my headache was
almost unbearably increasing. Returning to the palace, I lay down in
my bedroom, after writing a line to the Empress excusing myself from
tea. An hour later Tatiana came in, sympathetic as usual, but troubled
because Olga and Alexei were in bed with high temperatures and the
doctors still expected that they might be coming down with measles.

A week or two before some small cadets from the military school had spent the afternoon playing with Alexei, and one of these boys had a cough and such a flushed face that the Empress had called the attention of M. Gilliard to the child fearing illness. The next day we heard that he was ill with measles, but because our minds were so troubled with many other things none of us thought much of the danger of contagion.

As for me, even after Tatiana had told me that Olga and Alexei were suspected cases, it did not at once occur to me that I was going to be ill. Still my temperature went on rising and my headache was unrelieved. I lay in bed all the next day until the dinner.

That same day Tatiana fell ill, and now the Empress had four of us on her hands. Putting on her nurse's uniform, she spent all the succeeding days between her children's rooms and mine. Half conscious, I felt gratefully her capable hands arranging my pillows, smoothing my burning forehead, and holding to my lips medicines and cooling drinks. Already, as I heard vaguely, Maria and Anastasia had begun to cough, but this news disturbed me only as a passing dream.

Nicky to Alix – 23 February – Mogilev
My own beloved Sunny,

Loving thanks for your precious letter – you left in my compartment – I read it greedily before going to bed. It did me good, in my solitude, after two months being together, if not to hear your sweet voice, at least to be comforted by those lines of tender love!

I never went out until we arrived here. Today I feel much better, the voice is not hoarse and the cough is much less strong.

It was a sunny but cold day and I was met by the usual people – Alexeev at their head. He really looks all right and the face has an expression of rest and calm, which I have long not seen. We had a good talk for an hour; after that I arranged my rooms and got your wire about Olga's and Baby's measles. I could not believe my eyes – so unexpected was that news, especially after his own telegram where he says that he is feeling well! Anyhow it is very tiresome and rather troublesome for you, my Lovebird. Perhaps you will put off receiving so many people, as that is a lawful reason not to see so many, on account of their families.

In the 1st and 2nd Cadet Corps the number of boys who have got the measles is steadily rising.

I saw all the foreign generals at dinner – they were very sad to hear that news. It is so quiet in this house, no rumbling about, no excited shouts! I imagine he is asleep in the bedroom! All his tiny things, photos and toys are kept in good order in the bedroom and in the bow window-room! I need not!

On the other hand what a luck that he did not come with me now only to fall ill and lie in that small bedroom of ours. God grant the measles may continue with no complications and better all the children at once have it!

I miss my half an hour's work at the puzzle every evening. If I am free here I think I will turn to the domino again, because this silence around me is rather depressing. Of course if there is no work for me.

Old Ivanov was amiable and kind at dinner; my other neighbour was Sir N. Williams, who was delighted to have seen so many countrymen lately.

What you write about being firm – the master – is perfectly true. I do not forget it – be sure of that, but I need not bellow at the people right and left every moment. A quiet sharp remark or answer is enough very often to put the one or the other into the place.

Now, Lovy-mine, it is late. Good-night, God bless your slumber, sleep well without the animal-warmth.

24 February

My brain feels rested here – no ministers and no fidgety questions to think over – I think it does me good, but only the brain. The heart suffers from being separated and this separation I hate, during such time especially! I won't be long away – only to put all things as much as possible to rights here and then my duty will be done.

25 Febr[uary]   Just got your morning telegram – thank God no complications as yet. The first days the temp[erature] is always high and decreases slowly towards the end. Poor Ania – I can imagine what she feels and how much worse than the children!

Now before driving out for my walk I will peep into the monastery and pray for you and them to the virgin!

The last snowstorms, which ended yesterday along all our southwestern railway lines, have placed the armies into a critical situation. If the trains cannot begin moving at once – in 3 or 4 days real famine will break out among the troops. Quite horribly anguishing!

Goodbye, my own Love, my beloved little Wify, God bless you and the children. With tender love ever your own Huzy,

Nicky

Alix to Nicky – 25 February – Tsarskoe Selo
Precious, beloved Treasure,

8° and gently snowing – so far I sleep very well, but miss my love *more* than words can say. The rows in town and strikes are more than provoking and I send you Kalinin's letter to me, the paper is not worth while, and you will get a more detailed one for sure from the governor of the city.

It's a 'hooligan' movement, young boys and girls running about and screaming that they have no bread, only to excite – then the workmen preventing others from work – if it *were* very cold they would probably stay indoors. But this will all pass and quieten down – if the Duma would only behave itself – one does not print the worst speeches.

26 February Today I won't receive anybody, can't continue like that – tomorrow however must again. Told much about the disorders in town (I think over 200,000 people) – find that one does not keep good order. But I wrote all this yesterday, forgive me, I am foolish.

But *one ought* to arrange card system for bread (as in every country now) as one has it for sugar some time and all are quiet and got enough. Our people are idiots. A poor gendarme officer was killed by the crowd – a few other people too. That gaping public does harm, well dressed people, wounded soldiers and so on, *koursistki* [girl students], etc. who egg on others. Lili [Dehn][2] speaks to the *isvotchiki* [cabmen] to get news. They said that students came to them and said that if they come out in the morning, they will be shot.

I just took Marie to Znamenski [church] to place candles, went to our Friend's grave – now the Church so high I could kneel and pray there calmly for you all without being seen. Things were very bad yesterday in town – 120 arrests – 30 people, chief leaders and Lelianov drawn to account for speeches in the city's Duma. The ministers and some right members of the Duma had a council last night (Kalinin wrote at 4 in the morning) to take severe measures and they are full of hope that tomorrow it will be calm, they had intended to set up barricades etc.

Monday – I read a vile proclamation – but it seems to me it will be all right. The sun shines so brightly – and I felt such a peace and calm on His [Rasputin's] dear grave. He died to save us.

---

[2] Wife of the captain of the cruiser *Variag*, a close friend of Alix and Ania Vyrubova.

Nicky to Alix – 26 February – Mogilev

My own beloved One,

The trains are again all wrong; your letter came yesterday after 5.0, but today the last one N 647 arrived exactly before lunchtime.

Tender kisses for it. Please do not overtire yourself running across among the invalids.

See often Lily Dehn – a good reasonable friend.

I went yesterday to the Virgin's image and prayed hard for you, my Love, for the dear children and our country, also for Ania. Tell her that I saw her brooch fastened to the image and rubbed it with my nose while kissing!

Last evening I was in church; the old mother of the Bishop thanked for the money we gave.

This morning during service I felt an excruciating pain in the middle of my chest, which lasted for a quarter of an hour.

I could hardly stand and my forehead was covered with beads of sweat.

I cannot understand what it was, as I had no heart beating, but it came and left me at once, when I knelt before the Virgin's image!

God bless you, my Treasure, our children and her! I kiss you all very tenderly. Ever your own

Nicky

Chairman of the State Duma M. V. Rodzianko to Emperor Nicholas II – 26 February — Telegram

MOST HUMBLY I REPORT TO YOUR MAJESTY, THAT THE POPULAR DISTUR-BANCES WHICH HAVE BEGUN IN PETROGRAD ARE ASSUMING A SERIOUS CHARACTER AND THREATENING PROPORTIONS. THE CAUSES ARE A SHORTAGE OF BAKED BREAD AND AN INSUFFICIENT SUPPLY OF FLOUR, WHICH ARE GIV-ING RISE TO PANIC, BUT MOST OF ALL A COMPLETE LACK OF CONFIDENCE IN THE LEADERSHIP, WHICH IS INCAPABLE OF LEADING THE NATION OUT OF THIS DIFFICULT SITUATION. IN SUCH CIRCUMSTANCES THERE WILL UNDOUBTEDLY BE AN EXPLOSION OF EVENTS, WHICH IT MAY BE POSSIBLE TO CONTAIN TEM-PORARILY AT THE PRICE OF SHEDDING THE BLOOD OF INNOCENT CITIZENS, BUT WHICH IT WILL BE IMPOSSIBLE TO CONTROL IF THEY PERSIST. THE MOVE-MENT COULD SPREAD TO THE RAILWAYS, AND THE LIFE OF THE COUNTRY WILL COME TO A STANDSTILL AT SUCH A CRITICAL TIME. THE FACTORIES, WHICH ARE PRODUCING ARMAMENTS IN PETROGRAD, ARE COMING TO A HALT DUE TO LACK OF FUEL AND RAW MATERIALS, THE WORKERS ARE WITH-OUT JOBS, AND A HUNGRY UNEMPLOYED MASS IS BEING LAUNCHED ON THE ROAD TO ANARCHY, ELEMENTAL AND UNCONTROLLABLE ...

THE GOVERNMENT IS COMPLETELY PARALYSED, AND TOTALLY INCAPABLE OF RESTORING ORDER WHERE IT HAS BROKEN DOWN. YOUR MAJESTY, SAVE RUSSIA, HUMILIATION AND DISGRACE THREATEN. THE WAR CANNOT BE BROUGHT TO A VICTORIOUS END IN SUCH CIRCUMSTANCES, AS THE FERMENT HAS ALREADY AFFECTED THE ARMY AND THREATENS TO SPREAD, UNLESS THE AUTHORITIES PUT A DECISIVE END TO THE ANARCHY AND DISORDER. YOUR MAJESTY, WITHOUT DELAY SUMMON A PERSON WHOM THE WHOLE COUNTRY TRUSTS, AND CHARGE HIM WITH FORMING A GOVERNMENT, IN WHICH THE WHOLE POPULATION CAN HAVE CONFIDENCE. SUCH A GOVERNMENT WILL COMMAND THE SUPPORT OF THE WHOLE OF RUSSIA, WHICH WILL ONCE MORE REGAIN CONFIDENCE IN ITSELF AND IN ITS LEADERS. IN THIS HOUR, UNPRECEDENTED IN ITS TERROR AND THE HORROR OF ITS CONSEQUENCES, THERE IS NO OTHER WAY OUT AND THERE CAN BE NO DELAY.

Nicky, Diary – 27 February – Mogilev

Serious disturbances started in Petrograd several days ago; to make things worse, the troops have also joined in. It's a revolting sensation to be so far away and to receive only scraps of bad news! After dinner I decided to return to Tsarskoe Selo as soon as possible, and at one o'clock at night set out by train.

Nicky to Alix, Telegram No. 88
Sent from Likhoslavl, on 28 February 1917, 9.27 p.m.
Received in Tsarskoe Selo, on 28 February 1917, 10.10 p.m.

TO HER MAJESTY
THANKS FOR THE NEWS AM GLAD EVERYTHING IS ALL RIGHT WITH YOU HOPE TO BE AT HOME TOMORROW MORNING EMBRACING YOU AND THE CHILDREN GOD SAVE YOU

NICKY

Statement of the Interim Committee of the State Duma – 28 February

'In view of the grave situation of internal disorder, caused by measures taken by the old government, the Interim Committee of Members of the State Duma has found itself obliged to take into its own hands the restoration of state and public order. While recognizing the great responsibility of the decision they have taken, the Committee express their confidence, that the people and the army will give their support to the task of creating a new government, which will reflect the aspirations of the people and will be able to enjoy their confidence.'

Nicky, Diary – 28 February – in the train

I went to bed at 3.15, as I talked for a long time with [General] N..I. Ivanov, whom I am sending to Petrograd with troops to restore order.

Nicky to Alix – 28 February – Viasma – Telegram

LEFT THIS MORNING AT 5 THOUGHTS ALWAYS TOGETHER GLORIOUS WEATHER HOPE ARE FEELING WELL AND QUIET MANY TROOPS SENT FROM FRONT FONDEST LOVE

NICKY

King George V, Diary – 28 February – Buckingham Palace

Bad news from Russia, practically a revolution has broken out in Petrograd and some of the Guards regiments have mutinied and killed their Officers. This rising is against the Govt. not against the war. Nicky is at Headquarters.

Nicky, Diary – 1 March – on the train

At night we had to turn back from Malaia-Vichera as Liuban and Tosno turned out to be in the hands of the insurgents. Shame and dishonour! It isn't possible to get to Tsarskoe, although all my thoughts and feelings are constantly there! How difficult it must be for poor Alix to have to go through all this alone! Help us, Lord!

Sandro, Memoirs – 1 March

Nicky left last night for St Petersburg but the railway officials, obeying the orders of the Duma, have stopped his train at the station Dno and turned it in the direction of Pskov. He is practically alone aboard his train. A delegation of the members of the Duma are to see him in Pskov, submitting their ultimatum.

Felix Yusupov, Memoirs

The revolution did not shake the Grand Duchess Ella's strong spirit. On March 1st, a troop of revolutionary soldiers surrounded the convent, shouting: 'Where is the German spy?' The Grand Duchess came forward and replied very calmly:

'There is no German spy; this is a convent, of which I am the Mother Superior.'

Chief of Staff of the Supreme Command Gen. M. V. Alexeev to Emperor Nicholas II.

Sent from Mogilev and received in Pskov – 2 March – Telegram

I most humbly present to YOUR IMPERIAL MAJESTY the telegrams which I have received addressed to YOUR IMPERIAL MAJESTY:

From Grand Duke Nikolai Nikolaevich [Nikolasha]

ADJUTANT-GENERAL ALEXEEV HAS INFORMED ME OF THE UNPRECEDENTED AND FATAL SITUATION AND HAS ASKED ME TO SUPPORT HIS VIEW, THAT A VICTORIOUS END TO THE WAR, SO VITAL FOR THE WELL-BEING AND FUTURE OF RUSSIA, AS WELL AS THE SALVATION OF THE DYNASTY, REQUIRES EXTRAORDINARY MEASURES. AS A LOYAL SUBJECT, I FEEL IT MY NECESSARY DUTY OF ALLEGIANCE, AND IN THE SPIRIT OF MY OATH, TO BEG YOUR IMPERIAL MAJESTY ON MY KNEES TO SAVE RUSSIA AND YOUR HEIR, BEING AWARE OF YOUR SACRED FEELINGS OF LOVE FOR RUSSIA AND FOR HIM. MAKE THE SIGN OF THE CROSS AND HAND OVER TO HIM YOUR HERITAGE. THERE IS NO OTHER WAY. I ARDENTLY PRAY GOD AS NEVER BEFORE IN MY LIFE TO SUSTAIN AND GUIDE YOU.

From Adjutant-General Brusilov

I ASK YOU TO FORWARD TO HIS MAJESTY THE EMPEROR MY MOST HUMBLE REQUEST, FOUNDED ON MY DEVOTION AND LOVE FOR THE MOTHERLAND AND THE IMPERIAL THRONE, NAMELY THAT AT THE PRESENT TIME, ONLY ONE MEASURE CAN SAVE THE SITUATION AND MAKE IT POSSIBLE TO GO ON FIGHTING THE EXTERNAL ENEMY, WITHOUT WHICH RUSSIA WILL PERISH – THAT IS TO ABDICATE FROM THE THRONE IN FAVOUR OF HIS MAJESTY THE HEIR TSAREVICH UNDER THE REGENCY OF GRAND DUKE MIKHAIL ALEXANDROVICH. THERE IS NO OTHER ALTERNATIVE. BUT IT IS ESSENTIAL TO MAKE HASTE, TO QUELL THE POPULAR CONFLAGRATION WHICH HAS FLARED UP AND IS GAINING EVER LARGER PROPORTIONS, LEST IT ENTRAIN IN ITS WAKE IMMEASURABLY CATASTROPHIC CONSEQUENCES. SUCH AN ACT WILL SAVE THE DYNASTY IN THE PERSON OF THE LEGITIMATE HEIR.

From Adjutant-General Evert

YOUR IMPERIAL MAJESTY. THE CHIEF OF STAFF OF YOUR IMPERIAL MAJESTY HAS INFORMED ME OF THE SITUATION WHICH HAS ARISEN IN PETROGRAD, TSARSKOE SELO, THE BALTIC AND MOSCOW, AND OF THE RESULT OF TALKS

BETWEEN ADJUTANT-GENERAL RUZSKY[3] AND THE CHAIRMAN OF THE STATE DUMA. YOUR MAJESTY. IT IS NO LONGER POSSIBLE TO COUNT ON THE ARMY IN ITS PRESENT CONDITION TO SUPPRESS INTERNAL DISTURBANCES – IT CAN ONLY BE CONTROLLED IN THE NAME OF SAVING RUSSIA FROM CERTAIN ENSLAVEMENT BY OUR MORTAL ENEMY, AS IT IS IMPOSSIBLE TO CONTINUE THE STRUGGLE – I AM TAKING EVERY MEASURE TO ENSURE THAT NEWS OF THE PRESENT SITUATION IN THE CAPITALS DOES NOT LEAK OUT INTO THE ARMY, TO PROTECT IT FROM INEVITABLE AGITATION. THERE ARE NO MEANS WITH WHICH TO CRUSH REVOLUTION IN THE CAPITALS. AN IMMEDIATE DECISION IS ESSENTIAL, TO BRING AN END TO THE DISTURBANCES AND TO PRESERVE THE ARMY FOR THE FIGHT AGAINST THE ENEMY. IN THE PRESENT SITUATION, AND FINDING NO OTHER SOLUTION, AS A SUBJECT INFINITELY LOYAL TO YOUR MAJESTY, AND IN THE NAME OF SAVING THE COUNTRY AND THE DYNASTY, I BEG YOUR MAJESTY TO TAKE THE DECISION CONCURRING WITH THE STATEMENT OF THE CHAIRMAN OF THE DUMA, AND EXPRESSED BY HIM TO ADJUTANT-GENERAL RUZSKY, AND WHICH APPEARS TO BE THE ONLY ONE CAPABLE OF HALTING THE REVOLUTION AND SAVING RUSSIA FROM THE HORRORS OF ANARCHY.

From Adjutant-General Alexeev

IN HUMBLY PRESENTING THESE TELEGRAMS TO YOUR IMPERIAL MAJESTY, I BEG YOU TO TAKE WITHOUT DELAY THE DECISION WHICH THE LORD GOD WILL INDICATE TO YOU. DELAY THREATENS RUSSIA WITH RUIN. FOR THE MOMENT THE ARMY HAS BEEN SAVED FROM THE AFFLICTION WHICH HAS SEIZED PETROGRAD, MOSCOW, KRONSTADT AND OTHER TOWNS. BUT IT IS IMPOSSIBLE TO GUARANTEE THAT SUPREME DISCIPLINE CAN BE MAIN-TAINED. TO INVOLVE THE ARMY IN INTERNAL POLITICAL AFFAIRS WILL INEVITABLY LEAD TO THE END OF THE WAR, TO RUSSIA'S DISGRACE AND DESTRUCTION. YOUR IMPERIAL MAJESTY LOVES OUR COUNTRY, AND FOR THE SAKE OF ITS INTEGRITY AND INDEPENDENCE, FOR THE SAKE OF VICTORY, DEIGN TO TAKE THE DECISION, WHICH WILL PROVIDE A SAFE PEACEFUL RES-OLUTION OF THE PRESENT GRAVE SITUATION. I AWAIT YOUR ORDERS. 2 MARCH 1917

Maurice Paléologue, Memoirs – 2 March

Guchkov and Shulgin[4] left Petrograd at nine o'clock this morning. Thanks to the aid of an engineer attached to the railway service, they

---

[3] N. V. Ruzsky, commander-in-chief of the northern front.

[4] Guchkov, President of the War-Industry Committee; Shulgin, member of the Duma and President of the Military-Industrial Committee.

were able to get a special train without arousing the suspicions of the socialist committees.

Discipline is gradually being re-established among the troops. Order has been restored in the city and the shops are cautiously opening their doors again.

The Executive Committee of the Duma and the Council of Workmen's and Soldiers' Deputies have come to an agreement on the following points:

(1) Abdication of the Emperor; (2) Accession of the Tsarevich; (3) The Grand Duke Mikhail (the Emperor's brother) to be regent; (4) Formation of a responsible ministry; (5) Election of a constituent assembly by universal suffrage; (6) All races to be proclaimed equal before the law.

The young deputy Kerensky, who has gained a reputation as an advocate in political trials, is coming out as one of the most active and strong-minded organisers of the new order. His influence with the *Soviet*[5] is great. He is a man we must try to win over to our cause. He alone is capable of making the *Soviet* realize the necessity of continuing the war and maintaining the alliance. I have therefore telegraphed to Paris, suggesting to Briand [French Prime Minister] that an appeal from the French socialists to the patriotism of the Russian socialists should be sent through Kerensky.

But the whole of the interest of the day has been concentrated on the little town of Pskov, half-way between Petrograd and Dvinsk. It was there that the imperial train, which failed to reach Tsarskoe Selo, stopped at eight o'clock yesterday evening.

The Emperor, who left Mogilev on 27 February at 4.30 a.m., decided to go to Tsarskoe Selo, the Empress having begged him to return there at once. The news he had received from Moscow did not alarm him unduly. Of course it may be that General Voeikov kept part of the truth from him. About three o'clock in the morning of 28 February, as the engine of the imperial train was taking in water at the station of Malaia-Vichera, General Zabel, commander of His Majesty's Railway Regiment, took it upon himself to awaken the Emperor to tell him that the line to Petrograd had been closed and that Tsarskoe Selo was in the hands of the revolutionary forces. After giving vent to his surprise and irritation at not having been better informed, the Emperor is said to have replied: 'Moscow will remain faithful to me. We will go to Moscow!'

---

[5] 'Soviet' translates into English as 'Council'.

Then he is reported to have added, with his usual apathy: 'If the revolution succeeds, I shall abdicate voluntarily. I'll go and live at Livadia; I love flowers.'

But at the station of Dno it was learnt that the whole populace of Moscow had adhered to the revolution. Then the Emperor decided to seek a haven of refuge among his troops and selected the headquarters of the armies of the North, commanded by General Ruzsky at Pskov.

The imperial train arrived at Pskov at eight o'clock yesterday evening.

General Ruzsky came to confer with the Emperor at once and had no difficulty in demonstrating that his duty was to abdicate. He also invoked the unanimous opinion of General Alexeev and the army commanders, whom he had consulted by telegraph.

The Emperor instructed General Ruzsky to report to Rodzianko, the President of the Duma, his intention to renounce the throne.

This morning Pokrovsky resigned his office as Foreign Minister; he did so with that calm and unaffected dignity which makes him so lovable.

'My work is over,' he said to me. 'The President of the Council and all my colleagues have been arrested or are in flight. It is three days since the Emperor showed any sign of life and, to crown everything, General Ivanov, who was to bring us His Majesty's orders, has not arrived. In the circumstances it is impossible for me to carry out my duties; I am leaving my post and handing over its duties to my administrative deputy. In this way I avoid breaking my oath to the Emperor, as I have not entered into any sort of communication with the revolutionaries.'

During the evening, the leaders of the Duma have at last succeeded in forming a Provisional Government with Prince Lvov as president; he is taking the Ministry of the Interior. The other ministers are Guchkov (War), Milyukov (Foreign Affairs), Tereshchenko (Finance), Kerensky (Justice), etc.

The first cabinet of the new *regime* was only formed after interminable wrangling and haggling with the *Soviet*. The socialists have certainly realized that the Russian proletariat is still too inorganic and ignorant to shoulder the practical responsibilities of power; but they are anxious to be the power behind the scenes, so they have insisted on the appointment of Kerensky as Minister for Justice in order to keep an eye on the Provisional Government.

From Journal No. 1 of the Sitting of the Provisional Government on the Deportation of the Tsar's Family and Members of the Imperial Family Abroad – 2 March

In relation to the fate of members of the former imperial family, the Minister of Foreign Affairs [Milyukov] supported the necessity of deporting them beyond the frontiers of the Russian state, judging this measure to be essential both for political reasons, and because of the danger inherent in their continued presence in Russia. The provisional government considered that there were not sufficient grounds to extend such a measure to all members of the Romanov house, but that such a measure was absolutely essential and urgent in the case of the abdicated former emperor Nicholas II, as well as Grand Duke Mikhail, and their families. As far as the place of residence of such persons was concerned, there was no need to insist they leave Russia, and if they wished to stay in this country, it would only be necessary to limit their place of residence within certain boundaries and in the same way to limit their possibility of free movement.

Alix to Nicky – 2 March – Tsarskoe Selo

My own beloved, precious Angel, light of my life,

My heart breaks, thinking of you all alone going through all this anguish, anxiety and we know nothing of you and *you* neither of us, so I am sending off Soloviev and Grammatin each with a letter, trusting one may reach you at last. I wanted to send an airplane, but the men have gone. The young men will tell you *everything*, so that I won't say anything about the situation. It is so abnormally hideous and the rapidity colossal with which events go. But I have the firm belief, which *nothing* can shake that all will be well somehow, especially since I got your wire this morning, the first ray of sunshine in this swamp.

The children lie quiet in the dark, Baby lies with them for several hours after lunch and sleeps. I spend my days upstairs and receive there too – the lift does not work since 4 days, a pipe burst – Olga 37.7, T. 38.9 and ear begins to ache – An[astasia] 37.2 (because of medicine they gave her for her head). Baby still sleeping, Ania 36.6 – their illness has been very heavy – God for sure sent it for the good somehow! They are so brave the whole time. I shall go out and say good morning to the soldiers now in front of the house. Don't know what to write too many impressions, too much to say. Heart aches very much, but I don't need it, my spirits are quite up and I am like a cock. Only suffer too hideously for you.

Your Old Wify

Same day
Beloved, precious Light of my Life,

Grammatin and Soloviev are going off with 2 letters hoping that at least they can reach you to bring you and get news.

It's more than maddening not being together – but souls and hearts are more than ever – nothing can tear us apart, though they just wish this, that is why they won't let you see me until you have signed a paper of theirs – resp[onsible] min[isters] or Constitution.

The nightmare is that having no army behind you, you may be forced into it – but such a promise is 'null' when once in power again – they meanly caught you like a mouse in a trap – unheard of in history – and it kills me the vileness and humiliation: the young men will tell you clearly the whole situation which too complicated to write and I give only some letters which can be burned or easier hidden away.

All very weak and lie in the dark, knowing nothing about you nor the worst of all.

                                                                 Wify

Pierre Gilliard, Memoirs – 2 March
The Duma left the Tsar with the alternatives of abdicating or marching on Petrograd with the troops which remained faithful to him: the latter would mean civil war in the presence of the enemy. Nicholas II did not hesitate, and this morning he handed General Ruzsky a telegram informing the President of the Duma that he intended to abdicate in favour of his son.

A few hours later he summoned Professor Fedorov to his carriage and said:

'Tell me frankly, Sergei Petrovich. Is Alexei's malady incurable?'

Professor Fedorov, fully realizing the importance of what he was going to say, answered:

'Science teaches us, sire, that it is an incurable disease. Yet those who are afflicted with it sometimes reach an advanced old age. Still, Alexei Nikolaevich is at the mercy of an accident.'

The Tsar hung his head and sadly murmured:

'That's just what the Tsarina told me. Well, if that is the case and Alexei can never serve his country as I should like him to, we have the right to keep him ourselves.'

The day passed in an oppressive suspense. At 3.30 a.m. next morning Dr Botkin was called to the telephone by a member of the

Provisional Government, who asked him for news of Alexei Nikolaevich. (We heard subsequently that a report of his death had been circulating in the city.)

King George V, Diary – 2 March

[Grand Duke] Michael [Miche-Miche] came and I told all about the revolution in Petrograd, he was much upset, I fear Alicky is the cause of it all and Nicky has been weak. Heard from Buchanan that the Duma had forced Nicky to sign his abdication and Misha had been appointed Regent, and after he has been 23 years Emperor, I am in despair.

Nicky, Diary – 2 March – in the train

Ruzsky came in the morning and read me his long telephone conversation with Rodzianko. In his words, the situation in Petrograd is such, that at present a ministry from the Duma is powerless to do anything, because they are opposed by the social democrat party in the guise of the workers' committee.

My abdication is necessary. Ruzsky communicated his conversation to headquarters and Alexeev to all the commanders-in-chief.

By about 2.30 answers had arrived from all. The crux of the matter is that it is necessary to take this step, for the sake of Russia's salvation and of maintaining calm in the army at the front. I agreed.

The draft manifesto was sent out from headquarters. In the evening Gutchkov and Shulgin arrived from Petrograd, and after talking to them, I handed over the signed and recopied manifesto. I left Pskov at one o'clock at night, with a heavy heart. All around is betrayal, cowardice and deceit!

Abdication Manifesto of Nicholas II

By the grace of God, we, Nicholas II, Emperor of all the Russias, Tsar of Poland, Grand Duke of Finland, etc., etc., to all our faithful subjects make known:

In these days of terrible struggle against the foreign enemy who has been trying for three years to impose his will upon Our Fatherland, God has willed that Russia should be faced with a new and formidable trial. Troubles at home threaten to have a fatal effect on the ultimate course of this hard-fought war. The destinies of Russia, the honour of Our heroic army, the welfare of the nation and

the whole future of our dear country require that the war shall be
continued, cost what it may, to a victorious end.

Our cruel enemy is making his final effort and the day is at hand
when our brave army, with the help of our glorious allies, will over-
throw him once and for all.

At this moment, a moment so decisive for the existence of Russia,
Our conscience bids Us to facilitate the closest union of Our subjects
and the organisation of all their forces for the speedy attainment of
victory. For that reason We think it right – and the Imperial Duma
shares Our view – to abdicate the crown of the Russian State and
resign the supreme power.

As We do not desire to be separated from Our beloved son, We
bequeath Our inheritance to Our brother, the Grand Duke Michael
Alexandrovich, and give him Our blessing on his accession to the
throne. We ask him to govern in the closest concert with the repre-
sentatives of the nation who sit in the legislative assemblies and to
pledge them his inviolable oath in the name of the beloved country.

We appeal to all the loyal sons of Russia and ask them to do their
patriotic and sacred duty by obeying their Tsar at this moment of
painful national crisis and to help him and the representatives of the
nation to guide the Russian State into the path of prosperity and
glory.

May God help Russia!

NICHOLAS

Witnessed by Minister of the Imperial Court, Adjutant
General Count Fredericks
Pskov, 2 March 1917, 3.05 p.m.

Maurice Paléologue, Memoirs – 3 March
Nicholas II abdicated yesterday, shortly before midnight.

When the emissaries of the Duma, Guchkov and Shulgin, arrived
at Pskov about nine o'clock in the evening, the Emperor gave them
his usual simple and kindly reception.

In very dignified language and a voice which trembled somewhat,
Guchkov told the Emperor the object of his mission and ended with
these words:

'Nothing but the abdication of Your Majesty in favour of your son
can still save the Russian Fatherland and preserve the dynasty.'

The Emperor replied very quickly, as if referring to some perfectly
commonplace matter:

'I decided to abdicate yesterday. But I cannot be separated from my son; that is more than I could bear; his health is too delicate; you must realize what I feel. I shall therefore abdicate in favour of my brother, Mikhail.'

Guchkov at once bowed to the argument of fatherly affection to which the Tsar appealed and Shulgin also acquiesced.

The Emperor then went into his study with the Minister of the Court; he came out ten minutes later with the act of abdication signed. Count Fredericks handed it to Guchkov.

On reading this declaration, which was typed on an ordinary sheet of paper, the emissaries of the Duma were deeply stirred and could hardly speak as they took their leave of Nicholas II who was as unmoved as ever as he gave them a kindly handshake.

As soon as they left the carriage the imperial train started off for Dvinsk with a view to returning to Mogilev.

History can show few events so momentous, or so pregnant with possibilities and far-reaching in their effects. Yet of all those of which it has left any record, is there a single one which has taken place in such casual, commonplace and prosaic fashion, and above all with such indifference and self-effacement on the part of the principal hero?

Is it simply lack of interest in the Emperor's case? I think not. His abdication decree, over which he has pondered long if he did not actually word it himself, is inspired by the loftiest sentiments, and its general tone is nobility itself. But his moral attitude at this supreme crisis appears perfectly logical if it is admitted as I have often remarked, that for many months past the unhappy sovereign has felt himself lost and that he long ago made his sacrifice and accepted his fate.

The accession of the Grand Duke Mikhail to the throne has aroused the fury of the *Soviet*: 'No more Romanovs!' is the cry in all quarters: 'We want a republic!'

Maria Pavlovna [the younger], Memoirs
At four in the morning of 3 March, the new revolutionary commander of Tsarskoe Selo knocked at my father's house and announced the abdication of the Emperor, both for himself and for the Tsarevich, in favour of the Grand Duke Mikhail.

... my father went again to see the Empress. Incredible as it may seem, she did not know of the abdication. No one had found the courage to impart this news to her and my father was obliged to do it.

Olga Paley,[6] Memoirs – 3 March
The fall of the empire – for we all understood perfectly well that it
was the fall – appeared to us in all its horror. In vain we tried to convince ourselves that Grand Duke Mikhail would continue the tradition. We all knew him to be lacking in character and completely
under the malign influence of his wife, Madame Brassova, besides
which we loved 'our' emperor, chosen and anointed by God, and did
not wish for anyone else.

Grand Duke Pavel went to see the Empress at 11 o'clock.
Unbelievable though it may seem, the poor woman did not know of
her husband's abdication. None of her entourage had the courage to
deal her such a blow.

Grand Duke Pavel went in quietly and stood for a long time kissing her hand, unable to say a single word. His heart was breaking.
The Empress, in her simple nurse's uniform, struck him with her
calm and the serenity of her gaze. 'Dear Alix,' said the Grand Duke at
length, 'I wanted to be with you at such a difficult time ...'

The Empress looked him in the eyes. 'What is happening with
Nicky?' she asked. 'Nicky is well,' replied the prince hurriedly, 'but
you must be brave, as he is: today, 3rd March, at one o'clock in the
morning, he signed the act of abdication from the throne both for
himself and on behalf of Alexei.'

The Empress shuddered, lowering her head as if in prayer. Then she
straightened up and said: 'If Nicky did it, then it must have been necessary. I believe in God's mercy: God will not abandon us.' But at the
same time large tears trickled down her cheeks. 'I may no longer be
Empress,' she said with a sad smile, 'but I still remain a sister of
mercy. As Misha will now be Emperor, I shall look after the children,
the hospital, we will go to the Crimea ...'

Lily Dehn, Memoirs
Her face was distorted with agony, her eyes were full of tears. She tot-
tered rather than walked, and I rushed forward and supported her
until she reached the writing table between the windows. She leant
heavily against it, and taking my hand in hers she said brokenly,
'Abdiqué!' I could hardly believe my ears. I waited for her next words.
They were scarcely audible. At last: 'Poor darling – alone there and
suffering – My God! What he must have suffered!'

---

[6] Morganatic wife of Nicky's Uncle Pavel.

Pierre Gilliard, Memoirs – 3 March

No one can have any idea of what the Tsarina suffered during these days when she was despairing at her son's bedside and had no news of the Tsar. She reached the extreme limits of human resistance in this last trial, in which originated that wonderful and radiant serenity which was to sustain her and her family to the day of their death.

The Tsarina's despair almost defied imagination, but her great courage did not desert her. I saw her in Alexei's room that same evening. Her face was terrible to see, but, with a strength of will which was almost superhuman, she had forced herself to come to the children's rooms as usual so that the young invalids, who knew nothing of what had happened since the Tsar had left for GHQ, should suspect nothing.

Alix to Nicky – 3 March – Tsarskoe Selo

Beloved Soul of my Soul, my own Wee One, Sweet Angel, oh, me loves you so – always together, night and day – I feel what you are going through – and your poor heart. God have mercy, give you strength and wisdom. He won't forsake you. He will help, recompense this mad suffering and separation at such a time when one needs being together. Yesterday came a packet for you with maps from Headquarters, I have them safe.

Ah, whenever shall we be together again – utterly cut off in every way. Yet, their illness perhaps is a saving, one can't move him. Don't fear for him, we'll all fight for our Sunshine.

Such sunny weather, no clouds – that means, trust and hope – all is pitch black around, but God is above all; we know not His Way – nor how He will help – but he will harken unto all prayers.

Know nothing of the war, live cut off from the world – always new, maddening news – the last that Father declined to keep the place which he occupies 23 years. One might lose one's reason – but we won't – she shall believe in a future of sunshine, yet on earth remember that. Pavel just came – told me *all*.

I *fully* understand your action – my own hero! I *know* you could not sign against what you swore at your coronation – we know each other through and through and need no words – and, as I live, we shall see you back upon your throne, brought back by your people and troops to the glory of your reign.

You have saved your *Son's* reign and the country and your saintly purity and (Judas Ruzsky) you will be crowned by God on this earth, in your country. I hold you tight, tight in my arms and will never let them touch your shining soul. I kiss, kiss, kiss and bless you and always understand you,

Wify

Olga Paley, Memoirs – 3 March

At that moment Grand Duke Mikhail was in the Winter Palace in Petrograd. Very few people know that, when the commander of the troops, General Khabalov, saw the mass of people, he rushed to the palace and asked the Grand Duke whether he should fire at the crowd, relying on a few regiments that had remained loyal. Mikhail categorically rejected the idea, declaring that he 'did not wish to shed a single drop of Russian blood'. He left the palace secretly and hid in Millionnaya Street at the house of his friend Prince Putiatin.

While he was at Prince Putiatin's, Grand Duke Mikhail, who had been Tsar since one o'clock that morning, received visits from Prince Lvov, Guchkov, Rodzianko, Milyukov, Kerensky and others, all trying to convince him to abdicate the throne in favour of the people, who would in time themselves elect either him or somebody else. After a few minutes' hesitation this characterless prince gave in, to the great joy of those traitors to their country; and Kerensky, that marionette who by some error was taken seriously at the time, had a fit of hysterics.

Abdication Manifesto of Grand Duke Mikhail – 3 March[7]

A heavy burden has been placed on me by the will of my brother, who has transferred to me the Imperial Throne of all the Russias, at this time of unprecedented hostilities and civil disturbances.

Inspired, as are all our people, by the thought that the welfare of Russia must come above all else, I am firmly resolved to assume supreme power only if such is the will of our great people, who must now by universal suffrage and through their representatives in the Constituent Assembly establish a form of government and new fundamental laws for the Russian State.

Therefore, invoking the benediction of God, I call on all citizens of the Russian State to obey the Provisional Government, set up on the initiative of the State Duma and invested with full

---

[7] Penned by Vladimir Nabokov, father of the writer.

power, until such a time as a Constituent Assembly, summoned in the shortest possible delay on the basis of universal, fair, equal and secret elections, shall by its decision of a form of government, express the will of the people.

Mikhail

3/III – 1917

Petrograd

Ania Vyrubova, Memoirs

In that hour of supreme agony there was not a word spoken of the loss of a throne. Alexandra's whole heart was with her husband, her sole fears that he might be in danger and that their boy might be taken from them.

At once she began to send frantic telegrams to the Emperor begging him to come home as soon as possible. With the refinement of cruelty which marked the whole conduct of the Provisional Government in those days the telegrams were returned to the Empress marked in blue pencil: 'Address of person mentioned unknown.'

Not even this insolence nor all her fears broke the sublime courage of the Empress. When next morning she entered my sick room and saw by my tear-drenched face that I knew what had happened her only visible emotion was a slight irritation that other lips than her own had brought me the news. 'They should have known that I preferred to tell you myself,' she said. It was only when she had gone her rounds of the palace and was alone in her own bedroom that she finally gave way to her grief.

'Mama cried terribly,' little Grand Duchess Maria told me. 'I cried too, but not more than I could help, for poor Mama's sake.'

Maria to Nicky – 3 March – Tsarskoe Selo

Dear and beloved Father!

I'm always with You in my thoughts and prayers. Sisters are still lying in the dark room and Alexei is already bored with it so he is in the playing-room with the windows open. Today we moulded bullets from tin with Zilik [Gilliard] and he was very happy. I spend nearly all days with Mama because I'm now alone healthy and can walk. I also sleep with her to be nearby in case something must be said or someone wants to see her. Lily sleeps in the red room near the dining-room on the sofa where was Olga.

Dear beloved Father, we all greet and kiss You warmly. God protect You.

Your children

Nicky, Diary – 3 March – on the train

Slept long and deeply. Awoke far beyond Dvinsk. The day was sunny and frost. Talked with my people about yesterday. Read a lot about Julius Caesar. At 8.20 I arrived in Mogilev. All the staff of headquarters were on the platform. I received Alexeev in the compartment. By 9.30 I managed to get over to the house. Alexeev arrived with the latest news from Rodzianko.

It appears Misha has abdicated. His manifesto finishes with something about elections for a Constituent Assembly. God knows, who advised him to sign something so vile! In Petrograd the disturbances have ceased – may it continue that way.

King George V, Diary – 3 March

Went to M.H. [Marlborough House] and had a talk with Motherdear [Queen Alexandra] who is much distressed at the news from Russia.

Olga [sister], Memoirs

Sandro recalled that he had 'never seen Empress Marie in such a state. She could not sit still for a moment. She kept pacing the floor, and I saw that she was more angry than miserable. She understood nothing of what had happened. She blamed poor Alicky for everything.'

Nicky to General Alexeev – 4 March – Mogilev

For Communication with the Provisional Government

The following guarantees are demanded from the Provisional Government:

1) That I may proceed unimpeded to Tsarskoe Selo with the persons accompanying me.
2) That [we] may reside in safety at Tsarskoe Selo until the children's recovery, with those same persons.
3) That [we] may proceed unimpeded to Romanov-on-the-Murman [Murmansk] with the same persons.
4) That we may return to Russia at the end of the war to settle in the Crimea – in Livadia.

From Mogilev to Tsarskoe Selo – 4 March – Telegram
HER MAJESTY
THANKS DARLING AT LAST YOUR TELEGRAM COME DURING THIS NIGHT
DESPAIRING BEING AWAY GOD BLESS YOU ALL LOVE VERY TENDERLY   NICKY

Second Telegram – same day FOND THANKS WIRE MOTHERDEAR
ARRIVED FOR TWO DAYS SO KIND ALLOWING DINE WITH HER IN TRAIN
AGAIN SNOWSTORM THOUGHT PRAYERS ALWAYS TOGETHER   NICKY

Alix to Nicky – 4 March – Tsarskoe Selo
Sweet, beloved Treasure –
    The Lady leaves today instead of yesterday, so have occasion to
write again. *What* relief and joy it was to hear your precious voice
only one heard so badly and one listens now to all our conversations.
And your dear wire this morning. I wired to you yesterday evening
about 9½ and this morning before 1.
    Baby leans over the bed and tells me to kiss you. All 4 are lying in
the green room in the dark; Maria and I are writing scarcely seeing
anything with the curtains drawn. This morning only read the manifesto and then later another from Misha. People are beside themselves with misery and adoration for my Angel. A movement is
beginning amongst the troops. Fear nothing from Sunny, she does
not move – does not exist. Only I feel and foresee glorious sunshine
ahead.
    Am utterly disgusted with Ducky's husband [Grand Duke Kyril]![8]
One shuts up people right and left, officers of course. God knows
what goes on – here rifles choose their own Commanders and behave
abominably to them, don't salute, smoke in the faces of their officers.
Don't want to write all that goes on, so <u>hideous</u> it is. N.P. [Sabline]
shut up in town. Sailors come to fetch the others. The invalids
upstairs and downstairs know nothing of your decision – fear to tell
them and also yet unnecessary. Lily [Dehn] has been an angel and
helps one being like iron and me have not once broken down.
    You, my love, my Angel dear, cannot think of what you have and
are going through – makes me mad. Oh God; of course we will rec-

---

    [8] According to Maurice Paléologue: 'Forgetting the oath of fealty, and the office
of aide-de-camp which bind him to the Emperor, he went off about one o'clock
this afternoon to make obeisance to popular rule. In his naval captain's uniform he
was seen leading the marines of the Guard, whose commander he is, and placing
their services at the disposal of the rebels!'

ompense 100 fold for all your suffering. I won't write on that subject, one can't – how one has humiliated you sending those two brutes too – I did not know till you told me which of them have been. I feel that the army will stand up.

Revolution in Germany, W[illy] killed,[9] son wounded, one sees all over the freemasons movement. Now An[astasia]: temp. 38.6 and spots coming more out. Olga has pleurisy, Cow [Ania] too. T[atiana]'s ears better, Sunbeam better, and I doubt one would ever let us pass anywhere. Gibbes [tutor] saw Emma, Nini and their mothers in one room in an officers hosp. (English). Their rooms completely burned down; old woman very ill. Red cap still shut up. Live with you, love and adore you. Kiss and embrace so tenderly fondly. God bless and keep you now and ever. Get somebody to bring a line – have you plans more or less for the moment: God on high will help. Hold you tight, tight, your very own Wify.

Only *this morning* we knew that all given over to M[isha] and Baby now safe – such comfort.

Nicky, Diary – 4 March – on the train
Slept well. Went to receive the report. At 12 o'clock I went to the platform to meet dear Mama, who was arriving from Kiev [with Sandro]. I took her back home and lunched with her and our people. We sat and talked for a long time. Today at last I received two telegrams from dear Alix. The weather was foul cold and snowy. After tea I received Alexeev and Fredericks. At 8 o'clock I went to dine with Mama and sat with her until 11 o'clock.

Sandro, Memoirs
I dressed and went to break the heart of a mother. We ordered the train and left for the Stavka in the afternoon, as in the meanwhile we learnt that Nicky had received 'permission' to pay a farewell visit to GHQ.

Upon arrival in Mogilev our train was brought to the 'Imperial Platform', where the Tsar usually started on his trips to the capital. Nicky's motor car drew up to the station a minute later. He walked slowly along the platform, said good morning to the two Cossacks standing at the entrance to his mother's car, and went inside.

He was pale, but nothing otherwise disclosed his authorship of the

[9] Alix was misinformed.

horrible Manifesto. He remained closeted with the old Empress for two hours. She never told me the subject of their conversation. When I was invited to join them, she sat in a chair sobbing aloud, while he stood motionless, looking at his feet and, of course, smoking.

We embraced. I did not know what to say. The calmness of his demeanour showed his firm belief in the righteousness of his decision, although he did criticize his brother Misha for refusing to accept the throne and for leaving Russia without a ruler.

'Misha should not have done a thing like that,' he concluded sententiously. 'I wonder who could have given him such strange advice.'

This remark, coming from a man who had surrendered one-sixth of the earth's surface to a mob of drunken reservists and rioting workers left me speechless. After a painful pause he volunteered the casual explanation of the reasons that prompted his decision. He mentioned the three principal ones: 1, his unwillingness to plunge Russia into civil war; 2, his desire to keep the army out of politics and in a condition to help the Allies; 3, his belief that the Provisional Government would rule Russia better than he had.

Ania Vyrubova, Memoirs
Of his mother, who hurried from Kiev, accompanied by Grand Duke Alexander Mikhailovich [Sandro], to see him, he said that he was vastly comforted to have her near him, but that the sight of the Grand Duke was unendurable.

But what did he think was to become of him, of the Empress and the children? He did not know, but there was one prayer he should not be too proud to make to his enemies, and that was that they should not send him out of Russia.

'Let me live here in my own country, as the humblest and most obscure proprietor, tilling the land and earning the poorest living,' he exclaimed. 'Send us to any distant corner of Russia, but only let us stay.'

King George V to Nicky – 6 March – Buckingham Palace – Telegram, withheld by Provisional Government
EVENTS OF LAST WEEK HAVE DEEPLY DEPRESSED ME. MY THOUGHTS ARE CONSTANTLY WITH YOU AND I SHALL ALWAYS REMAIN YOUR TRUE AND DEVOTED FRIEND AS YOU KNOW I HAVE BEEN IN THE PAST.

Nicky, Diary – 7 March – Mogilev
Received two more letters from dear Alix, brought by two officers of the convoy. Went for a walk for about an hour. The weather was mild, but it snowed the whole day. After tea I started to pack my things. Dined with Mama and played bezique with her.

Journal No. 10, Provisional Government
7 March 1917
DISCUSSED:
The imprisonment of the abdicated Emperor Nicholas II and his Consort.
RESOLVED:
1) To declare the abdicated Emperor and his consort under arrest and to deliver the former Emperor to Tsarskoe Selo.
2) To instruct General Mikhail Vasilievich Alexeev to assemble a detail to guard the abdicated Emperor, at the disposal of the members of the State Duma dispatched to Mogilev.
3) To instruct the members of the State Duma sent to accompany the former Emperor from Mogilev to Tsarskoe Selo, to submit a written report when they have completed their assignment.
4) To promulgate the present resolution.

Count Benckendorff, Memoirs – 8 March
On the morning of the 8th March I was informed that General Kornilov, Commander-in-Chief was at Tsarskoe and that he was expected at the Palace at any moment. He told me that he wished to see the Empress in order to inform her of the decision of the Provisional Government. He gave me the document to read.
It was an order for the arrest of the Emperor, and, as has been said, of his wife. He added that this was a precautionary measure, and as soon as the health of the children allowed it, the Emperor's family would be sent to Murmansk where a British cruiser would await them and take them to England.
I went to inform the Empress of this visit, and she received [Kornilov] in the presence of Count Apraksin and myself. He read aloud the order of arrest which had been published the same day in the newspapers, after which he asked us to leave and remained alone with the Empress.
I learnt afterwards that he had given her the same assurance that he had given me, that is to say that it had been pointed out to him

that the arrest was solely a precautionary measure destined to be a safeguard against excesses that might be feared on the part of the troops. The latter, intoxicated, were out of control, disobeyed the officers and were under the influence of a Council of Workmen and Soldiers consisting of socialist elements. [Kornilov] indicated on a plan the doors which were to be closed, and gave the necessary orders before all of us. He told us that those persons who expressed a wish to remain at the Palace would be subject to the same order and that henceforth no person would be able to leave or enter.

Being questioned as to my intentions I declared that I desired to remain. After his departure I went to see the Empress. I found her calm, very brave, but with red eyes, she had wept a good deal.

I was able to announce to her the return of the Emperor on the morrow. She told me that he [Kornilov] had behaved well towards her. He assured her that the duration of the arrest would depend solely on the health of the children and that a British cruiser was already waiting at the port of Murmansk to take the imperial family to England. The last news was not true.

Pierre Gilliard, Memoirs – 8 March

At half past ten on the morning of the 8th Her Majesty summoned me and told me that General Kornilov had been sent by the Provisional Government to inform her that the Tsar and herself were under arrest and that those who did not wish to be kept in close confinement must leave the palace before four o'clock. I replied that I had decided to stay with them.

'The Tsar is coming back tomorrow. Alexei must be told everything. Will you do it? I am going to tell the girls myself.'

It was easy to see how she suffered when she thought of the grief of the Grand Duchesses on hearing that their father had abdicated. They were ill, and the news might make them worse.

I went to Alexei and told him that the Tsar would be returning from Mogilev next morning and would never go back there again.

'Why?'

'Your father does not want to be Commander-in-Chief any more.'

He was greatly moved at this, as he was very fond of going to GHQ.

After a moment or two I added:

'You know your father does not want to be Tsar any more?'

He looked at me in astonishment, trying to read in my face what had happened.

'What! Why?'

'He is very tired and has had a lot of trouble lately.'

'Oh yes! Mother told me they stopped his train when he wanted to come here. But won't papa be Tsar again afterwards?'

I then told him that the Tsar had abdicated in favour of the Grand Duke Mikhail, who had also renounced the throne.

'But who's going to be Tsar, then?'

'I don't know. Perhaps nobody now. '

Not a word about himself. Not a single allusion to his rights as the Heir. He was very red and agitated.

There was a silence, and then he said:

'But if there isn't a Tsar, who's going to govern Russia?'

At four o'clock the doors of the palace were closed. We were prisoners!

Sandro, Memoirs

General Alexeev invites us to assemble in the main hall of GHQ. Nicky is to address the members of his former staff. By eleven a.m. the hall is packed. Generals, officers, and persons in attendance on the Emperor are present.

Nicky enters – calm, reserved, bearing the semblance of a smile on his lips. He thanks the staff and begs them to continue their work 'with the same loyalty and in a spirit of self-sacrifice'. He invites them to forget all feuds, to serve Russia and lead our army to victory.

Then he says his adieus, in curt soldier-like sentences, avoiding words that could suggest pathos. His modesty makes a tremendous impression. We shout 'Hurray', as we never had in the last twenty-three years.

Elderly generals cry. A moment more, and someone is bound to step forward and implore Nicky to reconsider his decision. Such a move would be useless: the Tsar of Russia does not go back on his word.

Nicky bows and walks out. We lunch. We dine. Our conversation drags. We talk of the days of our childhood in the Crimean palace of Livadia ...

Nicky is trying to cheer up his mother. He expects to see her 'soon'. There is some talk of his going to England, although he would much rather stay in Russia. Quarter to four. His train is stationed opposite ours. We get up. He covers his mother's face with kisses.

He turns to me and we embrace. He goes out, crosses the platform and enters his saloon car. The gentlemen of the Duma, who came to the Stavka to escort Nicky to St Petersburg and incidentally to spy on his aides, shake hands with General Alexeev. They exchange cordial bows. No doubt, they have reasons to be grateful to the general.

Nicky's train whistles and commences to move slowly. He stands in the large mirrored window of his car. He smiles and waves his hand. His expression is infinitely sad. He is wearing a simple khaki blouse, with the cross of St George in its buttonhole. The old Empress cries unrestrainedly now that the Tsar's train has become a stream of smoke on the horizon.

[This was the last time Nicky and Sandro met.]

Nicky, Diary – 8 March – Mogilev

The last day in Mogilev. At 10.15 I signed my farewell statement to the army. At 10.30 I went to the duty office, where I said goodbye to all the staff of headquarters and administration. At home I took my leave of the officers and cossacks – my heart was nearly breaking!

At 12 o'clock Mama came into the carriage, I lunched with her and her suite and stayed with her until 4.30. I said goodbye to her, Sandro, Sergei, Boris and Alek [Alexeev]. Poor Nilov was not allowed to go with me. At 4.46 I left Mogilev, and was seen off by a touching crowd of people. 4 members of the Duma are travelling with me on the train!

I passed Orsha and Vitebsk.

The weather is frosty and windy.

It's sad, painful and depressing.

Count Benckendorff, Memoirs – 9 March – Tsarskoe Selo

About 11 o'clock in the morning, I went with Count Apraksin to the first entrance to await the arrival of the Emperor. The gate is about a hundred yards from the Palace.

Towards 11.15, the Emperor's motor-car arrived in front of the gate and was stopped by the sentry, who asked who was in it. After having received the answer of the chauffeur, he made the prearranged signal to the Commandant. The Commandant went down the steps and asked in a loud voice who was there. The sentry cried out, 'Nicholas Romanov'. 'Let him pass,' said the officer.

After this offensive comedy, the motor arrived at the steps and the Emperor and Dolgorukov[10] descended. The ante-chamber was full. He

---

[10] Prince Dolgorukov, a marshal of the court. His mother was married to Benckendorff.

walked through the crowd, saluting in military fashion, shook hands with me and with Apraksin, and entered the Empress's apartment without saying a word. Dolgorukov was moved to tears by this unexpected scene. I took him at once to his mother, and he told us all that had happened. His narrative was dramatic, and made a deep impression on us. It seemed to us inexplicable that the Emperor, who had never been able to make up his mind to grant a constitution and to appoint a responsible minister, had so quickly consented to abdicate. The part played by the Generals and the Staff seemed to us like treason.

Towards 2 o'clock I crossed the threshold of the room in which for so many years I had seen my sovereign at the height of mortal power. He himself was much moved, and embraced me very cordially, and at once began to tell me the vicissitudes of this dramatic event.

He showed me the telegrams of the Generals commanding the different fronts, who all, with one accord, had told him that the only means of saving the monarchy was to abdicate in favour of the Heir-Apparent. Nicholas was of this opinion and begged him on his knees. His Majesty complained bitterly of the almost rude insistence with which General Ruzsky had spoken to him. For several hours at a time General Ruzsky had argued with him without leaving him one moment for reflection. The Emperor as Supreme Commander of the army had, in the presence of the enemy, been betrayed by his Generals and had been forced to give way to pressure because the last support of the monarchy, the army, was going over to the revolutionaries.

The Emperor told me that he had first of all abdicated in favour of his son, and that he had already even put this act of abdication into the hands of General Ruzsky before the envoys of the Duma, Guchkov and Shulgin, had arrived at Pskov.

It was a conversation with Professor Fedorov which had caused him to change his mind. His Majesty had thought at first that it would be possible for him to retire with his family to Livadia, to keep his son with him and to look after his education. The Professor proved to him, and rightly, that the sovereign who has renounced his right to the throne could not in any case remain in the country; that events which would soon become tragic would oblige them to leave as soon as possible for abroad; that the new government would never allow him to educate the sovereign and that he should be prepared to be separated from him. Questioned as to the health of the heir, the Professor said that in his opinion, and in that of all the medical advisers who were looking after him the Heir-Apparent was incurable, that, thanks to care and precautions, it would be possible to prolong his life, but that he would never be a perfectly healthy man. Summing up his opinion Fedorov said that the Emperor, the Empress and the Grand Duchesses should leave as soon as possible, and that the Heir-Apparent should be left in the hands of the Regency which was to be formed. It was in consequence of this conversation that the Emperor decide to cancel his first act of abdication and without telling anybody, he drafted the act which he gave that evening to Guchkov, in virtue of which he abdicated in favour of his brother. The illegality of this act had not yet struck him.

Nicky, Diary – 9 March – Tsarskoe Selo

I arrived at Tsarskoe Selo quickly and without mishap – at 11.30. But God, what a difference, there were sentries on the street and in the park around the house, and ensigns of some sort in the entrance! I went upstairs and saw darling Alix and the dear children. She looked strong and well, but they were all lying in a darkened room. They are all feeling fine, except Maria who only developed measles a short time ago. We lunched and dined in Alexei's playroom. Saw dear Benckendorff. Went for a walk with Valia Dolg[orukov] and worked a little with him in the garden, as we aren't allowed to go further!! After tea I unpacked my things.

Ania Vyrubova, Memoirs

For a time at least the happiness of reunion blotted out the suspense of the past and the gloomy uncertainty of the future. But afterwards, alone, behind their own closed doors, the emotion of the betrayed and deserted Emperor completely overcame his self-control and he sobbed like a child on the breast of his wife. It was four o'clock in the afternoon before she could come to me, and when she came I read in her white, drawn face the whole story of the ordeal through which she had passed.

'He will not break down a second time,' she said with a brave smile. 'He is walking the garden now. Come to the window and see.' She helped me to the window and herself pulled aside the curtain.

Never, never while I live shall I forget what we saw, we two, clinging together in shame and sorrow for our disgraced country. Below in the garden of the palace which had been his home for twenty years stood the man who until a few days before had been Tsar of all the Russias. With him was his faithful friend Prince Dolgorukov

[Valia], and surrounding them were six soldiers, say rather six hooligans, armed with rifles.

With their fists and with the butts of their guns they pushed the Emperor this way and that as though he were some wretched vagrant they were baiting in a country road.

'You can't go there, Mr Colonel.' 'We don't permit you to walk in that direction', 'Stand back when you are commanded'.

The Emperor, apparently unmoved, looked from one of these coarse brutes to another and with great dignity turned and walked back towards the palace.

Pierre Gilliard, Memoirs – 9 March

The Emperor accepted all these restraints with extraordinary serenity and moral grandeur. No word of reproach ever passed his lips. The fact was that his whole being was dominated by one passion, which was more powerful even than the bonds between himself and his family – love of country. We felt he was ready to forgive anything to those who were inflicting such humiliations upon him so long as they were capable of saving Russia.

Lord Stamfordham,[11] note of meeting – 9 March – Buckingham Palace

I saw the Prime Minister this morning. He had not seen Sir George Buchanan's telegram received last evening reporting his conversation with Mr Miliukov [new Foreign Minister], in which the latter urged the earliest possible departure of the Emperor from Russia, and suggested that the King and British Government should offer His Imperial Majesty an asylum in this country.

I pointed out to Mr Lloyd George that naturally the King would wish to be consulted before his Government gave a definite reply to this suggestion.

After reading the telegram the Prime Minister discussed the alternative suggestion that the Emperor might go to Denmark. Mr Lloyd George, however, was strongly against this proposal. Denmark in his opinion is too near Germany, and there would be a serious danger of His Imperial Majesty becoming a focus of intrigue of Germany.

A counter Revolution in Russia is not at all improbable and as in France in the Great Revolution discontented Generals might encourage the Army to join in a plot to reinstate the Emperor.

---

[11] Private Secretary to King George V.

Although the Emperor might not encourage such schemes the Prime Minister did not feel at all certain that the Empress might not do so.

Lord Hardinge then joined us, and later Mr Bonar Law: the former recognized Mr Lloyd George's objections to Denmark, and it was generally agreed that the proposal that we should receive the Emperor in this country (having come from the Russian Government which we are endeavouring with all our powers to support) could not be refused.

I pointed out the King's apprehensions entailed in the sea voyage from Romanov. The Prime Minister asked why the Emperor should not come to Bergen. Lord Hardinge remarked that probably the Russian Government wished the Emperor to go to Romanov because he would be in their keeping until he was safe on board an English ship, whereas if he travelled to Bergen he would be free as soon as he crossed the Russian Frontier.

No doubt the present Russian Government are anxious as to the safety of the Emperor and Empress, and for that reason wish to expedite their departure.

I raised the question of the Emperor being provided with adequate means to live in this country.

Mr Lloyd George suggested that the King might be able to place at His Imperial Majesty's disposal one of his houses, but I reminded the Prime Minister that the King had got no houses except Balmoral, which would certainly not be a suitable residence at this time of year.

It was suggested that perhaps the British Government would make the Emperor an allowance, but at my suggestion Lord Hardinge thought it would be perfectly reasonable that Sir George Buchanan should in conveying to Monsieur Miliukov the British Government's willingness to provide an asylum for the Emperor in this country throw out a hint that the Russian Government should settle upon His Imperial Majesty sufficient means to enable him to live here with suitable dignity.

With regard to the Prime Minister's Message to the Russian Premier, which was dispatched yesterday, I said that the King thought it was a little strong to say 'that the *Revolution* is the greatest service which the Russian people have yet made to the cause for which the Allies are fighting'.

He explained that the message was framed to a considerable extent on the suggestions of Monsieur Nabokov at the Russian Embassy, who was anxious that we should emphasise the fact that responsible Government had been established, and that it was the establishment of a stable *Constitutional Government*, which appealed to us as one of the oldest Constitutional Governments, and Mr Lloyd George explained that the rest of the telegram was to a certain extent padding. I answered that the word 'Revolution' had a disagreeable sound coming from a good old Monarchical Government, but good humouredly the Prime Minister replied, 'No, an old *Constitutional Government*', and added that our present Monarch was founded upon a Revolution, which I could not deny.

Mr Lloyd George wished me to assure the King that the message was approved by the Cabinet, and he hoped His Majesty would interpret it in the sense above indicated.

Lord Hardinge undertook to draft an official telegram to Sir George Buchanan to the effect that the King and His Majesty's Government would be prepared to give effect to Monsieur Miliukov's request that the Emperor and his family should be received in this country.

It will be made clear that this proposal was initiated from the Russian Government itself and not from us.

A Private telegram is also to be sent at the Prime Minister's suggestion to point out to Sir George Buchanan the reasons why it is undesirable in the opinion of His Majesty's Government that Their Majesties should go to Denmark. The question of the Emperor's financial position will also be dealt with in this private message.

King George V, Diary – 10 March
Went over to M.H. [Marlborough House] and had a talk with Motherdear [Queen Alexandra] about Russia and Nicky, she is very much upset about it all.

Maurice Paléologue, Memoirs – 10 March
Last night Rasputin's coffin was secretly exhumed from its resting place in the chapel at Tsarskoe Selo and taken away to the Forest of Pargolovo, fifteen *versts* north of Petrograd.

In the midst of a clearing there, a number of soldiers, commanded by an engineer officer, had piled up a large quantity of pine logs.

After forcing off the coffin lid they drew the corpse out with sticks; they dare not touch it with their hands, owing to its putrefying condition, and they hoisted it, not without difficulty, on to the heap of logs. Then they drenched it in petrol and set it on fire. The process of cremation lasted until dawn, more than six hours.

In spite of the icy wind, the appalling length of the operation and the clouds of pungent and fetid smoke which rose from the pyre, several hundred *moujiks* crowded round the fire all night; silent and motionless, they gazed in horror-stricken stupor at the sacrilegious holocaust which was slowly devouring the martyred *staretz*, friend of the Tsar and Tsarina, the *Bojy tchelloviek*, 'Man of God'.

When the flames had done their work, the soldiers collected the ashes of the corpse and buried them under the snow.

Nicky, Diary – 11 March – Tsarskoe Selo
In the morning I received Benckendorff, and learned from him that we would be staying here for quite some time. That's good to know. Continued burning letters and papers. Anastasia's ears have started to ache – the same thing as with the others. From 3 to 4.30 I strolled and worked in the garden.

King George V, Diary – 11 March
Michael [Grand Duke, Miche-Miche] came to see me and we discussed the idea of poor Nicky coming to England.

Lord Stamfordham to A. J. Balfour[12] – 17 March
My dear Balfour,

The King has been thinking much about the Government's proposal that the Emperor Nicholas and his Family should come to England.

As you are doubtless aware the King has a strong personal friendship for the Emperor, and therefore would be glad to do anything to help him in this crisis. But His Majesty cannot help doubting, not only on account of the dangers of the voyage, but on general grounds of expediency, whether it is advisable that the Imperial Family should take up their residence in this country.

The King would be glad if you could consult the Prime Minister, as His Majesty understands no definite decision has yet been come to on the subject by the Russian Government.

Yours very truly, Stamfordham

---

[12] Secretary of State for Foreign Affairs.

Pierre Gilliard, Memoirs
Our captivity at Tsarskoe Selo did not seem likely to last long, and
there was talk about our imminent transfer to England.

Yet the days passed and our departure was always being postponed.
The fact was that the Provisional Government was obliged to deal
with the advanced wing and gradually felt that its authority was slipping away from it. Yet we were only a few hours by railway from the
Finnish frontier, and the necessity of passing through Petrograd was
the only serious obstacle.

Count Benckendorff, Memoirs
At the Palace the attitude of the soldiers on guard became more and
more provocative. Quarrels with the servants were an everyday
occurrence. They felt they had the right to criticise the mode of life
of their Majesties. They wandered about the Palace, walked into all
the rooms, and we were forced to lock the doors.

Pierre Gilliard, Memoirs – 19 March
Alexei feeling much better. We went to church this morning, where
we found Their Majesties, Olga and Tatiana, and the various members of the suite who are sharing our captivity. When the priest
prayed for the success of the Russian and Allied armies the Tsar and
Tsarina knelt down, the whole congregation following their example.

A few days ago, as I was leaving Alexei's room, I met ten soldiers
wandering about in the passage. I went up to them and asked what
they wanted.

'We want to see the Heir.'

'He's in bed and can't be seen.'

'And the others?'

'They are also unwell.'

'And where is the Tsar?'

'I don't know.'

'Will he be going out?'

'I don't know; but come, don't hang about here. There must be no
noise because of the invalids!'

They went back, walking on their toes and talking in low voices.
These are the soldiers depicted to us as wild revolutionaries hating
their ex-Tsar.

Ania Vyrubova, Memoirs

I passed the open door of Alexei's room, and this is what I saw.

Lying sprawled in a chair was the sailor Derevenko, for many years the personal attendant of the Tsarevich, and on whom the family had bestowed every kindness, every material benefit.

Bitten by the mania of revolution, this man was now displaying his gratitude for all their favours. Insolently he bawled at the boy whom he had formerly loved and cherished, to bring him this or that, to perform any menial service his mean lackey's brain could think of.

Dazed and apparently only half conscious of what he was being forced to do, the child moved about trying to obey. It was too much to bear. Hiding my face in my hands, I begged them to take me away from the sickening spectacle.

A. J. Balfour to Lord Stamfordham – 20 March – Foreign Office, London

My dear Stamfordham,

Many thanks for your letter of March 17.

As you are aware, the first suggestion that the Emperor Nicholas and his family should come to England was made by Milyukov to Sir G. Buchanan on March 20. On receipt of this telegram, Sir G. Buchanan was informed that we should be glad to see the Emperor leave Russia, and he was asked whether His Majesty had thought of either Denmark or Switzerland as a place of residence, since no invitation had been sent to His Majesty to come to England.

A further telegram was received from Sir G. Buchanan stating that M. Milyukov was most anxious that His Majesty should leave Russia at once, and that he would be grateful if the King and His Majesty's Government would at once offer the Emperor asylum in England. The question was therefore reconsidered by the Prime Minister, Lord Hardinge, and yourself, and it was decided that Sir G. Buchanan should be told that His Majesty's Government thought it preferable, the initiative having come from the Russian Government, that the Imperial family should come to England. M. Milyukov was informed accordingly, but the Russian Government have as yet come to no decision.

His Majesty's Ministers quite realize the difficulties to which you refer in your letter, but they do not think, unless the position changes, that it is now possible to withdraw the invitation which has been sent, and they therefore trust that the King will consent to adhere to the original invitation, which was sent on the advice of His Majesty's Ministers.

Arthur John Balfour

Nicky, Diary – 21 March – Tsarskoe Selo

This afternoon, Kerensky, the present Minister of Justice, suddenly arrived and walked through all the rooms, he requested to see us and spoke with me for five minutes, presented the new palace commandant, and then left.

He ordered that poor Ania be arrested and taken back to town together with Lily Dehn. This happened between 3 and 4 o'clock, while I was having my walk. The weather was foul, and corresponded exactly to our mood!

Count Benckendorff, Memoirs – 21 March – Tsarskoe Selo

At about 2 o'clock in the afternoon, the Minister of Justice of the Provisional Government, Kerensky, came to the Palace followed by fifteen people, officers and others.

He entered by the kitchen door, assembled the Guard in the passage, and made them an ultra-revolutionary speech, which shocked the officers of the Guard. He then spoke to a few servants who were assisting at this scene, and told them they no longer served their old masters, that they were paid by the people, and that their duty was to watch all that took place in the Palace and to consider themselves under the orders of the Commandant and the officers of the Guard.

The tone of this speech was as provocative as possible. He was dressed in a blue shirt buttoned to the neck, with no cuffs or collar, big boots, and he affected the air of a workman in his Sunday clothes. His manner was abrupt and nervous.

He did not walk, but ran through the rooms, talking very loudly, and even his expression was shifty, and his whole physiognomy, although energetic, disagreeable. He introduced himself and said, 'I have come here to see how you live, to inspect your Palace, and to talk to Nicholas.'

After having searched all their rooms, he had himself conducted to Madame Vyrubova.

[She] had gone to bed when she heard of Kerensky's arrival at the Palace. She had foolishly kept all her papers until the last moment, which she was at that moment burning in the fireplace. It was full of ashes of burnt paper. This did her a lot of harm. She at first refused to receive the Minister, but he insisted on an entry. After having asked after her health, he told her, without waiting for an answer, that she was to dress, take some luggage and follow him to the town. I could hear all that was said from the adjoining room. She answered in a trembling voice that she was ill and could not go out. He replied that he would talk to the doctors, but that in the meantime she was to get ready.

Ania Vyrubova, Memoirs – 21 March
Kerensky said: 'I am the Minister of Justice. You are to dress and go at once to Petrograd.'

I answered not a word but lay still on my pillows looking him straight in the face. This seemed to disconcert him somewhat for he turned to one of his officers and said nervously:

'Ask the doctors if she is fit to go. Otherwise she must be arrested and isolated in the palace.'

Count Benckendorff, who stood in the back of the room near the door, volunteered to see the doctor, and when he returned it was with the message that Dr Botkin gave them permission to take me.

Count Benckendorff, Memoirs – 21 March
After he stopped in Dr Derevenko's room, he ordered Dr Botkin to be summoned. He told me that after having spoken to the doctors, he wished to see Nicholas and Alexandra. I ran to the Emperor to warn him and to inform him of the arrest of Madame Vyrubova. His Majesty told me that he would receive Kerensky with the Empress in the children's schoolroom.

During this time, Kerensky questioned Drs. Botkin and Derevenko about Madame Vyrubova's health, and asked them whether they thought she could be taken to St Petersburg. Both of them answered that, from the medical point of view, there was nothing to prevent her leaving the Palace, and so the question was settled.

As he passed M. Gilliard's room he went in and, knowing him to be of Swiss nationality, he said to him familiarly, 'All is going well,' doubtless thinking that the establishment of a republic would give him real pleasure.

I went in first to the schoolroom to see if their Majesties were ready to receive him. As Kerensky entered he made a sort of bow and introduced himself as the Procurator-General. He was in a state of feverish agitation; he could not stand still, touched all the objects which were on the table and seemed like a madman. He spoke incoherently and to relieve his embarrassment he begged me to send for Dr Botkin.

As soon as Dr Botkin arrived Kerensky told him that the Queen of Denmark had telegraphed to the Provisional Government to enquire after the health of the Empress, and that he wished to ask the doctor to tell him what answer he could give. Botkin replied that Her Majesty had suffered for several years from an enlarged heart, that this condition was maintained, but that for the moment Her Majesty was as well as could be expected under the present circumstances, after the anxiety which the illness of her children had caused her. The Empress did not seem satisfied with the optimistic tone of this answer. The impression of this visit was painful ...

Madame Vyrubova was slowly dressing and a motor-car had been brought to take her to the station. I was bidden to give to the Empress a few images and objects which she did not wish to leave in her apartment, and to tell her that in a quarter of an hour Vyrubova would be brought to a room next door to take leave of her. The Emperor took no part in it. They exchanged but a few words, and after extremely tender farewells, Madame Vyrubova, on her crutches, and supported by two servants, was taken to her car. At St Petersburg she was taken to the Duma.

Ania Vyrubova, Memoirs – 21 March

Afterwards I learnt that the Empress reproached the doctor bitterly, saying over and over through her tears: 'How can you? How can you? You who have no children of your own.' But Dr Botkin was by this time a victim of craven fear and he was incapable of refusing any request of the Provisional Government.

They carried me downstairs to the motor, for I could neither walk nor stand, even with the help of my crutches. By this time I felt nothing, heard nothing. I was turned to stone.

[That was the last time Ania Vyrubova saw Nicky and Alix.]

Pierre Gilliard, Memoirs

It is worthy of note that Kerensky arrived at the palace in one of the Tsar's private cars, driven by a chauffeur from the Imperial garage.

Lord Stamfordham to A. J. Balfour – 21 March – Buckingham Palace

My dear Balfour,
    I have received and laid before the King your letter of the 2nd. inst.

respecting the proposal that the Emperor Nicholas and his family should come to England.

As His Majesty's Ministers are still anxious that the King should adhere to the original invitation sent on their advice His Majesty must regard the matter as settled, unless the Russian Government should come to any fresh decision on the subject.

Yours very truly, Stamfordham

Maurice Paléologue, Memoirs – 21 March

At five o'clock I went to see the Grand Duke Nikolai Mikhailovich in his palace, which is full of Napoleonic relics. It is the first time I have had the chance of a talk with him since the revolution.

He affected an optimism to which silence was my only reply. But he certainly carried it no further than the occasion warranted and, to prevent me thinking that he was entirely hoodwinked by the course of events, he concluded with this cautious reservation:

'As long as sensible and patriotic men like Prince Lvov, Milyukov and Guchkov are at the head of the government, I shall be hopeful enough. If they fall, we are in for a leap into the unknown.'

'In the first chapter of Genesis, that "unknown" is given a specific name.'

'Really! What?'

'The *Tohu-bohu*, which means "chaos".'

22 March   The Minister of Justice, Kerensky, yesterday paid a visit to Tsarskoe Selo to see for himself the arrangements made for guarding the ex-sovereigns. He found everything in order.

Count Benckendorff, Grand Marshal of the Court; Prince Dolgorukov, Marshal of the Court; Madame Naryschkin, Mistress of the Robes; Mlles. Buxhoeveden and Hendrikov,[13] Maids of Honour, and the Tsarevich's tutor, Gilliard, are sharing their monarch's captivity. Madame Vyrubova, who was also residing in the Alexander Palace, has been forcibly removed and confined in the Fortress of SS. Peter and Paul – in the famous Trubetskoi bastion.

Kerensky had a talk with the Emperor. In particular he asked him whether it were true, as the German papers have reported, that William II had frequently advised him to adopt a more liberal policy.

But the Empress was as frigid as she could be.

Madame Vyrubova's departure has not affected her, at any rate in

---

[13] A. Hendrikov. In 1918 she was arrested in Ekaterinburg and shot.

the way that might have been·expected. After all her passionate and jealous attachment to her, she has suddenly made her responsible for all the evils which have overtaken the Russian imperial family.

Xenia to Nicky – 23 March – St Petersburg

I have been sitting here in the hope that they would let me through to you, as my one wish was to see you. Now it has become clear it isn't feasible, and I leave for the Crimea on the 25th.

You will understand how painful and sad it is for me, but what can I do, I have to give up. I have been with you heart and soul during the dear children's illness, afraid from afar, without news, suffering as I suffer now for your sufferings, living everything with you. Today Mama, Sandro and Olga and her husband are going to the Crimea. They will be staying with us.

It will be very painful for poor Mama to return there, but at least we will all be together, and that is a real comfort at such a time! It is so sad that you cannot come and join us! I want to believe that everything will end well for Russia and the war will be brought to a victorious end.

My heart bleeds for you, for our country, for everything. But the God of the Russian land is great, and we have to believe and pray and put our faith in God's mercy. Please God we shall meet again in better circumstances – but where, when and how?

Nicky, Diary – 23 March – Tsarskoe Selo

I looked through my books and things, and started to put aside everything that I want to take with me, if we have to go to England.

25 March, The Annunciation We spent this feast day in unbelievable conditions – under arrest in our own house and without the slightest possibility of communicating either with Mama or our relatives!

Lord Stamfordham to A. J. Balfour – 24 March – Windsor Castle

My dear Balfour,

Every day the King is becoming more concerned about the question of the Emperor and Empress of Russia coming to this country.

His Majesty receives letters from people in all classes of life, known or unknown to him, saying how much the matter is being discussed, not only in Clubs but by working men, and that Labour Members in the House of Commons are expressing adverse opinions to the proposal.

As you know from the first the King has thought the presence of the Imperial Family (especially of the Empress) in this country would raise all sorts of difficulties, and I feel sure that you appreciate how awkward it will be for our Royal Family who are closely connected both with the Emperor and Empress.

You probably also are aware that the subject has become more or less public property, and that people are either assuming that it has been initiated by the King, or deprecating the very unfair position in which His Majesty will be placed if the arrangement is carried out.

The King desires me to ask you whether after consulting the Prime Minister, Sir George Buchanan should not be communicated with with a view to approaching the Russian Government to make some other plan for the future residence of Their Imperial Majesties?

Yours very truly, Stamfordham

Same day
My dear Balfour,

The King wishes me to write again on the subject of my letter of this morning. He must beg you to represent to the Prime Minister that from all he hears and reads in the Press, the residence in this Country of the Ex-Emperor and Empress would be strongly resented by the public, and would undoubtedly compromise the position of the King and Queen from whom it is already generally supposed the invitation has emanated.

I would particularly call your attention to an article in last Thursday's *Justice* by Hyndman who condemns the invitation, and implies that it has come from Their Majesties. And Hyndman is the person that Mr Henderson told the King he wished to send to Russia as one of the representatives of our Socialists in this Country!

Buchanan ought to be instructed to tell Milyukov that the opposition to the Emperor and Empress coming here is so strong that we must be allowed to withdraw from the consent previously given to the Russian Government's proposal.

Yours very truly, Stamfordham

Count Benckendorff, Memoirs – 27 March
On the 27th March during Mass, Kerensky arrived once more at the Palace. He said that the extreme parties demanded the removal of the

Emperor to a fortress to liberate him from the influence of the Empress who, it was everywhere said, was at the head of the so-called counter-revolutionary movement.

He wished to try and arrange matters, but in order to do this it was imperative that the Empress should be separated from the Emperor and the children and moved into the other wing of the Palace; so that all communication between them should be cut off and that they should only meet at Divine service and at meals, in the presence of the officer on duty.

Pierre Gilliard, Memoirs – 27 March

After Mass, Kerensky announced to the Tsar that he was obliged to separate him from the Tsarina – that he will have to live apart, only seeing Her Majesty at meals, and that on condition that only Russian is spoken. Tea, too, may be taken together, but in the presence of an officer, as no servants are present.

A little later the Tsarina came up to me in a great state of agitation, and said:

'To think of his acting like this to the Tsar, playing this low trick after his self-sacrifice and his abdication to avoid civil war; how mean, how despicable! The Tsar would not have had a single Russian shed his blood for him. He has always been ready to renounce all when he knew that it was for the good of Russia.'

A moment later she went on:

'Yes, this horrible bitterness must be endured too.'

Nicky, Diary – 27 March – Tsarskoe Selo

We started to fast, but this fast did not begin happily. After church, Kerensky arrived and asked us to limit our meetings to meal times and to sit separately from the children; this is apparently necessary to appease the famous Workers' Soviet and the Soldiers' Deputies! We had to agree, in order to avoid the use of force.

Maurice Paléologue, Memoirs

At Tsarskoe Selo a closer watch is being kept over the fallen sovereigns.

The Emperor still presents an extraordinary spectacle of indifference and imperturbability. He spends, in his calm and casual way, his day skimming the papers, smoking cigarettes, doing puzzles, playing

with his children and sweeping up snow in the garden. He seems to
find a kind of relief in being at length free of the burden of supreme
power.

Diocletian at Salona and Charles V at San Juste could not have
shown greater serenity.

The Empress, on the other hand, has taken to mystical exaltation;
she is always saying:

'It is God who has sent us this ordeal; I accept it thankfully for my
eternal salvation.'

But she cannot refrain from outbursts of indignation when she sees
how strictly those orders are carried out which deprive the Emperor
of all freedom of movement, even within the confines of the palace.
Sometimes a sentry refuses to allow him to pass into a gallery; sometimes the officer on duty, at the end of a meal taken in common,
gives him orders to retire to his room. Nicholas II always obeys, without a word of reproach. Alexandra Feodorovna rages and protests as
if she had been insulted; but she soon recovers herself and calms
down, murmuring:

'We must submit to this too. Did not Christ drink the cup to the
very dregs?'

Lord Stamfordham, note of meeting – 28 March – Windsor Castle
I saw the Prime Minister at 10 Downing Street, and tried to impress
upon him the King's strong opinion that the Emperor and Empress
of Russia should not come to this country, and that the Government
ought to inform Monsieur Miliukov that since they had agreed to his
proposal that Their Imperial Majesties should take up their residence
in this country public opinion here had become so stoutly opposed
to the idea that His Majesty's Government must withdraw the consent previously given.

I pointed out to Mr Lloyd George that it would be most unfair
upon the King, (who is closely related to both the Emperor and
Empress) if T.I.M.'s [Their Imperial Majesties] came here when popular feeling against their doing so is so pronounced.

I added that His Majesty is daily receiving communications,
anonymous and otherwise, from persons unknown to him as well as
from his friends, inveighing against an arrangement, which say what
the Government may, will be put down entirely to the King.

I reminded the Prime Minister about what has been said as to the
King's attitude regarding the King of Greece, and the exception taken
to His Majesty having received the Brothers of King Constantine

when they were in London. And I said that no doubt we should have similar complaints respecting the Emperor and Empress, who, of course, the King would see if they came to England: as not only are they His Majesty's relations, but the Emperor has been a staunch friend and Ally of this Country ever since he ascended the Throne twenty-three years ago.

I added that even if the Government publicly stated that they took the responsibility for T.I.M.'s coming here the PEOPLE would reply that this was done to screen the King.

I showed Mr Lloyd George an article by Mr Hyndman in last week's 'Justice', and quoted what other people had said as to the disastrous results which would inevitably accrue from the visit.

The Prime Minister admitted that evidently the matter was more serious than he was aware. He agreed that the South of France would be from our point of view a better place for the future residence of T.I.M.'s. As Monsieur Painlevé (the French Minister of War) was present, Mr Lloyd George asked him to join us, and we discussed the matter from the French point of view.

I asked Monsieur Painlevé whether public opinion in France was likely to object to such an arrangement, he said 'No', that French people had a personal regard for the Emperor who had been their Ally for some years. They had not the same feelings towards the Empress, but he did not anticipate any difficulty from the Public point of view: though the Government no doubt would recognize a certain responsibility in guarding the Emperor, and exercising vigilance as to H.I.M.'s actions. But Monsieur Painlevé quite appreciated the difference to us – a Monarchical Country – and especially as concerning the King who was so closely related to T.I.M.'s.

The Prime Minister is going to see Monsieur Ribot tomorrow and undertook to put the matter before him, with the hope of getting the French Government to offer the Emperor and Empress asylum on French territory.

I afterwards saw Mr Balfour and called attention to a telegram which I had just seen from Sir George Buchanan, who in his conversation with Monsieur Miliukov evidently took it for granted that the Emperor and Empress were coming to England, and that it was only a question of delay with regard to certain matters that had not been cleared up, which prevented an early start.

I told Mr Balfour that after what the King had written to him His Majesty expected that Sir George Buchanan would by now have been informed that the whole question was being reconsidered, and that our previous Agreement could no longer be held as binding. Mr

Balfour said that he would draft a telegram to Sir George Buchanan this afternoon and send it to the Prime Minister for his approval.

Count Benckendorff, Memoirs – 30 March

During the first days of Holy Week the work of digging a trench near the Chinese theatre was begun to bury the pretended victims of the revolution at Tsarskoe. The place chosen was where the Great Avenue which starts from the Grand Palais crosses with the avenue which faces the Alexander Palace, about 300 feet from the front.

On Maundy Thursday at 1 o'clock in the afternoon, the solemn funeral of the pretended victims took place. They were, in reality, six or seven drunkards who had died of drink on the day when the wine shops had been looted. There was a great display of troops, red flags, bands playing the 'Marseillaise' and other revolutionary tunes.

Nicky, Diary – 2 April, Easter Sunday – Tsarskoe Selo

Before lunch I kissed and exchanged greetings with all the servants, while Alix distributed china eggs, which were left over from our previous reserves. In all there were 135 people.

In the afternoon we began work by the bridge, but a large crowd of idlers soon gathered by the fence, so we had to move away and spend a boring time in the garden. Alexei and Anastasia went out into the fresh air for the first time.

Count Benckendorff, Memoirs – 2 April – Tsarskoe Selo

The Queen of Greece stopped at the door, sent for the officer on duty and asked him to give an Easter Egg to the Empress, which she had brought for her.

Nicky, Diary – 3 April – Tsarskoe Selo

After lunch, I went out into the park with Alexei and spent the time breaking the ice by our summer landing pier; a crowd of loiterers again stood by the railings and stared at us from start to finish.

Pierre Gilliard, Memoirs – 5 April

Whenever we go out, soldiers, with fixed bayonets and under the command of an officer, surround us and keep pace with us. We look like convicts with their warders. The instructions are changed daily, or perhaps the officers interpret them each in his own way!

This afternoon, when we were going back to the palace after our walk, the sentry on duty at the gate stopped the Tsar, saying:

'You cannot pass, sir.'

The officer with us intervened. Alexei blushed hotly to see the soldier stop his father.

Nicky, Diary – 7 April – Tsarskoe Selo
In the afternoon I worked with Tatiana and Alexei. The faces of the soldiers and their familiar appearance revolted everyone.

Count Benckendorff, Memoirs – 8 April – Tsarskoe Selo
On the 8th April the corps of the Guard of the 2nd regiment of rifles was more ill-disposed than usual. The arrogance of the soldiers was boundless. The officers were no better.

From the first, the commandants of the corps of the Guard had insisted, on taking over this duty, on being able to see the Emperor and the Empress, basing this on the regulation that an officer who takes charge of a prisoner should have the right to see him to make sure of his presence.

On this day, the officer commanding the incoming Guard was a former sergeant-major who, as soon as he had arrived at the Palace, had made himself conspicuous by his violence and his revolutionary opinions. He wished to search the Palace, threatening everyone with worse treatment if he found anything suspicious. When the Emperor held out his hand, he moved a step back, and said, 'Not for anything in the world.' Then the Emperor advanced a step and said, 'What have you got against me?'

He remained open-mouthed, turned on his heel and left the room. During the walk there were altercations between the officers and Dr Derevenko, because it was said that he did not walk quick enough, and with M. Gilliard because he spoke French with one of the Grand Duchesses.

Nicky, Diary – 8 April – Tsarskoe Selo
We found out why yesterday's guard were so disgusting: they were entirely composed of soldiers' deputies!

Count Benckendorff, Memoirs – 12 April – Tsarskoe Selo
Between 2 and 3 o'clock in the afternoon, Kerensky came to the palace. The Emperor was already out walking. He had the Empress warned that he wished to speak to her alone and begged her to come to the Emperor's study. The Empress answered that she was dressing and that she would receive him in her drawing-room.

The conversation dealt with the part the Empress had played in politics, her influence on the Emperor in the choice of ministers whom she often had received in the absence of the Emperor. Her Majesty answered that the Emperor and herself were the most united of couples, whose whole joy and pleasure was in their family life, and that they had no secrets from each other: that they discussed everything, and that it was not astonishing that in the last years which had been so troubled, they had often discussed politics.

Nicky, Diary – 12 April – Tsarskoe Selo
A cold day with a wind. Went for a walk for half an hour and then sat with the children, while Alix was at mass. In the afternoon Kerensky arrived and took me away from my work with the ice. At first he talked with Alix, then with me. After tea I read. In the evening we sat upstairs, had tea together and also slept together.

Maurice Paléologue, Memoirs – 14 April
The Princess [Paley] told me that as she was passing the railings of the Alexander park yesterday she had a distant glimpse of the Emperor and his daughters. He was passing the time by breaking the ice in a fountain with an iron-shod pole. He had been amusing himself thus for more than an hour! A number of soldiers who were also watching him through the railings, called out: 'What'll you be up to a few days hence, when the ice has melted?' But the Emperor was too far away to hear.

15 April   Russian society, by which I mean the highest society in the land, is a curious study at the present moment.

I have observed three currents of opinion, or rather three attitudes of mind, towards the revolution.

In principle, all the former *clientele* of tsarism, by which I mean all the families contributing, by virtue of birth or office, to the splendour of the imperial order, have remained loyal to the fallen sovereigns. But I have also observed that I hardly ever hear that loyalty expressed unless coupled with severe, acrimonious, angry and bitter criticisms of the weakness of Nicholas II, the errors of the Empress and the baneful intrigues of their *camarilla*.

Pierre Gilliard, Memoirs – 16 April
In the evening a long conversation with Their Majesties on the subject of Alexei's lessons. We must find a way out since we have no longer any tutors. The Tsar is going to make himself responsible for History and Geography, the Tsarina will take charge of his religious instruction. The other subjects will be shared between Baroness Buxhoeveden (English), Mlle. Schneider (Arithmetic), Dr Botkin (Russian) and myself.

Nicky, Diary – 18 April – Tsarskoe Selo
Abroad it's the 1st May today, so our blockheads decided to celebrate with street processions, musical choirs and red flags.[14] Apparently they came right into the park and placed wreaths on the tomb.

The weather changed for the worse during these celebrations, and thick wet snow started to fall! I went out for a walk at 3.45, when everything was over and the sun had come out. Worked for an hour and a half with Tatiana.

In the evening I started to read aloud to the children: *A Millionaire Girl*.

Count Benckendorff, Memoirs – Tsarskoe Selo
A soldier on duty reported that he had seen two officers, whom he named, kiss the hand of one of the Grand Duchesses. The 'Soviet' of this regiment made a fuss about it; the officers were accused of being counter-revolutionaries.

Maria Pavlovna [the younger], Memoirs
The day following my arrival [in St Petersburg] I watched, from the window of the drawing room looking out on the Neva, a procession which had been arranged to honour the victims of the revolution. The ceremony was civil. For the first time the clergy did not participate in a Russian affair of state. And this parade of mourning served

---

[14] May Day had not previously been celebrated in Russia.

another purpose; it was a display of power on the part of the new government.

But Petrograd rejoiced. The statesmen of the former regime were under lock in state buildings or in prisons; the newspapers sang laudatory hymns to the revolution and freedom and reviled the past with an astounding fury. Pamphlets with caricatures of the Tsars and with despicable and libellous hints and accusations were sold in the streets. Altogether new expressions became the fashion; the language was suddenly enriched with foreign words, imported to express more forcibly the enthusiasm of the moment.

But the practical life of the city had, in spite of all this revolutionary enthusiasm, become sluggish and colourless. The streets were carelessly cleaned. Crowds of idle, dissolute soldiers and sailors wandered continually about, while the well-dressed people who owned carriages and cars hid away in their homes. Police were not to be seen. Things ran themselves, and very badly.

Even those of our servants who had been in our service for many years, sometimes even for generations, were influenced by the new currents. They began to present demands, form committees. Few remained faithful to the masters who had in all times taken care of them, pensioned them in their old age, nursed them when they had been sick, and sent their children to school.

Petrograd frightened me.

Nicky, Diary – 1 May – Tsarskoe Selo

A wonderful warm day! In the morning had a good walk. From 12 o'clock gave a geography lesson to Alexei. In the afternoon we again worked on our orchard. The sun was quite hot, but the work progressed well. Read until dinner, and then aloud in the evening.

Yesterday we heard about the departure of general Kornilov from the post of commander-in-chief of the Petrograd military area, and today about the retirement of Guchkov, all because of the same irresponsible interference in the decisions of the military authorities by the Soviet of Workers' Deputies and some other even more left wing organizations.

What has providence in store for poor Russia? Let God's will be done!

3 May   Alexei's arm was hurting and he spent the day lying down.

Tatiana to P. Petrov[15] – 5 May – Tsarskoe Selo
Pyotr Vasilievich, my dear,

I feel so ashamed that I have not written to You before, but please don't think this shows I have forgotten You – absolutely not. After all, it's possible not to write to friends and yet keep them in mind – isn't that so? So, how are you feeling?

I was very upset, when I learnt about your illness. Do you have any news from your nephew – how is he? As you will have heard, we all try to keep busy here with some form of domestic activity – each one as he can. We are planting a kitchen garden. Do you really still have to stay in bed, or will you be able to go out onto the balcony once it gets warmer? Anyway, all my very best wishes. It's sad that we have not met for so long. Get well soon.

May God keep You.

Your old pupil, Tatiana

Nicky, Diary – 6 May – Tsarskoe Selo
I am 49 years old. Almost a half century! My thoughts are particularly with dear Mama.

It's terrible not even being able to correspond. I know nothing of her, except from stupid or revolting newspaper articles.

The day passed like a Sunday – mass, lunch upstairs, then a puzzle! Our congenial work in the orchard, where we started to dig flower beds, after tea, mass, dinner and in the evening reading – much more with my dear family than in normal years.

25 May   My dear Alix's birthday. May God send her good health and spiritual peace!

27 May   I forgot to mention yesterday that, after we had had dinner, Korovichenko asked to come in, to say goodbye, and brought with him his successor as commandant of the Tsarskoe Selo garrison regiment – Kobylinsky. None of us regret his departure, on the contrary everyone is delighted at the appointment of a new man.

From the report of the Special High Commissioner for Revision and Investigation of Ministers and other high personages of the Imperial Government – May 1917
A medical examination of Mme Vyrubova ordered by the Commission of Inquiry established the virginity of the woman.

---

[15] Teacher of Russian to all the children.

For Tatiana! from Alexei – 27 May [in English]

Old Mother Hubbard
Went to the cupboard
To seek her poor doggie a bone.
When she got there,
The Cupboard was bare,
And so the poor doggie got none.

Pierre Gilliard, Memoirs – 2 June
We finished our kitchen garden some time ago and it is now in splendid condition. We have every imaginable kind of vegetable, and five hundred cabbages. The servants, too, have made a garden on their side of the palace, where they can cultivate what they like. We went to help them dig it – the Tsar too.

To occupy our leisure now that we have finished our work on the garden, we have asked and obtained permission to cut down the dead tree in the park, so we go from place to place, followed by a guard which moves when we move. We are beginning to be quite skilful woodcutters. This will give us a supply of wood for next winter.

3 June Alexei was practising handling his little gun, which he thinks a lot of, as it was given to the Tsar when he was a boy by his father. An officer came up to us. He told me that the soldiers had decided to take the gun away from the Tsarevich, and were coming for it. When he heard this, Alexei put down his toy and joined the Tsarina, who was sitting on the grass a few yards from us. A moment later the officer on duty came with two soldiers and demanded that the 'weapon' should be given up. I tried to intervene and make them understand that the gun was not a weapon but a toy. It was no use: they took possession of it. Alexei began to sob. His mother asked me to make another attempt to convince the soldiers, but I did not succeed any better than the first time, and they went off with their prize.

Half an hour later the officer on duty took me aside and asked me to tell the Tsarevich that he was greatly distressed at what he had had to do. After trying in vain to dissuade the men, he had chosen to come with them to prevent any discourtesy on their part.

Colonel Kobylinsky was annoyed to hear of the incident, and brought back the little gun to Alexei piece by piece.

Nicky, Diary – 3 June – Tsarskoe Selo

After morning tea, Kerensky suddenly arrived from town by motor. He did not stay with me long: he asked me to send the investigating committee any papers or letters pertaining to domestic politics. After my walk, and up until lunch, I helped Korovichenko sort out these papers. After lunch he continued together with Kobylinsky. We finished sawing the tree trunks in the first place. During this time there was a *péché* with Alexei's rifle; he was playing with it on the island; some sentries, strolling in the garden, saw it and asked their officer to remove it, then took it back to the guard house. Apparently, for some reason they then sent it off to the town hall!

It's wonderful to have officers who don't dare to contradict the lower ranks!

9 June It's exactly three months since I came from Mogilev, and that we are here like prisoners. It's terribly hard to be without news of dear Mama, but as to the rest, I'm indifferent.

Pierre Gilliard, Memoirs – 9 June

As the Grand Duchesses were losing all their hair as the result of their illness, their heads have been shaved. When they go out in the park they wear scarves arranged so as to conceal the fact. Just as I was going to take their photographs, at a sign from Olga Nicolaevna they all suddenly removed their headdress.

I protested, but they insisted, much amused at the idea of seeing themselves photographed like this, and looking forward to seeing the indignant surprise of their parents. Their good spirits reappear from time to time in spite of everything. It is their exuberant youth.

Nicky, Diary – 10 June – Tsarskoe Selo

In the evening at about 11 o'clock a shot was heard in the garden, and a quarter of an hour later the head of the guard asked to come in, and explained that the sentry had fired because it appeared to him that someone was signalling with a red lamp from the window of the children's bedroom. One of the officers who came in with him realized what had happened, when he saw the position of the electric lamp and how Anastasia moved her head as she sat by the window, and after excusing themselves, they left.

15 June Benckendorff, Valia D[olgorukov] and the two ladies-in-waiting received notification that they are relieved of their duties.

Olga [daughter] to P. Petrov – 19 June – Tsarskoe Selo
Dear old P.V.P.

Thank you so much for your letter. I am so pleased that you are at last better and once again in Tsarskoe. After beastly Petrograd, the fresh air will of course do you good and restore your strength. As to how we spend our days, you will surely have heard from Zhilik [Gilliard].

We go for a walk in the afternoons from 2 o'clock until 5. We each do something in the garden. If it's not too close, Mama also comes out, and lies on a couch under the tree by the water. Papa goes (with several others) deep into the garden where he fells and saws up dead trees. Alexei plays on the 'children's island', runs around barefoot and sometimes swims.

Trina (Schneider) continues to weed and water the flower beds without respite. Sometimes we also help with the watering, including the roses which we have planted nearby, opposite Granny's windows. Lessons continue as normal. Maria and I are studying English together. She reads aloud to me, and if it's not too hot, will do a dictation. Twice a week she and I do Russian history. At the moment we are studying the heroes of folklore. Twice a week Anastasia and I study medieval history. It is much more difficult, as I have a terrible memory for all those events, though she isn't any better. I have myself assigned my free time to reading (boring things), history of art, French history, general history and Russian literature. There! I think that is everything. Mama sends you her regards and is glad you are better.

Everyone sends their greetings.

Your pupil no. 1, Olga
Thank you!

Nicky, Diary – 26 June – Tsarskoe Selo
The day was magnificent. Our good regimental commandant Kobylinsky asked me not to hold out my hand to the officers in front of others, and not to greet the sentries. There have been several occasions when they did not answer.

Gave Alexei a geography lesson. We cut down a huge pine tree not far from the orangerie fence. The sentries even wanted to help us.

In the evening I finished reading *The Count of Monte-Cristo*.

27 June I forgot to write that on the 26 June our troops made another breakthrough and captured: 131 officers, 7,000 lower ranks and 48 cannons, including 12 heavy ones. In the morning all the girls went out to collect the mown grass. I went for my usual walk.

In the afternoon we worked in the same place as yesterday. We cut down and sawed up two pine trees. Before dinner we spent half an hour in the orchard. In the evening I started to read aloud *Arsene Lupin contre Sherlock Holmes*.

28 June Yesterday we took Galich, together with 3,000 prisoners and about 30 cannons. Thank God!

Maria Pavlovna [the younger], Memoirs – June

I went to Moscow where I stopped at Aunt Ella's nunnery. I had not seen my aunt for several months. Nothing around her had changed, the atmosphere was still the same, but I was struck by her tired and ill appearance. She, who had always been on the go, now spent most of her time upon a wicker chaise-longue with a piece of embroidery or some knitting.

We talked at length of present events and of the causes that had brought them about. One evening when I was telling her about the life of the captive Emperor and his family, I added that if she wished to send them a letter I might find the means of having it delivered.

Her eyes turned hard and cold; her lips tightened. She replied somewhat sharply that she could not send a letter; she had nothing to say; she and her sister, the Empress, had long ago ceased to understand each other.

I kept silent. Nothing more was said.

[Maria Pavlovna and Ella never saw each other again.]

Nicky, Diary – 5 July – Tsarskoe Selo

It rained all morning, but towards 2 o'clock the weather cleared; in the evening it got cooler. We spent the day as usual. For the last few days there have been disturbances and firing in Petrograd. Yesterday a whole lot of soldiers and sailors arrived from Kronstadt, to march against the Provisional Government. What a mess! And where are the people who could take the situation in hand and stop the bloodshed and strife? The seed of all this evil is in Petrograd itself, not in Russia as a whole.

6 July Luckily, the overwhelming majority of the troops in

Petrograd remained faithful to their duty, and order has again been reestablished on the streets.

The weather was wonderful. Went for a good walk with Tatiana and Valia. In the afternoon we worked successfully in the woods – we cut down and sawed up four pine trees. In the evening I started *Tartarin de Tarascon*.

Count Benckendorff, Memoirs

Prince Lvov, having resigned, for several days we were without Government, and Kerensky had taken refuge with his family in the Grand Palais at Tsarskoe, giving dinners at the expense of the Court, driving about Pavlovsk in the Emperor's carriage.

P. Petrov to Grand Duchess Olga – 10 July – Tsarskoe Selo

The good Lord has allowed me to live until Your name-day, my dear unforgettable pupil, dearest Olga Nicolaevna!

If the good fairies of the stories really existed on this earth, I would ask them to bestow all the good wishes, which only those fantastical creatures are able to grant! I, as You are very well aware, am not a fairy, nevertheless from the depths of my heart and affection for you, I want to wish you the one thing, which is more precious than anything else on this earth: physical health and mental balance! Everything else will follow.

Goodbye until the next time! Please send my respectful greetings to Mama, Papa, Alexei Nikolaevich and your sisters. May God keep You!

Your old P.V.P.

Count Benckendorff, Memoirs

On the 11th we learnt that he [Kerensky] had accepted the post of President of the Council, formed his ministry, and was established in the rooms of the late Emperor Alexander II in the Winter Palace. On Sunday, the 11th July, at 11 o'clock in the morning, Kerensky came to the Emperor to report that the situation in the town had become alarming and he thought it would be more prudent for His Majesty and his family to leave, and to settle in the interior of the country.

He said that he himself and the Emperor were in great danger. The Bolsheviks 'are after me, and then will be after you'.

Nicky, Diary – 11 July – Tsarskoe Selo
In the morning I went for a walk with Alexei. On our return, I learnt of Kerensky's arrival. During our conversation, he mentioned our probable departure to the south, in view of the proximity of Tsarskoe Selo to the unrest in the capital.

13 July For the last few days, news from the south-western front has been bad. After our assault at Galich, many units, influenced by shameful defeatist propaganda, not only refused to advance further, but in some places even took flight without any pressure from the enemy. Taking advantage of these propitious circumstances, the Germans and Austrians managed to break through in southern Galicia with a small force, which could move the entire south-western front back to the east.

It's a shame and a disgrace! Today, at last, the Provisional Government has decreed that, anyone engaging in state treason in the theatre of war will face the death penalty. Let's hope these measures are not too late.

19 July It's three years since Germany declared war on us; it's as if we had lived a whole lifetime in those three years! Lord, help and save Russia!

21 July From the morning the weather was ideal; also a wonderful moon-lit night. In the morning we waited for Kerensky. It would be nice to know, at last, when and where we are going?

22 July Yesterday evening Kerensky suddenly appeared from town. It appears the government has fallen apart, he himself has resigned, and is awaiting the outcome of a meeting of the various parties who sit in the Winter Palace.

25 July A new Provisional Government has been formed with Kerensky at its head. Let's see whether he can do any better. The first task is to reestablish discipline in the army and revive its morale, as well as bringing some order to the internal situation in Russia!

28 July A wonderful day; enjoyed our walk. After lunch we learned from Benckendorff that we are not being sent to the Crimea, but to some remote provincial town three or four days' journey to the east!

Where exactly they haven't said – even the commandant doesn't know. And we were all counting on a long stay in Livadia!!

We cut down a huge pine tree where the paths cross. For a short time a warm rain fell.

In the evening I read aloud Conan Doyle's *A Study in Scarlet*.

29 July The same heavenly weather. During our morning walk, as we were passing the gates to the orangerie path, we noticed a sentry asleep on the grass. The officer accompanying us went over and removed his rifle.

30 July Our dear Alexei is thirteen years old today. May the Lord give him good health, patience and strength of body and mind in these difficult times!

Count Benckendorff, Memoirs – 31 July

Everything was ready at the Palace for the departure. After luncheon, their Majesties sent for my wife and myself to say goodbye. The Emperor was as calm and self-possessed as usual. We all went once more into the garden, and His Majesty took exercise and sawed wood as before. He told me to see that the vegetables and the wood that had been sawn and made ready in the park should be distributed among the servants who had taken part in the work. About 10.30 in the evening, I learned that the Commandant had ordered the Commandant of the Corps of the Guard by telephone to transfer the luggage into the round room and to employ fifty men for this duty. The Commandant of the Guard told me that his men refused to do this work for nothing and asked three roubles each.

Nicky, Diary – 31 July – Tsarskoe Selo

Our last day at Tsarskoe Selo. After dinner we waited for the time of our departure, which kept being put off. Kerensky suddenly appeared and announced that Misha was coming. And sure enough, at about 10.30 dear Misha walked in accompanied by Kerensky and the captain of the guard. It was wonderful to see him, but awkward to talk in front of outsiders.

Count Benckendorff, Memoirs – 31 July

The interview lasted ten minutes. The brothers were so moved and embarrassed at having to talk before witnesses that they found scarcely anything to say. The Grand Duke went out in tears and told

me that he had not even been able to notice whether the Emperor
was looking well or not.
[This was the last time Nicholas and Mikhail saw each other.]

Nicky, Diary – 31 July – Tsarskoe Selo
When he had left, the sentries started dragging our baggage into the
round hall. Benckendorff, the ladies in waiting, the girls and the servants were already sitting there. We walked to and fro, awaiting the
arrival of the vans. The secret of our departure was so tightly guarded
that the motors and the train were ordered only after the time designated for us to leave. Alexei wanted to go to sleep – he kept lying
down and getting up. There were several false alarms, when we put
on our coats and went out onto the balcony, only to return back into
the hall. It grew quite light. We had tea, and at last, at 5.15, Kerensky
appeared and said that we could go. We got into our two cars and
drove to Alexandrovsky station. From the park we were escorted by a
cavalry unit. At the train we were met by Tatischev[16] and two commissars from the government who were to accompany us to Tobolsk.
We set out towards Petrograd with a beautiful sunrise, and joined the
Northern line by a branch track. We left Tsarskoe Selo at 6.10 in the
morning.

Pierre Gilliard, Memoirs – 31 July
We were told to be ready by midnight; the train was ordered for one
o'clock. Final preparations. Farewell visit to the children's island,
kitchen garden, etc. We took leave of those of our fellow-captives
who could not leave with us.[17]

---

[16] General Tatischev held no Court appointment; he was one of the Tsar's aides-
de-camp, and escorted the Tsar's family to Tobolsk.

[17] 'Count and Countess Benckendorff, whom their great age and uncertain state
of health prevented from following us; Baroness Buxhoeveden, who was kept back
by illness and was to join us at Tobolsk as soon as she could, and a certain number
of servants. Kerensky had asked the Tsar whether he wished Count Benckendorff
to be replaced. The Tsar had replied that he would be very glad for General
Tatischev to come and share his captivity. On learning his Tsar's wish General
Tatischev only allowed himself time to put his affairs in order, and a few hours later
started, valise in hand, for Tsarskoe Selo. We found him in the train at the moment
of departure.' [Gilliard, Memoirs]

Count Benckendorff, Memoirs

Their Majesties chose the following persons: Baroness Buxhoeveden, Countess Hendrikov, Mlle. Schneider, Prince Valia Dolgorukov, Dr Botkin and M. Gilliard. Further, it was agreed that they should ask the Government's permission to replace me by someone else of the suite. Their choice fell on A.D.C. General Tatischev, who, on learning that the Emperor had chosen him, accepted without a moment's hesitation.

Maria Pavlovna [the younger], Memoirs

Their departure was accompanied by humiliations similar to those which had accompanied their life under arrest. They were told the night before to hold themselves ready for departure and were kept waiting, dressed, almost all night. Their departure left us with painful impressions, but we had no definite intimation of the tragedy that would put an end to their exile.

Nicky, Diary – 4 August – on the train

We advanced unbelievably slowly, in order to reach Tiumen late at night. There the train went right up to the jetty, so that we were able to get straight onto the steamer.

Ours is called *Russia*! They started loading our things, which took all night. God only knows when poor Alexei got to bed again? The bustle and noise went on all through the night and prevented me from getting to sleep. We left Tiumen at about 6 o'clock.

Pierre Gilliard, Memoirs – 5 August

We passed the native village of Rasputin, and the family, gathered on the deck, were able to observe the house of the *staretz*, which stood out clearly from among the *isbas*. There was nothing to surprise them in this event, for Rasputin had foretold that it would be so, and chance once more seemed to confirm his prophetic words.

Nicky, Diary – 5 August – sailing down the River Tura

Slept little. Alix, Alexei and I are in one cabin without any amenities, all the girls are together in another with five bunks, the suite next door along the corridor.

Pierre Gilliard, Memoirs – 6 August
On the 6th towards the end of the afternoon, we suddenly saw at a
bend in the river the crenellated silhouette of the Kremlin, which
dominates Tobolsk, and an hour later we reached our destination.

What reasons had the Council of Ministers for transporting the
Imperial family to Tobolsk?

It is difficult to say definitely. When Kerensky told the Tsar of the proposed transfer he explained the necessity by saying that the Provisional
Government had resolved to take energetic measures against the
Bolsheviks; this would result in a period of disturbance and armed conflict of which the Imperial family might be the first victims; it was therefore his duty to put them out of danger. It has been claimed in other
quarters that it was an act of weakness in face of the Extremists, who,
uneasy at seeing in the army the beginnings of a movement in favour
of the Tsar, demanded his exile to Siberia. However this may be, the
journey of the Imperial family from Tsarskoe Selo to Tobolsk was
effected under comfortable conditions and without any noteworthy
incident.

Nicky, Diary – 6 August – Sailing down the River Tobol
Got up late, having slept badly because of the general noise, whistles,
stops etc; during the night we came out of the Tura into the Tobol.
The river is wider, the banks higher. The morning was cool, but the
afternoon got quite warm when the sun came out. I forgot to mention that yesterday before dinner we went past the village of
Pokrovskoe – Grigory [Rasputin]'s home.

At 6.30 we arrived in Tobolsk, although we had been able to see it
for over an hour. There were a lot of people standing on the bank –
which means they knew of our arrival. As soon as the steamer
docked, they started to unload our baggage. Valia, the commissar and
the commandant went off to inspect the houses, which have been
assigned for us and our suite. When the first returned, we learnt that
the buildings are empty, dirty, without any furniture, and that it was
impossible to move into them. For this reason we stayed on the boat
and waited for them to bring back the luggage that we needed for the
night.

We had supper and joked about the surprising inability of people
to even arrange accommodation, then went to bed early.

13 August – Tobolsk We got up early and the last things were
immediately packed. At 10.30 the children and I went ashore with

the commandant and the officers and set off for our new home. We inspected the whole house from top to bottom. We have taken the first floor, the dining room is downstairs. At 12 o'clock there was a mass, and the priest sprinkled the rooms with holy water. We lunched and dined with our people. We went to look at the house where the suite is staying. Many of the rooms have still not been done, and look very unwelcoming. Then we went into the so-called garden, a paltry orchard, and looked at the kitchen and guard house. Everything looks old and neglected.

Valia Dolgorukov to his brother Pavel Dolgorukov – 14 August – Tobolsk

My dear Pavel

We arrived in Tobolsk at 6 in the evening. In order to see the house and find out what had been prepared, Makarov and I decided to go into town before the others and do a reconnaissance.

The picture was depressing in general, and in complete contrast to Ivan's description: a delightful farmhouse with a bakery, a confectionary, cellars etc! Nothing of the sort, but a dirty, boarded-up, smelly house consisting of 13 rooms, with some furniture, and terrible bathrooms and toilets. In the attic 5 rooms for servants. For those accompanying, Tatischev, Hendrikov, Botkin, Schneider, myself and the other officers (including Colonel Kobylinsky) there was the Kornilov house on the other side, quite spacious, but dirty and without any furniture, in other words a barn, but with parquet floors. I should tell you that both houses are situated in the centre of town, on the main 'Freedom' street.

This sight made an extremely depressing impression and we decided the same evening to climb up the hill to look at the bishop's house, and anything else that was suitable. Alas! The further we went on, the worse it was. We had to return and suggest that the whole family stay on board the steamboat a few more days until the house was made ready. I was struck by the carelessness and inefficiency of the local authorities for allowing such negligence.

This is the seventh day when we are cleaning, painting and getting the houses in order while we and the family are still on the steamboat *Russia*. The cabins are very small and the facilities, for women at least, miserable.

Alexei and Maria have caught cold. His arm is hurting a lot and he often cries at night. Gilliard has been lying in his cabin for the last eight days, he has some sort of boils on his arm and legs. And a slight fever. It is easier to get provisions here and significantly cheaper. Milk, eggs, butter and fish are plentiful.

The family is bearing everything with great sang-froid and courage. They apparently adapt to circumstances easily, or at least pretend to, and do not complain after all their previous luxury. Between us, Botkin has become a little careless. He did not think in time about disinfecting the house. His greatest preoccupation – how subsequently to accommodate his own family in Kornilov's house.

Your truly loving Valia

Nicky, Diary – 15 August – Tobolsk
As we are not allowed out in the street, and cannot go to church, a service was held at 1 o'clock in the hall.

18 August   In the morning Rita Khitrovo suddenly appeared in the street, having arrived from Petrograd, and went to see Nastenka Hend[rikov]. This was enough for them to search her quarters in the evening. The devil knows what for!

19 August   Because of yesterday's events, Nastenka was forbidden to go for a walk in the street for several days, and poor Rita Khitrovo had to take the evening steamer back!

22 August   Another heavenly day. It's infuriating not to be able to walk in the woods and along the river banks in such weather!

24 August   The bad news from the front has, unfortunately, been confirmed; today we heard that Riga has been abandoned, and that our troops have retreated far back to the northeast.

26 August   Worked in the garden. Alexei stayed in bed with a cold and an ear-ache. There is little news from the front, the newspapers arrive here six days late.

27 August   Today it got cooler. There was a service at 11 o'clock. We all very much like the priest who officiates for us; four nuns sing. Alexei stayed in bed as a precaution.

29 August   After dinner we read telegrams, one saying that general Kornilov had declared himself dictator, the other that he had been replaced as commander-in-chief, and general Klembovsky appointed in his place.

1 September The new commissar from the Provisional Government, Pankratov, arrived and installed himself in the suite's house, together with his assistant, a dishevelled ensign of some sort. He looks like – a worker or a poor school teacher. He will be the censor of our correspondence.

Misha [brother], Diary – 2 September

We woke up this morning to hear Russia proclaimed a democratic republic.

What does it matter what form of government will be, provided there is order and justice in the land.

Nicky, Diary – 4 September – Tobolsk

A magnificent summer's day. Spent a lot of time in the air. The last few days have brought a lot of unpleasantness in the sense of absence of plumbing. The downstairs W.C. overflowed with waste from the upstairs ones, and we had to stop using them or taking baths; all this because the septic pits are too small, and no one wanted to clean them out. I got Dr Botkin to draw this to the attention of commissar Pankratov, who was quite appalled by conditions here.

5 September Telegrams arrive here twice a day; many are so unclear, that it is difficult to believe what they say. It seems there is great confusion in Petrograd, and another change in the government. Apparently nothing came of Kornilov's attempt, he himself and the generals and officers who supported him have for the most part been arrested, and those troops who were marching on Petrograd have turned back. Wonderful, hot weather.

8 September We went for the first time to the church of the Annunciation, where our priest has served for a long time. But the pleasure was spoilt for me by the idiotic conditions in which we had to walk there. Sentries were posted all along the path of the town park, where there was no one, while there was a huge crowd at the church! I was deeply upset.

22 September A few days ago our dear bar[on] Bode arrived with a truck of further household items and some of our own things from Tsarskoe Selo.

23 September   Among these items were two or three crates of wine, which the soldiers got to hear about, and this created a whole commotion in the afternoon. They started to demand the destruction of all the bottles in the Kornilov house. After much admonishing on the part of the commissar and others, it was decided to take all the wine and pour it into the Irtysh. Before tea, from the window, we saw the departure of a cart containing the crates of wine, with the commissar's assistant sitting on top with an axe, followed by a whole escort of armed guards.

Pierre Gilliard, Memoirs

In September Commissary Pankratov arrived at Tobolsk, having been sent by Kerensky. He was accompanied by his deputy, Nikolsky – like himself, an old political exile. Pankratov was quite a well-informed man, of gentle character, the typical enlightened fanatic. He made a good impression on the Tsar and subsequently became attached to the children. But Nikolsky was a low type, whose conduct was most brutal. Narrow and stubborn, he applied his whole mind to the daily invention of fresh annoyances. Immediately after his arrival he demanded of Colonel Kobylinsky that we should be forced to have our photographs taken. When the latter objected that this was superfluous, since all the soldiers knew us – they were the same as had guarded us at Tsarskoe Selo – he replied: 'It was forced on us in the old days, now it's their turn.' It had to be done, and henceforward we had to carry our identity cards with a photograph and identity number.

The Tsar was suffering a great deal from lack of physical exercise. Colonel Kobylinsky, to whom he complained of this, had beech-trunks brought and bought some saws and axes, and we were able to cut the wood we required for the kitchen and stoves. This was one of our great outdoor distractions during our captivity at Tobolsk, even the Grand Duchesses becoming very keen on this new pastime.

The Tsar would often read aloud while the Grand Duchesses did needlework or played with us. The Tsarina regularly played one or two games of bezique with General Tatischev and then took up her work or reclined in her armchair. In this atmosphere of family peace we passed the long winter evenings, lost in the immensity of distant Siberia.

One of the greatest privations during our captivity at Tobolsk was the almost complete absence of news. Letters only reached us very irregularly and after long delay. As for newspapers, we were reduced to a nasty local rag printed on packing paper, which only gave us telegrams several days old and generally distorted and cut down.

Nicky, Diary – 24 September – Tobolsk
Because of yesterday's story, they did not allow us to go to church, fearing some sort of trouble.

25 September During the time of our walk, the commandant, the wretched commissar's assistant Nikolsky and three sentries searched the rooms of our house looking for wine. As they did not find anything, they came out after half an hour and went away.

29 September A few days ago Dr Botkin received a note from Kerensky, from which we learnt that we are allowed to take walks beyond the town. In answer to Botkin's question about when these could begin, Pankratov – the wretch – replied that there could be no question of it now because of some unexplained fear for our safety. Everyone was very upset by this answer.

2 October Now, any of our people who want to take a walk, have to go through the town accompanied by sentries.

6 October A bright, cold day. We learned of Mr Gibbes' [English tutor to Alexei] arrival yesterday, but have not seen him yet, probably because the letters and things he brought with him have not been searched!

7 October At night there were 9 degrees of frost. The day was clear, but quite cold, especially to the hands. At last Mr Gibbes appeared and told us many interesting things about life in Petrograd.

10 October Klavdia Bitner, who arrived two days ago, gave me a letter from Xenia.

Xenia to Nicky – undated – Ai-Todor
My dearest darling, what a joy to see your handwriting. I would give anything to see and be with you. How I envy my brother, even though your meeting was in the presence of witnesses, but even so! I asked again in March, but they did not let me, although they promised, and they didn't even forward my letter. We share everything with you in our thoughts and hearts, and pray fervently for you all, and for you in particular.

On the 12th Olga [sister] had a son. You can imagine her joy and happiness.

Olga [daughter] to P. Petrov – 10 October – Tobolsk

Your long letter reminded me that I have not once written to You, dear old Pyotr Vasilievich, for which I apologize.

We were very glad to learn that You are better. I hope it will stay that way. All is well with us; everyone is in good health. The weather is good.

Today it is sunny and thawing, while for the first few days of October it was almost hot, it changes so quickly. My brother and sisters have started lessons.

I am writing to you in the big hall, where the four of us have tea together. Our brother is playing with his soldiers at a separate table. M[aria] and A[nastasia] are reading at the window, Mama and Tatiana are playing at something, Papa is reading nearby. They all send their greetings, as do I. All my best wishes. We often remember with Zhilik [Gilliard] how we used to torment poor old P.V.P. during lessons, and so many other things.

Your pupil Nr. 1 Olga

Papa sends you his best regards.

Xenia to Nicky – 15 October – Ai-Todor

They have removed our guard, many sailors asked for leave, some asked to return to Sebastopol, i.e. they were 'thoroughly fed up' being here. At first we had many misunderstandings with them, but finally we all got used to each other and they understood that we are neither criminals, nor are we involved in propaganda! But the thought of how you must grieve and suffer for our poor dearly beloved country and army – makes my heart ache and bleed. What have they done to us? Why destroy everything?

Nicky, Diary – 20 October – Tobolsk

Today is the 23rd anniversary of dear Papa's death, what circumstances are we forced to live it in! God, how sad I feel for poor Russia!

22 October Went to church and the whole family took communion. What spiritual comfort in the times we are living.

Tatiana to P. Petrov – 23 October – Tobolsk
Dear Pyotr Vasilievich

I am very ashamed not to have written to You before now. I very much wonder if you would be able to get hold of my A Tolstoy books, they always used to stand on the first shelf of my cupboard, I don't know how it is now. I would be very grateful if you could get them, although I know how difficult it may be. You could send them with Iza if you are in time, otherwise by post addressed to Commissar Pankratov to be forwarded to me!

So there! We remember you often, and I hope you are quite better. There is still a lot of snow here, but it is not that cold. Lessons are going well, so that almost all our time is occupied and the day passes quickly – mainly because of the monotony.

Yesterday we took communion in church. It was wonderful.

All my best wishes. Everyone sends their warmest regards. May God keep You. I do not envy you being close to disgusting, filthy Petrograd.

                                                        Your pupil Nr. 2 Tatiana

Pierre Gilliard, Memoirs
About November 2, we learnt that the Provisional Government was overthrown and that the Bolsheviks had again come into power. But this event did not immediately react on our life, and it was not until some months later, as we shall see, that it occurred to them to turn their attention to us.

Nicky, Diary – 3 November – Tobolsk
Dear Olga is twenty-two years old; I feel sorry for her, poor thing, having to celebrate her birthday in such circumstances.

Nicky to Xenia – 5 November – Tobolsk
My dear sweet Xenia

I thank you with all my heart for your kind letter of the 15th October, which was a great joy.

You have now reassured me with everything that you write about Mama's health. May God grant that her full strength returns and that she looks after her health. We have just returned from church, which begins here at 8 o'clock in complete darkness.

In order to get to our church, we have to cross the town gardens and a road – in all it's 500 feet from the house. There are sentries standing in a serried line to the left and right and when we return home they gradually leave their places and follow behind, while others remain in the distance to the side, it all reminds us so much of being herded, that we always end up laughing by the time we reach our gate. I'm very glad they have removed your guard – it was understandably irksome both for them and for you.

Poor deluded people. I shall try to write to Misha. I have had no news of him, except from You.

The winter can't seem to get going; there is snow for two days with a light frost, then it all melts and the same thing happens again. But the air is remarkably clear, it's very good to breathe.

Here we live as on a ship at sea, the days are all very much alike, so I will tell You about our life in Tsarskoe Selo.

When I arrived from Mogilev, as You know, I found all the children very ill, especially Maria and Anastasia. I of course spent all day with them, dressed in a white gown. The doctors came to see them morning and evening at first, accompanied by an officer of the guard. A few of them came right into the bedroom and were present during the doctors' examination. A line of sentries stood round around the house, another around the pond and the railings of the little garden opposite Mama's rooms.

It was only possible to walk inside and along the second line.

Three weeks went by without any change. Then one fine day I was being followed by four sentries with bayonets; using this opportunity I said nothing but went on further into the park. From that time we began to take long daily walks in the park, and in the afternoon to fell and saw up dry trees. We all went out by the doors of the round hall, the keys being kept by the guards captain.

We didn't use the balcony once, as the door to it was locked.

Our outings into the garden with our people, to work either in the orchard or the woods, had something of being thrown to the wild beasts, as a crowd of sentries would gather next to the sentry box, by the exit from the round balcony, and mockingly observe our progress. We also had to return together at the same time, as the door was then locked. At first, from habit, I used to greet them, but then stopped, as they either replied rudely or not at all.

In the summer we were permitted to remain outdoors until 8 o'clock in the evening; I went bicycle riding with the girls and watered the orchard, as it was very dry. In the evening, we used to sit at the windows watching the sentries lying about on the lawn, smoking, reading, wrestling and singing.

I forgot to mention that during the March and April holidays there were processions in the streets (demonstrations), the music was the Marseillaise and always that same Chopin funeral march.

These processions ended without fail in our park at the grave of the 'Victims of the Revolution', which they dug in the alley opposite the round balcony. Because of these demonstrations we were only allowed out later than usual, when they had all left the park.

That unbearable funeral march stayed with us for a long time afterwards, we all kept whistling and singing it until it drove us to distraction.

The soldiers told us that they are also thoroughly tired of these demonstrations, which usually seem to end in foul weather and snow.

Of course in all this long time, we have experienced many amusing small occurrences, as well as some unpleasant ones, I can't write about them all but, God willing, one day I will be able to tell You everything in words.

I'm afraid I have bored You, dear Xenia, with this very long letter, yes and my hand is getting cramp.

My thoughts are always with you, with dear Mama and your family. I embrace you all warmly and love you.

The children kiss you tenderly.

May the Lord keep and bless you all.

How I wish we could all be together.

Goodbye my dear. With all my heart, your old

Nicky

Nicky, Diary – 11 November – Tobolsk

A lot of snow has fallen. For a long time now we have had no newspapers from Petrograd; the same thing with telegrams. It's very trying in such hard times. The girls played on the swings and jumped off them into the snow. There was a service at 9 o'clock.

17 November   The same unpleasant weather with a piercing wind. It makes you sick to read the newspaper descriptions of what happened two weeks ago in Petrograd and Moscow![18] It's worse and more shameful than events during the Time of Troubles.

18 November   We received the unbelievable news that three

---

[18] The Bolshevik Revolution.

deputies from our 5th army went to meet the Germans by Dvinsk and signed a preliminary peace agreement with them! I never expected such a nightmare. How could these bolshevik scoundrels have the effrontery to carry out their hidden dream of proposing peace to the enemy, without asking the opinion of the people, and while the enemy is occupying a large swathe of our country?

21 November We had to spend the feast of the Presentation of the Blessed Virgin without a service, as it did not please Pankratov to allow us one!

Empress Marie to Nicky – 22 November – Ai-Todor
My dear darling Nicky!

I have just received your dear letter of the 12th October, which made me terribly happy. I cannot find words to express it – I thank you from my heart, my dear. You know, that my thoughts and prayers never leave you – day and night I think of you all, sometimes it is so painful, that I can almost bear it no longer.

But God is merciful – He gives us strength during these terrible trials. Thank God, that you are all well, and at least are living cosily together. It's already a year since you and dear Alexei came to see me in Kiev. Who could have thought then what was in store and what we would have to live through. You simply can't believe it.

I live only by remembering the past and try, if possible, to forget the present nightmare. Misha also wrote to me about your last meeting in the presence of witnesses and about your nightmare departure, which was so distressing!

I am so terribly sorry that you are not allowed out to walk, I know how necessary it is for you and the dear children, it's simply incomprehensible cruelty! I am at last quite well after a long and tiresome illness and can again go out in the air after two months. The weather is wonderful, especially the last few days. We live very quietly and modestly, not seeing anyone as we are not allowed out of the estate, which is quite intolerable. Thank God at least that I am with dear Xenia, Olga and all my grandchildren, who take turns to lunch with me each day. My new grandson Tikhon [Kulikovsky] has been an immense joy to us all. He grows and gets fatter every day, and is so sweet and remarkably happy and quiet. It's a joy to see how happy Olga is and how she is enjoying her Baby, for whom she waited so long. They are very cosy living over the cellars.

She and Xenia come and see me every day and we drink cocoa

together as we are always hungry. It is so difficult to get provisions, I particularly miss white bread and butter, but sometimes kind people send me some, Felix's father crabs and butter – others white bread, for which I am very grateful.

I can imagine how pleasant it is for you to read our old letters and diaries, although these memoirs of happier times evoke such sadness in the heart. I do not even have that consolation, as during the searches in the spring they took everything, all your letters, everything that I received in Kiev, the children's letters, 3 diaries etc. and have so far not returned them, which is distressing, and you ask yourself, why?

Today is the 22nd November, dear Misha's birthday, apparently he is still confined in town. May God grant him health and happiness.

6 December All my thoughts be with you, my dear sweet Nicky, and I send you my dearest wishes. May the Lord protect you, and send you strength and spiritual peace, and may he not let Russia perish!

I embrace you warmly and tenderly. Christ be with you. Your deeply loving

Mama

Olga [daughter] to P. Petrov – 23 November – Tobolsk
I thank You dear old Pyotr Vasilievich for your letter, which I received today, a month after You sent it. It arrived in Tobolsk on 31st Oct[ober] (I saw it from the stamp) and I can't understand what it was doing until now. I have nothing of interest to tell you, as our life is quiet and monotonous. On Sundays we go to church at 8.30 in the morning, while vespers are held in the hall. The choir are amateurs, their voices aren't bad, only they sing in a concert style, which I can't abide, although many people admire it. They warned us so much about the harsh climate here, yet winter has still not settled in completely. One day there is a frost and a slight wind, the next it's two degrees and everything is thawing and unbelievably slippery. The sunrises are always very clear and beautiful, despite the overcast days. The Irtysh is long since frozen over. I think that is all the news.

We were intending to build a snow mountain, but there is still very little snow. Papa usually saws and stacks firewood, while Mama goes out when it is not too cold, otherwise it's difficult for her to breathe. Joy, Ortino and Jimmy [dogs] are flourishing. We have to spend the whole day chasing the first two out of the yard, where they have a wonderful time in the rubbish tip and eat all sorts of filth.

Well, it's time to end. Everyone here sends their best regards and wishes you good health. How is father? All my best wishes.

Pupil Nr. 1 Olga

Nicky, Diary – 26 November – Tobolsk

Today is the feast of St George. A dinner and other celebrations were arranged for the cavaliers of the town in the House of the People. There are several St George cavaliera among our guard from the 2nd regiment, but their comrades would not stand in for them, and made them report for duty in all their finery – even on such a day! Freedom!!! We went for a long, long walk, the weather was mild.

Xenia to Nicky – 30 November – Ai-Todor

I'm sorry my other letter never reached you. I sent it back in August in the name of the commandant. We have been in complete isolation for over a month, with no one allowed through to us, nor are we allowed out anywhere, so that like you, we have been stewing in our own juice, seeing no one, except those confined with us.

They only allow Irina [Yusupova] through, which is a good thing, otherwise we would have to spend the whole week apart: our commissar – Vershinin, who is known to us – is a very pleasant and kind man, but in view of the present situation he has lost the initiative and can decide or permit nothing without the Sebastopol committee. Our guard consists of a mere 14 men. Sometimes we chat with them when we meet (with the more pleasant ones!) and there are really some quite decent ones among them. They have allowed me to address them as 'thou' and we have all come to the conclusion that this is much nicer and more egalitarian.

Everything you write about your life in Tsarskoe Selo is so interesting. The heart bleeds at the thought of what you have gone through, what you have lived and are still living! At every step undeserved horrors and humiliations. But fear not, the Lord sees all. As long as you are healthy and well. Sometimes it all seems like a terrible nightmare, and that I will wake up and it will all be gone!

Poor Russia! What will happen to her? Everything has turned to dust, one just doesn't want to admit that any day the Germans can arrive and rule over us. What will they say then?

6 December And so the armistice has been declared ... from one hour to the next. It doesn't feel any better. We keep receiving horrible news about our estates – everything is being taken, and no one can say anything, soon we will all be quite destitute. We have been thinking about how we will live and earn our bread.

We have decided to open a hotel and have already allotted ourselves various functions: Sandro will be Director, Seriozha D. doorman, Sof(ia) Dm. – housekeeper, I – housemaid, Andrusha – chauffeur, Fogel – cashier, the younger children – lift boys or pages etc.

Mama has a chill.

We have had no news of Misha for over a month. He was arrested again and taken to P. but now it seems he has returned.

Everything is so sordid and cruel and painful. It would be better if it came from the Germans, not our own people.

Nicky, Diary – 7 December – Tobolsk
It dropped to 22 degrees of frost with a strong wind that cuts the face; nevertheless, we went out in the morning and the afternoon as usual. In my study, in the girls' room and in the hall it is very cold – 10 degrees, and for that reason I sit all day until the evening in a circassian infantry coat. Finished reading volume II of 'Universal History'.

Alix to Ania Vyrubova – 8 December – Tobolsk
My darling: In thoughts and prayers we are always together. Still it is hard not to see each other. My heart is so full, there is so much I would like to know, so many thoughts I should like to share with you. But we hope the time will come when we shall see each other, and all the old friends who now are scattered in different parts of the world.

We here live far from everybody and life is quiet, but we read of all the horrors that are going on. But I shall not speak of them. You live in their very centre, and that is enough for you to bear. Petty troubles surround us. The maids have been in Tobolsk four days and yet they are not allowed to come to our house, although it was promised that they should. How pitiful this everlasting suspicion and fear. Nobody is now allowed to approach us, but I hope they will soon see how stupid and brutal and unfair it is to keep them (the maids) waiting.

It is very cold – 24 degrees of frost. We shiver in the rooms, and there is always a strong draught from the windows. Your pretty jacket is so useful. We all have chilblains on our fingers. (You remember how you suffered from them in your cold little house?) I am writing this while resting before dinner. Little Jimmy lies near me while his mistress plays the piano. On the 6th Alexei, Marie, and Gilik [Gilliard] acted a little play for us. The others are committing to memory scenes from French plays. Excellent distraction and good for the memory. The evenings we spend together. He reads aloud to us, and I embroider. I am very busy all day preparing Christmas presents; painting ribbons for book markers, and cards.

On the 6th we had service at home, not being allowed to go to church on account of some kind of a disturbance. I have not been out in the fresh air for four weeks. I can't go out in such bitter weather because of my heart. Nevertheless church draws me almost irresistibly.

I am surrounded by their photographs and gifts – jackets, dressing gowns, slippers, silver dish, spoons, and ikons. How I would like to send you something, but I fear it would get lost. I kiss you tenderly, love, and bless you. We all kiss you. He was touched by your letter of congratulation. We pray for you, and we think of you, not always without tears.

Yours

A.

Tatiana to Ania Vyrubova – 9 December – Tobolsk

My darling: I often think and pray for you, and we are always remembering and speaking of you. It is hard that we cannot see each other, but God will surely help us, and we will meet again in better times. We wear the frocks your kind friends sent us, and your little gifts are always with us, reminding us of you. We live quietly and peacefully. The days pass quickly. In the morning we have lessons, walk from eleven to twelve before the house in a place surrounded for us by a high board fence. We lunch together downstairs, sometimes Mama and Alexei with us, but generally they lunch upstairs alone in Papa's study. In the afternoon we go out again for half an hour if it is not too cold. Tea upstairs, and then we read or write. Sometimes Papa reads aloud, and so goes by every day. On Saturdays we have evening service in the big hall at nine o'clock. Until that hour the priest has to serve in the church. On Sundays, when we are allowed, we go to a nearby church at eight o'clock in the morning. We go on foot through a garden, the soldiers who came here with us standing all around. They serve mass for us separately, and then have a mass for everybody. On holidays, alas, we have to have small service at home.

You remember how we used to tease you. Greetings to your old servants. Where are your brother and his wife? Have they got a baby? God bless you, my darling beloved. All our letters (permitted letters) go through the Kommissar.

Alix to Ania Vyrubova – 9 December – Tobolsk

The spirits of the whole family are good. God is very near us, we feel His support, and are often amazed that we can endure events and separations which once might have killed us. Although we suffer horribly still there is peace in our souls. I suffer most for Russia, and I suffer for you too, but I know that ultimately all will be for the best. Only I don't understand anything any longer. Everyone seems to have gone mad. I think of you daily and love you dearly. You are splendid and I know how wonderfully you have grown.

My love, burn my letters. It is better. I have kept nothing of the dear past. We all kiss you tenderly and bless you. God is great and will not forsake those encircled by His love. Dear child, I shall be thinking of you especially during Christmas. I hope that we will meet again, but where and how is in His hands. We must leave it all to Him who knows all better than we.

Nicky to Ania Vyrubova – 10 December – Tobolsk

Thank you so much for your kind wishes on my name day. Our thoughts and prayers are always with you, poor suffering creature. Her Majesty reads to us all your lines. Horrid to think all you had to go through. We are all right here. It is quite quiet. Pity you are not with us. Kisses and blessings without end from your loving friend,

N.

Give my best love to your parents.

Anastasia to Ania Vyrubova – 10 December – Tobolsk

My darling and dear: thank you tenderly for your little gift. It was so nice to have it, reminding me specially of you. We remember and speak of you often, and in our prayers we are always together. The little dog you gave is always with us and is very nice. We have arranged our rooms comfortably and all four live together.

We often sit in the windows looking at the people passing, and this gives us distraction. We have acted little plays for amusement. We walk in the garden behind high planks. God bless you.

An.

Nicky, Diary – 10 December – Tobolsk
Just before tea I was overjoyed to receive the first letter from dear Mama.

Alix to Ania Vyrubova – 15 December – Tobolsk
Dearest little one: Again I am writing to you.

It is bright sunshine and everything glitters with hoar frost. There are such moonlight nights, it must be ideal on the hills. But my poor unfortunates can only pace up and down the narrow yard. How I long to take Communion.

Some thoughts one is obliged to drive away, they are too poignant, too fresh in one's memory. All things for us are in the past, and what the future holds I cannot guess, but God knows, and I have given everything into His keeping. Pray for us and for those we love, and especially for Russia when you are at the shrine of the 'All-Hearing Virgin'. I love her beautiful face.

I am knitting stockings for the small one (Alexei). He asked for a pair as all his are in holes.

Mine are warm and thick like the ones I gave the wounded, do you remember? I make everything now. Father's trousers are torn and darned, the girls' under-linen in rags. Dreadful, is it not? I have grown quite grey.

Anastasia, to her despair, is now very fat, as Maria was, round and fat to the waist, with short legs. I do hope she will grow. Olga and Tatiana are both thin, but their hair grows beautifully so that they can go without scarfs.

I find myself writing in English, I don't know why. Be sure to burn all these letters as at any time your house may be searched again.

Valia Dolgorukov to his mother – December [no date] – Tobolsk
My very dear Mama

... She is often depressed, but in a rather gentle mood, and maintains the role she must play, calm, dignified, accepting all news and occurrences with equanimity. He is always the same, suffering morally, expressing himself openly, but has been able to retain his charm and affability.

Your devoted Valia,

Happy Christmas

Alexei to P. Petrov – 19 December – Tobolsk
My dear Pyotr Vasilievich

I send you my best wishes for the coming Christmas and first new year. I hope that you received my last letter. How are you keeping? For the moment we have very little snow, so it is difficult to make a mountain. Joy [the spaniel] is getting fatter every day as he keeps eating rubbish from the refuse pit. Everyone chases him away with sticks. He has a lot of friends in the town and is always running away.

I am writing to you during my French lesson, as I have almost no free time, but when I am on holiday I will write more often. Greetings and congratulations to the teachers. May the Lord keep you!

Your fifth pupil, Alexei

Nicky, Diary – 24 December – Tobolsk
Before our walk we prepared gifts for everyone and decorated the Christmas trees. At tea time – before five o'clock – Alix and I went to the guard house and prepared a tree for the first platoon of the 4th regiment. We sat with the sentries. After dinner it was the suite's turn to have a tree, and we had ours just before 8 o'clock. The service was very late as the father could not come earlier because of the service in the church. Those of the sentries who were free also attended.

Alix's Diary
Tobolsk. December 24. Sunday
Xmas Eve.
Arranged presents.
12. Service in the house.
Lunched downstairs.
Dressed the trees, placed the presents.
4½ Tea. Then went to the guard 14th inf[antry/rifles] R[egiment's]. Malishev, 20 men. I brought them a small Xmas tree and eatables – and a gospel each with a bookmarker I had painted – sat there.
7½. Dined downstairs with all, Kolia [Derevenko] too. One has forbidden Isa [Buxhoeveden] to come to us, or leave her house.
9. Xmas tree for the suite – all our people.
9½. Evening service: a large choir sang. Soldiers came too.

Nicky, Diary – 28 December – Tobolsk
We were most displeased to learn that our kind father Alexei [the priest] is being subjected to an investigation and held under house arrest.

It happened because during the Te Deum on December 25th, the deacon referred to us with our titles, and as there were many of the guards from the 2nd regiment in church, this inevitably caused a fuss, probably not without the participation of Pankratov and his cronies.

31 December Not too cold a day, with gusts of wind. Towards evening Alexei got up, as he was able to put on his shoe. After tea we all went our separate ways until it was time to meet the New Year. Lord! Save Russia!

1918

Nicky – ex-Emperor of Russia

Alix – ex-Empress of Russia

Xenia – Nicky's sister, husband of Sandro

Olga – eldest daughter of Nicky and Alix, aged twenty-three

Tatiana – second daughter of Nicky and Alix, aged twenty-one

Maria – third daughter of Nicky and Alix, aged nineteen

Anastasia – fourth daughter of Nicky and Alix, aged seventeen

Alexei – son of Nicky and Alix, aged fourteen

Georgie – King George V of England, first cousin of both Nicky and Alix

Prince Felix Yusupov – married to Irina, daughter of Xenia and Sandro

Ania Vyrubova – lady-in-waiting and close friend of Alix

Pierre Gilliard – Swiss tutor of Nicky and Alix's children

Valia Dolgorukov – a member of the imperial court

A. G. Beloborodov – Chairman of the Ural Regional Soviet

Y. M. Yurovsky – commander at the Ipatiev House

P. Medvedev – one of the assassins

A. V. Markov – President of the CHEKA at Perm

Ryabov – assassin of Ella

1918

DEMONS

In captivity – Tobolsk, then Ekaterinburg – The end.

Nicky, Diary – 1 January – Tobolsk
At 8 o'clock we went to church without Olga and Tatiana, who unfortunately both have a fever. The doctors think they probably have German measles.

2 January German measles has been confirmed, but fortunately they both feel all right today. The day was grey, not cold but with a strong wind. We go into the garden but there's no work to do – today I was bored to tears!

Pierre Gilliard, Memoirs – 2 January
At 2 p.m. there was a meeting of the committee of our garrison. It was decided by 100 votes to 85 to prohibit the wearing of epaulettes by officers and men.

Nicky, Diary – 3 January – Tobolsk
Alexei also started German measles, but quite mildly; Olga and Tatiana are feeling better, the latter even got up. It snowed all day. The detachment guards' committee instructed me to remove my epaulettes, in order to avoid being insulted or attacked in the town. It's beyond comprehension!

Alexei, Diary – 4 January – Tobolsk
Today I got even more spots. Played chequers with Nagorni all morning. Maria also got ill. She is also covered with spots. All the soldiers were ordered to remove their epaulettes, but Papa and I didn't.

Pierre Gilliard, Memoirs – 4 January
Colonel Kobylinsky came this morning. He wore mufti rather than wear his uniform without epaulettes.

Nicky, Diary – 5 January – Tobolsk
We talked with the guards from the 1st platoon of the 4th regiment about the removal of my epaulettes, and the behaviour of the 2nd regiment, of whom they are strongly critical.

Pierre Gilliard, Memoirs – 5 January
When it was Alexei's turn to kiss the cross held out by the priest the latter bent down and kissed his forehead. After dinner General Tatischev and Prince Dolgorukov came to beg the Tsar to remove his epaulettes in order to avoid a hostile demonstration by the soldiers. At first it seemed as though the Tsar would refuse, but, after exchanging a look and a few words with the Tsarina, he recovered his self-control and yielded for the sake of his family.

Alexei, Diary – 6 January – Tobolsk
Got up at 7. Had tea with Papa, Tatiana and Anastasia. We played cards. Maria is dressed and walking around the rooms. At 6 o'clock we played hide and seek and shouted and made a terrible noise.

Nicky to Xenia – 7 January – Tobolsk
My dear sweet Xenia
   You made me very happy with Your letter, and I thank You with all my heart. It is extremely difficult to live without news – papers arrive here but are not on sale in the streets every day, but they only tell of new horrors, being perpetrated in our poor Russia. It makes you sick to think how much our allies must despise us.
   For me, the night is the best part of the day, at least you can forget for a while. A few days ago our local committee discussed the ques-

tion of removing epaulettes and other distinctions, and it was decided by a very small majority not to wear them any more. There were two reasons: the fact that their regiments in Tsarskoe Selo had done the same thing, and another circumstance – attacks in the street by local soldiers and hooligans on individual sentries, with the aim of ripping off their epaulettes. All the real soldiers, who have spent three years at the front, have had to bow to this stupid order.

Everywhere it's the same story – one or two bad cavalry soldiers make trouble and lead on the others.

From the new year, all the children except Anastasia have had German measles, but now they are all over it.

The weather is splendid, nearly always sunny, a slight frost.

I embrace you warmly, also dear Mama and all the others. I am always with You all. With all my heart,

Your Nicky

Alexei, Diary – 7 January – Tobolsk
The whole day was just like yesterday.

Nicky, Diary – 9 January – Tobolsk
A splendid calm day with a light frost – 6 to 8 degrees. For the last two days I have been reading a book from the library of the local gymnasium *Tobolsk and its surroundings* by Golodnikov – with fascinating historical information.

I did some good work in the afternoon – I cleared the courtyard and then filled the little hut with firewood; I was helped by the kind old sentry from the 1st regiment, Orlov – formerly from the Preobrajensky.

Alexei, Diary – 9 January – Tobolsk
The whole day was just like yesterday.

10 January The whole day was just like yesterday. In the afternoon Kolia [Dr Derevenko's son] and I ran and jumped in the snow. We watered the mountain, fought and wrestled.

12 January The whole day was just like yesterday.

14 January The whole day was just like yesterday.

15 January   Anastasia has German measles. She spent the whole day in bed. The whole day was just like yesterday. Kolia had a cough and didn't come.

17 January   Everything is the same. Kolia still didn't come.

18 January   Everything is the same. Anastasia is up and dressed. 26 below. Boring!!!

Pierre Gilliard, Memoirs – 20 January
23° R. below zero. Prince Dolgorukov and I watered the snow mountain. We carried thirty buckets of water. It was so cold that the water froze on the way from the kitchen tap to the mountain. Our buckets and the snow mountain 'steamed'. Tomorrow the children can begin tobogganing.

Olga [daughter] to Ania Vyrubova – 22 January – Tobolsk
Dearest, we were so glad to hear from you. How cold it is these days, and what a strong wind. We have just come back from a walk. On our window it is written -'Anna darling' I wonder who wrote it. God bless you, dear. Be well.

Your Olga

Give my love to all who remember me.

Alexei, Diary – 22 January – Tobolsk
22 below – Storm. Snow whirling. It's still as boring.

24 January   In the afternoon I twirled a little stick in my hand and watched Papa working up on the roof cleaning snow and how they bring wood in the house.
   What a bore!!!

Tatiana to P. V. Petrov – 26 January – Tobolsk
Greetings dear Pyotr Vasilievich,
   Thank You so much for Your two letters. I was very touched that You should write so much. We are, thank God, in good health, and are living quietly as before, and strange though it may seem, none of those living with us have as yet quarrelled. There are lessons in the morning for two hours from 9–11, an hour's walk and then we study

for a further hour. After lunch we go for a walk again – usually until 4, but if the weather is good, for longer. We work until tea, or occupy ourselves in some way in our room. After tea until dinner there are rehearsals of some play. We have already put on three and are learning another, it's nevertheless a distraction and is good for our diction.

A small mountain has been built in our yard. When we get bored of walking to and fro we slide down it, there are often very amusing tumbles. Thus once Gilliard found himself sitting on my head. I begged him to get up, but he couldn't as he had twisted his foot and it was hurting. Somehow I managed to crawl free. It was terribly stupid and funny, though he had to lie up for a few days because of his foot.

Another time I slid down the mountain backwards and hit my head on the ice terribly hard. I thought there would be nothing of the mountain left, but as it turned out neither it nor my head were cracked or even hurt. I've got a tough old block, haven't I? Huh?

It has also been cold here, with a strong wind in particular, that cut the face terribly. It was very cold in the rooms. It was 5¾ degrees in the hall.

Keep well. We send everyone our warmest greetings.

Tatiana

Pierre Gilliard, Memoirs – 26 January
The soldiers' committee has today decided to replace Pankratov by a Bolshevik commissary from Moscow. Things are going from bad to worse. It appears that there is no longer a state of war between Soviet Russia and Germany, Austria, and Bulgaria. The army is to be disbanded, but Lenin and Trotsky have not yet signed the peace.

Alexei, Diary – 29 January – Tobolsk
Played with Kolia in the afternoon and slid down the hill. Hit the ankle on my right leg. Limped all evening. Put a compress at night.

30 January Slept very badly at night. My leg hurt. Had breakfast with Mama. Stayed in bed all day.

Xenia to Nicky – 31 January – Ai-Todor
I received your dear letter of the 27th, and am hurrying to thank you, dear Nicky and tell you what a joy it was. Thank God everyone is well

again, and that all is relatively quiet with you – which can't be said about our area, where at the present time everything is at boiling point.

Yes, you are absolutely right when you say that the best time is the night, when sleep makes you forget everything, and your soul can rest for a while. To watch and realize that our country is being destroyed, and so senselessly, is unbearable, and you simply wonder how you can go on living! You want to believe that everything is not yet lost, that people will be found to lead Russia out of this chaos and terrible impasse. What have they done with our unfortunate people? Will they come to their senses one day?

They don't allow anyone to see us, and we have not been allowed out of Ai-Todor for three months. We have not seen Irina since the 6th January.

By the way, a few sentences of your letter were crossed out – concerning the guard and mutual relations (for your information!) ('Nevertheless we read it all' – an Engl. saying, which cannot be translated into Russian, but it is all very upsetting). From this alone, it means the letters are being read.

I don't know how we are going to survive, everything is so madly expensive, and there's no money. For some days we have faced being without light, as there is no kerosene. But that isn't the point, we'll manage somehow, but you feel painfully sorry for poor Mama. Why should she have to suffer, and put up with such adversity, privations and insults at her age?

Nicky, Diary – 1/14 February[1] – Tobolsk
We learned that at the post they had received the order to change styles, and to count according to the foreign way as from February lst, i.e. today is already the 14th February. The misunderstanding and confusion will be endless.

5/18 and 6/19 Started reading the *Three Musketeers* of A. Dumas. This is the third day we have had tea in my study, as it is brighter and we can see the sunset, and the room is warmer.

Alexei, Diary – 5/18 February – Tobolsk
Everything the same. Had lessons.

---

[1] Henceforward both old and new style dates are given.

Nicky, Diary – 7/20 February – Tobolsk
Judging by the telegrams, the war with Germany has started up again, as the deadline for peace has run out; at the front, it seems, we have nothing, the army is demobilised, weapons and supplies are being abandoned to the whims of fate and the advancing enemy! It's disgraceful and appalling!

Alexei, Diary – 9/22 February – Tobolsk
Yesterday I hit my left leg on the ankle and had a compress all day.

I had both breakfast and dinner with Mama in Papa's study. In the afternoon I lay on the floor and drew caricatures.

Nicky, Diary – 12/25 February – Tobolsk
Today telegrams arrived informing us that the Bolsheviks, or as they call themselves the Sovnarkom, are obliged to agree to peace on the humiliating terms of the German government, in view of the fact that the enemy troops are pushing forward and there is no way of stopping them! A nightmare!

14/27 February   We are going to have to considerably reduce our expenditure on household supplies and staff, as the department of appanages is being closed down from March 1st, added to which we are only allowed to receive 600 roubles a month each from our personal capital. For the last few days we have been busy calculating the minimum that will allow us to make ends meet.

15/28 February   For this reason we will be forced to part with many of our people, as we are not able to keep on everyone who is with us in Tobolsk. It is of course very hard, but unavoidable. At our request, Tatischev, Valia D[olgorukov] and Mr Gilliard have taken charge of the household and the organization of those staff who have remained, with the valet Volkov under them.

Alexei, Diary – 19 February/4 March – Tobolsk
Spent the whole day like yesterday. In the afternoon I played with Kolia and made a wooden dagger with my knife, Kolia too, later we attacked each other. In the evening the soldiers destroyed the ice mountain, so we can't slide. We were told so by the commandant.

Nicky, Diary – 20 February/5 March
This morning we saw from the window that the little mountain has been destroyed; it appears that the idiotic detachment committee decided to do this, in order to stop us climbing up onto it and looking over the fence!

Alexei, Diary – 26 February/11 March – Tobolsk
I hit the toe on my right foot and could not put on my boot. So I had to stay at home.

27 February/12 March Spent the whole day indoors. There were pancakes for lunch, I ate nine.

Nicky, Diary – 28 February/13 March – Tobolsk
A similar day with 12 degrees of frost. I finished *Anna Karenina* and began reading Lermontov.
Sawed a lot of wood with Tatiana.
Over the last few days we have begun to receive butter, coffee, cakes for tea and jams, from various kind people who have heard that our expenditure on food has been reduced. How touching!

2/15 March I keep remembering these days last year in Pskov and on the train!
How much longer will our poor Russia be racked and torn apart by external and internal enemies! Sometimes it seems I no longer have the strength to go on, I don't even know what to pin my hopes on, what to wish for?
And yet there is no one like God!
Let His Sacred will be done!

Alexei, Diary – 2/15 March – Tobolsk
Everything the same. Did some drawing. Sig [Gibbes, English tutor] read aloud. Managed to put my boot on in the evening and went downstairs. There was a requiem service for great-grandfather [Alexander II] at 12 o'clock. Had a compress on my toe all afternoon. Pancakes for lunch.

Alix to Ania Vyrubova – 2/15 March – Tobolsk
Darling child: Thanks for all from Papa, Mama and the children.

How you spoil us all by your dear letters and gifts. I was very anxious going so long without news from you, especially as rumours came that you were gone. Alas, I can't write you as I could wish for fear that this may fall into other hands. We have not yet received all that you have sent, in jest I name it contraband. It comes to us little by little. Dear child, do be careful!

I have sat twice on the balcony and more often sit in the yard. My heart has been much better, but for a week I have had great pains in it again. I worry so much.

My God! How Russia suffers. You know that I love it even more than you do, miserable country, demolished from within, and by the Germans from without. Since the Revolution they have conquered a great deal of it without even a battle. If they created order now in Russia how dreadful would be the country's debasement – to have to be grateful to the enemy. They must never dare to attempt any conversations with Papa and Mama.

We live here on earth but we are already half gone to the next world. We see with different eyes, and that makes it often difficult to associate with people who are religious, but not completely.

My greatest sin is my irritability. The endless stupidity [of maid], for instance – she can't help being, she is so often untruthful, or else she begins to sermonize like a preacher and then I burst – you know how hot-tempered I am. It is not difficult to bear great trials, but these little buzzing mosquitoes are so trying.

I want to be a better woman, and I try. For long periods I am really patient, and then breaks out again my bad temper. We are to have a new confessor, the second in these seven months. I beg your forgiveness too, darling. Day after tomorrow is the Sunday before Lent when one asks forgiveness for all one's faults. Forgive the past, and pray for me. I long to warm and comfort others – but alas, I do not feel drawn to those around me here. I am cold towards them, and this, too, is wrong of me.

What a nightmare it is that it is Germans who are saving Russia and are restoring order. What could be more humiliating for us? With one hand the Germans give, and with the other they take away. Already they have seized an enormous territory. God help and save this unhappy country. Probably He wills us to endure all these insults, but that we must take them from the Germans almost kills me. During a war one can understand these things happening – but not during a revolution.

Now Batoum has been taken – our country is disintegrating into bits. I cannot think calmly about it. Such hideous pain in heart and soul. Yet I am sure God will not leave it like this. He will send wisdom and save Russia I am sure.

Alexei, Diary – 3/16 March – Tobolsk
Everything the same. Today at lunch I ate 16 pancakes. They were giving them for the last time. There was a service at 9 o'clock. The weather was cold and windy. I had a bath.

Pierre Gilliard, Memoirs – 4/17 March – Tobolsk
Today is Carnival Sunday. Everyone is merry. The sledges pass to and fro under our windows; sound of bells, mouth-organs, and singing. The children wistfully watch the fun. They have begun to grow bored and find their captivity irksome. They walk round the courtyard, fenced in by its high paling through which they can see nothing. Since the destruction of their snow mountain their only distraction is sawing and cutting wood.

The arrogance of the soldiers is inconceivable; those who have left have been replaced by a pack of blackguardly-looking young men.

In spite of the daily increase of their sufferings, Their Majesties still cherish hope that among their loyal friends some may be found to attempt their release. Never was the situation more favourable for escape, for there is as yet no representative of the Bolshevik Government at Tobolsk. With the complicity of Colonel Kobylinsky, already on our side, it would be easy to trick the insolent but careless vigilance of our guards. All that is required is the organised and resolute efforts of a few bold spirits outside. We have repeatedly urged upon the Tsar the necessity of being prepared for any turn of events. He insists on two conditions which greatly complicate matters: he will not hear of the family being separated or leaving Russian territory.

One day the Tsarina said to me in this connection: 'I wouldn't leave Russia on any consideration, for it seems to me that to go abroad would be to break our last link with the past, which would then be dead for ever.'

6/19 March After lunch the Treaty of Brest-Litovsk was discussed.[2] It has just been signed.

---

[2] Separate peace with Germany.

The Tsar was very depressed, saying: 'It is such a disgrace for Russia and amounts to suicide. I should never have thought the Emperor William and the German Government could stoop to shake hands with these miserable traitors. But I'm sure they will get no good from it; it won't save them from ruin!'

A little later, when Prince Dolgorukov remarked that the newspapers were discussing a clause in which the Germans demanded that the Imperial family should be handed over to them unharmed, the Tsar cried: 'This is either a manoeuvre to discredit me or an insult.'

The Tsarina added in a low voice: 'After what they have done to the Tsar, I would rather die in Russia than be saved by the Germans!'

Valia Dolgorukov to his mother – 6/19 March – Tobolsk

My very dear Mama

The family is well. They occupy themselves cutting wood in the courtyard. She goes out very little, as she cannot stand the cold. Little Alexei suffers from time to time with his leg. It comes and goes. He is very nice, but I think ambitious and authoritarian like his mother.

The family is very close and friendly. The soldiers' committee keeps making trouble. On one occasion they destroyed the snow mountain made for us in the yard, on another they prevented us from going to church.

Meals have been reduced to the minimum. No coffee or butter. Half a pound of sugar a month. For lunch soup and one dish. For dinner two dishes (no soup).

Your Valia

Alexei, Diary – 7/20 March – Tobolsk

We went to church at 8. After an hour we came home and had tea again. In the afternoon I piled up wood in the shed and tore my gloves. In the evening Mama and my sisters were singing. The rest like yesterday.

Nicky, Diary – 9/22 March – Tobolsk

It's a year today since I arrived in Tsarskoe Selo and my family and I were imprisoned in the Alexander Palace! It's difficult not to think about how difficult the last year has been! What more does the future hold in store for us? Everything is in the hands of God! He is our only recourse.

Alexei, Diary – 11/24 March – Tobolsk
Everything the same. At ¼ to 12 a short service. The choir sang. 10 degrees in the sun, zero in the shade. Everything is melting. In the afternoon Papa sawed wood, the sisters chopped logs and carried them into the shed. I threw snowballs.

Nicky, Diary – 14/27 March – Tobolsk
The local detachment was disbanded when the tours of duty expired. But as a detail of guards is still needed to patrol the town, a detachment has been sent from Omsk for this purpose. The arrival of this 'red guard', as every armed unit is now known, has given rise to all kinds of rumours and fears. It has even been quite amusing to listen to what has been said over the last few days. The commandant of our detachment was also, it seems, quite disturbed, and for the last two nights the guard has been strengthened and the machine gun in position from the evening! People really seem to trust each other in these times!

Alexei, Diary – 16/29 March – Tobolsk
Spent the whole day indoors. Had a bad cough. Snow storm outside. 10 below.

22 March/4 April Yesterday the sisters, me and others received a half-pound of sugar for the month. It's melting and in the evening a little rain. In the afternoon Kolia and I made a bow and arrow. Isn't it fun to shoot.

Nicky, Diary – 22 March/4 April – Tobolsk
In the morning, from the yard, we heard a band of rogue-bolsheviks from Tiumen, as they left Tobolsk in 15 *troikas*, with drums, whistling and shouting. The Omsk detachment had chased them out!

27 March/9 April It has suddenly turned cold with a north wind. The day was clear. Yesterday I started reading aloud Nilus's book about the Anti-Christ, to which are appended the 'protocols' of the jews and the masons – very topical reading.

RATION CARD

SURNAME	**Romanov**
FIRST NAME	**Nicholas**
PATRONYMIC	**Alexandrovich**
RANK	**Ex-Emperor**
STREET	**'Freedom'**
DEPENDENTS	**six**

TOB.CIT.FOOD.COM*

RATION CARD NO 54

Signature of Issuing Officer
Committee Chairman

RULES

1. The owner of this card can receive goods only on presentation in the City shop or in the cooperative shop "Self-conscience".

2. In case of loss of a card, the owner loses the right to a duplicate unless he can prove by official means the loss of the card.

3. Rations and prices are posted in the shops.

4. Transfer of cards to other persons prohibited.

OCTOBER

Flour	5 puds 10 lbs
Rye Flour	
Butter	7 lbs
Salt	
Candles	
Sugar	½ lb
Soap	
Cereals	
Oats	

*One of the first examples of Soviet 'New speech'

28 March/10 April There was some alarm in our detachment, caused by rumours of the arrival of more red guards from Ekaterinburg. The guard was doubled at night, the patrols reinforced and sentries posted in the street. There was talk of alleged danger to us in this house and of the need to move into the bishop's house on the hill. This was discussed all day in committees, but finally at night everything quietened down, which is what Kobylinsky came to tell me at 7 o'clock. Alix was even asked not to sit on the balcony for the next three days!

Alexei, Diary – 29 March/11 April – Tobolsk
[The last entry in Alexei's diary] Everything as before. In the evening
we shot at the target. It was a very interesting pastime. It's getting
warmer. During our morning walk, the extraordinary commissar
dropped in to look at our yard and garden. The Red Guards have
been here already one week.

Nicky, Diary – 30 March/12 April – Tobolsk
Everyday a new surprise! Today Kobylinsky brought a letter that he
received yesterday, addressed to our detachment from the Central
Executive Committee in Moscow, saying that everyone in the other
house is to be moved over to ours, and that we are to be considered
under arrest, as in Tsarskoe Selo. They immediately started moving
the chambermaids downstairs from one room into another, to make
room for the new arrivals.

Alexei developed a pain in the groin from his cough, and spent the
day in bed.

Alix to Ania Vyrubova – around 30 March/12 April – Tobolsk
Sunbeam has been ill in bed for the past week. I don't know whether
coughing brought on an attack, or whether he picked up something
heavy, but he had an awful internal haemorrhage and suffered fearfully. He is better now, but sleeps badly and the pains, though less
severe, have not entirely ceased. He is frightfully thin and yellow,
reminding me of Spala. Do you remember?

But yesterday he began to eat a little, and Dr Derevenko is satisfied
with his progress. The child has to lie on his back without moving,
and he gets so tired. I sit all day beside him, holding his aching legs,
and I have grown almost as thin as he.

It is certain now that we shall celebrate Easter at home because it
will be better for him if we have a service together. I try to hope that
this attack will pass more quickly than usual. It must, since all Winter
he was so well.

I have not been outside the house for a week. I am no longer permitted to sit on the balcony, and I avoid going downstairs. I am sorry
that your heart is bad again, but I can understand it. Be sure and let
me know well in advance if you move again. Everyone, we hear, has
been sent away from Tsarskoe. Poor Tsarskoe, who will take care of
the rooms now? What do they mean when they speak of an 'état de
siège' there?

Same day

Darling,

I want to talk to you again, knowing how anxious you will be for Sunbeam. The blood recedes quickly – that is why today he again had very severe pains. Yesterday for the first time he smiled and talked with us, even played cards, and slept two hours during the day. He is frightfully thin, with enormous eyes, just as at Spala. He likes to be read to, eats little – no appetite at all in fact. I am with him the whole day, Tatiana or Mr Gilliard relieving me at intervals.

Mr Gilliard reads to him tirelessly, or warms his legs with the Fohn apparatus. Today it is snowing again but the snow melts rapidly, and it is very muddy. I have not been out for a week and a half, as I am so tired that I don't dare to risk the stairs. So I sit with Alexei.

A great number of new troops have come from everywhere. A new Kommissar has arrived from Moscow, a man named Yakovlev, and today we shall have to make his acquaintance. It gets very hot in this town in summer, is frightfully dusty, and at times very humid. We are begging to be transferred for the hot months to some convent. I know that you too are longing for fresh air, and I trust that by God's mercy it may become possible for us all.

They are always hinting to us that we shall have to travel either very far away, or to the centre [of Siberia], but we hope that this will not happen, as it would be dreadful at this season.

Well, all is God's will. The deeper you look the more you understand that this is so. All sorrows are sent to free us from our sins or as a test of our faith, an example to others.

I should like to be a painter, and make a picture of this beautiful garden and all that grows in it. I remember English gardens, and at Livadia you saw an illustrated book I had of them, so you will understand.

Just now eleven more men have passed on horseback, good faces, mere boys – this I have not seen the like of for a long time. They are the guard of the new Kommissar.

Sometimes we see men with the most awful faces. I would not include them in my garden picture. The only place for them would be outside where the merciful sunshine could reach them and make them clean from all the dirt and evil with which they are covered.

Pierre Gilliard, Memoirs – 30 March/12 April

Alexei confined to bed, as since yesterday he has had a violent pain in the groin caused by a strain. He has been so well this winter. It is to be hoped it is nothing serious.

A soldier of our detachment who had been sent to Moscow has returned today and brought Colonel Kobylinsky a memorandum from the Central Executive Committee of the Bolshevik Government, ordering him to be much stricter with us. General Tatischev, Prince Dolgorukov, and Countess Hendrikova are to be transferred from our house and treated as prisoners. The arrival is also announced of a commissary with extraordinary powers, accompanied by a detachment of soldiers.

Nicky, Diary – 31 March/13 April – Tobolsk
The poor thing didn't sleep at all at night, and suffered greatly during the day. They brought over the furniture and things from the Kornilov house before lunch, while the inhabitants settled into their new quarters.

1/14 April   Today, implementing the order from Moscow, the local committee decreed that the people living in our house are also no longer allowed out on the street, i.e. in the town. The whole day there was talk of how to fit them all into our already overcrowded house, as it has meant moving seven people.

Everything is being done in a hurry, in view of the imminent arrival of a new detachment and a commissar, who will bring instructions with him. Our guards, therefore, want them to find us under a strict regime, in order to shield themselves from possible repercussions. Alexei lay in bed all day; the pains continued, but at greater intervals.

2/15 April   In the morning the commandant, together with an officers' commission and two sentries, went over our part of the house. The result of this 'search' was the confiscation of Valia and M. Gilliard's draughts set, and of my dagger!

Kobylinsky once more explained this measure as being necessary to pacify the sentries! Alexei was better, and he fell fast asleep from 7 in the evening. The weather was grey and calm.

Pierre Gilliard, Memoirs – 2/15 April – Tobolsk
Alexei Nicholaevich in great pain yesterday and today. It is one of his severe attacks of haemophilia.

Nicky, Diary – 5/18 April – Tobolsk
Alexei slept at intervals, the pain bothered him at times when he changed position in bed and sat up.

6/19 April   Today Alexei was in greater pain and only slept a little.

7/20 April   Alexei slept well, during the day the pains were less frequent.

8/21 April   The twenty-fourth anniversary of our engagement! The day was sunny with a cold wind, all the snow has melted.
   At 11.30 there was a service. Afterwards Kobylinsky showed me a telegram from Moscow, confirming the decree of the local committee ordering Alexei and myself to remove our epaulettes! I therefore decided not to wear them out for my walk, only at home. I will never forgive *them* this swinish action!

9/22 April   We learnt of the arrival of the extraordinary plenipotentiary from Moscow; he moved into the Kornilov house. The children were convinced that he would come and conduct a search today, so they burnt their letters, and Maria and Anastasia even their diaries. Alexei felt better and even slept two or three hours in the afternoon.

Pierre Gilliard, Memoirs – 9/22 April – Tobolsk
The commissary from Moscow arrived today with a small detachment; his name is Yakovlev. He has shown his papers to the commandant and soldiers' committee. In the evening he took tea with Their Majesties. Everyone is restless and distraught. The commissary's arrival is felt to be an evil portent, vague but real.

Nicky, Diary – 10/23 April – Tobolsk
At 10.30 in the morning, Kobylinsky appeared with Yakovlev and his suite. I received him in the hall with the girls. We were expecting him at 11 o'clock, which is why Alix was not ready. He came in, his face shaven, smiling and looking embarrassed, and asked me if I was satisfied with the accommodation and the guard.
   He then ran in to see Alexei, but without stopping, proceeded to look at the other rooms and, excusing himself for the inconvenience, went downstairs. He visited the others on the remaining floors just as quickly. Half an hour later he reappeared to present himself to Alix, dashed in again to see Alexei and downstairs.

Pierre Gilliard, Memoirs – 10/23 April
Commissary Yakovlev came at eleven o'clock. After an inspection of
the whole house he went to see the Tsar, who accompanied him to
the room of Alexei who is in bed. Not having been able to see the
Tsarina, who was not ready to receive him, he came again a little later
with the regimental doctor and paid a second visit to Alexei.

He wanted to be assured by his doctor that the boy was really ill.
As he was going away he asked the commandant whether we had
much luggage. Can this mean we are to move?

Alix, Diary – 10/23 April – Tobolsk
Baby had a bad night because of strong pains, 36.6. Snowing again.
In the morning the new Kommissar Yakovlev came to see us.
(Impression of an intelligent, highly nervous workman, engineer
etc.)

10½. Spent the day with Baby. Gay, played cards, read to him. Slept
from 5-7¼. 37.4. N. read to us in the evening.

11/24 April Baby had again a restless night with stronger pains.
36.6. Painted in bed and T[atiana] read to me. Spiritual Reading.
Spent the day with Baby, working, playing cards. Olga lunched and
dined with us. Lovely sunny day. Rested from 7–8. N[icky] read to us
in the evening.

Pierre Gilliard, Memoirs – 11/24 April – Tobolsk
We are all in a state of mental anguish. We feel we are forgotten by
everyone, abandoned to our own resources and at the mercy of this
man. Is it possible that no one will raise a finger to save the Imperial
family? Where are those who have remained loyal to the Tsar? Why
do they delay?

12/25 April Shortly before three o'clock, as I was going along the
passage, I met two servants sobbing. They told me that Yakovlev has
come to tell the Tsar that he is taking him away. What can be happening? I dare not go up without being summoned, and went back
to my room. Almost immediately Tatiana knocked at my door. She
was in tears, and told me Her Majesty was asking for me. I followed
her. The Tsarina was alone, greatly upset. She confirmed what I had
heard, that Yakovlev has been sent from Moscow to take the Tsar
away and is to leave tonight.

'The commissary says that no harm will come to the Tsar, and that if anyone wishes to accompany him there will be no objection. I can't let the Tsar go alone. They want to separate him from his family as they did before.

'They're going to try to force his hand by making him anxious about his family ... The Tsar is necessary to them; they feel that he alone represents Russia. Together we shall be in a better position to resist them, and I ought to be at his side in the time of trial. But the boy is still so ill ... Suppose some complication sets in ... Oh, God, what ghastly torture! ... For the first time in my life I don't know what I ought to do; I've always felt inspired whenever I've had to take a decision, and now I can't think. But God won't allow the Tsar's departure; it can't, it *must* not be. I'm sure the thaw will begin tonight.'

Tatiana here intervened:

'But mother, if father has to go, whatever we say, something must be decided ...'

I took up the cudgels on Tatiana's behalf, remarking that Alexei Nikolaevich was better, and that we should take great care of him.

Her Majesty was obviously tortured by indecision; she paced up and down the room, and went on talking, rather to herself than to us. At last she came up to me and said:

'Yes, that will be best; I'll go with the Tsar; I shall trust Alexei to you.'

A moment later the Tsar came in. The Tsarina walked towards him, saying:

'It's settled; I'll go with you, and Maria will come too.'

The Tsar replied: 'Very well, if you wish it.'

I came down to my room, and the whole day has been spent in getting ready. Prince Dolgorukov and Doctor Botkin will accompany Their Majesties, as also will Chemodurov, Anna Demidova, and Sednev.[3] It has been decided that eight officers and men of our guard are to go with them.

The family have spent the whole afternoon at the bedside of Alexei.

This evening at half past ten we went up to take tea. The Tsarina was seated on the divan with two of her daughters beside her. Their

---

[3] Terenty Ivanovich Chemodurov, the Tsar's valet; Anna Stefanova Demidova, the Tsarina's maid (also known as 'Nyuta'), and Leonid Ivanovich Sednev, footman to the Grand Duchesses, but pressed into service as kitchen-boy (also known as 'Lenka').

faces were swollen with crying. We all did our best to hide our grief and to maintain outward calm. We felt that for one to give way would cause all to break down. The Tsar and Tsarina were calm and collected. It is apparent that they are prepared for any sacrifices, even of their lives, if God in his inscrutable wisdom would require it for the country's welfare. They have never shown greater kindness or solicitude.

This splendid serenity of theirs, this wonderful faith, proved infectious.

Alix, Diary – 12/25 April – Tobolsk
Baby had a better night. 36.

12¼–1. Sat with Baby, played cards, worked.

After luncheon the Komm[issar] Yakovlev came, as I wanted to arrange about the visit to Church for Passion week. Instead of that he announced by the order of his government (Bolsheviki) that he has to take us away (when?). Seeing Baby is too ill, wished to take N[icky] alone (if not willing, then obliged to use force).

I had to decide to stay with ill Baby or accompany him. Settled to accompany him as can be of more need and too risky not knowing where and for what (we imagine Moscow). Horrible suffering. Maria comes with us, Olga will look after Baby, Tatiana – the household and Anastasia will cheer all up.

Took meals with Baby, put few things together, quite small luggage. Took leave of all our people after evening with all. Sat all night with the children. Baby slept and at 3 went to him till we left. Started at 4¼ in the morning. Horrid to leave precious children. 8 of our rifles went with us.

Nicky, Diary – 12/25 April – Tobolsk
After lunch Yakovlev arrived with Kobylinsky and explained that he had received the order to take me away, without saying where to? Alix decided to go with me, and to take Maria; there was no point in protesting. It is more than painful to leave the other children and Alexei – who is ill – and in such circumstances. We immediately started packing the basic necessities. Then Yakovlev said that he would return to fetch Olga, Tatiana, Anastasia and Alexei, and that we would probably see them in about three weeks. We spent a very sad evening; naturally no one could sleep at night.

Pierre Gilliard, Memoirs – 12/25 April – Tobolsk
At half past eleven the servants were assembled in the large hall.
Their Majesties and Maria took leave of them. The Tsar embraced
every man, the Tsarina every woman. Almost all were in tears. Their
Majesties withdrew; we all went down to my room.

At half past three the conveyances drew up in the courtyard. They
were the horrible *tarantass* [a simple type of carriage]. Only one was
covered. We found a little straw in the backyard and spread it on the
floor of the carriages. We put a mattress in the one to be used by the
Tsarina.

At four o'clock we went up to see Their Majesties and found them
just leaving Alexei's room. The Tsarina and the Grand Duchesses
were in tears. The Tsar seemed calm and had a word of encouragement for each of us; he embraced us. The Tsarina, when saying goodbye, begged me to stay upstairs with Alexei. I went to the boy's room
and found him in bed, crying.

A few minutes later we heard the rumbling of wheels. The Grand
Duchesses passed their brother's door on their way to their rooms,
and I could hear them sobbing.[4]

Nicky, Diary – 13/26 April – on the train
At four o'clock in the morning we said goodbye to the dear children
and climbed into the coaches, I – with Yakovlev, Alix – with Maria,
Valia with Botkin. The following of our people also came with us:
Nyuta Demidova, Chemodurov and Sednev, 8 sentries and a horse
convoy (red army) of 10 men. The weather was cold with an unpleasant wind, the road was very rough with terrible jolts from a seized-
up wheel.

Alix, Diary – 13/26 April
N[icky] with Komm[issar] Yakovlev. Maria and I in *tarantass*.

Cold, grey and windy, crossed the Irtysh. After changing horses at
8 and 12 stopped in a village and took tea with our cold provision.
Road perfectly atrocious, frozen ground, mud, snow, water up to the
horses stomachs, fearfully shaken, pains all over. After 4th change a
linchpin came off and we had to climb over another carriage.
Changed 5 times horses and got over into another *korsinka* [basket].
The others changed carriages every time. At 8 got to Ievlevo where

---

[4] This is the last Gilliard saw of Nicky and Alix.

we spent the night in a house where was the village shop before. We 3 slept in one room, we on our bed, M[aria] on the floor on her mattress, Nyuta in the sitting room where we eat our provisions and our luggage stood. Botkin and Chemodurov in one room, our men in another, all on the floors. Got to bed at 10, dead tired and aches all over.

One does not tell us where we are going from Tiumen some imagine Moscow, the little ones are to follow as soon as river free and Baby is well. By turn each carriage lost a wheel or something else smashed. Luggage always late. Heartaches enlarged, wrote to the children, through our first *yamtshik* [driver].

Nicky, Diary – 14/27 April – Tiumen
The day was splendid and very warm, the road became easier; but there were still strong jolts and I was afraid for Alix. In the open spaces it was very dusty, in the woods muddy. We had to change horses in the village of Pokrovskoe, which meant standing for a long time right opposite Grigory [Rasputin]'s house, and we saw his whole family looking through the window ... We arrived in Tiumen with a beautiful moon, and a whole squadron which surrounded our vehicles as we entered the town.

It was pleasant to get into the train, although it wasn't very clean. We ourselves and our things looked miserably dirty. We went to bed at 10 o'clock without undressing, I in the bunk over Alix, Maria and Nyuta in the next compartment.

15/28 April From the names of the stations, we realised we were going in the direction of Omsk. We started trying to guess: where would they take us after Omsk? To Moscow or Vladivostock? The commissars, of course, were saying nothing.

16/29 April In the morning we noticed that we had turned back. It seems they did not want to let us through Omsk!

Pierre Gilliard, Memoirs – 16/29 April – Tobolsk
The children received a letter from the Tsarina from Tiumen. The journey has been very trying. Horses up to their chests in water crossing the rivers. Wheels broken several times.

Nicky, Diary – 17/30 April – Ekaterinburg

At 8.40 we arrived in Ekaterinburg. We stood for three hours in one station. There was a heated dispute between the local commissars and our own. In the end, the first prevailed and the train was moved to another goods terminal. After standing there for an hour and a half, we got off the train. Yakovlev handed us over to the local regional commissar, with whom we drove by motor through empty streets to the accommodation which has been prepared for us – the Ipatiev house. Slowly our people and our things began to arrive, but they would not let Valia through.

The house is pleasant and clean. We have been given four large rooms. We were not able to unpack our things for a long time, as the commissar, the commandant and the guards captain had not had time to inspect our trunks. Then the inspection was like a customs search, just as strict, right down to the last capsule in Alix's travelling medicine kit. This annoyed me so much that I expressed my opinion sharply to the commissar. By 9 o'clock we had at last settled in.

This is how we installed ourselves: Alix, Maria and I together in the bedroom, sharing the dressing room, Demidova in the dining room, Botkin, Chemodurov and Sednev in the hall. The duty officer's room is by the entrance. In order to go to the bathroom or the W.C., it was necessary to go past the sentry at the door of the duty office. There is a very high wooden palisade built all around the house, about two *sajens* from the windows; all along there was a line of sentries, in the little garden also.

The Ural Regional Soviet to Chairman of the Council of People's Commissars V. I. Lenin and to Chairman of the Central Executive Committee Yakov M. Sverdlov, about the deportation of Nicholas II to Ekaterinburg – 17/30 April – Telegram

MILITARY. EXPRESS.
TO 2 ADDRESSES. MOSCOW.
TO CHAIRMAN OF THE COUNCIL OF PEOPLE'S COMMISSARS LENIN.
TO CHAIRMAN OF THE CENTRAL EXECUTIVE COMMITTEE SVERDLOV.

THIS DAY APRIL 30, AT 11 O'CLOCK PETROGRAD TIME, I TOOK CHARGE FROM COMMISSAR YAKOVLEV OF THE FORMER TSAR NICHOLAS ROMANOV, THE FORMER TSARINA ALEXANDRA AND THEIR DAUGHTER MARIA NICOLAEVNA. THEY HAVE ALL BEEN LODGED IN A GUARDED MANSION. CABLE YOUR QUESTIONS AND INSTRUCTIONS TO ME.

CHAIRMAN OF THE URAL REGION SOVIET BELOBORODOV

Maria to the sisters and brother in Tobolsk – 19 April/2 May – Ekaterinburg
Christ is Risen!

I kiss you tenderly three times my darling. My health is better today, but am still lying down. The others walked for an hour in the tiny garden, and were very pleased. The barrel has brought water, so now Papa can have 9 litres for his bath before dinner.

I rocked with Nyuta [Demidova] on the american swing and walked up and down with Papa. Mama is lying on her bed today, she is a little better, though her head and heart still ache. We have been asked to make a list of everyone who will be coming with you. I hope we have not forgotten anyone. We have to explain the presence of each person who is with us. Oh how complicated everything is now. We lived so peacefully for 8 months and now it's all started again, I feel so sorry for you having to pack and arrange everything alone. I hope to have news of you soon. May the Lord keep you.

Masha [Maria]

Nicky, Diary – 20 April/3 May, Good Friday – Ekaterinburg
For some reason our guard has not been changed for 48 hours. Now they are stationed on the lower floor, which is an undoubted advantage for us – we do not have to go to the bathroom and W.C. in front of everyone, and the dining room no longer smells of tobacco.

As on every day here, I read aloud the appropriate passages from the New Testament, morning and evening, in the bedroom. From the vague hints of those around us, it appears that poor Valia is no longer at liberty and that he faces an investigation, after which he will be released! There is no possibility of communicating with him, however hard Botkin tries.

21 April/4 May, Easter Sunday   All morning I read out loud, then added a few lines to a letter to the girls from Alix and Maria, and drew a plan of the house. At Botkin's request, they allowed a priest and a deacon in at 8 o'clock. They conducted the service quickly and well; it was a great comfort to pray even in such circumstances and to hear: 'Christ is Risen'. Ukraintzev, the commandant's assistant and the soldiers on guard were also present.

**Nicky and Maria to Olga – 22 April/5 May, Easter Monday –
Ekaterinburg**
Christ is Risen!

I kiss you three times in my mind, my dear Olga, and send you my
congratulations for Easter. I hope you spend the feast quietly. Please
give my greetings to everyone. I am writing to you sitting on Papa's
bed. Mama is still lying down as she is very tired and has her no. 3
heart. The three of us slept in a cosy white room with four large windows. The sun is shining as it does in our hall. The window is open
and we can hear the twittering of the birds and an electric tramway.
Everything around is quiet. In the morning the May 1st manifestation took place and we heard the music. We are living on the ground
floor, there is a wooden fence all round so we can only see the crosses
on the cupolas of the churches on the square. Nyuta is sleeping in
the dining room and Botkin, Sednev and Chemodurov in the large
drawing room. The prince [Valia] was not allowed to join us, I do not
know why and I feel very upset for him. They are sleeping on beds
brought yesterday for both them and the guards. The house is owned
by the Ipatievs. I kiss you tenderly and bless you my darling.

Your old Masha.

I am always with you in my thoughts, my dear Olga. The three of us
talk about you all constantly and what you are doing. The beginning
of the journey was unpleasant and depressing; it was easier once we
reached the train. We don't know how it will be here. May the Lord
keep you. I embrace you three times my darling.

Papa

Nyuta is darning stockings. Christ be with you.

Your M

**Pierre Gilliard, Memoirs – 22 April/5 May, Easter Sunday –
Tobolsk**
Still no news.

Nicky, Diary – 24 April/7 May – Ekaterinburg
Avdeev, the commandant, took out the plan of the house I had done
for the letter to the children three days ago, and kept it, saying it
could not be sent!

**Anastasia to her sister Maria and parents – 24 April/7 May –
Tobolsk**

He is risen indeed!

My dear Mashka, darling. We were so terribly glad to receive news, we kept on sharing our impressions! Forgive me for writing so crookedly, I'm just being stupid. Alexei is so sweet when he tries to do his best and eat (remember when you were there on the bench). We take turns to have breakfast with him and make him eat, although there are days when he does so without prompting. I am always with you dears in my thoughts. It's so terribly sad and lonely, I just don't know what to do. The Lord helps and will help.

We decorated the iconostasis terribly well for Easter, all in pine and flowers as is the custom here. We took our photograph, I hope it will come out. I continue to draw, they say rather well, which is pleasing.

We played on the swing, that was when I roared with laughter, the fall was so wonderful! Indeed! I told the sisters about it so many times yesterday that they got quite fed up, but I could go on telling it masses of times, only there's no one left. In fact I already have loads of things to tell you. My Jim [dog] has a cold and a cough, so he is staying at home and greeting everyone. What weather we've had! One could simply shout with joy.

Strangely enough I got more sunburnt than the others, like a real Arrrab! These last days I've been boring and ugly. It's cold and this morning we froze, although we did not of course return home.

I'm so sorry for forgetting to send You all, my dears, my congratulations for Easter, I kiss you all not three, but masses of times. Everyone thanks you, darling, for the letters. We also had demonstrations, but feeble. At the moment we are sitting together as always, but you are missing from the room.

I'm sorry of course for such a clumsy letter, you will understand that my thoughts keep racing ahead and I can't write everything down, I just grasp at whatever enters my noddle. We are going for a walk soon, summer still hasn't come and nothing is out, it's all very behind.

I want to see you so much it's depressing. I went out for a walk, but now I've come back, I'm sad and walking doesn't help. I played on the swing. The sun has come out but it's cold and my hand can hardly write.

Christ be with you, my golden ones. I embrace you all and kiss you
Anastasia

Nicky, Diary – 25 April/8 May – Ekaterinburg

The guard that arrived today was original both in its composition and its dress. There were several former officers and the majority of the soldiers were Letts, dressed in a variety of jackets and every conceivable kind of head gear. When we went out for a walk, all the off duty soldiers came in to the garden to look at us; they talked together in their language, walked around and wrestled together.

Before dinner I had a long talk with one of the former officers, a native of the Baikal region; he told me much of interest, as did the little captain of the guard who was standing next to us; he was from Riga. Ukraintzev brought us the first telegram from Olga before dinner. Thanks to this everyone in the house felt a little more cheerful.

Pierre Gilliard, Memoirs – 25 April/8 May – Tobolsk

The officers and men of our guard who accompanied Their Majesties have returned from Ekaterinburg. They say that on arrival at Ekaterinburg the Tsar's train was surrounded by Red Guards and that the Tsar, Tsarina, and Maria Nicolaevna have been incarcerated in Ipatiev's house. Prince Dolgorukov is in prison, and they themselves were only released after two days' detention.

Nicky, Diary – 26 April/9 May – Ekaterinburg

Today, from the morning, there was some kind of great disquiet around us, that is in the duty and guard rooms, with the telephone ringing all the time. Ukraintzev was away all day, although he should have been on duty. They did not, of course, tell us what had happened; perhaps the arrival here of some new unit alarmed the locals! In any case the sentries were in a good mood and very considerate.

The Ukrainian's place was taken by my enemy – 'Goggle-eye', who was supposed to accompany us on our walk. He was silent the whole time, as no one spoke to him. In the evening, while we were playing bezique he brought in another fellow, went round the rooms with him and then left.

Alix, Diary – 26 April/9 May – Ekaterinburg

Wrote 14th time to children.
Sun & clouds. Continue sleeping badly & having a headache.
N[icky] read the gospel to us & lesson for the day.
Every morning have to get out of bed for the commander of the

guard and commandant who come to see if we are there.
1 Sedn[ev] prepared my vermicelli.
2.18 At last brought the others their food.
Maria & Nyuta washed my hair.
Slightly snowing; & then sun appeared.
4½. The others went out.
5¼. Tea. Maria read to me. Spir[itual] Read[ing].
N[icky] read to us.
8. Supper wh. I took with the others.
Then played cards in Botkin's room.

Nicky, Diary – 27 April/10 May – Ekaterinburg

After tea, 'Goggle-eye' arrived and asked each of us in turn how much money we had? Then he asked us to write down the exact amounts and took everyone's spare money for safekeeping by the treasurer of the regional soviet! What an unpleasant story!

Maria, with additions by Alix, to the children in Tobolsk – 27 April/10 May – Ekaterinburg

We miss our quiet peaceful life in Tobolsk. Here practically every day brings unpleasant surprises. Members of the regional soviet have just been and asked how much money each of us has with them. We had to sign a paper. Since, as you know, Papa and Mama haven't a kopeck, they wrote down 'nothing', while I had 16 roubles 17 kopecks, which Anastasia gave me for the journey. They took everyone else's money into safekeeping with the committee, leaving them with only a very little – they gave them receipts. They have warned us we are not immune from further searches. Who could believe they would treat us this way after 14 months of detention. We hope things are better with you, as they were when we were there.

28 April/11 May Good morning my dears. We have just got up and lit the fire, as it has got cold in the rooms. The wood is crackling cosily, reminding us of frosty days in Tobolsk. Today we gave our dirty linen to the laundress. Nyuta has also become a laundress, she washed Mama's handkerchief and dusters, and extremely well. For the last few days we have had Letts as guards. It must be so grim for you, with everything already packed. Have you already packed my things? It seems as if you will soon be arriving now.

We know nothing of You and are very much awaiting a letter. I continue to draw from the book by Brem. Perhaps you might be able to buy some white paint. We have very little left. In the autumn Gilliard managed to find a good one somewhere, it was flat and round. Who knows, this letter might reach you on the eve of your departure. May the Lord bless your journey and keep you from all evil. We terribly want to know who will escort you. Tender thoughts and prayers surround you. If only we can all be together soon. I kiss you lovingly my sweet dears and send you my blessing. Warmest greetings to you and to all those who have stayed behind. I hope that Alexei is feeling stronger now and that the journey will not be too tiring for him.

Mama.

Maria   This morning we are going for a walk, as it is warm. Valia Dolgorukov is still not allowed to see us. Greetings to others. I'm so sorry I was not able to say goodbye. You must be very sad to leave Tobolsk, such a pleasant house etc; I remember the cosy rooms and the garden. Do you play on the swing, or has the plank already broken? Papa and I kiss you lovingly my dears. May God keep you. I send greetings to everyone in the house. Best wishes and a safe journey, if you are already leaving.

Your Maria

Nicky Diary – 1/14 May – Ekaterinburg
Today we were told by Botkin that we are only to be allowed one hour's walk a day; in answer to the question: why? the commandant's stand-in replied 'So that it should be more like a prison regime.' At least they have bought us a samovar, so we don't have to depend on the guards.

2/15 May   The 'prison regime' continues to be applied, and has resulted in our windows being white-washed over in the morning by the old painter. It looks as if there is a fog outside the windows. The captain of the guard did not talk to us, as there was always one of the commissars in the garden, watching us, him and the sentries. The weather was good, but it has become gloomy inside the rooms.

Alix, Diary – 2/15 May – Ekaterinburg
14 Wrote 20th time to the children.
N[icky] read as usual the gospel, acts to us.

Splendid weather, a nice breeze.

They were told not to go out this morning. An old man painted all the windows white from outside, so only at the top can see a bit of sky & it looks as tho' there were a thick fog, not at all cosy.

1½ Lunched. Sedn[ev] feels unwell & lies.

N[icky] read to us.

3¼ Were let into the garden for an hour.

N[icky] read again & we played patiences.

5 tea.

8 Supper.

cards.

Sednev infl: 38.6

3/16 May They smeared over the therm[ometer[, so can't see temp[erature], seems fine weather.

N[icky] read to us. Head continues aching.

1½ Luncheon

3-4 Sat in the garden.

5 tea

Wrote 21st time to the children

8½ Supper, 3 candles in glasses

cards – by light of one candle

Sedn[ev] half up.

Received coffee and chocolate from Ella. She has been sent out from Moscow and is at Perm (we read in the papers).

Felix Yusupov, Memoirs

In June 1918 the Grand Duchess Ella was arrested along with her faithful servant Varvara and taken to an unknown destination. Patriarch Tikhon tried in vain to trace her and have her set free. Finally, it became known that she was a prisoner in the small town of Alapaevsk, in the district of Perm, along with her cousin the Grand Duke Sergei Mikhailovich, Princes Ioann, Constantine and Igor, sons of the Grand Duke Konstantin Romanov [KR], and Prince Vladimir Paley, son of the Grand Duke Pavel Alexandrovich.

The Kaiser offered several times, through the Swedish Embassy, to give her shelter in Prussia, as he feared that Russia was on the eve of terrible happenings. None knew this better than he, as he was one of those responsible for them. But the Grand Duchess sent him word that she would never leave her convent, or Russia, of her own free will.

Maria to Ella – 4/17 May – Ekaterinburg
He is risen indeed!

We kiss you, dearest, three times. Thank you very much for the eggs, chocolate and coffee. Mama drank her first cup of coffee with great pleasure, it was very good. It's very good for her headaches, and as it happens we hadn't taken any with us. We learnt from the papers that you had been sent away from your convent, and were very sad for you. It's strange that we should all end up in the same province under arrest. We hope that you will be able to spend the summer somewhere out of town, in Verkhoturie or in some monastery. We have so missed having a church. My address: Ekaterinburg, The Regional Executive Committee, To the Chairman for transmission to me. May God keep you + Your loving god-daughter.

Nicky, Diary – 4/17 May – Ekaterinburg
We learned that the children have left Tobolsk, but Avdeev would not say when. In the afternoon he opened up the locked room, which we had assigned for Alexei. It turned out to be bigger and brighter than we expected, as it has two windows; our stove will soon warm it up.

Pierre Gilliard, Memoirs – 4/17 May – Tobolsk
The soldiers of our guard have been replaced by Red Guards brought from Ekaterinburg.

Nicky, Diary – 6/19 May – Ekaterinburg
We have received no news of the children, are beginning to wonder whether they have really left Tobolsk?

Pierre Gilliard, Memoirs – 5/18 May – Tobolsk
Vespers. The priest and nuns have been stripped and searched by order of the commissary.

6/19 May The Tsar's birthday. Our departure is fixed for tomorrow. The commissary refuses to allow the priest to come; he has forbidden the Grand Duchesses to lock their doors at night.

7/20 May At half past eleven we left the house and went on board the *Russia*. She is the boat which brought us here with the Tsar and Tsarina eight months ago. Baroness Buxhoeveden has been granted permission to rejoin us. We left Tobolsk at five o'clock.

Commissar Rodionov has shut Alexei in his cabin with Nagorni. We protested: the child is ill and the doctor ought to have access to him at any time.

Alix, Diary – 8/21 May – Ekaterinburg
Been pouring.
M[aria] Spir[itual] read[ing]. N[icky] reads as usual the gospel & lesson of the day.
3 weeks here today.
Lunched late.
Heard children come probably tomorrow or Thursday.
Have given us a room for Baby, 1 for the gentlemen and 1 for the men.
11 (where the guard was at first).
3½ N[icky] & M[aria] went out.
5 tea.
Sunshine after slight thunder at 3.
Maria took a bath.
8¾ Only had their supper.
cards.

Nicky, Diary – 10/23 May – Ekaterinburg
In the morning we were told within the space of an hour: that the children were a few hours from the town, then that they had reached the station, and finally that they had arrived at the house, although their train had been in the station since 2 o'clock at night. It was an immense joy to see them again and to embrace them after four weeks of separation and uncertainty.

There was no end to the mutual questions and answers. Very few letters had got through either way. The poor things had suffered a lot of anguish, both in Tobolsk and during their three day journey. Of those who accompanied them, only the cook Kharitonov and Sednev's nephew were allowed into the house. We waited in vain until the evening for them to bring beds and other necessities, but the girls ended up having to sleep on the floor. Alexei slept on Maria's bunk. In the evening, as if on purpose, he banged his knee and was in great pain the whole night, preventing us from getting to sleep.

The Guard's Duty Log Book – 10/23 May – Ekaterinburg
Arrival of four members of the Romanov family at the House of
Special Purpose [Ipatiev's house] Olga Nicolaevna, Tatiana
Nicolaevna, Anastasia Nicolaevna, Alexei Nikolaevich and with them
the cook Ivan Mikhailovich Kharitonov and the boy Leonid
Ivanovich Sednev.

Pavel Medvedev [guard]
On May 23 we were moved to new premises – the lower floor of the
Ipatiev house. As it happened, that day the whole family of the former emperor arrived. The emperor and his family settled in to the
upper floor of the house, the whole of the top [floor] being occupied
by them, with the exception of one room (to the left of the entrance)
which was reserved for the commandant and his assistants.

11/24 May I went into the corner room [the Tsar's bedroom], where
the following people were assembled: the emperor, his wife, son, and
four daughters, doctor Botkin, the cook, the footman and a young
boy, whose name I do not know. Having counted 12 people in all, we
left, without entering into any conversation with any of them. The
Tsar's daughters were lodged in the room next to the Tsar's bedroom.
For the first few days there were no beds in the room, but afterwards
beds were brought in. The regime within the house was at the discretion of the commandant, and those serving as guards only kept
watch. At first the guard had three shifts, then four.

Ania Vyrubova, Memoirs
I had a card a little later from Mr Gibbes saying that he and M.
Gilliard had brought the children from Tobolsk to Ekaterinburg and
that the family was again united. The card was written from the train
where he and M. Gilliard were living, not having been allowed to
join the family in their stockaded house. Mr Gibbes had an intuition
that both of these devoted tutors were soon to be sent out of the
country and such proved to be the case. This was my last news of my
Empress and of my Sovereigns, best of all earthly friends.

Alix, Diary – 11/24 May – Ekaterinburg
Ludwig's B.D. May's B.D.
Baby & I had our meals in our bedroom: his pains varied. Lunched at 2

– Vlad[imir] Nik[olaevich – Dr Derevenko] came to see Baby & change
his compresses, but in Avd[eev]'s presence so he cld. not say a word.
  Chemodurov left as not feeling well – was completely undressed &
searched before leaving the house. – After supper Nagorny and Trupp
(& Joy) came – 2 hours questioned & searched. All our other people
are being sent back to Tobolsk, only don't know where – Trina,
Nastenka, Tatischev & Volkov have been taken & Botkin wrote petition for Avdeev to take to the Oblast committee to beg for Gilliard as
absolutely indispensable, he shld. be with Baby, who suffers very
much. Baby slept in his room with Nagorny, the four girls next door,
not all beds brought yet. Baby had a bad night again.

Nicky, Diary – 12/25 May – Ekaterinburg
Through the good offices of Botkin we held talks with the chairman
of the regional soviet about allowing Mr Gilliard through to us. The
children got back their things after an unbelievably prolonged
inspection in the commandant's room.

The Guard's Duty Log Book – 13/26 May 5 p.m.
Received from Babichev in the presence of regional Soviet member
Avdeev and guard captain Glemer. Reception of the following during
exercise time: Nikolai Romanov, Alexandra Romanova, Maria
Romanova. doc. Botkin. The remainder: Chemodurov, Sednev, and
Demidova were indoors.

Nicky, Diary – 13/26 May
We all slept well except Alexei. His pains continued, but at longer
intervals. He lay on the bed in our room. There was no service. As in
recent days, Dr Derevenko came to examine Alexei; today he was
accompanied by a dark man, whom we realized must be a doctor.[5]
  After a short walk, we went with Com. Avdeev into the barn, where
our heavy baggage had been brought. Some open trunks were still
being inspected.

Alix, Diary – 14/27 May, Coronation Day – Ekaterinburg
Bright sunshine. Baby had again not good night, Botkin sat up part

---

[5] This was in fact Yurovsky, later responsible for organizing their murder.

of the night so as to let Nagorny sleep.

2 Lunch brought.

Baby spent the day in our room. Vl Nik [Dr Derevenko] did not come, don't know why.

Children darning linen with Nyuta.

At 6½ Sedn & Nagorny were taken off to the Region Kommissar, don't know the reason. The others played cards with Baby. On the whole better, tho' at times very strong pains.

Botkin spent the night with Baby.

18/31 May   Poured in the night.

Baby's night the same 36.9½

I remained in bed as feeling very giddy & eyes ache so.

Baby brought over at 1 to us

1.40 Luncheon

Slight rain, others went out.

Hammering hard, making wooden paling before Baby's windows higher. Vladimir Nikolaevich not let in as Avdeev was not there.

The others went out. Remained the whole day with shut eyes, head got worse towards the evening. Supper brought at 6 but they only eat it at 8, warmed up. Baby 37.6. After supper Baby was carried to his room – had rather cramps in his knee again.

19 May/1 June   Night better. Early morning sun.

Came over to me before luncheon.

I spent the day in bed, feeling weak & nasty in the head –

Baby 37.6. slept a little in the day.

12 The others went out.

Grey weather –

5½ Doctor & Avdeev came. After supper Baby was carried to his room. His head ached a little, but he went quickly to sleep.

The children washed handkerchiefs again –

Nicky, Diary – 20 May/2 June – Ekaterinburg

At 11 o'clock a service was held in the house; Alexei assisted, lying in bed. The weather is magnificent, and hot. It's unbearable to be locked up like this, and not to be able to go into the garden when we want to, or to spend a pleasant evening in the air. Prison regime!

The Guard's Duty Log Book – 20 May/2 June
A request from Nicholas Romanov, former tsar, to be given work:
clearing garden, sawing or cutting wood.

Nicky, Diary – 22 May/4 June – Ekaterinburg
It was hot and stuffy in the rooms. We only went for a walk in the
afternoon. There was a violent thunder storm around 5 o'clock and
another in the evening. Alexei is much better, his knee is very much
less swollen. I had pains in the small of my back and in my legs and
slept badly.

Alix, Diary – 23 May/5 June – Ekaterinburg
Got up at 6½, now 8½ by the water.
Glorious morning. Baby did not sleep well, leg ached probably more
because Vladimir Nikolaevich took it yesterday out of the ties which
held the knee firm. Botkin carried him out before the house & put
him in my wheeling chair & Tatiana & I sat out with him in the sun
before the entry with a paling erected around –
Back he went to bed as leg ached much from dressing & carrying
about.
Lunch only brought at 3 o'clock
Are putting yet higher planks before all the windows, so that not
even the tops of the trees can be seen – then one will have the
double windows taken out & at last we can open the windows.
4¼ The others went out.
6 Vladimir Nikolaevich & Avdeev came, made him again a plaster of
Paris as knee more swollen & hurts so again.
8 Supped at 8, but Baby only went to his room at 10 (8) as too light
to sleep.
Played bezique – to bed at 11 (9).

Nicky, Diary – 24 May/6 June – Ekaterinburg
I was in pain all day from my haemorrhoids, and for that reason lay
on the bed, as it made it easier to apply compresses. Alix and Alexei
spent half an hour in the fresh air, we went out for an hour after
them.
The weather was wonderful.

25 May/7 June Dear Alix spent her birthday in bed, with strong pains in her legs and other places! Over the next two days she got better, and was able to sit in a chair to eat.[6]

The Guard's Duty Log Book – 25 May/7 June
Doc. Derevenko was not received. Alexei was carried out for walk time. Were informed by doc. Botkin that, as a result of enlarged veins, Nikolai Romanov was unwell and had stayed in bed, where he was also fed.

Alix, Diary – 27 May/9 June – Ekaterinburg
Sunny morning.

Went out in the afternoon 3–4½ with the others, ideal weather – very strong. Back and leg aches from kidneys to belly. 2 days the others have no meat and live upon Kharitonov's Tobolsk remaining meagre provisions.

Took a bath. Bezique. They still find excuses not to bring Derevenko.

Nicky, Diary – 28 May/10 June – Ekaterinburg
A very warm day. In the barn, where our trunks are being kept, they keep opening boxes and taking out various objects and provisions from Tobolsk. And this without any reason being given.

All this leads one to suppose that anything that pleases can be taken away, and we will lose it! It's disgusting!

Outward relations have also changed over the last weeks: our jailers avoid talking to us, and they convey an impression of alarm or apprehension! We don't know why!

Alix, Diary – 28 May/10 June – Ekaterinburg
Komend[ant] invited to see us all at 10, but kept us waiting 20 minutes as was breakfasting and eating cheese. Won't permit us to have any more cream.

10½. Workmen turned up outside and put up iron railings before our one open window. Always fright of our climbing out or getting into contact with the sentry. Strong pains continue. Greyish weather. Brought meat for 6 days, but so little only suffice for putting in the

---

[6] From this day on Nicky no longer keeps his diary every day.

soup and was very rude to Kharitonov. Remained in bed all day,
lunched only as they brought the meat so late. Anastasia read to me
whilst the others went out. Lovely weather.

The Guard's Duty Log Book – 29 May/11 June
Sent to the laundry – washing of the former tsar Nikolai Romanov,
receipt no. 956.

Nicky, Diary – 31 May/13 June, Ascension day – Ekaterinburg
All morning we waited in vain for a priest to come and celebrate
mass: they were all busy in church. For some reason we were not
allowed into the garden in the afternoon. Avdeev[7] arrived and had a
long talk with Botkin.

According to him, both he and the regional soviet are afraid of an
attack by anarchists and for this reason, perhaps, we may have to
move out quickly – in all probability to Moscow! He asked us to prepare ourselves for such an eventuality. We immediately started to
pack, but quietly, in order to avoid attracting the attention of the
members of the guard, at Avdeev's express request.

At about 11 o'clock he returned and said that we would still be
remaining for a few days. Which is why we continued to camp on June
1st without unpacking anything.

Finally after dinner, Avdeev, looking somewhat happier, explained
that the anarchists had been detained, that the danger had passed
and our departure was cancelled! After all the preparations, it almost
seemed a pity!

The Guard's Duty Log Book – 4/17 June
Owing to Alexei Romanov's illness taking its normal course, Doctor
Derevenko was not received.

5/18 June For the first time Alexei Romanov was carried out for
walk time which lasted one hour. During doc. Derevenko's regular
examination of Alexei Romanov, in the presence of Commandant
Avdeev, Nikolai Romanov's wife talked in German to her daughters,[8]
in spite of it being forbidden to talk in foreign languages during doc.

---

[7] Commandant of the Ipatiev house, soon after replaced by Yurovsky.
[8] The daughters did not know German, only English.

Derevenko's visits. After this Commandant Avdeev issued a second warning.

Nicky, Diary – 5/18 June – Ekaterinburg

Dear Anastasia is 17 years old. The heat was great, both inside and out. I continued reading the third volume of Saltykov, which is interesting and clever. The whole family went for a walk before tea. Kharitonov has been cooking for us since yesterday, provisions are brought every two days.

The girls are helping him, kneading dough in the evening, which they cook in the morning – and we have bread! Not bad at all!

The Guard's Duty Log Book – 6/19 June

Doc. Derevenko was not received, Alexei was carried out for walk time.

Nicky, Diary – 9/22 June – Ekaterinburg

For the last few days the weather has been wonderful, but very hot; in our rooms it is very stuffy. Especially at night. Today before tea, six men came in, probably from the regional soviet to see which windows can be opened. Consideration of this problem has been going on for two weeks! Various types kept coming in and looking silently at the windows in our presence. The fragrance from all the town gardens is wonderful.

The Guard's Duty Log Book – 9/22 June

Nothing special happened during the day of June 9th, except that the sentry at post no. 5 detained a fellow, who upon being asked by the sentry to move on, answered with an obscenity, for which he was escorted to the Cheka.[9]

10/23 June The Romanov family's usual walk. A request from Nikolai Romanov for the windows to be opened to air the house, which was refused.

---

[9] The first Soviet secret service, precursor of the KGB.

MURDER OF MISHA

A. V. Markov [the assassin] – 13–14/26–7 June – Perm

The fact that he might decamp from Perm, or that Mikhail [Misha] Romanov might be kidnapped or hidden, made our small group of bolsheviks decide to 'take Mikhail Romanov out of circulation' by kidnapping him from the Korolev rooms where he was staying on Siberia street.

The kidnap plan was finally worked out. This is what was decided: we were to present ourselves at around 11 o'clock at night at the rooms, where he was staying, and present him with a document signed by comrade Malkov, ordering his immediate departure from Perm, as indicated by those persons presenting the mandate of departure.

If he kicked up a fuss, or refused to follow, we were to take him by force. I myself typed the document, we added a rather unclear seal and an illegible signature by comrade Malkov.

At around 11, we drove up to the entrance to the rooms in covered phaetons. Zhuzhgov and Kolpashikov went in. Mikhail Romanov refused to follow and demanded 'Malkov' (he spoke bad Russian) asking that he be contacted by telephone. When I then went into the building armed with a revolver and a grenade, the guards by the door completely lost their heads, and let me through without any hindrance, as they had the first two. I secured the corridor, so that no one could reach the phone, and went into the room where Romanov was living, he was continuing to resist, referring to his ill health, demanding a doctor. Then I demanded he be taken as he was.

They fell on him and grabbed him, then he came to his senses and asked whether he needed to take anything with him. I refused this, saying his things would be brought along later by others. Then he asked to be at least allowed to bring along his personal secretary Johnson – which was granted as we had already decided this among ourselves earlier. After this he hurriedly threw on a cloak. Zhuzhgov immediately grabbed him by the collar and ordered him out into the street, and he obeyed. Johnson went of his own free will out into the street, where the horses were waiting. We put Mikhail Romanov in the first carriage. Zhuzhgov sat behind the driver, and Ivanchenko next to Mikhail Romanov; I took Johnson with me, with Kolpashikov behind the driver, and thus we set off in covered phaetons (there was a freezing rain) along the road in the direction of Motovilicha.

When he estimated we were already beyond the town, comrade Drokin phoned in an official voice to say that unknown persons had appeared at the 'royal' rooms and taken Mikhail Romanov away in an unknown direction, and asked that the Kazan mounted police be immediately dispatched along the Siberia road. The same thing was reported to the Cheka. The manager of the rooms also conveyed the same message by phone to the Cheka and the police.

While this was all going on, we were far away by the Motovilicha factory.

From the beginning, our kidnap victims behaved quietly, and when we arrived at Motovilicha asked where they were being taken. We answered to the train, which was ready to depart, and that they would be taken on further in a special compartment; I also said I would only answer direct questions and refused to reply to any others.

In this way we drove past the kerosene depot some 5 *versts* from Motovilicha. We did not meet anyone on the way; a *verst* further on from the kerosene depot, we turned sharply to the right into the woods. After going another 100–120 feet Zhuzhgov shouted 'We're here – get out.' I quickly jumped out and demanded that my neighbour do the same. As soon as he started to get out of the phaeton – I shot him in the temple, he swayed and fell. Kolpashikov also fired, but his browning jammed. Zhuzhgov did the same thing, but only wounded Mikhail Romanov.

Romanov ran towards me with his arms open, asking to say goodbye to his secretary. At that very moment comrade Zhuzhgov's revolver also jammed. I had to fire a second time at Mikhail Romanov's head from fairly short range, and he immediately fell.

Zhuzhgov was swearing because his revolver had failed to fire, Kolpashikov also swore because the cartridge had got stuck in his browning; the first horse had taken flight at the first shots and bolted into the woods, and the carriage got knocked and overturned, comrade Ivanchenko ran after it and when he returned it was already all over.

It was beginning to get light. It was the 12th June and for some reason very cold. It was impossible to bury them as it was getting light rapidly and we were near the road. We dragged them together to the side of the road, covered them with branches and went off in the direction of Motovilicha.

On our return I drove with comrade Ivanchenko discussing the event, we both stayed calm only I was freezing as I was only in my soldier's blouse, with a watch on my left arm which is why, when we were at the rooms, I was mistaken for an officer, and why later the statements of those at the rooms said that Mikhail Romanov had been kidnapped by some officers. This was of course from fright and the speed of the kidnapping.

EKATERINBURG

The Guard's Duty Log Book – 13/26 June
The Romanov family's usual walk was cancelled. Doctor Derevenko was not received.

14/27 June The Romanov family's usual walk. Tatiana and Maria asked for a camera, explaining that they needed to take some plates, which was of course refused by the commandant.

Nicky, Diary – 14/27 June – Ekaterinburg
Our dear Maria is 19 years old. The weather was still as tropical, 26 degrees in the shade and 24 in the rooms, almost impossible to bear! We spent an anxious night and stayed awake fully dressed. This was because, a few days ago, we received two letters, one after the other, which informed us that we should prepare to be rescued by some people devoted to us! But the days passed and nothing happened, only the waiting and the uncertainty were torture.

Alix, Diary – 15/28 June – Ekaterinburg
At 8½ (6½) already 23½ in the room, later over 24. Tatted.
1 Lunched in our room.
2½–4½ the others went out, Olga stayed with me –
4½ tea
[Dr] Vladimir Nikolaevich came –
8 Supped with Baby –
All went earlier to bed as very tired & heat intense – 24½ room -
In the sun in the morning there were 30 dgr.
We hear the night sentry under our rooms being told quite particularly to watch every movement at our window – they have become again most suspicious, since our window is opened & don't allow one to sit on the sill even now.

Alexei to Kolia Derevenko – [no date] – Ekaterinburg
Dear Kolia
All the sisters send greetings to you, mother and grandmother. I feel

well myself. My head was aching all day, but now the pain has gone completely. I embrace you warmly. Greetings to Botkins from all of us.

Always yours

Alexei

The end.[10]

Alix, Diary – 20 June/3 July
Again glorious weather, yet warmer – 20 in the room at 9.
Everything as yesterday.
Tatiana stopped with me in the morning when they went out, & Olga in the afternoon, played bezique together – Baby begins making movements with his leg. Very hot & airless.
Before supper Maria & Nyuta washed my head.
10½ I took a bath –
In the night strong rain & thunderstorm.

Nicky, Diary – 21 June/4 July – Ekaterinburg
Today there was a change of commandant – Beloborodov arrived during dinner and explained that Yurovsky, the one we took for a doctor, has been appointed in place of Avdeev.

In the afternoon, before tea, he and his assistant made a list of all the gold things – both ours and the children's. They took most of it away with them (rings, bracelets etc.).

This they explained by the fact that there had been an unpleasant occurrence in our house and mentioned the sale of objects belonging to us. So my conviction, which I wrote about on 28th May, has been confirmed. I'm sorry for Avdeev, but he is guilty in that he did not prevent his people from stealing from the trunks in the barn.

23 June/6 July   Yesterday the commandant Yurovsky brought a casket with all the valuables he had taken, asked us to verify the contents and sealed it in front of us, leaving it with us for safekeeping. Yurovsky and his assistant are beginning to understand just *what* kind of people we were surrounded by, who stole from us as they guarded us.

25 June/8 July   Our life has not changed at all with Yurovsky. He comes into the bedroom to check the seal on the casket and looks through the open window. There are new Letts on guard inside the

---

[10] This is Alexei's last letter.

house, while outside they have remained the same – some soldiers, some workers! According to the rumours, some of Avdeev's men are already under arrest! The door to the barn with our things has been sealed. If only it had been done a month ago!

28 June/11 July In the morning at 10.30 three workmen came up to the open window, lifted up a heavy grill and fixed it to the outside of the frame – without any warning from Yurovsky. We like this man less and less!

30 June/13 July
Alexei took his first bath since Tobolsk; his knee is getting better, but he still cannot straighten it completely. The weather is warm and pleasant. We have absolutely no news from the outside.[11]

Yurovsky I started the preparations already on the 15th, as everything had to be done as quickly as possible.

I decided to use as many men as there were people to be shot, gathered them together and, after explaining the task, told them that everything had to be ready, so that when we received our final instructions we could carry everything out efficiently.

It has to be said, that it's no easy matter to arrange an execution, contrary to what some people may think. After all, this wasn't the front, but a so called 'peaceful' environment.

Here it wasn't simply a question of bloodthirsty people, carrying out the heavy duty of revolution. Which is why it was no coincidence that at the last moment two of the Letts backed out – they didn't have what it takes.

Medvedev I came on duty on the evening of July 16th, and soon after seven that same evening commandant Yurovsky ordered me to collect up and bring to him all the team's Nagan revolvers.

I removed the revolvers of those on duty and from a few others, there were 12 in all, and I took them to the commandant's office. Yurovsky then told me: 'Today they all have to be shot, tell the team not to be alarmed if they hear gunfire.'

Yurovsky On the morning of the 16th, I sent away the kitchen-boy Sednev, under the pretext of him meeting his uncle who had arrived. This caused disquiet among the detainees. The faithful go-between

---

[11] The last entry in Nicky's diary.

Botkin, and then one of the daughters tried to find out where, why and for how long Sednev had been taken away. On hearing the explanation, they went away seemingly reassured.

Twelve revolvers were prepared, and it was decided who would shoot at whom. Comrade Filipp [Goloschekin] informed me that a lorry would come at midnight, that the newcomers were to be admitted on giving the password, and the bodies handed over to them, to be taken away for burial.

Alix, Diary – 3/16 July, Irina's 23rd B.D. – Ekaterinburg

Grey morning, later lovely sunshine. Baby has a slight cold. All went out ½ hour in the morning, Olga & I arranged our medicines. Tatiana read Spiritual reading. They went out, Tatiana stayed with me & we read Book of prophet Amos and prophet Audios. Tatted. Every morning the Komendant comes to our rooms, at last after a week brought eggs again for Baby.
8 Supper.
Suddenly Lenka Sednev was fetched to go & see his Uncle & flew off – wonder whether it's true & we shall see the boy back again!
Played bezique with Nicky.
10½ to bed. 15 degrees.[12]

Yurovsky At about 11 o'clock at night I again called the men together, gave out the guns and informed them that we would soon be proceeding with the liquidation of the prisoners. Pavel Medvedev let me know that the interior and exterior guards had been carefully checked, that both he and the guards corporal were keeping the area surrounding the house under constant observation, as well as the house where the outside guard were quartered. The lorry only appeared at half past one.

When the automobile arrived, everyone was asleep. Botkin was woken up, and he roused all the others. The following explanation was given: 'In view of the unrest in the town, it is essential to move the Romanov family from the upper floor to the lower'. They got dressed in half an hour. Downstairs, a room with a plastered wooden partition had been chosen (to avoid ricochets), and all the furniture removed.

The squad were ready in the next room. The Romanovs did not suspect a thing.

---

[12] There are no further entries.

Medvedev Sometime after 1 am the tsar, Tsarina, and their four daughters emerged from their rooms; also the maid, the doctor, the cook and the valet.

The tsar carried the heir in his arms. The tsar and the heir were dressed in military blouses with caps. The empress and her daughters were in dresses with their heads uncovered. The emperor went first with the heir, after him the Tsarina, the daughters and the others.

They were escorted by Yurovsky, his assistant and the two members of the Extraordinary Commission I have already mentioned, I was also there. None of the family members asked anyone any questions in my presence, nor were there any tears or sobs. After taking the stairs leading from the second ante-room down to the lower floor, we emerged into the courtyard and from there entered the lower floor of the premises through the second door (counting from the gates).

Yurovsky led the way. He showed them into the corner room, next to the sealed store room. Yurovsky ordered chairs to be brought. His assistant brought three chairs. One chair was given to the empress, another to the emperor, the third – to the heir. The empress sat against the wall with the window, by the rear pillar of the arch; three of her daughters stood behind her (I know them all very well by face, as I saw them walking almost every day, but I am not exactly sure what each one was called). The heir and the emperor sat next to each other, almost in the centre of the room, behind the heir stood doctor Botkin; the maid, a tall woman, stood to the left of the door leading to the sealed store-room. With her stood one of the tsar's daughters (the fourth); the two servants stood in the corner to the left of the entrance, by the wall adjacent to the store.

Yurovsky Although I warned them through Botkin not to take anything with them, they nevertheless brought a few small things, pillows, handbags etc. and even a small dog.

After going down into the room (here by the entrance to the room, on the right, was a large window practically the length of the whole wall), I suggested they stand against the wall. At that moment, they evidently had no idea of what awaited them.

Alexandra said: 'There aren't even any chairs here.' Nicholas had carried Alexei down in his arms. Now he stood in the room holding him.

I then ordered two chairs to be brought, Alexandra sat on one of them, to the right of the entrance by the window, practically in the corner. Next to her, towards the left of the entrance, stood her daughters and Demidova. Alexei was also placed next to her on the other chair, and behind him came doctor Botkin, the cook and the others, while Nikolas remained standing opposite Alexei.

At the same time I arranged for the men to come down and ordered that everything should be prepared, and that each one be ready at his place when the order was given. Although he had put Alexei down, Nicholas was standing in a way that shielded him. Alexei was sitting in the corner of the room to the left of the entrance. At this point, I said roughly the following to Nicholas: that his royal relatives both at home and abroad were trying to liberate him, and that the Soviet of workers' deputies had ordered that they be shot.

Medvedev   The maid had a pillow, the tsar's daughters had also brought small cushions with them. One of these cushions was placed on the tsar's chair, another on the heir's.

Yurovsky   Nicholas turned away from the squad towards the family, then, as if remembering something, turned back with the question: 'What? What?'

The squad had already been told who was to fire at whom, and had been ordered to shoot straight at the heart, in order to avoid an excessive quantity of blood and to get it over with quickly. Nicholas said nothing more, turned again towards his family, the others made a few incoherent exclamations, the whole thing lasted a few seconds. Then the firing began.

I fired at him and killed him outright. He didn't even have the time to turn back to us for an answer. But now the gunfire became disorderly instead of methodical. Although the room was small, everyone could have fitted in and carried out the execution in an orderly manner. But many were evidently firing from the threshold, as the wall was stone and the bullets were ricocheting about, also the firing intensified with the cries of the victims. I had a lot of difficulty in stopping the shooting.

A bullet from one of the squad behind me flew past my head, and someone's hand, either the palm or the finger, was shot through and injured. When the firing stopped, it turned out that the daughters, Alexandra and apparently the lady-in-waiting Demidova, as well as Alexei, were still alive. I thought they had fallen down from fright, or perhaps on purpose, and had thus managed to stay alive. We then set about finishing them off.

Alexei was sitting as if frozen and I shot him. They were firing at the girls, but without much result, so Yermakov started with his bayonet, but it didn't help either, so we then shot them straight through the head. It was only in the forest that I discovered why it had been so difficult to shoot Alexandra and her daughters. The bayonet wouldn't go through their corsage.

Having checked that they were all dead, we started carrying them out. Here we realized that there would be traces of blood everywhere. So I ordered all the available soldier's cloth to be brought, put a piece at the bottom of the stretcher and used the rest to line the lorry. I had entrusted Mikhail Medvedev with removing the bodies, he's a former member of the Cheka and at present works with the security police.

They started carrying the bodies out and laying them in the automobile. Here the pilfering started: it became necessary to post 3 reliable comrades to guard the bodies, while the loading was completed (the bodies were brought out one by one). Under threat of the firing squad, everything that had been stolen was returned (a gold watch, a cigar box with diamonds etc).

The first intention had been to transport the bodies by automobile, and then from a certain point on with horses, as the automobile could not go any further. The place that had been chosen was a disused mine.

About five *versts* past the Upper-Isietsky factory, they came upon a whole encampment of some 25 men, horsemen, with carts etc. These were workers (members of the soviet, the executive committee etc) whom Yermakov had organized. The first thing they shouted was: 'What did you bring them to us dead for?!'

They had thought they would be entrusted with the execution of the Romanovs. They started to load the bodies onto the *droszkys*, as from then on carts were needed. It was very awkward. They immediately started to clean out the pockets – here again, it was necessary to threaten to shoot and to post sentries.

Here it became evident that Tatiana, Olga and Anastasia were wearing some kind of special bodices. It was decided to undress the corpses completely, but at the place of burial, not here. However, it turned out that nobody knew where the location of that mine was. It was getting light.

In the woods they found an old abandoned mine (at some point used to extract gold). There was an *arshin* of water in the shaft.

The commandant ordered that the corpses be stripped and a bonfire prepared, in order to burn everything. Riders were posted all round, to keep away any passers by. When they started to undress one of the girls, they realized that in the places where her corset had been torn by the bullets – diamonds could be seen. The men's eyes visibly lit up.

The commandant decided there and then to dismiss the whole company, retaining a few of the mounted sentries and 5 men from the squad. The rest dispersed. The squad started the task of undressing and burning. Alexandra turned out to have a whole belt of pearls, made up of several necklaces sewn into linen. Each of the girls had a portrait of Rasputin with the text of one of his prayers, in a little pouch around her neck. Diamonds were also ripped out from here.

In the process a few precious things were dropped (someone's brooch, Botkin's false teeth) and when they tried to make the mine cave in with the help of some grenades, obviously the corpses were disfigured and some of their upper limbs blown off.

It was decided to burn the corpses or to bury them in clay pits, filled with water, having previously disfigured them with sulphuric acid beyond all recognition.

A. G. Beloborodov to N. P. Gorbunov, Secretary of the Council of People's Commissars – 4/17 July – coded Telegram

THE KREMLIN. TO SECRETARY OF THE COUNCIL OF PEOPLE'S COMMISSARS N. P. GORBUNOV WITH RETURN VERIFICATION.

INFORM SVERDLOV THAT THE ENTIRE FAMILY SUFFERED THE SAME FATE AS THE HEAD, OFFICIALLY THE FAMILY WILL PERISH DURING THE EVACUATION.

BELOBORODOV

Protocol No. I of the sitting of the Presidium of the All Russian Central Executive Committee on the execution of the former Tsar Nicholas II – 5/18 July – Moscow

PRESENT: Ya. M. Sverdlov, L. S. Sosnovsky, A. P. Rosengoltz, Maksimov, M. F. Vladimirsky, Mitrofanov, G. I. Teodorovich, Rosen and V. A. Avanesov.

DISCUSSED: Information on the execution of Nicholas Romanov. (Telegram from Ekaterinburg).

RESOLVED: After deliberation the following resolution has been adopted:

The All Russian Central Executive Committee, in the persons of its Presidium, recognizes the decision of the Ural Regional Soviet as being correct.

Comrades Sverdlov, Sosnovsky and Avanesov are charged with drawing up an appropriate press-release. An announcement will be made about documents belonging to the former tsar now in the possession of the CEC (diary, letters etc).

Com. Sverdlov is charged with setting up a special commission for the examination of these papers and their publication.

Chairman of the ARCEC Ya. M.
Sverdlov
Secretary of the ARCEC V.
Avanesov.

MURDER OF ELLA

Ryabov [the assassin] – 4/17 July – Alapaevsk

We knew that the fate of the tsar and his family in Ekaterinburg, and of the other members of the imperial family in Alapaevsk, had already been decided in Moscow, and were only waiting for the order to carry out the sentence.

We had already been searching for a suitable place. We quickly found such a place, some twelve *versts* from the town, where their bodies would not be found immediately. We chose an abandoned half-flooded mine. Upon receiving the news of the execution of the tsar and all his family from Ekaterinburg we immediately put our plan into action, without losing a moment's time.

It was the night of the 17th to 18th July 1918. When we were sure the whole town was asleep, we quietly stole through the window into the school building. Nobody there noticed our presence, they were already all asleep. We entered through the unlocked door into the building where the women were sleeping, and woke them up, telling them quietly to get dressed at once, as they were to be taken to a safe place because of the possibility of an armed attack.

They obeyed without a murmur. We tied their hands behind their backs there and then, blindfolded them, and led them out to the cart, which was already waiting by the school, sat them in it and sent them off to their destination.

After that, we went into the room occupied by the men. We told them the same thing, as we had to the women. The young grand dukes Romanov [KR's sons] and Prince Paley [Vladimir] also obeyed meekly. We took them out into the corridor, blindfolded them, bound their hands behind their backs and put them in another cart.

We had decided earlier that the carts should not go together. The only one who tried to oppose us was the grand duke Sergei Mikhailovich.

Physically he was stronger than the rest. We had to grapple with him. He told us categorically that he was not going anywhere, as he knew they were all going to be killed! He barricaded himself behind the cupboard and our efforts to get him out were in vain. We only lost precious time. I finally lost my patience and shot at the grand duke.

However I only fired with the intention of wounding him slightly and frightening him into submission. I wounded him in the arm. He did not resist further. I bound his wound and covered his eyes. We put him in the last cart and set off. We were in a great hurry: the dawn already heralded the morning.

Along the way, grand duke Sergei Mikhailovich again repeated he knew they were all going to be killed.

'Tell me why?' he asked me. 'I have never been involved in politics. I loved sport, played billiards ... was interested in numismatics.'

I reassured him as best I could, although I was myself very agitated by everything I had been through that night.

Despite his wounded arms and the pain, the grand duke did not complain.

At last we arrived at the mine. The shaft was not very deep and, as it turned out, had a ledge on one side that was not covered by water.

First we led grand duchess Elizabeth [Ella] up to the mine. After throwing her down the shaft, we heard her struggling in the water for some time. We pushed the nun lay-sister Varvara down after her. We again heard the splashing of water and then the two women's voices. It became clear that, having dragged herself out of the water, the grand duchess had also pulled her lay-sister out. But, having no other alternative, we had to throw in all the men also.

None of them, it seems, drowned, or choked in the water and after a short time we were able to hear almost all their voices again.

Then I threw in a grenade. It exploded and everything was quiet. But not for long.

We decided to wait a little to check whether they had all perished. After a short while we heard talking and a barely audible groan. I threw another grenade.

And what do you think – from beneath the ground we heard singing! I was seized with horror. They were singing the prayer: 'Lord, save your people!'

We had no more grenades, yet it was impossible to leave the deed unfinished. We decided to fill the shaft with dry brushwood and set it alight. Their hymns still rose up through the thick smoke for some time yet.

When the last signs of life beneath the earth had ceased, we posted some of our people by the mine and returned to Alapaevsk by first light and immediately sounded the alarm in the cathedral bell tower. Almost the whole town came running. We told everyone that the grand dukes had been taken away by unknown persons!

Excerpt from Protocol No. 159 – Council of People's Commissars – 5/18 July
The extraordinary announcement by Ya. M. Sverdlov of the execution of Nicholas II
Chairman: V. Ilych Ulianov (Lenin)

PRESENT: Gukovsky, V. M. Bonch-Bruevich, Petrovsky, Semashko, Binokurov, Solovyov, Kozlovsky, Galkin, Smirnov, Dauge, Svidersky, Pravdin, Trotsky, Popov, Altfater, Stuchka, Rykov, Nogin, Skliansky, Petrovsky, Nevsky, Sereda, Podbielsky, Skomiakov, Yuriev, Briukhanov, Nikolaev, Miliutin, Popov (statistician), prof. Sirinov (for item 8), Chicherin, Karakhan.

DISCUSSED: 3. The extraordinary announcement by CEC chairman com. Sverdlov of the execution of the former tsar Nicholas II by decision of the Ekaterinburg Soviet of Deputies and the upholding of this decision by the Presidium of the CEC.

RESOLVED: to take note of the information

Chairman of the Council of People's Deputies
V. Ulianov (Lenin)
Secretary of the Council N. Gorbunov

EKATERINBURG

Yurovsky – 6/19 July
[After 48 hours of trying to dispose of the corpses, they are still in the wood]
At around 4.30 in the morning of the 19th of July, the motor finally

got completely stuck; the only option was to bury or incinerate, without reaching the mine. One comrade promised to undertake the latter, but left without fulfilling his promise.

They wanted to burn Alexei and Alexandra, but by mistake burned Alexei and the lady-in-waiting instead.

They then buried the remains right there under the bonfire, and lit another one, which completely covered up any traces of digging. At the same time they dug out a communal grave for the others.

The pit, measuring 3½ *arshins* square and 2½ *arshins* deep was ready by 7 in the morning. The corpses were laid in the pit, their faces and bodies in general covered with sulphuric acid to render them unrecognizable, and also to prevent any stench from the grave (the pit was not very deep).

Having covered it over with earth and brushwood, they laid down some sleepers and drove over it several times until no trace of the pit remained. The secret was preserved completely – the whites never found this grave.

LONDON

King George V, Diary – 25 July
May and I attended a Service at the Russian Church in Welbeck Street in memory of dear Nicky who I fear was shot last month by the Bolshevists, we can get no details, it was a foul murder, I was devoted to Nicky, who was the kindest of men, a thorough gentleman, loved his Country and his people.

ST PETERSBURG – 24 YEARS BEFORE

Nicky's Diary – 27 November 1894
[in Alix's hand] *No more separations. At last united, bound for life, and when this life is ended we meet again in the other world to remain together for all eternity. Yours, yours.*

HISTORICAL AFTERWORD

The future Emperor Nicholas II of Russia was born in 1868 on 6 May, the day the Russian Orthodox Church celebrates the memory of Job the Martyr. In later years many, including the Tsar himself, as his diaries show, were to see in this a grim prophecy of his future fate.

As if to contradict the portents, however, Nicholas spent an easy and carefree childhood and youth. All his life he was to feel the influence of his father, Emperor Alexander III, a man of strong will and stern temper. Indecisive by nature, Nicholas (known as Nicky), the eldest son, was instinctively drawn throughout his life to stronger characters and easily fell under their influence.

After the traditional education of a member of the Russian imperial family, Nicholas served with the Guards. His father died unexpectedly when he was twenty-six, leaving him utterly unprepared to succeed to the Russian throne. He had counted on another twenty years of peaceful existence before being called on to rule. But fate willed otherwise.

The constant need to deal with public life and, more importantly, that of taking decisions poisoned Nicholas's life. He suffered from his sense of duty and his obvious inability to settle complex political problems. This was well understood by his intimates. His mother, the Empress Maria Feodorovna, often complained that her son was lacking in character. His family and the Council of Ministers were all convinced that, whenever a complicated argument arose, Nicholas always sided with the last man who reported to him. His opinion would be the one finally officially approved by the Emperor.

Nicholas was best suited to a quiet family life. The British Prime Minister, David Lloyd George, once remarked that Nicholas would have escaped all reproach, gained the reputation of a fine man and lived a long and happy life, if only he had not been born an Emperor.

Nicholas was only sixteen when, in 1884, he met the young Princess Alice of Hesse for the first time. She had come to Russia for the marriage of her elder sister Ella to Alexander III's brother Grand Duke Sergei Alexandrovich. Nicholas immediately liked this twelve-year-old girl and on her return to Russia in 1889 they fell in love.

For five years they struggled to unite their lives. Nicholas loved Alice (whom he knew as Alix) fervently and she reciprocated his feelings. What then interfered with their plans of marriage? Above all, religion. Alice was a devout Protestant and could not bring herself to abandon her faith, whereas the wife of the heir to the Russian throne was required to profess the official Orthodox religion.

This conflict could have proved a fatal impediment, had it not been for the pressure of Ella, who did everything possible to bring about the love-match. Her own conversion to Orthodoxy after eight years of marriage provided Alice with the ultimate argument.

During the five long years of struggle for Alice's hand, Nicholas twice fell for the charms of other women. First there was a fleeting infatuation with the Russian princess, Olga Dolgorukaya. Then came a stormy romance with the ballerina Matilda Kshessinskaya, though both she and Nicholas understood perfectly that their relationship had no future. Nicholas left Kshessinskaya the moment he felt Alice would convert to Orthodoxy.

Nicholas and Alice became engaged in Coburg in April 1894. That spring and summer were full of happiness, as they planned their future family life. Alice was supposed to come to Russia to marry Nicholas in the autumn of that year.

She did indeed come to Russia, but found herself instead at the funeral of her future father-in-law. Alexander III died at Livadia in the Crimea, and it was here that Alice was received into the Orthodox faith and took the name of Alexandra Feodorovna, a few days after her arrival. The wedding took place in St Petersburg shortly after the funeral, on the birthday of Empress Maria Feodorovna, a day which permitted some relaxation of the rules of court mourning.

The public blamed the newly-weds for such haste, but Nicholas's desire to be with Alexandra was so strong that he ignored all conventions. Their marriage was unpretentious. Indeed, since they were not even photographed, it is difficult to know what they really looked like on that day. Thus, despite being in mourning, they began what proved to be a truly happy family life.

The early years of their marriage were, undoubtedly, the happiest of their life. Their mood was clouded only by the absence of an heir. With deplorable regularity Alexandra gave birth to one daughter after another – in 1895 to Olga, 1897 Tatiana, 1899 Maria and 1901 Anastasia. For Nicholas and his proud wife it was a terrible ordeal, given that any wife who is also a queen is expected to produce an heir to the throne.

Finally Alexandra became so neurotic that in 1902 she had a phantom pregnancy. Not only was she herself convinced that it was genuine, but she managed to persuade everyone else. The Court Ministry was already preparing suitable manifestos where only the name of the child was left blank. The Empress's self-deception was aided by her refusal to be examined by any doctor. This attitude to medicine could be the subject of a special study: the Empress was inclined to disbelieve doctors and accepted their services only when their opinions regarding her illnesses coincided with her own. This was linked to a certain extent with her growing passion for mysticism and one specifically Russian phenomenon – the *yurodivy* (God's fools). These dirty, barefoot men in shabby clothes, often defective in mind, appeared ever more frequently at the court with their incoherent prophecies.

Alexandra must have increasingly come to believe that only a miracle would allow her to conceive a son. This is the only explanation for the phenomenon of a certain Philippe, a butcher from Lyons, who was prosecuted in France for practising medicine without official permission. In Russia he rapidly became one of the Tsar's most intimate circle, and began to enjoy the complete confidence of the Empress, persuading her that he was able to change the sex of a child in the womb. Alexandra believed implicitly in Philippe's magic powers. She kept his present of a small icon with bells which, the charlatan had her believe, would ring at the approach of any evil power.

This passion for rogues and *yurodivy* was inseparably linked in Alexandra's soul with a sincere and profound religious faith. It is difficult to know to what extent her beliefs corresponded to the canons of Orthodoxy, but outwardly she kept strictly to all its formal traditions. In her desire to produce an heir, she wore herself out with prayers for a miracle. And finally her most fervent wish came true.

In 1903 the Orthodox church canonized Serafim Sarovsky. This was done, it was said, at the insistence of Nicholas, and on the advice of Philippe. Rumours spread that bathing at the source near the monastery, where Serafim had lived and died, cured people of ailments and brought the fulfilment of wishes. Alexandra and Nicholas made a pilgrimage to Sarov, where they visited the saint's abode and bathed in the pool. And a year afterwards, on 30 July 1904, their long-awaited son was born and given the name of Alexei.

The confinement was normal, but soon afterwards the baby began to bleed from the navel. This was the first – but not immediately recognized – sign that Alexei was afflicted by a terrible and incurable illness – haemophilia. Carried by women, but presenting a mortal danger only for men, this hereditary disease was transmitted by some of the female descendants of Queen Victoria. When Alexandra was only a year old, her brother Friedrich had died (he suffered from haemophilia); at eleven she saw the death of her uncle, Prince Leopold, a son of Queen Victoria. In 1904 her nephew, Heinrich, the four-year-old son of her sister, Iréne of Prussia, also died. We have no means of knowing when exactly Nicholas and Alexandra became aware of the threat that hung over their son. Most probably quite soon, because of one very obvious symptom of the illness – the failure of the blood to coagulate. Any important contusion, not to speak. of cut, led to internal haemorrhaging and the development of a haematoma which was difficult to cure and left no doubt as to its cause.

At the same time, it would be erroneous to think that all haemophiliacs were doomed to an early death. Another son of Irène of Prussia, Prince Waldemar, was also a victim of the disease, yet died only in 1945 at the age of fifty-six. It would be more correct to say that although Alexei was not necessarily condemned to an early death, he was nevertheless in constant mortal danger. He could have lived ten, twenty or thirty years, but equally, he could have died in a very short time while still a child. The agony Nicholas and Alexandra had to live through needs no explaining. For some time, they could not bring themselves to share their grief with anyone. The Tsar's sister Xenia states in her diary that it was only in 1912, when Alexei was already eight, that Alexandra told her of the terrible illness afflicting her son.

Misfortunes, as everyone knows, never come singly. The very year of Alexei's birth coincided with the start of Russia's war against Japan, which brought the crushing defeat of the imperial army and can now clearly be seen as the prologue to the first Russian revolution.

On 9 December 1905, soldiers opened fire on a peaceful demonstration heading for St Petersburg's Winter Palace with a petition asking the Tsar to improve the living conditions of ordinary people. That day is now known in history as 'Bloody Sunday'. At that time, Nicholas was in Tsarskoe Selo and the order to shoot was given by his uncle, the Grand Duke Vladimir Alexandrovich, but public opinion placed the responsibility firmly on the Tsar himself. The shooting provoked vigorous protests all over the country. In February 1905 another of the Tsar's uncles, Grand Duke Sergei Alexandrovich, was killed by an assassin. Rumours spread that terrorists were also preparing to murder Vladimir Alexandrovich. Frightened by these revolutionary events, the Tsar's family took refuge in Tsarskoe Selo and were not seen in public for over a year.

Meanwhile, the revolution gathered momentum. As strikes and peasants' revolts grew, the claims for the overthrow of tsarism and the establishment of a democratic republic became more and more persistent. Nicholas was forced to make concessions and on 17 October 1905 issued a manifesto giving the country freedom of speech, association and religion, while promising the election of a legislative-consultative Duma – a parliament in the Russian manner. It had not been easy for Nicholas to sign a document granting these political changes. He had done so under intense pressure from Grand Duke Nikolai Nikolaevich, who categorically insisted on his signature. But in his heart and soul Nicholas – and still more Alexandra – was never able to accept fully the need to break with the centuries-old tradition of autocracy in Russia. Even after the opening in 1906 of the first session of the Duma, he still thought of himself as 'Master of the Russian Land', which is how he defined his profession in the first all-Russian census of 1897.

The revolution of 1905–1907 came to an end, the peasant riots ceased. The country, firmly guided by Prime Minister Stolypin, seemed for the moment calm and peaceful. The agrarian reforms initiated by Stolypin allowed peasants to receive their own plots of land. Russia witnessed the gradual creation of a small and middle landowners' class. In an effort to reduce tension in the centre of the country, the Government encouraged the migration of peasants east to Siberia. The rate of industrial growth increased. Nothing heralded the forthcoming catastrophic events. After all the upheavals, the imperial family could return to the quiet life of the old days.

But appearances were deceptive. The life of the family was undermined not only by the successive deaths of the Tsar's uncles Alexei and Vladimir and the scandalous morganatic marriage of his brother Mikhail, but above all by the incurable hereditary disease afflicting the heir to the throne. Several times he was on the verge of death, and the situation was only aggravated by the decision to keep his illness a secret.

Peace in the country was also a delusion. Powerful underground revolutionary forces continued their work, which neither the secret police nor government repression was able to stop.

On 1 September 1910 in Kiev, Stolypin was fatally wounded by the student Bogrov in front of the Tsar. The new outburst of revolutionary activity awaited by the terrorists never occurred, but the event itself was a menacing warning that things were not going well.

During the last ten years of their lives, the Tsar and his family became increasingly isolated. Their circle of close friends was reduced, and two people appeared who were to play a tragic role in the fate of the Romanovs: Ania Vyrubova and Grigory Rasputin.

Vyrubova was the daughter of A. S. Taneev, an outstanding chief of the Tsar's private office, like his father and grandfather. Narrow-minded, plain, fat and clumsy – one of her nicknames was 'the cow' – Ania Taneeva had a failed marriage to Fleet-Lieutenant Vyrubov. Her struggle to obtain a divorce brought her close to the Empress, who actively supported her. In the course of time, Vyrubova became the most intimate – and in fact sole – friend of the Empress, who was painfully shy and never found it easy to get on with people. Vyrubova worshipped both the Emperor and the Empress and was infinitely devoted to them.

In the autumn of 1906 the Grand Duchess Militsa, wife of Grand Duke Pyotr Nikolaevich, brought to the imperial court a semi-literate Siberian *moujik*, Grigory Rasputin. It was Vyrubova who did every-thing in her power to make Nicholas and Alexandra revere the new *staretz* (holy man) as a saint until the end of their lives. His very name became synonymous with the degradation of Russia's state and society at the beginning of the twentieth century. *Rasputinshina* was a symbol of the fall of the Romanov dynasty. The police reports pre-served in the archives, as well as the testimonies of Rasputin's con-temporaries and eye-witness accounts of his debaucheries, leave us in no doubt as to the real life of the 'saintly *staretz*' as he was called by the Tsar's family. Night-revels, whore-houses, bribes, the promotion to the highest state posts of people obliged to Rasputin or his inti-mates – these are only some of his 'heroic deeds'. He was thought to belong to the *Khlisty* sect, whose devotions ended in an orgy of col-lective sexual intercourse. Yet he became a close friend – 'Our Friend' is his usual designation in the Romanovs' letters – of the Tsar's fam-ily and therefore had a major influence on the destiny of the Empire.

How can one explain the intimacy of a libertine peasant with the profoundly religious Emperor and Empress? The most frequent explanation is Rasputin's ability to stop Alexei's haemorrhages. We reject any suggestion of a sexual relationship between the Empress and Rasputin, because it is quite unfounded. Rasputin undoubtedly possessed an impressive hypnotic power and could in all probability relieve Alexei's pain. In his book *Nicholas and Alexandra* Robert Massie describes a mechanism by which modern medical science can explain the cessation of bleeding under hypnosis. We can be certain that the ability to relieve Alexei's suffering was an important factor in Rasputin's growing influence. But it was not the only one.

By the nature of court life, Nicholas and Alexandra were cut off from reality, and deprived of the true image of the Russian peasant. To them, Rasputin came to represent that primordial Russian, who was in fact their reason for governing the Empire. The arrival of the huge *moujik*, who always wore peasant clothes and who addressed the Tsar and Tsaritsa as 'Thou' and 'Father' and 'Mother', was bound to have a profound effect on Nicholas and Alexandra. To them, Rasputin personified the Russian people as they believed them to be: strongly devout, faithful to the throne, and the guarantors of Russia's prosperity. Deeply and mystically religious, the Empress believed in the prophecies of the *staretz* to the point of fanaticism. Shrewd contemporaries were quick to notice that Rasputin never opposed the imperial family's wishes but cunningly made them appear as his own prophecies.

Blinded by their faith, Nicholas and Alexandra dismissed every hostile word about Rasputin as slander. It never occurred to them that the man whose company they enjoyed might turn out to be a swindler and a debauchee. Fanaticism deprives an individual of reason, and this is unfortunately what happened to Nicholas and Alexandra. Everyone who dared speak the truth about Rasputin was banished – such as S.I. Tiutcheva, the imperial children's governess, and even Alexandra's sister Grand Duchess Ella, who was never again admitted into the imperial presence after her attempt to talk about the *staretz* in 1916.

Rasputin in effect split the imperial family: on one side Nicholas and Alexandra, on the other the rest of the ruling dynasty, headed by Empress Marie. The failure of several attempts to persuade Nicky to distance himself from Rasputin eventually led to the conspiracy which ended in the death of the *staretz*. Two of the key participants were the Emperor's beloved young cousin Dmitri Pavlovich, and Prince Felix Yusupov, son-in-law of Nicholas's sister Xenia. With Rasputin's murder in 1916, society believed the monarchy in Russia was living its last months.

One striking coincidence must be mentioned. In order to strengthen his position at court, Rasputin constantly repeated to Nicholas and Alexandra that as long as he remained alive their son would live and the dynasty survive; but his own death would inevitably bring the end of the Romanovs. And this is in fact what happened.

The last decade of Nicholas's reign saw some very grandiose anniversary celebrations. In 1913 the country solemnly celebrated three hundred years of Romanov rule. Nicholas, Alexandra and their children undertook a long tour of Russia, including a voyage on the

Volga and a visit to Kostroma, the native city from where the Romanovs had been summoned to rule Russia.

In 1909 there were festivities to mark the battle of Poltava, where Peter the Great had defeated the Swedish army of King Charles XII, and in 1912 others to mark the centenary of the battle of Borodino which, despite the defeat of the Russian army and the evacuation of Moscow, was seen as the beginning of the eventual victory over Napoleon.

The huge crowds present for these events and the demonstrations of patriotic sentiment once again helped convince Nicholas and Alexandra that the simple Russian people were true supporters of the autocracy. The extent to which they were led astray was only revealed in 1917.

The year 1914 witnessed a sharp deterioration of the international situation. Political considerations superseded the traditional bonds of kinship between the Russian court, the German principalities and Emperor Wilhelm II himself. Russia, which since the time of Alexander II had favoured friendship with the French, found herself among the enemies of Germany and Austro-Hungary. In August 1914 Germany and then Austro-Hungary declared war on Russia.

The Tsar's family behaved with great dignity. The Empress founded a hospital for the wounded at Tsarskoe Selo and personally financed several hospital trains. As well as visiting the sick, both she and her daughters worked as simple nurses.

The first Commander-in-Chief of the Russian troops was Grand Duke Nikolai Nikolaevich, but in September 1915, yielding to strong pressure from the Empress, the Emperor took the fatal decision to assume command of the army himself. He ignored the pleas of both the Chairman of the Duma, M. V. Rodzianko, and of his own ministers, who begged him not to take personal responsibility for everything that happened at the front. But Nicholas was convinced that as autocrat and anointed sovereign he had to assume responsibility in times of crisis.

He took his young son to the front, even though he understood quite clearly the risks this posed for the boy. He spent many sleepless nights at Alexei's bedside at his headquarters in Mogilev. When, in December 1915, Alexei suffered a severe haemorrhage from the nose, the Tsar was forced to return to Tsarskoe Selo. For a time the situation seemed hopeless, but the illness eventually subsided.

Although Nicholas could have been a good officer, he was quite evidently inept as Commander-in-Chief. In 1915 the Russian army suffered major defeats. Even the successful offensive in the spring of

1916 failed to bring any strategic advantage because of the Tsar's interference in military affairs.

The general situation in the country began to worsen, with food shortages and rising prices. Waves of strikes hit even the armaments factories. Troops sent to quell the protests proved unreliable. The possibility of insubordination became more and more apparent.

Anti-German feeling grew stronger. Rumours began to circulate suggesting that the defeats of the Russian army were due to treason by the highest officials. People reminded themselves of Alexandra's German origins. The most improbable rumours were circulated in a whisper – that a secret cable had been laid between Tsarskoe Selo and Berlin, which allowed the Empress to exchange secrets with the Kaiser.

The air was heavy with revolution. Perhaps the only place where it was not noticed was in the Tsar's family. How to explain otherwise that the events of February 1917 came as a total surprise to them?

Powerful demonstrations in St Petersburg, the refusal of local troops to open fire on the rioters, the political activity of the Duma and the creation of its Provisional Committee, the proposal to the Emperor that he should abdicate – these were some of the events which completely changed the course of Russian history.

Nicholas left his headquarters and tried to reach St Petersburg, but his train was detained by the troops and on 2 March he was forced to sign the manifesto of abdication for himself and his son in favour of his brother Mikhail. One day later Mikhail in turn abdicated. It was the end of the Romanov dynasty.

With the formation of a Provisional Government, the last period in the lives of Nicholas and his family began. On 9 March Nicholas returned from Mogilev to Tsarskoe Selo, where he was reunited with Alexandra.

Nicholas hoped at first that his family would be able to leave Russia for exile in Britain. But despite the consent of the Provisional Government an unexpected obstacle arose – his cousin, King George V, concerned by opposition to this proposal within Britain, deemed it inadvisable. The talks between the Provisional Government and the British Foreign Office failed. Nevertheless, George V continued to seek assurances through the British ambassador concerning Nicholas's safety.

By that time anti-government feelings in the capital had reached a peak. Many meetings ended with a call to do away with the 'bloody butcher'. The Petrograd soviet of workers and soldiers continued to call for Nicholas and Alexandra to be put on trial. In an effort to ease the tension, the Provisional Government decided to move the Tsar and his family to the remote city of Tobolsk in Siberia.

Nicholas, Alexandra and their children displayed striking courage in the tragedy of their new situation. The letters, diaries and memoirs of those who were in contact with them during the last year and a half of their life unanimously attest to this.

In October 1917 the Provisional Government was overthrown and political power fell into the hands of the Bolsheviks. The denouement was not far away. The country meanwhile was ravaged by civil war.

In May 1918 the family was transferred to Ekaterinburg in the Urals. By mid-summer White Russian troops began to make advances against the Bolsheviks. By the beginning of July Ekaterinburg found itself threatened with capture.

Even today, the circumstances surrounding the Bolsheviks' decision to execute the Romanov family are far from clear. Why were they shot without trial? Who actually took the decision to shoot the family? Lenin? Sverdlov? Local Bolsheviks? Why also shoot Dr Botkin and the servants?

But do we really need an answer? We know how the slaughter was carried out. Following the discovery near Ekaterinburg, in the summer of 1991, of the place where the remains of Nicholas, Alix, the children, Dr Botkin and the servants were buried, we know for certain that all the family perished and there were no survivors.

One month later other members of the imperial family were murdered: Nicholas's brother Mikhail in Perm, and in Alapaevsk Alexandra's sister Grand Duchess Ella, Grand Duke Sergei Mikhailovich, three of KR's children and Prince Vladimir Paley.

Nicholas's mother the Dowager Empress Marie managed to escape. In the spring of 1919, she was evacuated from the Crimea on the British cruiser *Marlborough*, together with her daughter Xenia and her husband Sandro, their daughter Irina and her husband Felix Yusupov, the family of Grand Duke Nikolai Nikolaevich and other relatives. Empress Marie spent the last years of her life in Denmark, where she died in 1928. An era had ended.

SERGEI MIRONENKO

SOURCES

The following documents used in this book are preserved in the State Archive of the Russian Federation: the diaries of both Nicholas II and Alexandra, those of Nicholas's sister Xenia, of Grand Duke Konstantin Konstantinovich, Nicholas and Alexandra's letters to each other and to their children and relatives, the correspondence of the Grand Dukes and their families, as well as the official papers of the Provisional Government and the highest organs of Soviet power, who decided the fate of the Romanovs after the 1917 Revolution.

Both the letters of Kalyaev from prison in 1905, which are contained in the unpublished manuscript of Boris Savinko, and the memoirs of A. A. Mordvinov, aide-de-camp, are held in the State Archive of the Russian Federation.

The Editors have also used the letters of Nicholas II's sister Xenia to Princess Obolensky, which are preserved in the manuscript department of the State Museum of History in Moscow. In addition the State Archive of the Russian Federation also holds the originals of some of the letters quoted from Queen Victoria, King George V and Kaiser Wilhelm II. Some letters addressed by members of the Imperial family to their British relatives are held in the Royal Archives at Windsor.

The Editors and the Publishers acknowledge the gracious permission of Her Majesty Queen Elizabeth II to quote from letters of Queen Victoria, King George V, Lord Stamfordham and A. J. Balfour.

Although every effort has been made, it has not always been possible to locate copyright owners in works quoted in the book. The Editors and Publishers apologize for any inconvenience caused and will be pleased to make appropriate acknowledgement in any future editions.

The Editors have consulted and drawn on material from the following books:

Grand Duke Alexander, *Once a Grand Duke*. Cassell, London; Doubleday, Garden City, New York, 1932.

Paul Benckendorff, *Last Days at Tsarskoie Selo*. Heinemann, London, 1927.

Lily Dehn, *The Real Tsaritsa*. Thornton, Butterworth, London, 1922

Pierre Gilliard, *Thirteen Years at The Russian Court*. Hutchinson, London; Doran, New York, 1921.

Grand Duchess Marie of Russia, *Things I Remember*. Cassell, London, 1930. US title: *Education of a Princess*.

Maurice Paléologue, *An Ambassador's Memoirs*, three volumes. Hutchinson, London; Doran, New York, 1923–5.

V. Poliakoff, *The Tragic Bride – The Story of the Empress Alexandra of Russia*. Appleton, New York and London [no date].

V. M. Purishkevich, *Dnevnik* (reissue). Moscow, 1990.

V. V. Shulgin, *Dni*, 1920 (reissue). Moscow, 1990.

Ian Vorres, *The Last Grand Duchess*. Hutchinson, London, 1964; Scribner, New York, 1965.

Anna Vyrubova, *Memories of the Russian Court*. Macmillan, New York, 1923.

Felix Yusupov, *Lost Splendour*. Cape, London, 1953.

Felix Yusupov, *Rasputin*. Dial, New York, 1927; *La Fin De Raspoutine*. Paris, 1927.

ACKNOWLEDGEMENTS

First of all we would like to thank our publisher and editor, Ion Trewin, for his vision, commitment, wisdom and patience. Also we would like to thank our agent, Mark Lucas of Peters, Fraser & Dunlop who made this project possible.

We are infinitely indebted to Sarah Zhitomirzskaya, whose unique knowledge and experience with documents were invaluable to us. We are also indebted to Olga Barkovets, whose knowledge of the later Romanovs was a major contribution. We would like to thank Princess Anne Trubetskoy for her enthusiasm and long nights with Empress Alexandra's letters. We are deeply grateful to Yanni Petsopoulos and John Stuart for their help, advice and friendship; also to Philippe Solar and Mayfair Intercontinental Hotel for accommodation.

Without the invaluable help of the staff of the State Archives of the Russian Federation this book would not have been possible. In particular we would like to thank the following: Yevgeny Lunacharsky, Galina Kuznetsova, Olga Edelman, Vladimir Khrustalev, Zinaida Peregudova, Lubov Tutunik, Vera Khitrova, Sergei Samokhvalov, Elena Kitlova.

Our warmest thanks to the staff of the Royal Archives at Windsor Castle, whose knowledge and admirable professionalism also made this book possible. We are deeply indebted to Oliver Everett and Lady de Bellaigue.

For the pictorial illustrations we would like to thank the following people and museums in Russia: at the Hermitage, Mikhail Piotrovsky, Georgy Vilinbakhov, Augusta Pobedinskaya and Galina Mirolubova; at the Russian Museum, Vladimir Gusev, Grigory Goldovsky, Svetlana Janchenko; at the Pavlovsk Museum, Alexei Guzanov; at the Pskov Art Museum, Vladimir Galitsky; at the Pushkinsky Dom, Valentina Loginova. Also Alexander Margolis from The Revival of St Petersburg Foundation and Svetlana Khval from Slavia Interbook publishing house.

We would like to thank the following people for making available to us unique documents or information: Prince Hans-Adam II of Lichtenstein, Kyrill Zinoviev, Sonia Goodman, Xenia Sfiri, Prince Rostislav Romanov, Yuri Kovalenko, Anton Kozlov, the Russian daily newspaper in New York, *Novoe Russkoe Slovo*.

For friendship, help and moral support we would like to thank Andreas Palffy, Charlotte Petsopoulos, Nancy Mitchell, Silvia Rella, Vladimir Soloviev, Alyona Mileeva and Vladimir Boutslov and special thanks to Gordon von Abben.

Finally we thank the staff at Weidenfeld & Nicolson, in particular Cassia Joll, Elizabeth Blumer, Coralie Hepburn, Lesley Baxter and Richard Hussey; and to Douglas Matthews for his index.

INDEX